OCCASIONS

for

PHILOSOPHY

JAMES C. EDWARDS
Furman University

DOUGLAS M. MacDONALD
Furman University

Prentice-Hall, Inc., Englewood Cliffs, New Jersey 07632

Library of Congress Cataloging in Publication Data

Main entry under title:

Occasions for philosophy.

Includes bibliographical references.
1. Philosophy—Collected works. 2. Life—
Collected works. I. Edwards, James C., 1943-
II. MacDonald, Douglas M., 1941-
B21.025   108   78-25577
ISBN   0-13-629287-9

Printed in the United States of America

10 9 8 7 6 5 4 3 2 1

Editorial/production supervision and interior design by Cynthia Marione
Cover design by Michael Clane Graves
Manufacturing buyer: Harry P. Baisley

PRENTICE-HALL INTERNATIONAL, INC., *London*
PRENTICE-HALL OF AUSTRALIA PTY. LIMITED, *Sydney*
PRENTICE-HALL OF CANADA, LTD., *Toronto*
PRENTICE-HALL OF INDIA PRIVATE LIMITED, *New Delhi*
PRENTICE-HALL OF JAPAN, INC., *Tokyo*
PRENTICE-HALL OF SOUTHEAST ASIA PTE. LTD., *Singapore*
WHITEHALL BOOKS LIMITED, *Wellington, New Zealand*

This book is dedicated to Martha and to Willis

CONTENTS

2
PHILOSOPHY
and
HUMAN NATURE

3
PHILOSOPHY, EDUCATION
and the
LIBERAL ARTS

4
PHILOSOPHY
and
PERSONAL RELATIONS

Marriage   277

5
PHILOSOPHY
and the
CLAIMS of RELIGION

What is Religion?   316

Religious Epistemology: Reason   355

6
DEATH
and the
MEANING of LIFE

individual and the significance of life

ACKNOWLEDGMENTS

Since we began to teach philosophy at Furman University in 1970 our students have been constant in their superior abilities, in their demands for excellence, and in their charities to strugglers. Their enthusiasm for learning has, time and again, challenged us to think anew and has shamed us when we were tempted to settle for easy half-truths or apparently profound obscurities. It is because of these students, and particularly because of a special few, who know who they are, that this anthology exists. Extraordinary thanks are due the Fall, 1977, introductory class that we team-taught using these materials.

Certain individuals and groups have aided us very directly in this endeavor. A grant from the W. K. Kellogg Foundation to Furman University provided the initial opportunity to redesign our introductory philosophy course, and a grant from Furman's Research and Professional Growth Committee provided a summer's freedom in which to consolidate our thought into this anthology. Our grateful thanks to both groups. The Kellogg grant enabled us to bring to Furman as a consultant J. B. Schneewind, Provost of Hunter College, CUNY; and his insights and suggestions are acknowledged with gratitude. Bryan McKown, our Prentice-Hall representative and a Furman graduate, has been stalwart in his support and generous in his praise; we thank him. Thanks also to Bud Therien, Philosophy Editor at Prentice-Hall, to Cindy Marione, our production editor, and to the anonymous reviewers of the manuscript for their excellent suggestions.

Judy Leavell and Nancy Yacobi were always cheerful and splendidly efficient as they typed, retyped, copied, and collated enormous quantities of paper. They have our most sincere gratitude and admiration. Martha Edwards, who spent a broiling August Saturday laboring over a hot Xerox machine, is due our thanks, and has them. The academic administration, from our department chairman Tom Buford to our deans Stuart Patterson and Frank Bonner, has been consistently supportive of our efforts; thanks to them all.

Finally, we wish to acknowledge the debts—of every variety—implied in our dedications. "Whereof one cannot speak, thereof must one be silent."

January, 1978   JAMES C. EDWARDS
                                                   DOUGLAS M. MACDONALD

INTRODUCTION

Another introductory philosophy anthology? Yes, for what we believe are very good reasons.

Three main sorts of introductory philosophy courses, with textbooks to match, are found in American universities today. There are, first of all, historical introductions, which study representative great philosophers in historical sequence, hoping to introduce the student to philosophy through its historical dialectic. Then there are "problems" courses, which isolate a number of major philosophical issues—usually in epistemology, metaphysics, and value theory—and deploy around these some readings from classical and contemporary philosophers. While both sorts of courses can sometimes serve as excellent introductions to philosophy, they have more frequently been charged with a glaring defect—a lack of perceived connection between the material read and the lives of the students and teachers who read it. Students often leave such courses with the distinct (if unfounded) impression that what philosophers have written is of little use to "real" life, that the problems philosophers worry about are not, for all their difficulty and historical patina, problems that ought to concern any thinking person. The problems of philosophy are historical curiosities, and the study of philosophy is the dusty unwrapping of these thought-mummies.

The concern for freshness and clear human interest in introductory philosophy courses is sharpened since such courses are usually taught as part of the general education sequence of a college curriculum. At most schools the student's general education requirements are met by taking a certain number and distribution of the introductory courses of various academic departments, philosophy among them; so introductory philosophy courses are thereby asserted to be relevant to the student's general education as well as being introductory of the discipline *per se*. But are they? Does a straightforward introduction, whether historical or problems-oriented, contribute most significantly to the general education of the student who will, in all likelihood, never take another philosophy course?

Spurred by such questions, a third type of introductory philosophy course has recently arisen. Its avowed aim has been *relevance*, bridging the gap between the student's concerns and the traditional concerns of philosophers. Anthologies have been produced which include standard philosophical pieces alongside readings from contemporary political statements, pop psychology, the new religions, and the like. ("Immanuel Kant, say hello to Carlos Castaneda.") But large problems still remain. In the first place, the philosophical interest of the "bridge" material is frequently negligible. Furthermore, the connections between such material and the included philosophy selections are often either very slight or else buried too deep for the beginning student to appreciate. And third, today's guru is tomorrow's blank look; a course that seeks relevance the easy way courts very swift obsolescence. How can one demonstrate some connections between philosophy and a student's very real and immediate human concerns without the fluff and strained relevance one finds in the pop texts and courses?

We intend that this anthology serve as the basis for a course that is both an introduction to *philosophy* and a significant part of the student's general education. We believe that an introductory philosophy course, especially one that claims to serve the purposes of general education, ought to exhibit clear connections with issues fundamental to any thoughtful human life; and in selecting topics and readings we have tried to show that philosophical reflection does have a substantial (indeed, essential) place in such a life. We do this, not by including bits of ephemeral non-philosophical material, but by showing what powerful philosophers have had to say on issues that are of perennial human interest no matter what the political, social, and aesthetic climate—issues like death and the threat it poses to life's meaning, the nature and significance of our varied personal relations, the possibility of religious belief. Such issues are of intrinsic concern to any thoughtful person, and philosophers have had much interesting and useful to say about them.

We wish to emphasize our concern with *doing philosophy*. All the selections in this book have substantial philosophical content; their authors are among the finest classical and contemporary thinkers: Plato, Aristotle, Aquinas, Kierkegaard, James, and Nagel. As is clear from the first section, we model a first encounter with philosophy on the figure of Socrates.

Our selections are analytical and critical, not constructive and speculative. In an introductory course students respond best to the challenge of critically investigating their own presuppositions, and for that task there could hardly be a better model than Socrates. Rather than scatter-shoot, we have included relatively few major topics, with deeper analysis of each. Philosophy is argument; so we have, as best we can, arranged our selections dialectically. And we have tried to leave each issue with the student; philosophy shouldn't end with the course.

So, here is our anthology. We, of course, think it is a good book; but the proof of the pudding is in the eating. Teaching philosophy well is enormously difficult, but its rewards are commensurate with its difficulty. If this book in any way mitigates the difficulty without diminishing the rewards, it will have justified itself. We wish it, and you, well.

1

PHILOSOPHY

and the

SOCRATIC MODEL

What is philosophy? According to one philosopher it is the attempt "to understand how things in the broadest possible sense of the term hang together in the broadest possible sense of the term"; [1] for another it is "a battle against the bewitchment of our intelligence by means of language." [2] The trouble with such definitions is that they are either so vague as to be almost meaningless or so specific as to exclude what some other philosophers consider to be vital to the subject. The specification of the nature of philosophy is itself a major philosophical task; thus we will not begin this book by trying to capture the essence of philosophy in a single, all-inclusive verbal definition. Rather, in this first section of readings philosophy is defined *ostensively*, that is, it is demonstrated by example, not by a discussion. By presenting one exemplary philosopher —Socrates—we intend to introduce the aims, techniques, and values specific to philosophical activity itself.

What, then, do we see the philosopher Socrates doing? We see him talking and talking and talking. But rather than being idle chatter, the Socratic dialogues are conversations with a man who is intelligent, rational, playful, and unwilling to accept another's opinions at face value. In the *Euthyphro*, for example, we see Socrates conversing with a man who believes himself to be the paradigm of piety, a man who is so sure of his righteousness that he is willing to prosecute his own father. In his dialogue with the self-satisfied Euthyphro, Socrates himself is *never* satisfied: He tries repeatedly to make Euthyphro define what he means by

1

"piety" and to make him assess the arguments on which his self-righteous-ness rests. Socrates shows himself to be a skeptic of a sort; but his critical questioning of received opinion is not an end in itself; it is a means to truth. While much of Socrates' philosophical activity is destructive, he sees the razing of illusion as the necessary first step in attaining wisdom.

The *Euthyphro* ends on a disquieting note; the discussion concludes practically where it began. Is this also a characteristic of philosophical investigation—that it goes nowhere? Perhaps the message (albeit unin-tended) of the *Euthyphro* is that philosophy is unimportant to the dis-covery of public truth; perhaps, even more radically, public truth is itself an illusion, and we are thrown back on opinions, of which those of one person are just as good as those of another. Or perhaps the message of the dialogue is just that truth is always difficult to grasp and that its at-tainment requires a great deal more persistence and intellectual integrity than Euthyphro offers.

The *Apology*, ostensibly the story of Socrates' trial for treason, is also his defense of the philosophical life itself. Then, as now, many people saw philosophy as corrosive of the social framework essential to their contentment; the *Apology* forces us to consider whether philosophy has any real virtue for the individual or for society. In his defense Socrates urges that we have arguments for our beliefs, actions, and attitudes; that we be willing to examine and reexamine our life to discover whether its structure has justification. He forcefully opposes any form of intellectual dogmatism. For him philosophy is an *activity*, not a body of sterile doc-trine—an activity appropriate to all of one's life. Without philosophy, an individual is condemned to live in illusion, condemned not to know the true sense of his or her life. A society without philosophers is like a city of slaves; it is a prisoner of ignorance, prejudice, tradition, and passion.

For Socrates, the activity of philosophy is integral to being fully hu-man; merely having a human body doesn't guarantee having a genuinely human life. The distinction of human beings is *autonomy*, one's control of one's own life. Animals cannot be autonomous; their actions are con-trolled either by innate behavioral mechanisms or by reinforced environ-mental patterns. They are in bondage to their genes and their habitats. We human beings seem to be able to determine for ourselves (at least some of) our actions. We can, it appears, *reason* about what we are to do; we can direct our behavior internally, not always have it imposed from without. Autonomy, however, is something to be won; if we don't strug-gle, we will still be ruled externally by ignorance, tradition, and illusion. For Socrates, philosophy is the way to autonomy, the way to a life that is distinctively human.

Furthermore, philosophical autonomy has an important social dimen-sion. A person's actions are based (consciously or unconsciously) on be-liefs which he or she holds—about the nature of the world, about moral-ity, about religion—and in our social contacts it doesn't take us long to realize just how diverse these beliefs are. Since our lives don't always allow us the luxury of ignoring these diversities, disagreement and conflict arise; and these disputes can be resolved by force, bribery, or rational persuasion. Physical force has always been an effective way of getting people to change their actions, if not their minds; and much of modern advertising is a form of bribery. ("Want a date this Saturday night? Use our toothpaste and . . .") But these forms of persuasion are not respecters of the person; they externally compel assent. A person's beliefs and actions are changed, not by compulsion for truth, but by *fear*—fear of pain, fear of not being loved.

The Socratic appeal to reason, on the other hand, is a recognition of personal autonomy. It asks us to believe only that for which there are good reasons, and it encourages us to give up those beliefs which we cannot rationally support. Neither is easy; for as difficult as it often is to specify good reasons for our beliefs, it is even harder to abandon those cherished propositions for which we have been unable to find a rational basis. Yet, hard or easy, the Socratic ideal is an ideal worthy of the *individual*; it fully allows for autonomy. We want to be allowed to make up our own mind; simple justice demands that we allow others the same. If we care about autonomy, then the Socratic conception of philosophical activity seem to be essential to us in our desire for individual freedom and for a just basis of social cooperation.

The Socratic model of the philosopher, the person committed to the critical examination of his life, shapes this book. The selections raise issues vital to any thoughtful, sensitive person; the intent is not to raise senseless questions or to criticize for the sake of criticism, but to provoke us into truth. But truth is hard to get, and very easy to confuse with other things. It is sometimes, for instance, confused with rhetorical skill and argumentative facility.

> Just as a vagrant accused of stealing a carrot from a field stands before a comfortably seated judge who keeps up an elegant flow of queries, comments, and witticisms while the accused is unable to stammer a word, so truth stands before an intelligence which is concerned with the elegant manipulation of opinions.[3]

~ WaRNiNG

Caveat: The study of philosophy often seems to help one in the elegant manipulation of opinions; it is rare that it actually gives one the truth.

A final word of caution: The Socratic model of philosophy requires the criticism of beliefs, attitudes, and actions. As much as Socrates was critical of others, he was, ironically, even more critical of himself. He was never more sincere than when he proclaimed to Athens his own ignorance. We would be poor students of Socrates if we were to accept his critical model of philosophy uncritically. Although the Socratic model certainly shapes this book, the selections by Vlastos and Nietzsche raise—in very different ways—some hard questions about this conception of philosophy and about Socrates' use of it.

What, then, is philosophy? Surely, in part, philosophy is what Socrates did, and what, after his example, we now do. For philosophy is, finally, something that is *done*; we do not study philosophical texts to try to emulate point by point the great philosophers like Socrates. Rather, the texts in which we encounter him and his descendents are *occasions* for philosophy, for *our* philosophy, the reflective examination of our own life here and now.

NOTES

1. Wilfrid Sellars, *Science, Perception and Reality* (London: Routledge and Kegan Paul, 1963), p. 1.
2. Ludwig Wittgenstein, *Philosophical Investigations,* trans. G. E. M. Anscombe (Oxford: Basil Blackwell, 1953), sec. 109.
3. Simone Weil, *Selected Essays 1934–1943,* trans. Sir Richard Rees (London: Oxford University Press, 1965), p. 13.

Euthyphro

Plato

CHARACTERS

Socrates

Euthyphro

Scene—The Hall of the King

Euthyphro: What in the world are you doing here in the king's hall, Socrates? Why have you left your haunts in the Lyceum? You surely cannot have a suit before him, as I have.

Socrates: The Athenians, Euthyphro, call it an indictment, not a suit.

Euth.:   What? Do you mean that someone is prosecuting you? I cannot believe that you are prosecuting anyone yourself.

Socr.:   Certainly I am not.

Euth.:   Then is someone prosecuting you?

Socr.:   Yes.

Euth.:   Who is he?

Socr.:   I scarcely know him myself, Euthyphro; I think he must be some

From *Euthyphro, Apology, Crito,* trans. F. J. Church (Indianapolis: The Library of Liberal Arts, Bobbs-Merrill, 1956), pp. 1-20. Reprinted by permission of the publisher.

unknown young man. His name, however, is Meletus, and his district Pitthis, if you can call to mind any Meletus of that district— a hook-nosed man with lanky hair and rather a scanty beard.

Euth.: I don't know him, Socrates. But tell me, what is he prosecuting you for?

Socr.: What for? Not on trivial grounds, I think. It is no small thing for so young a man to have formed an opinion on such an important matter. For he, he says, knows how the young are corrupted, and who are their corrupters. He must be a wise man who, observing my ignorance, is going to accuse me to the state, as his mother, of corrupting his friends. I think that he is the only one who begins at the right point in his political reforms; for his first care is to make the young men as good as possible, just as a good farmer will take care of his young plants first, and, after he has done that, of the others. And so Meletus, I suppose, is first clearing us away who, as he says, corrupt the young men growing up; and then, when he has done that, of course he will turn his attention to the older men, and so become a very great public benefactor. Indeed, that is only what you would expect when he goes to work in this way.

Euth.: I hope it may be so, Socrates, but I fear the opposite. It seems to me that in trying to injure you, he is really setting to work by striking a blow at the foundation of the state. But how, tell me, does he say that you corrupt the youth?

Socr.: In a way which sounds absurd at first, my friend. He says that I am a maker of gods; and so he is prosecuting me, he says, for inventing new gods and for not believing in the old ones.

Euth.: I understand, Socrates. It is because you say that you always have a divine guide. So he is prosecuting you for introducing religious reforms; and he is going into court to arouse prejudice against you, knowing that the multitude are easily prejudiced about such matters. Why, they laugh even at me, as I were out of my mind, when I talk about divine things in the assembly and tell them what is going to happen; and yet I have never foretold anything which has not come true. But they are resentful of all people like us. We must not worry about them; we must meet them boldly.

Socr.: My dear Euthyphro, their ridicule is not a very serious matter. The Athenians, it seems to me, may think a man to be clever without paying him much attention, so long as they do not think that he teaches his wisdom to others. But as soon as they think that he makes other people clever, they get angry, whether it be from resentment, as you say, or for some other reason.

Euth.: I am not very anxious to test their attitude toward me in this matter.

Socr.: No, perhaps they think that you are reserved, and that you are not anxious to teach your wisdom to others. But I fear that they may think that I am; for my love of men makes me talk to everyone whom I meet quite freely and unreservedly, and without payment.

Indeed, if I could I would gladly pay people myself to listen to me. If then, as I said just now, they were only going to laugh at me, as you say they do at you, it would not be at all an unpleasant way of spending the day—to spend it in court, joking and laughing. But if they are going to be in earnest, then only prophets like you can tell where the matter will end.

Euth.:   Well, Socrates, I dare say that nothing will come of it. Very likely you will be successful in your trial, and I think that I shall be in mine.

Socr.:   And what is this suit of yours, Euthyphro? Are you suing, or being sued?

Euth.:   I am suing.

Socr.:   Whom?

Euth.:   A man whom people think I must be mad to prosecute.

Socr.:   What? Has he wings to fly away with?

Euth.:   He is far enough from flying; he is a very old man.

Socr.:   Who is he?

Euth.:   He is my father.

Socr.:   Your father, my good man?

Euth.:   He is indeed.

Socr.:   What are you prosecuting him for? What is the accusation?

Euth.:   Murder, Socrates.

Socr.:   Good heavens, Euthyphro! Surely the multitude are ignorant of what is right. I take it that it is not everyone who could rightly do what you are doing; only a man who was already well advanced in wisdom.

Euth.:   That is quite true, Socrates.

Socr.:   Was the man whom your father killed a relative of yours? But, of course, he was. You would never have prosecuted your father for the murder of a stranger?

Euth.:   You amuse me, Socrates. What difference does it make whether the murdered man were a relative or a stranger? The only question that you have to ask is, did the murderer kill justly or not? If justly, you must let him alone; if unjustly, you must indict him for murder, even though he share your hearth and sit at your table. The pollution is the same if you associate with such a man, knowing what he has done, without purifying yourself, and him too, by bringing him to justice. In the present case the murdered man was a poor laborer of mine, who worked for us on our farm in Naxos. While drunk he got angry with one of our slaves and killed him. My father therefore bound the man hand and foot and threw him into a ditch, while he sent to Athens to ask the priest what he should do. While the messenger was gone, he entirely neglected the man, thinking that he was a murderer, and that it would be no great matter, even if he were to die. And that was exactly what happened; hunger and cold and his bonds killed him before the messenger returned. And now my father and the rest of my family are indignant with me because I am prosecuting my father for the murder of this murderer. They assert that he did not kill the man at all; and they say that, even if he had killed him over and over again, the man himself was a murderer, and that I ought not to concern myself about such a person because it is impious for a son to prosecute his father for murder. So little, Socrates, do they know the divine law of piety and impiety.

Socr.: And do you mean to say, Euthyphro, that you think that you understand divine things and piety and impiety so accurately that, in such a case as you have stated, you can bring your father to justice without fear that you yourself may be doing something impious?

Euth.: If I did not understand all these matters accurately, Socrates, I should not be worth much—Euthyphro would not be any better than other men.

Socr.: Then, my dear Euthyphro, I cannot do better than become your pupil and challenge Meletus on this very point before the trial begins. I should say that I had always thought it very important to have knowledge about divine things; and that now, when he says that I offend by speaking carelessly about them, and by introducing reforms, I have become your pupil. And I should say, "Meletus, if you acknowledge Euthyphro to be wise in these matters and to hold the correct belief, then think the same of me and do not put me on trial; but if you do not, then bring a suit, not against me, but against my master, for corrupting his elders—namely, myself whom he corrupts by his teaching, and his own father whom he corrupts by admonishing and punishing him." And if I did not succeed in persuading him to release me from the suit or to indict you in my place, then I could repeat my challenge in court.

Euth.: Yes, by Zeus! Socrates, I think I should find out his weak points if he were to try to indict me. I should have a good deal to say about him in court long before I spoke about myself.

Socr.: Yes, my dear friend, and knowing this I am anxious to become your pupil. I see that Meletus here, and others too, seem not to notice you at all, but he sees through me without difficulty and at once prosecutes me for impiety. Now, therefore, please explain to me what you were so confident just now that you knew. Tell me what are righteousness and sacrilege with respect to murder and everything else. I suppose that piety is the same in all actions, and that impiety is always the opposite of piety, and retains its identity, and that, as impiety, it always has the same character, which will be found in whatever is impious.

Euth.: Certainly, Socrates, I suppose so.

Socr.: Tell me, then, what is piety and what is impiety?

Euth.: Well, then, I say that piety means prosecuting the unjust individual who has committed murder or sacrilege, or any other such crime, as I am doing now, whether he is your father or your mother or whoever he is; and I say that impiety means not prosecuting him. And observe, Socrates, I will give you a clear proof, which I have already given to others, that it is so, and that doing right means not letting off unpunished the sacrilegious man, whosoever he may be. Men hold Zeus to be the best and the most just of the gods; and they admit that Zeus bound his own father, Cronos, for wrongfully devouring his children; and that Cronos, in his turn, castrated his father for similar reasons. And yet these same men are incensed with me because I proceed against my father for doing wrong. So, you see, they say one thing in the case of the gods and quite another in mine.

Socr.:   Is not that why I am being prosecuted, Euthyphro? I mean, because I find it hard to accept such stories people tell about the gods? I expect that I shall be found at fault because I doubt those stories. Now if you who understand all these matters so well agree in holding all those tales true, then I suppose that I must yield to your authority. What could I say when I admit myself that I know nothing about them? But tell me, in the name of friendship, do you really believe that these things have actually happened?

Euth.:   Yes, and more amazing things, too, Socrates, which the multitude do not know of.

Socr.:   Then you really believe that there is war among the gods, and bitter hatreds, and battles, such as the poets tell of, and which the great painters have depicted in our temples, notably in the pictures which cover the robe that is carried up to the Acropolis at the great Panathenaic festival? Are we to say that these things are true, Euthyphro?

Euth.:   Yes, Socrates, and more besides. As I was saying, I will report to you many other stories about divine matters, if you like, which I am sure will astonish you when you hear them.

Socr.:   I dare say. You shall report them to me at your leisure another time. At present please try to give a more definite answer to the question which I asked you just now. What I asked you, my friend, was, What is piety? and you have not explained it to me to my satisfaction. You only tell me that what you are doing now, namely, prosecuting your father for murder, is a pious act.

Euth.:   Well, that is true, Socrates.

Socr.:   Very likely. But many other actions are pious, are they not, Euthyphro?

Euth.:   Certainly.

Socr.:   Remember, then, I did not ask you to tell me one or two of all the many pious actions that there are; I want to know what is characteristic of piety which makes all pious actions pious. You said, I think, that there is one characteristic which makes all pious actions pious, and another characteristic which makes all impious actions impious. Do you not remember?

Euth.:   I do.

Socr.: Well, then, explain to me what is this characteristic, that I may have it to turn to, and to use as a standard whereby to judge your actions and those of other men, and be able to say that whatever action resembles it is pious, and whatever does not, is not pious.

Euth.: Yes, I will tell you that if you wish, Socrates.

Socr.: Certainly I do.

Euth.: Well, then, what is pleasing to the gods is pious, and what is not pleasing to them is impious.

Socr.: Fine, Euthyphro. Now you have given me the answer that I wanted. Whether what you say is true, I do not know yet. But, of course, you will go on to prove that it is true.

Euth.: Certainly.

Socr.: Come, then, let us examine our statement. The things and the men that are pleasing to the gods are pious, and the things and the men that are displeasing to the gods are impious. But piety and impiety are not the same; they are as opposite as possible—was not that what we said?

Euth.: Certainly.

Socr.: And it seems the appropriate statement?

Euth.: Yes, Socrates, certainly.

Socr.: Have we not also said, Euthyphro, that there are quarrels and disagreements and hatreds among the gods?

Euth.: We have.

Socr.: But what kind of disagreement, my friend, causes hatred and anger? Let us look at the matter thus. If you and I were to disagree as to whether one number were more than another, would that make us angry and enemies? Should we not settle such a dispute at once by counting?

Euth.: Of course.

Socr.: And if we were to disagree as to the relative size of two things, we should measure them and put an end to the disagreement at once, should we not?

Euth.: Yes.

Socr.: And should we not settle a question about the relative weight of two things by weighing them?

Euth.: Of course.

Socr.: Then what is the question which would make us angry and enemies if we disagreed about it, and could not come to a settlement? Perhaps you have not an answer ready; but listen to mine. Is it not the question of the just and unjust, of the honorable and the dishonorable, of the good and the bad? Is it not questions about these matters which make you and me and everyone else quarrel, when we do quarrel, if we differ about them and can reach no satisfactory agreement?

Euth.: Yes, Socrates, it is disagreements about these matters.

Socr.: Well, Euthyphro, the gods will quarrel over these things if they quarrel at all, will they not?

Euth.:   Necessarily.

Socr.:   Then, my good Euthyphro, you say that some of the gods think one thing just, the others another; and that what some of them hold to be honorable or good, others hold to be dishonorable or evil. For there would not have been quarrels among them if they had not disagreed on these points, would there?

Euth.:   You are right.

Socr.:   And each of them loves what he thinks honorable, and good, and just; and hates the opposite, does he not?

Euth.:   Certainly.

Socr.:   But you say that the same action is held by some of them to be just, and by others to be unjust; and that then they dispute about it, and so quarrel and fight among themselves. Is it not so?

Euth.:   Yes.

Socr.:   Then the same thing is hated by the gods and loved by them; and the same thing will be displeasing and pleasing to them.

Euth.:   Apparently.

Socr.:   Then, according to your account, the same thing will be pious and impious.

Euth.:   So it seems.

Socr.:   Then, my good friend, you have not answered my question. I did not ask you to tell me what action is both pious and impious; but it seems that whatever is pleasing to the gods is also displeasing to them. And so, Euthyphro, I should not be surprised if what you are doing now in punishing your father is an action well pleasing to Zeus, but hateful to Cronos and Uranus, and acceptable to Hephaestus, but hateful to Hera; and if any of the other gods disagree about it, pleasing to some of them and displeasing to others.

Euth.:   But on this point, Socrates, I think that there is no difference of opinion among the gods: they all hold that if one man kills another unjustly, he must be punished.

Socr.:   What, Euthyphro? Among mankind, have you never heard disputes whether a man ought to be punished for killing another man unjustly, or for doing some other unjust deed?

Euth.:   Indeed, they never cease from these disputes, especially in courts of justice. They do all manner of unjust things; and then there is nothing which they will not do and say to avoid punishment.

Socr.:   Do they admit that they have done something unjust, and at the same time deny that they ought to be punished, Euthyphro?

Euth.:   No, indeed, that they do not.

Socr.:   Then it is not the case that there is nothing which they will not do and say. I take it, they do not dare to say or argue that they must not be punished if they have done something unjust. What they say is that they have not done anything unjust, is it not so?

Euth.:   That is true.

Socr.:   Then they do not disagree over the question that the unjust individual must be punished. They disagree over the question, who is unjust, and what was done and when, do they not?

Euth.: That is true.

Socr.: Well, is not exactly the same thing true of the gods if they quarrel about justice and injustice, as you say they do? Do not some of them say that the others are doing something unjust, while the others deny it? No one, I suppose, my dear friend, whether god or man, dares to say that a person who has done something unjust must not be punished.

Euth.: No, Socrates, that is true, by and large.

Socr.: I take it, Euthyphro, that the disputants, whether men or gods, if the gods do disagree, disagree over each separate act. When they quarrel about any act, some of them say that it was just, and others that it was unjust. Is it not so?

Euth.: Yes.

Socr.: Come, then, my dear Euthyphro, please enlighten me on this point. What proof have you that all the gods think that a laborer who has been imprisoned for murder by the master of the man whom he has murdered, and who dies from his imprisonment before the master has had time to learn from the religious authorities what he should do, dies unjustly? How do you know that it is just for a son to indict his father and to prosecute him for the murder of such a man? Come, see if you can make it clear to me that the gods necessarily agree in thinking that this action of yours is just; and if you satisfy me, I will never cease singing your praises for wisdom.

Euth.: I could make that clear enough to you, Socrates; but I am afraid that it would be a long business.

Socr.: I see you think that I am duller than the judges. To them, of course, you will make it clear that your father has committed an unjust action, and that all the gods agree in hating such actions.

Euth.: I will indeed, Socrates, if they will only listen to me.

Socr.: They will listen if they think that you are a good speaker. But while you were talking, it occurred to me to ask myself this question: suppose that Euthyphro were to prove to me as clearly as possible that all the gods think such a death unjust, how has he brought me any nearer to understanding what piety and impiety are? This particular act, perhaps, may be displeasing to the gods, but then we have just seen that piety and impiety cannot be defined in that way; for we have seen that what is displeasing to the gods is also pleasing to them. So I will let you off on this point, Euthyphro; and all the gods shall agree in thinking your father's action wrong and in hating it, if you like. But shall we correct our definition and say that whatever all the gods hate is impious, and whatever they all love is pious; while whatever some of them love, and others hate, is either both or neither? Do you wish us now to define piety and impiety in this manner?

Euth.: Why not, Socrates?

Socr.:   There is no reason why I should not, Euthyphro. It is for you to consider whether that definition will help you to teach me what you promised.

Euth.:   Well, I should say that piety is what all the gods love, and that impiety is what they all hate.

Socr.:   Are we to examine this definition, Euthyphro, and see if it is a good one? Or are we to be content to accept the bare statements of other men or of ourselves without asking any questions? Or must we examine the statements?

Euth.:   We must examine them. But for my part I think that the definition is right this time.

Socr.:   We shall know that better in a little while, my good friend. Now consider this question. Do the gods love piety because it is pious, or is it pious because they love it?

Euth.:   I do not understand you, Socrates.

Socr.:   I will try to explain myself: we speak of a thing being carried and carrying, and being led and leading, and being seen and seeing; and you understand that all such expressions mean different things, and what the difference is.

Euth.:   Yes, I think I understand.

Socr.:   And we talk of a thing being loved, of a thing loving, and the two are different?

Euth.:   Of course.

Socr.:   Now tell me, is a thing which is being carried in a state of being carried because it is carried, or for some other reason?

Euth.:   No, because it is carried.

Socr.:   And a thing is in a state of being led because it is led, and of being seen because it is seen?

Euth.:   Certainly.

Socr.:   Then a thing is not seen because it is in a state of being seen: it is in a state of being seen because it is seen; and a thing is not led because it is in a state of being led: it is in a state of being led because it is led; and a thing is not carried because it is in a state of being carried: it is in a state of being carried because it is carried. Is my meaning clear now, Euthyphro? I mean this: if anything becomes or is affected, it does not become because it is in a state of becoming; it is in a state of becoming because it becomes; and it is not affected because it is in a state of being affected: it is in a state of being affected because it is affected. Do you not agree?

Euth.:   I do.

Socr.:   Is not that which is being loved in a state either of becoming or of being affected in some way by something?

Euth.:   Certainly.

Socr.:   Then the same is true here as in the former cases. A thing is not loved by those who love it because it is in a state of being loved; it is in a state of being loved because they love it.

Euth.:   Necessarily.

Socr.: Well, then, Euthyphro, what do we say about piety? Is it not loved by all the gods, according to your definition?

Euth.: Yes.

Socr.: Because it is pious, or for some other reason?

Euth.: No, because it is pious.

Socr.: Then it is loved by the gods because it is pious; it is not pious because it is loved by them?

Euth.: It seems so.

Socr.: But, then, what is pleasing to the gods is pleasing to them, and is in a state of being loved by them, because they love it?

Euth.: Of course.

Socr.: Then piety is not what is pleasing to the gods, and what is pleasing to the gods is not pious, as you say, Euthyphro. They are different things.

Euth.: And why, Socrates?

Socr.: Because we are agreed that the gods love piety because it is pious, and that it is not pious because they love it. Is not this so?

Euth.: Yes.

Socr.: And that what is pleasing to the gods because they love it, is pleasing to them by reason of this same love, and that they do not love it because it is pleasing to them.

Euth.: True.

Socr.: Then, my dear Euthyphro, piety and what is pleasing to the gods are different things. If the gods had loved piety because it is pious, they would also have loved what is pleasing to them because it is pleasing to them; but if what is pleasing to them had been pleasing to them because they loved it, then piety, too, would have been piety because they loved it. But now you see that they are opposite things, and wholly different from each other. For the one is of a sort to be loved because it is loved, while the other is loved because it is of a sort to be loved. My question, Euthyphro, was, What is piety? But it turns out that you have not explained to me the essential character of piety; you have been content to mention an effect which belongs to it—namely, that all the gods love it. You have not yet told me what its essential character is. Do not, if you please, keep from me what piety is; begin again and tell me that. Never mind whether the gods love it, or whether it has other effects: we shall not differ on that point. Do your best to make clear to me what is piety and what is impiety.

Euth.: But, Socrates, I really don't know how to explain to you what is in my mind. Whatever statement we put forward always somehow moves round in a circle, and will not stay where we put it.

Socr.: I think that your statements, Euthyphro, are worthy of my ancestor Daedalus. If they had been mine and I had set them down, I dare say you would have made fun of me, and said that it was the consequence of my descent from Daedalus that the statements which I construct run away, as his statues used to, and will not stay where they are put. But, as it is, the statements are yours, and the joke would have no point. You yourself see that they will not stay still.

Euth.:   Nay, Socrates, I think that the joke is very much in point. It is not my fault that the statement moves round in a circle and will not stay still. But you are the Daedalus, I think; as far as I am concerned, my statements would have stayed put.

Socr.:   Then, my friend, I must be a more skillful artist than Daedalus; he only used to make his own works move, while I, you see, can make other people's works move, too. And the beauty of it is that I am wise against my will. I would rather that our statements had remained firm and immovable than have all the wisdom of Daedalus and all the riches of Tantalus to boot. But enough of this. I will do my best to help you to explain to me what piety is, for I think that you are lazy. Don't give in yet. Tell me, do you not think that all piety must be just?

Euth.:   I do.

Socr.:   Well, then, is all justice pious, too? Or, while all piety is just, is a part only of justice pious, and the rest of it something else?

Euth.:   I do not follow you, Socrates.

Socr.:   Yet you have the advantage over me in your youth no less than your wisdom. But, as I say, the wealth of your wisdom makes you complacent. Exert yourself, my good friend: I am not asking you a difficult question. I mean the opposite of what the poet said, when he wrote:

"You shall not name Zeus the creator, who made all things: for where there is fear there also is reverence."

Now I disagree with the poet. Shall I tell you why?

Euth.:   Yes.

Socr.:   I do not think it true to say that where there is fear, there also is reverence. Many people who fear sickness and poverty and other such evils seem to me to have fear, but no reverence for what they fear. Do you not think so?

Euth.:   I do.

Socr.:   But I think that where there is reverence there also is fear. Does any man feel reverence and a sense of shame about anything, without at the same time dreading and fearing the reputation of wickedness?

Euth.:   No, certainly not.

Socr.:   Then, though there is fear wherever there is reverence, it is not correct to say that where there is fear there also is reverence. Reverence does not always accompany fear; for fear, I take it, is wider than reverence. It is part of fear, just as the odd is a part of number, so that where you have the odd you must also have number, though where you have number you do not necessarily have the odd. Now I think you follow me?

Euth.:   I do.

Socr.: Well, then, this is what I meant by the question which I asked you. Is there always piety where there is justice? Or, though there is always justice where there is piety, yet there is not always piety where there is justice, because piety is only a part of justice? Shall we say this, or do you differ?

Euth.: No, I agree. I think that you are right.

Socr.: Now observe the next point. If piety is a part of justice, we must find out, I suppose, what part of justice it is? Now, if you had asked me just now, for instance, what part of number is the odd, and what number is an odd number, I should have said that whatever number is not even is an odd number. Is it not so?

Euth.: Yes.

Socr.: Then see if you can explain to me what part of justice is piety, that I may tell Meletus that now that I have been adequately instructed by you as to what actions are righteous and pious, and what are not, he must give up prosecuting me unjustly for impiety.

Euth.: Well, then, Socrates, I should say that righteousness and piety are that part of justice which has to do with the careful attention which ought to be paid to the gods; and that what has to do with the careful attention which ought to be paid to men is the remaining part of justice.

Socr.: And I think that your answer is a good one, Euthyphro. But there is one little point about which I still want to hear more. I do not yet understand what the careful attention is to which you refer. I suppose you do not mean that the attention which we pay to the gods is like the attention which we pay to other things. We say, for instance, do we not, that not everyone knows how to take care of horses, but only the trainer of horses?

Euth.: Certainly.

Socr.: For I suppose that the skill that is concerned with horses is the art of taking care of horses.

Euth.: Yes.

Socr.: And not everyone understands the care of dogs, but only the huntsman.

Euth.: True.

Socr.: For I suppose that the huntsman's skill is the art of taking care of dogs.

Euth.: Yes.

Socr.: And the herdsman's skill is the art of taking care of cattle.

Euth.: Certainly.

Socr.: And you say that piety and righteousness are taking care of the gods, Euthyphro?

Euth.: I do.

Socr.: Well, then, has not all care the same object? Is it not for the good and benefit of that on which it is bestowed? For instance, you see that horses are benefited and improved when they are cared for by the art which is concerned with them. Is it not so?

Euth.:   Yes, I think so.

Socr.:   And dogs are benefited and improved by the huntsman's art, and cattle by the herdsman's, are they not? And the same is always true. Or do you think care is ever meant to harm that which is cared for?

Euth.:   No, indeed; certainly not.

Socr.:   But to benefit it?

Euth.:   Of course.

Socr.:   Then is piety, which is our care for the gods, intended to benefit the gods, or to improve them? Should you allow that you make any of the gods better when you do a pious action?

Euth.:   No indeed; certainly not.

Socr.:   No, I am quite sure that that is not your meaning, Euthyphro. It was for that reason that I asked you what you meant by the careful attention which ought to be paid to the gods. I thought that you did not mean that.

Euth.:   You were right, Socrates. I do not mean that.

Socr.:   Good. Then what sort of attention to the gods will piety be?

Euth.:   The sort of attention, Socrates, slaves pay to their masters.

Socr.:   I understand; then it is a kind of service to the gods?

Euth.:   Certainly.

Socr.:   Can you tell me what result the art which services a doctor serves to produce? Is it not health?

Euth.:   Yes.

Socr.:   And what result does the art which serves a shipwright serve to produce?

Euth.:   A ship, of course, Socrates.

Socr.:   The result of the art which serves a builder is a house, is it not?

Euth.:   Yes.

Socr.:   Then tell me, my good friend: What result will the art which serves the gods serve to produce? You must know, seeing that you say that you know more about divine things than any other man.

Euth.:   Well, that is true, Socrates.

Socr.:   Then tell me, I beg you, what is that grand result which the gods use our services to produce?

Euth.:   There are many notable results, Socrates.

Socr.:   So are those, my friend, which a general produces. Yet it is easy to see that the crowning result of them all is victory in war, is it not?

Euth.:   Of course.

Socr.:   And, I take it, the farmer produces many notable results; yet the principal result of them all is that he makes the earth produce food.

Euth.:   Certainly.

Socr.:   Well, then, what is the principal result of the many notable results which the gods produce?

Euth.:   I told you just now, Socrates, that accurate knowledge of all these matters is not easily obtained. However, broadly I say this: if any man knows that his words and actions in prayer and sacrifice are acceptable to the gods, that is what is pious; and it preserves the state, as it does private families. But the opposite of what is acceptable to the gods is sacrilegious, and this it is that undermines and destroys everything.

Socr.: Certainly, Euthyphro, if you had wished, you could have answered my main question in far fewer words. But you are evidently not anxious to teach me. Just now, when you were on the very point of telling me what I want to know, you stopped short. If you had gone on then, I should have learned from you clearly enough by this time what piety is. But now I am asking you questions, and must follow wherever you lead me; so tell me, what is it that you mean by piety and impiety? Do you not mean a science of prayer and sacrifice?

Euth.: I do.

Socr.: To sacrifice is to give to the gods, and to pray is to ask of them, is it not?

Euth.: It is, Socrates.

Socr.: Then you say that piety is the science of asking of the gods and giving to them?

Euth.: You understand my meaning exactly, Socrates.

Socr.: Yes, for I am eager to share your wisdom, Euthyphro, and so I am all attention; nothing that you say will fall to the ground. But tell me, what is this service of the gods? You say it is to ask of them, and to give to them?

Euth.: I do.

Socr.: Then, to ask rightly will be to ask of them what we stand in need of from them, will it not?

Euth.: Naturally.

Socr.: And to give rightly will be to give back to them what they stand in need of from us? It would not be very skillful to make a present to a man of something that he has no need of.

Euth.: True, Socrates.

Socr.: Then piety, Euthyphro, will be the art of carrying on business between gods and men?

Euth.: Yes, if you like to call it so.

Socr.: But I like nothing except what is true. But tell me, how are the gods benefited by the gifts which they receive from us? What they give is plain enough. Every good thing that we have is their gift. But how are they benefited by what we give them? Have we the advantage over them in these business transactions to such an extent that we receive from them all the good things we possess, and we give them nothing in return?

Euth.: But do you suppose, Socrates, that the gods are benefited by the gifts which they receive from us?

Socr.: But what *are* these gifts, Euthyphro, that we give the gods?

Euth.: What do you think but honor and praise, and, as I have said, what is acceptable to them.

Socr.:   Then piety, Euthyphro, is acceptable to the gods, but it is not profitable to them nor loved by them?

Euth.:   I think that nothing is more loved by them.

Socr.:   Then I see that piety means that which is loved by the gods.

Euth.:   Most certainly.

Socr.:   After that, shall you be surprised to find that your statements move about instead of staying where you put them? Shall you accuse me of being the Daedalus that makes them move, when you yourself are far more skillful than Daedalus was, and make them go round in a circle? Do you not see that our statement has come round to where it was before? Surely you remember that we have already seen that piety and what is pleasing to the gods are quite different things. Do you not remember?

Euth.:   I do.

Socr.:   And now do you not see that you say that what the gods love is pious? But does not what the gods love come to the same thing as what is pleasing to the gods?

Euth.:   Certainly.

Socr.:   Then either our former conclusion was wrong or, if it was right, we are wrong now.

Euth.:   So it seems.

Socr.:   Then we must begin again and inquire what piety is. I do not mean to give in until I have found out. Do not regard me as unworthy; give your whole mind to the question, and this time tell me the truth. For if anyone knows it, it is you; and you are a Proteus whom I must not let go until you have told me. It cannot be that you would ever have undertaken to prosecute your aged father for the murder of a laboring man unless you had known exactly what piety and impiety are. You would have feared to risk the anger of the gods, in case you should be doing wrong, and you would have been afraid of what men would say. But now I am sure that you think that you know exactly what is pious and what is not; so tell me, my good Euthyphro, and do not conceal from me what you think.

Euth.:   Another time, then, Socrates. I am in a hurry now, and it is time for me to be off.

Socr.:   What are you doing, my friend! Will you go away and destroy all my hopes of learning from you what is pious and what is not, and so of escaping Meletus? I meant to explain to him that now Euthyphro has made me wise about divine things, and that I no longer in my ignorance speak carelessly about them or introduce reforms. And then I was going to promise him to live a better life for the future.

The Apology

Plato

CHARACTERS

Socrates

Meletus

Scene—The Court of Justice

Socrates: I do not know what impression my accusers have made upon you, Athenians. But I do know that they nearly made me forget who I was, so persuasive were they. And yet they have scarcely spoken one single word of truth. Of all their many falsehoods, the one which astonished me most was their saying that I was a clever speaker, and that you must be careful not to let me deceive you. I thought that it was most shameless of them not to be ashamed to talk in that way. For as soon as I open my mouth they will be refuted, and I shall prove that I am not a clever speaker in any way at all—unless, indeed, by a clever speaker they mean someone who speaks the truth. If that is their meaning, I agree with them that I am an orator not to be compared with them. My accusers, I repeat, have said little or nothing that is true, but from me you shall hear the whole truth. Certainly you will not hear a speech, Athenians, dressed up, like theirs, with fancy words and phrases. I will say to you what I have to say, without artifice, and I shall use the first words which come to mind, for I believe that what I have to say is just, so let none of you expect anything else. Indeed, my friends, it would hardly be right for me, at my age, to come before you like a schoolboy with his concocted phrases. But there is one thing, Athenians, which I do most earnestly beg and entreat of you. Do not be surprised and do not interrupt with shouts if in my defense I speak in the same way that I am accustomed to speak in the market place, at the tables of the money-changers, where many of you have heard me, and elsewhere. The truth is this: I am more than seventy, and this is the first time that I have ever come before a law court; thus your manner of speech here is quite strange to me. If I had really been a stranger, you would

From *Euthyphro, Apology, Crito,* trans. F. J. Church (Indianapolis: The Library of Liberal Arts, Bobbs-Merrill 1956), pp. 21-49. Reprinted by permission of the publisher.

have forgiven me for speaking in the language and the manner of my native country. And so now I ask you to grant me what I think I have a right to claim. Never mind the manner of my speech—it may be superior or it may be inferior to the usual manner. Give your whole attention to the question, whether what I say is just or not? That is what is required of a good judge, as speaking the truth is required of a good orator.

I have to defend myself, Athenians, first against the older false accusations of my old accusers, and then against the more recent ones of my present accusers. For many men have been accusing me to you, and for very many years, who have not spoken a word of truth; and I fear them more than I fear Anytus and his associates, formidable as they are. But, my friends, the others are still more formidable, since they got hold of most of you when you were children and have been more persistent in accusing me untruthfully, persuading you that there is a certain Socrates, a wise man, who speculates about the heavens, who investigates things that are beneath the earth, and who can make the worse argument appear the stronger. These men, Athenians, who spread abroad this report are the accusers whom I fear; for their hearers think that persons who pursue such inquiries never believe in the gods. Besides they are many, their attacks have been going on for a long time, and they spoke to you when you were most ready to believe them, since you were all young, and some of you were children. And there was no one to answer them when they attacked me. The most preposterous thing of all is that I do not even know their names: I cannot tell you who they are except when one happens to be a comic poet. But all the rest who have persuaded you, from motives of resentment and prejudice, and sometimes, it may be, from conviction, are hardest to cope with. For I cannot call any one of them forward in court to cross-examine him. I have, as it were, simply to spar with shadows in my defense, and to put questions which there is no one to answer. I ask you, therefore, to believe that, as I say, I have been attacked by two kinds of accusers—first, by Meletus and his associates, and, then, by those older ones of whom I have spoken. And, with your leave, I will defend myself first against my old accusers, since you heard their accusations first, and they were much more compelling than my present accusers are.

Well, I must make my defense, Athenians, and try in the short time allowed me to remove the prejudice which you have been so long a time acquiring. I hope that I may manage to do this, if it be best for you and for me, and that my defense may be successful; but I am quite aware of the nature of my task, and I know that it is a difficult one. Be the outcome, however, as is pleasing to god, I must obey the law and make my defense.

Let us begin from the beginning, then, and ask what is the

accusation that has given rise to the prejudice against me, on which Meletus relied when he brought his indictment. What is the prejudice which my enemies have been spreading about me? I must assume that they are formally accusing me, and read their indictment. It would run somewhat in this fashion: "Socrates is guilty of engaging in inquiries into things beneath the earth and in the heavens, of making the weaker argument appear the stronger, and of teaching others these same things." That is what they say. And in the comedy of Aristophanes you yourselves saw a man called Socrates swinging around in a basket and saying that he walked on air, and sputtering a great deal of nonsense about matters of which I understand nothing at all. I do not mean to disparage that kind of knowledge if there is anyone who is wise about these matters. I trust Meletus may never be able to prosecute me for that. But the truth is, Athenians, I have nothing to do with these matters, and almost all of you are yourselves my witnesses of this. I beg all of you who have ever heard me discussing, and they are many, to inform your neighbors and tell them if any of you have ever heard me discussing such matters at all. That will show you that the other common statements about me are as false as this one.

But the fact is that not one of these is true. And if you have heard that I undertake to educate men, and make money by so doing, that is not true either, though I think that it would be a fine thing to be able to educate men, as Gorgias of Leontini, and Prodicus of Ceos, and Hippias of Elis do. For each of them, my friends, can go into any city, and persuade the young men to leave the society of their fellow citizens, with any of whom they might associate for nothing, and to be only too glad to be allowed to pay money for the privilege of associating with themselves. And I believe that there is another wise man from Paros residing in Athens at this moment. I happened to meet Callias, the son of Hipponicus, a man who has spent more money on sophists than everyone else put together. So I said to him (he has two sons), "Callias, if your two sons had been foals or calves, we could have hired a trainer for them who would have trained them to excel in doing what they are naturally capable of. He would have been either a groom or a farmer. But whom do you intend to take to train them, seeing that they are men? Who understands the excellence which a man and citizen is capable of attaining? I suppose that you must have thought of this, because you have sons. Is there such a person or not?" "Certainly there is," he replied. "Who is he," said I, "and where does he come from, and what is his fee?" "Evenus, Socrates," he replied, "from Paros, five minae." Then I thought that Evenus was a fortunate person if he really understood this art and could teach so cleverly. If I had possessed knowledge of that kind, I should have been conceited and disdainful. But, Athenians, the truth is that I do not possess it.

Perhaps some of you may reply: "But, Socrates, what is the trouble with you? What has given rise to these prejudices against you? You must have been doing something out of the ordinary. All these rumors and reports of you would never have arisen if you had not been doing something different from other men. So tell us what it is, that we may not give our verdict arbitrarily." I think that that is a fair question, and I will try to explain to you what it is that has raised these prejudices against me and given me this reputation. Listen, then. Some of you, perhaps, will think that I am joking, but I assure you that I will tell you the whole truth. I have gained this reputation, Athenians, simply by reason of a certain wisdom. But by what kind of wisdom? It is by just that wisdom which is perhaps human wisdom. In that, it may be, I am really wise. But the men of whom I was speaking just now must be wise in a wisdom which is greater than human wisdom, or else I cannot describe it, for certainly I know nothing of it myself, and if any man says that I do, he lies and speaks to arouse prejudice against me. Do not interrupt me with shouts, Athenians, even if you think that I am boasting. What I am going to say is not my own statement. I will tell you who says it, and he is worthy of your respect. I will bring the god of Delphi to be the witness of my wisdom, if it is wisdom at all, and of its nature. You remember Chaerephon. From youth upwards he was my comrade; and also a partisan of your democracy, sharing your recent exile and returning with you. You remember, too, Chaerephon's character—how impulsive he was in carrying through whatever he took in hand. Once he went to Delphi and ventured to put this question to the oracle—I entreat you again, my friends, not to interrupt me with your shouts—he asked if there was anyone who was wiser than I. The priestess answered that there was no one. Chaerephon himself is dead, but his brother here will witness to what I say.

Now see why I tell you this. I am going to explain to you how the prejudice against me has arisen. When I heard of the oracle I began to reflect: What can the god mean by this riddle? I know very well that I am not wise, even in the smallest degree. Then what can he mean by saying that I am the wisest of men? It cannot be that he is speaking falsely, for he is a god and cannot lie. For a long time I was at a loss to understand his meaning. Then, very reluctantly, I turned to investigate it in this manner: I went to a man who was reputed to be wise, thinking that there, if anywhere, I should prove the answer wrong, and meaning to point out to the oracle its mistake, and to say, "You said that I was the wisest of men, but this man is wiser than I am." So I examined the man— I need not tell you his name, he was a politician—but this was the result, Athenians. When I conversed with him I came to see that, though a great many persons, and most of all he himself, thought that he was wise, yet he was not wise. Then I tried to prove to him that he was not wise, though he fancied that he was. By so doing I made him indignant, and many of the bystanders. So when I went away, I thought to myself, "I am wiser than this man: neither of us knows anything that is really worth knowing, but he thinks that he has knowledge when he has not, while I, having no knowledge, do not think that I have. I seem, at any rate, to be a little wiser than he is on this point: I do not think that I know what I do not know." Next I went to another man who was reputed to be still wiser than the last, with exactly the same result. And there again I made him, and many other men, indignant.

Then I went on to one man after another, realizing that I was arousing indignation every day, which caused me much pain and anxiety. Still I thought that I must set the god's command above everything. So I had to go to every man who seemed to possess any knowledge, and investigate the meaning of the oracle. Athenians, I must tell you the truth; I swear, this was the result of the investigation which I made at the god's command: I found that the men whose reputation for wisdom stood highest were nearly the most lacking in it, while others who were looked down on as common people were much more intelligent. Now I must describe to you the wanderings which I undertook, like Herculean labors, to prove the oracle irrefutable. After the politicians, I went to the poets, tragic, dithyrambic, and others, thinking that there I should find myself manifestly more ignorant than they. So I took up the poems on which I thought that they had spent most pains, and asked them what they meant, hoping at the same time to learn something from them. I am ashamed to tell you the truth, my friends, but I must say it. Almost any one of the bystanders could have talked about the works of these poets better than the poets themselves. So I soon found that it is not by wisdom that the poets create their works, but by a certain instinctive inspiration, like soothsayers and prophets, who say many fine things, but understand nothing of what they say. The poets seemed to me to be in a similar situation. And at the same time I perceived that, because of their poetry, they thought that they were the wisest of men in other matters too, which they were not. So I went away again, thinking that I had the same advantage over the poets that I had over the politicians.

Finally, I went to the artisans, for I knew very well that I possessed no knowledge at all worth speaking of, and I was sure that I should find that they knew many fine things. And in that I was not mistaken. They knew what I did not know, and so far they were wiser than I. But, Athenians, it seemed to me that the skilled artisans had the same failing as the poets. Each of them believed himself to be extremely wise in matters of the greatest importance because he was skillful in his own art: and this presumption of theirs obscured their real wisdom. So I asked myself, on behalf of the oracle, whether I would choose to remain as I was, without either their wisdom or their ignorance, or to possess both, as they did. And I answered to myself and to the oracle that it was better for me to remain as I was.

From this examination, Athenians, has arisen much fierce and bitter indignation, and as a result a great many prejudices about me. People say that I am "a wise man." For the bystanders always think that I am wise myself in any matter wherein I refute another. But, gentlemen, I believe that the god is really wise, and that by this oracle he meant that human wisdom is worth little or nothing. I do not think that he meant that Socrates was wise. He only made use of my name, and took me as an example, as though he would say to men, "He among you is the wisest who, like Socrates, knows that his wisdom is really worth nothing at all." Therefore I still go about testing and examining every man whom I think wise, whether he be a citizen or a stranger, as the god has commanded me. Whenever I find that he is not wise, I point out to him, on the god's behalf, that he is not wise. I am so busy in this pursuit that I have never had leisure to take any part worth mentioning in public matters or to look after my private affairs. I am in great poverty as the result of my service to the god.

Besides this, the young men who follow me about, who are the sons of wealthy persons and have the most leisure, take pleasure in hearing men cross-examined. They often imitate me among themselves; then they try their hands at cross-examining other people. And, I imagine, they find plenty of men who think that they know a great deal when in fact they know little or nothing. Then the persons who are cross-examined get angry with me instead of with themselves, and say that Socrates is an abomination and corrupts the young. When they are asked, "Why, what does he do? What does he teach?" they do not know what to say. Not to seem at a loss, they repeat the stock charges against all philosophers, and allege that he investigates things in the air and under the earth, and that he teaches people to disbelieve in the gods, and to make the worse argument appear the stronger. For, I suppose, they would not like to confess the truth, which is that they are shown up as ignorant pretenders to knowledge that they do not possess. So they have been filling your ears with their bitter prejudices for a long time, for they are ambitious, energetic, and numerous; and they speak vigorously and persuasively against me. Relying on this, Meletus, Anytus, and Lycon have attacked me. Meletus is indignant with me on behalf of the poets, Anytus on behalf of the artisans and politicians, and Lycon on behalf of the orators. And so, as I said at the beginning, I shall be surprised if I am able, in the short time allowed me for my defense, to remove from your minds this prejudice which has grown so strong. What I have told you, Athenians, is the truth: I neither conceal nor do I suppress anything, trivial or important. Yet I know that it is just this outspokenness which rouses indignation. But that is only a proof that my words are true, and that the prejudice against me, and the causes of it, are what I have said. And whether you investigate them now or hereafter, you will find that they are so.

What I have said must suffice as my defense against the charges of my first accusers. I will try next to defend myself against Meletus, that "good patriot," as he calls himself, and my later accusers. Let us assume that they are a new set of accusers, and read their indictment, as we did in the case of the others. It runs thus: Socrates is guilty of corrupting the youth, and of believing not in the gods whom the state believes in, but in other new divinities. Such is the accusation. Let us examine each point in it separately. Meletus says that I am guilty of corrupting the youth. But I say, Athenians, that he is guilty of playing a solemn joke by casually bringing men to trial, and pretending to have a solemn interest in matters to which he has never given a moment's thought. Now I will try to prove to you that this is so.

Come here, Meletus. Is it not a fact that you think it very important that the young should be as good as possible?

Meletus: It is.

Socrates: Come, then, tell the judges who improves them. You care so much, you must know. You are accusing me, and bringing me to trial, because, as you say, you have discovered that I am the corrupter of the youth. Come now, reveal to the gentlemen who improves them. You see, Meletus, you have nothing to say; you are silent. But don't you think that this is shameful? Is not your silence a conclusive proof of what I say—that you have never cared? Come, tell us, my good man, who makes the young better?

Mel.: The laws.

Socr.: That, my friend, is not my question. What man improves the young, who begins by knowing the laws?

Mel.: The judges here, Socrates.

Socr.: What do you mean, Meletus? Can they educate the young and improve them?

Mel.: Certainly.

Socr.: All of them? Or only some of them?

Mel.: All of them.

Socr.: By Hera, that is good news! Such a large supply of benefactors! And do the members of the audience here improve them, or not?

Mel.: They do.

Socr.: And do the councilors?

Mel.: Yes.

Socr.: Well, then, Meletus, do the members of the assembly corrupt the young or do they again all improve them?

Mel.: They, too, improve them.

Socr.: Then all the Athenians, apparently, make the young into good men except me, and I alone corrupt them. Is that your meaning?

Mel.:   Certainly, that is my meaning.

Socr.:   You have discovered me to be most unfortunate. Now tell me: do you think that the same holds good in the case of horses? Does one man do them harm and everyone else improve them? On the contrary, is it not one man only, or a very few—namely, those who are skilled with horses—who can improve them, while the majority of men harm them if they use them and have anything to do with them? It is not so, Meletus, both with horses and with every other animal? Of course it is, whether you and Anytus say yes or no. The young would certainly be very fortunate if only one man corrupted them, and everyone else did them good. The truth is, Meletus, you prove conclusively that you have never thought about the young in your life. You exhibit your carelessness in not caring for the very matters about which you are prosecuting me.

Now be so good as to tell us, Meletus, is it better to live among good citizens or bad ones? Answer, my friend. I am not asking you at all a difficult question. Do not the bad harm their associates and the good do them good?

Mel.:   Yes.

Socr.:   Is there anyone who would rather be injured than benefited by his companions? Answer, my good man; you are obliged by the law to answer. Does anyone like to be injured?

Mel.:   Certainly not.

Socr.:   Well, then, are you prosecuting me for corrupting the young and making them worse, voluntarily or involuntarily?

Mel.:   For doing it voluntarily.

Socr.:   What, Meletus? Do you mean to say that you, who are so much younger than I, are yet so much wiser than I that you know that bad citizens always do evil, and that good citizens do good, to those with whom they come in contact, while I am so extraordinarily ignorant as not to know that, if I make any of my companions evil, he will probably injure me in some way? And you allege that I do this voluntarily? You will not make me believe that, nor any-one else either, I should think. Either I do not corrupt the young at all or, if I do, I do so involuntarily, so that you are lying in either case. And if I corrupt them involuntarily, the law does not call upon you to prosecute me for an error which is involuntary, but to take me aside privately and reprove and educate me. For, of course, I shall cease from doing wrong involuntarily, as soon as I know that I have been doing wrong. But you avoided associating with me and educating me; instead you bring me up before the court, where the law sends persons, not for education, but for punishment.

The truth is, Athenians, as I said, it is quite clear that Meletus has never cared at all about these matters. However, now tell us, Meletus, how do you say that I corrupt the young? Clearly, according to your indictment, by teaching them not to believe in the gods the state believes in, but other new divinities instead. You mean that I corrupt the young by that teaching, do you not?

Mel.: Yes, most certainly I mean that.

Socr.: Then in the name of these gods of whom we are speaking, explain yourself a little more clearly to me and to these gentlemen here. I cannot understand what you mean. Do you mean that I teach the young to believe in some gods, but not in the gods of the state? Do you accuse me of teaching them to believe in strange gods? If that is your meaning, I myself believe in some gods, and my crime is not that of complete atheism. Or do you mean that I teach other people not to believe in them either?

Mel.: I mean that you do not believe in the gods in any way whatever.

Socr.: You amaze me, Meletus! Why do you say that? Do you mean that I believe neither the sun nor the moon to be gods, like other men?

Mel.: I swear he does not, judges. He says that the sun is a stone, and the moon earth.

Socr.: My dear Meletus, do you think that you are prosecuting Anaxagoras? You must have a very poor opinion of these men, and think them illiterate, if you imagine that they do not know that the works of Anaxagoras of Clazomenae are full of these doctrines. And so young men learn these things from me, when they can often buy them in the theater for a drachma at most, and laugh at Socrates were he to pretend that these doctrines, which are very peculiar doctrines, too, were his own. But please tell me, do you really think that I do not believe in the gods at all?

Mel.: Most certainly I do. You are a complete atheist.

Socr.: No one believes that, Meletus, not even you yourself. It seems to me, Athenians, that Meletus is very insolent and reckless, and that he is prosecuting me simply out of insolence, recklessness, and youthful bravado. For he seems to be testing me, by asking me a riddle that has no answer. "Will this wise Socrates," he says to himself, "see that I am joking and contradicting myself? Or shall I deceive him and everyone else who hears me?" Meletus seems to me to contradict himself in his indictment: it is as if he were to say, "Socrates is guilty of not believing in the gods, but believes in the gods." This is joking.

Now, my friends, let us see why I think that this is his meaning. You must answer me, Meletus, and you, Athenians, must remember the request which I made to you at the start, and not interrupt me with shouts if I talk in my usual manner.

Is there any man, Meletus, who believes in the existence of things pertaining to men and not in the existence of men? Make him answer the question, gentlemen, without these interruptions. Is there any man who believes in the existence of horsemanship and not in the existence of horses? Or in flute playing and not in flute players? There is not, my friend. If you will not answer, I will tell both you and the judges. But you must answer my next question. Is there any man who believes in the existence of divine things and not in the existence of divinities?

Mel.: There is not.

Socr.: I am very glad that these gentlemen have managed to extract an answer from you. Well then, you say that I believe in divine things, whether they be old or new, and that I teach others to believe in them. At any rate, according to your statement, I believe in divine things. That you have sworn in your indictment. But if I believe in divine things, I suppose it follows necessarily that I believe in divinities. Is it not so? It is. I assume that you grant that, as you do not answer. But do we not believe that divinities are either gods themselves or the children of the gods? Do you admit that?

Mel.: I do.

Socr.: Then you admit that I believe in divinities. Now, if these divinities are gods, then, as I say, you are joking and asking a riddle, and asserting that I do not believe in the gods, and at the same time that I do, since I believe in divinities. But if these divinities are the illegitimate children of the gods, either by the nymphs or by other mothers, as they are said to be, then, I ask, what man could believe in the existence of the children of the gods, and not in the existence of the gods? That would be as absurd as believing in the existence of the offspring of horses and asses, and not in the existence of horses and asses. You must have indicted me in this manner, Meletus, either to test me or because you could not find any act of injustice that you could accuse me of with truth. But you will never contrive to persuade any man with any sense at all that a belief in divine things and things of the gods does not necessarily involve a belief in divinities, and in the gods.

But in truth, Athenians, I do not think that I need say very much to prove that I have not committed the act of injustice for which Meletus is prosecuting me. What I have said is enough to prove that. But be assured it is certainly true, as I have already told you, that I have aroused much indignation. That is what will cause my condemnation if I am condemned; not Meletus nor Anytus either, but that prejudice and resentment of the multitude which have been the destruction of many good men before me, and I think will be so again. There is no prospect that I shall be the last victim.

Perhaps someone will say: "Are you not ashamed, Socrates, of leading a life which is very likely now to cause your death?" I should answer him with justice, and say: "My friend, if you think that a man of any worth at all ought to reckon the chances of life and death when he acts, or that he ought to think of anything but whether he is acting justly or unjustly, and as a good or a bad man would act, you are mistaken. According to you, the demigods who died at Troy would be foolish, and among them Achilles, who thought nothing of danger when the alternative was disgrace. For when his mother—and she was a goddess—addressed him, when he was resolved to slay Hector, in this fashion, 'My son, if you avenge the death of your comrade Patroclus and slay Hector, you will die yourself, for fate awaits you next after Hector.' When he heard this, he scorned danger and death; he feared much more to live a coward and not to avenge his friend. 'Let me punish the evildoer and afterwards die,' he said, 'that I may not remain here by the beaked ships jeered at, encumbering the earth.' " Do you suppose that he thought of danger or of death? For this, Athenians, I believe to be the truth. Wherever a man's station is, whether he has chosen it of his own will, or whether he has been placed at it by his commander, there it is his duty to remain and face the danger without thinking of death or of any other thing except disgrace.

When the generals whom you chose to command me, Athenians, assigned me my station during the battles of Potidaea, Amphipolis, and Delium, I remained where they stationed me and ran the risk of death, like other men. It would be very strange conduct on my part if I were to desert my station now from fear of death or of any other thing when the god has commanded me—as I am persuaded that he has done—to spend my life in searching for wisdom, and in examining myself and others. That would indeed be a very strange thing. Then certainly I might with justice be brought to trial for not believing in the gods, for I should be disobeying the oracle, and fearing death and thinking myself wise when I was not wise. For to fear death, my friends, is only to think ourselves wise without really being wise, for it is to think that we know what we do not know. For no one knows whether death may not be the greatest good that can happen to man. But men fear it as if they knew quite well that it was the greatest of evils. And what is this but that shameful ignorance of thinking that we know what we do not know? In this matter, too, my friends, perhaps I am different from the multitude. And if I were to claim to be at all wiser than others, it would be because, not knowing very much about the other world, I do not think I know. But I do know very well that it is evil and disgraceful to do an unjust act, and to disobey my superior, whether man or god. I will never do what I know to be evil, and shrink in fear from what I do not know to be good or evil. Even if you acquit me now, and do not listen to Anytus' argument that, if I am to be acquitted, I ought never to have been brought to trial at all, and that, as it is, you are bound to put me to death because, as he said, if I escape, all your sons will be utterly corrupted by practicing what Socrates teaches. If you were therefore to say to me, "Socrates, this time we will not listen to Anytus. We will let you go, but on the condition that you give up this investigation of yours, and philosophy. If you are found following these pursuits again, you shall die." I say, if you offered to let me go on these terms, I should reply: "Athenians, I hold you in the highest regard and affection, but I will be persuaded by the god rather than you. As long as I have breath and strength I will not give up philosophy and exhorting you and declaring the truth to every one of you whom I meet, saying, as I am accustomed, 'My good friend, you are a citizen of Athens, a city which is very great and very famous for its wisdom and power—are you not ashamed of caring so much for the making of money and for fame and prestige, when you neither think nor care about wisdom and truth and the improvement of your soul?' " If he disputes my words and says that he does care about these things, I shall not at once release him and go away: I shall question him and cross-examine him and test him. If I think that he has not attained excellence, though he says that he has, I shall reproach him for undervaluing the most valuable things, and overvaluing those that are less valuable. This I shall do to everyone whom I meet, young or old, citizen or stranger, but especially to citizens, since they are more closely related to me. This, you must recognize, the god has commanded me to do. And I think that no greater good has ever befallen you in the state than my service to the god. For I spend my whole life in going about and persuading you all to give your first and greatest care to the improvement of your souls, and not till you have done that to think of your bodies or your wealth. And I tell you that wealth does not bring excellence, but that wealth, and every other good thing which men have, whether in public or in private, comes from excellence. If then I corrupt the youth by this teaching, these things must be harmful. But if any man says that I teach anything else, there is nothing in what he says. And therefore, Athenians, I say, whether you are persuaded by Anytus or not, whether you acquit me or not, I shall not change my way of life; no, not if I have to die for it many times.

Do not interrupt me, Athenians, with your shouts. Remember the request which I made to you, and do not interrupt my words. I think that it will profit you to hear them. I am going to say something more to you, at which you may be inclined to protest, but do not do that. Be sure that if you put me to death, I who am what I have told you that I am, you will do yourselves more harm than me. Meletus and Anytus can do me no harm: that is impossible, for I am sure it is not allowed that a good man be injured by a worse. He may indeed kill me, or drive me into exile, or deprive me of my civil rights. Perhaps Meletus and others think those things great evils. But I do not think so. I think it is a much greater evil to do what he is doing now, and to try to put a man to death unjustly. And now, Athenians, I am not arguing in my own defense at all, as you might expect me to do, but rather in yours in order you may not make a mistake about the gift of the god to you by condemning me. For if you put me to death, you will not easily find another who, if I may use a ludicrous comparison, clings to the state as a sort of gadfly to a horse that is large and well-bred but rather sluggish because of its size, so that it needs to be aroused. It seems to me that the god has attached me like that to the state, for I am constantly alighting upon you at every point to arouse, persuade, and reproach each of you all day long. You will not easily find anyone else, my friends, to fill my place; and if you are persuaded by me, you will spare my life. You are indignant, as drowsy persons are when they are awakened, and, of course, if you are persuaded by Anytus, you could easily kill me with a single blow, and then sleep on undisturbed for the rest of your lives, unless the god in his care for you sends another to arouse you. And you may easily see that it is the god who has given me to your city; for it is not human, the way in which I have neglected all my own interests and allowed my private affairs to be neglected for so many years, while occupying myself unceasingly in your interests, going to each of you privately, like a father or an elder brother, trying to persuade him to care for human excellence. There would have been a reason for it, if I had gained any advantage by this, or if I had been paid for my exhortations; but you see yourselves that my accusers, though they accuse me of everything else without shame, have not had the shamelessness to say that I ever either exacted or demanded payment. To that they have no witness. And I think that I have sufficient witness to the truth of what I say—my poverty.

Perhaps it may seem strange to you that, though I go about giving this advice privately and meddling in others' affairs, yet I do not venture to come forward in the assembly and advise the state. You have often heard me speak of my reason for this, and in many places: it is that I have a certain divine guide, which is what Meletus has caricatured in his indictment. I have had it from childhood. It is a kind of voice which, whenever I hear it, always turns me back from something which I was going to do, but never urges me to act. It is this which forbids me to take part in politics. And I think it does well to forbid me. For, Athenians, it is quite certain that, if I had attempted to take part in politics, I should have perished at once and long ago without doing any good either to you or to myself. And do not be indignant with me for telling the truth. There is no man who will preserve his life for long, either in Athens or elsewhere, if he firmly opposes the multitude, and tries to prevent the commission of much injustice and illegality in the state. He who would really fight for justice must do so as a private citizen, not as a political figure, if he is to preserve his life, even for a short time.

I will prove to you that this is so by very strong evidence, not by mere words, but by what you value more—actions. Listen, then, to what has happened to me, that you may know that there is no man who could make me consent to commit an unjust act from the fear of death, but that I would perish at once rather than give way. What I am going to tell you may be commonplace in the law court; nevertheless, it is true. The only office that I ever held in the state, Athenians, was that of councilor. When you wished to try the ten admirals who did not rescue their men after the battle of Arginusae as a group, which was illegal, as you all came to think afterwards, the executive committee was composed of members of the tribe Antiochis, to which I belong. On that occasion I alone of the committee members opposed your illegal action and gave my vote against you. The orators were ready to impeach me and arrest me; and you were clamoring and urging them on with your shouts. But I thought that I ought to face the danger, with law and justice on my side, rather than join with you in your unjust proposal, from fear of imprisonment or death. That was when the state was democratic. When the oligarchy came in, The Thirty sent for me, with four others, to the council-chamber, and ordered us to bring Leon the Salaminian from Salamis, that they might put him to death. They were in the habit of frequently giving similar orders to many others, wishing to implicate as many as possible in their crimes. But then I again proved, not by mere words, but by my actions, that, if I may speak bluntly, I do not care a straw for death; but that I do care very much indeed about not doing anything unjust or impious. That government with all its power did not terrify me into doing anything unjust. When we left the council-chamber, the other four went over to Salamis and brought Leon across to Athens; I went home. And if the rule of The Thirty had not been overthrown soon afterwards, I should very likely have been put to death for what I did then. Many of you will be my witnesses in this matter.

Now do you think that I could have remained alive all these years if I had taken part in public affairs, and had always maintained the cause of justice like a good man, and had held it a paramount duty, as it is, to do so? Certainly not, Athenians, nor could any other man. But throughout my whole life, both in private and in public, whenever I have had to take part in public affairs, you will find I have always been the same and have never yielded unjustly to anyone; no, not to those whom my enemies falsely assert to have been my pupils. But I was never anyone's teacher. I have never withheld myself from anyone, young or old, who was anxious to hear me converse while I was making my investigation; neither do I converse for payment, and refuse to converse without payment. I am ready to ask questions of rich and poor alike, and if any man wishes to answer me, and then listen to what I have to say, he may. And I cannot justly be charged with causing these men to turn out good or bad, for I never either taught or professed to teach any of them any knowledge whatever. And if any man asserts that he ever learned or heard anything from me in private which everyone else did not hear as well as he, be sure that he does not speak the truth.

Why is it, then, that people delight in spending so much time in my company? You have heard why, Athenians. I told you the whole truth when I said that they delight in hearing me examine persons who think that they are wise when they are not wise. It is certainly very amusing to listen to. And, as I have said, the god has commanded me to examine men, in oracles and in dreams and in every way in which the divine will was ever declared to man. This is the truth, Athenians, and if it were not the truth, it would be easily refuted. For if it were really the case that I have already corrupted some of the young men, and am now corrupting others, surely some of them, finding as they grew older that I had given them bad advice in their youth, would have come forward today to accuse me and take their revenge. Or if they were unwilling to do so themselves, surely their relatives, their fathers or brothers, or others, would, if I had done them any harm, have remembered it and taken their revenge. Certainly I see many of them in court. Here is Crito, of my own district and of my own age, the father of Critobulus; here is Lysanias of Sphettus, the father of Aeschines; here is also Antiphon of Cephisus, the father of Epigenes. Then here are others whose brothers have spent their time in my company—Nicostratus, the son of Theozotides and brother of Theodotus—and Theodotus is dead, so he at least cannot entreat his brother to be silent; here is Paralus, the son of Demodocus and the brother of Theages; here is Adeimantus, the son of Ariston, whose brother is Plato here; and Aeantodorus, whose brother is Aristodorus. And I can name many others to you, some of whom Meletus ought to have called as witnesses in the course of his own speech; but if he forgot to call them then, let him call them now—I will yield the floor to him—and tell us if he has any such evidence. No, on the contrary, my friends, you will find all these men ready to support me, the corrupter who has injured their relatives, as Meletus and Anytus call me. Those of them who have been already corrupted might perhaps have some reason for supporting me, but what reason can their relatives have who are grown up, and who are uncorrupted, except the reason of truth and justice—that they know very well that Meletus is lying, and that I am speaking the truth?

Well, my friends, this, and perhaps more like this, is pretty much all I have to offer in my defense. There may be some one among you who will be indignant when he remembers how, even in a less important trial than this, he begged and entreated the judges, with many tears, to acquit him, and brought forward his children and many of his friends and relatives in court in order to appeal to your feelings; and then finds that I shall do none of these things, though I am in what he would think the supreme danger. Perhaps he will harden himself against me when he notices this; it may make him angry, and he may cast his vote in anger. If it is so with any of you—I do not suppose that it is, but in case it should be so— I think that I should answer him reasonably if I said: "My friend, I have relatives, too, for, in the words of Homer, I am 'not born of an oak or a rock' but of flesh and blood." And so, Athenians, I have relatives, and I have three sons, one of them nearly grown up, and the other two still children. Yet I will not bring any of them forward before you and implore you to acquit me. And why will I do none of these things? It is not from arrogance, Athenians, nor because I lack respect for you—whether or not I can face death bravely is another question—but for my own good name, and for your good name, and for the good name of the whole state. I do not think it right, at my age and with my reputation, to do any-thing of that kind. Rightly or wrongly, men have made up their minds that in some way Socrates is different from the multitude of men. And it will be shameful if those of you who are thought to excel in wisdom, or in bravery, or in any other excellence, are going to act in this fashion. I have often seen men of reputation behaving in an extraordinary way at their trial, as if they thought it a terrible fate to be killed, and as though they expected to live for ever if you did not put them to death. Such men seem to me to bring shame upon the state, for any stranger would suppose that the best and most eminent Athenians, who are selected by their fellow cit-izens to hold office, and for other honors, are no better than women. Those of you, Athenians, who have any reputation at all ought not to do these things, and you ought not to allow us to do them. You should show that you will be much more ready to condemn men who make the state ridiculous by these pathetic performances than men who remain quiet.

But apart from the question of reputation, my friends, I do not think that it is right to entreat the judge to acquit us, or to escape condemnation in that way. It is our duty to each and persuade him. He does not sit to give away justice as a favor, but to pronounce judgment; and he has sworn, not to favor any man whom he would like to favor, but to judge according to law. And, therefore, we ought not to encourage you in the habit of breaking your oaths; and you ought not to allow yourselves to fall into this habit, for then neither you nor we would be acting piously. Therefore, Athenians, do not require me to do these things, for I believe them to be neither good nor just nor pious; especially, do not ask me to do them today when Meletus is prosecuting me for impiety. For were I to be successful and persuade you by my entreaties to break your oaths, I should be clearly teaching you to believe that there are no gods, and I should be simply accusing myself by my defense of not believing in them. But, Athenians, that is very far from the truth. I do believe in the gods as no one of my accusers believes in them; and to you and to the god I commit my cause to be decided as is best for you and for me.

(He is found guilty by 281 votes to 220.)

I am not indignant at the verdict which you have given, Athenians, for many reasons. I expected that you would find me guilty; and I am not so much surprised at that as at the numbers of the votes. I certainly never thought that the majority against me would have been so narrow. But now it seems that if only thirty votes had changed sides, I should have escaped. So I think that I have escaped Meletus, as it is; and not only have I escaped him, for it is perfectly clear that if Anytus and Lycon had not come forward to accuse me, too, he would not have obtained the fifth part of the votes, and would have had to pay a fine of a thousand drachmae.

So he proposes death as the penalty. Be it so. And what alternative penalty shall I propose to you, Athenians? What I deserve, of course, must I not? What then do I deserve to pay or to suffer for having determined not to spend my life in ease? I neglected the things which most men value, such as wealth, and family interests, and military commands, and public oratory, and all the civic appointments, and social clubs, and political factions, that there are in Athens; for I thought that I was really too honest a man to preserve my life if I engaged in these affairs. So I did not go where I should have done no good either to you or to myself. I went, instead, to each one of you privately to do him, as I say, the greatest of benefits, and tried to persuade him not to think of his affairs until he had thought of himself and tried to make himself as good and wise as possible, nor to think of the affairs of Athens until he had thought of Athens herself; and to care for other things in the same manner. Then what do I deserve for such a life? Something good, Athenians, if I am really to propose what I deserve; and something good which it would be suitable for me to receive. Then what is a suitable reward to be given to a poor benefactor who requires leisure to exhort you? There is no reward, Athenians, so suitable for him as receiving free meals in the prytaneum. It is a much more suitable reward for him than for any of you who has won a victory at the Olympic games with his horse or his chariots. Such a man only makes you seem happy, but I make you really happy; he is not in want, and I am. So if I am to propose the penalty which I really deserve, I propose this—free meals in the prytaneum.

Perhaps you think me stubborn and arrogant in what I am saying now, as in what I said about the entreaties and tears. It is not so, Athenians. It is rather that I am convinced that I never wronged any man voluntarily, though I cannot persuade you of that, since we have conversed together only a little time. If there were a law at Athens, as there is elsewhere, not to finish a trial of life and death in a single day, I think that I could have persuaded you; but now it is not easy in so short a time to clear myself of great prejudices. But when I am persuaded that I have never wronged any man, I shall certainly not wrong myself, or admit that I deserve to suffer any evil, or propose any evil for myself as a penalty. Why should I? Lest I should suffer the penalty which Meletus proposes when I say that I do not know whether it is a good or an evil? Shall I choose instead of it something which I know to be an evil, and propose that as a penalty? Shall I propose imprisonment? And why should I pass the rest of my days in prison, the slave of successive officials? Or shall I propose a fine, with imprisonment until it is paid? I have told you why I will not do that. I should have to remain in prison, for I have no money to pay a fine with. Shall I then propose exile? Perhaps you would agree to that. Life would indeed be very dear to me if I were unreasonable enough to expect that strangers would cheerfully tolerate my discussions and arguments when you who are my fellow citizens cannot endure them, and have found them so irksome and odious to you that you are seeking now to be relieved of them. No, indeed, Athenians, that is not likely. A fine life I should lead for an old man if I were to withdraw from Athens and pass the rest of my days in wandering from city to city, and continually being expelled. For I know very well that the young men will listen to me wherever I go, as they do here. If I drive them away, they will persuade their elders to expel me; if I do not drive them away, their fathers and other relatives will expel me for their sakes.

Perhaps someone will say, "Why cannot you withdraw from Athens, Socrates, and hold your peace?" It is the most difficult thing in the world to make you understand why I cannot do that. If I say that I cannot hold my peace because that would be to disobey the god, you will think that I am not in earnest and will not believe me. And if I tell you that no greater good can happen to a man than to discuss human excellence every day and the other matters about which you have heard me arguing and examining myself and others, and that an unexamined life is not worth living, then you will believe me still less. But that is so, my friends, though it is not easy to persuade you. And, what is more, I am not accustomed to think that I deserve anything evil. If I had been rich, I would have proposed as large a fine as I could pay: that would have done me no harm. But I am not rich enough to pay a fine unless you are willing to fix it at a sum within my means. Perhaps I could pay you a mina, so I propose that. Plato here, Athenians, and Crito, and Critobulus, and Apollodorus bid me propose thirty minae, and they guarantee its payment. So I propose thirty minae. Their security will be sufficient to you for the money.

(He is condemned to death.)

You have not gained very much time, Athenians, and at the price of the slurs of those who wish to revile the state. And they will say that you put Socrates, a wise man, to death. For they will certainly call me wise, whether I am wise or not, when they want to reproach you. If you had waited for a little while, your wishes would have been fulfilled in the course of nature; for you see that I am an old man, far advanced in years, and near to death. I am saying this not to all of you, only to those who have voted for my death. And to them I have something else to say. Perhaps, my friends, you think that I have been convicted because I was wanting in the arguments by which I could have persuaded you to acquit me, if I had thought it right to do or to say anything to escape punishment. It is not so. I have been convicted because I was wanting, not in arguments, but in impudence and shamelessness—because I would not plead before you as you would have liked to hear me plead, or appeal to you with weeping and wailing, or say and do many other things which I maintain are unworthy of me, but which you have been accustomed to from other men. But when I was defending myself, I thought that I ought not to do anything unworthy of a free man because of the danger which I ran, and I have not changed my mind now. I would very much rather defend myself as I did, and die, than as you would have had me do, and live. Both in a lawsuit and in war, there are some things which neither I nor any other man may do in order to escape from death. In battle, a man often sees that he may at least escape from death by throwing down his arms and falling on his knees before the pursuer to beg for his life. And there are many other ways of avoiding death in every danger if a man is willing to say and to do anything. But, my friends, I think that it is a much harder thing to escape from wickedness than from death, for wickedness is swifter than death. And now I, who am old and slow, have been overtaken by the slower pursuer: and my accusers, who are clever and swift, have been overtaken by the swifter pursuer—wickedness. And now I shall go away, sentenced by you to death; they will go away, sentenced by truth to wickedness and injustice. And I abide by this award as well as they. Perhaps it was right for these things to be so. I think that they are fairly balanced.

And now I wish to prophesy to you, Athenians, who have condemned me. For I am going to die, and that is the time when men have most prophetic power. And I prophesy to you who have sentenced me to death that a far more severe punishment than you have inflicted on me will surely overtake you as soon as I am dead. You have done this thing, thinking that you will be relieved from having to give an account of your lives. But I say that the result will be very different. There will be more men who will call you to account, whom I have held back, though you did not recognize it. And they will be harsher toward you than I have been, for they will be younger, and you will be more indignant with them. For if you think that you will restrain men from reproaching you for not living as you should, by putting them to death, you are very much mistaken. That way of escape is neither possible nor honorable. It is much more honorable and much easier not to suppress others, but to make yourselves as good as you can. This is my parting prophesy to you who have condemned me.

With you who have acquitted me I should like to discuss this thing that has happened, while the authorities are busy, and before I go to the place where I have to die. So, remain with me until I go: there is no reason why we should not talk with each other while it is possible. I wish to explain to you, as my friends, the meaning of what has happened to me. An amazing thing has happened to me, judges—for I am right in calling you judges. The prophetic guide has been constantly with me all through my life till now, opposing me even in trivial matters if I were not going to act rightly. And now you yourselves see what has happened to me—a thing which might be thought, and which is sometimes actually reckoned, the supreme evil. But the divine guide did not oppose me when I was leaving my house in the morning, nor when I was coming up here to the court, nor at any point in my speech when I was going to say anything; though at other times it has often stopped me in the very act of speaking. But now, in this matter, it has never once opposed me, either in my words or my actions. I will tell you what I believe to be the reason. This thing that has come upon me must be a good; and those of us who think that death is an evil must needs be mistaken. I have a clear proof that that is so; for my accustomed guide would certainly have opposed me if I had not been going to meet with something good.

And if we reflect in another way, we shall see that we may well hope that death is a good. For the state of death is one of two things: either the dead man wholly ceases to be and loses all consciousness or, as we are told, it is a change and a migration of the soul to another place. And if death is the absence of all consciousness, and like the sleep of one whose slumbers are unbroken by any dreams, it will be a wonderful gain. For if a man had to select that night in which he slept so soundly that he did not even dream, and had to compare with it all the other nights and days of his life, and then had to say how many days and nights in his life he had spent better and more pleasantly than this night, I think that a private person, nay, even the Great King of Persia himself, would find them easy to count, compared with the others. If that is the nature of death, I for one count it a gain. For then it appears that all time is nothing more than a single night. But if death is a journey to another place, and what we are told is true—that all who have died are there—what good could be greater than this, my judges? Would a journey not be worth taking, at the end of which, in the other world, we should be delivered from the pretended judges here and should find the true judges who are said to sit in judgment below, such as Minos and Rhadamanthus and Aeacus and Triptolemus, and the other demigods who were just in their own lives? Or what would you not give to converse with Orpheus and Musaeus and Hesiod and Homer? I am willing to die many times if this be true. And for my own part I should find it wonderful to meet there Palamedes, and Ajax the son of Telamon, and the other men of old who have died through an unjust judgment, and to compare my experiences with theirs. That I think would be no small pleasure. And, above all, I could spend my time in examining those who are there, as I examine men here, and in finding out which of them is wise, and which of them thinks himself wise when he is not wise. What would we not give, my judges, to be able to examine the leader of the great expedition against Troy, or Odysseus, or Sisyphus, or countless other men and women whom we could name? It would be an inexpressible happiness to converse with them and to live with them and to examine them. Assuredly there they do not put men to death for doing that. For besides the other ways in which they are happier than we are, they are immortal, at least if what we are told is true.

And you too, judges, must face death hopefully, and believe this one truth, that no evil can happen to a good man, either in life or after death. His affairs are not neglected by the gods; and what has happened to me today has not happened by chance. I am persuaded that it was better for me to die now, and to be released from trouble; and that was the reason why the guide never turned me back. And so I am not at all angry with my accusers or with those who have condemned me to die. Yet it was not with this in mind that they accused me and condemned me, but meaning to do me an injury. So far I may blame them.

Yet I have one request to make of them. When my sons grow up, punish them, my friends, and harass them in the same way that I have harassed you, if they seem to you to care for riches or for any other thing more than excellence; and if they think that they are something when they are really nothing, reproach them, as I have reproached you, for not caring for what they should, and for thinking that they are something when really they are nothing. And if you will do this, I myself and my sons will have received justice from you.

But now the time has come, and we must go away—I to die, and you to live. Which is better is known to the god alone.

The Paradox of Socrates *

Gregory Vlastos

The Socrates of this book is the Platonic Socrates, or, to be more precise, the Socrates of Plato's early dialogues. That this figure is a faithful, imaginative recreation of the historical Socrates is the conclusion of some very reputable scholars, though not of all. It is the conclusion I would be prepared to defend myself. To try to do this in detail would be out of place in this essay. All I can do here is to indicate the main consideration which has led me to this conclusion.

There is one, and only one, serious alternative to Plato's Socrates, and that is Xenophon's.[1] The two are irreconcilable at certain points, and these are crucial.

> Xenophon's is a Socrates without irony and without paradox. Take these away from Plato's Socrates, and there is nothing left.
>
> Xenophon's Socrates is so persuasive that, "whenever he argued," Xenophon declares, "he gained a greater measure of assent from his hearers than any man I have ever known" (*Memorabilia* 4.6.16). Plato's Socrates is not persuasive at all. He wins every argument, but never manages to win over an opponent. He has to fight every inch of the way for any assent he gets, and gets it, so to speak, at the point of a dagger.
>
> Xenophon's Socrates discourses on theology and theodicy, argues for the existence of a divine mind that has created man and ordered the world for his benefit. Plato's refuses to argue over anything other than man and human affairs.
>
> Plato's Socrates maintains that it is never right to repay evil with evil. He says this in studied defiance of the contrary view, axiomatic in Greek morality from Hesiod down, and fixes here the boundary-line between those who can agree with him on fundamentals and those who can't. Xenophon's Socrates has never heard of the boundary-line. He stands on the wrong side, the popular side, parrots the common opinion that the good man will "excel in rendering benefits to his friends and injuries to his enemies" (*Memorabilia* 2.6.35).

* This essay is adapted from an address to a meeting of the Humanities Association of Canada at Ottawa on June 13, 1957. I make no apologies for the style and form of the presentation. If the reader should like to see how I try to ground interpretations of Socrates on a close reading of Plato's text, he may consult other papers of mine.

What does this prove? If Plato and Xenophon cannot both be right, why must Plato be right? That his Socrates is incomparably the more interesting of the two figures, in fact the only Socrates worth talking about, proves nothing. We cannot build history on wish-fulfillment. Fortunately there is another consideration that proves a great deal. It is that Plato accounts, while Xenophon does not, for facts affirmed by both and also attested by others. For example: that Critias and Alcibiades had been companions of Socrates; or again: that Socrates was indicted and condemned on the charge of not believing in the gods of the state and of corrupting its youth. Xenophon's portrait will not square with either of these. Not with the first, for his Socrates could not have attracted men like Critias and Alcibiades, haughtily aristocrats both of them, and as brilliant intellectually as they were morally unprincipled. Xenophon's Socrates, pious reciter of moral commonplaces, would have elicited nothing but a sneer from Critias and a yawn from Alcibiades, while Plato's Socrates is just the man who could have gotten under their skin. As for the second, Plato, and he alone, gives us a Socrates who could have plausibly been indicted for subversion of faith and morals. Xenophon's account of Socrates, apologetic from beginning to end, refutes itself: had the facts been as he tells them, the indictment would not have been made in the first place.

How far can we then trust Plato? From the fact that he was right on some things it does not follow, certainly, that he was right in all his information on Socrates, or even on all its essential points. But we do have a check.[2] Plato's *Apology* has for its *mise en scène* an all-too-public occasion. The jury alone numbered 501 Athenians. And since the town was so gregarious and Socrates a notorious public character, there would have been many more in the audience. So when Plato was writing the *Apology*, he knew that hundreds of those who might read the speech he puts into the mouth of Socrates had heard the historic original. And since his purpose in writing it was to clear his master's name and to indict his judges, it would have been most inept to make Socrates talk out of character. How could Plato be saying to his fellow citizens, 'This is the man you murdered. Look at him. Listen to him,'[3] and point to a figment of his own imagining? This is my chief reason for accepting the *Apology* as a reliable recreation of the thought and character of the man Plato knew so well. Here, as before, I speak of *recreation*, not reportage. The *Apology* was probably written several years after the event. This, and Plato's genius, assures us that it was not journalism, but art. Though the emotion with which Plato had listened when life and death hung on his master's words must have branded those words into his mind, still, that emotion recollected in tranquillity, those remembrances recast in the imagination, would make a new speech out of the old materials, so that those who read it would recognize instantly the man they had known without having to scan their own memory and ask, 'Did he open with that remark? Did he really use that example?' or any such question. This is all I claim for the veracity of the *Apology*. And if this is conceded, the problem of our sources is solved in principle. For we may then use the *Apology* as a touchstone of the like veracity of the thought and character of Socrates depicted in Plato's other early dialogues. And when we do that, what do we find?

We find a man who is all paradox. Other philosophers have talked *about* paradox. Socrates did not. The paradox in Socrates is Socrates. But unlike later paradoxes, Scandinavian, German, and latterly even Gallic, this Hellenic paradox is not meant to defeat, but to incite, the human reason. At least a part of it can be made quite lucid, and this is what I shall attempt in the main part of this essay. For this purpose I must point out the roles whose apparently incongruous junction produces paradox:

In the *Apology* (29D–E) * Socrates gives this account of his lifework:

> So long as I breathe and have the strength to do it, I will not cease philosophizing, exhorting you, indicting whichever of you I happen to meet, telling him in my customary way:

> Esteemed friend, citizen of Athens, the greatest city in the world, so outstanding in both intelligence and power, aren't you ashamed to care so much to make all the money you can, and to advance your reputation and prestige—while for truth and wisdom and the improvement of your soul you have no care or worry?

This is the Socrates Heinrich Maier had in mind when he spoke of "the Socratic gospel." [4] If this makes us think of the Christian gospel, the evocation is not inappropriate at this point. Socrates could have taken over verbatim the great question of our gospels, "What shall it profit a man, if he gain the whole world, and lose his own soul?"

The only gloss I need add here is a caution that one should not be misled by the other-worldly associations with which the word "soul" is loaded in our own tradition and which were nearly as heavy in the Greek. If there is anything new in the way Socrates uses the word "soul" it is that he quietly narrows down its meaning to something whose supernatural origin or destiny, if any, is indeterminate, and whose physical or metaphysical structure, if any, is also indeterminate, so that both theological and anti-theological, mystical and physicalistic doctrines of the soul become inconsequential. His is a gospel without dogma. You may hold any one of a great variety of beliefs about the soul, or none of them, without either gaining or losing any essential part of what Socrates wants you to think about and care for when he urges you to "care for your soul." In particular you don't have to believe in the immortality of the soul. Socrates himself does believe in it,[5] but for this faith he has no argument. In the *Apology* he muses on how pleasant it would be *if* it

* References to Plato are usually cited by means of *Stephanus numbers*, as in '*Apology* 29 D-E.' These are derived from the pagination and page subdivisions of the 1578 edition of Plato by Henri Estienne (Stephanus).—Eds.

were true, the soul carrying along to Hades all its intellectual equipment, so it could carry on Socratic arguments with no more fear of interruption. Such a life, he says, would make him "unspeakably happy." But he does not say this is a good reason for believing in it, or that there is some other good reason. He says nothing to exclude the alternative he mentions: total extinction of consciousness; death could mean just this, and if it did, there would be nothing in it to frighten a good man, or dissuade him from the "care of the soul." The soul is as worth caring for if it were to last just twenty-four more hours, as if it were to outlast eternity. If you have just one more day to live, and can expect nothing but a blank after that, Socrates feels that you would still have all the reason you need for improving your soul; you have yourself to live with that one day, so why live with a worse self, if you could live with a better one instead?

How then is the soul improved?—Morally, by right action; intellectually, by right thinking; the two being strictly complementary, so that you can't have one without the other and, if you do have either you will be sure to have the other. This, of course, is his famous doctrine, that 'virtue is knowledge,' which means two things:

First, that there can be no virtue without knowledge. This is what gives such intensity to Socrates' arguments, such urgency to his quests for definition. He makes you feel that the failure to sustain a thesis or find a definition is not just an intellectual defeat, but a moral disaster. At the end of the *Euthyphro* that gentleman is as good as told that his failure to make good his confident claim to know "exactly" (5A, 15D) what piety is, means not just that he is intellectually hard up, but that he is morally bankrupt. I am stating what Socrates believes in as extreme a form as Plato allows us to see it. One of the many things for which we may be grateful to Plato is that, as Boswell said of his own treatment of Johnson, he "did not make a cat out of his tiger." Unlike Xenophon's cat, Plato's tiger stands for the savage doctrine that if you cannot pass the stiff Socratic tests for knowledge you cannot be a good man.

No less extreme is the mate to this doctrine, that if you do have this kind of knowledge, you cannot fail to *be* good and *act* as a good man should, in the face of any emotional stress or strain. The things which break the resolution of others, which seduce or panic men to act in an unguarded moment contrary to their best insights—"rage, pleasure, pain, love, fear" (*Prt.* 352B)—any one of them, or all of them in combination, will have no power over the man who has Socratic knowledge. He will walk through life invulnerable, sheathed in knowledge as in a magic armor which no blow from the external world can crack or even dent. No saint has ever claimed more for the power of faith over the passions than does Socrates for the power of knowledge.

So here is one side of Socrates. He has an evangel to proclaim, a great truth to teach: Our soul is the only thing in us worth saving, and there is only one way to save it: to acquire knowledge.

What would you expect of such a man? To propagate his message, to disseminate the knowledge which is itself the elixir of life. Is this what he does? How *could* he, if, as he says repeatedly in the dialogues, he does not have that knowledge? Plato makes him say this not only in the informality of private conversation but also in that most formal speech of all, the *Apology*. If he is wiser than others, Socrates there declares (21D), it is only because he does not *think* he has the knowledge which others think they have but haven't.[6]

Could this be true? If it were, then on his own teaching, he too would be one of the damned. But no man ever breathed greater assurance that his feet were planted firmly on the path of right. He never voices a doubt of the moral rightness of any of his acts or decisions, never betrays a sense of sin. He goes to his death confident that "no evil thing can happen to a good man" (*Apology* 41D)—that "good man" is himself. Can this be the same man who believes that no one can be good without knowledge, and that he has no knowledge?

But there is more to the paradox. It is not merely that Socrates *says* things—as in his disclaimer of moral knowledge—which contradict the role of a preacher and teacher of the care of the soul, but that he *acts* in ways which do not seem to fit this role. Socrates' characteristic activity is the *elenchus*, literally, "the refutation." You say *A*, and he shows you that *A* implies *B*, and *B* implies *C*, and then he asks, 'But didn't you say *D* before? And doesn't *C* contradict *D*?' And there he leaves you with your shipwrecked argument, without so much as telling you what part of it, if any, might yet be salvaged. His tactics seem unfriendly from the start. Instead of trying to pilot you around the rocks, he picks one under water a long way ahead where you would never suspect it and then makes sure you get all the wind you need to run full-sail into it and smash your keel upon it.

This sort of thing happens so often in Plato's Socratic dialogues and is so perplexing, that one can't help wondering whether the historical Socrates could have been really like that. I have had to ask myself more than once whether this pitiless critic, this heartless intellectual, this man who throws away his chances to preach a gospel so he may push an argument instead, is not, after all, only a Platonic projection, and tells us more about the youthful Plato than about the aged Socrates. As often as this doubt has reared its head in my mind, I have chopped it down by going back to the *Apology*. Here, where Socrates' evangelistic mission is stated so emphatically, it is most distinctly implied that his customary conduct did not fit the evangelist's role. I am thinking, of course, of that story [7] about the supposed oracle of Delphi that no one was wiser than Socrates; this supposedly started Socrates on his search for someone wiser than himself, trying everyone who had the reputation for wisdom, first the statesmen, then the poets, then, scraping the bottom of the barrel, even the artisans, only to find that the wisdom of all these people, from top to bottom, was worse than zero, a minus quantity. What to make of this whole story is itself a puzzle for the scholar, and I will not try to crack it here. But whatever the Pythian priestess may or may not have said in the first place, and whatever Socrates may or may not have thought about whatever she did say, the one thing which is certain is this: the story frames a portrait of Socrates whose day-in, day-out role was known to his fellow-citizens as that of a destructive critic, whose behavior looked from the outside like that of a man who saw nothing in his interlocutors but balloons of pretended knowledge and was bent on nothing else but to puncture them. So the *Apology* confirms the conduct which presents our paradox. It tells of a Socrates who says the care of the soul is the most important thing in the world, and that his mission in life is to get others to see this. And yet it also as good as says that if you were going down the Agora and saw a crowd around Socrates you could take three to one bets that Socrates would not be saying anything about the improvement of the soul, nor acting as though he cared a straw for the improvement of his interlocutor's soul, but would be simply arguing with him, forcing him into one corner after another, until it became plain to all the bystanders, if not the man himself, that his initial claim to know this or that was ridiculously false.

Here then is our paradox. But it is no use looking for the answer until we have taken into account still another side to Socrates: the role of the *searcher.* "Don't think," he says to the great sophist Protagoras, "that I have any other interest in arguing with you, but that of clearing up my own problems as they arise" (*Prt.* 348C). Or again, when that nasty intellectual, Critias, accuses him of just trying to refute him instead of advancing the argument, Socrates replies:

> And what if I am? How can you think that I have any other interest in refuting you, but what I should have in *searching myself*, fearing lest I might fool myself, thinking I know something, when I don't know (*Chrm.* 166C–D)?

Moments of self-revelation like these are rare in the dialogues. Socrates is not a character out of Chekhov introspecting moodily on the public stage. He is a man whose face is a mask, whose every word is deliberate, and seems calculated to conceal more than to reveal. One gets so used to this artful exterior, that one is left unprepared for moments like these, and is apt to discount them as irony. I speak for myself. This is the way I used to take them. And so long as I did, I could find no way through the paradox of which I have been speaking. But then it occurred to me that in the statements I have just cited Socrates means to be taken at his word, and in this one too:

> Critias, you act as though I professed to know the answers to the questions I ask you, and could give them to you if I wished. It isn't so. I inquire with you . . . because I don't myself have knowledge (*Chrm.* 165D).

Can he really mean this? He can, if in such passages he is using "knowledge" in a sense in which the claim to know something implies the conviction that any further investigation of its truth would be superfluous. This is the sense in which the word "knowledge" is used in formal contexts by earlier philosophers, and nothing gives us a better sense of the dogmatic certainty implied by their use of it than the fact that one of them, Parmenides, presented his doctrine in the guise of a divine revelation. In doing this Parmenides did not mean in the least that the truth of his philosophy must be taken on faith. He presented his system as a purely rational deductive argument which made no appeal to anything except the understanding. What he meant rather is that the conclusions of this argument have the same certainty as that which the devotees of mystic cults would attach to the poems of Orpheus or of some other divinely inspired lore. This, I suggest, is the conception of wisdom and knowledge Socrates has in mind in those contexts where he disclaims it. When he renounces "knowledge" he is telling us that the question of the truth of anything *he* believes can always be sensibly re-opened; that any conviction he has stands ready to be re-examined in the company of any sincere person who will raise the question and join him in the investigation.

Consider his great proposition that it is never right to harm the enemy. Would you not think that if there is anything Socrates feels he *knows*, this is it; else how could he have taken his stand on it, declaring that for those who believe it and those who do not "there can be no common mind, but they can only despise each other when they confront each other's counsels" (*Crt.* 49D)? But even this he is prepared to re-examine. He continues to Crito:

> So consider very carefully whether you too are on my side and share my conviction, so we can start from this: that neither doing nor returning wrong nor defending oneself against evil by returning the evil is ever right? Or do you dissent and part company with me here? For myself this is what I have long believed and still do. But if you think differently, go ahead, explain, show me (49D–E).

You would think this hardly the time and place to re-open this issue, but Socrates is quite willing. And I suggest that he is always willing; that he goes into every discussion in just this frame of mind. Previous reflection has led him to many conclusions, and he does not put them out of his mind when jumping into a new argument. There they all are, and not in vague or jumbled up form, but in a clear map, on which he constantly relies to figure out, many moves in advance, the direction in which he would like to press an argument. But clear as they are, they are not finally decided; every one of them is open to review in the present argument, where the very same kind of process which led to the original conclusion *could* unsettle what an earlier argument may have settled prematurely, on incomplete survey of relevant premises, or by faulty deductions. Nor is it only a matter of re-examining previously reached conclusions; it is no less a matter of hoping for new insights which may crop up right in this next argument and give the answer to

For Socrates there is no knowledge that is fixed for all times, no longer subject to reexamination

some hitherto unanswered problem. And if this is the case, Socrates is not just the fighter he appears to be on the surface, intent on vindicating predetermined results by winning just one more victory in an ordeal by combat. He is the investigator, testing his own ideas in the course of testing those of his interlocutor, watching the argument with genuine curiosity to see whether it will really come out where it should if the results of previous arguments were sound, and scanning the landscape as he goes along, looking for some new feature he failed to notice before.

Does this show a way out of our paradox? I think it does. It puts in a new light the roles that seemed so hard to reconcile before. Socrates the *preacher* turns out to be a man who wants others to find out his gospel so far as possible by themselves and for themselves. Socrates the *teacher* now appears as the man who has not just certain conclusions to impart to others, but a *method of investigation*—the method by which he reached these results in the first place, and which is even more important than the results, for it is the means of testing, revising, and going beyond them. Socrates the *critic* is much more than a mere critic, for he exhibits his method by putting it to work; even if not a single positive result were to come out of it in this or that argument, the method itself would have been demonstrated, and those who saw how it works could put it to work for themselves to reach more positive conclusions. Even Socrates the *professed* agnostic becomes more intelligible. His 'I don't know' is a conscientious objection to the notion that the conclusions of any discussion are secure against further testing by further discussion. Seen in this way, Socrates no longer seems a bundle of incompatible roles precariously tied together by irony. He seems one man, unified in his diverse activities by the fact that in all of them he remains the searcher, always pursuing his own search and seeking fellow-seekers.

May I offer a particular illustration, for I would not like to leave this solution hanging in generality. I take the *Euthyphro*, though almost any one of Plato's early dialogues would do. On your first reading of this dialogue you come to the end with a sense of disappointment that after all this winding and unwinding of argument no positive result seems to be reached, and Socrates is ready, as he says, "to begin all over again" with the original question, "What is piety?" As you watch Euthyphro hurry off, this is what you feel like telling Socrates: 'I don't believe you really care for that man's soul, for if you did, how could you have let him go with his head still stuffed with his superstitions? You know that the pollution he fears has nothing to do with the only piety you think worth talking about, the kind that will improve what *you* call the soul. Why then not tell him this, and show him the difference between religion and magic?'

But if you go back and re-read the dialogue more carefully, you can figure out Socrates' reply:

'That is what I did try to show him. But I wanted him to find it out for himself. For this purpose it would have been no use telling him his notion of piety was all wrong, which would not even have been true. It was *not* all wrong, but a jumble of right and wrong beliefs, and my job was to help him see that he could not hold both sets at once. If he could see this, he would become his own critic, his own teacher, even his own preacher, for if this man could see the implications of some things he already believes, I would not have to preach to him that he should care for his soul as it should be cared for. He would be doing his own preaching to himself.'

Socrates might then add that though he failed in this objective, the fault was not entirely his own. For sheer sluggishness of intellect it would be hard to beat this complacent fanatic whom Plato ironically calls *Euthyphro*, "Straight-thinker." How straight he thinks on matters of religion we may judge by his response when Socrates shows him that, on his view, religion is a business-relationship between men and gods, a barter of divine favors for human offerings. Faced with this consequence our Mr. Straight-thinker sees nothing positively wrong with it: "Yes, you may call it (piety) a commercial art, if you like" (14E). Yet even with such unpromising material on his hands, Socrates tries hard, and makes good headway, coming at one point within a stone's throw of success: He gets Euthyphro to admit that piety cannot be defined as "that which is pleasing to the gods," i.e., as obedience to any demand the gods might happen to make on men; the demand must itself be *just*, and piety must consist of discharging services we *owe* the gods. Socrates then pushes Euthyphro to say what sort of services these might be. Why do the gods *need* our services, he presses; what is that "wonderful work" (13E) the gods can only achieve through our own cooperating efforts? I suppose it was too much to expect Euthyphro to see the answer once Socrates has led him so far, and say to himself, in line with Socrates' reasoning, with all of which he agrees: since the gods are great and powerful past all imagining, they surely don't need our services to improve *their* estate; and since they are also good and benevolent, they do desire what is best for us—and what can this be, but the improvement of our souls? Isn't this then the object of piety, this the discharge of the highest obligation we owe the gods? Socrates evidently thought this was *not* too much to hope that Euthyphro would have seen for himself on the strength of the Socratic prodding. When Euthyphro went hopelessly off the track in a wordy tangent, Socrates remarked:

> Certainly, Euthyphro, you could have answered my main question in far fewer words, if you had wished. . . . Just now when you were on the very edge of telling me what I want to know, you turned aside (14B–C).

Clearly Socrates has *not* been playing a cat-and-mouse game with Euthyphro in this dialogue, putting questions to him only to pounce on the answers and claw them to pieces. He has been doing his best to lead Euthyphro to the point where he could see for himself the right answer. What he positively refuses to do is to *tell* Euthyphro this answer, and this, not because he does not think Euthyphro's soul worth the saving, but because he believes there is only one way to save it and that Euthyphro himself must do the job by finding this one right way, so that he too becomes a searcher. Whether or not you think Socrates was right in this, I trust you will agree with me that he was at least consistent.

But *was* Socrates right? On some fundamental points I think him wrong.

I do not think the Socratic way is the only way to save a man's soul. What Socrates called "knowledge" he thought both necessary and sufficient for moral goodness. I think it neither. Not necessary, for the bravest men I ever met would surely have flunked the Socratic examination on courage. Why this should be so would take long to unravel, and I have no confidence I could do it successfully. But I don't need to for the point at issue. For this I need only stick to the fact: that a man can have great courage, yet make a fool of himself when he opens his mouth to explain what it is that he has. I am not saying that it would not be a fine thing if he could talk better, and know more. I am not depreciating Socratic knowledge. I am only saying it is not necessary for what Socrates did think it necessary. And I would also say that it is not sufficient. For this I need no better example than that famous saying of his, in the *Apology*, (29A–B) that the fear of death is the pretense of wisdom. 'Why do we fear death?—Because we think we know it is a great evil. But do we *know* this?—No. We don't know anything about death. For all we know to the contrary, it might be a great good.' So argues Socrates, and implies confidently that if you saw all this, your fear of death would vanish. Knowledge—in this case, knowledge of your ignorance of what death is and what, if anything, comes after it—would dissipate your fear. You couldn't fear death or anything else unless you knew it to be evil. But why couldn't you? 'Because it would be absurd,' Socrates would say. But could it not be absurd, and exist just the same? Aunt Rosie is afraid of mice, but she knows quite well that a mouse can do her no great harm. She knows she runs a far graver risk to life and limb when she drives her car down Main Street, but she is not a bit afraid of that, while she is terrified of mice. This is absurd, but it happens; and her knowing that it is absurd does not prevent it from happening either, but only adds shame and guilt to fear. This is not evidence of a high order; it is just a *fact* that does not square with Socrates' theory.

But Socratic knowledge has all too little interest in facts. That is the main trouble with it. Socrates' model for knowledge was what we would call deductive knowledge now-a-days. The knowledge he sought, and with such marked success, is that which consists in arranging whatever information one has in a luminous, perspicuous pattern, so one can see at a glance where run the bright lines of implication and where the dark ones of contradiction. But of the other way of knowing, the empirical way, Socrates had little understanding, and he paid for his ignorance by conceit of knowledge, failing to understand the limitations of his knowledge of fact generally, and of the fact of knowledge in particular. Had he so much as felt the need of investigating knowledge itself as a fact in human nature, to determine just exactly what, as a matter of fact, happens to a man when he has or hasn't knowledge, Socrates might have come to see that even his own dauntless courage in the face of death he owed not to knowledge but to something else, more akin to religious faith.

But to explain Socrates' failure merely in this way would be itself to concede more to Socrates' theory than the facts allow, for it would be to explain it as only a failure of knowledge. I will put all my cards on the table and say that behind this lay a failure of love. In saying this I am not taking over-seriously the prickly exterior and the pugilist's postures. I have already argued that he does care for the souls of his fellows. But the care is limited and conditional. If men's souls are to be saved, they must be saved his way. And when he sees they cannot, he watches them go down the road to perdition with regret but without anguish. Jesus wept for Jerusalem. Socrates warns Athens, scolds, exhorts it, condemns it. But he has no tears for it. One wonders if Plato, who raged against Athens, did not love it more in his rage and hate than ever did Socrates in his sad and good-tempered rebukes. One feels there is a last zone of frigidity in the soul of the great erotic; had he loved his fellows more, he could hardly have laid on them the burdens of his "despotic logic," [8] impossible to be borne.

Having said all this, let me now add that grave as these complaints are, they do not undermine his greatness. Let me try to say why, in spite of this or a longer bill of particulars which might be drawn against him, he is still great.

Let me start where I just left off: his character. To be different in some way or other from everyone else one need not be a great man; one need only be a man. But to find in this difference the material for a personal creation wherewith to enrich the common life of humanity —this is a difficult achievement for anyone, and was exceptionally so for Socrates, for his initial endowment was so discouraging: physical ugliness. This he had to live with among a people who adored beauty. Socrates solved the problem classical antiquity would have judged insoluble. In the world of the fine arts—plastic, graphic, auditory—classical antiquity just took it for granted that if the product is to be fine the materials must be beautiful to begin with. Socrates proved this was not so in the medium of personal life. He showed how there at least art could fashion beauty out of ugliness. He did this by stylizing his deformity, making an abstract mask out of it, and so detaching himself from it, while he could never put it off, he could always laugh at it as from a great distance with his mind. And as a good artist does not drop an image once he gets hold of it, but puts it to new and surprising uses, so Socrates with this theme of ugliness as a comic mask. He made his words common and vulgar, like his face. He said he could not make fine speeches, or even understand the fine ones others made. His memory, he said, was short, he could only take things in a sentence or two at a time; nor could his wits move fast, so everything must be explained to him in painfully slow, dragging steps. His manners, too, he said, were poor; he must be forgiven if he could not be as polite in argument as other men. With this cumulative renunciation of ornaments of culture and graces of mind he built his character. Its surface traits, uncouth, ludicrous to the casual eye, were so severely functional, so perfectly adapted to the work he had to do, that men with the keenest eye for beauty, men like Alcibiades and Plato, found more of it in Socrates than in anyone they had ever known. The test of art is: Will it last? And for this kind of art: Will it last in adversity? Socrates' art passed this test. The self behind the mask was never shown up as just another mask. He was the same before his judges as he had been in the market-place. When he took the poison from the hands of the executioner there was "no change of colour or expression on his face" (*Phd.* 117B).

Second, Socrates was great as a reformer of morality: not a social reformer, but a reformer of the conscience which in the very long run has power to make or break social institutions. A poet like Aristophanes sensed this, without really understanding it; so did Callicles in the *Gorgias* (481C), when he asked Socrates:

> If you're serious, and what you say is really true, won't human life have to be turned completely upside down?

I trust that even some of the incidental illustrations I have used here will document the truth of this rhetorical question. Think of the answer to 'What is piety?' Socrates is fishing for in the *Euthyphro*. How could Athenian piety remain the same, or how could ours for that matter, if Socrates is right on this, if man's obligation to the gods is one he would have to his own self, even if there were no gods: to improve his own soul? Again, how many practices or sentiments in Socrates' world or ours would remain intact if his conviction that it is never right to return evil for evil were taken seriously as really true?

There is another change Socrates wrought in the texture of the moral conscience, one which is scarcely mentioned in the books about him. I cannot hope to remedy this deficiency here. But I can at least remind you that Greek morality still remained to a surprising extent a class-morality. The conviction that high-grade moral virtue was possible only for a man who was well born and rich or, at least, moderately well off, ran wide and deep. The disinheritance of a majority of the urban population—not only the slaves, but the free-born manual workers—from the life of virtue is a reasoned belief in Aristotle. Even that radical refashioner of the social fabric, Plato, did not reject the dogma; he only sublimated it. Socrates did reject it. He expunged it from the universe of moral discourse when he made the improvement of the soul as mandatory, and as possible, for the manual worker as for the gentlemen of leisure, when he redefined all the virtues, and virtue itself, in such a way as to make of them, not class attributes, but human qualities.

But even this is not his greatest contribution. If my solution of the paradox of Socrates is correct, then certainly Socrates himself would have attached far more importance to his method of moral inquiry than to any of its results. If we could get past the palaver of his mock-humility and make him say in simple honesty what he thought was his greatest achievement he would certainly have put that method far above anything else. I cannot now argue further for this point which is as crucial to my estimate of Socrates' greatness as it was to the resolution of the paradox. I can only point out that if what I am now contending were not true, that paradox would not have been there. Had he valued the results of his method above the method itself, he would have been just a preacher and teacher of moral truths, not also the professed agnostic, the tireless critic, examiner and re-examiner of himself and of others; in other words, he would not have been the Socrates of the Platonic dialogues and of this book.

Why rank that method among the great achievements of humanity? Because it makes moral inquiry a common human enterprise, open to every man. Its practice calls for no adherence to a philosophical system, or mastery of a specialized technique, or acquisition of a technical vocabulary. It calls for common sense and common speech. And this is as it should be, for how man should live is every man's business, and the role of the specialist and the expert should be only to offer guidance and criticism, to inform and clarify the judgment of the layman, leaving the final decision up to him. But while the Socratic method makes moral inquiry open to everyone, it makes it easy for no one. It calls not only for the highest degree of mental alertness of which anyone is capable, but also for moral qualities of a high order: sincerity, humility, courage. Socrates expects you to say what you really believe about the way *man* should live; which implies, among other things, about the way *you* should live. His method will not work if the opinion you give him is just *an* opinion; it must be *your* opinion: the one you stand ready to live by, so that if that opinion should be refuted, your own life or a part of it will be indicted or discredited, shown up to be a muddle, premised on a confusion or a contradiction. To get into the argument when you realize that this is the price you have to pay for it —that in the course of it your ego may experience the unpleasant sensation of a bloody nose—takes courage. To search for moral truth that may prove your own life wrong takes humility that is not afraid of humiliation. These are the qualities Socrates himself brings to the argument, and it is not entirely clear that he realizes how essential they are to protect it against the possibility that its dialectic, however rigorous, would merely grind out, as it could with impeccable logic, wild conclusions from irresponsible premises.

But is there not still a residual risk, you may ask, in making the Socratic method the arbiter of moral truth, inviting thereby every man to take, on its terms, a place in the supreme court which judges questions of morality? Certainly there is a risk, and a grave one. For though the method has some built-in protection against moral irresponsibility —the one I have just mentioned—it offers no guarantee whatever that it will always lead to truth. On this Socrates himself, if the foregoing interpretation of his agnosticism was correct, is absolutely clear. His 'I don't know' honestly means 'I could be mistaken in results reached by this method.' And if Socrates could be mistaken, how much more so Tom, Dick, and Harry. Why then open it to them? Socrates' answer is clear: Because each of them is a man, and "the unexamined life is not worth living by man" (*Apology* 38A). I could not go so far as he did at this point. I believe that many kinds of life are worth living by man. But I do believe that the best of all is the one in which every man does his own examining. I have dissented earlier from Socrates' assumption that his is the only way by which any man's soul can be saved. But I can still give wholehearted assent to Socrates' vision of man as a mature, responsible being, claiming to the fullest extent his freedom to make his own choice between right and wrong, not only in action, but in judgment. I do not see how man can reach the full stature of his manhood unless he claims the right to make his own personal judgments on morality; and if he is to claim this right, he must accept the implied chance of misjudgment as a calculated risk. This is the price he must pay for being free. I am using now very un-Socratic language, and I will compound the offense by adding that this vision of human freedom, of which the Socratic method is an expression, could not be appropriately described as knowledge, and that the best name for it is faith. That the man who had this faith to a supreme degree should have mistaken it for knowledge, is yet another part of the paradox of Socrates.

NOTES

1. Why the Aristophanic portrait, though composed much earlier than either Plato's or Xenophon's, offers no basis for correcting Plato's, will be clear to anyone who goes through Kenneth Dover's masterly study, "Socrates in the *Clouds*," in this volume. As for the Aristotelian references to Socrates (on which see Section V of A. R. Lacey's "Our Knowledge of Socrates" in this volume; for more detailed treatment see Th. Deman, *Le Temoignage d'Aristote sur Socrate* [Paris, 1942]), they tally completely with the portrait of Socrates in Plato's early dialogues, supporting the latter at every point on which it differs from the Aristophanic or the Xenophonean portraits or from both.
2. In a fuller discussion I would have added other checks, notably Aristotle's testimony.
3. Here and throughout this introduction I use single quotation marks to indicate an *imaginary* quotation, reserving regular quotation marks for citations from the texts.
4. *Sokrates* (Tuebingen, 1913), pp. 296 ff.

5. The question is left open in the *Apology*. But see *Cr.* 54 B–C.
6. And see especially *Grg.* 506A, 508E–509A.
7. *Ap.* 20E–21A.
8. I borrow here from Nietzsche, who called Socrates "this despotic logician" (*Birth of Tragedy*, Section XIV; translation by Francis Golffing, New York, 1956, p. 90).

The Problem of Socrates

Friedrich Nietzsche

1

Concerning life, the wisest men of all ages have judged alike: it is *no good.* Always and everywhere one has heard the same sound from their mouths—a sound full of doubt, full of melancholy, full of weariness of life, full of resistance to life. Even Socrates said, as he died: "To live—that means to be sick a long time: I owe Asclepius the Savior a rooster." Even Socrates was tired of it. What does that evidence? What does it evince? Formerly one would have said (—oh, it has been said, and loud enough, and especially by our pessimists): "At least something of all this must be true! The consensus of the sages evidences the truth." Shall we still talk like that today? *May* we? "At least something must be *sick* here," *we* retort. These wisest men of all ages—they should first be scrutinized closely. Were they all perhaps shaky on their legs? late? tottery? decadents? Could it be that wisdom appears on earth as a raven, inspired by a little whiff of carrion?

2

This irreverent thought that the great sages are *types of decline* first occurred to me precisely in a case where it is most strongly opposed by both scholarly and unscholarly prejudice: I recognized Socrates and Plato to be symptoms of degeneration, tools of the Greek dissolution, pseudo-Greek, anti-Greek (*Birth of Tragedy*, 1872). The consensus of the sages—I comprehended this ever more clearly—proves least of all that they were right in what they agreed on: it shows rather that they themselves, these wisest men, agreed in some *physiological* respect, and hence adopted the same negative attitude to life—*had to* adopt it. Judgments, judgments of value, concerning life, for it or against it, can, in the end, never be true: they have value only as symptoms, they are worthy of consideration only as symptoms; in themselves such judgments are stupidities. One must by all means stretch out one's fingers and make the attempt to grasp this amazing finesse, *that the value of life cannot be estimated.* Not by the living, for they are an interested party, even a bone of contention, and not judges; not by the dead, for a different reason. For a philosopher to see a problem in the value of life is thus an objection to him, a question mark concerning his wisdom, an un-wisdom. Indeed? All these great wise men—they were not only decadents but not wise at all? But I return to the problem of Socrates.

3

In origin, Socrates belonged to the lowest class: Socrates was plebs. We know, we can still see for ourselves, how ugly he was. But ugliness, in itself an objection, is among the Greeks almost a refutation. Was Socrates a Greek at all? Ugliness is often enough the expression of a development that has been crossed, *thwarted* by crossing. Or it appears as *declining* development. The anthropologists among the criminologists tell us that the typical criminal is ugly: *monstrum in fronte, monstrum in animo.* But the criminal is a decadent. Was Socrates a typical criminal? At least that would not be contradicted by the famous judgment of the physiognomist which sounded so offensive to the friends of Socrates. A foreigner who knew about faces once passed through Athens and told Socrates to his face that he *was* a *monstrum*—that he harbored in himself all the bad vices and appetites. And Socrates merely answered: "You know me, sir!"

4

Socrates' decadence is suggested not only by the admitted wantonness and anarchy of his instincts, but also by the hypertrophy of the logical faculty and that *sarcasm of the rachitic* which distinguishes him. Nor should we forget those auditory hallucinations which, as "the *daimonion* of Socrates," have been interpreted religiously. Everything in him is exaggerated, *buffo,* a caricature, everything is at the same time concealed, ulterior, subterranean. I seek to comprehend what idiosyncrasy begot that Socratic equation of reason, virtue, and happiness: that most bizarre of all equations, which, moreover, is opposed to all the instincts of the earlier Greeks.

5

With Socrates, Greek taste changes in favor of dialectics. What really happened there? Above all, a *noble* taste is thus vanquished; with dialectics the plebs come to the top. Before Socrates, dialectic manners were repudiated in good society: they were considred bad manners, they were compromising. The young were warned against them. Furthermore, all such presentations of one's reasons were distrusted. Honest things, like honest men, do not carry their reasons in their hands like that. It is indecent to show all five fingers. What must first be proved is worth little. Wherever authority still forms part of good bearing, where one does not give reasons but commands, the dialectician is a kind of buffoon: one laughs at him, one does not take him seriously. Socrates was a buffoon who *got himself taken seriously:* what really happened there?

6

One chooses dialectic only when one has no other means. One knows that one arouses mistrust with it, that it not very persuasive. Nothing is easier to erase than a dialectical effect: the experience of every meeting at which there are speeches proves this. It can only be *self-defense* for those who no longer have other weapons. One must have to *enforce* one's right: until one reaches that point, one makes no use of it. The Jews were dialecticians for that reason; Reynard the Fox was one—and Socrates too?

7

Is the irony of Socrates an expression of revolt? Of plebian *ressentiment?* Does he, as one oppressed, enjoy his own ferocity in the knife-thrusts of his syllogisms? Does he *avenge* himself on the noble people whom he fascinates? As a dialectician, one holds a merciless tool in one's hand; one can become a tyrant by means of it; one compromises those one conquers. The dialectician leaves it to his opponent to prove that he is no idiot: he makes one furious and helpless at the same time. The dialectician renders the intellect of his opponent powerless. Indeed? Is dialectic only a form of *revenge* in Socrates?

8

I have given to understand how it was that Socrates could repel: it is therefore all the more necessary to explain his fascination. That he discovered a new kind of *agon,*[1] that he became its first fencing master for the noble circles of Athens, is one point. He fascinated by appealing to the agonistic impulse of the Greeks—he introduced a variation into the wrestling match between young men and youths. Socrates was also a great *erotic.*

9

But Socrates guessed even more. He saw *through* his noble Athenians; he comprehended that his own case, his idiosyncrasy, was no longer exceptional. The same kind of degeneration was quietly developing everywhere: old Athens was coming to an end. And Socrates understood that all the world *needed* him—his means, his cure, his personal artifice of self-preservation. Everywhere the instincts were in anarchy; everywhere one was within five paces of excess: *monstrum in animo* was the general danger. "The impulses want to play the tyrant; one must invent a *counter-tyrant* who is stronger." When the physiognomist had revealed to Socrates who he was—a cave of bad appetites—the great master of irony let slip another word which is the key to his character. "This is true," he said, "but I mastered them all." *How* did Socrates become master over *himself?* His case was, at bottom, merely the extreme case, only the most striking instance of what was then beginning to be a universal distress: no one was any longer master over himself, the instincts turned *against* each other. He fascinated, being this extreme case; his awe-inspiring ugliness proclaimed him as such to all who could see: he fascinated, of course, even more as an answer, a solution, an apparent *cure* of this case.

10

When one finds it necessary to turn *reason* into a tyrant, as Socrates did, the danger cannot be slight that something else will play the tyrant. Rationality was then hit upon as the savior; neither Socrates nor his "patients" had any choice about being rational: it was *de rigeur,* it was their last resort. The fanaticism with which all Greek reflection throws itself upon rationality betrays a desperate situation; there was danger, there was but one choice: either to perish or—to be *absurdly rational.* The moralism of the Greek philosophers from Plato on is pathologically conditioned; so is their esteem of dialectics. Reason-virtue-happiness, that means merely that one must imitate Socrates and counter the dark appetites with a permanent daylight—the daylight of reason. One must be clever, clear, bright at any price: any concession to the instincts, to the unconscious, leads *downward.*

11

I have given to understand how it was that Socrates fascinated: he seemed to be a physician, a savior. Is it necessary to go on to demonstrate the error in his faith in "rationality at any price"? It is a self-deception on the part of philosophers and moralists if they believe that they are extricating themselves from decadence when they merely wage war against it. Extrication lies beyond their strength: what they choose as a means, as salvation, is itself but another expression of decadence; they change its expression, but they do not get rid of decadence itself. Socrates was a misunderstanding; *the whole improvement-morality, including the Christian, was a misunderstanding.* The most blinding daylight; rationality at any price; life, bright, cold, cautious, conscious, without instinct, in opposition to the instincts—all this too was a mere disease, another disease, and by no means a return to "virtue," to "health," to happiness. To *have* to fight the instincts—that is the formula of decadence: as long as life is *ascending,* happiness equals instinct.

12

Did he himself still comprehend this, this most brilliant of all self-outwitters? Was this what he said to himself in the end, in the *wisdom* of his courage to die? Socrates *wanted* to die: not Athens, but he himself chose the hemlock; he forced Athens to sentence him. "Socrates is no physician," he said softly to himself; "here death alone is the physician. Socrates himself has merely been sick a long time."

NOTE

1. "Contest."

Based on his idea of
slave morality as opposed
to master morality.
The Dionysian & Apollonian

2

PHILOSOPHY

and

HUMAN NATURE

In everything we think, say, or do, we assume—consciously or unconsciously, for good or for ill—a particular picture of human nature. Beneath everything, we order our lives by a conception of what we are, a picture of what is possible and necessary for human beings. Consider for example a woman trying to decide whether to try for admission to medical school, knowing that the studying necessary would require a sacrifice of her other pleasures. She wants very much to become a physician; at the same time, she knows that competition for places in medical schools is intense and that without high grades and excellent examination scores she would have little chance for admission. Such grades and scores require much time and effort, and their pursuit would force her to forego other things that seem important. For example, it would not be possible for her to maintain a wide circle of friends, nor would she be able to continue her volunteer work tutoring children with learning disabilities. Furthermore, she might wonder whether, given the rigors of her study program, she would have to give up any hopes of romantic involvement until she has her degree. These are difficult choices. How does one decide whether to sacrifice the satisfactions of the present for the (possible) rewards of the future? How does one balance the value of meaningful work (assuming one can get it) against the values of close personal relationships and immediate service to others in need? More often than we would like to admit, we are all faced by these or equally difficult questions.

How do we make such awful choices? Often, of course, we do not *make* them. We *drift into* them, ingeniously refusing to face them squarely. In spite of our great capacities for procrastination and self-deception, sometimes we *do* make these decisions. Women sometimes decide to try for admission to medical school, and sometimes they decide not to. What is the basis for such decisions?

The ultimate basis seems to be a conception of one's nature as a human being. To see this it is necessary to distinguish the real basis from all the apparent ones. Our hypothetical woman may insist, quite sincerely, that she made her decision without any "philosophical" thought about human nature. She may say that she decided to try for admission to medical school because she thought she'd hate herself if she didn't, or she thought it was the morally right thing to do, or after prayer she decided it was God's will for her life. Still, all these replies rest on profound conceptions of human nature. If she goes to medical school to seek satisfaction and avoid distress, she is assuming a picture of what a person is and ought to be (roughly, a creature of appetite and aversion). If she goes out of ethical duty or religious conviction, a different conception of the person is involved. Any substantial ethical theory will rest its account of the "good life" on a theory of human nature; likewise, a theology necessarily includes an account of mankind in relation to God.

Here we can begin to see one level of meaning in the familiar Socratic injunction to "Know thyself." Until one knows oneself, not just in the sense that one knows one's own individual traits and capacities but also in the sense that one knows one's deepest nature, one cannot live the appropriate life. Without this essential knowledge of self, a life of virtue —a life of distinctively human excellence—is impossible. Without a clear conception of human being, one cannot intelligently make the decisions that determine happiness or misery for oneself and others. To decide well, our imaginary woman must have self-knowledge in the most profound sense.

Naturally, it is rare that one clear conception of human nature dominates throughout life or even at a particular moment of decision. Our self-understanding is usually confused, with rival accounts of our nature vigorously claiming parts of our allegiance. We might perceive ourselves as pleasure-seeking, pain-avoiding mechanisms; at the same time, we might think of ourselves as free moral agents or as children of God. These incompatible self-conceptions clash, inevitably making our most important decisions matters of darkness and strife.

Such a situation provides a significant occasion for philosophy. If an understanding of our nature is the basis for our most important decisions, and if our self-conceptions are typically unconscious, confused, and inconsistent, then a philosophical investigation of human nature seems essential to the rational autonomy valued so highly by Socrates. Unless we become conscious of the self-images which shape our thoughts and actions, and clarify these images, looking to see on what evidence they rest, we will continue to live under the spell of piecemeal and often fantastic self-conceptions, forfeiting any chance to order our lives on rational principle. We will repeat past errors and condemn ourselves to the rat-runs built by confusion and illusion.

In this section we have presented readings which express some of the major philosophical conceptions of human nature. Some philosophers identify reason as the fundamental human quality; others emphasize passion and appetite. We have also included philosophers who reject the idea of a definite human nature as a compromise of our self-creative impetus. As with all the topics in this anthology, our philosophical impulse here is Socratic: we present these views of human nature as *occasions* for philosophy. Rather than a body of sterile doctrine, Socratic philosophy is an activity aiming at self-knowledge; it is the attempt to achieve autonomy through self-critical investigation. These competing views of human nature are not just objects of intellectual interest; rather, they profoundly determine quite different individual and social ideals. Our acceptance or rejection of them is not simply an "academic" matter. For the Socratic philosopher, an occasion for philosophy is an occasion which determines the quality of his or her life.

Persons as Essentially Rational Beings

Plato

Socrates: The just man then, if we regard the idea of justice only, will be like the just State?

Glaucon: He will.

Socrates: And a State was thought by us to be just when the three classes in the State severally did their own business; and also thought to be temperate and valiant and wise by reason of certain other affections and qualities of these same classes?

Glaucon: True.

Socrates: And so of the individual; we may assume that he has the same three principles in his own soul which are found in the State; and he may be rightly described in the same terms, because he is affected in the same manner?

From the *Republic,* from *The Dialogues of Plato,* trans. by Benjamin Jowett, Vol. III, 1892.

Glaucon: Certainly.

Socrates: Once more then, O my friend, we have alighted upon an easy question—whether the soul has these three principles or not?

Glaucon: An easy question! Nay, rather, Socrates, the proverb holds that hard is the good.

Socrates: Very true; and I do not think that the method which we are employing is at all adequate to the accurate solution of this question; the true method is another and a longer one. Still we may arrive at a solution not below the level of the previous enquiry.

Glaucon: May we not be satisfied with that?—under the circumstances, I am quite content.

Socrates: I too shall be extremely well satisfied.

Glaucon: Then faint not in pursuing the speculation.

Socrates: Must we not acknowledge that in each of us there are the same principles and habits which there are in the State; and that from the individual they pass into the State?—how else can they come there? Take the quality of passion or spirit;—it would be ridiculous to imagine that this quality, when found in States, is not derived from the individuals who are supposed to possess it, e.g., the Thracians, Scythians, and in general the northern nations; and the same may be said of the love of knowledge, which is the special characteristic of our part of the world, or of the love of money, which may, with equal truth, be attributed to the Phoenicians and Egyptians.

Glaucon: Exactly so.

Socrates: There is no difficulty in understanding this.

Glaucon: None whatever.

Socrates: But the question is not quite so easy when we proceed to ask whether these principles are three or one; whether, that is to say, we learn with one part of our nature, are angry with another, and with a third part desire the satisfaction of our natural appetites; or whether the whole soul comes into play in each sort of action—to determine that is the difficulty.

Glaucon: Yes; there lies the difficulty.

Socrates: Then let us now try and determine whether they are the same or different.

Glaucon: How can we?

Socrates: The same thing clearly cannot act or be acted upon in the same part or in relation to the same thing at the same time, in contrary ways; and therefore whenever this contradiction occurs in things apparently the same, we know that they are really not the same, but different.

Glaucon: Good.

Socrates: For example, can the same thing be at rest and in motion at the same time in the same part?

Glaucon: Impossible.

Socrates: Still, let us have a more precise statement of terms, lest we should hereafter fall out by the way. Imagine the case of a man who is standing and also moving his hands and his head, and suppose a person to say that one and the same person is in motion and at rest at the same moment—to such a mode of speech we should object, and should rather say that one part of him is in motion while another is at rest.

Glaucon: Very true.

Socrates: And suppose the objector to refine still further, and to draw the nice distinction that not only parts of tops, but whole tops, when they spin round with their pegs fixed on the spot, are at rest and in motion at the same time (and he may say the same of anything which revolves in the same spot), his objection would not be admitted by us, because in such cases things are not at rest and in motion in the same parts of themselves; we should rather say that they have both an axis and a circumference; and that the axis stands still, for there is no deviation from the perpendicular; and that the circumference goes round. But if, while revolving, the axis inclines either to the right or left, forwards or backwards, then in no point of view can they be at rest.

Glaucon: That is the correct mode of describing them.

Socrates: Then none of these objections will confuse us, or incline us to believe that the same thing at the same time, in the same part or in relation to the same thing, can act or be acted upon in contrary ways.

Glaucon: Certainly not, according to my way of thinking.

Socrates: Yet, that we may not be compelled to examine all such objections, and prove at length that they are untrue, let us assume their absurdity, and go forward on the understanding that hereafter, if this assumption turn out to be untrue, all the consequences which follow shall be withdrawn.

Glaucon: Yes, that will be the best way.

Socrates: Well, would you not allow that assent and dissent, desire and aversion, attraction and repulsion, are all of them opposites, whether they are regarded as active or passive (for that makes no difference in the fact of their opposition)?

Glaucon: Yes, they are opposites.

Socrates: Well, and hunger and thirst, and the desires in general, and again willing and wishing,—all these you would refer to the classes already mentioned. You would say—would you not?—that the soul of him who desires is seeking after the object of his desire; or that he is drawing to himself the thing which he wishes to possess: or again, when a person wants anything to be given him, his mind, longing for the realization of his desire, intimates his wish to have it by a nod of assent, as if he had been asked a question?

Glaucon: Very true.

Spirit = animating force in body

Socrates: And what would you say of unwillingness and dislike and the absence of desire; should not these be referred to the opposite class of repulsion and rejection?

Glaucon: Certainly.

Socrates: Admitting this to be true of desire generally, let us suppose a particular class of desires, and out of these we will select hunger and thirst, as they are termed, which are the most obvious to them?

Glaucon: Let us take that class.

Socrates: The object of one is food, and of the other drink?

Gaucon: Yes.

Socrates: And here comes the point: is not thirst the desire which the soul has of drink, and of drink only; not of drink qualified by anything else; for example, warm or cold, or much or little, or, in a word, drink of any particular sort: but if the thirst be accompanied by heat, then the desire is of cold drink; or, if accompanied by cold, then of warm drink; or, if the thirst be excessive, then the drink which is desired will be excessive; or, if not great, the quantity of drink will also be small: but thirst pure and simple will desire drink pure and simple, which is the natural satisfaction of thirst, as food is of hunger?

Glaucon: Yes; the simple desire is, as you say, in every case of the simple object, and the qualified desire of the qualified object.

Socrates: But here a confusion may arise; and I should wish to guard against an opponent starting up and saying that no man desires drink only, but good drink, or food only, but good food; for good is the universal object of desire, and thirst being a desire, will necessarily be thirst after good drink; and the same is true of every other desire.

Glaucon: Yes, the opponent might have something to say.

Socrates: Nevertheless I should still maintain, that of relatives some have a quality attached to either term of the relation; others are simple and have their correlatives simple.

Glaucon: I do not know what you mean.

Socrates: Well, you know of course that the greater is relative to the less?

Glaucon: Certainly.

Socrates: And the much greater to the much less?

Glaucon: Yes.

Socrates: And the sometime greater to the sometime less, and the greater that is to be to the less that is to be?

Glaucon: Certainly.

Socrates: And so of more and less, and of other correlative terms, such as the double and the half, or again, the heavier and the lighter, the swifter and the slower; and of hot and cold, and of any other relatives;—is not this true of all of them?

Glaucon: Yes.

Socrates: And does not the same principle hold in the sciences? The

Soul = essence of humanity   iRRaTioNal — 3 parts
Life-giving force — spirit +
appetite
Persons as Essentially Rational Beings   65   Takes
us off
in different
direction

object of science is knowledge (assuming that to be the true definition), but the object of a particular science is a particular kind of
knowledge; I mean, for example, that the science of house-building
is a kind of knowledge which is defined and distinguished from
other kinds and is therefore termed architecture.

Glaucon: Certainly.

Socrates: Because it has a particular quality which no other has?

Glaucon: Yes.

Socrates: And it has this particular quality because it has an object of
a particular kind; and this is true of the other arts and sciences?

Glaucon: Yes.

Socrates: Now, then, if I have made myself clear, you will understand
my original meaning in what I said about relatives. My meaning
was, that if one term of a relation is taken alone, the other is taken
alone; if one term is qualified, the other is also qualified. I do not
mean to say that relatives may not be disparate, or that the science
of health is healthy, or of disease necessarily diseased, or that the
sciences of good and evil are therefore good and evil; but only that,
when the term science is no longer used absolutely, but has a qualified object which in this case is the nature of health and disease,
it becomes defined, and is hence called not merely science, but the
science of medicine.

Glaucon: I quite understand, and I think as you do.

Socrates: Would you not say that thirst is one of these essentially relative terms, having clearly a relation—

Glaucon: Yes, thirst is relative to drink.

Socrates: And a certain kind of thirst is relative to a certain kind of
drink; but thirst taken alone is neither of much nor little, nor of
good nor bad, nor of any particular kind of drink, but of drink
only?

Glaucon: Certainly.

Socrates: Then the soul of the thirsty one, in so far as he is thirsty,
desires only drink; for this he yearns and tries to obtain it?

Glaucon: That is plain.

Socrates: And if you suppose something which pulls a thirsty soul away
from drink, that must be different from the thirsty principle which
draws him like a beast to drink; for, as we were saying, the same
thing cannot at the same time with the same part of itself act in
contrary ways about the same.

Glaucon: Impossible.

Socrates: No more than you can say that the hands of the archer push
and pull the bow at the same time, but what you say is that one
hand pushes and the other pulls.

Glaucon: Exactly so.

Socrates: And might a man be thirsty, and yet unwilling to drink?

Glaucon: Yes, it constantly happens.

Socrates: And in such a case what is one to say? Would you not say

Reason directs these 2 to a desired good
Plato sought to make a work off and
with one's life

that there was something in the soul bidding a man to drink, and something else forbidding him, which is other and stronger than the principle which bids him?

Glaucon: I should say so.

Socrates: And the forbidding principle is derived from reason, and that which bids and attracts proceeds from passion and disease?

Glaucon: Clearly.

Socrates: Then we may fairly assume that they are two, and that they differ from one another; the one with which a man reasons, we may call the rational principle of the soul, the other, with which he loves and hungers and thirsts and feels the flutterings of any other desire, may be termed the irrational or appetitive, the ally of sundry pleasures and satisfactions?

Glaucon: Yes, we may fairly assume them to be different.

Socrates: Then let us finally determine that there are two principles existing in the soul. And what of passion, or spirit? Is it a third, or akin to one of the preceding?

Glaucon: I should be inclined to say—akin to desire.

Socrates: Well, there is a story which I remember to have heard, and in which I put faith. The story is, that Leontius, the son of Aglaion, coming up one day from the Piraeus, under the north wall on the outside, observed some dead bodies lying on the ground at the place of execution. He felt a desire to see them, and also a dread and abhorrence of them; for a time he struggled and covered his eyes, but at length the desire got the better of him; and forcing them open, he ran up to the dead bodies, saying, Look, ye wretches, take your fill of the fair sight.

Glaucon: I have heard the story myself.

Socrates: The moral of the tale is, that anger at times goes to war with desire, as though they were two distinct things.

Glaucon: Yes; that is the meaning.

Socrates: And are there not many other cases in which we observe that when a man's desires violently prevail over his reason, he reviles himself, and is angry at the violence within him, and that in this struggle, which is like the struggle of factions in a State, his spirit is on the side of his reason;—but for the passionate or spirited element to take part with the desires when reason decides that she should not be opposed, is a sort of thing which I believe that you never observed occurring in yourself, nor, as I should imagine, in any one else?

Glaucon: Certainly not.

Socrates: Suppose that a man thinks he has done a wrong to another, the nobler he is the less able is he to feel indignant at any suffering, such as hunger, or cold, or any other pain which the injured person may inflict upon him—these he deems to be just, and, as I say, his anger refuses to be excited by them.

Glaucon: True.

Socrates: But when he thinks that he is the sufferer of the wrong, then he boils and chafes, and is on the side of what he believes to be justice; and because he suffers hunger or cold or other pain he is only the more determined to persevere and conquer. His noble spirit will not be quelled until he either slays or is slain; or until he hears the voice of the shepherd, that is, reason, bidding his dog bark no more.

Glaucon: The illustration is perfect; and in our State, as we were saying, the auxiliaries were to be dogs, and to hear the voice of the rulers, who are their shepherds.

Socrates: I perceive that you quite understand me; there is, however, a further point which I wish you to consider.

Glaucon: What point?

Socrates: You remember that passion or spirit appeared at first sight to be a kind of desire, but now we should say quite the contrary; for in the conflict of the soul spirit is arrayed on the side of the rational principle.

Glaucon: Most assuredly.

Socrates: But a further question arises: Is passion different from reason also, or only a kind of reason; in which latter case, instead of three principles in the soul, there will only be two, the rational and the concupiscent; or rather, as the State was composed of three classes, traders, auxiliaries, counsellors, so may there not be in the individual soul a third element which is passion or spirit, and when not corrupted by bad education is the natural auxiliary of reason?

Glaucon: Yes, there must be a third.

Socrates: Yes, if passion, which has already been shown to be different from desire, turn out also to be different from reason.

Glaucon: But that is easily proved:—We may observe even in young children that they are full of spirit almost as soon as they are born, whereas some of them never seem to attain to the use of reason, and most of them late enough.

Socrates: Excellent, and you may see passion equally in brute animals, which is a further proof of the truth of what you are saying. And we may once more appeal to the words of Homer, which have been already quoted by us,

'He smote his breast, and thus rebuked his soul;' [1]

for in this verse Homer has clearly supposed the power which reasons about the better and worse to be different from the unreasoning anger which is rebuked by it.

Glaucon: Very true.

Socrates: And so, after much tossing, we have reached land, and are fairly agreed that the same principles which exist in the State exist also in the individual, and that they are three in number.

Glaucon: Exactly.

Socrates: Must we not then infer that the individual is wise in the same way, and in virtue of the same quality which makes the State wise?

Glaucon: Certainly.

Socrates: Also that the same quality which constitutes courage in the State constitutes courage in the individual, and that both the State and the individual bear the same relation to all the other virtues?

Glaucon: Assuredly.

Socrates: And the individual will be acknowledged by us to be just in the same way in which the State is just?

Glaucon: That follows of course.

Socrates: We cannot but remember that the justice of the State consisted in each of the three classes doing the work of its own class?

Glaucon: We are not very likely to have forgotten.

Socrates: We must recollect that the individual in whom the several qualities of his nature do their own work will be just, and will do his own work?

Glaucon: Yes, we must remember that too.

Socrates: And ought not the rational principle, which is wise, and has the care of the whole soul, to rule, and the passionate or spirited principle to be the subject and ally?

Glaucon: Certainly.

Socrates: And, as we were saying, the united influence of music and gymnastic will bring them into accord, nerving and sustaining the reason with noble words and lessons, and moderating and soothing and civilizing the wildness of passion by harmony and rhythm?

Glaucon: Quite true.

Socrates: And these two, thus nurtured and educated, and having learned truly to know their own functions, will rule over the concupiscent, which in each of us is the largest part of the soul and by nature most insatiable of gain; over this they will keep guard, lest, waxing great and strong with the fulness of bodily pleasures, as they are termed, the concupiscent soul, no longer confined to her own sphere, should attempt to enslave and rule those who are not her natural-born subjects, and overturn the whole life of man?

Glaucon: Very true.

Socrates: Both together will they not be the best defenders of the whole soul and the whole body against attacks from without; the one counselling, and the other fighting under his leader, and courageously executing his commands and counsels?

Glaucon: True.

Socrates: And he is to be deemed courageous whose spirit retains in pleasure and in pain the commands of reason about what he ought or ought not to fear?

Glaucon: Right.

Socrates: And him we call wise who has in him that little part which rules, and which proclaims these commands; that part too being supposed to have a knowledge of what is for the interest of each of the three parts and of the whole?

Glaucon: Assuredly.

Socrates: And would you not say that he is temperate who has these same elements in friendly harmony, in whom the one ruling principle of reason, and the two subject ones of spirit and desire are equally agreed that reason ought to rule, and do not rebel?

Glaucon: Certainly, that is the true account of temperance whether in the State or individual.

Socrates: And surely, we have explained again and again how and by virtue of what quality a man will be just.

Glaucon: That is very certain.

Socrates: And is justice dimmer in the individual, and is her form different, or is she the same which we found her to be in the State?

Glaucon: There is no difference in my opinion.

Socrates: Because, if any doubt is still lingering in our minds, a few commonplace instances will satisfy us of the truth of what I am saying.

Glaucon: What sort of instances do you mean?

Socrates: If the case is put to us, must we not admit that the just State, or the man who is trained in the principles of such a State, will be less likely than the unjust to make away with a deposit of gold or silver? Would any one deny this?

Glaucon: No one.

Socrates: Will the just man or citizen ever be guilty of sacrilege or theft, or treachery either to his friends or to his country?

Glaucon: Never.

Socrates: Neither will he ever break faith where there have been oaths or agreements.

Glaucon: Impossible.

Socrates: No one will be less likely to commit adultery, or to dishonor his father and mother, or to fail in his religious duties?

Glaucon: No one.

Socrates: And the reason is that each part of him is doing its own business, whether in ruling or being ruled?

Glaucon: Exactly so.

Socrates: Are you satisfied then that the quality which makes such men and such states is justice, or do you hope to discover some other?

Glaucon: Not I, indeed.

Socrates: Then our dream has been realized; and the suspicion which we entertained at the beginning of our work of construction, that some divine power must have conducted us to a primary form of justice, has now been verified?

Glaucon: Yes, certainly.

Socrates: And the division of labour which required the carpenter and the shoemaker and the rest of the citizens to be doing each his own business, and not another's, was a shadow of justice, and for that reason it was of use?

Glaucon: Clearly.

Socrates: But in reality justice was such as we were describing, being concerned however, not with the outward man, but with the inward, which is the true self and concernment of man: for the just man does not permit the several elements within him to interfere with one another, or any of them to do the work of others,—he sets in order his own inner life, and is his own master and his own law, and at peace with himself; and when he has bound together the three principles within him, which may be compared to the higher, lower, and middle notes of the scale, and the intermediate intervals —when he has bound all these together, and is no longer many, but has become one entirely temperate and perfectly adjusted nature, then he proceeds to act, if he has to act, whether in a matter of property, or in the treatment of the body, or in some affair of politics or private business; always thinking and calling that which preserves and co-operates with this harmonious condition, just and good action, and the knowledge which presides over it, wisdom, and that which at any time impairs this condition, he will call unjust action, and the opinion which presides over it ignorance.

Glaucon: You have said the exact truth, Socrates.

Socrates: Very good; and if we were to affirm that we had discovered the just man and the just State, and the nature of justice in each of them, we should not be telling a falsehood?

Glaucon: Most certainly not.

Socrates: May we say so, then?

Glaucon: Let us say so.

Socrates: And now, I said, injustice has to be considered.

Glaucon: Clearly.

Socrates: Must not injustice be a strife which arises among the three principles—a meddlesomeness, and interference, and rising up of a part of the soul against the whole, an assertion of unlawful authority, which is made by a rebellious subject against a true prince, of whom he is the natural vassal,—what is all this confusion and delusion but injustice, and intemperance and cowardice and ignorance, and every form of vice?

Glaucon: Exactly so.

Socrates: And if the nature of justice and injustice be known, then the meaning of acting unjustly and being unjust, or, again, of acting justly, will also be perfectly clear?

Glaucon: What do you mean?

Socrates: Why, they are like disease and health; being in the soul just what disease and health are in the body.

Glaucon: How so?

Socrates: Why, that which is healthy causes health, and that which is unhealthy causes disease.

Glaucon: Yes.

Socrates: And just actions cause justice, and unjust actions cause injustice?

Glaucon: That is certain.

Socrates: And the creation of health is the institution of a natural order and government of one by another in the parts of the body; and the creation of disease is the production of a state of things at variance with this natural order?

Glaucon: True.

Socrates: And is not the creation of justice the institution of a natural order and government of one by another in the parts of the soul, and the creation of injustice the production of a state of things at variance with the natural order?

Glaucon: Exactly so, he said.

Socrates: Then virtue is the health and beauty and well-being of the soul, and vice the disease and weakness and deformity of the same?

Glaucon: True.

Socrates: And do not good practices lead to virtue, and evil practices to vice?

Glaucon: Assuredly.

Socrates: Still our old question of the comparative advantage of justice and injustice has not been answered: Which is the more profitable, to be just and act justly and practise virtue, whether seen or unseen of gods and men, or to be unjust and act unjustly, if only unpunished and unreformed?

Glaucon: In my judgment, Socrates, the question has now become ridiculous. We know that, when the bodily constitution is gone, life is no longer endurable, though pampered with all kinds of meats and drinks, and having all wealth and all power; and shall we be told that when the very essence of the vital principle is undermined and corrupted, life is still worth having to a man, if only he be allowed to do whatever he likes with the single exception that he is not to acquire justice and virtue, or to escape from injustice and vice; assuming them both to be such as we have described?

Socrates: Yes, the question is, as you say, ridiculous. Still, as we are near the spot at which we may see the truth in the clearest manner with our own eyes, let us not faint by the way.

Glaucon: Certainly not.

Socrates: Come up hither, and behold the various forms of vice, those of them, I mean, which are worth looking at.

Glaucon: I am following you, proceed.

Socrates: The argument seems to have reached a height from which, as from some tower of speculation, a man may look down and see that virtue is one, but that the forms of vice are innumerable; there being four special ones which are deserving of note.

Glaucon: What do you mean?

Socrates: I mean that there appear to be as many forms of the soul as there are distinct forms of the State.

Glaucon: How many?

Socrates: There are five of the State, and five of the soul, I said.

Glaucon: What are they?

Socrates: The first is that which we have been describing, and which may be said to have two names, monarchy and aristocracy, accordingly as rule is exercised by one distinguished man or by many.

Glaucon: True.

Socrates: But I regard the two names as describing one form only; for whether the government is in the hands of one or many, if the governors have been trained in the manner which we have supposed, the fundamental laws of the State will be maintained.

Glaucon: That is true.

NOTE

1. Od. xx. 17, quoted supra, III. 390 D.

Persons as Creatures of Appetite and Aversion

Thomas Hobbes

Men by Nature Equal

Nature hath made men so equal, in the faculties of the body, and mind; as that though there be found one man sometimes manifestly stronger in body, or of quicker mind than another; yet when all is reckoned together, the difference between man, and man, is not so considerable, as that one man can thereupon claim to himself any benefit, to which another may not pretend, as well as he. For as to the strength of body, the weakest has strength enough to kill the strongest, either by secret machination, or by confederacy with others, that are in the same danger with himself.

From Thomas Hobbes, the *Leviathan.*

And as to the faculties of the mind, setting aside the arts grounded upon words, and especially that skill of proceeding upon general, and infallible rules, called science; which very few have, and but in few things; as being not a native faculty, born with us; not attained, as prudence, while we look after somewhat else, I find yet a greater equality amongst men, than that of strength. For prudence, is but experience; which equal time, equally bestows on all men, in those things they equally apply themselves unto. That which may perhaps make such equality incredible, is but a vain conceit of one's own wisdom, which almost all men think they have in a greater degree, than the vulgar; that is, than all men but themselves, and a few others, whom by fame, or for concurring with themselves, they approve. For such is the nature of men, that howsoever they may acknowledge many others to be more witty, or more eloquent, or more learned; yet they will hardly believe there be many so wise as themselves; for they see their own wit at hand, and other men's at a distance. But this proveth rather that men are in that point equal, than unequal. For there is not ordinarily a greater sign of the equal distribution of any thing, than that every man is contented with his share.

From Equality Proceeds Diffidence — *Lacking confidence*

From this equality of ability, ariseth equality of hope in the attaining of our ends. And therefore if any two men desire the same thing, which nevertheless they cannot both enjoy, they become enemies; and in the way to their end, which is principally their own conservation, and sometimes their delectation only, endeavour to destroy, or subdue one another. And from hence it comes to pass, that where an invader hath no more to fear, than another man's single power; if one plant, sow, build, or possess a convenient seat, others may probably be expected to come prepared with forces united, to dispossess, and deprive him, not only of the fruit of his labour, but also of his life, or liberty. And the invader again is in the like danger of another.

From Diffidence War

man builds his power in anticipation of some one taking his

And from this diffidence of one another, there is no way for any man to secure himself, so reasonable, as anticipation; that is, by force, or wiles, to master the persons of all men he can, so long, till he see no other power great enough to endanger him: and this is no more than his own conservation requireth and is generally allowed. Also because there be some, that taking pleasure in contemplating their own power in the acts of conquest, which they pursue farther than their security requires; if others, that otherwise would be glad to be at ease within modest bounds, should not by invasion increase their power, they would not be able, long time, by standing only on their defence, to subsist. And by consequence,

we seek safety

IF someone is satisfied with what they have + doesn't increase it, then they won't last.

such augmentation of dominion over men being necessary to a man's conservation, it ought to be allowed him.

Again, men have no pleasure, but on the contrary a great deal of grief, in keeping company, where there is no power able to over-awe them all. For every man looketh that his companion should value him, at the same rate he sets upon himself: and upon all signs of contempt, or under-valuing, naturally endeavours, as far as he dares, (which amongst them that have no common power to keep them in quiet, is far enough to make them destroy each other), to extort a greater value from his contemners, by damage; and from others, by the example.

So that in the nature of man, we find three principal causes of quarrel. First, competition; secondly, diffidence; thirdly, glory.

The first, maketh men invade for gain; the second, for safety; and the third, for reputation. The first use violence; to make themselves masters of other men's persons, wives, children, and cattle; the second, to defend them; the third, for trifles, as a word, a smile, a different opinion, and any other sign of undervalue, either direct in their persons, or by reflec-tion in their kindred, their friends, their nation, their profession or their name.

Out of Civil States, There Is Always War of Every One Against Every One

Hereby it is manifest, that during the time men live without a common power to keep them all in awe, they are in that condition which is called war; and such a war, as is of every man, against every man. For WAR, con-sisteth not in battle only, or the act of fighting; but in a tract of time, wherein the will to contend by battle is sufficiently known: and therefore the notion of *time,* is to be considered in the nature of war; as it is in the nature of weather. For as the nature of foul weather, lieth not in a shower or two of rain; but in an inclination thereto of many days to-gether: so the nature of war, consisteth not in actual fighting; but in the known disposition thereto, during all the time there is no assurance to the contrary. All other time is PEACE.

The Incommodities of Such a War

Whatsoever therefore is consequent to a time of war, where every man is enemy to every man; the same is consequent to the time, wherein men live without other security, than what their own strength, and their own invention shall furnish them withal. In such condition, there is no place for industry; because the fruit thereof is uncertain: and consequently no culture of the earth; no navigation, nor use of the commodities that may be imported by sea; no commodious building; no instruments of moving, and removing, such things as require much force; no knowledge of the face of the earth; no account of time; no arts; no letters; no society; and which is worst of all, continual fear, and danger of violent death; and the life of man, solitary, poor, nasty, brutish, and short.

It may seem strange to some man that has not well weighed these things; that nature should thus dissociate, and render men apt to invade, and destroy one another: and he may therefore, not trusting to this inference, made from the passions, desire perhaps to have the same confirmed by experience. Let him therefore consider with himself, when taking a journey, he arms himself, and seeks to go well accompanied; when going to sleep, he locks his doors; when even in his house he locks his chests; and this when he knows there be laws, and public officers, armed, to revenge all injuries shall be done him; what opinion he has of his fellow-subjects, when he rides armed; of his fellow citizens, when he locks his doors; and of his children, and servants, when he locks his chests. Does he not there as much accuse mankind by his actions, as I do by my words? But neither of us accuse man's nature in it. The desires, and other passions of man, are in themselves no sin. No more are the actions, that proceed from those passions, till they know a law that forbids them: which till laws be made they cannot know: nor can any law be made, till they have agreed upon the person that shall make it.

It may peradventure be thought, there was never such a time, nor condition of war as this; and I believe it was never generally so, over all the world: but there are many places, where they live so now. For the savage people in many places of America, except the government of small families, the concord whereof dependeth on natural lust, have no government at all; and live at this day in that brutish manner, as I said before. Howsoever, it may be perceived what manner of life there would be, where there were no common power to fear, by the manner of life, which men that have formerly lived under a peaceful government, use to degenerate into, in a civil war.

But though there had never been any time, wherein particular men were in a condition of war one against another; yet in all times, kings, and persons of sovereign authority, because of their independency, are in continual jealousies, and in the state and posture of gladiators; having their weapons pointing, and their eyes fixed on one another; that is, their forts, garrisons, and guns upon the frontiers of their kingdoms; and continual spies upon their neighbours; which is a posture of war. But because they uphold thereby, the industry of their subjects; there does not follow from it, that misery, which accompanies the liberty of particular men.

In Such a War Nothing Is Unjust

To this war of every man, against every man, this also is consequent; that nothing can be unjust. The notions of right and wrong, justice and injustice have there no place. Where there is no common power, there is no law: where no law, no injustice. Force, and fraud, are in war the two cardinal virtues. Justice, and injustice are none of the faculties neither of the body, nor mind. If they were, they might be in a man that were alone in the world, as well as his senses, and passions. They are qualities, that relate to men in society, not in solitude. It is consequent also to the same condition, that there be no propriety, no dominion, no *mine* and *thine* distinct; but only that to be every man's, that he can get: and for so long, as he can keep it. And thus much for the ill condition, which man by mere nature is actually placed in; though with a possibility to come out of it, consisting partly in the passions, partly in his reason.

The Passions that Incline Men to Peace

The passions that incline men to peace, are fear of death; desire of such things as are necessary to commodious living; and a hope by their industry to obtain them. And reason suggesteth convenient articles of peace, upon which men may be drawn to agreement. These articles, are they, which otherwise are called the Laws of Nature.

Persons as Products of Social Conditioning

B.F. Skinner

MAN A MACHINE

Behavior is a primary characteristic of living things. We almost identify it with life itself. Anything which moves is likely to be called alive—especially when the movement has direction or acts to alter the environment. Movement adds verisimilitude to any model of an organism. The puppet comes to life when it moves, and idols which move or breathe smoke are especially awe-inspiring. Robots and other mechanical creatures entertain us just because they move. And there is significance in the etymology of the *animated* cartoon.

Machines seem alive simply because they are in motion. The fascination of the steam shovel is legendary. Less familiar machines may actually be frightening. We may feel that it is only primitive people who mistake them for living creatures today, but at one time they were unfamiliar to everyone. When Wordsworth and Coleridge once passed a steam engine,

From B. F. Skinner, *The Self as an Organized System of Responses*, from *Science and Human Behavior* (New York: The Free Press, 1965). Copyright © 1953 by Macmillan Publishing Co., Inc.

Wordsworth observed that it was scarcely possible to divest oneself of the impression that it had life and volition. "Yes," said Coleridge, "it is a giant with one idea."

A mechanical toy which imitated human behavior led to the theory of what we now call reflex action. In the first part of the seventeenth century certain moving figures were commonly installed in private and public gardens as sources of amusement. They were operated hydraulically. A young lady walking through a garden might step upon a small concealed platform. This would open a valve, water would flow into a piston, and a threatening figure would swing out from the bushes to frighten her. René Descartes knew how these figures worked, and he also knew how much they seemed like living creatures. He considered the possibility that the hydraulic system which explained the one might also explain the other. A muscle swells when it moves a limb—perhaps it is being inflated by a fluid coming along the nerves from the brain. The nerves which stretch from the surface of the body into the brain may be the strings which open the valves.

Descartes did not assert that the human organism always operates in this way. He favored the explanation in the case of animals, but he reserved a sphere of action for the "rational soul"—perhaps under religious pressure. It was not long before the additional step was taken, however, which produced the full-fledged doctrine of "man a machine." The doctrine did not owe its popularity to its plausibility—there was no reliable support for Descartes's theory—but rather to its shocking metaphysical and theoretical implications.

Since that time two things have happened: machines have become more lifelike, and living organisms have been found to be more like machines. Contemporary machines are not only more complex, they are deliberately designed to operate in ways which resemble human behavior. "Almost human" contrivances are a common part of our daily experience. Doors see us coming and open to receive us. Elevators remember our commands and stop at the correct floor. Mechanical hands lift imperfect items off a conveyor belt. Others write messages of fair legibility. Mechanical or electric calculators solve equations too difficult or too time-consuming for human mathematicians. Man has, in short, created the machine in his own image. And as a result, the living organism has lost some of its uniqueness. We are much less awed by machines than our ancestors were and less likely to endow the giant with even one idea. At the same time, we have discovered more about how the living organism works and are better able to see its machine-like properties.

THE SELF

What is meant by the "self" in self-control or self-knowledge? When a man jams his hands into his pockets to keep himself from biting his nails, *who* is controlling *whom*? When he discovers that a sudden mood must be due to a glimpse of an unpleasant person, *who* discovers *whose* mood to be due to *whose* visual response? Is the self which works to facilitate the recall of a name the same as the self which recalls it? When a thinker teases out an idea, is it the teaser who also eventually has the idea?

The self is most commonly used as a hypothetical cause of action. So long as external variables go unnoticed or are ignored, their function is assigned to an originating agent within the organism. If we cannot show what is responsible for a man's behavior, we say that he himself is responsible for it. The precursors of physical science once followed the same practice, but the wind is no longer blown by Aeolus, nor is the rain cast down by Jupiter Pluvius. Perhaps it is because the notion of personification is so close to a conception of a behaving individual that it has been difficult to dispense with similar explanations of behavior. The practice resolves our anxiety with respect to unexplained phenomena and is perpetuated because it does so.

Whatever the self may be, it is apparently not identical with the physical organism. The organism behaves, while the self initiates or directs behavior. Moreover, more than one self is needed to explain the behavior of one organism. A mere inconsistency in conduct from one moment to the next is perhaps no problem, for a single self could dictate different kinds of behavior from time to time. But there appear to be two selves acting simultaneously and in different ways when one self controls another or is aware of the activity of another.

The same facts are commonly expressed in terms of "personalities." The personality, like the self, is said to be responsible for features of behavior. For example, delinquent behavior is sometimes attributed to a psychopathic personality. Personalities may also be multiple. Two or more personalities may appear in alternation or concurrently. They are often in conflict with each other, and one may or may not be aware of what the other is doing.

Multiple selves or personalities are often said to be systematically related to each other. Freud conceived of the ego, superego, and id as distinguishable agents within the organism. The id was responsible for behavior which was ultimately reinforced with food, water, sexual contact, and other primary biological reinforcers. It was not unlike the selfish, aggressive "Old Adam" of Judeo-Christian theology, preoccupied with the basic deprivations and untouched by similar requirements on the parts of others. The superego—the "conscience" of Judeo-Christian theology—was responsible for the behavior which controlled the id. It used techniques of self-control acquired from the group. When these were verbal, they constituted "the still small voice of conscience." The superego and the id were inevitably opposed to each other, and Freud conceived of them as often in violent conflict. He appealed to a third agent—the ego—which, besides attempting to reach a compromise between the id and the superego, also dealt with the practical exigencies of the environment.

We may quarrel with any analysis which appeals to a self or personality as an inner determiner of action, but the facts which have been represented with such devices cannot be ignored. The three selves or personalities in the Freudian scheme represent important characteristics of behavior in a social milieu. Multiple personalities which are less systematically related to each other serve a similar function. A concept of self is not essential in an analysis of behavior, but what is the alternative way of treating the data?

THE SELF AS AN ORGANIZED SYSTEM OF RESPONSES

The best way to dispose of any explanatory fiction is to examine the facts upon which it is based. These usually prove to be, or suggest, variables which are acceptable from the point of view of scientific method. In the present case it appears that a self is simply a device for representing *a functionally unified system of responses*. In dealing with the data, we have to explain the functional unity of such systems and the various relationships which exist among them.

The Unity of a Self

A self may refer to a common *mode of action*. Such expressions as "The scholar is Man Thinking" or "He was a better talker than plumber" suggest personalities identified with *topographical subdivisions of behavior*. In a single skin we find the man of action and the dreamer, the solitary and the social spirit.

On the other hand, a personality may be tied to a particular type of occasion—when a system of responses is organized around a given *discriminative stimulus*. Types of behavior which are effective in achieving reinforcement upon occasion A are held together and distinguished from those effective upon occasion B. Thus one's personality in the bosom of one's family may be quite different from that in the presence of intimate friends.

Responses which lead to a common reinforcement, regardless of the situation, may also comprise a functional system. Here the principal variable is *deprivation*. A motion to adjourn a meeting which has run through the lunch hour may show "the hungry man speaking." One's personality may be very different before and after a satisfying meal. The libertine is very different from the ascetic who achieves his reinforcement from the ethical group, but the two may exist side by side in the same organism.

Emotional variables also establish personalities. Under the proper circumstances the timid soul may give way to the aggressive man. The hero may struggle to conceal the coward who inhabits the same skin.

The effects of *drugs* upon personality are well known. The euphoria of the morphine addict represents a special repertoire of responses the strength of which is attributable to an obvious variable. The alcoholic wakes on the morrow a sadder and wiser man.

It is easy to overestimate the unity of a group of responses, and unfortunately personification encourages us to do so. The concept of a self may have an early advantage in representing a relatively coherent response system, but it may lead us to expect consistencies and functional integrities which do not exist. The alternative to the use of the concept is simply to deal with demonstrated covariations in the strength of responses.

Relations Among Selves

Organized systems of responses may be related to each other in the same way as are single responses and for the same reasons. For example, two response systems may be incompatible. If the relevant variables are never present at the same time, the incompatibility is unimportant. If the environment of which behavior is a function is not consistent from moment to moment, there is no reason to expect consistency in behavior. The pious churchgoer on Sunday may become an aggressive, unscrupulous businessman on Monday. He possesses two response systems appropriate to different sets of circumstances, and his inconsistency is no greater than that of the environment which takes him to church on Sunday and to work on Monday. But the controlling variables may come together; during a sermon, the churchgoer may be asked to examine his business practices, or the businessman may engage in commercial transactions with his clergyman or his church. Trouble may then arise. Similarly, if an individual has developed different repertoires with family and friends, the two personalities come into conflict when he is with both at the same time. Many of the dramatic struggles which flood the literature on multiple personalities can be accounted for in the same way.

More systematic relations among personalities arise from controlling relations. In self-control, for example, the responses to be controlled are organized around certain immediate primary reinforcements. To the extent that competition for reinforcement makes this behavior aversive to others—and to this extent only—we may refer to an anti-social personality, the id or Old Adam. On the other hand, the controlling behavior engendered by the community consists of a selected group of practices evolved in the history of a particular culture because of their effect upon anti-social behavior. To the extent that this behavior works to the advantage of the community—and again to this extent only—we may speak of a unitary conscience, social conscience, or superego. These two sets of variables account, not only for the membership of each group of responses, but for the relation between them which we describe when we say that one personality is engaged in controlling the other. Other kinds of relations between personalities are evident in the processes of making a decision, solving a problem, or creating a work of art.

An important relation between selves is self-knowledge. The behavior which we call knowing is due to a particular kind of differential reinforcement. In even the most rudimentary community such questions as "What did you do?" or "What are you doing?" compel the individual to respond to his own overt behavior. Probably no one is completely unselfconscious in this sense. At the other extreme an advanced and relatively nonpractical society produces the highly introspective or introverted individual, whose repertoire of self-knowledge extends to his covert behavior—a repertoire which in some cultures may be almost nonexistent. An extensive development of self-knowledge is common in certain Eastern cultures and is emphasized from time to time in those of the West—for example, in the *culte du moi* of French literature. An efficient repertoire of this sort is sometimes set up in the individual for purposes of therapy. The patient under psychoanalysis may become highly skilled in observing his own covert behavior.

When an occasion arises upon which a report of the organism's own behavior, particularly at the covert level, is likely to be reinforced, the personality which makes the report is a specialist trained by a special set of contingencies. The self which is concerned with self-knowing functions concurrently with the behavioral system which it describes. But it is sometimes important to ask whether the selves generated by other contingencies "know about each other." The literature on multiple personalities raises the question as one of "continuity of memory." It is also an important consideration in the Freudian scheme: to what extent, for example, is the superego aware of the behavior of the id? The contingencies which set up the superego as a controlling system involve stimulation from the behavior of the id, but they do not necessarily establish responses of knowing about the behavior of the id. It is perhaps even less likely that the id will know about the superego. The ego can scarcely deal with conflicts between the other selves without responding to the behavior attributed to them, but this does not mean that the ego possesses a repertoire of knowing about such behavior in any other sense.

THE ABSENCE OF SELF-KNOWLEDGE

One of the most striking facts about self-knowledge is that it may be lacking. Several cases deserve comment.

A man may not know that *he has done something*. He may have behaved in a given way, perhaps energetically, and nevertheless be unable to describe what he has done. Examples range all the way from the unnoticed verbal slip to extended amnesias in which large areas of earlier behavior cannot be described by the individual himself. The possibility that the behavior which cannot be described may be covert raises an interesting theoretical problem, since the existence of such behavior must be inferred, not only by the scientist, but by the individual himself. We have seen that a mathematician frequently cannot describe the process through which he solves a problem. Although he may report the preliminary stages of his investigation, his arrangement of materials, and many tentative solutions, he may not be able to describe the self-manipulation which presumably preceded the required response which he suddenly emits. It is not always necessary to infer that other behavior has actually occurred, but under certain circumstances this inference may be justified. Since authenticated overt behavior sometimes cannot be reported by the individual, we have no reason to question the possibility of a covert parallel.

A man may not know that *he is doing something.* Absent-minded conduct, unconscious mannerisms, and mechanically habitual behavior are common examples. More dramatic is automatic writing, in which behavior taking place at the moment cannot be described by the "rest of the organism."

A man may not know that *he tends to, or is going to, do something.* He may be unaware of aggressive tendencies, of unusual predilections, or of the high probability that he will follow a given course of action.

A man may not recognize *the variables of which his behavior is a function.* In the Verbal Summator, for example, the subject often supposes himself to be repeating a verbal stimulus when it is easy to identify variables lying elsewhere in his environment or history which account for the behavior. Projective tests are used for diagnostic purposes just because they reveal variables which the individual himself cannot identify.

These phenomena are often viewed with surprise. How can the individual fail to observe events which are so conspicuous and so important? But perhaps we should be surprised that such events are observed as often as they are. We have no reason to expect discriminative behavior of this sort unless it has been generated by suitable reinforcement. Self-knowledge is a special repertoire. The crucial thing is not whether the behavior which a man fails to report is actually observable by him, but whether he has ever been given any reason to observe it.

Self-knowledge may, nevertheless, be lacking where appropriate reinforcing circumstances have prevailed. Some instances may be dismissed without extended comment. For example, the stimuli supplied by behavior may be weak. One may be "unaware" of a facial expression because of the inadequacy of the accompanying self-stimulation. The subject in an experiment on muscle-reading may not be aware of the slight responses which the reader detects and uses in getting the subject to "tell" him the location of a hidden object. The functional relation between behavior and a relevant variable is especially likely to be of subtle physical dimensions. A face in the crowd may be clear enough as a stimulus to generate a mood, but the fact that it has done so may still not be noted. This does not mean that the stimuli are below threshold, for they may be brought into control in other ways. When we point out some part of the behavior of an individual, an occasion is established under which special reinforcement is accorded a discriminative reaction. The fact that the individual then responds to his behavior is what we mean by saying that he was "able to do so" in the first place.

Another case of "not knowing what one is doing" is explained by the principle of prepotency. In the heat of battle there may be no time to observe one's behavior, since strong responses conflict with the discriminative response. Self-knowledge may also be lacking in certain states of satiation and in sleep. One may talk in one's sleep or behave in other ways "without knowing it." Behavior under the influence of drugs—for example, alcohol—may also occur with a minimum of self-observation. The effect of alcohol in reducing the behavior of self-knowledge may be similar to that in reducing the response to the conditioned aversive stimuli characteristic of guilt or anxiety.

It has been argued that one cannot describe behavior after the fact which one could not have described at the time. This appears to explain our inability to recall the events of infancy, since the behavior of the infant occurs before a repertoire of self-description has been set up and therefore too soon to control such a repertoire. The same explanation should apply to behavior unnoticed in the heat of battle. However, it is possible that the rearousal of response on the pattern of the conditioned reflex may supply the basis for a description. In any case it is sometimes impossible to describe earlier behavior which could have been described, and perhaps was described, at the time it was emitted. An important reason why a description may be lacking has still to be considered.

Repression. We have seen that punishment makes the stimuli generated by punished behavior aversive. Any behavior which reduces that stimulation is subsequently reinforced automatically. Now, among the kinds of behavior most likely to generate conditioned aversive stimuli as the result of punishment is the behavior of *observing* the punished act or of observing the occasion for it or any tendency to execute it. As the result of punishment, not only do we engage in other behavior to the exclusion of punished forms, we engage in other behavior to the exclusion of *knowing about* punished behavior. This may begin simply as "not liking to think about" behavior which has led to aversive consequences. It may then pass into the stage of not thinking about it and eventually reach the point at which the individual denies having behaved in a given way, in the face of proof to the contrary.

The result is commonly called repression. The individual may repress behavior simply in the sense of engaging in competing forms, but we must now extend the meaning of the term to include the repression of knowing about punished behavior. This is a much more dramatic result, to which the term "repression" is sometimes confined. The same formulation applies, however. We do not appeal to any special act of repression but rather to competing behavior which becomes extremely powerful because it avoids aversive stimulation.

It is not always knowledge of the form of a response which is repressed, because punishment is not always contingent upon form.

Aggressive behavior, for example, is not punished in warfare. Imitative behavior is not often punished so long as it is actually under the control of similar behavior on the part of others. For example, when we emit obscene or blasphemous behavior in testifying to an instance of it on the part of someone else, our testimony may not be entirely free of conditioned aversive consequences, and we may avoid testifying if possible; but the aversive stimulation will be much less than that aroused by the same behavior when it is not imitative. In experiments with the Verbal Summator a subject will often emit aggressive, ungrammatical, obscene, or blasphemous responses so long as he remains convinced that he is correctly repeating speech patterns on a phonograph record. He has been told to repeat what he hears and punishment is not contingent upon the form of his behavior under these circumstances, especially if a few objectionable samples are first presented clearly. As soon as he is told that there are no comparable speech patterns on the record, however, this type of response usually becomes much less frequent. The individual must now, so to speak, take the responsibility for the aggression, obscenity, and so on. In other words, his behavior is now of a form and under a controlling relation upon which punishment is contingent. In such a case the subject will often refuse to acknowledge that earlier stimuli were not of the form he reported.

A variation on the repression of a controlling relationship is sometimes called "rationalization." The aversive report of a functional relation may be repressed by reporting a fictitious relationship. Instead of "refusing to recognize" the causes of our behavior, we invent acceptable causes. If an aggressive attack upon a child is due to emotional impulses of revenge, it is usually punished by society; but if it is emitted because of supposed consequences in shaping the behavior of the child in line with the interests of society, it goes unpunished. We may conceal the emotional causes of our aggressive behavior, either from ourselves or from others, by arguing that the child ought to learn what sort of effect he is having on people. We spank the child "for his own good." In the same way we may delight in carrying bad news to someone we dislike "because the sooner he knows it the better." It is not the aggressive response which is repressed, but the response of knowing about the aggressive tendency. The rationalization is the repressing response which is successful in avoiding the conditioned aversive stimulation generated by punishment.

Persons as Self-Creators

Jean-Paul Sartre

I should like on this occasion to defend existentialism against some charges which have been brought against it.

First, it has been charged with inviting people to remain in a kind of desperate quietism because, since no solutions are possible, we should have to consider action in this world as quite impossible. We should then end up in a philosophy of contemplation; and since contemplation is a luxury, we come in the end to a bourgeois philosophy. The communists in particular have made these charges.

On the other hand, we have been charged with dwelling on human degradation, with pointing up everywhere the sordid, shady, and slimy, and neglecting the gracious and beautiful, the bright side of human nature; for example, according to Mlle. Mercier, a Catholic critic, with forgetting the smile of the child. Both sides charge us with having ignored human solidarity, with considering man as an isolated being. The communists say that the main reason for this is that we take pure subjectivity, the *Cartesian I think,* as our starting point; in other words, the moment in which man becomes fully aware of what it means to him to be an isolated being; as a result, we are unable to return to a state of solidarity with the men who are not ourselves, a state which we can never reach in the *cogito.*

From the Christian standpoint, we are charged with denying the reality and seriousness of human undertakings, since, if we reject God's commandments and the eternal verities, there no longer remains anything but pure caprice, with everyone permitted to do as he pleases and incapable, from his own point of view, of condemning the points of view and acts of others.

I shall try today to answer these different charges. Many people are going to be surprised at what is said here about humanism. We shall try to see in what sense it is to be understood. In any case, what can be said from the very beginning is that by existentialism we mean a doctrine which makes human life possible and, in addition, declares that every truth and every action implies a human setting and a human subjectivity.

As is generally known, the basic charge against us is that we put the emphasis on the dark side of human life. Someone recently told me of a lady who, when she let slip a vulgar word in a moment of irritation, ex-

Jean-Paul Sartre, "Existentialism" from *Extentialism and Human Emotions,* trans. B. Frechtman (New York: Philosophical Library, 1957), pp. 9-32. Reprinted by permission of the publisher.

cused herself by saying, "I guess I'm becoming an existentialist." Consequently, existentialism is regarded as something ugly; that is why we are said to be naturalists; and if we are, it is rather surprising that in this day and age we cause so much more alarm and scandal than does naturalism, properly so called. The kind of person who can take in his stride such a novel as Zola's *The Earth* is disgusted as soon as he starts reading an existentialist novel; the kind of person who is resigned to the wisdom of the ages—which is pretty sad—finds us even sadder. Yet, what can be more disillusioning than saying "true charity beings at home" or "a scoundrel will always return evil for good"?

We know the commonplace remarks made when this subject comes up, remarks which always add up to the same thing: we shouldn't struggle against the powers-that-be; we shouldn't resist authority; we shouldn't try to rise above our station; any action which doesn't conform to authority is romantic; any effort not based on past experience is doomed to failure; experience shows that man's bent is always toward trouble, that there must be a strong hand to hold him in check, if not, there will be anarchy. There are still people who go on mumbling these melancholy old saws, the people who say, "It's only human!" whenever a more or less repugnant act is pointed out to them, the people who glut themselves on *chansons réalistes;* these are the people who accuse existentialism of being too gloomy, and to such an extent that I wonder whether they are complaining about it, not for its pessimism, but much rather its optimism. Can it be that what really scares them in the doctrine I shall try to present here is that it leaves to man a possibility of choice? To answer this question, we must re-examine it on a strictly philosophical plane. What is meant by the term *existentialism?*

Most people who use the word would be rather embarrassed if they had to explain it, since, now that the word is all the rage, even the work of a musician or painter is being called existentialist. A gossip columnist in *Clartés* signs himself *The Existentialist,* so that by this time the word has been so stretched and has taken on so broad a meaning, that it no longer means anything at all. It seems that for want of an advance-guard doctrine analogous to surrealism, the kind of people who are eager for scandal and flurry turn to this philosophy which in other respects does not at all serve their purposes in this sphere.

Actually, it is the least scandalous, the most austere of doctrines. It is intended strictly for specialists and philosophers. Yet it can be defined easily. What complicates matters is that there are two kinds of existentialist; first those who are Christian, among whom I would include Jaspers and Gabriel Marcel, both Catholic; and on the other hand the atheistic existentialists, among whom I class Heidegger, and then the French existentialists and myself. What they have in common is that they think that existence precedes essence, or, if you prefer, that subjectivity must be the starting point.

Just what does that mean? Let us consider some object that is manufactured, for example, a book or a paper-cutter: here is an object which has been made by an artisan whose inspiration came from a concept. He referred to the concept of what a paper-cutter is and likewise to a known method of production, which is part of the concept, something which is, by and large, a routine. Thus, the paper-cutter is at once an object produced in a certain way and, on the other hand, one having a specific use; and one can not postulate a man who produces a paper-cutter but does not know what it is used for. Therefore, let us say that, for the paper-cutter, essence—that is, the ensemble of both the production routines and the properties which enable it to be both produced and defined—precedes existence. Thus, the presence of the paper-cutter or book in front of me is determined. Therefore, we have here a technical view of the world whereby it can be said that production precedes existence.

When we conceive God as the Creator, He is generally thought of as a superior sort of artisan. Whatever doctrine we may be considering, whether one like that of Descartes or that of Leibnitz, we always grant that will more or less follows understanding or, at the very least, accompanies it, and that when God creates He knows exactly what He is creating. Thus, the concept of man in the mind of God is comparable to the concept of paper-cutter in the mind of the manufacturer, and, following certain techniques and a conception, God produces man, just as the artisan, following a definition and a technique, makes a paper-cutter. Thus, the individual man is the realization of a certain concept in the divine intelligence.

In the eighteenth century, the atheism of the *philosophes* discarded the idea of God, but not so much for the notion that essence precedes existence. To a certain extent, this idea is found everywhere; we find it in Diderot, in Voltaire, and even in Kant. Man has a human nature; this human nature, which is the concept of the human, is found in all men, which means that each man is a particular example of a universal concept, man. In Kant, the result of this universality is that the wild-man, the natural man, as well as the bourgeois, are circumscribed by the same definition and have the same basic qualities. Thus, here too the essence of man precedes the historical existence that we find in nature.

Atheistic existentialism, which I represent, is more coherent. It states that if God does not exist, there is at least one being in whom existence precedes essence, a being who exists before he can be defined by any concept, and that this being is man, or, as Heidegger says, human reality. What is meant here by saying that existence precedes essence? It means that, first of all man exists, turns up, appears on the scene, and, only afterwards, defines himself. If man, as the existentialist conceives him is indefinable, it is because at first he is nothing. Only afterward will he be something, and he himself will have made what he will be. Thus, there is no human nature, since there is no God to conceive it. Not only is man what he conceives himself to be, but he is also only what he wills himself to be after this thrust toward existence.

Man is nothing else but what he makes of himself. Such is the first principle of existentialism. It is also what is called subjectivity, the name we are labeled with when charges are brought against us. But what do we mean by this, if not that man has a greater dignity than a stone or table? For we mean that man first exists, that is, that man first of all is the being who hurls himself toward a future and who is conscious of imagining himself as being in the future. Man is at the start a plan which is aware of itself, rather than a patch of moss, a piece of garbage, or a cauliflower; nothing exists prior to this plan; there is nothing in heaven; man will be what he will have planned to be. Not what he will want to be. Because by the word "will" we generally mean a conscious decision, which is subsequent to what we have already made of ourselves. I may want to belong to a political party, write a book, get married; but all that is only a manifestation of an earlier, more spontaneous choice that is called "will." But if existence really does precede essence, man is responsible for what he is. Thus, existentialism's first move is to make every man aware of what he is and to make the full responsibility of his existence rest on him. And when we say that a man is responsible for himself, we do not only mean that he is responsible for his own individuality, but that he is responsible for all men.

The word subjectivism has two meanings, and our opponents play on the two. Subjectivism means, on the one hand, that an individual chooses and makes himself; and, on the other, that it is impossible for man to transcend human subjectivity. The second of these is the essential meaning of existentialism. When we say that man chooses his own self, we mean that every one of us does likewise; but we also mean by that that in making this choice he also chooses all men. In fact, in creating the man that we want to be, there is not a single one of our acts which does not at the same time create an image of man as we think he ought to be. To choose to be this or that is to affirm at the same time the value of what we choose, because we can never choose evil. We always choose the good, and nothing can be good for us without being good for all.

If, on the other hand, existence precedes essence, and if we grant that we exist and fashion our image at one and the same time, the image is valid for everybody and for our whole age. Thus, our responsibility is much greater than we might have supposed, because it involves all mankind. If I am a workingman and choose to join a Christian trade-union rather than be a communist, and if by being a member I want to show that the best thing for man is resignation, that the kingdom of man is not of this world, I am not only involving my own case—I want to be resigned for everyone. As a result, my action has involved all humanity. To take a more individual matter, if I want to marry, to have children; even if this marriage depends solely on my own circumstances or passion or wish, I am involving all humanity in monogamy and not merely myself. Therefore, I am responsible for myself and for everyone else. I am creating a certain image of man of my own choosing. In choosing myself, I choose man.

This helps us understand what the actual content is of such rather grandiloquent words as anguish, forlornness, despair. As you will see, it's all quite simple.

First, what is meant by anguish? The existentialists say at once that man is anguish. What that means is this: the man who involves himself and who realizes that he is not only the person he chooses to be, but also a law-maker who is, at the same time, choosing all mankind as well as himself, can not help escape the feeling of his total and deep responsibility. Of course, there are many people who are not anxious; but we claim that they are hiding their anxiety, that they are fleeing from it. Certainly, many people believe that when they do something, they themselves are the only ones involved, and when someone says to them, "What if everyone acted that way?" they shrug their shoulders and answer, "Everyone doesn't act that way." But really, one should always ask himself, "What would happen if everybody looked at things that way?" There is no escaping this disturbing thought except by a kind of double-dealing. A man who lies and makes excuses for himself by saying "not everybody does that," is someone with an uneasy conscience, because the act of lying implies that a universal value is conferred upon the lie.

Anguish is evident even when it conceals itself. This is the anguish that Kierkegaard called the anguish of Abraham. You know the story: an angel has ordered Abraham to sacrifice his son; if it really were an angel who has come and said, "You are Abraham, you shall sacrifice your son," everything would be all right. But everyone might first wonder, "Is it really an angel, and am I really Abraham? What proof do I have?"

There was a madwoman who had hallucinations; someone used to speak to her on the telephone and give her orders. Her doctor asked her, "Who is it who talks to you?" She answered, "He says it's God." What proof did she really have that it was God? If an angel comes to me, what proof is there that it's an angel? And if I hear voices, what proof is there that they come from heaven and not from hell, or from the subconscious, or a pathological condition? What proves that they are addressed to me? What proof is there that I have been appointed to impose my choice and my conception of man on humanity? I'll never find any proof or sign to convince me of that. If a voice addresses me, it is always for me to decide that this is the angel's voice; if I consider that such an act is a good one, it is I who will choose to say that it is good rather than bad.

Now, I'm not being singled out as an Abraham, and yet at every moment I'm obliged to perform exemplary acts. For every man, everything happens as if all mankind had its eyes fixed on him and were guiding itself by what he does. And every man ought to say to himself, "Am I really the kind of man who has the right to act in such a way that humanity might guide itself by my actions?" And if he does not say that to himself, he is masking his anguish.

There is no question here of the kind of anguish which would lead to quietism, to inaction. It is a matter of a simple sort of anguish that anybody who has had responsibilities is familiar with. For example, when a military officer takes the responsibility for an attack and sends a certain number of men to death, he chooses to do so, and in the main he alone makes the choice. Doubtless, orders come from above, but they are too broad; he interprets them, and on this interpretation depend the lives of ten or fourteen or twenty men. In making a decision he can not help having a certain anguish. All leaders know this anguish. That doesn't keep them from acting; on the contrary, it is the very condition of their action. For it implies that they envisage a number of possibilities, and when they choose one, they realize that it has value only because it is chosen. We shall see that this kind of anguish, which is the kind that existentialism describes, is explained, in addition, by a direct responsibility to the other men whom it involves. It is not a curtain separating us from action, but is part of action itself.

When we speak of forlornness, a term Heidegger was fond of, we mean only that God does not exist and that we have to face all the consequences of this. The existentialist is strongly opposed to a certain kind of secular ethics which would like to abolish God with the least possible expense. About 1880, some French teachers tried to set up a secular ethics which went something like this: God is a useless and costly hypothesis; we are discarding it; but, meanwhile, in order for there to be an ethics, a society, a civilization, it is essential that certain values be taken seriously and that they be considered as having an *a priori* existence. It must be obligatory, *a priori*, to be honest, not to lie, not to beat your wife, to have children, etc., etc. So we're going to try a little device which will make it possible to show that values exist all the same, inscribed in a heaven of ideas, though otherwise God does not exist. In other words—and this, I believe, is the tendency of everything called reformism in France—nothing will be changed if God does not exist. We shall find ourselves with the same norms of honesty, progress, and humanism, and we shall have made of God an outdated hypothesis which will peacefully die off by itself.

The existentialist, on the contrary, thinks it very distressing that God does not exist, because all possibility of finding values in a heaven of ideas disappears along with Him; there can no longer be an *a priori* Good, since there is no infinite and perfect consciousness to think it. Nowhere is it written that the Good exists, that we must be honest, that we must not lie; because the fact is we are on a plane where there are only men. Dostoievsky said, "If God didn't exist, everything would be possible." That is the very starting point of existentialism. Indeed, everything is permissible if God does not exist, and as a result man is forlorn, because neither within him nor without does he find anything to cling to. He can't start making excuses for himself.

If existence really does precede essence, there is no explaining things away by reference to a fixed and given human nature. In other words, there is no determinism, man is free, man is freedom. On the other hand, if God does not exist, we find no values or commands to turn to which legitimize our conduct. So, in the bright realm of values, we have no excuse behind us, nor justification before us. We are alone, with no excuses.

That is the idea I shall try to convey when I say that man is condemned to be free. Condemned, because he did not create himself, yet, in other respects is free; because, once thrown into the world, he is responsible for everything he does. The existentialist does not believe in the power of passion. He will never agree that a sweeping passion is a ravaging torrent which fatally leads a man to certain acts and is therefore an excuse. He thinks that man is responsible for his passion.

The existentialist does not think that man is going to help himself by finding in the world some omen by which to orient himself. Because he thinks that man will interpret the omen to suit himself. Therefore, he thinks that man, with no support and no aid, is condemned every moment to invent man. Ponge, in a very fine article, has said, "Man is the future of man." That's exactly it. But if it is taken to mean that this future is recorded in heaven, that God sees it, then it is false, because it would really no longer be a future. If it is taken to mean that, whatever a man may be, there is a future to be forged, a virgin future before him, then this remark is sound. But then we are forlorn.

To give you an example which will enable you to understand forlornness better, I shall cite the case of one of my students who came to see me under the following circumstances: his father was on bad terms with his mother, and, moreover, was inclined to be a collaborationist; his older brother had been killed in the German offensive of 1940, and the young man, with somewhat immature but generous feelings, wanted to avenge him. His mother lived alone with him, very much upset by the half-treason of her husband and the death of her older son; the boy was her only consolation.

The boy was faced with the choice of leaving for England and joining the Free French Forces—that is, leaving his mother behind—or remaining with his mother and helping her to carry on. He was fully aware that the woman lived only for him and that his going-off—and perhaps his death—would plunge her into despair. He was also aware that every act that he did for his mother's sake was a sure thing, in the sense that it was helping her to carry on, whereas every effort he made toward going off and fighting was an uncertain move which might run aground and prove completely useless; for example, on his way to England he might, while passing through Spain, be detained indefinitely in a Spanish camp; he might reach England or Algiers and be stuck in an office at a desk job. As a result, he was faced with two very different kinds of action: one, concrete, immediate, but concerning only one individual; the other concerned an incomparably vaster group, a national collectivity, but for that very reason was dubious, and might be interrupted en route. And, at the same time, he was wavering between two kinds of ethics. On the one hand, an ethics of sympathy, of personal devotion; on the other, a broader ethics, but one whose efficacy was more dubious. He had to choose between the two.

Who could help him choose? Christian doctrine? No. Christian doctrine says, "Be charitable, love your neighbor, take the more rugged path, etc., etc." But which is the more rugged path? Whom should he love as a brother? The fighting man or his mother? Which does the greater good, the vague act of fighting in a group, or the concrete one of helping a particular human being to go on living? Who can decide *a priori*? Nobody. No book of ethics can tell him. The Kantian ethics says, "Never treat any person as a means, but as an end." Very well, if I stay with my mother, I'll treat her as an end and not as a means; but by virtue of this very fact, I'm running the risk of treating the people around me who are fighting, as means; and, conversely, if I go to join those who are fighting, I'll be treating them as an end, and, by doing that, I run the risk of treating my mother as a means.

If values are vague, and if they are always too broad for the concrete and specific case that we are considering, the only thing left for us is to trust our instincts. That's what this young man tried to do; and when I saw him, he said, "In the end, feeling is what counts. I ought to choose whichever pushes me in one direction. If I feel that I love my mother enough to sacrifice everything else for her—my desire for vengeance, for action, for adventure—then I'll stay with her. If, on the contrary, I feel that my love for my mother isn't enough, I'll leave."

But how is the value of a feeling determined? What gives his feeling for his mother value? Precisely the fact that he remained with her. I may say that I like so-and-so well enough to sacrifice a certain amount of money for him, but I may say so only if I've done it. I may say "I love my mother well enough to remain with her" if I have remained with her. The only way to determine the value of this affection is, precisely, to perform an act which confirms and defines it. But, since I require this affection to justify my act, I find myself caught in a vicious circle.

On the other hand, Gide has well said that a mock feeling and a true feeling are almost indistinguishable; to decide that I love my mother and will remain with her, or to remain with her by putting on an act, amount somewhat to the same thing. In other words, the feeling is formed by the acts one performs; so, I can not refer to it in order to act upon it. Which means that I can neither seek within myself the true condition which will impel me to act, nor apply to a system of ethics for concepts which will permit me to act. You will say, "At least, he did go to a teacher for advice." But, if you seek advice from a priest, for example, you have chosen this priest; you already knew, more or less, just about what advice he was going to give you. In other words, choosing your adviser is involving yourself. The proof of this is that if you are a Christian, you will say, "Consult a priest." But some priests are collaborating, some are just marking time, some are resisting. Which to choose? If the young man chooses a priest who is resisting or collaborating, he has already decided on the kind of advice he's going to get. Therefore, in coming to see me he knew the answer I was going to give him, and I had only one answer to give: "You're free, choose, that is, invent." No general ethics can show you what is to be done; there are no omens in the world. The Catholics will reply, "But there are." Granted—but, in any case, I myself choose the meaning they have.

When I was a prisoner, I knew a rather remarkable young man who was a Jesuit. He had entered the Jesuit order in the following way: he had had a number of very bad breaks; in childhood, his father died, leaving him in poverty, and he was a scholarship student at a religious institution where he was constantly made to feel that he was being kept out of charity; then, he failed to get any of the honors and distinctions that children like; later on, at about eighteen, he bungled a love affair; finally, at twenty-two, he failed in military training, a childish enough matter, but it was the last straw.

This young fellow might well have felt that he had botched everything. It was a sign of something, but of what? He might have taken refuge in bitterness or despair. But he very wisely looked upon all this as a sign that he was not made for secular triumphs, and that only the triumphs of religion, holiness, and faith were open to him. He saw the hand of God in all this, and so he entered the order. Who can help seeing that he alone decided what the sign meant?

Some other interpretation might have been drawn from this series of setbacks; for example, that he might have done better to turn carpenter or revolutionist. Therefore, he is fully responsible for the interpretation. Forlornness implies that we ourselves choose our being. Forlornness and anguish go together.

As for despair, the term has a very simple meaning. It means that we shall confine ourselves to reckoning only with what depends upon our will, or on the ensemble of probabilities which make our action possible. When we want something, we always have to reckon with probabilities. I may be counting on the arrival of a friend. The friend is coming by rail or street-car; this supposes that the train will arrive on schedule, or that the street-car will not jump the track. I am left in the realm of possibility; but possibilities are to be reckoned with only to the point where my action comports with the ensemble of these possibilities, and no further. The moment the possibilities I am considering are not rigorously involved by my action, I ought to disengage myself from them, because no God, no scheme, can adapt the world and its possibilities to my will. When Descartes said, "Conquer yourself rather than the world," he meant essentially the same thing.

The Marxists to whom I have spoken reply, "You can rely on the support of others in your action, which obviously has certain limits because you're not going to live forever. That means: rely on both what others are doing elsewhere to help you, in China, in Russia, and what they will do later on, after your death, to carry on the action and lead it to its fulfillment, which will be the revolution. You even *have* to rely upon that, otherwise you're immoral." I reply at once that I will always rely on fellow-fighters insofar as these comrades are involved with me in a common struggle, in the unity of a party or a group in which I can more or less make my weight felt; that is, one whose ranks I am in as a fighter and whose movements I am aware of at every moment. In such a situation, relying on the unity and will of the party is exactly like counting on the fact that the train will arrive on time or that the car won't jump the track. But, given that man is free and that there is no human nature for me to depend on, I can not count on men whom I do not know by relying on human goodness or man's concern for the good of society. I don't know what will become of the Russian revolution; I may make an example of it to the extent that at the present time it is apparent that the proletariat plays a part in Russia that it plays in no other nation. But I can't swear that this will inevitably lead to a triumph of the proletariat. I've got to limit myself to what I see.

Given that men are free and that tomorrow they will freely decide what man will be, I can not be sure that, after my death, fellow-fighters will carry on my work to bring it to its maximum perfection. Tomorrow, after my death, some men may decide to set up Fascism, and the others may be cowardly and muddled enough to let them do it. Fascism will then be the human reality, so much the worse for us.

Actually, things will be as man will have decided they are to be. Does that mean that I should abandon myself to quietism? No. First, I should involve myself; then, act on the old saw, "Nothing ventured, nothing gained." Nor does it mean that I shouldn't belong to a party, but rather that I shall have no illusions and shall do what I can. For example, suppose I ask myself, "Will socialization, as such, ever come about?" I know nothing about it. All I know is that I'm going to do everything in my power to bring it about. Beyond that, I can't count on anything. Quietism is the attitude of people who say, "Let others do what I can't do." The doctrine I am presenting is the very opposite of quietism, since it declares, "There is no reality except in action." Moreover, it goes further, since it adds, "Man is nothing else than his plan; he exists only to the extent that he fulfills himself; he is therefore nothing else than the ensemble of his acts, nothing else than his life."

3

PHILOSOPHY,

EDUCATION,

and the

LIBERAL ARTS

In the first section of this text we met Euthyphro, a man who claimed to know the nature of piety. Upon closer examination by Socrates, however, Euthyphro was shown to have only a shallow conception of piety and its proper place in life. Just as piety plays a dominant role in Euthyphro's life, education plays an important role in our own. During an average lifetime of seventy years, most of us spend at least sixteen years, approximately twenty-three percent of our lives, in formal education. Like Euthyphro, we probably believe we understand what education is and what value it brings to our lives. Have we ever stopped, however, to consider it reflectively, to articulate and defend the role of education in a rational life plan? Probably not.

For the first sixteen years of our lives, education is mandatory. Our compulsory education laws leave a young person no alternative but to be in school. When one is left no option, the natural tendency is to simply do what is required, not to examine that requirement or investigate its possible justifications. Moreover, most young people, lacking intellectual maturity, have not developed a rational life plan to provide them with the perspective necessary to define for themselves the nature and value of education. In our culture, the choice of whether to go to college is typically the first occasion for considering formal education as a living option. A young person must not only decide whether to continue formal schooling past high school, he or she must also decide what sort of higher education—a technical school, a professional education like forestry, or a liberal arts degree—is worth pursuing. In many cases, however, these choices are not made through rational reflection. Instead, parental and peer-group pressures combine to make higher education another requirement, not an option to be chosen autonomously.

As a result of these pressures, many students matriculate at a college and spend at least four years there, investing large amounts of time, effort, and money. They pursue a degree without any deep understanding of what they are pursuing, or why. In the process they become masters at playing the educational game. Note-taking skills are honed to a razor edge; test-taking and writing papers are just hurdles on the way to a degree. The student becomes adept at "psyching" his teachers —finding out what they want and giving it to them in the required form. Information is gathered, memorized, and regurgitated on final exams. Like rats learning to run a maze, students become skilled at performing the required tasks; many, if not most, graduate untouched and unchanged by their exposure to college. From their point of view, one more hurdle has been cleared; now it is time to move on to the more important things in life. The sad fact is that students and society are frequently under the illusion that in this process *education* has taken place.

If students were to encounter Socrates, and were asked to pause in their frantic pursuit of grades and a degree long enough to offer a rational justification of their activities, many would probably assert that higher education is a means to an end. The end at which many aim is success in one's work: the high paying job, and the material pleasures that our consumer society provides. Perhaps a few would reject the goal of material rewards and would claim instead that college is a means to a humanly satisfying vocation.

Yet nagging doubts may undermine these instrumental justifications of higher education. In years past there was a direct correlation between the amount of higher education one received and the financial rewards that one obtained. In today's economic world, this correlation may not always hold true. Many "blue collar" workers now earn as much as college graduates. Although a college degree may provide one with a passport to a meaningful vocation, it is far from certain that upon graduation a student will obtain employment in his chosen profession. It is not unknown for a college graduate (or the holder of a Ph.D. degree) to work as a store clerk, waiter, or taxi driver, simply because he or she could not find employment in a chosen profession.

Such uncomfortable facts shake the foundations of instrumental justifications of higher education and ought to provide educators and students with an occasion to critically examine the nature and value of higher education. The articles in this section begin such an examination by raising and trying to answer the following questions. What is a Liberal Arts education? What role should it play in the life of a person who comes under its influence? How does it foster a fuller and more satisfactory, if not materially richer, life? Moreover, are instrumental lines of reasoning appropriate means of justifying the time, effort, and money that we invest in education? Finally, are there widespread presuppositions about education, presuppositions linked to powerful societal forces, that threaten the very nature of liberal education? If we are content to leave these fundamental questions unexamined, we are—like Euthyphro—condemning ourselves to a superficial understanding of an ideal that occupies a significant and enduring place in our lives.

The Justification of Education

R.S. Peters

INTRODUCTION

To be educated is thought by many to be a desirable condition of mind, but it obviously does not encompass all that is desirable. Uneducated people can be compassionate and courageous and there is surely some value in such mental dispositions. On the other hand educated people often lack perseverance and integrity, which are also generally thought to be valuable. So even though there may be value in being educated it must be associated with some specific types of value. What then are the values which are specific to being educated and what sort of justification can be given for them? It is to these limited questions that I propose to address myself in this article rather than to wider questions of value with which I was concerned in *Ethics and Education*, and with which, in places, I confused these limited questions—owing perhaps to certain inadequacies in the analysis of the concept of "education" with which I was then working.

1. THE VALUES SPECIFIC TO EDUCATION

What, then, are the values which are specific to being educated? This depends on whether 'education' is being used in a general or in a

From *The Philosophy of Education,* edited by R. S. Peters, © Oxford University Press, 1973. Reprinted by permission of the author and Oxford University Press.

My thanks are due to colleagues and friends who helped me by their criticism of early versions of this paper, especially Paul Hirst and A. Phillips Griffiths. The author's views are further developed and clarified in a symposium with R. K. Elliott in *Proceedings of the Philosophy of Education Society of Great Britain,* July 1977.

specific sense.[1] There is a general concept of 'education' which covers almost any process of learning, rearing, or bringing up. Nowadays, when we speak of education in this general way, we usually mean going to school, to an institution devoted to learning. In this sense of 'education' almost any quality of mind can be deemed a product of it—compassion and perseverance included. To say that such qualities of mind are the product of education is to say that they are learned. Education, in this sense, can be accorded any kind of instrumental value and so is not of any significance for its valuative suggestions.

Of more relevance is the specific concept of 'education' which emerged in the nineteenth century as a contrast to training. Various processes of learning came to be termed 'educative' because they contribute to the development of an educated man or woman. This was an ideal which emerged in opposition both to narrow specialization and to the increasingly instrumental view of knowledge associated with the development of technology. It was, of course, as old as the Greeks, though it was not previously picked out by the concept of an 'educated man.' Thus (a) the educated man is not one who merely possesses specialized skills. He may possess such specific know-how but he certainly also possesses a considerable body of knowledge together with understanding. He has a developed capacity to reason, to justify his beliefs and conduct. He knows the reason why of things as well as that certain things are the case. This is not a matter of just being knowledgeable; for the understanding of an educated person transforms how he sees things. It makes a difference to the level of life which he enjoys; for he has a backing for his beliefs and conduct and organizes his experience in terms of systematic conceptual schemes. (b) There is the suggestion, too, that his understanding is not narrowly specialized. He not only has breadth of understanding but is also capable of connecting up these different ways of interpreting his experience so that he achieves some kind of cognitive perspective. This can be exhibited in two sorts of ways. Firstly he is not just embedded in one way of reacting to what he encounters. He can, for instance, combine a knowledge of how a car works with sensitivity to its aesthetic proportions, to its history, and to its potentiality for human good and ill. He can see it as a problem for town-planners as well as a fascinating machine. Secondly he is ready to pursue the links between the different sorts of understanding that he has developed. Any moral judgement, for instance, presupposes beliefs about people's behaviour and many moral judgements involve assessments of the consequences of behaviour. An educated person, therefore, will not rely on crude, unsophisticated interpretations of the behaviour of others when making moral judgements; he will not neglect generalizations from the social sciences, in so far as they exist, about the probable consequences of types of behaviour. If these are at all sophisticated he will have to bring to bear some rudimentary understanding of statistics. Similarly, as a scientist he will not be oblivious of the moral presuppositions of scientific activity nor of the aesthetic features of theories; neither will he be insensitive to the relevance of his findings to wider issues of belief and action.

(c) In contrast, too, to the instrumentality so often associated with specialized knowledge, the educated person is one who is capable, to a certain extent, of doing and knowing things for their own sake. He can delight in what he is doing without always asking the question 'And where is this going to get me?' This applies as much to cooking as it does to chemistry. He can enjoy the company of a friend as well as a concert. And his work is not just a chore to be carried out for cash. He has a sense of standards as well as a sense of the setting of what he is doing between the past and the future. There are continuities in his life which reflect what he cares about. He takes care because he cares.

(d) *Processes of education.* Processes of education are processes by means of which people become this way, by means of which they are gradually initiated into this form of life. They are not to be regarded strictly as means to being educated, if 'means' is taken as indicating a process which is both valuatively neutral and related to the end purely causally as taking a drug might be related to a tranquil state of mind. For these processes are processes of learning, and this always involves some kind of content to be mastered, understood, remembered. This content, whether it is a skill, an attitude, an item of knowledge, or a principle to be understood must be intimated, perhaps in embryonic form, in the learning situation. There must, therefore, be some link of a logical rather than a causal sort between the 'means' and the 'end' if it is to be a process of learning. If anyone, for instance, is to learn to think mathematically or morally, the learning situations must include some kind of experiences of a mathematical or a moral sort. Learning may be aided by the temperature of the room, by constant repetition, by smiling at the learner or rewarding him. Some of these conditions of learning may be of a causal type. But there must be some kind of logical link between the content to which the learner is introduced in the learning situation and that which is constitutive of his performance when he has learnt.

Because of this logical type of relationship between means and ends in education it is not appropriate to think of the values of an educational process as contained purely in the various attainments, which are constitutive of being an educated person. For in most cases the logical relationship of means to ends is such that the values of the product are embryonically present in the learning process. Suppose, for instance, that children learn to think scientifically by being set simple problems to solve in chemistry and physics. Some of the values of scientific thinking—for instance being clear and precise, looking for evidence, checking results and not cooking them—are instantiated in the learning situation.[2] This would suggest that, from the point of view of value, there is little difference between the learning situation and that of the exercise of what has been learnt. This has led thinkers such as Dewey to claim that the values of living are no different from those of education. For both the learner and the liver exhibit the virtues of critical, open-ended, disciplined inquiry.

On the other hand there is the type of difference to which Aristotle drew attention in his paradox of moral education which is really the paradox of all education. This is that in order to develop the dispositions of a just man the individual has to perform acts that are just, but the acts which contribute to the formation of the dispositions of the just man are not conceived of in the same way as the acts which finally flow from his character, once he has become just. Similarly doing science or reading poetry at school contribute to a person being educated. But later on, as an educated person, he may conceive of them very differently. He may do them because he is drawn to their underlying point or because he sees their relevance to some issue of belief or conduct. This makes the justification of values immanent in such activities very complicated. However, nothing yet has been said about the justification of any of the values of being educated.

2. INSTRUMENTAL JUSTIFICATIONS OF EDUCATION

The most all-pervading type of justification for anything in our type of society is to look for its use either to the community or to the individual; for basically our society is geared to consumption. Even the work of the artist, for instance, is not always valued for the excellences which are intrinsic to it. Rather it is valued because it attracts more people to a public place, because it provides a soothing or restful atmosphere for people who are exposed to it, or because of the prestige of the artist which rubs off on to the body which commissions him. Music is piped into railway stations and air terminals to make people feel cheerful just as heat is piped through radiators to make them warm. Art and music can be thought of in this way irrespective of how the artists or musicians conceive of what they are doing. The same sort of thing can happen to education, though there are difficulties in thinking of education in this way if all its criteria are taken into account. To make this point I will consider its aspects separately.

(a) Knowledge and Understanding

It can be argued cogently that the development of knowledge, skill, and understanding is in both the community's and the individual's interest because of other types of satisfaction which it promotes, and because of distinctive evils, which it mitigates. Skills are an obvious case in point. Whatever their intrinsic value as forms of excellence the learning of them is obviously necessary for the survival of a community. Many of them also provide an individual with a living and hence with food, shelter, and a range of consumer satisfactions.

A strong instrumental case can also be made for the passing on of knowledge and understanding. Knowledge, in general, is essential to the survival of a civilized community in which processes of communication are very important. For 'knowledge' implies at least (i) that what is said or thought is true and (ii) that the individual has grounds for what he says or thinks. It is no accident that all civilized societies have such a concept. As far as (i) is concerned, most forms of communication would be impossible if people did not, in general, say what they thought was true. It is socially important, therefore, to have a special word to mark out communications drawing attention to what is true. (ii) The evidence condition is also socially very important because of the value of reliability and predictability in social life. Most of human behaviour depends on beliefs which are expressed and transmitted by means of language. If such beliefs were entirely based on guesses, on feelings which people had in their stomachs, or on various forms of divination, a predictable form of social life would be difficult to imagine. It is no accident, therefore, that civilized societies have the special word 'knowledge' which signals that the person who uses it has good grounds for what he says or thinks.

'Understanding' is equally important, for it suggests that a particular event can be explained in terms of a general principle or shown to fit into some kind of pattern or framework. This permits a higher degree of predictability because of the recourse to generality or to analogy. The context of predictability is thus widened. And, needless to say, the development of knowledge and understanding has an additional social benefit because it permits better control over and utilization of the natural world for human purposes as was emphasized by thinkers such as Bacon, Hobbes, and Marx. Hence the social value of highly specialized knowledge with the development of industrialism.

The development of understanding is particularly important in a modern industrialized society in which the skills required change rapidly. Industrialists do not demand that the schools should provide a lot of specialized technical training. They prefer to do this themselves or to arrange courses in technical colleges for their employees. If people just serve an apprenticeship in a specialized skill and if they are provided only with a body of knowledge which is necessary to the exercise of that skill under specific conditions, then they will tend to be resistant to change and will become redundant when there is no longer need for this particular skill. If, on the other hand, they have also some understanding in depth of what they are about, they will, at least, be more flexible in their approach and more ready to acquire new techniques. This applies also to social understanding, some degree of which is necessary for working with others; for, as Marx showed, changes in techniques bring with them changes in social organization. If a builder or a teacher is both limited in his understanding and rigid in his attitudes, he is not likely to be good at adapting to changes in organization brought about by changes in techniques.

(b) Breadth of Understanding

The importance of social understanding suggests an instrumental type of argument for the other aspect of being educated which is incompatible with narrow specialization, namely that of 'breadth'. But what kind of case, in terms of providing services, can be made for typists, dentists, and shop stewards being aesthetically sensitive, and alive to their historical situation and religious predicament? A case can be made for such breadth of understanding as being an important aspect of political education in a democracy. It is, however, often said that such people make more efficient employees than those with a narrow training. But if this is true, which is questionable, it may not be due to the breadth of their understanding and sensitivity but to the fact that, in studying various subjects, they become practised in the generalizable techniques of filing papers and ideas, mastering and marshalling other people's arguments, of presenting alternatives clearly and weighing them up, of writing clearly and speaking articulately, and so on. Their academic training in the administration of ideas may prepare them for being administrators.

Of course it may be argued that educated people are of benefit to the professions and to industry because the breadth of their sensitivities helps to make their institutions more humane and civilized. But this is to abandon the instrumental form of argument in which qualities of mind are regarded purely as contributing to the efficiency of the service provided judged by some obvious criterion such as profit, number of patients cured, amount of food produced, and so on. As soon as industry or the professions come to be looked at not simply as providing profit, goods for consumption, or services to the public, but as being themselves constitutive of a desirable way of life, then the values associated with consumption begin to recede. And this introduces the third aspect of being educated.

(c) Non-instrumental Attitude

It is difficult to make explicit quite what is involved in this non-instrumental attitude. The key to it is that regard, respect, or love should be shown for the intrinsic features of activities. This can be exemplified in at least the following ways. Firstly it involves doing things for reasons that are reasons for doing this sort of thing rather than for reasons that can be artificially tacked on to almost anything that can be done. By that I mean that most things can be done for profit, for approval, for reward, to avoid punishment, for fame, for admiration. Such reasons are essentially extrinsic, as distinct from intrinsic reasons which are internal to the conception of the activity. If, for instance, a teacher changes his methods because his pupils seem too bored to learn, that is a reason intrinsic to the activity; for 'teaching' implies the intention to bring about learning.

Secondly, if things are done for some end which is not extrinsic in this sense, the features of the means matter. If, for instance, someone wants to get to another town or country and is absolutely indifferent to the merits of different ways of travelling, save in so far as he arrives quickly at his destination, then he has an instrumental attitude to travelling.

Thirdly, well established activities such as gardening, teaching, and cooking have standards which are constitutive of performing them well. These are usually related to the point of the activity. If the individual cares about the point of the activity he will therefore care about the standards which are related to its point. If, for instance, he is committed to an inquiry because he genuinely wants to find something out, he will value clarity, will examine evidence carefully, and will attempt to eliminate inconsistencies.

The ingenious could, no doubt, give arguments from the outside in terms of benefits to consumers for the capacity for doing and making things out of love for the job rather than for some extrinsic reason. It could be claimed, for instance, that bricklayers or doctors in fact render better service to the public if they approach their tasks with this attitude rather than with their minds on their pay packet or someone else's satisfaction. But this is like the utilitarian argument in favour of encouraging religious belief if it comforts the believer and ensures his social conformity. In both cases the practice is looked at without any regard to its intrinsic nature. It is assessed from the outside purely in terms of its actual results, not at all in terms of how it is conceived by its participants. This, of course, is not an entirely irrelevant or immoral way of looking at a practice. But if it predominates a widespread and insidious type of corruption ensues. For the point of view of participants in a practice becomes of decreasing importance. They are regarded basically as vehicles for the promotion of public benefit, whose queer attitudes may sometimes promote this, though no thought of it ever enters their heads. This is the manipulator's attitude to other human beings, the 'hidden hand' in operation from the outside.

3. THE INCOMPLETENESS OF INSTRUMENTAL JUSTIFICATIONS

All these arguments for education deriving from social benefit could also be put in terms of individual benefit with equal plausibility or lack of it. For it merely has to be pointed out that if certain types of knowledge and skill are socially beneficial, then it will be in the individual's interest to acquire some of them; for he has to earn a living and he will be likely to get prestige and reward for his possession of skills and knowledge that are socially demanded. He is afloat in the pool of relevantly trained manpower. There is also a lot of knowledge which will help him spend and consume more wisely—e.g. about types of food, house purchase, income tax, and so on. So the same kind of limited instrumental case can be made for education when it is looked at externally from the individual's point of view as when it is looked at from the point of view of social benefit. But there is an obvious incompleteness about these sorts of social justification, even if they are quite convincing—e.g. the justification for specialized knowledge. For what, in the end, constitutes social benefit? On what is the individual going to spend his wages? If approval is the lure, why should some things rather than others be approved of? What account is to be given of the states of affairs in relation to which other things are to be thought of as instrumental?

The answer of those whose thoughts veer towards consumption is that social benefit is constituted by various forms of pleasure and satisfaction. This, however, is an unilluminating answer; for pleasure and satisfaction are not states of mind supervenient on doing things. Still less is happiness. They are inseparable from things that are done, whether this be swimming, eating a beef-steak, or listening to a symphony. And if it is said that such things are pleasures or done for the pleasure or satisfaction that they give, this is at least to suggest that they are done in a non-instrumental way. The reasons for doing them arise from the intrinsic features of the things done. So this is to repeat that they need no instrumental justification, they are indeed the sorts of things for the sake of which other things are done. It can then be asked why some pleasures rather than others are to be pursued. For many the pursuit of knowledge ranks as a pleasure. So this is no more in need of justification than any other form of pleasure and no less.

The question, therefore, is whether knowledge and understanding have strong claims to be included as one of the goods which are *constitutive* of a worth-while level of life and on what considerations their claims are based. This is a particularly pertinent question in the context of the value of education. For it was argued that the instrumental arguments for the breadth of knowledge of the educated man are not very obvious. Also it has been claimed that the educated person is one who is capable, to a certain extent, of a non-instrumental outlook. This would suggest that he does not think of his knowledge purely in terms of the uses to which he can put it. How then can it be justified?

4. NON-INSTRUMENTAL JUSTIFICATIONS OF EDUCATION

Questions about the intrinsic value of states of mind and of activities are often put by asking whether they are 'worth while.' This term is often used, of course, to raise questions of extrinsic value. If a man is asked whether gardening is worth while he may take it to be a question about its cash value. The term, too, is often used to draw attention to an individual's benefit, or lack of it, from something—e.g. 'It simply is not worth while for him to change his job just before he retires.' But even in its intrinsic uses it has ambiguities. (*a*) It can be used to indicate that an activity is likely to prove absorbing, to be an enjoyable way of passing the time. (*b*) Alternatively it can point to 'worth' that has little to do with absorption or enjoyment. Socrates obviously regarded questioning young men as being worth while; for it was an activity in which they came to grasp what was true, which, for him was a state of mind of ultimate value. But at times he may have found it a bit boring. Let us therefore explore the 'worthwhileness' of education in these two senses.

(a) Absence of Boredom

An educated person is one who is possessed of a range of dispositions connected with knowledge and understanding. These will be revealed in what he says, in his emotional expressions, and in what he does. Of particular importance are the activities on which he spends time and the manner in which he engages in them. Activities can be more or less interesting, absorbing, or fascinating, depending on the dispositions and competences of the agent and the characteristics of the activity in question. Fishing, for instance, is more absorbing in one respect for a man who depends on fish for his meals or livelihood than for one who does it for sport; but in another respect the interest depends not so much on the urgency of the objective as on the skill there is in it. The more occasions there are for exercising skill in dealing with the unexpected, the more fascinating it becomes as an activity.

Some activities are absorbing because of their palpable and pleasurable point, such as eating, sexual activity, and fighting. But erected on this solid foundation of want is often an elaborate superstructure of rules and conventions which make it possible to indulge in these activities with more or less skill, sensitivity, and understanding. Such activities become 'civilized' when rules develop which protect those engaged in them from brutal efficiency in relation to the obvious end of the exercise. Eating could consist in getting as much food into the stomach in the quickest and most efficient way—like pigs at a trough. Civilization begins when conventions develop which protect others from the starkness of such 'natural' behaviour. The development of rules and conventions governing the manner in which these activities are pursued, because of the joys involved in mastery, generates an additional source of interest and pleasure.

To take part in activities of this civilized type requires considerable knowledge and understanding. The possession of it at least makes life less boring, as well as making possible levels of boredom beyond the ken of the uneducated. A case may be made, therefore, for the possession of knowledge in so far as it transforms activities by making them more complex and by altering the way in which they are conceived. This can take place in the pursuit of pleasures like those of the palate; it can also take place in spheres of duty which are sometimes regarded as boring. And in spheres like those of politics, or administration, which can be looked at both as pleasures and as duties, the degree of knowledge with which the activities are conducted makes a marked difference. For what there is in politics, administration, or business depends to a large extent on what a person conceives of himself as doing when he engages in them.

Another way in which knowledge can exert a transforming influence on conduct is in the sphere of planning—not just in the planning of means to ends within activities but in the avoidance of conflict between activities. This is where talk of happiness, integration, and the harmony of the soul has application. The question is not whether something should be indulged in *for the sake* of something else but whether indulging in some activity to a considerable extent is compatible with indulging in another which may be equally worth while. A man who wants to give equal expression to his passions for golf, gardening, and girls is going to have problems, unless he works out his priorities and imposes some sort of schedule on the use of his time. The case for the use of reason in this sphere of planning is not simply that by imposing coherence on activities conflict, and hence dissatisfaction, are avoided; it is also that the search for order and its implementation in life is itself an endless source of satisfaction. The development of knowledge is inseparable from classification and systematizing. In planning there is the added satisfaction of mastery, of imposing order and system on resistant material. Children begin to delight in this at the stage of concrete operations, and, when more abstract thought develops, it is a potent source of delight. The love of order permeates Plato's account of reason and Freud regarded it as one of the main effective sources of civilization.

The mention of the pursuit of knowledge introduces another type of justification for knowledge and hence for education. For so far the case for knowledge in relation to the avoidance of boredom has been confined to its transforming influence on other activities. A strong case can be made for it, however, as providing a range of activities which are concerned with its development as an end in itself and which provide an endless source of interest and satisfaction in addition to that concerned with the love of order.

Philosophers from Plato onwards have made strong claims for the pursuit of knowledge as providing the most permanent source of satisfaction and absorption. They have claimed, not altogether convincingly, that the ends of most activities have certain obvious disadvantages when compared with the pursuit of truth. The ends of eating and sex, for instance, depend to a large extent on bodily conditions which are cyclic in character and which limit the time which can be spent on them; there are no such obvious limitations imposed on theoretical activities. Questions of scarcity of the object cannot arise either; for no one is prevented from pursuing truth if many others get absorbed in the same quest. There is no question either, as Spinoza argued so strongly, of the object perishing or passing away.

Theoretical activities could also be defended in respect of the unending opportunities for skill and discrimination which they provide. Most activities consist in bringing about the same state of affairs in a variety of ways under differing conditions. One dinner differs from another just as one game of bridge differs from another. But there is a static quality about them in that they both have either a natural or a conventional objective which can be attained in a limited number of ways. In science or history there is no such attainable objective. For truth is not an object that can be attained; it is an aegis under which there must always be progressive development. To discover something, to falsify the views of one's predecessors, necessarily opens up fresh things to be discovered, fresh hypotheses to be falsified. There must therefore necessarily be unending opportunities for fresh discrimination and judgment and for the development of further skills. An educated person, therefore, who keeps learning in a variety of forms of knowledge, will have a variety of absorbing pursuits to occupy him. The breadth of his interests will minimize the likelihood of boredom.

These arguments carry weight, but they are not entirely convincing. Even an educated person might claim that they are one-sided. In relation to the nature of the ends of activities he might argue that evanescence is essential to the attraction of some pursuits. What would winetasting or sexual activity be like if the culminating point was too permanent and prolonged? And is there not something to be said for excursions into the simple and brutish? Does not intensity of pleasure count as well as duration? In relation, too, to the arguments in terms of the open-endedness and progressive features of the pursuit of knowledge, it might well be said that the vision of life presented is altogether too exhausting. It smacks too much of John Dewey and the frontier mentality. It takes too little account of the conservative side of human nature, the enjoyment of routines, and the security to be found in the well-worn and the familiar.

(b) The Values of Reason

The major objection to these types of argument for the pursuit of knowledge, or for the transformation of other activities by the development of knowledge, is not to be found, however, within these dimensions or argument. It is rather to exclusive reliance on this form of argument. It is to the presupposition that, leaving aside straightforward moral arguments in terms of justice or the common good, science or wisdom in polities have to be defended purely hedonistically. This is not to say that arguments for education in terms of absorption and satisfaction are not important. Of course they are especially with the increase in leisure time in modern society and the boring character of so many jobs. It is only to say that this is only one way of justifying education. To gain a fuller perspective we must turn to the other sense of 'worth while'.

In section 2(a) the connection between 'knowledge' and 'truth' was spelled out. To 'know' implies that what is said or thought is true and that the individual has grounds for what he says or thinks. The utilitarian case both for having a concept of knowledge and for the importance of knowledge in the life of the society and of the individual was briefly indicated. But being concerned about truth has another type of worth. It can be regarded as having a worth which is independent of its benefit. Indeed the state of mind of one who is determined to find out what is true and who is not obviously deluded or mistaken about how things are can be regarded as an ultimate value which provides one of the criteria of benefit. This was the central point of Socrates's answer to Callicles in Plato's *Gorgias*. Someone who values truth in this way may find the constant effort to free his mind from prejudice and error painful; he may sometimes find it wearisome and boring; but it matters to him supremely, even if he falls short of the ideal which he accepts.

Three points must be briefly made to explain further this ideal. Firstly no finality is assumed or sought for. It is appreciated that error is always possible. Value attaches as much to the attempt to eradicate error as it does to the state of not being in error. Secondly no positivistic view of truth is being assumed, which claims that true statements can only be made in the realms of empirical science, logic, and mathematics. Rather the term is being used widely to cover fields such as morals and understanding other people in which some kind of objectivity is possible, in which reasons can be given which count for or against a judgement. Thirdly there is a group of virtues which are inseparable from any attempt to decide questions in this way. They are those of truth-telling and sincerity, freedom of thought, clarity, non-arbitrariness, impartiality, a sense of relevance, consistency, respect for evidence, and for people as the source of it—to mention the main ones. These must be accepted as virtues by anyone who is seriously concerned with answering questions by the use of reason.

How, then, is this concern for truth relevant to the attempt to justify knowledge and understanding? Surely because the activity of justification itself would be unintelligible without it. If a justification is sought for doing X rather than Y, then firstly X and Y have to be distinguished in some way. To distinguish them we have to rely on the forms of discrimination which are available, to locate them within some kind of conceptual scheme. For instance, if the choice is between going into medicine or going into business some understanding of these activities is a prerequisite. Understanding such activities is an open-ended business depending upon how they are conceived and how many aspects of them are explored. So an open-ended employment of various forms of understanding is necessary. And such probing must be conducted at least on the presupposition that obvious misconceptions of what is involved in these activities are to be removed. There is a presumption, in other words, that it is undesirable to believe what is false and desirable to believe what is true.

Secondly, if a reason is to be given for choosing X rather than Y, X has to be shown to have some feature which Y lacks which is relevant to its worth or desirability. If smoking in fact is a threat to health and chewing gum is not, these are relevant considerations, given the assumption that health is desirable. And this, in its turn, presupposes two types of knowledge, one about the effects of smoking as distinct from chewing gum, and the other about the desirability of health. Further questions can, of course, be raised about the desirability of health, which may lead to questions in moral philosophy about the existence and epistemological status of ultimate ends. But whatever the outcome of such explorations they too are part of the quest for further clarity and understanding. Maybe the inquirer will be chary of saying that what he ends up with is 'knowledge', but at least he may claim to have eliminated some errors and to have obtained more clarity and understanding of the issues involved. Arbitrary assertions will have been rejected, irrelevant considerations avoided, and generalizations queried for their evidential basis. These procedures, which are constitutive of the search for truth, are not those for which some individual might have a private preference; they are those which he must observe in rational discussion. This would be unintelligible as a public practice without value being ascribed at least to the elimination of muddle and error.

It might be admitted that there are links of this sort between justification and forms of knowledge in that to ask for reasons for believing or doing anything is to ask for what is only to be found in knowledge and understanding. But three sorts of difficulties might be raised about ascribing value to this concern for what is true. Firstly, the value of justification itself might be queried. Secondly, it might be suggested that this does not establish the value of *breadth* of knowledge. Thirdly, it might be argued that this only establishes the instrumental value of attempts to discover what is true. These three types of difficulty must be dealt with in turn.

(i) *The value of justification.* The difficulty about querying the value of justification is that any such query, if it is not frivolous, presupposes its value. For to discuss its value is immediately to embark upon reasons for or against it, which is itself a further example of justification. This is not, as might be thought, a purely *ad hominem* argument which might be produced to confound a reflective sceptic. For to give reasons why unreflective people should concern themselves more with what they do, think, and feel is to accept the very values that are at issue. No reason, therefore, can be given for justification without presupposing the values which are immanent in it as an activity.

It might be thought that this smacks of arbitrariness. But this is not so; for 'arbitrariness' is a complaint that only has application within a context where reasons can be given. To pick out the values presupposed by the search for reasons is to make explicit what gives point to the charge of arbitrariness. There is an important sense, too, in which anyone who denies the value of justification, not by making a case against it, which is to presuppose it, but by unreflectively relying on feelings in his stomach or on what other people say, is himself guilty of arbitrariness; for human life is a context in which the demands of reason are inescapable. Ultimately they cannot be satisfied by recourse to such methods. So anyone who relies on them is criticizable in the sense that he adopts procedures which are inappropriate to demands that are admitted, and must be admitted by anyone who takes part in human life.

To explain this point properly would require a treatise on man as a rational animal. All that can be here provided is a short sketch of the broad contours of the demand for justification that is immanent in human life. Human beings, like animals, have from the very start of their lives expectations of their environment, some of which are falsified. With the development of language these expectations come to be formulated and special words are used for the assessment of the content of these expectations and for how they are to be regarded in respect of their epistemological status. Words like 'true' and 'false' are used, for instance, to appraise the contents, and the term 'belief' for the attitude of mind that is appropriate to what is true. Perceiving and remembering are distinguished by their built-in truth claims from merely imagining. Knowledge is similarly distinguished from opinion. In learning we come up to standards of correctness as a result of past experience. Our language, which is riddled with such appraisals, bears witness to the claims of reason on our sensibility. It reflects our position as fallible creatures, beset by fears and wishes, in a world whose regularities have laboriously to be discovered.

The same sort of point can be made about human conduct. For human beings do not just veer towards goals like moths towards a light; they are not just programmed by an instinctive equipment. They conceive of ends, deliberate about them and about the means to them. They follow rules and revise and assess them. Assessment indeed has a toehold in every feature of this form of behaviour which, in this respect, is to be contrasted with that of a man who falls off a cliff or whose knee jerks when hit with a hammer. Words like 'right', 'good', and 'ought' reflect this constant scrutiny and monitoring of human actions.

Man is thus a creature who lives under the demands of reason. He can, of course, be unreasonable or irrational; but these terms are only intelligible as fallings short in respect of reason. An unreasonable man has reasons, but bad ones; an irrational man acts or holds beliefs in the face of reasons. But how does it help the argument to show that human life is only intelligible on the assumption that the demands of reason are admitted, and woven into the fabric of human life? It helps because it makes plain that the demands of reason are not just an option available to the reflective. Any man who emerges from infancy tries to perceive, to remember, to infer, to learn, and to regulate his wants. If he is to do this he must have recourse to some procedure of assessment. For how else could he determine what to believe or do? In their early years all human beings are initiated into human life by their elders and rely for a long time on procedures connected with authority and custom. They believe what they are told and do what others do and expect of them. Many manage most of their lives by reliance on such procedures. This fact, however, is a reflection of human psychology rather than of the logic of the situation; for ultimately such procedures are inappropriate to the demand that they are meant to serve. For belief is the attitude which is appropriate to what is true, and no statement is true just because an individual or a group proclaims it. For the person whose word is believed has himself to have some procedure for determining what is true. In the end there must be procedures which depend not just on going on what somebody else says but on looking at the reasons which are relevant to the truth of the statement. The truth of a lot of statements depends upon the evidence of the senses; and all men have sense-organs. Similarly reasons for action are connected with human wants; and all men have wants. There may be good reasons, in certain spheres of life, for reliance on authorities; but such authorities, logically speaking, can only be regarded as provisional. They cannot be regarded as the ultimate source of what is true, right, and good. This goes against the logic of the situation.

Thus those who rely permanently and perpetually on custom or authority are criticizable because they are relying on procedures of assessment which are not ultimately appropriate to the nature of belief and conduct. To say, therefore, that men ought to rely more on their reason, that they ought to be more concerned with first-hand justification, is to claim that they are systematically falling down on a job on which they are already engaged. It is not to commit some version of the naturalistic fallacy by basing a demand for a type of life on features of human life which make it distinctively human. For this would be to repeat the errors of the old Greek doctrine of function. Rather it is to say that human life already bears witness to the demands of reason. Without some acceptance by men of such demands their life would be unintelligible. But given the acceptance of such demands they are proceeding in a way which is inappropriate to satisfying them. Concern for truth is written into human life. There are procedures which are ultimately inappropriate for giving expression to this concern.

This is not to say, of course, that there are not *other* features of life which are valuable—love for others, for instance. It is not even to say that such other concerns may not be more valuable. It is only to say that at least some attempt must be made to satisfy the admitted demands that reason makes upon human life. If, for instance, someone is loved under descriptions which are manifestly false, this is a fault. If, too, a person is deluded in thinking that he loves someone—if, for instance, he mistakes love of being loved for loving someone, this too is a criticism.

This argument, which bases the case for the development of knowledge and understanding on its connection with justification, does not make a case for the pursuit of any kind of knowledge. It only points to the importance of knowledge that is relevant to the assessment of belief, conduct, and feeling. It does not show, for instance, that there is value in amassing a vast store of information, in learning by heart every tenth name in a telephone directory. And this accords well with the account of the sort of knowledge that was ascribed to an educated person. For to be educated is to have one's view of the world transformed by the development and systematization of conceptual schemes. It is to be disposed to ask the reason why of things. It is not to have a store of what Whitehead called 'inert ideas'.

(ii) *The case for breadth.* It might still be claimed, however, that this type of argument only shows the value of some sort of knowledge; it does not establish the value of the breadth of understanding characteristic of the educated man. A man might just look for grounds of a certain sort of beliefs—e.g. empirical grounds. He might only value philosophy.

The case for breadth derives from the original link that was claimed between justification and forms of knowledge. For if a choice has to be made between alternatives these have both to be sampled in some way and discriminated in some way. It is not always possible to do the former but the latter must be done for this to rank as a choice. The description of possible activities open to anyone and hence the discussion of their value is not a matter of mere observation. For they depend, in part, on how they are conceived, and this is very varied. If the choice is, for instance, between an activity like cooking or one like art or science, what is going to be emphasized as characterizing these activities? Many such activities—chess, for instance, or mathematics—are difficult to understand without a period of initiation. But they cannot simply be engaged in; they have to be viewed in a certain way. And this will depend upon the forms of understanding that are available and the extent to which the individual has been initiated into them. It would be unreasonable, therefore, to deprive anyone of access in an arbitrary way to forms of understanding which might throw light on alternatives open to him. This is the basic argument for breadth in education.

In the educational situation we have positively to put others in the way of such forms of understanding which may aid their assessment of options open to them. It is of great importance in a society such as ours in which there are many life-styles open to individuals and in which they are encouraged to choose between them, and to make something of themselves. But this value accorded to autonomy, which demands criticism of what is handed on and some first-hand assessment of it, would be unintelligible without the values immanent in justification. Indeed it is largely an implementation of them. For it demands not only critical reflection on rules and activities, with the search for grounds that this involves, but also a genuineness which is connected with the rejection of second-hand considerations. By that I mean that a conventionally minded person goes on what others say. If he has reasons for doing things these are connected with the approval which he will get if he does them and the disapproval if he does not. These are reasons of a sort but are artificially related to what is done. They are reasons for doing a whole variety of things, not this thing in particular. If, for instance, people refrain from smoking because they are disapproved of if they do, this is not connected with smoking in the way in which the probability of lung cancer is connected. As Hume put this point in the context of morality: 'no action can be virtuous or morally good unless there be in human nature some motive to produce it distinct from the sense of its morality'. The same sort of point can be made about other forms of judgement—e.g. aesthetic, scientific, religious. So if the individual is to be helped to discriminate between possibilities open to him in an authentic, as distinct from a second-hand way, he has to be initiated into the different forms of reasoning which employ different criteria for the relevance of reasons.

A corollary of this type of argument for breadth of understanding would be that some forms of knowledge are of more value from the point of view of a 'liberal education' than others, namely those which have a more far-reaching influence on conceptual schemes and forms of understanding. There are forms of understanding such as science, philosophy, literature, and history which have a far-ranging cognitive content. This is one feature which distinguishes them from 'knowing how' and the sort of knowledge that people have who are adept at games and at practical skills. There is a limited amount to know about riding bicycles, swimming, or golf. Furthermore, what is known sheds little light on much else.

Science, history, literary appreciation, and philosophy, on the other hand, have a far-ranging cognitive content which gives them a value denied to other more circumscribed activities. They consist largely in the explanation, assessment, and illumination of the different facets of life. They can thus insensibly change a man's view of the world. The point, then, about activities such as science, philosophy, and history is that they need not, like games, be isolated and confined to set times and places. A person who has pursued them systematically can develop conceptual schemes and forms of appraisal which transform everything else that he does.

(iii) *An instrumental type of argument?* But, it might be said, this shows only the *instrumental* value of breadth of understanding and imagination. It does not show that a variety of forms of knowledge should be pursued for any other reason, particularly if they are rather boring. This argument also shows the great importance of physical education. For without a fit body a man's attempts to answer the question 'Why do this rather than that?' might be sluggish or slovenly. So it provides, it seems, a transcendental deduction of the principle of physical fitness! The seeming correctness of such a deduction, if the empirical connection were to be shown, does not establish that physical exercise has any value except of an instrumental sort.

There is, however, a confusion in this comparison between physical exercise and the pursuit of knowledge in their relations to justification; for the former is suggested as an empirically necessary condition and hence is properly regarded as instrumental, whereas the latter is connected by logical relationships such as those of 'relevance', 'providing evidence', 'illuminating', and 'explaining'. Indeed the latter is an educational type of relationship to justification in that it suggests avenues of learning which are relevant to choice, and this is not properly conceived of as an instrumental relationship, as was argued in section 1(d). In engaging in the activity of justification the individual is envisaged as exploring the possibilities open to him by developing the ways of discriminating between them that are available to him—i.e. through the different forms of understanding such as science, history, literature which the human race has laboriously developed. This process of learning is logically, not causally related, to the questioning situation. He will be articulating, with increasing understanding and imagination, aspects of the situation in which he is placed, and in pursuing various differentiated forms of inquiry he will be instantiating, on a wider scale, the very values which are present in his original situation—e.g. respect for facts and evidence, precision, clarity, rejection of arbitrariness, consistency, and the general determination to get to the bottom of things. If, for instance, he considers one of the possibilities open to him as desirable he must, as has already been argued, view this under a certain description. The question then arises whether this description is really applicable and whether there is any other way of looking at this possibility which might be relevant. The ethical question immediately articulates itself into other sorts of questions. The values of reason, such as those of consistency, relevance, and clarity, inherent in such educational explorations are the values of the starting point 'writ large.'

It is important to stress the values of reason which are immanent in such attempts to discriminate alternatives with more clarity and precision rather than the 'means–end' type of link between questioning and forms of knowledge that can often be both logical, and of the means-end type, as in the case of the relationship between learning to read and reading George Eliot, previously explained (p. 121, note 2). Socrates, it seems, gave up his pursuit of knowledge in the physical sciences in favour of devotion to ethics and psychology. It could be argued that, leaving aside *other* questions to do with what he found absorbing, he could well have thought that he ought to study psychological questions deeply only because of their logical links with ethical questions. He had reason to engage in such a disinterested inquiry but did not value this form of knowledge 'for its own sake'. But this is to misconceive the way in which the value of concern for truth enters into both answering justificatory questions *and* into asking them. The point is that value is located in the procedures necessary to explicate what is meant by *justification.* In other words the value is not in the acquisition of knowledge *per se* but in the demands of reason inherent both in answering questions of this sort and in asking them. Evidence should be produced, questions should be clearly put, alternatives should be set out in a clear and informed way, inconsistencies and contradictions in argument should be avoided, relevant considerations should be explored, and arbitrariness avoided. These monitoring and warranting types of relationships, which are characteristic of the use of reason, are not instrumental types of relationship. They are articulations of the ideal implicit in thought and action. We are drawn towards this ideal by what I have elsewhere called the 'rational passions'.[3] And this ideal may draw us towards types of inquiry which we do not find particularly absorbing in their own right.

To put this point in another way: much has been said in this section about the 'concern for truth' and 'the demands of reason'. The value picked out by these expressions is not to be thought of as a kind of consumer value which bestows importance on the accumulation of countless true propositions. Devotion to the pursuit of knowledge, in this sense, may also be fascinating, and a case can be made for it in terms of the first sense of 'worth while'. But that type of argument is not now being used either. Value rather is being ascribed to the quality of knowledge rather than to its amount or to its capacity to mitigate boredom. It is being claimed that what is valuable is inherent in the demand that what is done, thought, or felt should be rationally scrutinized.

It will not do to suggest that this concern for truth is instrumentally valuable just because people need to know in order to satisfy their wants, including their desire for knowledge itself, unless 'want' is used in a very general sense which makes it a conceptual truth that anything which people can value must be, in some sense, what they want. For, firstly, to want is always to want under some description that involves belief; hence wants can be more or less examined. Secondly, one of the most perplexing questions of conduct is whether, in any ordinary sense of 'want', people ought to do what they want to do. Thirdly, the very notion of 'instrumentality' presupposes the demand of reason. For, as Kant put it, taking a means to an end presupposes the axiom of reason that to will the end is to will the means. Thus the demands of reason are presupposed in the form of thought which might lead us to think of its value as being instrumental.

On the other hand the demand for truth is not an absolute demand in the sense that it can never be over-ridden. It sometimes can be, if, in some situation, some other value is more pressing. In general, for instance, it is undesirable that people should ignore facts about themselves or about others which are relevant to what they should do. But on a particular occasion, when someone's suffering is manifestly at stake for instance, it might be argued that it is just as well for a person not to be too persistent in his demand for truth, if satisfying this demand would occasion great suffering. The values of reason are only one type of value. As has been argued from the start, there are other values, e.g. love for others, the avoidance of suffering. But situations like this, in which there is a conflict of values, do not affect the general status of the concern for truth. As E. M. Forster put it: 'Yes, for we fight for more than Love or Pleasure: there is Truth. Truth counts. Truth does Count.'[4]

This type of argument for the value of knowledge helps to explain the value inherent in being educated not only of breadth of knowledge, as previously explained, but also of what was called 'cognitive perspective'. What was suggested is that an educated person is not one who has his mind composed of *disconnected* items of knowledge. What he knows and understands should be seen to be interrelated in terms of consistency, relevance, evidence, implication, and other such rational connections. If his knowledge is linked together in this way it is 'integrated' in one sense of the term. It may well be, too, that certain studies such as philosophy, which explicitly examines grounds for different types of knowledge and their interrelationship, and literature, which imaginatively depicts people in situations in which they have to make complex judgments and respond emotionally to perplexing situations, contribute to the development of this cognitive perspective.

Those who favour certain educational methods might argue that the exploration of literature, of history, and of philosophy should not begin until children begin to be troubled or curious about various aspects of the human condition. And certainly, if inquiries and explorations move outwards from a centre of puzzlement and concern, they are more likely to be genuine and to instantiate the values immanent in justification in a first-hand way. Others, however, might argue that one way of generating such concern and puzzlement in people is to initiate them into our human heritage. This kind of imaginative situation may be necessary to make people more alive to their position in the world as believers and choosers. But there is the danger of the second-hand in this approach. There is also the possibility that individuals may fail to connect, to transfer values learnt in a specialized context to wider contexts. A person, for instance, may be ruthless in demanding evidence for assumptions when learning history or social science. But he may not show the same ruthlessness when having to make up his mind about policies presented to him by politicians. This raises questions which are, in part, empirical about transfer of learning. But it does not, I think, affect the basic point about the non-instrumental features of the relationship between justification, and the forms of understanding which contribute to it.

In a purely philosophical context it might be said, then, that the demand for justification presupposes the acceptance of the values implicit in it. In an educational context, however, children must be initiated somehow into those forms of understanding which are of particular relevance to justification. It is, of course, no accident that there should be these two ways of explicating this relationship. For processes of education are processes by means of which people come to know and to understand. These are implementations, through time, by means of learning, of the values and procedures implicit in justification. Education, properly understood, is the attempt to actualize the ideal implicit in Socrates' saying that the unexamined life is not worth living.

5. THE NON-INSTRUMENTAL ATTITUDE

An educated person, it was argued, is characterized not just by his abiding concern for knowledge and understanding but also by the capacity to adopt, to a certain extent, a non-instrumental attitude to activities. How can this attitude be justified? This is not difficult; for the justification of it is implicit in what has already been said. It is presupposed by the determination to search for justification. Anyone who asks the question about his life 'Why do this rather than that?' has already reached the stage at which he sees that instrumental justifications must reach a stopping place in activities that must be regarded as providing end-points for such justifications. To ask of his pattern of life 'What is the point of it all?' is to ask for features internal to it which constitute reasons for pursuing it. A stage has been reached at which the ordinary use of 'point' has no application—unless, that is, the same types of question are transferred to an afterlife or to the life of future generations. So a person who asks this type of question seriously demonstrates that he is not a stranger to this attitude. To what extent it will in fact transform his way of going about particular activities within his life cannot be inferred from this capacity for reflection. It is, to a certain extent, an empirical question—but not entirely empirical, because of the logical connection between the general capacity to reflect and particular instantiations of it.

In so far, however, as he values knowledge and understanding he values one very important ingredient in the non-instrumental attitude; for this attitude requires attention to the actual features of that with which he is confronted, as distinct from tunnel vision determined by his own wants. He is concerned about what is 'out there'. Even at the crudest level a person who *just* regards a piece of fish as a way of satisfying his hunger, or a glass of wine as a way of satisfying his thirst, ignores a range of features. He fails to discriminate the variety of tastes. Conversely he will think nothing of using a beautiful glass to house his tooth-brush—unless, of course, he thinks that it is worth a lot of money and that he might break it. In sexual activity, too, he will regard a woman as a necessary object for satisfying his lust; he will be indifferent to her idiosyncrasies and point of view as a person. He will only listen to people in so far as they share his purposes or provide, by their remarks, springboards for his own self-display. His interest in people and things is limited to the use he can make of them. He lacks interest in and concern for what is 'out there'.

A person, on the other hand, who presses the question 'Why do this rather than that?' already accepts the limitations of his egocentric vision. He is not satisfied with a life geared to unexamined wants. He wonders whether some of the things that he wants are really worth wanting or whether he really wants them. He wonders about the relevance of his wants. In attempting to find out what is the case he may reveal features of situations that in no way serve his wants and which indeed may run counter to them. An unreflective businessman, for instance, might visit an undeveloped country with a view to setting up a factory. But, on going into all the details of what this would involve, he might become more and more aware of the disruption of a way of life that is entailed. He might 'not want to know' or he might begin to question the whole enterprise. And if he began to question this particular feature of business life he might begin to query the way of life more generally.

Another aspect of the instrumental attitude is the view of time that goes with it. For the instrumentally minded good lies always in future consumption. The present has to be hurried through for the sake of what lies ahead. It is not to be dwelt in and its aspects explored. To a person who uses his reason this attitude is just as unreasonable as the opposed cult of instancy. For, as Sidgwick put it, to a rational person, 'Hereafter as such is to be regarded neither more nor less than now.' [5] Reasons have to be given for instant or delayed gratification other than temporal position—e.g. 'If you wait you won't be able to have it at all' or 'If you wait there will be more of it.' The important thing for a man is to connect, to grasp the features of objects and situations and the relationships which structure his life. It is not, therefore, the fact that the pleasure of smoking is to be had now or in five minutes that matters; it is rather how it is to be conceived and its relation to other things in life. Can smoking, like sexual activity, be conceived of not simply as a physical pleasure, but also as an expression of love? Can it be done with skill and grace like dancing? And are its relationships to other human activities other than detrimental?

To ascribe a non-instrumental attitude to a person is not, of course, to lay down that he will indulge in some activities rather than others. It is only to indicate the way in which he will go about activities and conceive them. He will not always do things for the sake of some extrinsic end. He will, first of all, enjoy performing well according to the standards required. He will have an attitude of care in other words. But this care will be related to the point of the activity. He will feel humility towards the givenness of the features of the activity, towards the impersonal demands of its standards. And he will have a sense of its connection with other things in life, a wary consciousness of the past and the future and of the place of what is being done in the passage through the present. Indeed, as Spinoza put it, he should be capable of viewing what he does 'under a certain aspect of eternity'.

6. CONCLUDING PROBLEM

There is a major outstanding problem to which this approach to justification gives rise. Two types of value have been distinguished, which underpin the life of an educated person, leaving aside moral values such as justice, and the minimization of suffering, which structure the interpersonal realm of conduct. These are (i) values relevant to the avoidance of boredom, in relation to which the pursuit of knowledge was accorded a high place, and (ii) values implicit in the demands of reason which give rise to virtues such as humility, hatred of arbitrariness, consistency, clarity, and so on. If a reasonable person examines his beliefs or conduct these virtues govern his conduct of the inquiry; but he does not necessarily find this kind of examination enjoyable or absorbing.·

Now, for reasons that were explained in Section 1(d), when dealing with processes of education, a person can only *become* educated if he pursues theoretical activities such as science and literature and/or practical activities which require a fair degree of understanding; but why, having become educated, should he devote himself much to activities of this sort? Why should he choose to spend much of his time in reading, taking part in discussions, or in demanding practical activities such as engineering? On occasions, of course, in acknowledgement of the demands of reason, he may feel obliged to enlighten himself on some issue, to seek information which is relevant to his beliefs and action. And while so doing he submits to the standards of such a disinterested pursuit. But why should he seek out *any* such pursuits? To take a parallel in the moral sphere: why should a person who accepts the principle of justice, and who acknowledges its demands on his life by relevant actions and inquiries when occasions arise, pursue the promotion of justice as an *activity*—e.g. by working as a judge or as a social reformer? Similarly in this sphere of worth-while pursuits why should not an educated man settle for an undemanding job which allows him plenty of time for playing golf which is the one activity which he really enjoys apart from eating, sun-bathing, and occasionally making love to his wife? He is, of course, capable of seeing point in a more Dewey type of life of expanding experience and understanding. He is not a philistine; neither is he particularly instrumental in his outlook. He just loves his game of golf more than any of the more intellectually taxing types of pursuits. Golf is to him what he presumes science is to the other fellow.

Could the answer be connected with the fact, already pointed out, that the use of reason itself exemplifies the two types of value? On the one hand is the absorption springing from curiosity and from the love of order, etc. Human beings, it might be said, 'naturally' find discrepancies between what they expect and what they experience intolerable. This is what leads them to learn according to cognitive theories of motivation stemming from Piaget. On the other hand there are the normative demands connected with the use of reason. Inconsistencies and confusions in thought ought to be removed; evidence ought to be sought for and arbitrariness avoided. Is it conceivable that the latter type of value could be accepted by a person who was unmoved by curiosity and by the desire to sort things out? Is this not like saying, in the moral sphere, that respect for persons, as a moral attitude, could exist without some natural sympathy for them?

There may well be some relationships, which are not merely contingent, between the 'natural' and the normative aspects of the use of reason, which may parallel those between sympathy and respect, but it would require another paper to elucidate them. The doubt, as far as this paper goes, is whether such connections need be strong enough to carry the required weight. It might be shown that acceptance of the demands of reason presupposes certain 'natural' passions such as curiosity and the love of order, but would it show enough to make it necessarily the case that an educated person must not only proceed in a rational way with regard to his beliefs and conduct but must also adopt some pursuits for their own sake which provide ample scope for curiosity or which are taxing in relation to the level of understanding that they require? Does not Dewey's educational method, which requires that learning should always be harnessed to spontaneous interest and curiosity, seem appropriate because so many people emerge from school and university with some degree of sophistication and capacity for rational reflection, but with a singular lack of enthusiasm either for further theoretical pursuits or for practical activities that make frequent and open-ended demands on their understanding? Could not his methods be seen as an attempt to close the gap between the two types of value? And does not this suggest that, as closing this gap depends upon empirical conditions underlying methods of learning, the connection in question is an empirical connection? Indeed is not one of the main tasks of the educator the devising of procedures which are likely to minimize this type of gap?

This sounds plausible but a nagging doubt remains. The problem can be summarized as follows:

> (i) There are activities such as science, engineering, the study of literature, etc., by engaging in which a person becomes an educated person— one who has breadth and depth of understanding and who is prepared to examine his beliefs and conduct.
>
> (ii) As an educated person he may, later on, see reason to pursue such activities on occasions, if he sees their relevance to some issue of belief and conduct, though he may not find them particularly absorbing. Such exercises will be manifestations of his acceptance of the demands of reason.
>
> (iii) But, as an educated person, he will do *some* things for their own sake. Whatever he does will be, to a certain extent, transformed by his level of understanding, but will he necessarily pursue, for their own sake, some activities of the sort that he pursues or has pursued in contexts (i) and (ii), which make demands on his understanding? Is it intelligible that he should both be educated and find *all* such activities too frustrating or boring to pursue for their own sake? Would such a man be any more intelligible than Kant's moral being who is virtuous only out of respect for

the law? Socrates may have sometimes regarded his pursuit of truth with others as a boring duty, though we know that he did not always find it so. But does it not seem inconceivable that he could *always* have found it boring? And is this *simply* because of the empirical fact that he spent a lot of time that way?

NOTES

1. R. S. Peters, 'Education and the Educated Man', *Proceedings of the Philosophy of Education Society of Great Britain,* Vol. 4 (Jan. 1970).
2. In other cases, however, the logical relationship of the learning process to the product is that of being a necessary preliminary rather than a full-blooded instantiation. Reading, for instance, is often taught as a kind of discrimination skill. Practising such discriminations may be thought of as instantiating little that is valuable. It is valuable only as a necessary preliminary to reading poetry with sensitivity and expression, or to reading George Eliot's novels.
3. See R. S. Peters, 'Reason and Passion', in G. Vezey (ed.), *The Proper Study,* Royal Institute of Philosophy (London: Macmillan, 1971).
4. E. M. Forster, *A Room with a View* (Harmondsworth: Penguin Books, 1955), p. 218.
5. H. Sidgwick, *The Methods of Ethics* (Papermac ed., London: Macmillan, 1962), p. 381.

The Uses of a Liberal Education

Brand Blanshard

Our higher education has two types. One of them is represented by schools of engineering and law, medicine and journalism. The other is represented by the liberal arts colleges. About the first I am going to say almost nothing, since for most of us professional studies need no defense. But liberal studies, the sort of studies that are pursued for their own sake rather than for their utility, do stand in need of defense. To put it bluntly, if they have no use, what is the use of them? Each

B. Blanshard, "The Uses of a Liberal Education," from *The Uses of a Liberal Education,* pps. 27-43. By permission of The Open Court Publishing Company, La Salle, Illinois, 1973, and the author.

wave of students, considering how they are to budget their lives, must ask that question anew. On the answer they give to it will depend not only the course of their education, but very possibly the course of their lives. Furthermore, it is a question on which there are two sides. Many people take the view that in these days when the getting of a living is so sternly competitive a business and in all the professions there is so much to learn, liberal studies should be regarded as merely the parsley on the roast, or if you prefer, the frosting on the cake, or the sugar coating on the educational pill. The dean of a well-known medical school told me that he would be just as happy over a good halfback among his applicants as over a Phi Beta Kappa in the liberal arts. Such studies in his view did supply a buttonhole bouquet which, worn with a careless grace, might help a young gentleman through conversational evenings, particularly if the talk happened to veer toward T. S. Eliot or Jean Paul Sartre. But he regarded them as decorative merely. They did not supply the vitamins and calories of the educational feast; they were something added as garnishing.

I want to raise the question whether he is right. He certainly has a case. And in order not to be unfair, I will begin by stating and stressing some of the arguments commonly used against liberal education.

First, there is an argument that often stirs as a vague protest in the subliminal mind of students, the argument from the price you have to pay for it, not merely the price in money, though that is high and going higher, but also the price in freedom. For many young people the opening of college is the time when shades of the prison house begin to fall, when life must be abjured for books. Four years of it, too! Four years when the sap is rising in one's veins, and adventure calls, and the urge to do things is at its strongest, given over to the companionship of—whom? Primarily not human beings at all, but books—dusty books, dead books, by authors dead and dry as nails. Four years of forcing a reluctant attention, of sitting in dreary classrooms, of dragging the academic ball and chain, while beyond the prison walls the skies are blue and open roads are inviting to the larger world where things are happening.

And what are the books about? Perhaps economics, described by Carlyle as the dismal science, in which all men are supposed to be scrambling for wealth at the expense of their neighbors. Or mathematics, described by a great mathematician as the science in which nobody ever knows what he means, or whether what he says is true. Or history, which is the record, according to Dean Inge, either of events that probably never happened or of events that do not matter. Or philosophy, defined by one practitioner as the finding of bad reasons for what we believe on instinct, and by another as an inverted filter into which whatever goes in clear comes out cloudy. Now people have been known to offer themselves a living sacrifice because they thought that sooner or later a reward would be conferred on them for their high disregard of the flesh, as St. Simeon Stylites chose to divorce himself from the world by living on top of a pillar where normal comforts and contacts were out of the question. But who believes nowadays that one must buy the abundant life with asceticism? Youth was not made for gazing at print through premature glasses; it was made for action and high spirits. We your teachers would vote for the books, but of course with a professional bias—and besides just look at us. The poet's voice is more understanding:

> Gather ye rosebuds while ye may,
> Old time is still a-flying:
> And this same flower that smiles today,
> Tomorrow will be dying.

That is the first argument, the argument from the dreariness of academic drudgery. The second argument is stronger. If the drudgery brought proportionate rewards, it would and should be borne in patience. But it does not. These years of the treadmill, it is said, are on the whole wasted effort. To be sure we hear on all sides that a college education is the condition of getting on. In some fields the statement is plausible. If one is going to be a physician or dentist or engineer, one needs a technical training, and if one wants to form connections with future secretaries of state, experience reveals that it is the part of prudence to go to Yale. But even in fields where the argument seems strongest, as in engineering, there seem to be plenty of contrary cases. Robert Fulton, Thomas A. Edison, Henry Ford, have left firm footprints on the sands of time, but those footprints never passed across the threshold of a college. And if even a technical degree can be dispensed with, how much more readily can one in the liberal arts, which hardly pretend to usefulness. One can no longer take the high line of the Cambridge don of story, who, after demonstrating a very abstruse mathematical theorem, added: "And the best of this, gentlemen, is that this theorem is pure theory with no sort of application anywhere." But if John Dewey is right, there are still fossil remains among us of those academics of old time who thought of an education rather as an aristocratic adornment than as a thing of utility. The Greek aristocrat and the young gentleman of Victorian Oxford had no need to bother their handsome heads about earning a living; a liberal education was for them an aid to the graceful employment of leisure; and some people seem to conceive it so still.

We no longer feel happy about such a view, but the critics tell us that we really have little more to offer. They point out that the classicists staved off the inevitable for a while by insisting that their subjects had transfer value, so that the habits formed in studying them could be applied to other subjects. But the psychologists have undercut this argument by showing that habits are far less transferable than was supposed. And the suggestion that these subjects are widely applicable is met by the critic with an embarrassing insistence that this be shown specifically. You are studying mathematics, for example, often described as a tool subject. Just how often in the past year, or in all your years, have you had occasion to use a trigonometrical theorem or an algebraic equation? And even if you have done so occasionally, was the advantage worth some hundreds of hours of work? You are proposing to study French. How often in the future do you expect to be in a position where the information or ideas you need are inaccessible in English? You are studying Spanish. What is the likelihood of your taking up residence in Spain or in South America, where Spanish will be necessary? You are studying history. Do not even the historians now admit that not one law can be derived from history that will make possible the prediction of any single event? How well have historians done in prophesying American depressions, war, or elections? As for philosophy, the utility of that distinguished subject was suggested very early when the first Western philosopher, Thales, wandering about with his head in the clouds, fell into a well, to the mirth of his more practical neighbors and all their derisive progeny. They have put their view on the matter in the proverb that philosophy bakes no bread. And so of the other subjects. If you ask your father and mother how well they remember and how often they have used the physics and chemistry, the political or economic theory, the astronomy or zoology, the knowledge of *Beowulf* or *Paradise Lost* that they picked up in college, the answer will be strangely hesitant.

The skeptic could say more if we let him. He could point out that students' interest even in Shakespeare may be dulled by enforced study, so that they never read a page of him later, that some of the humanities, poetry for example, are better grasped in maturity than in youth; that college puts off the apprenticeship in practical life which will in any case be necessary; that a passing grade of seventy is ill preparation for a world of competitive business where you will go under with less than eighty. But I have said enough to indicate the main line of attack. It is simply that a liberal education calls for a great outlay in time, money, and effort, for which little or nothing useful is gained in return.

What is to be said on the other side? Unfortunately the argument in defense of liberal studies is harder to state. But I will try to put it in the following steps. To begin with, I will ask you to examine with me what usefulness really means. When we have got clear about this, I will argue that the studies in question are enormously useful in three ways. First, they are useful *directly* because they satisfy some of the deepest wants in our nature. Secondly, they are useful *indirectly* through enabling us to borrow the best insights and standards of others. Thirdly, if taken seriously, they may permeate with their influence all our thought and feeling and action.

First, then, let us ask the critics a question. You are insisting that the college prove its usefulness: just what do you mean by usefulness? You imply that a thing is useful when it contributes to success, but how do you measure success? Is it success, for example, to make a great deal of money? That is certainly not the whole story, for money is not an end in itself; it too is prized because it is useful, that is, because it is a means to something beyond. Money in itself has no value. If you were on an island, cut finally off from civilization, and your pockets were bulging with bills of large denominations, what would the money be worth? A little, perhaps, it would save one the trouble of gathering leaves if one wanted to build a fire; but that would be about all. Money is literally not worth keeping; its only value is that we can get rid of it in exchange for other things. Well, what are these other things? A better house, we say, a better car, the chance to travel. But then we prize these too for their usefulness, for the something further that they bring us. The ampler house brings us comfort and rest and quiet and a sense of freedom and dignity; the car brings to our family the pleasures of the open road, and their pleasure is reflected in ours; travel enriches us with new impressions and ideas. These are the ulterior things, the self-validating things, that make money and possessions useful. Comfort and quiet and richness of mind are not good because they are good *for* something; they are simply good, good in their own right. And you will notice that all these values are goods of the spirit, goods that lie not in things but in the minds that enjoy them. In the end all useful things are useful because they produce these useless goods that are valued for nothing further; or if you wish, it is precisely the useless things of the world that in the end alone are useful, since only they will give us what we want.

We are now ready to deal with the question whether a liberal education has use. It is clear that the issue is not whether an education will increase our income or our efficiency; it may very well do that; but if it fails to do so, it is not thereby proved to be useless. The issue is a deeper one. It is whether an education does or does not contribute substantially to those ultimate goods on which all usefulness depends. I do not think many of us would hesitate here. It contributes enormously.

It does so in the first place by satisfying directly some of our elemental hungers. One of these is the hunger to know. To be sure, I have sometimes wondered how elemental this is when I have observed how skilful some students are in avoiding the banquets spread before them. "The love of truth," said A. E. Housman, "is the faintest of human passions." And there is no doubt that much that passes as the love of knowledge is really something else, such as the love of finding some place off the beaten track where one can excel, or a mere hobby like that of a friend of mine who collects languages, or a frankly avowed means to a further end, as it is in the subscriber to the *Wall Street Journal*. But when all the impurities have been washed away, there remains, I think, a genuine golden residuum of interest in truth itself.

I am a teacher of philosophy, which is commonly held to be one of the most difficult as well as most useless of all fields of study. Students prowling about in search of what they may most painlessly devour have often asked me what was the use of studying the subject. I have come to see that when they do, it is a radical blunder to stutter out something about how helpful philosophy is in solving business and personal problems. I do not for a moment deny that it is thus helpful. But that is not the real reason why men philosophize. They philosophize because they want to understand the world they live in. I believe that, in some degree or other, everyone wants this. Everyone is a budding philosopher, not perhaps in the sense that he wants to spoil a great many pages with very large words, but in the sense that he is genuinely interested in the great metaphysical problems.

Take one or two of these at random. The old question of free will is the question whether, if I knew all about your body and mind at this moment, I could tell what you would do or say five minutes from now, or whether, so to speak, you could double-cross me by doing something incalculable. One of the clearest heads that ever wrote on the problem, Henry Sidgwick, said that a solution one way or the other would make no practical difference; and yet the problem has fascinated men's thought for thousands of years, and, if Milton is to be believed, is eagerly canvassed by the angels in such spare time as they have. Or take body and mind. I find it impossible to doubt that at the present moment something called ideas in my mind are causing movements of tiny particles in the cells of my head, which movements in turn cause messages to be sent down to my lips and make them move. But how is it done? How can an idea, which has no mass or shape or motion, push solid particles about in a very solid head? If any student can write a paper on this which gives a tenable answer, I should be glad to propose him for a Nobel prize.

Of course if one has no interest in questions of this kind, the effort to answer them will be a dreary business. But the dreariness will belong less to philosophy than to one's own soul. Certainly the great thinkers have not found philosophy a dreary business. As Josiah Royce said, "You cannot think the truth without loving it; and the dreariness which we often impute to metaphysics is merely the dreariness of not understanding the subject—a sort of dreariness for which indeed there is no help except learning to understand." This desire to understand rises in some persons to a passion. Professor Montague of Columbia remarked that "man began to think in order that he might eat; he has now evolved to the point where he eats in order that he may think." Perhaps not many of us could say that of ourselves, but certainly some people can. I like the story that Alcibiades tells in Plato's *Symposium* about his companion in a military campaign, a strange ugly soldier whose immense physical strength was matched only by the delight he took in the play of ideas. "One morning," says Alcibiades, "he was thinking about something that he could not resolve, and he would not give up, but continued thinking from early dawn until noon—there he stood fixed in thought; and at noon attention was drawn to him, and the rumour ran through the wondering crowd that Socrates had been standing and thinking about something ever since the break of day. At last in the evening after supper, some Ionians out of curiosity . . . brought out their mats and slept in the open air that they might watch him and see whether he would stand all night. There he stood all night as well as the day . . . and with the return of light he offered up a prayer to the sun, and went his way." The Western world has never been quite the same since this strange figure stood that way in thought. He showed men an ideal city and gave them the key. Even the tough campaigners who poked fun at him did so with a puzzled respect, for they knew that he had the freedom of that city, and in an instant, from the midst of business or the crowd, could go for refreshment to far places where they could not follow.

But the field of truth is as wide as the world, and philosophy is only one part of it. The mind that wants to know can find fascination along a hundred avenues. Darwin will spend countless fascinated hours in watching the behavior of earthworms, Heisenberg the behavior of atoms, Shapley the behavior of nebulae, Jane Goodall the behavior of apes. One of the most remarkable lectures I ever heard was given by Karl von Frisch, the Austrian zoologist, whose particular interest was bees. He discovered that when a bee finds a new bed of flowers, it is able to report its find to the hive and to supply its colleagues with accurate directions as to the distance, the direction, and the kind of nectar to look for. Von Frisch set out to solve the intricate problem of how it did this, and was able to prove beyond doubt that it was done by a dance that the discoverer performed for its neighbors, in which it indicated the point of the compass by dancing in the right direction, the distance by the number of wiggles, and the nectar by supplying whiffs from a specially collected sample. If you were to ask these scientists what was the use of such knowledge, they might reply, as Faraday did to the person who asked the use of his early studies in electricity, "What is the use of a child? It grows to be a man." But probably in their own minds they would silently register one more philistine. If one wants as much as they do to know the secrets of things, one would not need to ask the question; if one does not, their answer would be unintelligible. Knowledge was their profession; and it has been said that while a trade is something one follows in order to live, a profession is something one lives in order to follow.

This passion of the scholar and the scientist, this love of truth for its own sake, is a quality beyond price. "To love truth for truth's sake," said John Locke in his wise old age, "is the principal part of human perfection in this world, and the seed-plot of all other virtues." This may appear extravagant praise. There seems to be nothing very heroic in ferreting out the facts about bees and earthworms. But put this same pure light, this love of uncolored truth, in one of those fields that are rendered murky by human bias, and "how far that little candle throws its beams." "Things and actions are what they are," said Bishop Butler, "and the consequences of them will be what they will be; why then should we desire to be deceived?" But apparently we do. "We are past masters in the art of throwing dust in our own eyes." How many of the millions who read about Women's Liberation or black militancy can look at the issue with an eye wholly single to the truth of the matter? How often does one find a person who can see in perspective not only the cruelty and intolerance of the system behind the Iron Curtain, but also that which makes it so seductive to millions the world over? A man or a society with a genuine interest in truth is like a gyroscope that may wobble crazily for a while, but will right itself in the end. What seems to some of us most sinister in the reports from behind the Curtain is not so much the suppression of mercy, heavy-fisted as that is, as the suppression of objectivity, the discouragement of the very desire to see things straight. When it is decreed that the issue between Lysenko and Mendel, or between the religious man and the atheist is to be settled by an appeal not to the facts or to reflection, but to the party line, the love of truth itself becomes an offense. And when the love of truth is banished, justice and honor too are on the way out. Archbishop Whately was right that "it makes all the difference in the world whether we put truth in the first place or in the second place."

Now the true defense of the educated mind is that it alone has at once the desire and the discipline to see the truth. This truth may or may not have applications in practice; that is not the test of its value. We even have it on good authority that he that increaseth knowledge increaseth sorrow and makes men sadder as well as wiser. Even so, would you, if you had the choice, prefer to be happier at the cost of living among illusions? You have come to see, perhaps, that the theory of evolution is true, and that its truth renders impossible your old interpretation of Genesis and of much else that you once believed. With the passing of those beliefs there has gone something of your old assurance and peace of mind. But would you be willing to buy back that old assurance at the cost of the knowledge you have gained? I suspect not. There is something wrong with the man who would sell his intellectual maturity for the sake of a return to childhood with its irresponsibilities. "In the long run," as Augustine Birrell says, "even a gloomy truth is better company than a cheerful falsehood." The mature mind, the mind that has escaped the straitjacket of prejudice, superstition and ignorance, the mind that knows the truth about itself and its world and by knowing the truth has been made free, is itself the highest value that education can confer. The courageous clinging to that value by a comparatively few men—Socrates, for example, Galileo, Erasmus, Newton, Darwin—brought our Western intellectual world into being. The Irish poet "AE" has given us their quiet injunction:

No blazoned banner we unfold—
One charge alone we give to youth,
Against the sceptered myth to hold
The golden heresy of truth.

I have mentioned only one of the direct satisfactions that liberal studies bring us, the satisfaction of an understanding mind. But of course there are many others. We are told that a thing of beauty is a joy forever, and many people have testified to this in the province of beauty that they have made their own: the province of poetic speech, or of line and color, or that purest of the arts, music. Again, one of our deepest desires is to be liked by other people. There are no classes in college on the art of social intercourse, yet every day of college life provides discipline in that high art. Oscar Wilde said of Bernard Shaw that he had no enemies, but was much disliked by his many friends. College will not teach you how to avoid enemies; such avoidance is hardly open to one with the strong convictions that an educated mind should have. But it will give you a hundred lessons in the important business of making friends and keeping them.

In theory it is possible to satisfy all these hungers, hungers for the best that has been thought and said and acted and painted and composed in the world, without going to college at all; indeed it has actually been done. John Stuart Mill was one of the best educated men of his century, but he was never entered as a student in school, college, or university. But it is sad to think of how few Mills there are, how few people succeed in educating themselves merely by efforts after hours. They find that the noblest and purest pleasures are the results of an acquired taste which itself must be won laboriously. That is what college is for: to help one acquire the tastes that make possible the deeper delights. Those who can really hear Bach—and their numbers are not great—tell us that they are transported by him into another and serener world; but to hear Bach is not a matter of walking into a concert hall and sitting down; it is a matter of years, not minutes. So of all truly fine art. Probably much that nowadays passes as such has a streak of charlatanry in it; but only those who have served an honest apprenticeship in these things have the right to bring the charge. And even if Eliot and Picasso are all that their admirers say they are, we shall not find it out by approaching them jauntily and demanding that they stand and deliver. We cannot see till we have eyes to see, and perhaps also some mental spectacles. "Mr. Whistler," said a lady to whom the painter had shown one of his pictures, "I never saw a sunset like that." "Madam," he answered, "don't you wish you could?"

But it is not only the direct enjoyment of the greater values of life that a liberal training gives us; it is also, and secondly, a large indirect enjoyment. Other minds are sounding boards that enlarge our own powers of response. The psychologist William McDougall reminded us that it is an exciting experience to sit in the grandstand with ten thousand other people through the wind and rain of an autumn day and watch a football game, but that if you had to watch that same game sitting in the grandstand in wind and rain alone, it would be a dreary business. Indeed many things remain simply invisible till we see them through others' eyes. This was brought home to me vividly when I first visited Venice. Venice is by any estimate an extraordinary city, but by a double stroke of luck it became for me an enchanted city. The small pension where I was staying happened to be a house where John Ruskin had lived when he was writing *The Stones of Venice,* and on one of its shelves was a battered old copy of this wonderful book. It was just what an unobservant descendant of Thales needed, and from then on I went gaping about the streets of Venice with the book open in my hands, gazing at the Doge's palace and St. Mark's and the Rialto through eyes many times more discerning than my own. Thanks to Ruskin, Venice has been to me ever since a sort of fairy city.

Fortunately, it is not only others' sense of sight that we can borrow, but also something more important, their sense of values. Education, someone has said, is a process of learning to like the right things. Our likes, then, should change as our education proceeds. It is natural that a boy of eight should regard Superman as the creation of genius; if he holds this opinion at eighteen, he is suffering from arrested development; if he holds it at fifty-eight, he is suffering from premature senility. Unhappily, the growth of a formed and independent taste calls, in this country, for exceptional courage and self-reliance. One reason for this, whose relevance is perhaps not at once plain, is that America is the largest market in the world. A company that can produce the right refrigerator or cookbook or washing machine for the average American family has its fortune assured, for the two hundred-odd millions of us are mainly average people with average income and average tastes. This means that America is the paradise of mass production; Dr. Stringfellow Barr has said that mass production is one of our two main contributions to civilization, the other being the idea of a federal union of states. Now mass production is an admirable thing, which is here to stay; but its results are not equally admirable in all fields. In the field of taste it is a catastrophe. The artist or novelist or Hollywood producer who has original gifts knows that if he consults his own idea of what is first-rate, he is not unlikely to wind up in bankruptcy, while if he can manage to hit the dead center of taste, he may make a fortune. No doubt there are persons who, like Henry Clay, "would rather be right than be President," and get their choice; but the pressure on an American artist to compromise his integrity is almost irresistible.

The result is what we see all around us; moving pictures, for example. Our moving pictures alone might make us believe Professor Terman's pronouncement that the average mental age of American adults is fourteen years. What do Americans read? Dean Mott of the Missouri School of Journalism reminded us some years ago of the name of "the most popular author in the annals of American publishing." What would be your guess as to that name? Not Hawthorne or Melville or Henry James, of course, but perhaps Mark Twain or Harriet Beecher Stowe? No, it would take you several guesses more. It was Mrs. E. D. E. N. Southworth, nearly all of whose fifty novels sold more than 100,000 copies, and two of them more than 2,000,000 each. What, one wonders, are the standards of a reading public that would place books of this kind on such a pedestal? Sentimentality, sex, and excitement find it all too easy a business to palm themselves off as artistic worth. Nor is it only in art and literature that counterfeits are common. President Davidson of Union College spoke wisely, I think, when he said, "Americans need to be warned about . . . words and ideas which look much alike, but have different effects. For example, Americans often confuse size with importance, . . . speed with progress, . . . money with wealth, . . . authority with wisdom, . . . religion with theology, . . . excitement with pleasure. . . ." Goethe once spoke of "was uns alle bändigt, das Gemeine," of what enslaves us all, the commonplace. Commonplaceness, the surrender to the average, that good which is not bad but still the enemy of the best—that is our besetting danger.

The danger is the greater because it is so largely invisible and connected so intimately with what is best in American life. In our country the common man rules, and until we can achieve the Platonic utopia, that is perhaps as good a plan as can be devised. But it is fatally easy to go from the proposition that political power should follow the majority to the proposition that taste should follow the majority, a conclusion both false and fallacious. If you accept it, even implicitly, the probable result will be the drowning out of any budding distinction or individuality you may possess. In the great volume of voices you cannot, as the saying goes, hear yourself think; and before long you cease to have any thought worth hearing. How is one to escape mass suffocation? One must get outside the mass to some point from which it can be looked at in detachment. And the best and highest of those points is one that we shall never reach unaided, because the only guides that can take us there are those great spirits of the race who themselves hewed out the trail.

When we look back from such a peak, we see what little lives we were living. We begin to see ourselves as we are. Nobody who has read Meredith's *The Egoist* sees himself again in quite the same light. Nobody can take his motives at face value after reading Freud. Nobody can place himself at the same point in the moral scale after following the long slow advance toward purity of heart in the Old and New Testaments. Of course if the change in perspective meant a disillusionment with the old with no compensating devotion, it would be better to go on with the bleak life of the wasteland. The snob and the pedant are restless creatures because they can neither like what other people like, nor get much from their own sterile idolatries; Sinclair Lewis's Mrs. Dodsworth gives the type. True advance in taste or morals is that in which one falls in love with something better, and therefore is no longer tempted by the old. If you want the doctrine worked out on its moral side, you will find it in a classic sermon by Thomas Chalmers on "The Expulsive Power of a New Affection." Many years ago, when I was doing an obscure turn with the army in France, we had a song that was not quite refined in some of its interpretations, but enormously popular in spite of, or perhaps because of, that. It ran, "How're you going to keep them down on the farm after they've seen Paree?" There is philosophy in that song. Podunk and Zenith do look different as seen from the porches of the Louvre.

This brings us to the last value in liberal studies that I set out to remark on. They give us great direct satisfactions. They serve us indirectly by enabling us to share the insights and standards of first-order minds. Finally, they infuse a new quality into our thought, feeling, and action. It seems to be implied in the ditty that once you have seen Paree, you are ruined as a farmhand. Many people think of a liberal education as a means of escape into a white-collar job and otherwise useless. How often have I been told that all you can do with philosophy is to teach it! Now it is true that to rest the defense of philosophy or history or literature on applicability, in the sense that the theory of gas engines is applicable, is to blunder badly. The main value of philosophy and history and literature lies in what they supply directly, a deeper understanding, a wider knowledge, a finer power of response. But to say that this is their main value does not imply that they lack values in use. These they have abundantly.

The reason they have such uses is that a mind is built, not like a rockpile, but like an organism. If you can add a stone or a thousand stones to the rockpile, none of the original stones will take the least notice or perhaps stir one inch from its place. But you cannot add to your mind an understanding of Plato or Milton or modern Europe and leave the rest of your mind what it was; everything you think or feel or do will be affected by it. It is said that Mendelssohn was once scheduled to give an organ concert, but was delayed; a local organist took his place and did what he could against a sea of inattentive conversation in the hall. Mendelssohn at last arrived, and, slipping unobserved onto the organist's seat, took over the piece he was playing. Suddenly the conversation was hushed and the audience was all ears. It was the same instrument and the same score, but there was one great unmistakable difference. Mendelssohn was at the keys.

I like to think of that incident which, according to Vasari, brought to light the genius of Giotto. The Pope wanted a supreme craftsman to help in making the old church of St. Peter a thing of beauty. He sent his envoy round to the studios of the Italian painters asking for samples of their work. When his envoy came to Giotto in Florence, so the story goes, the painter halted his work briefly and told the envoy to watch. Taking a large sheet of paper, he drew a perfect circle on it with a single stroke of his hand. "Take that to the Pope," he said; "he will understand." The Pope did understand, and Giotto got the appointment. Both knew that genuine mastery can reveal itself not only in a vast spread of painted wall, but in the drawing of a single line.

Now the educated mind is the mind that has achieved mastery of his own powers, and such mastery is reflected through all the detail of one's living. A liberal education impractical? Why there is nothing in the range of our speech or thought, our feeling or action, that it leaves quite as it was! Because the educated man knows the difference between knowledge and opinion, his thought on everything—on his business, on his creed, on the devaluation of the dollar—will be more self-critical and more precise. Because speech is the reflection of thought, his talk on all these matters will have more point and precision and weight. Again, right feeling is largely a matter of right thinking; if a man is honestly convinced that racial discrimination is wrong, the struggle for right feeling is two-thirds won. And besides, feeling is as educable as thought. The person who has really entered into "Rabbi Ben Ezra" or Burns on the field-mouse, or Stephen Benét's *John Brown's Body* can never feel about old age, or four-footed things, or black people, as he did before.

And if his thought and feeling are affected, so surely will his action be. I have been reading lately Thornton Wilder's *The Ides of March*. I felt about his hero, Julius Caesar, though with some reservations, as I felt long ago in reading Froude and Mommsen, that there is something not only fascinating but almost frightening in the man. That extraordinary intelligence so permeated everything he did that the ablest statesmen and generals of his time, when they tried to oppose him, looked as you or I would look if we played chess against Bobby Fischer. He was a great man of action, but he was so because his action embodied the precise and lucid mind that wrote the *Gallic War*, a mind that saw every detail, saw them all in perspective, seized the essential as if by instinct, and conducted a campaign with the economy of a superb artist. And through it all there was so little sign of strain that Caesar almost seemed to be lounging through life. With that serene intelligence sitting on the inner throne, he was not only adequate, but almost effortlessly adequate, to every situation. To corner him was not to defeat him; it was only to give his infinite resourcefulness its chance.

To educate a human mind is not merely to add something to it, but to do something to it. It is to transform it at a vital point, the point where its secret ends reside. Change what a man prizes and you change him as a whole, for the essential thing about him is what he wants to be. Samuel Butler said that there were two rules about human life, a general rule and a special one. The general rule was that everyone could make of himself what he wanted to be, and the special rule was that everyone was more or less an exception to the general rule. Yes, but only more or less an exception. It remains true that as a man thinketh in his heart, so is he. He may cut a wide swath socially, financially, politically, and be a midget. He may be a humble doctor of black people on the rim of the African jungle and be, in the opinion of discerning

— I'm not so sure

Raise a question

people, the greatest man alive. What is significant about a person or a people is the invisible things about them, the place where they keep their treasure stored, the unseen sun behind the clouds that determines the orbit of their lives. And curiously enough, it is these unseen things that are most nearly eternal. The educators of the West were those restlessly active people, the Greeks. But not one ship or bridge, not one palace or fortress or temple that their impatient activity erected has come down to us except as a ruin; and the state they built so proudly was already a ruin two thousand years ago. Does anything of them remain? Yes, the Greek spirit remains. The thought of Plato remains, the art of Sophocles, the logic and ethics of Aristotle. Literature, it has been said, is the immortal part of history. No doubt there were hard-headed practical men in Athens who stopped before the door of Plato's Academy and asked what was the use of it all. They and their names have vanished; the little Academy became a thousand academies among nations then unborn. There is a moral, I think, in this history. It is the usefulness, the transcendent usefulness, of useless things.

Work, Labour, and University Education

Peter Herbst

The central idea of this paper is to apply a distinction of Hannah Arendt's[1] to the educational scene; the distinction is between work and labour. The thesis is briefly that education is work rather than labour, and that to educate well is to work, as well as to teach people to work. Some critical conclusions will then be drawn about contemporary education and some unflattering remarks made about contemporary universities.

The work-labour distinction may be interpreted as an application of certain theories in the philosophy of action. The relevant investigations have mainly occupied continental philosophers, existentialists, and phenomenologists for instance. The Marxists and neo-Wittgensteinians have also contributed. The theme of these philosophers is that human

From *The Philosophy of Education*, edited by R. S. Peters, © Oxford University Press, 1973. Reprinted by permission of the author and Oxford University Press.

A revised version of a paper, first written in 1967 as a contribution to a symposium on education in the Australian National University.

actions are subject to certain characteristic defects which make them less characteristically actions and which make the agents less characteristically human. Such defects are variously called alienation, bad faith, viscosity, anomie, and so on. People who elect life-styles which involve them in habitually defective action are sometimes said to lack authenticity, or to be dehumanized.

Roughly speaking, work is conceived to be a species of unalienated action, labour is activity tending to alienation. (It must be conceded from the outset that the distinction between work and labour cannot be made very sharp. More than one criterion for distinguishing them will need to be introduced, and there will be cases which will answer to one criterion, but not to another.)

Work and labour have this in common, that they consume the time and energies of people, and that, being directed to a purpose, they may be done more or less quickly, or more or less competently, or more or less conscientiously, and so on. Also, and for these reasons, both work and labour tend to exclude other human pursuits. They call for a certain discipline or self-direction, and so, whether you work, or whether you labour at a task, you cannot at the same time make love or engage in sport.

Both work and labour are commonly directed to production, though not everything which is produced is a commodity, or a negotiable possession. For present purposes we must subsume the provision of services, and the tasks of planning, administration, and exchange under the heading of production, even though, in an obvious sense, much labour is quite unproductive. An instance is the labour which is expended in the service of the war-industry.

The products of work are works. I am sorry that the only available English word is so weak and colourless. I shall use the Latin word 'opus' instead. The opus, as I conceive it, is the point of the workman's work; if the opus is well done, he has not worked in vain. I shall argue that in order to work well, a workman needs to love or value that at which he works and if so, he aims at good workmanship. The excellence of an opus will be sharply distinguished from its instrumental goodness, and in particular, from its propensity to procure satisfaction for consumers. At the same time it is not denied that in objects which belong to a telic species, what counts as their excellence may depend on their telos. For instance, because a chair may be defined as something for sitting on, being comfortable is a virtue in chairs.

The satisfaction of consumers is not a measure of the excellence of a product. This seems pretty evident, particularly if the consumers themselves have been exposed to sales talk. Thus efficient advertising induces consumers positively to prefer shoddy to good workmanship, and sometimes, to regard all goods as being made purely for consumption, so that, unlovely and unmemorable, they will have served their turn, if, by being consumed, they perish.

Palmström, a creation of the German poet Morgenstern, did not share this attitude. He had a handkerchief of such exquisite beauty and workmanship, that, meaning to blow his nose in it, he was overawed by its grandeur. The handkerchief was re-folded, the nose betrayed. I mention him because he illustrates the mistaken idea that if the telos of an opus is not utilitarian satisfaction, the object must become a mere museum piece.

Labour is toil, labour is hardship. It is the price which we pay for whatever advantages the rewards of labour will buy. A typist who neither understands nor cares for the material which she is typing, is hired to work in an office. She accepts the inconvenience of having to perform an uncongenial task for the sake of keeping body and soul together and for the sake of the activities and amusements which her wages and her social contacts at work bring within her reach. If she could obtain these advantages without having to type, that would be better, but typing is better than forgoing the advantages. It is a ledger-calculation.

Labour may in some circumstances cause us to have pleasurable experiences, and very commonly, it puts us into a position to buy pleasures. But, if it is not justified puritanically, as the *aspera* which are involved in the pursuit of *astra,* it must be justified by the pleasures or satisfactions to which it is a means. Work need not similarly cause or give us pleasure; congenial work on the contrary *is* a pleasure. The pleasure consists in doing the work, not in some consequence, or state of mind, produced by the work. The pleasure of labour on the other hand (if any) is always extrinsic to it.

The view of happiness on which the argument relies is Aristotelian. Happiness *consists in* activities: it is not compounded of pleasures which are *produced by* activities. Activities conceived as pleasure-producers are labour. Activities conceived as happiness-constituents are work.

Labour is contingently related to its product. Artifacts of the same kind may be produced by radically different productive processes. Human labour may be made more productive, more efficient, by being aided or even supplanted by machines. The process of production and the product are conceptually distinct. Many process-workers do not even know to what product their labour contributes: the finished arti-fact is no concern of theirs.

Work is non-contingently related to its product. The description of the process and the description of the product are part of a single con-ceptual scheme. The excellences of the product may be described in terms of workmanship, the productive work as aiming at these excel-lences.[2] Education is a case in hand. To be educated, is to bear the marks of having been through the educational process. Thus finished product and productive processes are correlatively understood.

The adequacy of work and the excellence of its product are *judged* together. If the unified conceptual scheme is abandoned, this advantage is lost and the point of the work is no longer clear. It is then, poor

Pleasure of work is intrinsic

thing, fed into the machine of means and ends and justified by the calculus of satisfactions. The ironic outcome is that the workman comes to hate his work, or in bad faith, to invent a myth in order to persuade himself that he likes it, and thus its fruits are mortgaged, even before they have been gathered. The workman then becomes a labourer.

A simple, but perhaps not over-simple account of unalienated action is that the aims and purposes of the agent, as a person, accord with the general telos of his enterprise. Unalienated work is a case in hand; there has to be some enterprise in which an opus of a certain kind is produced, subject to standards of excellence for *that kind* of work, and such that the workman desires to produce that kind of work under a description such that these standards of excellence are appropriate, which he endorses in any case.

The view that work, unlike labour, must have a point which the workman can endorse, and a purpose with which he can associate himself, has been apparently bypassed by some doctrines, recently orthodox, in the philosophy of action. The position which I have in mind is that any performance or activity may be described in indefinitely many ways of which none is more basic or more revealing than another, and it is held that the frustration of not being free to do as one purposes is avoided, provided that one endorses what one does under some description which one's exertions will bear. Thus, for instance, since much labour is correctly described as making money and most labourers are keen on making money, it seems that, except through their failure to make money, they cannot be frustrated.

The theory of multiple descriptions is also used to deflect the point of the remark that the frustration of labour arises as much from the absence of standards of excellence to which the labourer can aspire, as from the lack of a real object in labouring. In certain situations, especially under conditions of modern advertising, there may be a performance which is a bad way of earning money but a good way of building a house, or a good way of achieving promotion in a university but a bad way of teaching pupils. Here again it will be argued that if the labourer really wants money and promotion, then he can take a pride of workmanship in his endeavours, provided that they are adequately described as successful money-getting or promotion-earning. Thus, according to this relativist thesis, conceptions of skill and excellence of workmanship vary with different descriptions of the same activity, and the labourer will not go without reward if he conceptualizes his activities under some description under which they come out well.

These arguments seem to be nothing better than sophistries. It is clearly wrong to say that people *care* about making money or achieving status; they *desire* these things. The concept of care connects with the idea that there are some things which we cherish, and to which we devote ourselves. We care for things lovingly, or tenderly, or devotedly, but except in bad faith we pursue our interests quite unsentimentally.

The workman then *cares* for his opus, and he will have a reason for proceeding thus rather than thus, in terms of the qualities and excellences at which he aims in the finished product. Thus his performance bears a description under which it is a condition of quality in his product, there being a description of his product under which he wants to make it, and to make it well.

Now it is not evident that these conditions can be met by activities of which the point is money-making, or some such other extrinsic end. The money which a man earns is not his product, but rather what he gets in exchange for his product. Money is not an opus. One lot of money differs from another lot of money only by way of more or less; money does not bear the marks of craftsmanship. Similarly, the activities which are addressed to the task of money-making have the qualities and excellences of which they are capable only relative to some opus which is saleable, or some purpose from the pursuit of which an income happily results.

Let us meet the critics of our viewpoint who proceed from the theory of multiple descriptions by experimenting with an example. Consider a man who, being a devoted builder, has conceptions of excellence in houses, and under these conceptions cares about what and how he builds. Incidentally, he wants to earn a living out of building. Now let us attempt to invert the example. Thus we get a man who, being a devoted money-getter, has conceptions of excellence in money-getting, and under these conceptions cares for the sums of money which he makes, and for what he does by way of getting them. Incidentally, what he does by way of money-getting is house-building.

Now it makes sense to suppose that a man builds houses, no matter whether well or badly, in order to obtain money, but it does not make the same sense to suppose that a man makes money, no matter whether well or badly, in order to obtain a house. The only interpretation which we can place on that suggestion is that he makes money in order to be in a position to *buy* a house, and if so, he had better do well at money-making, because the house of his choice may turn out expensive.

There seems to be a confusion between constitution and instrumentality in the arguments of the cynics. Good workmanship is constitutive of a good work, but (with good luck) only a means of obtaining rewards. Good workmanship on the other hand is as little constitutive of rewards as it is instrumental to a well-made opus. By these tests not all descriptions under which a man may be said to be acting when he makes something come out equal. For instance "earning a living," "making a reputation for himself," "earning promotion," "serving his company," "doing his duty," cannot be descriptions of work, while "building a house," "composing a quartet," "working at a philosophical problem," and "educating a student" may serve as work descriptions proper. A workman is one who avowably acts under such a description.

Universities, despite the composition of their councils, are, by and large, self-governing institutions still, but more than the armed forces, or the institutionalized professions, the pressures of society affect them everywhere. Governments hold the purse-strings; they do not find it difficult to persuade universities to volunteer research in areas deemed useful, nor do they hesitate to encourage subject-areas and educational techniques to produce students who will accept the roles envisaged by the official planners. The media and the politicians, not to mention the representatives of business interests and the trade unions, are forever admonishing universities not to abuse their positions of privilege, but to shoulder their social responsibilities, and to assist in the accomplishment of some task which, at the time, is conceived to be essential to progress, or to the country's well-being (or to that of the nation, mankind, society, or some other likely recipient of people's fundamental loyalties). The funds and the support which universities receive from the public purse are insufficient for their needs, however, and thus they must seek the assistance of industry, and trade, and the professions to enable them to branch out into areas of research on which their prestige depends. It seems likely that funds would no longer be readily available if the interests of learning and the interests of the donors came to be in serious conflict. Situations in which the consciences of individual university teachers conflict with the interests of a donor are now increasingly common, specially in the ecological field. The results will need to be studied.

Some university people feel slightly guilty about the pursuit of learning: the image of the ivory tower puts them on the defensive. In such a mood they are anxious to stress the continuity of their outlook with that of society at large, and they become active in organizations to which the idea of thought, directed to the telos of truth, is alien, but in which they can prove themselves good fellows.

The attachment of some university teachers to their institutions, and to the traditions and ideals of universities, is often only partial. Take a department in a vocational branch of university teaching: law, for instance. Some of its most distinguished members are fully functioning members of their profession, perhaps on temporary loan to a university. The department as a whole has its moorings at least as much in chambers and in the law-courts as in the cloisters, it invites distinguished counsel, judges, and attorneys general for talks and dinners: in return its members sit on committees which make them influential in the profession, and are allowed to appear in an advisory capacity on various bodies designed to solve the legal problems of governments, banks, trade unions, and public corporations. The interests of the legal profession, however, are no more guaranteed to coincide with the interests of the students in acquiring an education than the interests of General Motors are guaranteed to accord with those of the American nation. Thus, for a teacher who has the education of his students at heart (as distinct from their careers) there may be a tension, a case of divided loyalties. The students themselves undoubtedly often feel this tension, and the disinterested desire to emerge as educated men and women struggles with the desire for a meal ticket. What it is to receive an education remains to be discussed below.

The professions and the institutions to whose service students are destined have influence, not only through their members or nominees on university councils, grants commissions, research foundations and such bodies which control universities and their work, but also because they have it in their power to employ or to reject graduates. This power is great, and to many, fearful.

Thus, for many reasons, and not least, because it is a universal tendency for people to rationalize the pressures upon them and to contrive an ideology designed to make these pressures bearable, universities reflect the ethos of the societies in which they operate, even where this ethos is incompatible with the enterprise of teaching and research. That seems to be the present situation in the technologically advanced affluent societies of the western world. Some remarks about this ethos are called for.

To begin with a cliché: we live in a society of consumers. It is true, the pundits and the politicians are forever exhorting us to production, and seem to regard the indefinite expansion of production as the greatest good, but production is conceived of as a mere correlative of consumption. We produce either what we anticipate that we will consume, or we produce the means of accelerated production, machines, that is to say. Sometimes we even produce the means of accelerated consumption, as in the advertising industry. Society as a whole is here conceived to be acting on the supposition that consumption is the only worth-while human function, and that the indefinite expansion of the production-consumption cycle, together with the unhampered freedom to produce and consume, are the only worth-while ends of action.

The greater part of our political energy is devoted to economic matters, to welfare, the enhancement of the standard of living, the expansion of output, the procurement of "jobs," and the provision of common services which otherwise would have to be purchased by the individual. To this we must add our preoccupation with stability and security, the protection of our vast and infinitely complex system of production, administration, commerce, and organized consumption against organic imbalances, and against internal and external foes. The question whether the ideological emphasis in our society is on production or consumption is bound up with whether we are concerned with the health and stability of the system, growth-rates for instance, employment opportunities and the avoidance of slumps, or whether, concerned to advertise the benefits of the system, we point to the bonanza of an indefinitely rising "standard of living." It seems clear that, despite the emphasis on growth-rates, few believe in production for its own sake. Our consciences are ruffled when the alleged needs of the stability of the system cause us to dump foodstuffs in the sea, even without the thought of the starving millions of Bangla Desh.

To consume a commodity is so to put it to use that in the process it disappears or perishes. Thus a commodity is given in exchange for a service or a satisfaction. Not all consumer commodities are as ephemeral as food: some, the so-called durable consumer goods, are consumed slowly. There are also consumer services (banking, for instance); and there are those objects which are not, in any obvious way, consumed at all, but which are produced, bought, sold, and disposed of as if they were consumer goods. I mean "desirable residences," gardens, jewels, and the palpable artifacts of learning and art (books, paintings, stereo, etc.).

It has been remarked that the central ethos of capitalist production is puritanism, that is, justification by achievement wrought from self-sacrifice, self-discipline, frugality, and labour. Paradoxically enough, the central ethos of capitalist consumption is utilitarianism,[3] that is, the doctrine that the discipline and toil of the productive process can only by justified by the personal satisfactions of the consumers. Since the most successful producers acquire wealth, they also become major consumers, and thus we have that grotesque historical joke, the tycoon who practises frugality in luxury, and who pursues his pleasures in the same spirit of grim determination in which he approaches his managerial role. The puritan ethos is irreducibly individualistic, no man can hope to win merit for another, none can assuage his conscience through the sacrifices or exertions of another man. The utilitarian ethos on the other hand is social and impersonal. Any man may glean satisfactions from consuming a commodity, no matter who produced it, and society as a whole is conceived to be in a state of well-being if the majority is happy, that is, according to that ideology, if the level of consumption is high.

The early philosophers and economists who set the intellectual tone of our system of production saw one thing very clearly: the destiny of a consumer-good is to be consumed, and there is no point in consuming it unless one derives some pleasure or satisfaction from doing so. Thus we produce in order that we may consume, and we consume for the sake of the satisfactions to be derived from doing so; thus our satisfactions alone are an end, and everything else, the goods themselves, the productive process of which they are the fruit, and the labour which is expended in the process are but means. Viewed from this standpoint nothing has intrinsic value but human satisfactions, and the best life is that in which the capacity for consumption is maximized, and the opportunities do not lag behind.

From our point of view the crucial thing about the consumer ideology is its indifference to the opus, the work which a workman makes. Since the opus is conceived to be a mere means, a cog in a process of which the end-product is pleasure or satisfaction, there are no conceptions of excellence for it as such; its goodness becomes a relational property; to be good it must be such that out of its consumption the consumers derive satisfactions. Thus art is debased to amusement, literature to journalism, the serious and rational debate of public issues to image-building and gimmickry, and that part of learning which is not a mere service industry for trade, industry, government, or the professions is made to provide a cultural varnish for the young barbarians whom the system needs and nourishes.

The labourer is a social being.[4] He subserves the "needs of society," and, if properly socialized, conceives of himself as subserving these needs. If society cannot consume his products, he has laboured in vain. If his products are not good to consume, or if they are inefficiently produced, or produced at too great a cost to society, he has laboured badly. Labourers, as I here conceive them, include some of the most highly paid men in the kingdom, and most of our society consists of labourers.

The things which we value or love engage our interest: we care about them and they concern us. We cannot *care* about what touches us only through its effects or its potential uses. A key for instance, common and undistinguished, is unlikely to be something about which we care, even if it puts a fortune within our reach. The attitudes of interest, concern, or care depend on the intrinsic properties of an object. If an object touches us only because we can use it, or because we want what it will bring about, then we do not care about it as such. Our attitude to it will then be commercial. That which is treated exclusively as a means, commercially that is to say, is thereby degraded if it is degradable. The time-honoured example is a prostitute. Even if no money changes hands, the girl's dignity is undermined if, viewing her only as an instrument of sexual gratification, we do not care whether she be happy or unhappy, religious or atheistical, interested in mountaineering or politics, and so on. In the commercial state of mind we do not even care whether she likes or abominates her partner, nor will we be concerned about her subsequent fate.

The consumer's society degrades whatever it touches, work, nature, art, its own history and traditions, and the creations of men of genius. Work (being confused with labour) is but toil, the process of production is distinct from and merely instrumental to the product; it is the product and, beyond it, a satisfaction which are desired, not the process. Since the process of producing is troublesome, we abandon it with relief and turn to its natural counter-pole, which is play (or fun as the newspapers now call it). This increasingly becomes the really serious business of our lives; besides, it has the advantage of opening up quite unlimited new opportunities for consumption.

The ideological producer for consumption, despite his rockets to the moon, is the world's most unambitious creature and also the most destructive. All, or nearly all, the immense array of ingenious and amazing objects to the manufacture of which his intelligence is harnessed are made for consumption. At the same time, as the opportunities for consumption magnify, so does the consumer's appetite, until, as things stand now, the earth itself stands in danger of being devoured. He destroys the beauty of nature, the animal kingdom is expended for his satisfaction, he destroys whole cultures and traditions to stimulate trade, and finally he destroys men themselves. I do not mean in warfare only, which is nothing peculiar to our times, but by a process of depersonalization which results from being made a means to an end.

It is time we returned to the universities. Universities do not fit in well in a consumer's society. I do not mean that the structure and fabric of a university cannot survive in such a society; that would clearly be wrong. Universities are growing still. They receive unprecedented attention from the mighty, and a degree has become a passport to worldly success as never before.

Nevertheless universities do not flourish in a consumer's society without suffering a sea change. The ethos of a university has in the past been principally an ethos of work, and the objects to the achievement of which universities used to be committed were conceived as of intrinsic worth. These objects were twofold, namely the pursuit of learning (or inquiry as I propose to call it) and the education of the young. They seem to me to be the proper aims of universities still. Unfortunately they are in danger of being lost. If they are lost, it will not be as a result of an open change, but imperceptibly, ostensibly under the old ethos still. They will be lost, like liberty in a society grown totalitarian in the defence of liberty. Even in 1984, the academic credo affirming the pursuit of learning and the education of the young will be intoned. But it seems that the pursuit of learning will be transmuted into the pursuit of skills and know-how, and that education will become training or instruction. It seems probable that the matter of education will increasingly be parcelled out into one or other of two broad categories, on the one hand essential knowledge, that is, knowledge which is good for some socially acceptable purpose, and luxury knowledge, a sort of prestigious top-dressing on the other. It is possible even that the pursuit of luxury knowledge will altogether disappear from the syllabus, and that activities which fall within its sphere will become extra-curricular. There will be concerts, exhibitions, poetry-readings, and meditation-sessions, and these will be calculated to perform a function in that parcel of life which is now called leisure.

We are sufficiently imbued with the ethos of our era for the thought that universities are primarily for the service of society to be natural to us. Thus we conceive of our role in terms of the satisfaction of social needs. We provide society with trained men for the professions, with experts to advise government and industry, and we produce persons with cultural graces to dignify our voracity. When we think of university expansion, we naturally look at the market to see what graduates it will absorb, and we plan research training as immediately addressed to social needs.

Thus we become a factory for making a certain kind of equipment which society needs, people as well as computers. But perhaps this account of the matter may strike you as too pessimistic. There is a current development which seems to belie it; I mean the expansion of research in universities, and the prestige which it enjoys.

Research is surely work. Many of us, perhaps a majority, regard it as the real business of universities, and think of the advancement of knowledge as the ultimate aim. Teaching is viewed as a slightly inferior activity, necessary, alas, both because society demands it and for the perpetuation of academic institutions, but an imposition on a true man of learning. Adapting Plato's famous simile, academic people have to earn a place in the sun of pure research by a temporary sojourn in the cave of education. They do their duty, earn their release, and go off on sabbatical leave.

There are few images as appealing as the image of ourselves adding to the sum of human knowledge. Knowledge seems to us like a vast impersonal edifice, to which, by the sheer exercise of our industry and wit, we can add a brick. What could be a more enduring monument than this? Our knowledge is not and cannot be consumed, neither could it conceivably have accrued from some activity generically different from inquiry. It is therefore non-contingently related to the activity from which it results. Our claims to knowledge are tested by the tools of logic and the resources of experiment and these alone provide the tests of workmanship.

This image is pretty, but it does more than justice to most contemporary academic research. There is a sense of course in which all knowledge is enduring. Copies of our monographs and journals will continue to accumulate in our libraries at an ever-expanding rate, but much of this work is undertaken as labour rather than work.

The idea that work may be undertaken in the spirit of labour presents no difficulty. Analogously a puritan may debauch himself in the spirit of duty, and an intending lover may trade his affections in the spirit of a ledger-clerk. In each case the conception which the agent has of his act ill accords with its point, and this argues confusion or self-deception on his part. The agent does not know what he is about: he acts katatelically.

Research-labourers do research katatelically, though not necessarily without results, if "results" are a kind of pay-off to society or to some interest represented in it. (Discoveries of genuine interest to intellectuals are not excluded.) A research-labourer works in the spirit of labour. He puts his highly trained labour-force at the disposal of society or its agencies. He works in its interests, and conceives that to be its point. The beneficiaries generally reward him, but not from love of the intellectual enterprise. The beneficiaries use him, even as he will presently use his students, or prepare them for social use after they have obtained their "qualification." The beneficiaries accept useful results, whether or not they have accrued from intellectually reputable work. They know what they want: unfortunately he generally does not.

Inquiry absorbs a man. It is an extension of his personality. Roughly, if a man is content to engage in a piece of research from nine to five as a job, he will not engage in it as inquiry. The workman is involved in his work. The sort of involvement which I have in mind is not unlike what is called commitment. One cannot change one's work as one can change one's job. The workman who is deprived of his work is deprived *tout court*.

Research, it seems, has become a sort of independent empire. There is indeed a myth that people who have gone through the research-mill make good university teachers, and if the function of a good university teacher is simply to train people in the techniques of research, it may not be a myth entirely. The belief that research produces good teachers adds to our notion of its utility.

Research begets research. Much of it is addressed to the expansion of the research-culture, which nobody, not even the research workers, regards as intrinsically valuable. We tend the dog, clip its fur, polish its teeth, publish its pedigree, and enter it for every available dog-show, but we are not really fond of animals.

Now we come to teaching. This presents us with our thorniest problem. It is in our attitudes to students that we most clearly show whether we accept or reject the ethos of consumption. Our traditions demand that we should educate our students. Education is one of the excellences of which human beings are capable, and just as the excellence of a painting cannot be defined in terms of its monetary value or in terms of its social usefulness, so also the state of being educated cannot be defined in careerist or social-utility terms.

An educated student is one in whom certain potentialities are developed, including the potentiality for work in a certain field. Students are intelligent or stupid before they enroll, but good teachers develop their intelligence and teach them to use it, to apply it, to delight in its exercise. An educated man is sensitive, perceptive, daring in imagination, subtle in distinction, lucid and powerful in reasoning, and articulate. An educated student understands the enterprise of inquiry. This may take the form of reflection, discussion, or internal dialectic, it need not consist in writing articles. For instance, the preparation of a creative lecture is also part of the enterprise. Often the kind of inquiry which most obviously lends itself to publication is from the point of education, infertile. For this reason, among others, the greater part of our journal literature is almost at birth embedded in the sedimentary deposits of the academy, and will never be looked at again.

The education of a student is an end in itself, and the making of him is our noblest work. This work requires no further justification, and by attempting to justify it further, in terms of the values of the consumer society, we only succeed in undermining it.

We educate students by working with them in a field or discipline. One cannot do everything at once, and a certain concentration in a field ensures that work is done in depth and discourages superficiality. But the field is never more than the locus in which the work of education is accomplished. Competence in a field is not the aim of education, but only one of its expedients. The emphasis on a field as against the potentialities which work in a field makes actual is inimical to the enterprise of education.

The consumer mentality makes education wellnigh impossible. First a relatively mild and engaging variant, the idea that it is our task to equip students to earn a livelihood, or to make a position for themselves in society. If a teacher is fond of his students, he will not wish them to come to grief in life, and thus he may skimp their education in order to increase their value in the market.

The more insidious forms of consumer education mould the student, not in his own material interests but in the alleged interests of society. The student and his skills are debased into a means for the achievement of social ends. The student becames a capital investment. He is there for the performance of certain kinds of labour which will procure satisfactions for his fellow citizens, and the teachers are there in order to train him in the skills which will make him a useful instrument in procuring these satisfactions. *He* ceases to matter, provided only that he performs the part which the diviners of social needs have cast for him. The diviners of social needs are roughly men in authority, with their academic advisers.

The replacement of education by instruction is a serious matter. It naturally goes hand in hand with the abandonment of any real interest in students or their maturation, which in turn is the inevitable result of the mass-production techniques which are now being forced on us. Instruction is a practical enterprise in which a set skill, or a standard quota of information is imparted for a purpose. The point of instruction is to suit the subject to a task. Thus soldiers are instructed in the use of weapons, and trainee-policemen are instructed in their duties. Instruction is standardized, uncritical, undialectical, and it discourages speculation about ends and means alike. Some university courses seem to be almost pure instruction. All available teaching time is parcelled out into segments each of which is devoted to imparting some particular item of information, or to allow time for the practice of some particular skill. Directives to tutors are printed in detailed cyclostyled sheets; these ensure that all tutorials will operate in parallel. The student is there to absorb this material. He contributes nothing and his intellect remains unengaged. The teachings of some psychologists have aggravated this state of affairs.

Educational is a dialectical enterprise, critical, discursive, and largely idiosyncratic on the teacher's and the student's side alike. It is true that education presupposes the mastery of some skills and the possession of some information. These are ancillary to education. In the consumer's society, however, they tend to replace it. One cannot educate a student well at a distance. Education is a meeting of two intellects, and therefore of two persons, and this requires a common life. But in the contemporary academy the teacher is becoming ever more inaccessible. Many students do not even know their lecturers by name.

The students who are subjected to this sort of pseudo-education are not fully conscious of what is happening, but they are dimly aware that they are being used for purposes not of their own choosing. Many feel cheated. They came to the university for an education, and find themselves being moulded for the purposes of a society of which the official representatives often strike them as unadmirable. "Society" speaks to them through members of the establishment.

The view that their teachers lack capacity, or knowledge, or skill is not essential to this state of mind, and it is not the principal cause of discontent. On the contrary, student disaffection is often associated with a sense of inferiority. Students feel that their teacher's interest in them is inauthentic. The jargon-word "alienation" is not easily banished from one's lips.

To sum up, the danger in modern universities is that students will be regarded as capital equipment and that by being "instructed" they will be conditioned to take their place in the technical, commercial, or administrative machinery of a society which recognizes no values but consumption. They will therefore be made ready for being used. When that happens, the university will have played a part in the production of highly skilled and (unless there is an oversupply) extremely precious labourers, but it will not have taught them to work, albeit both their well-being and that of society depends on their capacity for action, which, in the productive field, is work. Neither is the producing of such young men and women anything but labour, and thus some of the most imaginative and ingenious men and women in the land are reduced to the status of labourers. Thus, given the tedious absurdities of the research-empire, especially in subjects which are insecure in their standing and seek to prove that they too are hard-headed and "scientific," the university and its *raison d'être* pass each other by.

The idea that universities should subserve social needs, as these are understood in the dominant ideology, has been disparaged in this essay, and the traditional values of men of learning have been defended in opposition to ideological, economic, and political demands. Society, in so far as it can be said to have judgement and articulation, is a poor judge of its own needs, and universities sacrifice a good to promote an evil if they think themselves committed to the utilitarian objectives (or the ideologically inspired projects) which worldly spokesmen advocate. The consumer's ethos does not serve its exponents well. By undermining the human personality, it deprives people of the power of happiness. True, it provides us with the technical means of abolishing the miseries of disease and want, but it also destroys that capacity for love and care, and that freedom of the spirit, which vouchsafe fulfilment, and which are a condition of the enjoyment of worldly things.

We do no service to society by making ourselves into its servants.

A society is not better than the persons who compose it. If by education we produce men and women of excellence, we have no need of a higher aim.

NOTES

1. Hannah Arendt, *The Human Condition* (Chicago: University of Chicago Press, 1958), chs. 3 and 4.
2. The view that work does not play a part in the *causation* of opera (assuming its intelligibility) is not expressed here, and must not be ascribed to the author.
3. The popular, not the "philosophical" variant is intended.
4. A thesis of Mrs. Arendt's.

4

PHILOSOPHY and PERSONAL RELATIONS

Would you, right now, trade your life for the life of Robinson Crusoe, shipwrecked and alone on a desolate island? No matter how unsatisfactory and hassled we feel our present lives to be, very few of us would willingly choose Crusoe's solitary existence. Why? Part of the answer is our awareness of how short a time we would survive outside the complex technologies that provide our food, water, shelter, and other necessities. An even larger part of the answer, however, is our powerful hunger for the company of other people. Human life lived to its fullest is a complex network of personal relations. Many of our greatest joys, as well as our most profound sorrows, would be impossible without relationships binding us to others. What would one's life be like without the possibilities of friendship, love, and sexual union? Hobbes' phrase is perfect: "solitary, poor, nasty, brutish, and short."

How many of us have seriously reflected on the personal relations that give human life its savor? We can, on a moment's consideration, feel their value, but can we truly understand their value to us without first understanding their natures? In this section we have chosen readings that explore in philosophical depth some major forms of the relationships that are essential to our happiness.

One fundamental personal relation is *friendship*. Most of us are friends; we befriend, and we are befriended. What does it mean to be someone's friend? Is friendship, as some maintain, a relationship that can exist only between equals? What could *equality* mean in this context?

149

Is friendship a single specific relationship, or are there various modes of being a friend? We may immediately think that we can make certain demands on friends that we cannot make on strangers or mere acquaintances, but is that so? What are the limits of those demands? Can one ask a friend to lie, to cheat, to break the law? Finally, what exactly does friendship add to human life? In what sense are we potentially more virtuous because we are friends? The selections we have chosen explore some of these large and important questions.

Ours is a society that is constantly talking about *love;* the word is on everyone's lips, from pop singers to preachers and TV pitchmen. What is this love that everyone extols? For many people, the paradigm that comes immediately to mind is romantic love between men and women. But this is to nourish oneself with a one-sided diet of examples; there are many other kinds of love as well. It is unfortunate that love has more often claimed the attention of the poet than of the philosopher, for there are significant philosophical questions to be answered: What are the various kinds of love, and what are their relationships to one another? What is the connection between love and sexual desire? What kind of person must one be to love? Is love a passion, something over which we have no control, or can we rationally choose to grant or withhold our love? The three selections we have included atttempt to provide a philosophical basis for answering some of these questions. That raises a further question: Is love analyzed love understood and enriched, or love destroyed?

We do not need to be told that we are sexual beings; our bodies make us well aware of that dominating factor in our existence. To be a sexual being, however, does not require that we understand our sexuality or that we have placed it in proper relationship to other aspects of our lives. Is there such a thing as a purely sexual relationship, and if so, can it be a source of human happiness? Many moralists work with an expression theory of sexual behavior: sexual relationships are properly the expression of other sorts of relations, love, for example. Must this be so? This raises the issue of the connections between sex and morality. Is there a distinctively sexual morality? Can it be argued that good sex promotes human virtue? The essays by Nagel, Ruddick, and Goldman address these questions and others that are equally important.

The most common long-term relationship among individuals in our society is marriage; it is also an institution under attack from within and without. As commonly understood, marriage is a lifetime commitment: "What God has joined together, let not man put asunder." We know, however, that one in three American marriages ends in divorce. Marriage is also usually considered to demand sexual exclusivity from the partners, but adultery is certainly not uncommon in this society. Is traditional monogamous marriage doomed; more importantly, *ought* it to be doomed? Does marriage add something to the quality of human life that is not to be found in other sorts of personal relations, or is it an institution that inevitably constricts and distorts individuals? The essays of McMurtry, Bayles, and Wasserstrom present a wide range of reasoned opinion on the nature, purpose, and value of marriage.

When Socrates said that the unexamined life is not worth living, part of what he must have meant was that failure to understand those aspects of human life that are the sources of good is to forgo any reasonable chance to attain that good. As we rightfully reject the solitary life of Robinson Crusoe, we also need to recall the character in Sartre's *No Exit* who exclaims, "Hell is—other people." Our personal relations can be sources of good; they can be springs of distress and evil as well. Perhaps philosophical reflection cannot guarantee that our personal relations will yield good rather than evil, but surely a rational investigation of such complex and varied phenomena will heighten our possibilities for fulfillment in these important dimensions of human life.

FRIENDSHIP

Friendship and Its Forms

Aristotle

BOOK VIII

After what we have said, a discussion of friendship would naturally follow, since it is a virtue or implies virtue, and is besides most necessary with a view to living. For without friends no one would choose to live, though he had all other goods; even rich men and those in possession of office and of dominating power are thought to need friends most of all; for what is the use of such prosperity without the opportunity of beneficence, which is exercised chiefly and in its most laudable form towards friends? Or how can prosperity be guarded and preserved without friends? The greater it is, the more exposed is it to risk. And in poverty and in other misfortunes men think friends are the only refuge. It helps the young, too, to keep from error; it aids older people by ministering to their needs and supplementing the activities that are failing from weakness; those in the prime of life it stimulates to noble actions—'two

From "Nichomachean Ethics," trans. by W. D. Ross, in *The Oxford Translation of Aristotle*, edited by W. D. Ross, Vol. IX, 1925. Reprinted by permission of Oxford University Press.

going together'—for with friends men are more able both to think and to act. Again, parent seems by nature to feel it for offspring and offspring for parent, not only among men but among birds and among most animals; it is felt mutually by members of the same race, and especially by men, whence we praise lovers of their fellowmen. We may see even in our travels how near and dear every man is to every other. Friendship seems too to hold states together, and lawgivers to care more for it than for justice; for unanimity seems to be something like friendship, and this they aim at most of all, and expel faction as their worst enemy; and when men are friends they have no need of justice, while when they are just they need friendship as well, and the truest form of justice is thought to be a friendly quality.

But it is not only necessary but also noble; for we praise those who love their friends, and it is thought to be a fine thing to have many friends; and again we think it is the same people that are good men and are friends.

Not a few things about friendship are matters of debate. Some define it as a kind of likeness and say like people are friends, whence come the sayings 'like to be like', 'birds of a feather flock together', and so on; others on the contrary say 'two of a trade never agree'. On this very question they inquire for deeper and more physical causes, Euripides saying that 'parched earth loves the rain, and stately heaven when filled with rain loves to fall to earth', and Heraclitus that 'it is what opposes that helps' and 'from different tones comes the fairest tune' and 'all things are produced through strife'; while Empedocles, as well as others, expresses the opposite view that like aims at like. The physical problems we may leave alone (for they do not belong to the present inquiry); let us examine those which are human and involve character and feeling, e.g. whether friendship can arise between any two people or people cannot be friends if they are wicked, and whether there is one species of friendship or more than one. Those who think there is only one because it admits of degrees have relied on an inadequate indication; for even things different in species admit of degree. We have discussed this matter previously.

The kinds of friendship may perhaps be cleared up if we first come to know the object of love. For not everything seems to be loved but only the lovable; and this is good, pleasant, or useful; but it would seem to be that by which some good or pleasure is produced that is useful, so that it is the good and the useful that are lovable as ends. Do men love, then, *the* good, or what is good for *them*? These sometimes clash. So too with regard to the pleasant. Now it is thought that each loves what is good for himself, and that the good is without qualification lovable, and what is good for each man is lovable for him; but each man loves not what is good for him but what seems good. This however will make no difference; we shall just have to say this is 'that which seems lovable'. Now there are three grounds on which people love; of the love of lifeless objects we do not use the word 'friendship'; for it is not mutual love, nor is there a wishing of good to the other (for it would surely be ridiculous to wish wine well; if one wishes anything for it, it is that it may keep, so that one may have it oneself); but to a friend we say we ought to wish what is good for his sake. But to those who thus wish good we ascribe only goodwill, if the wish is not reciprocated; goodwill when it *is* reciprocal being friendship. Or must we add 'when it is recognized'? For many people have goodwill to those whom they have not seen but judge to be good or useful; and one of these might return this feeling. These people seem to bear goodwill to each other; but how could one call them friends when they do not know their mutual feelings? To be friends, then, they must be mutually recognized as bearing goodwill and wishing well to each other for one of the aforesaid reasons.

Now these reasons differ from each other in kind; so, therefore, do the corresponding forms of love and friendship. There are therefore three kinds of friendship, equal in number to the things that are lovable; for with respect to each there is a mutual and recognized love, and those who love each other wish well to each other in that respect in which they love one another. Now those who love each other for their utility do not love each other for themselves but in virtue of some good which they get from each other. So too with those who love for the sake of pleasure; it is not for their character that men love ready-witted people, but because they find them pleasant. Therefore those who love for the sake of utility love for the sake of what is good for *themselves,* and those who love for the sake of pleasure do so for the sake of what is pleasant to *themselves,* and not in so far as the other is the person loved but in so far as he is useful or pleasant. And thus these friendships are only incidental; for it is not as being the man he is that the loved person is loved, but as providing some good or pleasure. Such friendships, then, are easily dissolved, if the parties do not remain like themselves; for if the one party is no longer pleasant or useful the other ceases to love him.

Now the useful is not permanent but is always changing. Thus when the motive of the friendship is done away, the friendship is dissolved, inasmuch as it existed only for the ends in question. This kind of friendship seems to exist chiefly between old people (for at that age people pursue not the pleasant but the useful) and, of those who are in their prime or young, between those who pursue utility. And such people do not live much with each other either; for sometimes they do not even find each other pleasant; therefore they do not need such companionship unless they are useful to each other; for they are pleasant to each other only in so far as they rouse in each other hopes of something good to come. Among such friendships people also class the friendship of host and guest. On the other hand the friendship of young people seems to aim at pleasure; for they live under the guidance of emotion, and pursue above all what is pleasant to themselves and what is immediately before them; but with increasing age their pleasures become different. This is why they quickly become friends and quickly cease to be so; their friendship changes with the object that is found pleasant, and such pleasure alters quickly. Young people are amorous too; for the greater part of the friendship of love depends on emotion and aims at pleasure; this is why they fall in love and quickly fall out of love, changing often within a single day. But these people do wish to spend their days and lives together; for it is thus that they attain the purpose of their friendship.

Perfect friendship is the friendship of men who are good, and alike in virtue; for these wish well alike to each other *qua* good, and they are good in themselves. Now those who wish well to their friends for their sake are most truly friends; for they do this by reason of their own nature and not incidentally; therefore their friendship lasts as long as they are good—and goodness is an enduring thing. And each is good without qualification and to his friend, for the good are both good without qualification and useful to each other. So too they are pleasant; for the good are pleasant both without qualification and to each other, since to each his own activities and others like them are pleasurable, and the actions of the good *are* the same or like. And such a friendship is as might be expected permanent, since there meet in it all the qualities that friends should have. For all friendship is for the sake of good or of pleasure— good or pleasure either in the abstract or such as will be enjoyed by him who has the friendly feeling—and is based on a certain resemblance; and to a friendship of good men all the qualities we have named belong in virtue of the nature of the friends themselves; for in the case of this kind of friendship the other qualities also are alike in both friends, and that which is good without qualification is also without qualification pleasant, and these are the most lovable qualities. Love and friendship therefore are found most and in their best form between such men.

But it is natural that such friendships should be infrequent; for such men are rare. Further, such friendship requires time and familiarity; as the proverb says, men cannot know each other till they have 'eaten salt together'; nor can they admit each other to friendship or be friends till each has been found lovable and been trusted by each. Those who quickly show the marks of friendship to each other wish to be friends, but are not friends unless they both are lovable and know the fact; for a wish for friendship may arise quickly, but friendship does not.

This kind of friendship, then, is perfect both in respect of duration and in all other respects, and in it each gets from each in all respects the same as, or something like what, he gives; which is what ought to happen between friends. Friendship for the sake of pleasure bears a resemblance to this kind; for good people too are pleasant to each other. So too does friendship for the sake of utility; for the good are also useful to each other. Among men of these inferior sorts too, friendships are most permanent when the friends get the same thing from each other (e.g. pleasure), and not only that but also from the same source, as happens between ready-witted people, not as happens between lover and beloved. For these do not take pleasure in the same things, but the one in seeing the beloved and the other in receiving attentions from his lover; and when the bloom of youth is passing the friendship sometimes passes too (for the one finds no pleasure in the sight of the other, and the other gets no attention from the first); but many lovers on the other hand are constant, if familiarity has led them to love each other's characters, these being alike. But those who exchange not pleasure but utility in their amour are both less truly friends and less constant. Those who are friends for the sake of utility part when the advantage is at an end; for they were lovers not of each other but of profit.

For the sake of pleasure or utility, then, even bad men may be friends of each other, or good men of bad, or one who is neither good nor bad may be a friend to any sort of person, but for their own sake clearly only good men can be friends; for bad men do not delight in each other unless some advantage come of the relation.

The friendship of the good too and this alone is proof against slander; for it is not easy to trust any one's talk about a man who has long been tested by oneself; and it is among good men that trust and the feeling that 'he would never wrong me' and all the other things that are demanded in true friendship are found. In the other kinds of friendship, however, there is nothing to prevent these evils arising.

For men apply the name of friends even to those whose motive is utility, in which sense states are said to be friendly (for the alliances of states seem to aim at advantage), and to those who love each other for the sake of pleasure, in which sense children are called friends. Therefore we too ought perhaps to call such people friends, and say that there are several kinds of friendship—firstly and in the proper sense that of good men *qua* good, and by analogy the other kinds; for it is in virtue of something good and something akin to what is found in true friendship that they are friends, since even the pleasant is good for the lovers of pleasure. But these two kinds of friendship are not often united, nor do the same people become friends for the sake of utility and of pleasure; for things that are only incidentally connected are not often coupled together.

Friendship being divided into these kinds, bad men will be friends for the sake of pleasure or of utility, being in this respect like each other, but good men will be friends for their own sake, i.e. in virtue of their goodness. These, then, are friends without qualification; the others are friends incidentally and through a resemblance to these.

As in regard to the virtues some men are called good in respect of a state of character, others in respect of an activity, so too in the case of friendship; for those who live together delight in each other and confer benefits on each other, but those who are asleep or locally separated are not performing, but are disposed to perform, the activities of friendship; distance does not break off the friendship absolutely, but only the activity of it. But if the absence is lasting, it seems actually to make men forget their friendship; hence the saying 'out of sight, out of mind'. Neither old people nor sour people seem to make friends easily; for there is little that is pleasant in them, and no one can spend his days with one whose company is painful, or not pleasant, since nature seems above all to avoid the painful and to aim at the pleasant. Those, however, who approve of each other but do not live together seem to be well-disposed rather than actual friends. For there is nothing so characteristic of friends as living together (since while it is people who are in need that desire benefits, even those who are supremely happy desire to spend their days together; for solitude suits such people least of all); but people cannot live together if they are not pleasant and do not enjoy the same things, as friends who are companions seem to do.

The truest friendship, then, is that of the good, as we have frequently said, for that which is without qualification good or pleasant seems to be lovable and desirable, and for each person that which is good or pleasant to him; and the good man is lovable and desirable to the good man for both these reasons. Now it looks as if love were a feeling, friendship a state of character; for love may be felt just as much towards lifeless things, but mutual love involves choice and choice springs from a state of character; and men wish well to those whom they love, for their sake, not as a result of feeling but as a result of a state of character. And in loving a friend men love what is good for themselves; for the good man in becoming a friend becomes a good to his friend. Each, then, both loves what is good for himself, and makes an equal return in goodwill and in pleasantness; for friendship is said to be equality, and both of these are found most in the friendship of the good.

Between sour and elderly people friendship arises less readily, inasmuch as they are less good-tempered and enjoy companionship less; for these are thought to be the greatest marks of friendship and most productive of it. This is why, while young men become friends quickly, old men do not; it is because men do not become friends with those in whom they do not delight; and similarly sour people do not quickly make friends either. But such men may bear goodwill to each other; for they wish one another well and aid one another in need; but they are hardly *friends* because they do not spend their days together nor delight in each other, and these are thought the greatest marks of friendship.

One cannot be a friend to many people in the sense of having friendship of the perfect type with them, just as one cannot be in love with many people at once (for love is a sort of excess of feeling, and it is the nature of such only to be felt towards one person); and it is not easy for many people at the same time to please the same person very greatly, or perhaps even to be good in his eyes. One must, too, acquire some experience of the other person and become familiar with him, and that is very hard. But with a view of utility or pleasure it is possible that many people should please one; for many people are useful or pleasant, and these services take little time.

Of these two kinds that which is for the sake of pleasure is the more like friendship, when both parties get the same things from each other and delight in each other or in the same things, as in the friendships of the young; for generosity is more found in such friendships. Friendship based on utility is for the commercially minded. People who are supremely happy, too, have no need of useful friends, but do need pleasant friends; for they wish to live with *some one* and, though they can endure for a short time what is painful, no one could put up with it continuously, nor even with the Good itself if it were painful to him; this is why they look out for friends who are pleasant. Perhaps they should look out for friends who, being pleasant, are also good, and good for them too; for so they will have all the characteristics that friends should have.

People in positions of authority seem to have friends who fall into distinct classes; some people are useful to them and others are pleasant, but the same people are rarely both; for they seek neither those whose pleasantness is accompanied by virtue nor those whose utility is with a view to noble objects, but in their desire for pleasure they seek for ready-witted people, and their other friends they choose as being clever at doing what they are told, and these characteristics are rarely combined. Now we have said that the *good* man *is* at the same time pleasant and useful; but such a man does not become the friend of one who surpasses him in station, unless he is surpassed also in virtue; if this is not so, he does not establish equality by being proportionally exceeded in both respects. But people who surpass him in both respects are not so easy to find.

However that may be, the aforesaid friendships involve equality; for the friends get the same things from one another and wish the same things for one another, or exchange one thing for another, e.g. pleasure for utility; we have said, however, that they are both less truly friendships and less permanent. But it is from their likeness and their unlikeness to the same thing that they are thought both to be and not to be friendships. It is by their likeness to the friendship of virtue that they seem to be friendships (for one of them involves pleasure and the other utility, and these characteristics belong to the friendship of virtue as well); while it is because the friendship of virtue is proof against slander and permanent, while these quickly change (besides differing from the former in many other respects), that they appear *not* to be friendships; i.e. it is because of their unlikeness to the friendship of virtue.

But there is another kind of friendship, viz. that which involves an inequality between the parties, e.g. that of father to son and in general of elder to younger, that of man to wife and in general that of ruler to subject. And these friendships differ also from each other; for it is not the same that exists between parents and children and between rulers and subjects, nor is even that of father to son the same as that of son to father, nor that of husband to wife the same as that of wife to husband. For the virtue and the function of each of these is different, and so are the reasons for which they love; the love and the friendship are therefore different also. Each party, then, neither gets the same from the other, nor ought to seek it; but when children render to parents what they ought to render to those who brought them into the world, and parents render what they should to their children, the friendship of such persons will be abiding and excellent. In all friendships implying inequality the love also should be proportional, i.e. the better should be more loved than he loves, and so should the more useful, and similarly in each of the other cases; for when the love is in proportion to the merit of the parties, then in a sense arises equality, which is certainly held to be characteristic of friendship.

But equality does not seem to take the same form in acts of justice and in friendship; for in acts of justice what is equal in the primary sense is that which is in proportion to merit, while quantitative equality is secondary, but in friendship quantitative equality is primary and proportion to merit secondary. This becomes clear if there is a great interval in respect of virtue or vice or wealth or anything else between the parties; for then they are no longer friends, and do not even expect to be so. And this is most manifest in the case of the gods; for they surpass us most decisively in all good things. But it is clear also in the case of kings; for with them, too, men who are much their inferiors do not expect to be friends; nor do men of no account expect to be friends with the best or wisest men. In such cases it is not possible to define exactly up to what point friends can remain friends; for much can be taken away and friendship remain, but when one party is removed to a great distance, as God is, the possibility of friendship ceases. This is in fact the origin of the question whether friends really wish for their friends the greatest goods, e.g. that of being gods; since in that case their friends will no longer be friends to them, and therefore will not be good things for them (for friends *are* good things). The answer is that if we were right in saying that friend wishes good to friend for his sake, his friend must remain the sort of being he is, whatever that may be; therefore it is for him only so long as he remains a man that he will wish the greatest goods. But perhaps not *all* the greatest goods; for it is for himself most of all that each man wishes what is good.

Most people seem, owing to ambition, to wish to be loved rather than to love; which is why most men love flattery; for the flatterer is a friend in an inferior position, or pretends to be such and to love more than he is loved; and being loved seems to be akin to being honoured, and this is what most people aim at. But it seems to be not for its own sake that people choose honour, but incidentally. For most people enjoy being honoured by those in positions of authority because of their hopes (for they think that if they want anything they will get it from them; and therefore they delight in honour as a token of favour to come); while those who desire honour from good men, and men who know, are aiming at confirming their own opinion of themselves; they delight in honour, therefore, because they believe in their own goodness on the strength of the judgement of those who speak about them. In being loved, on the other hand, people delight for its own sake; whence it would seem to be better than being honoured, and friendship to be desirable in itself. But it seems to lie in loving rather than in being loved, as is indicated by the delight mothers take in loving; for some mothers hand over their children to be brought up, and so long as they know their fate they love them and do not seek to be loved in return (if they cannot have both), but seem to be satisfied if they see them prospering; and they themselves love their children even if these owing to their ignorance give them nothing of a mother's due. Now since friendship depends more on loving, and it is those who love their friends that are praised, loving seems to be the characteristic virtue of friends, so that it is only those in whom this is found in due measure that are lasting friends, and only their friendship that endures.

It is in this way more than any other that even unequals can be friends; they can be equalized. Now equality and likeness are friendship, and especially the likeness of those who are like in virtue; for being steadfast in themselves they hold fast to each other, and neither ask nor give base services, but (one may say) even prevent them; for it is characteristic of good men neither to go wrong themselves nor to let their friends do so. But wicked men have no steadfastness (for they do not remain even like to themselves), but become friends for a short time because they delight in each other's wickedness. Friends who are useful or pleasant last longer; i.e. as long as they provide each other with enjoyments or advantages. Friendship for utility's sake seems to be that which most easily exists between contraries, e.g. between poor and rich, between ignorant and learned; for what a man actually lacks he aims at, and one gives something else in return. But under this head, too, might bring lover and beloved, beautiful and ugly. This is why lovers sometimes seem ridiculous, when they demand to be loved as they love; if they are equally lovable their claim can perhaps be justified, but when they have nothing lovable about them it is ridiculous. Perhaps, however, contrary does not even aim at contrary by its own nature, but only incidentally, the desire being for what is intermediate; for that is what is good, e.g. it is good for the dry not to become wet but to come to the intermediate state, and similarly with the hot and in all other cases. These subjects we may dismiss; for they are indeed somewhat foreign to our inquiry.

Another question that arises is whether friendships should or should not be broken off when the other party does not remain the same. Perhaps we may say that there is nothing strange in breaking off a friendship based on utility or pleasure, when our friends no longer have these attributes. For it was of these attributes that we were the friends; and when these have failed it is reasonable to love no longer. But one might complain of another if, when he loved us for our usefulness or pleasantness, he pretended to love us for our character. For, as we said at the outset, most differences arise between friends when they are not friends in the spirit in which they think they are. So when a man has deceived himself and has thought he was being loved for his character, when the other person was doing nothing of the kind, he must blame himself; but when he has been deceived by the pretences of the other person, it is just that he should complain against his deceiver; he will complain with more justice than one does against people who counterfeit the currency, inasmuch as the wrongdoing is concerned with something more valuable.

But if one accepts another man as good, and he turns out badly and is seen to do so, must one still love him? Surely it is impossible, since not everything can be loved, but only what is good. What is evil neither can nor should be loved; for it is not one's duty to be a lover of evil, nor to become like what is bad; and we have said that like is dear to like. Must the friendship, then, be forthwith broken off? Or is this not so in all cases, but only when one's friends are incurable in their wickedness? If they are capable of being reformed one should rather come to the assistance of their character or their property, inasmuch as this is better and more characteristic of friendship. But a man who breaks off such a friendship would seem to be doing nothing strange; for it was not to a man of this sort that he was a friend; when his friend has changed, therefore, and he is unable to save him, he gives up.

But if one friend remained the same while the other became better and far outstripped him in virtue, should the latter treat the former as a friend? Surely he cannot. When the interval is great this becomes most plain, e. g. in the case of childish friendships; if one friend remained a child in intellect while the other became a fully developed man, how could they be friends when they neither approved of the same things nor delighted in and were pained by the same things? For not even with regard to each other will their tastes agree, and without this (as we saw) they cannot be friends; for they cannot live together. But we have discussed these matters.

Should he, then, behave no otherwise towards him than he would if he had never been his friend? Surely he should keep a remembrance of their former intimacy, and as we think we ought to oblige friends rather than strangers, so to those who have been our friends we ought to make some allowance for our former friendship, when the breach has not been due to excess of wickedness.

Goodwill is a friendly sort of relation, but is not *identical* with friendship; for one may have goodwill both towards people whom one does not know, and without their knowing it, but not friendship. This has indeed been said already. But goodwill is not even friendly feeling. For it does not involve intensity or desire, whereas these accompany friendly feeling; and friendly feeling implies intimacy while goodwill may arise of a sudden, as it does towards competitors in a contest; we come to feel goodwill for them and to share in their wishes, but we would not *do* anything with them; for, as we said, we feel goodwill suddenly and love them only superficially.

Goodwill seems, then, to be a beginning of friendship, as the pleasure of the eye is the beginning of love. For no one loves if he has not first been delighted by the form of the beloved, but he who delights in the form of another does not, for all that, love him, but only does so when he also longs for him when absent and craves for his presence; so too it is not possible for people to be friends if they have not come to feel goodwill for each other, but those who feel goodwill are not for all that friends; for they only *wish* well to those for whom they feel goodwill, and would not do anything with them nor take trouble for them. And so one might by an extension of the term friendship say that goodwill is inactive friendship, though when it is prolonged and reaches the point of intimacy it becomes friendship—not the friendship based on utility nor that based on pleasure; for goodwill too does not arise on those terms. The man who has received a benefit bestows goodwill in return for what has been done to him, but in doing so is only doing what is just; while he who wishes some one to prosper because he hopes for enrichment through him seems to have goodwill not to him but rather to himself, just as a man is not a friend to another if he cherishes him for the sake of some use to be made of him. In general, goodwill arises on account of some excellence and worth, when one man seems to another beautiful or brave or something of the sort, as we pointed out in the case of competitors in a contest.

The question is also debated, whether a man should love himself most, or some one else. People criticize those who love themselves most, and call them self-lovers, using this as an epithet of disgrace, and a bad man seems to do everything for his own sake, and the more so the more wicked he is—and so men reproach him, for instance, with doing nothing of his own accord—while the good man acts for honour's sake, and the more so the better he is, and acts for his friend's sake, and sacrifices his own interest.

But the facts clash with these arguments, and this is not surprising. For men say that one ought to love best one's best friend, and a man's best friend is one who wishes well to the object of his wish for his sake, even if no one is to know of it; and these attributes are found most of all in a man's attitude towards himself, and so are all the other attributes by which a friend is defined; for, as we have said, it is from this relation that all the characteristics of friendship have extended to our neighbours. All the proverbs, too, agree with this, e.g. 'a single soul', and 'what friends have is common property', and 'friendship is equality', and 'charity begins at home'; for all these marks will be found most in a man's relation to himself; he is his own best friend and therefore ought to love himself best. It is therefore a reasonable question, which of the two views we should follow; for both are plausible.

Perhaps we ought to mark off such arguments from each other and determine how far and in what respects each view is right. Now if we grasp the sense in which each school uses the phrase 'lover of self', the truth may become evident. Those who use the term as one of reproach ascribe self-love to people who assign to themselves the greater share of wealth, honours, and bodily pleasures; for these are what most people desire, and busy themselves about as though they were the best of all things, which is the reason, too, why they become objects of competition. So those who are grasping with regard to these things gratify their appetites and in general their feelings and the irrational element of the soul; and most men are of this nature (which is the reason why the epithet has come to be used as it is—it takes its meaning from the prevailing type of self-love, which is a bad one); it is just, therefore, that men who are lovers of self in this way are reproached for being so. That it is those who give themselves the preference in regard to objects of this sort that most people usually call lovers of self is plain; for if a man were always anxious that he himself, above all things, should act justly, temperately, or in accordance with any other of the virtues, and in general were always to try to secure for himself the honourable course, no one will call such a man a lover of self or blame him.

But such a man would seem more than the other a lover of self; at all events he assigns to himself the things that are noblest and best, and gratifies the most authoritative element in himself and in all things obeys this; and just as a city or any other systematic whole is most properly identified with the most authoritative element in it, so is a man; and therefore the man who loves this and gratifies it is most of all a lover of self. Besides, a man is said to have or not to have self-control according as his reason has or has not the control, on the assumption that this is the man himself; and the things men have done on a rational principle are thought most properly their own acts and voluntary acts. That this is the man himself, then, or is so more than anything else, is plain, and also that the good man loves most this part of him. Whence it follows that he is most truly a lover of self, of another type than that which is a matter of reproach, and as different from that as living according to a rational principle is from living as passion dictates, and desiring what is noble from desiring what seems advantageous. Those, then, who busy themselves in an exceptional degree with noble actions all men approve and praise; and if *all* were to strive towards what is noble and strain every nerve to do the noblest deeds, everything would be as it should be for the common weal, and every one would secure for himself the goods that are greatest, since virtue is the greatest of goods.

Therefore the good man should be a lover of self (for he will both himself profit by doing noble acts, and will benefit his fellows), but the wicked man should not; for he will hurt both himself and his neighbours, following as he does evil passions. For the wicked man, what he does clashes with what he ought to do, but what the good man ought to do he does; for reason in each of its possessors chooses what is best for itself, and the good man obeys his reason. It is true of the good man too that he does many acts for the sake of his friends and his country, and if necessary dies for them; for he will throw away both wealth and honours and in general the goods that are objects of competition, gaining for himself nobility; since he would prefer a short period of intense pleasure to a long one of mild enjoyment, a twelvemonth of noble life to many years of humdrum existence, and one great and noble action to many trivial ones. Now those who die for others doubtless attain this result; it is therefore a great prize that they choose for themselves.

They will throw away wealth too on condition that their friends will gain more; for while a man's friend gains wealth he himself achieves nobility; he is therefore assigning the greater good to himself. The same too is true of honour and office; all these things he will sacrifice to his friend; for this is noble and laudable for himself. Rightly then is he thought to be good, since he chooses nobility before all else. But he may even give up actions to his friend; it may be nobler to become the cause of his friend's acting than to act himself. In all the actions, therefore, that men are praised for, the good man is seen to assign to himself the greater share in what is noble. In this sense, then, as has been said, a man should be a lover of self; but in the sense in which most men are so, he ought not.

Should we, then, make as many friends as possible, or—as in the case of hospitality it is thought to be suitable advice, that one should be 'neither a man of many guests nor a man with none'—will that apply to friendship as well; should a man neither be friendless nor have an excessive number of friends?

To friends made with a view to *utility* this saying would seem thoroughly applicable; for to do services to many people in return is a laborious task and life is not long enough for its performance. Therefore friends in excess of those who are sufficient for our own life are superfluous, and hindrances to the noble life; so that we have no need of them. Of friends made with a view to *pleasure*, also, few are enough, as a little seasoning in food is enough.

But as regard *good* friends, should we have as many as possible, or is there a limit to the number of one's friends, as there is to the size of a city? You cannot make a city of ten men, and if there are a hundred thousand it is a city no longer. But the proper number is presumably not a single number, but anything that falls between certain fixed points. So for friends too there is a fixed number—perhaps the largest number with whom one can live together (for that, we found, is thought to be very characteristic of friendship); and that one cannot live with many people and divide oneself up among them is plain. Further, they too must be friends of one another, if they are all to spend their days together; and it is a hard business for this condition to be fulfilled with a large number. It is found difficult, too, to rejoice and to grieve in an intimate way with many people, for it may likely happen that one has at once to be happy with one friend and to mourn with another. Presumably, then, it is well not to seek to have as many friends as possible, but as many as are enough for the purpose of living together; for it would seem actually impossible to be a great friend to many people. This is why one cannot love several people; love is ideally a sort of excess of friendship, and that can only be felt towards one person; therefore great friendship too can only be felt towards a few people. This seems to be confirmed in practice; for we do not find many people who are friends in the comradely way of friendship, and the famous friendships of this sort are always between two people. Those who have many friends and mix intimately with them all are thought to be no one's friend, except in the way proper to fellow-citizens, and such people are also called obsequious. In the way proper to fellow-citizens, indeed, it is possible to be the friend of many and yet not be obsequious but a genuinely good man; but one cannot have with many people the friendship based on virtue and on the character of our friends themselves, and we must be content if we find even a few such.

Do we need friends more in good fortune or in bad? They are sought after in both; for while men in adversity need help, in prosperity they need people to live with and to make the objects of their beneficence; for they wish to do well by others. Friendship, then, is more necessary in bad fortune, and so it is useful friends that one wants in this case; but it is more noble in good fortune, and so we also seek for good men as our friends, since it is more desirable to confer benefits on these and to live with these. For the very presence of friends is pleasant both in good fortune and also in bad, since grief is lightened when friends sorrow with us. Hence one might ask whether they share as it were our burden, or—without that happening—their presence by its pleasantness, and the thought of their grieving with us, make our pain less. Whether it is for these reasons or for some other that our grief is lightened, is a question that may be dismissed; at all events what we have described appears to take place.

But their presence seems to contain a mixture of various factors. The very seeing of one's friends is pleasant, especially if one is in adversity, and becomes a safeguard against grief (for a friend tends to comfort us both by the sight of him and by his words, if he is tactful, since he knows our character and the things that please or pain us); but to see him pained at our misfortunes is painful; for every one shuns being a cause of pain to his friends. For this reason people of a manly nature guard against making their friends grieve with them, and, unless he be exceptionally insensible to pain, such a man cannot stand the pain that ensues for his friends, and in general does not admit fellow-mourners because he is not himself given to mourning; but women and womanly men enjoy sympathisers in their grief, and love them as friends and companions in sorrow. But in all things one obviously ought to imitate the better type of person.

On the other hand, the presence of friends in our *prosperity* implies both a pleasant passing of our time and the pleasant thought of their pleasure at our own good fortune. For this cause it would seem that we ought to summon our friends readily to share our good fortunes (for the beneficent character is a noble one), but summon them to our bad fortunes with hesitation; for we ought to give them as little a share as possible in our evils—whence the saying 'enough is *my* misfortune'. We should summon friends to us most of all when they are likely by suffering a few inconveniences to do us a great service.

Conversely, it is fitting to go unasked and readily to the aid of those in adversity (for it is characteristic of a friend to render services, and especially to those who are in need and have not demanded them; such action is nobler and pleasanter for both persons); but when our friends are prosperous we should join readily in their activities (for they need friends for these too), but be tardy in coming forward to be the objects of their kindness; for it is not noble to be keen to receive benefits. Still, we must no doubt avoid getting the reputation of kill-joys by repulsing them; for that sometimes happens.

The presence of friends, then, seems desirable in all circumstances.

Does it not follow, then, that, as for lovers the sight of the beloved is the thing they love most, and they prefer this sense to the others because on it love depends most for its being and for its origin, so for friends the most desirable thing is living together? For friendship is a partnership, and as a man is to himself, so is he to his friend; now in his own case the consciousness of his being is desirable, and so therefore is the consciousness of his friend's being, and the activity of this consciousness is produced when they live together, so that it is natural that they aim at this. And whatever existence means for each class of men, whatever it is for whose sake they value life, in *that* they wish to occupy themselves with their friends; and so some drink together, others dice together, others join in athletic exercises and hunting, or in the study of philosophy, each class spending their days together in whatever they love most in life; for since they wish to live with their friends, they do and share in those things which give them the sense of living together. Thus the friendship of bad men turns out an evil thing (for because of their instability they unite in bad pursuits, and besides they become evil by becoming like each other), while the friendship of good men is good, being augmented by their companionship; and they are thought to become better too by their activities and by improving each other; for from each other they take the mould of the characteristics they approve—whence the saying 'noble deeds from noble men'. So much, then, for friendship; our next task must be to discuss pleasure.

Friendship

Simone Weil

There is however a personal and human love which is pure and which enshrines an intimation and a reflection of divine love. This is friendship, provided we keep strictly to the true meaning of the word.

Preference for some human being is necessarily a different thing from charity. Charity does not discriminate. If it is found more abundantly in any special quarter, it is because affliction has chanced to provide an occasion there for the exchange of compassion and gratitude. It is equally available for the whole human race, inasmuch as affliction can come to all, offering them an opportunity for such an exchange.

Preference for a human being can be of two kinds. Either we are seeking some particular good in him, or we need him. In a general way all possible attachments come under one of these heads. We are drawn toward a thing, either because there is some good we are seeking from it, or because we cannot do without it. Sometimes the two motives coincide. Often however they do not. Each is distinct and quite independent. We eat distasteful food, if we have nothing else, because we cannot do otherwise. A moderately greedy man looks out for delicacies, but he can easily do without them. If we have no air we are suffocated, we struggle to get it, not because we expect to get some advantage from it but because we need it. We go in search of sea air without being driven by any necessity, because we like it. In time it often comes about automatically that the second motive takes the place of the first. This is one of the great misfortunes of our race. A man smokes opium in order to attain to a special condition, which he thinks superior; often, as time goes on, the opium reduces him to a miserable condition which he feels to be degrading; but he is no longer able to do without it. Arnolphe bought Agnès [1] from her adopted mother, because it seemed to him it would be an advantage to have a little girl with him, a little girl whom he would gradually make into a good wife. Later on she ceased to cause him anything but a heart-rending and degrading torment. But with the passage of time his attachment to her had become a vital bond which forced this terrible line from his lips:

"Mais je sens là-dedans qu'il faudra que je crève——" [2]

Harpagon started by considering gold as an advantage. Later it became nothing but the object of a haunting obsession, yet an object of which the loss would cause his death. As Plato says, there is a great difference between the essence of the Necessary and that of the Good.

There is no contradiction between seeking our own good in a human being and wishing for his good to be increased. For this very reason, when the motive which draws us towards anybody is simply some advantage for ourselves, the conditions of friendship are not fulfilled. Friendship is a supernatural harmony, a union of opposites.

When a human being is in any degree necessary to us, we cannot desire his good unless we cease to desire our own. Where there is necessity there is constraint and domination. We are in the power of that of which we stand in need, unless we possess it. The central good for every man is the free disposal of himself. Either we renounce it, which is a crime of idolatry, since it can only be renounced in favour of God, or we desire that the being we stand in need of should be deprived of it.

Any kind of mechanism may join human beings together with bonds of affection which have the iron hardness of necessity. Mother-love is often of such a kind; so at times is paternal love, as in *Le Père Goriot* of Balzac; so is carnal love in its most intense form as in *L'Ecole des Femmes* and in *Phèdre;* so also, very frequently, is the love between husband and wife, chiefly as a result of habit. Filial and fraternal love are more rarely of this nature.

There are moreover degrees of necessity. Everything is necessary in some degree if its loss really causes a decrease of vital energy. (This word is here used in the strict and precise sense which it might have if the study of vital phenomena were as far advanced as that of falling bodies.) When the degree of necessity is extreme, deprivation leads to death. This is the case when all the vital energy of one being is bound up with another by some attachment. In the lesser degrees, deprivation leads to a more or less considerable lessening of energy. Thus a total deprivation of food causes death, whereas a partial deprivation only diminishes the life force. Nevertheless the necessary quantity of food is considered to be that required if a person is not to be weakened.

The most frequent cause of necessity in the bonds of affection is a combination of sympathy and habit. As in the case of avarice or drunkenness, that which was at first a search for some desired good is transformed into a need by the mere passage of time. The difference from avarice, drunkenness and all the vices, however, is that in the bonds of affection the two motives—search for a desired good, and need—can very easily co-exist. They can also be separated. When the attachment of one being to another is made up of need and nothing else it is a fearful thing. Few things in this world can reach such a degree of ugliness and horror. There is always something horrible whenever a human being seeks what is good and only finds necessity. The stories which tell of a beloved being who suddenly appears with a death's head best symbolise this. The human soul possesses a whole arsenal of lies with which to put up a defence against this ugliness and, in imagination, to manufacture sham advantages where there is only necessity. It is for this very reason that ugliness is an evil, because it conduces to lying.

Speaking quite generally, we might say that there is affliction whenever necessity, under no matter what form, is imposed so harshly that the hardness exceeds the capacity for lying of the person who receives the impact. That is why the purest souls are the most exposed to affliction. For him who is capable of preventing the automatic reaction of defence which tends to increase the soul's capacity for lying, affliction is not an evil, although it is always a wounding and in a sense a degradation.

When a human being is attached to another by a bond of affection which contains any degree of necessity, it is impossible that he should wish autonomy to be preserved both in himself and in the other. It is impossible by virtue of the mechanism of nature. It is however made possible by the miraculous intervention of the supernatural. This miracle is friendship.

"Friendship is an equality made of harmony," said the Pythagoreans. There is harmony because there is a supernatural union between two opposites, that is to say necessity and liberty, the two opposites which God combined when he created the world and men. There is equality because each wishes to preserve the faculty of free consent both in himself and in the other.

When anyone wishes to put himself under a human being or consents to be subordinated to him, there is no trace of friendship. Racine's Pylades is not the friend of Orestes. There is no friendship where there is inequality.

A certain reciprocity is essential in friendship. If all good will is entirely lacking on one of the two sides, the other should suppress his own affection, out of respect for the free consent which he should not desire to force. If on one of the two sides there is not any respect for the autonomy of the other, this other must cut the bond uniting them out of respect for himself. In the same way, he who consents to be enslaved cannot gain friendship. But the necessity contained in the bond of affection can exist on one side only, and in this case there is only friendship on one side, if we keep to the strict and exact meaning of the word.

A friendship is tarnished as soon as necessity triumphs, if only for a moment, over the desire to preserve the faculty of free consent on both sides. In all human things, necessity is the principle of impurity. All friendship is impure if even a trace of the wish to please, or the contrary desire to dominate is found in it. In a perfect friendship these two desires are completely absent. The two friends have fully consented to be two and not one, they respect the distance which the fact of being two distinct creatures places between them. Man has the right to desire direct union with God alone.

Friendship is a miracle by which a person consents to view from a certain distance, and without coming any nearer, the very being who is necessary to him as food. It requires the strength of soul that Eve did not have; and yet she had no need of the fruit. If she had been hungry at the moment when she looked at the fruit, and if in spite of that she had remained looking at it indefinitely without taking one step towards it, she would have performed a miracle analogous to that of perfect friendship.

Through this supernatural miracle of respect for human autonomy, friendship is very like the pure forms of compassion and gratitude called forth by affliction. In both cases the contraries which are the terms of the harmony are necessity and liberty, or in other words subordination and equality. These two pairs of opposites are equivalent.

From the fact that the desire to please and the desire to command are not found in pure friendship, it has in it, at the same time as affection, something not unlike a complete indifference. Although it is a bond between two people it is in a sense impersonal. It leaves impartiality intact. It in no way prevents us from imitating the perfection of our Father in heaven who freely distributes sunlight and rain in every place. On the contrary, friendship and this distribution are the mutual conditions one of the other, in most cases at any rate. For, as practically every human being is joined to others by bonds of affection which have in them some degree of necessity, he cannot go towards perfection except by transforming this affection into friendship. Friendship has something universal about it. It consists of loving a human being as we should like to be able to love each soul in particular of all those who go to make up the human race. As a geometrician looks at a particular figure in order to deduce the universal properties of the triangle, so he who knows how to love directs upon a particular human being a love which is universal. The consent to preserve an autonomy within ourselves and in others is essentially of a universal order. As soon as we wish for this autonomy to be respected in more than just one single being we desire it for everyone, for we cease to arrange the order of the world in a circle whose centre is here below. We transport the centre of the circle beyond the heavens.

Friendship does not have this power if the two beings who love each other, through an unlawful use of affection, think they only form one. But then there is not friendship in the true sense of the word. That is what might be called an adulterous union, even though it comes about between husband and wife. There is not friendship where distance is not kept and respected.

The simple fact of having pleasure in thinking in the same way as the beloved being, or in any case the fact of desiring such an agreement of opinion, attacks the purity of the friendship at the same time as its intellectual integrity. It is very frequent. But at the same time pure friendship is rare.

When the bonds of affection and necessity between human beings are not supernaturally transformed into friendship, not only is the affection of an impure and low order, but it is also combined with hatred and repulsion. That is shown very well in *L'Ecole des Femmes* and in *Phèdre*. The mechanism is the same in affections other than carnal love. It is easy to understand this. We hate what we are dependent upon. We become disgusted with what depends on us. Sometimes affection does not only become mixed with hatred and revulsion, it is entirely changed into it. The transformation may sometimes even be almost immediate, so that hardly any affection has had time to show; this is the case when necessity is laid bare almost at once. When the necessity which brings people to-gether has nothing to do with the emotions, when it is simply due to circumstances, hostility often makes its appearance from the start.

When Christ said to his disciples: "Love one another," it was not attachment he was laying down as their rule. As it was a fact that there were bonds between them due to the thoughts, the life and the habits they shared, he commanded them to transform these bonds into friend-ship, so that they should not be allowed to turn into impure attachment or hatred.

Since, shortly before his death, Christ gave this as a new commandment to be added to the two great commandments of the love of our neighbour and the love of God, we can think that friendship which is pure, like the love of our neighbour, has in it something of a sacrament. Christ per-haps wished to suggest this with reference to Christian friendship when he said: "Where there are two or three gathered together in my name there am I in the midst of them." Pure friendship is an image of that original and perfect friendship which belongs to the Trinity and which is the very essence of God. It is impossible for two human beings to be one while scrupulously respecting the distance which separates them, unless God is present in each of them. The point at which parallels meet is infinity.

NOTES

1. Characters in Molière's *L'Ecole des Femmes*. Harpagon, below, is a character in Molière's *L'Avare*.
2. But I feel in all this that I shall be torn asunder.

Friendship

Elizabeth Telfer

It is often said that friendships are among the most important constit-uents of a worth-while life. I wish to examine this view by trying to answer three questions about friendship: what it is, how morality bears on it, and why it is thought to be important.

From Elizabeth Telfer, *Friendship,* from *Proceedings of the Aristotelian Society,* Vol. 71 (1970-71), pp. 223-41.

THE NATURE OF FRIENDSHIP

We can begin our answer to the first question with the obvious point that there is a certain type of activity which all friends, *qua* friends, engage in: the performing of services of all kinds for some other person. Suppose, however, that a man fetches coal and shopping and clears the snow for the lonely old lady next door. This kind of case would not really be one of friendship, for, while she might say, 'My neighbour's been a real *friend* to me this winter', we would normally distinguish between 'befriending' or 'being a friend to' and 'being friends' or 'being a friend of'. In the situation described we would not speak of the existence of a friendship or say that the pair were friends or that he was a friend of hers (as distinct from a friend to her). His conduct is in some ways like that of a friend, but the situation is not one of *friendship*, and it is the latter concept with which we are concerned.

It might be suggested that what is missing in the example is reciprocity. But the old lady and her neighbour do not become friends simply because in return for his fetching and shovelling she knits him socks. What are missing are two other types of activity, which are not so much reciprocal as actually *shared*: those activities the main point of which is that they involve contact with the friend, such as talking together or exchanging letters; and joint engagement in pursuits which the friends would in any case perform quite apart from the friendship—notably leisure pursuits, but also sometimes work, worship and so on. My thesis, then, is that there are three types of activity which are all necessary conditions of friendship: reciprocal services, mutual contact and joint pursuits. I shall henceforth refer to these necessary conditions collectively, as the 'shared activity' condition for friendship.

The 'shared activity' condition, however, is not a sufficient condition for friendship. This becomes clear if we imagine a case where the condition is fulfilled. Consider, for example, the situation where two neighbours, each living alone, perform services for each other, go to the pictures together, and drop in on each other to chat in the evenings. Would we be able to say that the pair were friends, simply on the strength of this situation? I think it is clear that we would not, on the ground that friendship depends, not only on the performance of certain *actions*, but also on their being performed for certain specific *reasons*— out of friendship, as we say, rather than out of duty or pity or indeed self-interest. These reasons can, I think, be seen as a set of long-term *desires*, which motivate and hence explain actions done out of friendship. My contention is that the existence of the relevant desires is a second necessary condition for friendship. Let us examine these desires— which we may call the *passions* of friendship—in more detail.

The first element in the passions of friendship is affection; friends must have affection for, or be fond of, each other. (This passion is not of course peculiar to friendship; for example, it is also felt by colleagues of long standing, or by members of the same family.) I define 'affection'

as a desire for another's welfare and happiness *as a particular individual.*
This desire is thus to be distinguished both from sense of duty and from
benevolence. For these motives prompt us to seek others' good in general, whereas we want to say that those who feel affection feel a concern
for another which they do not feel for everyone. It is this concern which
normally motivates services performed out of friendship, whereas befriending is motivated by benevolence, pity or sense of duty. This special concern for friends also gives rise to reactions of special pleasure
at their good fortune, pain at their misfortune, anger with those who
injure them, and so on.

Two points about affection may be briefly noted before we consider
other passions of friendship. The first concerns its relation with benevolence and sense of duty. We have said that benevolence and sense of
duty are to be distinguished from affection because affection is for the
individual. But surely, it may be argued, the benevolent and the dutiful
man also concern themselves with the individual? The answer here is
to distinguish between two kinds of concern for the individual. To
say that the benevolent or dutiful man concerns himself with the individual is to say that he sees each individual as making separate claims
which may not only compete with the majority interest but also differ
in content from those of other individuals. But the concern of affection
is not for *each* individual, but for *this* individual rather than others.

The second point I wish to make about affection is that it does not
seem to have any necessary connexion with the particular character of
him for whom it is felt. If asked to explain why we are fond of someone, we *may* mention characteristics in him which stimulate affection,
but it makes equally good sense to give an historical explanation—'I've
known him for a long time' or 'I looked after him when he was ill'—or
a biological one such as 'He's my brother, after all'. Affection is in this
sense *irrational,* and because of this may survive radical changes in the
character of its object. Thus we often continue to be fond of someone
when we no longer like or respect him, and such a situation is not considered in any way odd.

The second element in the passions which are part of friendship, and
one which distinguishes it from many other relationships which involve
affection, is a desire on the part of the friends for each other's company,
as distinct from a desire for company as such. It will normally be this
desire which leads friends to seek contact with each other and to share
pursuits, and which also gives rise to our pleasure when we see friends,
regret at parting, and so on. It is the presence of this desire which distinguishes a case of friendship from those where a man keeps company
with another out of loneliness, or pity, or sense of duty.

Is this desire for another's company irrational in the same way as
affection is? I think not, at least where it is part of *friendship* and not
of being in love, infatuation, *etc.* These latter states also involve a desire
for the other's company. But whereas it is characteristic of them that
a sufferer from them may intelligibly say 'I don't know what it is about

him/her that draws me, but I cannot be without him/her' we would not speak of friendship unless the friends are prepared to *explain* the desire for each other's company, and to do so in terms of two particular attitudes towards each other: liking, and the sense of a bond or of something in common.

Now both these attitudes are rational, in the sense that they are necessarily based on beliefs about the nature of the friend; we *like* a person and feel we *are like* him because of what we think he is *like*. The degree of rationality which this involves, however, is rather limited. For even where we *can* give our reasons for liking someone or feeling a bond with him, we cannot further justify these reasons, or always explain why they operate in one case and not in another apparently similar. And we may find it very difficult to *state* our reasons at all. In such a case the most we might be prepared to say is that there must be qualities in the friend, even if we cannot 'pin them down', such that if he ceased to have them we would cease to like or feel akin to him. Let me say a little more about these two attitudes.

Liking is a difficult phenomenon to analyse. Although it is a *reason* for seeking someone's company, it is not simply *equivalent* to enjoyment of his company, as might at first seem, as we can for a time enjoy the company of people whom we do not basically like—indeed, certain kinds of unpleasant people have their own fascination. It seems rather to be a quasi-aesthetic attitude, roughly specifiable as 'finding a person to one's taste', and depends partly on such things as his physical appearance, mannerisms, voice and speech, and style of life; partly on his traits of character, moral and other. The relative importance of these features as a basis for liking obviously depends on the liker.

This account of liking tends to suggest that before we can like someone we have to tot up items in his nature and strike a balance between the attractive and the unattractive aspects of it. But in reality our reaction, like a reaction to a picture, is to a whole personality seen as a unified thing. This is why we often find it very difficult to say what it is we like about a person. Sometimes what we like is partly the way in which everything about the person seems to 'hang together' and be part of a unified style; sometimes we enjoy a contrast, for example that between a mild unassuming exterior and an iron determination. Of course, the fact that we like a personality as a unity or whole does not rule out the possibility that we may dislike some individual features intensely. But in such a case we characteristically feel that these features are not merely objectionable in themselves, but also somehow mar, or intrude upon, a whole that is otherwise pleasing; and this fact sharpens our vexation.

The sense of a bond, or the sense that we have something in common with another person, is a quite separate reason for seeking his company from the existence of liking. For people can be ill-at-ease with those whom they like, and explain why they are *not* friends with them, contrary to others' expectation, by saying 'I like him, but I can't seem to communicate with him' or 'We don't talk the same language' or 'We don't seem to have much in common'. The bond may be shared interests or enthusiasms or views, but it may also be a similar style of mind or way of thinking which makes for a high degree of empathy.

In the light of this discussion we can I think reject the notion that we need to think of our friends as good people, as Plato and Aristotle sometimes seem to assume. For there seems no *necessary* incompatibility between fondness, liking, and a sense of a bond, on the one hand, and disapproval of some qualities in a person, on the other. (Indeed, we can even have a kind of admiration or liking for the very qualities of which we at the same time disapprove.) On the other hand, some moral defects arouse distaste as well as disapproval and so prevent liking. And one of the strongest bonds may well be, even if not matched virtue and mutual admiration as in Aristotle, at least similar moral seriousness and shared moral purpose. Again, to say that we need not think of our friends as good people is not to say that friendship with a thoroughly bad person is morally permissible, or to deny that some moral defects may make a person incapable of friendship.

One reason why Aristotle insists that friendship (at any rate, the truest form of friendship) must be between good men is that he thinks that to care for someone because he is virtuous is to care for him for his own sake, whereas to care for him because he is useful or pleasant is not.[1] Now if Aristotle means merely that it is not true friendship to care for someone for what you can get out of him, we agree. But he seems rather to mean that to care for a man because of his virtue is to care for him 'in himself,' rather than because of contingent and changeable facts about him, and that 'caring for him in himself' in this sense is one of the requirements of friendship.

Now it is clear that Aristotle is mistaken in supposing that a man's virtue is not a contingent and changeable fact—as indeed he later admits.[2] But his other assumption—that we care for friends 'in themselves' rather than for any contingent facts about them—has a certain plausibility. How far is it valid? It is false if it means that qualities in the friend cannot be *reasons* for friendship. For liking and the sense of a bond, which are necessary conditions of friendships, both depend on the friend's nature. It follows that if the friends change in such a way that they cease to like each other or to have anything in common, the friendship is at an end —not in the sense that it would be wise or usual to break it off, but by definition. It may be that 'Love is not love which alters when it alteration finds'; but friendship, which is based on and dependent on reasons, is different.

But there are two senses in which Aristotle's requirement *is* valid, as can be seen in the light of my earlier discussion. First, there is an element in friendship—affection—which does not have the same dependence on the nature of the friend as liking and sense of a bond. It *may* fade if the friend alters, but there is no logical reason why it should do so, and often it in fact does not. Secondly, even liking, although it depends on qualities which others may also have, is nevertheless a reaction to an individual, not a type. Thus if I like James because he is witty, gentle, and good at making things, I like him, not as one example of a witty, gentle and craftsmanlike person, for whom another such might be substituted, but as an individual whose uniqueness defies complete classification.[3]

My account so far of friendship is in terms of two necessary conditions: shared activities and the passions of friendship. But it might well be objected that this account fails to do justice to an important aspect of friendship, that of commitment and choice. Indeed, an objector might go further, and say that to give the status of a necessary condition to the passions of friendship is *incompatible* with the plain fact that we can speak of choosing to be someone's friend. His argument is that since we can speak of choosing to be someone's friend, but cannot choose our feelings, the presence of certain feelings cannot be a necessary condition for friendship. Their rôle, he would maintain, is rather that of *reasons* for friendship, reasons why I might choose to be someone's friend. Similarly, if my inclinations alter, this may be a reason for breaking off the friendship, but it does not *mean* that the friendship is broken off. Such an objector might compare friendship in this respect to marriage, which is normally entered upon on the basis of certain feelings but which exists whether or not these feelings obtain. He might go on to say that in friendship, as in marriage, it makes sense to ask which feelings do justify entering upon the friendship, and again which changes of feelings (if any) justify breaking it off.

My reply to this objection is first of all to recall the case where the usual passions of friendship do not obtain, but the behavior does—where, for example, A helps B and does things with him, not out of spontaneous inclination, but out of pity or sense of duty. My claim is that if B comes to realise A's real motives he would naturally say, not 'You shouldn't have become my friend', but 'You don't really regard me as a friend at all'. Again, if A ceases to like B or to feel any bond with him, but goes on acting as before 'for auld lang syne', as it were, B on becoming aware of the situation would I think say 'You don't really think of me as a friend any more'.

To some extent, of course, I am stipulating, rather than reporting, that the presence of the inclinations is a necessary part of friendship. I think the word may sometimes be used to describe a relationship analogous to marriage. But perhaps I can make the stipulation more palatable by pointing out that, even on my analysis so far, choice necessarily enters into friendship. For although the right passions are a necessary condition of friendship they are not by themselves a sufficient condition. A man who possesses these passions has still to act on them—actually to help instead of merely wanting to, for example—and insofar as he acts he is necessarily making choices. In this way my two necessary conditions are compatible with, and themselves imply, *choice* in friendship—though they also imply that we cannot choose to be a friend of just anyone, since the relevant passions cannot be summoned up at will.

It might plausibly be maintained, however, that we speak of choosing our friends in a stronger sense than that already covered by the two necessary conditions of shared activities and passions of friendship. For the existence of what I have called shared activities need not imply more than a series of unconnected choices, not seen by the chooser as forming any pattern. But choosing a friend seems to mean forming a long-term *policy* of action: making one decision to act in general in the ways we have described, not making many decisions on particular occasions.

Is it a necessary condition of friendship that we should choose our friends, in this stronger sense? It seems clear that we need not (though we may) make a conscious decision of the kind I have just described; we can speak of people as gradually *becoming* friends, or of friendship as *springing up*, thus suggesting that there need not be any definite beginning to the friendship. But nevertheless I would claim that a weaker version of this condition *is* necessary: namely, that the existence of the passions of friendship in both parties, and the practice on both sides of acting on them, once established, be *acknowledged* by the parties. This acknowledgement involves, not so much the *formation* of a policy, as endorsement of or consent to a policy which is by then enshrined in practice. This is part of what is meant by *commitment* in friendship.

I have claimed that there are three necessary conditions for friendship: shared activities, the passions of friendship, and acknowledgement of the fulfilment of the first two conditions, constituting an acknowledgement of and consent to the special relationship. I now add that I regard these as not only individually necessary but also jointly sufficient for friendship.

FRIENDSHIP AND DUTY

But friends can also be said to be committed in a quite different sense from that which I have been discussing: friendship is seen as giving rise to *duties* and correponding rights. Examples of such duties, as commonly conceived, are: to help the friend when under attack (physical or verbal) or in need or trouble of any kind; to proffer advice and criticism, not only when asked for but also when not asked for but needed. The notion of duties to friends, however, is by no means unproblematic, and before I can consider these duties further I must discuss three arguments to the effect that it does not make sense to speak of duties to friends.

The first argument can be dismissed fairly briskly. It is to the effect that friendship is an involuntary relationship, and no duties can be founded on an involuntary relationship. I have already denied that friendship is involuntary in the relevant sense. But in any case we should query the assumption that no duties can arise from an involuntary relationship. Cannot children be said to have duties to their parents, or siblings to each other?

The second reason for rejecting the notion of duties to friends is more problematic. It is that to speak of duty implies the possibility that the action may be against the grain, whereas we spontaneously want to help our friends. We cannot meet this difficulty simply by saying that we can often speak of duties in situations where we also in fact wish to do the actions, as in the case of duties to family. For whether or not we wish to help our families is a contingent matter, whereas I have made it part of the very definition of friendship that we should want to help our friends.

This difficulty about duties to friends can I think be circumvented by stressing two points. First, the existence of friendship, while it implies general goodwill, need not imply that the friends wish each other well at all times and in all respects. Thus it is quite compatible with friendship for a man to lose concern temporarily for a friend—perhaps as the result of a quarrel—or to find that some aspect of his friend's behaviour always tries his patience. In these cases it makes perfectly good sense to say that caring for his friend goes against the grain. Secondly, some of our duties to our friends are extremely disagreeable (such as telling them unpleasant 'home truths'). There is thus a point in speaking of duty in that our natural concern for our friends' welfare, though prompting us in the right direction, is not so strong that all the required actions come easily to us.

The third objection which may be raised to the conception that we have duties to friends is that duties belong to impersonal relationships, whereas friendship is a personal relationship. The force of this objection, however, obviously depends on what sense of 'personal' and 'impersonal' is in question. Let us therefore consider in what senses friendship may be said to be personal, and whether any of them preclude us from speaking of 'duties of friendship'.[4]

First, friendship is personal in that it necessarily involves knowledge by acquaintance. But in this it does not differ from many relationships which obviously involve duties: for example, that of husband and wife.

Secondly, friendship is personal in that it necessarily involves what we may call a 'reactive' attitude: that which regards another human being, not as an object to be manipulated causally, but as a *person, i.e.,* a rational agent capable of self-determination.[5] But our relationships with all adult sane human beings should be, and normally are, personal in this sense; it therefore cannot be incompatible with the existence of duties.

Thirdly, we may say that friendship is personal in that it is 'part of one's private life'. But the notion of private life itself needs elucidation. It may mean anything which is not connected with one's work. In this sense relationships with one's family, friends, fellow-churchmen, fellow-clubmen, mistress, are all part of one's private life. Or one may use the term in a sense relative to one's interlocutor, meaning roughly 'whatever I choose to keep apart from you'. In this sense family life may be private life to one's colleagues, friendships and love affairs to one's family. But 'private life' in both these senses can include relationships in which we normally speak of duties, so we cannot base an argument against the conception of duties to friends on the idea that friendship is part of private life.

Fourthly, we may say that friendship is personal in that it is part of one's 'non-official life', as contrasted with 'official life' in which what to do is in some way fixed or laid down. It might then be argued that the official sphere (which would include not only work, or most forms of it, but also membership of organizations such as clubs, churches and political parties, and of relationships which are governed by law and convention such as marriage and parenthood) is that in which it makes sense to speak of duty. The non-official sphere, on the other hand, to which belong friendships, companionships and acquaintanceships, and love affairs, is outside the scope of duty. This argument from the non-official nature of friendship seems to have a certain plausibility. But it in fact comprises two different claims, which must be considered separately.

First, then, the claim may be that duties belong to conventional or institutional relationships, whereas friendship is a natural relationship. To support the claim examples are adduced of relationships involving duties: for example, that of husband to wife (and *vice versa*), schoolmaster to pupils, treasurer of club to club members, and so on. In all these cases the rôle is *defined* in terms of a set of duties: one cannot explain what a husband is without explaining the rights and duties of marriage. But friendship can be explained entirely in natural terms (in the kind of way we explained it in our first section). Hence, it may be argued, friendship is not a duty-relationship.

But this argument is confused. For there are cases of *natural* relationships, such as that between parent and child, which give rise to duties just as much as do the conventional relationships. The difference is that, whereas the statement that husbands have duties to wives is analytic, the statement that parents have duties to children is synthetic. If then friendship is a natural relationship, it may well involve duties in the same way as parenthood does—duties whose precise content will depend on the nature of the particular society. We incur these duties as a result of making friends just as we incur the duties of parents as a result of having children.

The second claim based on the non-official nature of friendship may be developed as a criticism of our reply to the first. It may be argued that parenthood, although like friendship in being a natural rather than a conventional relationship, is nevertheless official in a sense in which friendship is not, because society *recognizes* the duties of parenthood. This recognition is shown both by the legal enforcement of some very important duties, and by the more informal sanctions of disapproval which are brought to bear on parents who neglect non-legal duties to their children. Nothing of this kind—the argument goes on—happens in the case of friendship, and therefore we cannot speak of duties to friends.

This second argument assumes that duties are always dependent on the attitudes of society. But this assumption does not seem to be correct. We may grant that the precise content of one's duties may vary from society to society, since people's needs vary in different societies and are met in different ways by different social arrangements. But it does not follow that we have no duties except those recognized by society. For example it makes sense to say that parents had a duty to educate their daughters as well as their sons, even at the time when society did not recognize this duty, because the daughters had a need which was not being met at all. In the same way we might have duties to friends, which society does not recognize, in view of some need which is not otherwise met.

I conclude then that the personal nature of friendship, however this is interpreted, does not rule out the possibility of our having duties to friends.

It is possible, however, to attack the notion of duties to friends from a quite different point of view. This attack would grant that it *makes sense* to speak of duties to friends, but hold that we are *mistaken* in thinking that we in fact have such duties, because the alleged duties to friends cannot be properly grounded or justified. It might of course be retorted that further defence of the view that friends have special duties to each other is neither possible nor necessary; it is just an ultimate moral principle that we have special duties to friends. But it does not seem to be self-evident that we have special duties to a small group of people, simply because we care about them and seek their company. In any case, those who oppose the idea of duties to friends might well go on to argue that friendship seems *prima facie* to involve a kind of *injustice,* in that it means giving preferential treatment to those who differ neither in need nor in desert—in other words that, so far from being duties, our services to friends might be construed as positively immoral.

Faced with these arguments, the defenders of the duties of friendship will point out first of all that not all services to friends are in any sense exclusive of services to others. Thus we can distinguish between the expenditure on our friends of time or money which might otherwise have been spent on others, and the proffering of advice or criticism which is *not* thereby rendered unavailable for others. It is only in the first type of case that the issue of the morality of preferential treatment for friends arises sharply. And even there the alleged duties to help our friends are acknowledged to be severely restricted in various ways by the demands of other specific duties.

But these restrictions still leave an area in which no duty arising out of another rôle is in question but in which there may be a choice between helping a friend and helping a stranger. Suppose, for example, a man could spend an evening helping to decorate either a friend's flat or that of an old age pensioner, or could spend spare cash either on a loan to friends or on contributions to Oxfam. Most people would say that the friends had, if not a prior claim, at least a competing claim, and our present problem is to defend this view.

A plausible line of defence seems to be an appeal to a Rule-Utilitarian position. Thus it might be argued that many sets of rights and duties which set up special claims not obviously required by justice, are justified by the conduciveness of their observance to the general good. If for example a parent is asked why he should support his child, he will reply that it is one of the duties of a parent. If he is then asked *why* parents should be held to have special duties to their children, instead of their being the responsibility of the State or of grand-parents, he will say that it is best for all concerned that parents should have special responsibility for children. In the same way, then, we may suggest that the general welfare is best served by our regarding friends as having a special claim on us. We may defend this view on the grounds that more happiness overall is produced if each man makes the welfare of a few others his special concern, for two reasons: he will be able to be more effective if he concentrates his energies, and he will be able to know more precisely what the needs of a small group are.

Now the first of these arguments does not by itself support the view that we have special duties to *friends*, but only the view that we should choose *a* small group as special recipients of our benevolence. But if we add the second argument, about the knowledge of needs, we can defend the view that the special group we choose should be that of our friends. It is not only that we have a good deal of contact with our friends and get to know their needs that way, for this fact applies equally to our family or to colleagues at work. But we also have a special understanding of our friends' needs, in virtue not only of the *rapport* which by definition exists between friends but also of a sharpened *awareness*, which results from the special concern friends in any case have for each other.

We can thus advance beyond the point made earlier, that there is nothing self-contradictory in the idea of duties towards those for whom we already feel a special concern, and assert that the existence of this concern is part of the *justification* for the claim that we have special duties to friends. As we have just seen, a special concern, in making us especially aware of others' needs, gives us the duties that are attendant on special knowledge of needs. But it also gives us a special degree of *power* to help, and in this way also gives us special duties. This is because a man can have a duty to do only what he is able to do, and in some cases he is able, as a result of the strength of his concern for a friend, to do for him what he *could* not do (and hence could not have a duty to do) for anyone else.

It might be argued at this point that I have not met the objection that it is *unjust* to view friends as having special claims; for since friendship is, and is bound to be, very unevenly distributed, the rights which it confers will also be unevenly distributed. I think the only possible answer is that this is a case where the utility of a practice is high enough to compensate for the fact that some measure of injustice is involved in it. But in any case when we speak of duties to friends we are clearly speaking of *prima facie* duties, which would be overridden by a stronger claim.

I can now briefly sum up the conclusions of this section. I have tried to show that various arguments, purporting to show that it does not make sense to speak of duties to friends, are not cogent: those from the alleged involuntariness of friendship, from the constraining nature of duty, and from the personalness, in either the 'knowledge by acquaintance' or the 'reactive' or the 'private life' sense, of the relationship of friendship. I considered at more length the notion that friendship is separated from duty by being personal in the sense of 'non-official'. I suggested there that we could speak of the duties of friendship even though they are both non-institutional and unsupported by social sanctions. I then raised a new type of problem, that of *grounding* the alleged duties to friends. I have tried to show that this can be done in terms of the general good.

THE VALUE OF FRIENDSHIP

It may be said that the train of thought so far has been that, *if* we have friends, *then* we have certain duties to them. But this does not constitute a demonstration of the value of friendship itself, any more than it shows the value of parenthood to say that if people produce children then they have a duty towards them.

Now some people will say that there is no point in raising the question what the *good* of friendship is, since people cannot help having friends in any case. But this is not strictly true, as we have seen; commitment to friendship is a voluntary matter. It may be true that people cannot help forming vaguer and looser associations, and that they cannot help having the *passions* of friendship towards various other people. But this does not amount to the inevitability of friendship itself.

It may be said that if our emotional make-up is such as to incline us to want to make friends, then this in itself constitutes a *prima facie* case for the goodness of friendship. For how can we show something to be good (it may be maintained) except by showing that it meets deep-seated desires?

But this argument is cogent only if the desires in question—the passions of friendship—are unavoidable; whereas it seems clear that, even if we cannot ourselves get rid of them once we have them, we can foster or inhibit their development in children. Certain kinds of early environment make people less inclined to form strong attachments later, and whether this is a good or bad thing depends on whether friendship itself is a good or a bad thing. Nor can we settle the question by saying that a person who cannot make friends is considered psychologically unhealthy. For we would not include a capacity for friendship in our requirement for psychological health unless we already assumed that friendship is a good thing, so we cannot defend friendship in the name of mental health without going round in a circle.

Why, then, is friendship always considered a good thing—perhaps one of the chief blessings of life? Part of the reason has been given already in my previous section. It is true that my account of the duties of friendship did not raise the question of the value of friendship itself, but rather asked whether, given that we have friends, we are to regard ourselves as having duties to them. But we can use the conclusions of the account as part of a justification of friendship itself. Friendship, we may say, promotes the general happiness by providing a degree and kind of consideration for others' welfare which cannot exist outside it, and which compensates by its excellence for the 'unfairness' of the unequal distribution of friendship. For even those who have no friends are (we may suppose) better off than they would be if there were no such thing as friendship, since the understanding developed by it and the mutual criticism involved in it will improve the way friends deal with people outside the relationship.

But we value friendship for reasons other than its general service-ability to society. To see what these are, we may start from Aristotle's account of why the happy man needs friends [6]—though he tends to assume, as we have seen, that friendship worthy of the name must be between good people. He suggests first that friends are *useful* to a man both to help him in his need and to be recipients of his beneficence in his prosperity. These points have both been partially dealt with earlier; but we would say, not that a man must have friends in order to receive or give *any* help (as Aristotle seems to suggest) but rather that there are particular services which a man can receive only from friends and perform only for them.

Secondly, Aristotle suggests friendship is *pleasant*. He sees this pleasure mainly in terms of the *good* man's pleasure at his equally good friend's virtuous actions. But the joys of friendship are many and various. Notably, of course, there is the pleasure of the friend's company and of shared activity with someone of kindred outlook. Nor need the fact that we gain this pleasure mean that the friendship is 'for the sake of pleasure'. We may begin a friendship because we enjoy someone's company, but soon we enjoy his company because he is a friend.

Now an appeal to pleasure as a justification of friendship may not seem to be on very safe ground, for friendship, like any other attachment we may form, increases our potentiality for pain as well as for pleasure. It could well be argued that from the point of view of the balance of pleasure over pain we would do better to play safe by eschewing friendship. But this pessimistic view does not take into account the full range of the pleasures of friendship. It is true that we can set the pleasure of making a new friend against the sorrow of losing an old one, or the pleasure of a friend's company against the pain of his absence, or the pleasure of discovering his excellences against the pain of dis-illusionment with him. But there are some pleasures of friendship which have no corresponding pains. These are the pleasures which arise from doing things with a friend, as opposed to doing them alone or with others. What we are doing may be in any case enjoyable—playing games, playing music, conversation, philosophy—in which case the presence of the friend enhances the pleasure. Or what we do may in itself be un-attractive, but become fun—indeed, be turned into a kind of game—when shared with a friend: for example, spring-cleaning or moving house.

This discussion of the pleasures of friendship points to a third value in friendship, noted indirectly by Aristotle: friendship is *life-enhancing*, it makes us have life 'more abundantly'. This happens in various ways. First, it increases our stake in the world, and hence our capacity for emotions. We have already noticed this point in terms of the increased capacity for pleasure and pain, but it applies also to the whole range of emotions: hope, fear, anger, pride and so on. Friendship makes us 'more alive' because it makes us *feel* more.

Secondly, friendship enhances many of our *activities*, by intensifying our absorption in them, and hence the quality of our performance of them. The increased absorption is partly a by-product (or rather per-haps an aspect) of the increased pleasure which joint activity with friends produces, since (as Aristotle says) pleasure taken in an activity intensifies it. But I think collaboration with friends may also produce an increased emotional commitment to the activity which is separable from the effects of enhanced pleasure.

Thirdly, friendship enlarges our *knowledge*. I have already spoken of the increased knowledge of human needs and wishes which springs from close association with some one other person. But friendship can enlarge our knowledge throughout the whole gamut of human experi-ence, by enabling us in some measure to adopt the viewpoint of another person through our sympathetic identification with him. Through friendship we can know what it is like to feel or think or do certain things which we do not feel, think or do ourselves. And our knowledge is not merely knowledge by description, but knowledge by acquaintance, derived from our sympathetic sharing of his experience.

We might compare this effect of friendship with that of reading a great work of literature. C. S. Lewis, trying to answer the question, 'What is the good of Literature?', says "We want to be more than our-selves . . . we want to see with other eyes, to imagine with other imaginations, to feel with other hearts, as well as with our own.

". . . It is not a question of knowing [in the sense of gratifying our rational curiosity about other people's psychology] at all. It is *connaître* not *savoir*; it is *erleben*: we become these other selves." [7] This empathy with the authors of literature is exactly like the empathy with friends which I have tried to describe, and indeed C. S. Lewis himself compares in this respect for effects of love with those of literature.

Friendship, then, contributes to the well-being of society and to the profit, pleasure and life-enhancement of the friends. But this strong justification of friendship need not show that a particular person is mistaken in deciding it is not for him. He might legitimately do this either because he feels that his temperament makes him unlikely to be a satisfactory friend or because he feels called upon to embark on some absorbing project which will leave no time or energy for friendship.

Perhaps I might conclude by pointing out that too much dwelling on the values of friendship has its own dangers. It may lead people to concentrate on looking for *friendships* rather than friends, and to value the other person as a possible term in a relationship rather than as himself. But it may well be that this attitude, which is wrong in itself and hurtful if detected, is also self-defeating: in other words, that we attain the valuable relationship of friendship only when we cease to think about it and concentrate on the friend himself.

NOTES

1. Aristotle, *Nicomachean Ethics,* 1156a 10-19, 1156b 6-12.
2. *Op. cit.,* 1165b 12-22.
3. This discussion of liking owes much to W. G. Maclagan, "Respect for Persons as a Moral Principle", Part I, *Philosophy,* 1960.
4. This discussion of senses of "personal" and "impersonal" is based on that in R. S. Downie, *Roles and Values,* pp. 134-8 (Methuen, 1971).
5. For the notion of a reactive attitude see P. F. Strawson, "Freedom and Resentment", *Proceedings of the British Academy,* 1962.
6. Aristotle, *op. cit.,* 1169b-1170b 19.
7. C. S. Lewis, *An Experiment in Criticism,* pp. 137, 139 (Cambridge University Press, 1961).

LOVE

A Conceptual Investigation of Love

W. Newton-Smith

Concepts like love, which we use in describing, explaining and ordering the personal relations of ourselves and others, have received scant attention in the recent Anglo-American philosophical tradition. This contrasts decidedly with philosophical interests on the continent. The difference may be explained in part by the fact that here interests have lain in different areas. More interestingly, perhaps, this difference may reflect disagreement about the connection between such an account and more basic issues in epistemology and the philosophy of mind and about the import of a philosophical account of, say, love. For example, Sartre, when discussing relations with others in *Being and Nothingness*, concludes at the end of something bearing at least a family resemblance to an argument, that it follows from his account of the relation between mind and body that an attempt to love is bound to fail. The acceptance of Sartre's argument would have clear import for someone who regulated his or her sex life according to the principle that sex without love was not permissible. A person who accepted the argument and who was unwilling to adopt a chaste life would seem to be compelled either to violate or to revise his or her principles. Clearly, if one accepts that an account of the relation between mind and body might entail conclusions of this force, one would be interested, to say the least, in working out the entailments.

On a conception of philosophy which has had some currency in the recent Anglo-American tradition such conclusions would not be expected. For, on this view, philosophy is seen as a sort of second-order discipline, which seeks to give a descriptive, and possibly systematic, account of the concepts we employ in dealing with the world. Philosophy presupposes a linguistic practice which it describes and leaves untouched. Within this framework it is highly unlikely that someone would argue that something which we took, at the level of common sense, to be the case was not in fact the case. In the presence of Sartre's strong and

From *Philosophy and Personal Relations: An Anglo-French Study*, ed. Alan Montefiore (Montreal: McGill-Queen's University Press, 1973), pp. 113-36. Reprinted by permission of the publisher.

An obvious debt of gratitude is owed to all those who participated in the discussions that led to this volume. I would like especially to thank Derek Parfit, Alan Montefiore and my wife for many stimulating discussions.

counter-intuitive conclusion that love is not possible, it would be argued via paradigm cases that love is indeed possible and that consequently Sartre's account of the relation between mind and body is shown, by *reductio ad absurdum*, to be false. While these few remarks have done justice neither to Sartre nor to the practitioners of this linguistic conception of philosophy, they do suggest an important contrast between these traditions with regard to their expectations of the possible fruits of a philosophical account of concepts such as love.

In this paper I will seek both to provide an account of our concept of love and to explore the possible practical bearing of such an account for our thinking and acting in the context of personal relations. The first part of the paper will involve an attempt to determine some of the features which mark the concept off from certain related concepts. Within the confines of this paper, this treatment can only be provided in detail sufficient to suggest the general structure of the concept. A more detailed tracing of the multifarious web of connections will, I hope, come later. In the second part of the paper a number of hypothetical situations in which the protagonists appear to be disagreeing about matters of love will be considered. This will allow us to test the adequacy of the philosophical account of love in terms of its power to account for these disputes. These cases will also be used to determine what relevance the philosophical account might have for us in our personal relations with others. That there may be some practical relevance is suggested by the following considerations.

Any complete account of the state of a relation between persons, as opposed to objects, must take account of what the persons involved take the state of the relationship to be. The state of a personal relationship between business colleagues, Smith and Jones, may be a function more of how Smith sees Jones (i.e. as dishonest) than of how Jones actually is (i.e. honest). Similarly, the practical course of a relationship between Joe and Joel, which they both see as one of love, might be in part a function of what they take love to be or to involve. A philosophical account of love which ruled out one of their ways of thinking of love would then be relevant. Whether this philosophical intervention was for the better is entirely another matter. Rather than defend or amplify this thesis here, it will be left until we consider some hypothetical personal relationships.

Before proceeding further it will be helpful to introduce the following methodological distinctions. As well as speaking of the concept of x, I will talk of someone's conception of x. Someone's conception of x refers to how that person uses the term 'x'. The concept of x refers to those features which anyone's conception of x must possess in order to count as a conception of x at all. This distinction is intended as a device to avoid prejudging the issue concerning the existence of a precise, determinate, public concept of x. That is, different persons might draw the boundaries of their concepts somewhat differently but not so differently that they cannot be said to be speaking of the same thing.

For instance, two persons might be said to have the same concept of x in virtue of an agreement about paradigm cases of x but to have slightly different conceptions of x in virtue of making different decisions about borderline cases. I will also speak of someone's picture of x. By this I mean the answer the person would give to the question 'What is x?'. Roughly, then, someone's picture of x is the account he would offer of x. This is intended as a distinction between someone's possessing a certain concept where this is displayed through the correct application of the concept and the person's being able to say in virtue of what features he applies the concept. Someone may possess a concept, x, but have no picture of x at all. If we ask him 'What is x?' he draws a blank or can only point to examples. Someone's picture of x might be a full-blown philosophical analysis of x. It might also be incompatible with the actual use he makes of the concept.

Use will also be made of the following distinction between two sorts of non-contingent truth. If, for example, it should be a necessary truth that *all* cases of love must involve sexual desire, I will speak of a necessary connection between love and sexual desire. And if it should be a necessary truth that *generally* cases of love involve sexual desire I will speak of a g-necessary connection. A particular case lacking a g-necessary feature of x-hood, will count as a case of x only in the presence of some special explanation. Obviously this paper is not the place to enter into a discussion of the nature of necessary truth, and I can here offer no defence of this distinction beyond attempt to display its fruitfulness in application.

I

This study cannot deal with all our uses of 'love'. We speak of loving persons, food, countries, art, hypothetical divine beings, and so on. In this paper I will be interested only in cases where the object of a love is some one or more persons. It would seem fairly clear that this is, as it were, the home territory of the concept of love and that the use of 'love' in conjunction with objects other than persons is best understood as an extension of this use. Having distinguished a kind of love in terms of a kind of object, namely persons, of a love relation, it is necessary to narrow the field of investigation further. And so attention will be confined to cases of love which involve sexuality. For the balance of this paper then, 'love' is to be understood as implying this restriction. 'Sexuality' is used here as a generic term whose species are sexual feelings, desires, acts and so on. Thus the stipulation excludes from present consideration cases of fraternal love, paternal love, and other cases not involving sexuality.

While this restriction is not intended as a substantial point about love, neither is it purely arbitrary. Rather it is intended to reflect a rough distinction that we do make between kinds of love between persons. Cases of love between persons cluster around certain paradigms.

On the one hand we have a group of paradigms which includes Romeo and Juliet, Abelard and Helöise, and Caesar and Cleopatra. Jules and Jim provide another set of paradigms; the heroine of Gorky's *Mother* and the father of the prodigal son still another. It would seem that sexuality can serve as a criterial mark for picking out those cases that cluster around our first set of paradigms. Thus for instance, given a parent that loves a child, the occurrence of a prolonged, active and intense desire for sexual relations with the child on the part of the parent would lead us to regard the love, all things being equal, as not purely maternal. Analogously, the absence of sexuality between two persons of the opposite sex whom we think of as loving each other may incline us to describe the love as platonic or aesthetic. Anyone who thinks that this requirement of sexuality does not capture what is the essential delimiting feature of the romantic paradigms, can regard the requirement as simply a device for selecting a more manageable set of cases for this preliminary investigation.

A brief word about the status of these paradigms is in order. One way of displaying in part what someone's conception of, say, O is, is by displaying what he would regard as paradigm instances of O. While the cases given above would be offered as paradigms by a large number of persons, there is no proper set of paradigms. By this I mean that while the conceptual features of love to be given below rule out certain things as not possibly being paradigms of love, it is possible for different individuals to have different paradigms. In what follows I hope to display what we must think of a relationship in order to think of it as a relationship of love at all. I will suggest that this leaves considerable range for the construction of competing paradigms. This divergence in paradigms leaves room for interesting psychological and sociological investigations in the variations in paradigms from person to person, for instance, or from class to class, or historical era to historical era. And, given the normative aspect of a conception of love, these paradigms take on the character not just of clear examples but of ideals. Some of the consequences of this will be seen in the second half of this paper.

It is not suggested that the sexuality requirement provides any precise distinction. It seems likely that there is not a precise distinction to be marked. For we might wish to allow some feelings of a sexual sort to enter into a case of basically maternal love. And we might allow some aspects of homosexual love in the close relationship between the officer and men of a marine platoon without the relationship ceasing to be basically a fraternal one. However, things are different if the officer is continually wanting to get to bed with one particular soldier. Thus while there may be no precise distinction here, there is nonetheless a distinction. To be any more definite than this would require an exploration of sexuality that cannot be undertaken here.[1]

It might be objected on the basis of certain psychoanalytic theories that all personal relations involve sexuality, and hence sexuality could not be used as the distinguishing feature of a kind of personal relation.

The grounds on which such a claim would rest are not uncontroversial. In any event, their acceptance involves the hypothesizing of repressed sexual feelings. This in turn does not invalidate our distinction but rather requires us to draw it in terms of a contrast between repressed and unrepressed sexuality rather than in terms of a contrast between the presence and absence of sexuality. In fact, Freud, in *Civilization and its Discontents*, contrasted aim-inhibited love in which the sexual component is suppressed and sexual love in which it is not suppressed. Freud took this distinction to divide the field roughly as we have done. Thus acceptance of certain psychoanalytic theories would require only the recasting, and not the abandoning, of our sexuality requirement.

The preceding modification would be required if a psychoanalytic theory which claimed that *all* relations involve a form of sexuality was adopted. More plausibly perhaps, it might be argued that in some relationships with no apparent sexuality involved, some form of suppressed sexuality was present. That is, given a psychoanalytic theory of genuine explanatory power, we might want to hypothesize on the basis of, say, some form of aberrant behaviour, the presence of repressed sexuality in a relationship apparently devoid of sexuality. In this case we would have a non-analytic counter-factual to the effect that the removal of repression would lead to explicit sexuality. If such a theory is produced our sexuality requirement will have to be extended to include both explicit and repressed sexuality.

It might also be objected to my sexuality requirement that while instances of courtly love belong with our romantic paradigms, not only was sexuality absent in courtly love relations, it was thought to be incompatible with true (courtly) love. Now evidence of the chastity of courtly lovers is decidedly absent. But in any case, courtly lovers must be thought of as possessing sexual feelings which they set aside. This is implicit in their thinking of themselves as noble for not expressing sexual feelings. There would be no trick to it, and hence no nobility involved, if they simply did not have sexual feelings or inclinations at all.

Having defined the field of investigation, we can now sketch the concepts analytically presupposed in our use of 'love'. An idea of these concepts can be gained by sketching a sequence of relations, the members of which we take as relevant in deciding whether or not some given relationship between persons A and B is one of love. These are not relevant in the sense of being evidence for some further relation 'love' but as being, in part at least, the material of which love consists. The sequence would include at least the following:

(1) A knows B (or at least knows something of B)
(2) A cares (is concerned) about B
    A likes B
(3) A respects B
    A is attracted to B

A feels affection for **B**
(4) A is committed to **B**
A wishes to see **B**'s welfare promoted

The connection between these relations which we will call 'love-comprising relations' or 'LCRs', is not, except for 'knowing about' and possibly 'feels affection for', as tight as strict entailment. While perhaps in certain paradigm cases of love these relations would all be satisfied to a high degree, they are not jointly necessary. In a particular case which we are inclined to regard as one of love, some LCRs may be satisfied to only a low degree or not satisfied at all. For there is no contradiction involved in speaking of, say, love without commitment or love without respect. There would of course be a contradiction involved in asserting that some relationship was one of love while denying that any of the LCRs were satisfied. Thus we have a g-necessary truth that love involves the satisfaction of the LCRs to an as yet unspecified degree.

That the LCRs listed are non-contingently involved in love seems fairly obvious and for that reason not particularly interesting. We would not countenance the claims of A to love B if A had neither met B nor knew anything about B.. I will argue below when discussing the limitations of the sorts of reasons A can have for loving B in particular that there are certain sorts of things that A must know about B. The items in group 2 embody the fact that love involves having certain pro-attitudes to the object of the love. Group 3 embodies the condition that the lover sees the object of his love as having in his eyes at least meritorious features. In love it is not just the case that the lover holds the relations of groups 2 and 3 to the object of his love, these relations are held to such a degree that the lover is inclined to act on behalf of his beloved in ways that he is not inclined to act for arbitrary strangers or the general run of the mill acquaintances. Suppose that someone has the unhappy choice of saving either his putative beloved or an arbitrary stranger from drowning. If the putative lover elects to save the stranger, then, all things being equal, the relation is not one of love. Acting out of panic or just after a quarrel, among other possibilities, might show that all things were not equal. This feature of love is captured by the items of group 4.

It may seem frivolous to have introduced this thought experiment to prove such an obvious point. However, that the element of commitment is important in marking off love from other related relations can be seen if we vary the parameters in the thought experiment. Suppose the putative lover has to choose between saving his beloved and a group of strangers. In the event of a choice between a single stranger or a large group of strangers, we clearly think that we should opt for the larger number. Does the commitment element entail that the lover place the welfare of his beloved above the welfare of a group of strangers? Or can he call across to her as he saves the strangers, 'I love you, but unfortunately there are more of them'?

A similar dilemma arises if we imagine a putative lover having to choose between his putative beloved and adherence to his ethical or political principles. In fiction anyway, lovers frequently test the devotion of one another by asking if they would steal etc. for their sake. In *Middlemarch*, for example, Rosamund thinks that if Lydgate does in fact love her, he ought to be willing to set aside his moral scruples for her sake. She wants him to withhold large debts owed to the tradesmen in order to sustain her luxurious standard of living. And in Moravia's *Bitter Honeymoon*, Giacome and Simona are portrayed as being in love and as thinking themselves in love. Simona is a committed communist. Giacome describes himself as an 'individualist'. The following interchange takes place:

Giacome: 'For instance, if a communist government comes to power and I say something against it, you'll inform on me. . . .'
It was true then, he thought to himself, since she didn't deny it, then she would inform on him. He gripped her arm tighter almost wishing to hurt her. 'The truth is that you don't love me.'
Simona: 'I wouldn't have married you except for love.'

These examples are not meant to imply any thesis to the effect that in 'true' love, commitment to the beloved must take preference over all other commitments. The significant conceptual point of the examples is that in the case of love there are these tensions, and this displays the extent to which love involves a commitment. This marks off love from, for example, relations of just 'liking' or 'being attracted to', where these tensions do not arise. We would not, I think, be tempted to redescribe an apparent relation of liking or being attracted to as not being a relation of liking or being attracted to, just because the protagonists did not tend to place the other party on a par with political or ethical commitments.

It has been suggested that love involves holding the LCRs to the beloved. If someone holds these relations to another, he will hold them to the person under certain descriptions of the person. For a relation to count as one of love these descriptions must be of certain sorts. A's saving his putative beloved, B, from drowning only because she is wearing his watch or has just won the pools, may be incompatible with A's thinking of the relationship as being one of love. Of course motives on a particular isolated occasion are not necessarily conclusive determinants of the kind of relationship one way or the other. But there are general limitations on the sorts of ways in which A thinks of the object of his affections where the ways in question are the grounds of his affection for the person. Very roughly, A must, say, care about B for herself, A must be attracted to B on her own account. That is, not all properties which A sees B as possessing can serve as the grounds for loving B.

Of the descriptions which A sees as applying to B, I will call those which can be the grounds of A's loving B, intrinsic descriptions of B.

Descriptions which cannot play this role will be called extrinsic descriptions. Clearly there are some extrinsic and some intrinsic descriptions. Suppose we have an apparent love relation between A and B where B is very wealthy. Suppose B's wealth suddenly evaporates. If A's interest in B should also evaporate, we conclude that, all things being equal, the relation had not been one of love. We might say that A loved not B but B's money. A was interested in B not for her own sake but for the sake of her money. A liked B-the-wealthy-woman and not B *per se*. Of course it is simplistic to speak as I have been doing, as if one isolated incident would lead us to revise our description of a particular personal relation. The complexity of these situations is such that no one incident is likely to be decisive one way or the other. All that is required for the argument is that these incidents give cause to reconsider the descriptions given.

Suppose on the other hand we have an apparent love relation between A and B. A claims to love B largely on account of certain features of her personality and character. But one day, perhaps as the result of some traumatic accident, B undergoes a radical personality transformation. B no longer has those attributes that A loved her for. A, realizing this, can, we suppose, no longer love B. Here we are not so inclined to revise our descriptions of the relation as we were in the case above. We might say that A had indeed loved B but that this was no longer the case as B is no longer the person she once was.

In attempting to draw this distinction I am assuming that it is not a necessary condition of a relationship's being one of love that the lover's attitude to the beloved remain unchanged through all possible changes in the beloved. This question of constancy in love will be taken up later in one of our case studies. The classification of features as extrinsic or intrinsic depends on our attitude to inconstancy, given that the feature in question changed. That is, if A claims to love B in part at least because of her being $\emptyset$, and if A's attitude to B would be negatively affected should B cease to be $\emptyset$ (or, should A cease to see B as being $\emptyset$) then, if we count this inconstancy as evidence against the relationship's having been one of love, $\emptyset$ is an extrinsic property of B; otherwise $\emptyset$ is an intrinsic property. This places no limitations whatsoever on the features which initially attracted A to B. B's money may have been the initial lure. But, if the relationship is to count as one of love, the money cannot be the sustaining feature. In some cases there may be an intimate causal relation between extrinsic and intrinsic factors. In our previous example, B may have been a dynamic capitalist entrepreneur whose personality is intimately bound up with the acquisition of wealth. Financial failure might bring about a personality change. However, only intrinsic factors matter for themselves. The extrinsic factors are relevant only in as much as they are evidence for intrinsic factors.

It was suggested that features of personality and character clearly count as intrinsic and that the state of someone's bank balance was clearly extrinsic. Not all features are so easily classified. Consider the details of the beloved's physical make-up. Traditionally lovers are enraptured with dainty ears, firm thighs and so on. The general acceptance of these sorts of features as grounds for loving suggests that they are to be counted as intrinsic. But, on the other hand, if the moment the ears thicken or the thighs soften the lover falters, we may well have doubts about his alleged love. This suggests that we consider physical features to be extrinsic ones. Perhaps the most that we can say is that someone might love another solely or chiefly because of his or her physical features but that such cases will not be as near to our paradigms of a love relation as cases in which the beloved is loved solely or chiefly for attributes of his or her personality and character. That is, while physical features can be offered as reasons for loving (indeed our sexuality requirement would entail this), we tend to consider relations, which are not also grounded on regard for aspects of the personality and character of the object of the relation, as lacking certain dimensions. A person having as his chief or only reasons for loving another, regard for their physical attributes, would seem to be regarding the object of his love as being less than a person. Persons are not just bodies, they are at least bodies which think and act.

Any attempt to distinguish between physical characteristics as more extrinsic than features of personality and character is complicated by the problematic status of the role of physical features in determining personality and character. Clearly we identify some personality features via physical features—the look of the eyes, the character of the smile. The possession of some, though certainly not all, personality traits may be tied to the possession of certain physical characteristics. Perhaps some properties, for instance, elegance, while not being entirely physical attributes, can only be possessed by someone with certain physical attributes. I mention this as a question of some interest requiring a detailed consideration which cannot be given here.

That someone might love another for certain of her features suggests a problem. Suppose someone else should appear who also instantiates these properties. If the possession of these properties is someone's reason for loving one, reasons being universalizable, he will have equal reason to love the other as well. Perhaps the second person more perfectly embodies those properties which the lover previously lauded in the first. According to Gellner,[2] if someone in this kind of context should divide his affection between the two persons, neither relationship can be counted as a relationship of love. (We will have reasons to challenge this assumption later.) In most actual cases the universalizability of reasons will not require a person, A, to extend his affection to cover both B and C where C is a second embodiment of those features which A lauded in B. For, often A's reasons for loving B will involve reference to what B has done for him, to what they have done together. If A has been socially interacting with B, he is likely to have reasons of this character and these reasons would not be grounds for loving C as well.

However, suppose A falls in love with B from a distance and has no social contact with B. Even here, one of A's reasons for loving B may be that it was B that first excited this passion in him. A might recognize that C would have done the same, if he had first known of C. But, A first met B and B generated the passion. A may now love B for having been the generator of the passion.

Of course it is possible that reasons of this sort are not among A's reasons for loving B and that either A does not love B for the reasons he thought he did, or that A will transfer his affection. I shall argue (part II) that if A extends his affection in this way, he may nonetheless love both B and C. If A does not think of himself as having any reasons for loving B that do not equally apply to C, and if A does not have any inclination to extend his affection to C, this provides us with the grounds for supposing that A is simply mistaken about his reasons for loving. That is, we would, I think, suppose that there is some present feature of B, or some feature of B's history or their history together, that was important to A and was part of A's reasons for loving B whereas the feature in question is not shared by C.

There are two sorts of intriguing and subtle kinds of cases which might seem to suggest that we have been assuming too readily that there is no problem in identifying who the object of a love is. The first relates to the suggestion, to be found in Stendhal, that one never really loves another person but one loves rather some creation of one's imagination based on, but usually bearing little resemblance to, the actual person one appears to love. Following Stendhal, I will refer to this theory as the 'crystallization' theory of love. Stendhal thought of the actual object of a love as an imaginary creation built on and transforming a few true perceptions of the apparent object of the love, in a manner analogous to the growth of crystals on a branch placed in the Salzburg salt mines. Lawrence Durrell, in *Clea*, provides a model of what I take Stendhal to have in mind. Here Darley is presented as suddenly realizing that he never loved Justine. He concludes that he loved some 'illusory creation' of his own based on Justine. The revelation comes to him on Justine's informing him that it was pointless for her to return to him after their separation, for it was not *her* Darley loved. As the case is presented, Darley thinks of himself as loving Justine because of certain intrinsic features. But the features do not apply to Justine.

Darley thinks of himself as loving Justine for a sequence $\phi_1, \ldots, \phi_n$ of features which he takes to apply to Justine. If the following counterfactual is true, the case is easily dealt with. If Darley would feel as strongly about Justine should he come to see that she does not possess the properties in question, he does in fact, all things being equal, love her. He has simply been radically mistaken about her. Perhaps when he discovers what she is really like, his attraction for her will actually increase. Suppose on the other hand, Darley would not think of himself as loving Justine if he came to realize his mistake. In this case he never loved anyone at all and to speak of having loved an 'illusory creation' is, at best, a metaphorical way of saying that he mistakenly thought of himself as loving someone as a result of radically misunderstanding the sort of person she was.

The 'crystallization' theory draws our attention to the notorious fact that we often misapprehend the properties of persons and often act in personal relationships on the basis of our beliefs about persons which are wrong and sometimes radically so. But as a theory to the effect that we never love other persons, it is just wrong. We are not always mistaken about other persons. In many cases the beloved will in fact have some of the properties on the basis of which the lover loves. Even in cases of grave error, the lover may, as I argued above, be said to love in spite of being mistaken.

The other intriguing case concerning the real object of a love arises in psychoanalytic theory. Aberrant behaviour on the part of a person A, who appears to love person B, might be thought explicable in some contexts on the hypothesis that A does not in fact love B but really loves, say, a parental figure. B is a sort of stand-in in an elaborate fantasy. This seems like a misleading description of the case. For, it is towards B and not towards, say, his mother, that A performs the action appropriate in a context of love. Perhaps it is therefore best to say that A does love B while admitting the existence of a causal connection between his attitude towards his mother and his attitude towards B. Perhaps A would not care for B at all if he had not had a certain attitude towards his mother. Or, perhaps A's loving B depends on his thinking of B in ways appropriate to thinking of a mother.

It has been argued that love involves having certain kinds of relations (the LCRs) to some person, and that it also involves thinking of the object of these relations in certain ways. In addition love is essentially reciprocal. Stendhal reports André le Chapelain as writing in his twelfth-century Code of Love 'No one can love unless bidden by the hope of being loved'. It does seem to be a g-necessary truth that if A loves B, A wishes to be loved by B. We can see that this is a conceptual fact and not just a matter of fact about lovers, by seeing what would be involved in imagining a case where A loves B but does not wish to be loved in return. The following situation, drawn with adaptation, from Dickens' *Little Dorrit* seems to provide the sort of case we want. A loves B who is already married to another. A is particularly concerned for the welfare and happiness of B. A knows that B would not be happy loving him. For, if B loved A in return B would suffer extreme guilt feelings at taking on another affection while committed in marriage to another. B has, let us suppose, a loving husband and children. A, being magnanimous, does not reveal his love for B, for fear that the mere revelation would precipitate reciprocated love and subsequent unhappiness for B. In one sense the lover does wish for reciprocated love. He would wish it if all things were equal. But given the circumstances as they are, he does not wish it. No doubt we would countenance the lover's denial of any wish for reciprocated love in the circumstances. But to render this plausible we had to imagine a case where the reciprocated love would be an unhappy love. Other cases can be provided if the lover is imagined to be masochistic or to be involved in some form of self-abasement. In the absence of such a background we would simply fail to understand a denial of a wish for reciprocated love. If someone claims to love another, we understand him as wishing to be loved in return. We do not have to ask, 'And do you wish her to love you?' The inference to a wish for reciprocated love is blocked only if the background is filled out in certain ways. Loving entails, *ceteris paribus,* the desire for reciprocated love.

This essential reciprocity interestingly delimits love from many other concepts used in describing personal relations. A clear case in point is that of worship. A's worshipping B does not, *ceteris paribus,* entail that A wishes to be worshipped by B. Quite the contrary in fact. For, in wishing to be worshipped by B, A would be demeaning B from the elevated position relative to himself, that A accords to B, in thinking of B as an object of worship. Perhaps 'liking' is a more pertinent example for our present purposes. We do not take someone's claim to like another as implying a wish on his part to be liked by the other person. He may or may not. Perhaps we do take him as wishing not to be disliked but this is not the same as wishing to be liked. The reciprocal factor is similarly absent in the case of a commitment outside the context of a love relation (except possibly in the context of a contractual relation). A claim to be committed to my party leader does not imply a wish that he commit himself to me (I may think of myself as a lowly pawn not deserving such a commitment) in the way that a claim to be committed to my beloved does.

It is not suggested that the features of the concept of love which have been given provide anything like a calculus for deciding, objectively, whether or not any given relationship is one of love. The term 'love' has undeniable emotive force. Different individuals may require that the LCRs be satisfied to different degrees before awarding the epithet love to a relationship. It is not uncommon [3] to find the requirements placed so high as to make relationships that count as relationships of love a very rare commodity. The account of love given is intended to display only what one must think of as involved in thinking of a relationship as love. For instance, it is g-necessary that a case of love involves concern. The person who thinks of himself as loving another, and who at some time sees himself as having failed to act as concern requires, must (g-necessarily) think of himself as having failed. He must see himself as being under a *prima facie* obligation to make excuse. If the person does not see the relation as one of love, he may not see his failure to display concern as anything for which excuse need be made. One does not have an obligation to display to just any acquaintance the sort of concern that loving involves. While we can thus display what is involved in thinking of a relationship under the concept of love, we have no criterial test for 'love' simply because there are no public, objective standards as to the degree of concern, respect, etc., that is required to constitute love. In the case studies that follow we will see something of the consequences of this fact.

II

Case One: Love and Responsibility

This first case will be constructed around conflicting theories or 'pictures' of love. On one picture of love, a picture most prominent in the romantic tradition, love is seen as a feeling or emotion which simply overcomes one with an all-conquering force. The lover is held to be a victim of his passion. And, if the lover can avoid giving in to his passion, it is not genuine. This picture will be called the involuntaristic one.

I have referred to the above as a 'picture' of love. The reason for so doing is to avoid begging the question that the term is used or could consistently be used by those who would offer this picture in a manner consistent with the picture. For instance, someone might claim that 'red' is the name of a kind of purely private mental impression. It might be argued that no one uses the term in this way and that no one could use a term in this way. In my terminology this could be summed up by saying that this person has an erroneous picture of the concept he in fact possesses.

According to another picture, call this one the 'voluntaristic' picture, love is seen as a deliberate, volitional commitment to another. It is this sort of picture that has at times been appealed to in justifying arranged marriage. The partners once selected and brought together will, it is felt, come to love one another if they make a sincere exercise of will.

We can see how subscribing to one of these pictures can have a practical impact on one's personal relationship. For, on the involuntaristic picture, to be in love is to be in a state of diminished responsibility. Once one is in the grip of love, one may act out of passion in ways that one cannot help. The picture is rarely held in this categorical form. Most commonly on this picture, love is taken as a force, difficult to resist, which comes not of the agent's choice and brings not total absence of responsibility but the diminishing of culpability for acts done out of love. This picture is to be found in the writings of George Sand. Interesting illustrations of the effects of adopting it can be found in the far from simple relations of the Herzens to the Herweghs (and others). Under the sway of George Sand, the protagonists, in what can only be described as an eternal polygon, followed courses of action which they themselves regarded as *prima facie* undesirable, involving as they did considerable unpleasantness for other parties. But acting out of love and seeing love in terms of the involuntaristic picture, they saw themselves as not culpable for these consequences. Or, more accurately, they saw themselves as less culpable than they would have seen themselves if the acts had not been done in the throes of love.

One possible impact of the voluntaristic picture is seen in the context of unobtainable love. In the merry-go-round of relationships in Iris Murdoch's *Bruno's Dream*, one of the protagonists, Lisa, is smitten with love for Miles who is unobtainable. Danby, who is presented as seeing love in an involuntaristic manner, loves Lisa. Lisa emphatically does not love him. However, Lisa, presented as subscribing to a voluntaristic picture, simply decides, when it becomes clear that Miles is indeed unobtainable, to cure herself by taking up with Danby and by coming to love Danby. Of course, when she reveals this to Danby, with his rather more romantic picture of things, he is, to say the least, puzzled and sceptical. Danby thinks that either she loves Miles, and if so cannot volitionally pull off what she is attempting, or that she can pull this off and hence does not love Miles. Lisa thinks of herself as both genuinely and passionately loving Miles and as capable of transferring this sort of affection volitionally to another.

Both of these pictures have some basis in the conceptual facts about love as a look at the LCRs will reveal. For instance, among the LCRs are the relations of respect, affection and attraction. The involuntaristic picture calls attention to these. One may identify the presence of affection, attraction and respect in terms partly of patterns of volitions. A crude example of this would be concluding that someone is attracted to another because he regularly does things with the intent of being in the presence of this person. But there is a sense in which these feelings are not subject to volitions. For, I cannot here and now decide to feel or not to feel attraction for some given person. I can decide to try and see the girl next door, I cannot decide to be attracted to her. Of course, my deciding to go and see her may be evidence of a degree of attraction. Being attracted involves wanting. I do not decide my wants, I have them and decide on the basis of them to do or not to do various actions. I might decide to give these sorts of feelings the best chance of developing. I focus my attention on the given person, I get to know them intimately, I try to dwell on their good points, and so on. Whether this will lead to attraction, only time will tell. Similarly, I can attempt to put myself in the worst position for the continuation of current feelings of attraction. I join the foreign legion, I associate intimately with other persons, I focus on the given person's worst characteristics and so on. Time and effort may bring success.

Attention to other of the LCRs will bring out the conceptual basis of the voluntaristic picture. For instance, consider commitment. A commitment is something that I can here and now decide to take up. I can promise to commit myself forever to another, I can promise always to be concerned. I cannot, in the same way, promise to be always attracted to another.

On the basis of the account given of love, we can reject any 'picture' which allows only voluntaristic elements or only involuntaristic elements. But granted this, different individuals are free to give different stress to the importance of different LCRs in their conception of love. Someone can give more prominence to the aspects of love involving attraction, than to commitment. This is likely to reveal itself in the selection of paradigms this person would offer. Someone else can give more importance to commitment. There is no conceptual resolution of the question as to which features are more important. The concept is not determinate in this way. We can uncover the features which anyone's conception of love must have in order to be a conception of love at all. However, within these confines one is free to stress passion or commitment.

Case Two: Constancy of Love

Suppose that Jude and Jan are two persons of the same or opposite sex who have been having an intense affair over a period of time. Mutual declarations of love have been made and all concerned regard the relationship as entirely satisfactory. Until, that is, Jude announces the demise of his love for Jan. The following dialogue ensues:

Jan: 'What do you mean, you don't love me anymore! Have I done anything, said anything?'

Jude: 'No, it's just that my feelings for you have changed.'

Jan: 'Why? I don't understand. Have I changed in your eyes? Have you changed? What is it?'

Jude: 'No. It's not anything like that. We're still the same people. It's just that . . . well, the old intensity of feeling just isn't there anymore, that's all."

Jan: 'You flirt! You never really loved me at all. It's just been an adventure. Look, read this, this is what love is: "Love is not a feeling. Love is put to the test, pain not. One does not say: 'That was not true pain or it would not have gone off so quickly.' " [4]

To this Jude replies with a recitation of 'A Woman's Constancy' and 'The Broken Heart' in which Donne describes 'true' love which flourishes and passes in a single day. Jude adds: 'You admit that there was nothing in my former behaviour and attitude to suggest a lack of love. What has time got to do with it? Love isn't any less true for having been short-lived.'

It may make a difference to Jan whether she (he) decides that Jude did or did not love her. Deciding that it was love may incline her to view the current situation just with regret for the passing of Jude's love. Deciding that Jude never loved may incline her to think of Jude as having operated under false pretences and to see herself as having been trifled with. As we shall see, the various LCRs differ in their temporal aspects. Thus it may be that Jude and Jan are in a sense disagreeing at cross purposes in that they may be operating with conceptions of love that give different stress to the importance of particular LCRs. Some LCRs, like respect and affection, may be imagined to flourish and pass in a relatively short period of time. Some act or feature of a person might call forth feelings of respect or affection. Some later revelations may reveal that things are not as they appeared, thus ending the respect or affection. If the time span is sufficiently long, I think we would allow that affection can simply fade away without there being any particular occurrence which is seen as ending the affection. Perhaps Jude found some things about Jan intriguing which lose their mystery on constant exposure. However, if the time span during which affection is .thought to be involved is short enough, we have to think of some things having happened, some realization having occurred, which can be described as the reason for the withdrawal of affection. If an apparent affection begins in the evening and evaporates in the morning and if the person involved cannot point to something real or imagined which serves as a reason for the withdrawal of affection, we would be inclined to view the affection as merely apparent.

Concern and commitment, on the other hand, seem significantly different in this respect from respect and affection. For it would seem that genuine concern or commitment cannot be terminated simply by some revelation about or change in the object of that concern or commitment. We are inclined to accept: 'I felt affection for her so long as I thought she was pure and innocent' but not, 'I was really concerned for her welfare so long as I thought she was pure and innocent.' Being genuinely concerned or committed seems to involve a willingness on my part to extend that concern or commitment to the person even if I have been mistaken about that person with regard to some feature of her that led to the concern, and even if that person ceases to have those features that led me to be concerned or committed to her. I do not want to suggest that there is a total asymmetry between these pairs of relations. But to some extent, one measure of the degree of concern or commitment at a time, is the time it extends and its constancy in the face of alteration. And the measure of affection at a time is more the way it disposes me to act at that time and not through some period of time.

To return to Jude and Jan. It may be that Jude has a picture of love which construes love as just a feeling which can come and go. In declaring his love he did not think of himself as taking on any commitments. If the account of love provided in this paper is at all near the mark, we see that he has failed to see what the concept involves and has possibly misled Jan in his declarations. Or, it may be the case that while Jude and Jan both see that love involves the satisfaction of the LCRs they have different conceptions, Jude giving less stress to affection than commitment than Jan does. As we saw in case 1, there is no conceptual resolution of this sort of difference. Allowing this freedom to legislate within certain bounds does not mean that each conception is equally appropriate. Concepts are tied to forms of life. Just as our concept of love is tied to the fact that we are sexual beings, it is also tied to general facts about social organization. Thus, someone like Donne in opting for a short-range conception of love would appear to be opting for a form of life in which personal relations are diverse, changing and not closely tied to long-term responsibilities. In a society which institutionalizes personal relations and attempts to tie them to long-term responsibilities in the form of children, it is not surprising that many opt for long-range conceptions of love which lay stress on commitment.

Case Three: Multiple Person Love

Much is made of the particularity of love. It seems commonly felt that if A is in intimate realtions with both B and C, whatever the state of that relationship is, it is not one of love. We have this on authority as diverse as André le Chapelain and E. A. Gellner.[5] Apparently proposition 3 of le Chapelain's code of love was: no one can give himself to two loves. I want to consider whether anything in the concept of love rules out multiple person love relations. By a multiple person love relation, or MPLR, I mean some social set-up in which a person is in intimate relations with more than one person, each of whom he *claims* to love. According to Fromm, Jaspers and other moralists, MPLRs are ruled out as relations of love by the 'very nature (or essence) of love'. This seems rather strong. What we have here in fact is an attempt for normative purposes to enforce a range of paradigms, i.e. those which do not involve MPLRs. I will suggest that there is nothing in the concept of love which rules out MLPRs as relations of love. Any move to rule out the MPLRs will be a legislative one.

No doubt there are severe practical difficulties involved in staging a MPLR. The protagonist in such a situation is apt to find himself spread a little thin if he attempts to provide the sort of concern, interest, commitment and so on which we take love to involve. In his paper on sexual perversion Nagel has elaborated on some of the complexities involved in staging a multiple person sexual relationship that would approach the paradigms of non-multiple person sexual relations. Such complexities are bound to increase dramatically in any MPLR. But, that it will be difficult to bring off does not show that it is in principle impossible. And there may be those like the carpenter in Agnes Varda's film *Le Bonheur* who find it as easy to do for two persons as for one, what love requires.

Difficulties are most apt to arise if the set-up is not mutual all round. By being mutual all round I mean that each person in the set-up claims to love each other person involved. Suppose Jude thinks of himself as loving both Jan and Joe. Jude, Jan and Joe may be of the same or different sex. Jan and Joe not only loathe each other, they are most unhappy about Jude's divided affection. We may feel that Jude cannot be really concerned for both Jan and Joe if he continues this relationship in a manner which clearly distresses them. But probably all that is required for Jude to be thought of as loving both Jan and Joe is that he be thought of as distressed at their distress. Jude may think, say, that more happiness is to be had all around by this shared affection than by one of them having his whole concern and affection. In any event, to show that love is not so exclusive as to rule out multiple love relationships we need only imagine a set-up that is mutual all round.

For those like Jaspers, who claims in his *Philosophie* that 'He only does love at all who loves one specific person', we might suggest the following thought experiment. Consider that all factors involved in loving, excepting any reference to numbers, are satisfied to a high degree by the pair of persons, A and B, and by the pair, C and D. What grounds could one have for retracting a description of these cases as cases of love when it is discovered that B and D are the same person? The only grounds for ruling out such a case would seem to be an *ad hoc* rule that love is necessarily a one to one relationship. While Jaspers and Fromm are entitled to make up their own rule here, should they wish, it cannot be presented as a fact about the nature or essence of love. Of course, the desirability of multiple love does not follow from its possibility.

I have tried in this paper to sketch some conceptual features of love and to illustrate the role these features, and pictures of these features, play in judgments about personal relations. And if my account of the case studies is at all plausible, coming to accept a philosophical analysis of the concept of love may bear on how we think about our personal relations and may, in affecting how we think about them, affect the state of the relationship itself, though the affects are unlikely to be of a Sartrian magnitude. The variability in possible conceptions of love has ruled out the sort of precise and determinate conceptual relations that philosophers are prone to seek. Because of this indeterminacy, how one must (conceptually) think about love drifts imperceptibly into how one does generally think about love. Crossing this boundary can give rise to the worst sort of arm-chair psychology. But then to shy away from the boundary for fear of crossing is not entirely satisfactory either.

One final, and perhaps pessimistic, note. To show that an analysis of love is relevant to practical dealings in personal relations, would not in any way demonstrate that beneficial results would accrue for the lover or the beloved from the utilization of such knowledge. Ibsenian life lies may be productive of the greater happiness.[6]

NOTES

1. Some beginnings towards such an explication can be found in Thomas Nagel's paper, 'Sexual Perversion', *Journal of Philosophy*, 66, 1969, pp. 5-17.
2. E. A. Gellner, 'Ethics and Logic', *Proceedings of the Aristotelian Society*, 55, 1955, pp. 157-78.
3. In this regard see Erich Fromm's *The Art of Loving*, London, Allen & Unwin, 1957 and José Ortega y Gasset's *On Love . . . Aspects of a Single Theme*, trans. Toby Talbot, London, Jonathan Cape, 1967.
4. L. Wittgenstein, *Zettel*, Berkeley, University of California Press, 1967, p. 89e.
5. Gellner, op. cit., p. 159.
6. Since this paper was written I have come to regard this account of love as in many ways too simplistic.

Personal Love

Robert R. Ehman

In the measure that we detach ourselves from our roles in immediate social life and develop our own subjectivity and our sensitivity to the subjectivity of others, we become aware of ourselves and others as unique personalities and thereby become touched by the possibility and appeal of personal love. Personal love is the most radical attempt to transcend the solitude of our separate self and to participate in an intimate common life with another self. For this reason, it presupposes an awareness of the separate self both in our own case and in the case of another. The mere child is incapable of personal love in the full sense even though the full and wondrous unity of parent and child recollected from our earliest days serves as a model of love; and in one respect love can be seen as an attempt to recover the closeness of childhood familial life. While there are many who never realize personal love in their own life, they nevertheless feel its absence as a peculiar lack and are in this sense involved with it. Those who anxiously turn away from love and protect themselves against it witness to its peculiar power in their very evasion of it. In its inescapable relevance to the human self, it is as fundamental as morality, work, play, and death. The understanding of personal love is on this account essential to an understanding of the self.

However, although personal love fulfills an otherwise unavoidable lack in our life, it opens us to radical pain and suffering and never fulfills the whole of its promise. Hence, while it promises the highest personal happiness and for many persons is an essential ingredient in genuine happiness, it often delivers us over to sorrow and disappointment for which it has no defense or comfort. Moreover, although the lover hopes to achieve an untroubled security in his relation to another on the model of his idealized recollection of childhood, he in fact finds himself confronted with and at the mercy of the independent attitude of the other. Further, the lover might fail to recognize the intrinsic limits of love since there is nothing in love itself to announce them. He might in the blindness of his love shatter himself against the ultimate limits of union with another and be thrown back upon himself with a more acute sense of loneliness and isolation than anyone else. He will find that however close he comes to his beloved, he still feels distant and alone and can never bridge the gap between himself and the other. The lover attempts to put his love above the usual scale of values and to free it from the relativity

From *The Personalist,* Vol. 49 (Winter, 1968), pp. 116-141. Reprinted by permission of the author and the editor.

of being merely one value commensurable with others. However, he can never escape from the demands of the other dimensions of his social life or from the appeal of other values; and he cannot fully carry out his aim of putting the relation to his beloved above all else. Finally, the lover seeks a relationship with his beloved that cuts beneath the roles and functions in terms of which he ordinarily comports himself toward others and seeks to relate to his beloved as she is in her uniqueness behind roles and masks. However, in the same manner as others, the beloved tends to vanish behind roles and masks; and the lover can never be sure that he relates to her as she really is. Even when they attempt to strip off their masks for one another and disclose their naked selves, both the lover and beloved tend to fall into simply another role and to present a facade rather than their unique self. From the point of view of love, other modes of social life appear superficial and constraining; from the point of view of these other modes, personal love appears as a threat since it puts itself outside of them and fails to respect the limits of their forms and rules.

The main philosophical interpretations of love view it as an instance of a more general project with a basis and aim which are species of the basis and aim of more generic modes of existence. Thus classical and Christian philosophers regard love as essentially an ethical relationship and interpret the basis and aim as falling under those of ethical relationships in general. For thinkers in both of these traditions, love reduces to lust in the measure that it forgets or conflicts with valid ethical principles. They deny that love is autonomous. Hence, while they admit that the original choice of a beloved is not based solely on ethical considerations, they hold that love is fulfilled only in marriage or some other institution that is regulated by the valid rules of society and objectively based on the respect for the other as an ethical person. Freud and Sartre in recent times have sought for more fundamental categories in which to interpret the distinctive nature of love. However, they too deny the autonomy and irreducibility of the erotic. For Freud, love is a form of sexual desire to be understood primarily from the perspective of biological sexual drives in their interaction with social reality. In the measure that love appears to transcend mere sexual desire, it is simply a "sublimated" and modified version of sexual desire. The basis of love on the Freudian view is the sexual attractiveness of the object; and the aim is the sexual act. For Sartre, on the other side, love is one of several alternative projects by which we attempt to come to terms with our being for others. The basis is the other's threat to our freedom; and the aim is the recovery and mastery of our being for the other.[1]

In this paper, I shall put radically into question the claim that personal love is a mere species of either ethical relationships, sexual desire, or the dialectical struggle to dominate the other. In the first part of my discussion, I shall describe the distinctive basis and aim of personal love and show that these are irreducibly other than those of the other forms of relationship to which love is subordinated in the traditional discussions. I shall argue that the basis is the unique individual style of life and feeling of the beloved and that the aim is a sharing of the private and intimate dimension of life. The distinctive basis and aim of love bestow central importance on precisely the dimensions of the self which are incidental from other perspectives. In the second part of my discussion, I shall turn to the dilemmas that arise in the realization of love. The full phenomenon of love is not found in its mere meaning but includes in addition the tensional relation between the meaning and the concrete fulfillment. The description of the dilemmas that arise in the concrete realization provide further evidence for our interpretation of the meaning and at the same time point up the ultimate limits of love. Only by attending to the relation between the aim and the concrete realization is it possible to understand the anxiety, frustration, and disillusionment that arise from the radical attempts to fulfill the erotic ideal.

In asserting our love for a person, we single out the person and raise her above the field of the social relations and obligations in terms of which we comport ourselves toward others. The assertion of love implies that the beloved has a value for the lover above that of others and that the lover regards his relation to his beloved as more important than his other relationships. In the measure that the lover fulfills the ideal demands of love, he is forced to concentrate his love on a single person. For although he might put two or more persons ahead of all others, he cannot put two persons absolutely first in his life; and this is what love demands. The beloved ought to have a *unique* place in his life. When a person finds that she shares love with others, she feels jealous and deceived, not because she is selfish or possessive, but because this goes against the ideal of love itself. The distinctive joy of being loved is that of finding oneself singled out as a unique individual for special evaluation. When the lover admits that his beloved is merely one of several whom he counts as equal, he takes back his claim to love her.

In the presence of our beloved, we feel in the presence of a supreme and wondrous value. The emotional affection for the beloved is not a mere blind force but a disclosure of the person as is evidenced by the fact that we feel as though we know the person we love more intimately than we know others. The love appears to be an experience of the most concrete personal reality of the beloved. The idea that love is a gratuitous or arbitrary commitment or a blind passion fails to do justice to the feeling of value in the presence of the beloved. If love were simply an arbitrary commitment, faithfulness to the beloved would reduce to faithfulness to our own commitments, and the beloved would be a mere occasion for us to prove our own consistency. On the other hand, if love were blind passion, it would not even make sense to demand faithfulness since in this case it would be a mere aberration without valuational basis which would come and go as an illness or hypnotic spell. The ideal faithfulness of love is based on the permanence of the value at the root of our love. In the measure that a person's love develops and focuses on a single person to the exclusion of others, he will feel that the basis is something unique to his beloved and goes beyond all repeatable qualities that the person shares with others. For this reason, he will not be satisfied with attempts to provide reasons for his love or to describe the valuational basis. He will tend to claim that his love is based on nothing less than the unique personality and style of the beloved. However, even though this be the case, repeatable traits will be relevant and will be the grounds of the initial attraction. Moreover, even the lover cannot fully reveal the unique concrete personality of his beloved; and although this might be the ideal basis of his love, it will always transcend his grasp, and his actual attitude toward his beloved will be rooted in more general and less concrete values. He might *mean* to love the person only for what she is in her peculiar individual reality but he will always in fact love her for qualities that are in some degree general.

In raising the issue of the role of repeatable qualities, it is important to distinguish the grounds of initial attraction from the grounds of deeper love, even though we never escape from repeatable qualities even in deeper love. The repeatable intellectual, moral, social, aesthetic, and sexual traits of a person are fundamental to our initial attraction even though we do not necessarily choose the person who is most desirable from the perspective of any of them. Hence, we might single out a person because of his moral goodness, his high station, his intelligence, or his good looks or again because of his daring immorality, his low station, his slowness, or his ugliness. The role of sexual attractiveness is in every case central; and in the initial stages, there is no clear distinction between love and sexual desire. The traits that erotically attract us to the person are traits that make him sexually attractive, even though sexual attractiveness is not reducible to the possession of any given traits. The person is perceived as having certain sexual potentialities and has a distinct value as a sexual object which is not wholly dependent on other traits, even though there might be important correlations. When we select a brilliant, handsome person as an erotic object, envy and esteem and aesthetic sensitivity play an important role; when, on the other side, we choose someone without these qualities, sympathy, benevolence, and desire to dominate play important roles. The notorious difficulty that we have in the effort to persuade someone to love (or not to love) a certain person by pointing to his personal qualities does not imply that these are irrelevant and that the lover has insight into something more fundamental; it is rather a result of the fact that given qualities do not play a constant or predictable role. The same qualities that attract one person to another repel a third.

However, although the general qualities are relevant to our initial attraction, they are too changeable and too general to serve as the basis for love in the full sense; and the lover attempts to penetrate beneath them to the unique personality of the beloved. The fact that love is ideally independent of fundamental changes in the repeatable qualities

of a person has led to the claim that our love is altogether unconditioned by any empirical considerations and is addressed to the person
in his ideal personal value. However, to regard love in this manner is
abstract. The promise to love a person *no matter what* would be a blind
and fanatical commitment to a person in his abstract identity rather
than in his full concreteness. If no change in or action of the person
were relevant to our love for him, our love would be directed toward an
abstract idea and not a real concrete person. While in the deepest forms
of love, we continue to love a person in spite of fundamental changes
in his age, appearance, health, social position, and even talents and
moral character, we would feel that our love is baseless if we were no
longer able to communicate our intimate feelings with her, no longer
felt that we were "close" to her and "attuned" to her, and no longer
shared the same "sensitivity" to things or the same "tastes." In order to
love a person, we must delight in her presence and in the peculiar
manner that she responds to us and to other things. There is a serious
question as to whether we can continue to love a person for whom we
no longer feel sexual desire. The sexual desire follows from our love;
and the very features of her personal style that lead us to love a person
will lead us to desire her even though in some cases we might no longer
be able to fulfill our desire. In illness, age, or other disability, it might
no longer be possible to become sexually united with the person we
love. However, a genuine lover will feel this as a lack; and he will still
desire union even when it is impossible. The lover indeed will still
desire the beloved after her death. The sexual is a fundamental mode
in which we participate in the personal being of the beloved and share
our life with her.

The basis of our love for a person therefore shows itself to be the
distinctive manner in which the person responds to us and to the world
that we share. The style of the person is realized in ever-changing
circumstances and occasions and is made up of countless individual
responses and gestures that we can never fully describe. The general
descriptions that we give of the person always fall short of the concrete
actions and manner of life which we feel in her presence and which
ever again arouses our love for her and leads us to desire to be with
her. The very fact that it takes time to reveal the individual style of
life of a person means that we can never in the strict sense love a
person at first sight. The basis of genuine love takes time to be revealed. At first sight, we might indeed be sexually attracted to the
person and impressed with her in numerous other ways; we might even
catch a glimpse of her whole manner of life and find that we enjoy
being with her. However, in order to raise this initial attraction to
genuine love, we must put it to the test of time and see whether the
attraction lasts and is based on something more fundamental than some
quality that is easily seen and which is liable soon to vanish. The deeper
and purer our love for a person the more deeply it is based on the
qualities of the person that are at once most unique and most per-

manent. The personal identity of the beloved as beloved is the identity of her personal style of responding to the feelings and actions of
her lover and to the things that they share with one another.

In the same way that there is in the strict sense no love at first sight,
there is no purely unrequited love. If a lover has never had the opportunity to share his life with his beloved, has never been able to establish
an emotional and valuational attunement with her, he cannot in the
full sense love her. He might, to be sure, desire to know her and feel
assured that if only she would open herself up to him, he could love
her. However, in this case, he is in fact in love with an idealized version
of the person, not the actual person herself. For he does not and cannot
love her as she actually is but only as he imagines she might be. The
sorrow in this case is not in the strict sense sorrow over non-reciprocity
but sorrow over the failure of the other to be a person we can love.
While we might long for a person who turns away from us and feel
that life is worthless without her, we are in fact longing only for an
ideal and not for an actual reality. In the same manner as an insane
person, we give the imaginary an even higher emotional value than
the real. Thus while reciprocity is not a condition of our desiring a
person and even wishing to love her, it is nevertheless a condition of
genuine love and even of the experience of the person which can put
our original desire for her to the test and distinguish illusion from
reality in respect to it.

While our love for a person is certainly a factor in determining our
concrete obligations to her, it is already evident that the basis of love
is irreducibly other than that of moral obligation. For the basis of love
is the unique concrete personality of the beloved and the basis of moral
obligation is our respect for the person as a person. The fundamental
requirement of love is to raise the beloved above others and to give
her a privileged status in our life so long as she retains the personal
style of life which serves as the ground of our love for her. The fundamental requirement of morality in contrast is to treat all persons as having equal worth and to justify all special treatment of a person by
reference to universally valid principles. In putting the beloved ahead
of others, the lover might at any time find himself in conflict with
acknowledged obligations to others; and there is always something immoral in the privilege and attention that the lover gives to the beloved
at the expense of others who might have an even higher moral claim
on the beloved. The lover finds himself torn between the demands of
his love and the demands of his moral obligations to others which count
for nothing from the point of view of his love. The lover might indeed
demonstrate his love by violating moral demands in his treatment of
others in order to give his beloved a special place in his life. There are
even some cases, as we shall have occasion to discuss, in which the lover
remains with the beloved even though he morally ought to renounce
the relationship and the relationship is morally degrading. A person
might find that he is closer to another than to anyone else and finds

more delight in her company than in the company of others even though the other degrades him and causes him pain and suffering. The pain and suffering of the lover at the hands of his beloved might be the manner in which he shares in her life and realizes his love for her. The personal style that he adores might be one that causes him pain.

Moral deliberations ideally take into account *all* of the empirical factors relevant to a given decision, action, or relationship to another; love takes into account only the factors that constitute the personal style of life of the beloved and motivate our love for her. Morality must take into account a wide range of factors precisely because it forbids our treating one person in the same empirical situation and status in a more favorable manner than others. In order to assure that we treat each person according to principles valid for all, we must take into account all relevant factors. Love neglects factors that play a part in morality because it cares nothing for general principles and fairness; it singles out an individual for special concern simply on the basis of her personality and of the delight that we take in being close to her. For love, all persons are not equal and the beloved simply as an individual is more important than others. For morality, on the other hand, the individual in his mere individuality is incidental. Hence, even when the lover acts in a manner compatible with moral demands, his actions are as such independent of them. In the measure that he takes love seriously, he cannot be counted on to act on moral principles even when he is a man of sound moral character. When a man "falls in love," his character is deeply altered and together with his beloved he retreats to a world that stands apart from the universal ethical reality. *Not sure I agree*

In its very respect for the person as a person, morality is in a peculiar sense impersonal since it fails to acknowledge the uniqueness of the individual and to place the importance on his feeling and moods that he himself or his lover does. When a person is treated merely in accordance with morality, he feels that he is treated impersonally and abstractly without full consideration for his individual reality. Fairness, justice, and respect come to him simply as a person; and he is aware that insofar as they are genuinely moral, they apply him in the same way as to others. The special delight that comes from being loved arises from the recognition that the lover singles us out and affirms us in our unique personality and not simply as a human person in general. Friendship might seem to be an exception to the principle that moral relationships fail to focus on our individual personality. However, friendship is not supreme and incommensurate with our other public relationships in the manner of personal love and is in principle open to all those with whom we share the same values and interests. The ideal of friendship does not permit us to take the personal style of life of the other and our delight in sharing his personal life as the sole basis of friendship. Friendship is based on respect for the other as a person specified by a sharing of common interests and ends. The personal style of the friend is merely one factor; and the choice of a friend is properly a moral choice: anyone with a certain character and under certain conditions ought to be accepted as a friend. The moment that a person takes the sharing of the personal side of the life of his friend as his ultimate motive in his relationship and puts his relation to his friend simply as the individual he is beyond the sphere of his other relationships, he moves beyond friendship to genuine personal love; and he dramatically reveals the distinction between friendship and love.

While friendship rules out personal love, marriage does not, and, for this reason, the relation between love and marriage is more complex than that between love and friendship. However, although we might fulfill love in marriage and in this manner bring love into conformity with ethical reality, marriage is nevertheless independent of love and love is independent of marriage. For as an ethical relationship, marriage is based on the commitment and obligation to care for, remain faithful to, and to live with a person who reciprocally fulfills the same obligation with respect to us. Marriage is essentially an ethical agreement; and although love might be a relevant condition, it is never the sole basis of the obligation to maintain the agreement and persons might be obligated to remain married even when they no longer or never did love one another and even when they love someone else. The absence of love would in every case invalidate marriage if marriage were *simply* an institutional fulfillment of love. In a given society, it might be hard to realize love apart from marriage. However, this does not in the least imply that the *valuational* basis of the two is the same or that marriage enters essentially into the ideal of love. The independence of love and marriage is dramatically brought to the fore in homosexual love. There is nothing in the pure ideal of love itself to rule out love between those of the same sex. The sexuality of the person is simply one factor; and it is possible to take an equal delight in sharing the personal life of a person of the same sex as in sharing the life of a person of the opposite sex. The sexual attraction for a person of the same sex might be even more intense than for a person of the opposite sex. If sexuality itself transcends the natural law that opposites attract, it is certainly possible for love to do so. There is nothing erotically wrong with homosexual love even though it might be morally or socially wrong. The erotic and moral evaluations are independent. The denial of homosexual love and the attempt to restrict love to courtship and marriage is an effort on the part of the ethical reality to subordinate love to ethics and to deny its autonomy. The result in many cases is radical conflict. The very concern of morality to subordinate love to itself betrays an implicit awareness that love is an independent reality.

There is a wondrous and inseparable connection between love and sexual desire, as we have already had occasion to remark. However, there is nothing in sexual desire alone or in its interaction with social reality to explain the ideal of love for a single person. The sexual drive is originally highly indiscriminate and admits of a wide range of objects. The restriction to a narrow range comes as a result of a long process of repression. However, the repression might not go so far as to repress desire for all but a single person; and in any case, the *ideal* of exclusive love cannot be accounted for as simply a product of repression. The repression might lead us to limit our sexual desires in accordance with it but it cannot generate the ideal. Moreover, the ideal exists even when there is no social pressure to conform to it and might itself be a factor in the repression and restriction of sexual desire; it is certainly not in every case a mere consequence of repression. The lover might have to inhibit and restrict his sexual impulses in order to fulfill the ideal demands of his love.

While love might take the sexual up into itself, there remains a clear distinction between the basis of sexual desire by itself and the basis of genuine love. The basis of the one is found in momentary qualities that might at any time be shared by a plurality of diverse persons. The most important of these qualities are physical appearance and style of sexual conduct. The basis of love, on the other side, is found only in the concrete style of the personal life of the person which can only be revealed over time and is distinctive of the single person. From the perspective of sexual desire, the other person is of value only as a sexual object; and the person motivated by sexual desire alone has no further interest in the other person. There is nothing in sexuality to lead to permanence in the relationship; and indeed from a purely sexual point of view, a series of new and even more exciting sexual partners is more desirable than faithfulness to one. When we attempt to interpret love as a mere form of sexual desire, we find ourselves unable to do justice to the exclusiveness, permanence, and concern for the other in his full concreteness that are essential to genuine love.

When we put to Sartre the question of the basis of love, the answer might at first sight appear to be the freedom of the other. The freedom of the other is the power to make us an object, to transcend and outstrip us, and to put our own being into question. The disclosure of his freedom motivates our attempt to recover the dimension of our being that he holds under his control by making ourselves a supreme value in his world and a limit and final end of his freedom. However, although the freedom of the other is a necessary condition of the project of love, it is not the valuational basis. The freedom of the other is not a value but a *threat* that we seek to master. The valuational basis of love for Sartre is not located in the other at all but is a value of our own being: it is the value of being affirmed as a supreme value and of recovering our alienated being for the other. The lover therefore seeks the supreme valuation for himself that he ought to give to the beloved and is concerned with the value of his own self, not with that of the other. The beloved becomes incidental. Thus Sartre fails to account for the feeling of adoration and even worship that the lover has for his beloved and therefore fails to account for the value that the lover attributes to his beloved. Moreover, although Sartre has no difficulty accounting for the desire of the lover to be the sole object of the beloved, he cannot account for the demand on the lover to give his love to a single person. There is nothing in Sartre's view to prohibit a person's projecting love in relation to numerous persons; indeed for Sartre love appears to be simply a basic mode in which we relate to the other in general. The beloved might be anyone for whom we exist.

When we raise the issue of the aim of love, we must take as our clue what we have already discovered as the basis of love. If the basis is the personal intimate style of action and feeling of the beloved, the aim must be to participate in and share in the personal life of the beloved. In the same manner as a friend will seek to pass his time with and be in the presence of his friends, the lover will seek to pass his time with and be in the presence of his beloved; and he will fulfill his love by being with the beloved. However, while the lover will comport himself toward the person he loves in much the same manner that he does toward a friend, there will be something distinctive about his relationship. Unless there is a special aim and content to their relationship, the claim of lovers to be something more for one another than they are for anyone else would be empty and vacuous, a mere claim without reality and truth. The demand that we reserve our love for a single person alone would be meaningless since we could not relate to him in any other manner than we relate to a plurality of persons.

The requirement that the relationship to the person we love be reserved for her alone means that the essential aim of their behavior toward one another must be set apart from aims that can be fulfilled with a plurality of persons. There is no necessary limit in the number of persons with whom we might co-operate in the fulfillment of such universal ends as civic projects, business, art, or knowledge and for this reason, these cannot be the distinctive aims of lovers, even though the lovers might also incidentally pursue them together. Their aim will be to share those aspects of their life which they share with no one else and to constitute a "world" together which is their own alone and in and through which they can share each other's moods and feelings, hopes, and dreams in a manner more intimate than they do with others. In order to fulfill this aim, they will seek to be alone and will cover their relationship in secrecy. They will reveal to each other the side of their self that they reveal to no one else. They will always attempt to express more to each other than they do to others; and for this reason, in the measure that they successfully achieve their aim, a third person will feel left out. He will find that the lovers live in a private world of their own which he cannot fully decipher and in which gestures, words, and things have meanings for them that they do not have for him. From his point of view, the lovers see "too much" in things and make "much ado" about nothing.

In sharing their privacy, lovers give a significance to whims, desires, and moods that receive no recognition in the larger social world. The lover caters to and makes an issue of the purely personal tastes of his beloved and tries to please her simply to please her and not for any further motive. He gives her things, treats her attentively, and is sensitive to her moods and feelings and shows her in countless ways that she counts more for him than others do. There is playfulness in the relation of lovers in that their whole comportment is simply for its own sake and has no further end, is free of fixed universal rules, and is spontaneous, light, and full of delight and transforms the world in which it occurs into a magic world where the beloved is the center. While others might attend to the personal moods and wishes of a person, they do so for some ulterior motive; and a criterion of love is the lack of any further motive in the attention that we pay to the person. For the lover, there is not even a moral ground for making his beloved the center of attention and indeed his action might even go against his moral obligations to others. In many cases, one acts as though one were in love with a person with whom one is not in love in order to manipulate him, seduce him, or to win his favor. The pretense of love in this case is successful in its aim precisely because it is a semblance of the real thing and the real thing is a delight to the person who receives it. There is no one who is totally untouched by the charm of being loved since it fulfills a lack and neglect that is present in other domains of life. Part of the satisfaction of being important and rich is that one receives a semblance of that concern for one's personal whims and feelings that is found in personal love. While the important and rich might in fact be hated, they are treated as though they were loved.

The aim of love is achieved when the lovers retreat by themselves to a personal world apart from the world of everyday social and moral life. They constitute their world by their language, moods, gestures, and actions that have a meaning for them beyond what they have in the everyday world. There is no lover so prosaic and unimaginative that he cannot in some degree transcend the world of the everyday and give a new nuance and tone to the common words with which he expresses his love. When lovers retreat into their own world of meaning, they attain the security and mutual affirmation they fail to find in the public world. However, in this very retreat into a personal world, they show that the aim of love is independent of and even opposed to the moral aim. There are, of course, a wide variety of interpretations of the moral aim but most would agree that one component is the attempt to constitute a common social world in which each person is recognized as being of intrinsically equal worth and treated in a manner valid for anyone in the same circumstances. Morality is in principle opposed to a retreat into a private world in which personal whims, feelings, and moods take precedence over universal obligations. Morality finds a place for love only within the institution of marriage and family life. From the perspective of morality, the aim of love is marriage and children; and both of these are extrinsic from the purely erotic point of view. The aims of morality and love might come into sharp and irreconcilable conflict in cases where the aims of marriage and family life conflict with the pure erotic aim. The conflict might arise when a person loves someone else than the person to whom he is married or loves someone already married to another. In other cases, it arises within marriage when the partners fail to fulfill the ethical duties toward their children or other members of the family because of their retreat into an erotic world that they share alone. They might show their love to one another by putting each other above their children and devaluing their children in favor of their own aims. The presence of children in any case poses a problem for love since it threatens to turn the parents away from each other toward children and to reduce their relationship to a purely ethical project that pursues the common goal of rearing children. From the perspective of love, children are outsiders in the same manner as others. The distinctive aim and fulfillment of love is found in the mutual relation of the lovers themselves and has no room for a third.

While it is impossible to interpret the aim of love in terms of sexuality alone, the fulfillment of the sexual aim is a central act by which lovers achieve their aim of participating in the personal life of each other. The gestures and words of lovers as well as all forms of their bodily contact have a sexual significance in that they point towards the sexual union as the most complete form of the very same personal unity toward which these words, gestures, and actions are themselves directed. In the sexual union itself persons do not come together merely at the "ideal" level of language and meaning but come together in their concrete bodily reality. They become as far as possible one body, and in the measure that the person is his body, they become one person. The significance of sexual union depends on the significance of a person's body; and in the measure that one regards his body as himself, sexual union will be the highest form of personal union. Unless one detaches himself altogether from his body, he will regard sexual union as a vital form of personal union. The sexual union, to be sure, in some cases reduces to a mere means of pleasure or even a means of livelihood as in prostitution. For this reason, we cannot identify the sexual aim with the aims of love; the sexual aim is in any case simply a moment of the full erotic aim. However, the sexual union is never altogether without the significance of a personal union and is always a semblance of love. The peculiar satisfaction that it brings and its peculiar attraction arise in part from the fact that it is never merely a physical union or merely a physiological process but always a sharing in the intimate life of another. The prostitute or other person who must engage in sexual acts without having any attraction for the partner must for this reason detach herself from her body and her sexual life and regard them as alien. However, even she will find in the sexual union an image of genuine participation. The *merely* sexual is a limiting case.

For Sartre, the sexual act and other modes of action by which the lover participates in the life of the person he loves are not a fulfillment of the aim of love. They are merely strategies by which he pursues his proper aim of making himself a supreme value for the beloved and a limit on her freedom. The sexual is taken up as a mere phase of the struggle to dominate the other who threatens our own freedom. In regarding the aim of love as a state of being affirmed and being made a supreme end, Sartre takes it as a state rather than as a manner of life and action and fails to see that the very actions by which we are with our beloved are in fact the fulfillment of our love for him. The lover on Sartre's view never really transcends the circle of his own selfhood and is never genuinely concerned about sharing his loneliness and private selfhood with the person he loves. He is so concerned about himself and so involved in a struggle for domination that he is oblivious to the joy of being together. The lover is in fact concerned about the attitude of the beloved toward him; but not, as Sartre thinks, primarily because he is threatened by her and feels himself alienated by virtue of his existence for her, but rather because he already seeks to be with her and to share his life with her. From the perspective of the aim of love, we find the same failure to recognize the genuinely transcending and ecstatic character of love that we saw in Sartre's account of the object and basis of love.

Given his premises, there is nothing surprising in Sartre's conclusion that the aim of love is unattainable. The aim is selfish and has no place for the reciprocity that is essential to love. For Sartre, love reduces wholly to the desire to be loved; and therefore in the strict sense there is neither a lover nor a beloved. Nevertheless, Sartre's whole account operates with a conception of love as the supreme valuation of the person; and the fact that on Sartre's view, we seek this only for ourselves and never bestow it on another does not in the least mean that he does not conceive of love as supreme valuation. The basic mistake of Sartre is not in his interpretation of the ideal meaning of love but in the attempt to fit love into the general struggle for domination. The very fact that love cannot be realized within the sphere of this struggle ought to lead Sartre to re-examine the framework of his discussion. From the point of view of the struggle for domination, love reduces to pure self-love and leads to the futility that Sartre describes. However, this simply goes to show that love transcends this struggle. In the act by which we perceive the unique value of a person and take delight in her presence and receive back from her our invitation to share the intimate dimension of our life, we leave behind the struggle to dominate and enter into a world of playful freedom. The lovers do not feel alienated by the look of the beloved but rather feel affirmed. They find themselves in each other and abandon all aims in respect to one another but the playful sharing of their inmost life.

When we turn from the pure ideal to the actual reality, we find the inevitable shadow that falls between the ideal and the real. In the pursuit of the aim of his love, the lover comes up against the independence and freedom of his beloved and up against the inescapable demands of the other irreducible dimensions of his social life. The person he loves might fail to reciprocate his initial gestures of love, might turn away after initial acceptance or might use his love as a means of degrading him in favor of herself. Moreover, the beloved might at any time die and leave her beloved alone. The public dimension of our life demands our attention and prevents us from giving ourselves wholly to our relation to the person whom we love. From the perspective of love, there is no answer to the problems posed by the failure of reciprocity and no means to adjudicate the conflict between the claims of love and of the other sides of life. For love, there are no limits of love; and it always experiences limits as an alien necessity against which it thrusts itself in futile pain and suffering. The impulse of love is to persist in its aim in the face of reality even at the cost of a distortion of personality. This naiveté of love is the ultimate ground of the perversions to which it is open and the threat it poses to the dignity and integrity of the person. In its relation to a wider reality, love is fanatical.

While love in its initial immediacy goes out to the beloved without an explicit demand of reciprocity, reciprocity need only be called into question in order for the love itself to be put into question. In the absence of reciprocity, it is not only impossible to fulfill the erotic aim but also impossible to test the truth of the erotic claim. The truth of a claim to love a person can only be shown in the process by which the lover participates over time in the life of his beloved. The unrequited lover may make a show of loving, but in fact he loves a mere unrealized ideal; and to remain faithful to that is not the same as remaining faithful to a concrete person. The mournful longing for another might indeed be easier than actually living with the other since the ideal is without the flaws of reality. The ideal picture of the beloved we can never attain is more perfect than any person we can ever concretely love; and the higher our ideal, the more difficult to love an actual person.

When a person turns away from us, we can at least hope that she will turn back to us and make it possible to put our professed love to the test of actual reality. However, when the beloved dies, we can no longer share in her life. The dead are inaccessible, remote, and unresponsive in a manner more radical than the coldest and most distant living person. There is no hope of ever again communicating with the dead within the horizon of the present life. However, the distance of the dead is not self-imposed. The separation of death is in most cases not deliberate, as another's rejection of our love. The deceased person might have loved us with all her heart and soul right up to the end. From the point of view of love, she is therefore no less worthy of our love after her death than she was during her life. The death of a person does not make her less worthy of our respect and affection since death is in most cases simply something that overtakes a person and therefore does not affect her inner worth. However, from the moment of death, our love for a person reduces to a mere longing and can only be expressed in gestures of respect, in mourning and sorrow, and in turning away from others to the solitude of our being with the dead. There is now loneliness and silence instead of communion and animate speech. In a way, love makes the dead present but the presence is in the form of a heartfelt absence. Love is no comfort for the loss of the dead and holds no answer for it; on the contrary, love makes it the harder to bear. If the lover turns away from his beloved, he will feel that he has betrayed her and allowed her to die a second time; on the other side, when he remains faithful to her, he finds that his love becomes increasingly empty and abstract and finally reduces to a futile gesture. In death, love experiences the absurd negation of its own reality.

There are cases between the full non-reciprocity of absolute rejection or death and the full reciprocity of ideal love. These perverse forms illustrate in a dramatic manner the independence of love and morality. From the point of view of love, they in part fulfill its aim even though from a moral point of view they might be degrading and reprehensible. These are cases in which the beloved uses the love of the beloved in order to dominate and exercise her power over her lover and to receive affirmation at his hands. Her motives belong to the domain of the struggle for power; and they might be understood along the lines that Sartre proposes. The motives of the degraded lover are on the other side quite different. He shares in the personal life of his beloved and therefore in part attains the erotic aim. He has no alternative to degradation but to give up the project of love altogether. The conduct of the sadist toward her lover in this perverted relationship is the precise reverse of that by which she would reciprocate his love and in this respect belongs to the same sphere of life. The sadist does not degrade and humiliate her partner on the level of his public self but on the level of his most intimate personal self. Instead of doing and saying the things that she knows will please him, she does and says those that she knows will hurt him; instead of tenderness and reverence, she shows him cruelty and disdain. She attempts to make him act in an obscene manner; and she abuses him sexually. However, in this very behavior, she shares with him an aspect of her own intimate selfhood and shares in personal life with him. The very pain that she causes him is a source of pleasure to him insofar as it is a mode in which he participates in her life. To give up his pain in this case would be to give up being with his beloved.

The active partner in this cruel game might at first sight appear to be the independent essential reality. For in every act by which her lover humiliates himself in front of her and accepts her abuse, she finds a proof of her own supremacy in the eyes of the lover. However, there is a dialectic in the relationship which makes it less one-sided than it initially appears to be. The beloved appears to maintain her independence and superiority over the lover in the behavior by which she devalues and degrades him. However, she is dependent on her lover for the position that she enjoys. She can put herself above him and subordinate him only so long as he allows it. He might at any time declare his independence and turn her abuse into a futile gesture that no longer strikes home. Moreover, he is himself in some measure aware of his power over his beloved, and this makes the relationship tolerable to him. In the very act by which he submits to her abuse, he plays something of an active role; and in the very interest that she shows in subordinating him, she is dependent on his love for her.

In some cases the sadist loves her victim as much as he loves her; and in these cases she degrades and subordinates him not merely in order to test the love of her beloved but also to try to escape from putting herself in the position he is in. She attempts to prove both to herself and to the other that she is superior to the power of love and is not open to the pain and degradation of being rejected. This futile defensive move arises from the painful realization that a lover is at the mercy of his beloved and is open to being hurt by him. The lover in this case is driven by anxiety in the fact of the possibility of her own humiliation and pain to humiliate and hurt the very person who has the power to humiliate and hurt her. Sadistic love is troubled and reflective and is torn between the ecstatic attraction for the other and anxious self-concern. First love is never sadistic; sadistic love is never naive.

In the same manner that moral and communal domains attempt to subjugate personal love to their own values and ends, personal love endeavors to subordinate these to its own distinctive value and end. In its purity, the ideal of love demands of lovers that they put their relationship to each other first in their lives and devalue other persons, values, and projects in favor of their own personal union. From the perspective of love, personal union with the beloved is the supreme value of life; and in the measure that one is serious about love, one will find oneself in a conflict with the demands of other persons and the demands of other values and tasks. From the perspective of these other realms, love has only a limited validity and is merely *one* relationship on the scale with others. The lover is in fact never *merely* a lover, even though he might desire to be; nor, on the other side, is the person in love fully a moral agent or a member of the larger community. He is torn between both and is inescapably involved with both; and in practice, he is forced to compromise with regard to the demands of both and in this manner falls short of all ideals. In the measure that he attempts to do full justice to the ideal requirements of love, he will turn away from communal life and give up the attempt to make a substantial recognized achievement in the public world; on the other side, in the measure that he attempts to fulfill his moral requirements and contribute to larger goals, he will fail to give his beloved the attention that his love for her demands. If he goes too far toward the pole of the private world of the erotic, he volatilizes his life by cutting himself off from the serious work of the community and morality in favor of the play of mood and sexuality that constitutes the main content of the pure erotic life. If, on the other side, he goes too far toward the pole of the public world of civic and professional life, he neglects his beloved and allows his love to reduce to a mere claim. The very demand that lovers make the purely personal side of their lives the center of focus prevents them from resolving the conflict between substantial achievement and moral responsibility, on the one side, and their love for one another, on the other side, by co-operating on common ventures and projects that have a significance beyond their personal relationship. In the measure that they make something beyond themselves their fundamental aim, they pass beyond the pure erotic. Their love dissolves into the general ethical reality.

From the present perspective, we may conclude with a brief remark regarding the role of personal love in disclosing our own self and the self of the other. In a more radical manner than other forms of experience, personal love reveals the value and uniqueness of the individual person. When a person loves another, he penetrates beneath the public self defined by interchangeable tasks, roles, and functions to the unique style of feeling and action by which the individual fulfills them and the inward life into which he withdraws from them. In aiming at the concrete individual personality of the beloved, the lover, at the same time reveals her personality to the beloved herself and thereby helps to constitute and realize her personality. The beloved first becomes radically aware of her own uniqueness through the eyes of her lover. In this respect, love gives us an affirmation and recognition beyond that which we receive in other forms of relationship. When she reciprocates love, the beloved does the same for her lover in this regard that her lover does for her and thus leads him to a fuller awareness of his own individual being. The lovers teach each other who they are and serve as a conscience for each other. The individuality of a person is covered over and hidden in the general conduct of everyday public life where one tends to become anonymous and to conceive of oneself and be conceived in terms of one's function and status alone. The individual, of course, is not denied in the public life but is rather passed over as insignificant. The individual first becomes central and fully present in personal love.

However, the very individuality of the beloved puts her at a distance since an individual stands apart from everyone else with a center of personal freedom and a perspective all her own. In the measure that the lover becomes aware of the radical uniqueness of his beloved, he will feel separation from her. The separation arises both from his own freedom and from the freedom of the other. They both discover that the dimension of their selves which they share with the other and which constitutes the substance of their relationship is merely an aspect. They are always both something more for themselves and for others than they are for each other even though they might both aim to be the whole world for each other and to put themselves wholly into their personal relationship. They both open to a wider world which relativizes the personal world that they constitute together and both retreat even from that personal world into personal worlds of their own. They never fully succeed in moving wholly out of the public world to the world that they share with each other nor wholly out of the private world of their own unexpressed feelings, desires, and emotions. Hence, while the lovers come together on the level of their concrete individual being and share in the personal side of their lives, opening themselves to each other and treating the other as being as important as their own self, they fall short of full union and in fact reveal their irreducible otherness. The sexual act, where they come closest to full union, is momentary and ephemeral. The magic spell of their union is over at the very point where it appears to have taken the lovers fully outside of themselves and made them really one. The sexual union provides an ecstatic release from the privacy of our own self; and yet its fulfillment throws us back again into the recesses of that very privacy. Not surprisingly, the apartness of persons reveals itself most dramatically in the most radical attempt to transcend it. In revealing the apartness, love reveals the loneliness of our own self and the uniqueness and distinct value of the other which serve as the subjective and objective grounds of its own reality.

NOTE

1. For Sartre's account of love, see *Being and Nothingness* (Translated by Hazel Barnes) Philosophical Library, New York, 1956, pp. 364-379.

On the Christian Concept of Love

D.Z. Phillips

This chapter is selective, and to that extent, arbitrary. There are many concepts of love (despite the Freudian view) and I do not touch on most of them. There is the love involved in lust, romantic love, the love of average respectable marriages, love of friendship, love of beauty, love of God, and so on. I make no attempt to prove the reality of these ideas of love. I take that for granted. What I want to do is to set out certain

D. Z. Phillips, "On the Christian Concept of Love" from *Faith and Philosophical Inquiry* (London: Routledge and Kegan Paul, 1970). Reprinted by permission of the author and the publisher.

problems which arise from *one* idea of love—namely, that found in the Christian commandment to love our fellow men. Certain interpretations of this idea are open to serious moral objections. There is one interpretation of the commandment which avoids these objections, but even this has little, if anything, to say about problems which arise from the nature of human love in certain contexts.

It would be a misunderstanding to look for *the* answer to the problems which I mention in this chapter, since people's answers will be as different as their loves.

Can I be commanded to love? Can I have a duty to love? Kant seemed to think that acting from a sense of duty is acting from the highest motive. But does it make sense to say that I can love a woman out of a sense of duty? Is not this the same as saying that I do not love her at all? True, we often have occasion to point out a husband's obligations to his wife, the parents' obligations to their children, the friend's obligations to his friend. But the occasions on which these reminders are given are those where the relationships referred to have broken down in some way or other: 'You have a duty to your wife. You can't leave her.'—'Yes, I see that. But I can't love her.'

It is one thing to say that these relationships entail obligations, but quite another thing to say that a sense of duty can be the motive for the love which in ideal cases makes these relationships what they are. Again, duties arise and can be met within these relationships ('No. I'd better not stay. I've promised to take my wife out tonight'), but this is not to say that the relationship can be participated in out of a sense of duty.

In what sense, then, do Christians say that we are commanded to love our fellow men? How can we regard love as a duty? Clearly, I am not called upon to love all women as I love my wife, to love all children as I love my own, to love everyone as I love my friends. But if not, what am I called upon to do when told to love my fellow men?

One cannot understand the Christian love of others unless one understands its connection with love of God. The Christian concept of love is very different from the love found in the relationships we have mentioned, where the love depends on the particularity of the relationship. What does this particularity refer to? Consider marriage: 'Wilt thou have *this* woman . . . ?' Am I saying that there is only one girl for you in the world? No! It is not that *this* woman *is* different from all others, but that she *becomes* different from all others in becoming *your wife*. Similarly, my friends are different from other people because they are my friends. But according to Christian teaching, I must love all men because *all men are the same*. They are children of God. But what kind of love is this? '. . . "Thou shalt love." It consists first and foremost in the fact that you must not love in such a way that the loss of the beloved would reveal the fact that you were desperate, that is, that you simply must not love despairingly.' [1]

When the person I love is *this* person rather than another, the death of the beloved is the worst that can happen. This is not so in Christian love of others, since they are loved, not because of their being *these persons* rather than others, but simply because of their *being*. 'The neighbour is your equal. The neighbour is not your beloved for whom you have a passionate partiality. . . . The neighbour is every man. . . . He is your neighbour through equality with you before God. . . .'[2] And again, 'Belief in the existence of other human beings as such is *love*.'[3]

Christian love of fellow men seems to have little in common with the love that exists between husband and wife, parents and children, friend and friend. In many outstanding examples of Christian love—say, St. Peter Claver or St. Vincent de Paul—charity is shown to those whom the charitable person did not know.

What conclusions can be drawn from these differences between the way the concept of love is used in the Christian commandment and the way it is used elsewhere? What I want to do now is to show how certain possible, if not necessary, implications of the Christian concept of love are open to moral and religious objections, and at the same time try to point to an alternative interpretation of the concept which is free from such censure.

Christianity seeks that which is essential in all men. There are inessential things, but in the last analysis, these can be ignored. But what is this essential thing which all men have in common? Their identity as children of God.

> The difference is the confusion of the temporal existence which marks every man differently, but the neighbour is the mark of the eternal—on every man. Take a number of sheets of paper, write something different on each of them so that they do not resemble each other, but then take again each individual sheet, do not be confused by the different inscriptions, hold it up to the light, and then you can see a common mark in them all. And so the neighbour is the common mark, but you see it only by the light of the eternal, when it shines through the differences.[4]

But what is the mark of the eternal? That is the difficult problem. Christians hold that 'the eternal' has been captured in certain specific propositions about God—for example, that God became incarnate in Jesus of Nazareth. It follows, according to them, that what is of eternal importance is that they should try to get all men to give assent to this special revelation of God. As a matter of fact, this conclusion does not follow at all. Even if you believe that you have eternal truth, it does not follow that you ought to proselytize. One may say that something is the eternal truth, but at the same time stress the importance of each man's coming to it for himself. Many Christians seem to think that men have a duty to follow *this* way of life rather than another. This is difficult to understand from a moral point of view. Certainly, we often condemn those who hold moral opinions which are different from our own. We say they are wrong in holding such views. But when the views and actions in question are tied up with a culture different from our own, the position is altered. If I hear that one of my neighbours has killed another neighbour's child, given that he is sane, my condemnation is immediate. (There are exceptions. See Faulkner's *Requiem for a Nun*.) But if I hear that some remote tribe practises child sacrifice, what then? I do not know what sacrifice means for the tribe in question. What would it mean to say I condemned it when the 'it' refers to something I know nothing about? If I did condemn it I would be condemning murder. But murder is not child sacrifice. 'The ethical expression of Abraham's action is that he wished to murder Isaac: the religious expression is that he wished to sacrifice him.' [5]

My moral opinions are bound up with the way of life I lead. Various influences have helped to shape my morality. This does not mean that when I make moral judgments I say anything about the way of life I lead or that the meaning of the moral judgments can be expressed in terms of the influences which, in part, account for them. For example, a person brought up in the Welsh Nonconformist tradition is likely to have strong views on what activities should be allowed on a Sunday—views either in sympathy with or in reaction against the tradition. When he makes his moral judgment on this matter, however, he is not saying anything about the tradition, but about what activities ought to be allowed on a Sunday. I must, on the other hand, understand the significance of actions before I can judge them.[6] My understanding is not limited by one tradition, I understand something of the other traditions within the same culture, however vague my grasp of them may be. For example, in belonging to one tradition of Christian worship one usually has some idea of the other traditions as well. When we consider different cultures, however, the position is altered radically. What should Buddhists do on Sunday? When I do not understand ways of life and worship different from my own, I had better refrain from judging.

But do Christians need to understand? Sometimes they speak as if even within the same culture there were only one morality; as if all one has to determine is whether what one judges is the same as or different from what one believes. If what one judges is the same, it is true; if different, it is false. The question is whether Christianity allows a *serious* consideration of competing moralities and religions. Must it not say that these are part of the inessential in man, the confusing inscriptions which hide from us the common mark in all men—their identity as children of God? But can one speak of competing moralities as incidental and peripheral? Are they not rooted and grounded in the actual ways of life that men pursue?

> The first point to be made is just that there are different moralities, opposing sets of rules of human behaviour. This is because there are different ways of life, different 'movements', each with its own rules of procedure for its members. Such rules, it may be noted, need not have been formulated; but the more important point is that formulated or unformulated, they are not

to be regarded as preceptual or mandatory . . . the moral question is of
how people do behave and not of their 'obeying the moral law'; obedience,
or the treating of something as an authority, is just one particular way of
behaving, the moral characterization of which has still to be given. The
phrase 'how people do behave' may be misleading here. It is not a question
of taking any type of activity in isolation; we do not have a morality until
we have a way of life, a number of ways of behaving that hang together,
that constitute a system—and it is in the conflict of such systems that rules
come to be formulated. From this point of view it might be best to say that
a morality *is* a way of life or a movement; and in that case the person who
spoke in the name of 'morality' would be neglecting to specify the movement he represented.[7]

But am I mistaken in thinking that Christianity does speak in the name
of 'morality', *the* way, *the* truth, and *the* life? These other beliefs and
ways of life must consist of what is inessential. But how far is one justified in ridding men of the inessential in order that they gain the essential
truth? How high a price can be put on truth? If you say that no price is
too high, the logic of persecution is complete. The end justifies the means.
To torture or to kill (the means) is justified by the resultant confession
(the end). On the other hand, you may say that some prices are too high.
Christians say that only free confession is worthwhile. But it is notoriously difficult to know where to draw the line. Persecutors are obsessed
by the idea that a free confession is just out of reach: 'A little more . . . a
little longer . . . and then perhaps . . .' [8] and so on. Because of the supposition that most men confess belief at the hour of death ('Who is to
know what a man says to his God at such a time?') one can never tell
whether the end justified the means. Camus notes that Scheler sees Christian neighbour-love and humanitarianism as two sides of the same coin.
Such love is an excuse for oppression, and Scheler claims that it is always
accompanied by misanthropy. 'Humanity is loved in general in order to
avoid loving anybody in particular.' [9]

But as Camus points out, there is another kind of love of humanity. It
does not involve elevating 'the essential' above all else. It is the love of
humanity of which Ivan Karamazov speaks. Each individual is accepted
as he is. The death of *one* child is too high a price for *harmony*. If anything is essential, it is 'the individual good' as opposed to 'the common
good', 'eternal truth', etc. As Kant expressed the matter, human beings
should be treated '*never merely as means,* but in every case *at the same
time as ends in themselves*'.[10]

Is there an interpretation of the Christian concept of love which is not
open to the moral objections we have mentioned? I think there is. To
show this, it is necessary, of course, to deny that what we have considered
hitherto is the Christian concept of love. Think of Kierkegaard's remark
concerning the concept, 'The neighbour is every man. . . . He is your
neighbour through equality with you before God.' The kind of relationship between believer and unbeliever which we have considered is not a

relationship of equality, but of inequality: one had the truth while the other had nothing. The 'truth' is considered to be so important that any treatment of the unbeliever is justified if it leads to assent to the truth. For Simone Weil, this is a distortion of the Christian concept of love. The special revelation is loved more than the neighbour; love of dogma replaces love of man. It is in this way that atrocities are committed in the name of love. The kind of religion one supports depends on whether one loves dogma or whether one loves man. The way towards love of God cannot begin with the former.

Simone Weil calls love of man a 'form of the implicit love of God'. She contrasts this with the moral distinction between justice and charity. Simone Weil considers the account of Thucydides of the ultimatum the Athenians gave to the people of Melos when they asked them to join them in their war against Sparta. The men of Melos invoked justice, 'imploring pity for the antiquity of their town'. The Athenians brush aside this reference to justice, saying:

> 'Let us treat rather of what is possible. . . . You know it as well as we do; the human spirit is so constituted that what is just is only examined if there is equal necessity on both sides. But if one is strong and the other weak, that which is possible is imposed by the first and accepted by the second.'
> The men of Melos said that in the case of a battle they would have the gods with them on account of the justice of their cause. The Athenians replied that they saw no reason to suppose so:
> 'As touching the gods we have the belief, and as touching men the certainty, that always by a necessity of nature, each one commands wherever he has the power. We did not establish this law, we are not the first to apply it; we found it already established, we abide by it as something likely to endure for ever; and that is why we apply it. We know quite well that you also, like all the others, once you reached the same degree of power, would act in the same way.' [11]

According to Simone Weil, most people have gone a step further than the Athenians, who at least recognized that they were brushing aside considerations of justice in accepting as justice what one can be reasonably expected to do or what one can reasonably expect to receive in a given situation. If one's conception of justice varies with the circumstances, then it is likely that whenever one has the power to command, one will do so. When such a concept of justice is found in religion, it tends to be located in the so-called justice of a cause—the cause of a particular religion. No atrocity can be an injustice if it can be shown to further the cause. Simone Weil accuses the Hebrew religion of this distortion: confusing love of man with love of the cause. 'The religions which represent divinity as commanding wherever it has the power to do so are false. Even though they are monotheistic they are idolatrous.' [12]

True religion, for Simone Weil, is the religion which manifests true love. But what is this idea of love? If we hold the relativistic concept of justice, we shall regard charity as a supererogatory act: as something we need not have done. According to Simone Weil, the Christian concept of love does not recognize this distinction. It equates justice and charity. How does this come about?

To answer the above question one must distinguish between two important concepts in Simone Weil's thought: 'attachment' and 'detachment'. 'Attachment' belongs to all relationships of inequality: the strong and the weak, the conqueror and the conquered, employer and employee, and so on. Justice in these relationships is what the strong, for instance, can reasonably be expected to give, and what the weak can reasonably expect to receive. Charity would then be giving more than one is expected to give as an employer, let us say: 'Beyond a certain degree of inequality in the relations of men of unequal strength, the weaker passes into a state of matter and loses his personality. The men of old used to say: "A man loses half his soul the day he becomes a slave." ' [13]

On rare occasions, however, we find a person not using his power, but instead, having compassion on the person to whom he stands in a relationship of inequality. Simone Weil calls this 'the supernatural virtue of justice', and says that it 'consists of behaving exactly as though there were equality when one is the stronger in an unequal relationship'.[14] This is where 'detachment' is important. It is the possibility of acting in a way which is not determined by the relative criteria of reasonableness which function in unequal relationships. It is the possibility of detaching oneself from one's special status, and seeing the other as an equal. Simone Weil says that 'He who treats as equals those who are far below him in strength really makes them a gift of the quality of human beings, of which fate had deprived them'.[15] We recall her other remark: 'Belief in the existence of other human beings as such is *love.*' [16]

Compassion is not easy to achieve. It is easy enough to give bread to the starving, money to the needy or clothes to the naked. It is not surprising that a person does these things. 'What is surprising,' as Simone Weil says, 'is that he should be capable of doing so with so different a gesture from that with which we buy an object. Alms-giving when it is not supernatural is like a sort of purchase. It buys the sufferer.' [17]

It is difficult to act from compassion partly because it involves a contemplation of other people as one's equal. This contemplation is akin to another form of the implicit love of God which Simone Weil talks about—namely, the love of the beauty of the world. In some ways, this is easier to understand because it is a more common experience. For example, when ambition threatens to destroy us, and we have come to regard everyone and everything as instruments for our own use, what Simone Weil calls 'The love we feel for the splendour of the heavens, the plains, the sea and the mountains, for the silence of nature' can give us is something which cannot be used—namely, the beauty of the world. One cannot use beauty; one can only contemplate it, since, as Simone Weil says, 'it only gives itself, it never gives anything else'.[18] By this kind of contemplation one's self-centredness is destroyed. One is able 'to see the true centre outside the world'. This contemplation of the beauty of the world—cf. Wittgenstein: 'Not *how* the world is, is the mystical, but *that* it is' [19]—has a parallel in the love of one's neighbour. People can be seen not in relation to my needs and uses, but as human beings—not *how* they are (rich, poor, educated, ignorant, useful, useless, etc.), but *that* they are. Simone Weil says that this act of contemplation 'places the Good outside this world, where are all the sources of power'.[20] Her own life illustrates the kind of powers of courage and endurance given to those who possess this love.

It is important to note that Simone Weil did not think it necessary that those who possessed this love should attribute it to God. She did think, however, that such love is religious and the result of divine activity. This was partly due to her insistence that this love could not be achieved by an effort of will; it only comes by contemplation. That is why she calls it a gift; for her, a gift from God. One has a duty to wait on God, but one cannot have a duty to receive. Simone Weil also thought that this form of implicit love of God leads to a more explicit love of God. It is outside my present task to discuss the difficult question of how this is brought about. All I have been concerned to show is that there is one interpretation of the Christian concept of love which is free from the moral objections we have considered hitherto.

Why do I call Simone Weil's treatment of the concept of love an *interpretation* of the Christian concept? I do so because some of the implications of her standpoint are contrary to orthodox Christian teaching. One of the most important implications of her analysis is that it leaves no place of priority for any one religion. The third form of implicit love of God Simone Weil considers is the love of religious practices. She holds the view that the kind of contemplation she has been considering takes place most naturally within the religion of one's own land and culture. 'All religions pronounce the name of God in their particular language.' [21]

A man can call on God best in his own language and idiom. There should be no searching for words in such worship. Simone Weil cannot give assent to the Christian desire and policy to change men's religious allegiances. Can Christianity take other religions seriously? It is not a case of Christianity being a *better* religion. This would assume the existence of an objective religious norm. But is the norm any more than what we believe in? If any part of the beliefs of other religions is true, it is regarded as *an approximation to Christian truth*. Christians then say that it follows that a love of men involves the desire to bring them from approximate to complete truth. Hence missionaries. It is the identification of complete truth with Christian truth which has inspired religious protests like that of Simone Weil:

> Personally, I should never give as much as a sixpence towards any missionary enterprise. I think that for any man a change of religion is as dangerous a thing as a change of language is for a writer. It may turn out a success, but it may have disastrous consequences. . . .

> The various authentic religious traditions are different reflections of the same truth, and perhaps equally precious. But we do not realize this, because each of us lives only one of these traditions and sees the others from the outside.[22]

The claim of any religion to have the whole truth distorts love of man into love of dogma. Simone Weil recognizes the difficulty of comparative religion as a study, since each religion must be understood from the inside. Understanding can only come, if at all, through a sympathetic bond with the religion in question. But, as Simone Weil says: 'This scarcely ever happens, for some have no faith, and the others have faith exclusively in one religion and bestow upon the others the sort of attention we give to strangely shaped shells.'[23] Simone Weil is not, of course, advocating a rejection of allegiance to particular religions. She sees too clearly how so-called impartiality can lead to a vague and empty religiosity. What she is saying is that such allegiance need not lead one to make claims to possess the entire truth. Sympathetic understanding of other religions is the necessary condition for retracting such a claim.

On the other hand, *all* religions are not suited for what Simone Weil calls, 'calling on the name of the Lord'. We have seen already how love of dogma, and belief in the infallibility of a cause can lead to a religion very different from the kind she advocates. Dostoevsky called such a religion the religion of the devil. His Grand Inquisitor says to Christ, who has re-visited the earth:

> 'We are not working with Thee, but with *him*—that is our mystery. It's long—eight centuries—since we have been on *his* side and not on Thine. Just eight centuries ago, we took from him what Thou didst reject with scorn, that last gift he offered Thee, showing Thee all the kingdoms of the earth. We took from him Rome and the sword of Caesar, and proclaimed ourselves sole rulers of the earth, though hitherto we have not been able to complete our work. But whose fault is that? Oh, the work is only beginning, but it has begun. It has long to await completion and the earth has yet much to suffer, but we shall triumph and shall be Caesars, and then we shall plan the universal happiness of man.'[24]

By what criterion does Simone Weil call such religion false? How is she able to judge that 'The true God is the God we think of as almighty, but as not exercising His power everywhere'?[25] She says that 'Those of the Athenians who massacred the inhabitants of Melos had no longer any idea of such a God'.[26] All right, but they did have an idea of God. How can one prove that this idea of God is wrong? Simone Weil answers as follows: 'The first proof that they were in the wrong lies in the fact that, contrary to their assertion, it happens, though extremely rarely, that a man will forbear out of pure generosity to command where he has the power to do so. That which is possible for man is possible also for God.'[27]

In this answer, Simone Weil is profoundly right. What other proof of the truth of a religion could one ever ask for or hope to possess?

Before ending, I want to consider another major difficulty. I said at the outset that even the interpretation of the Christian concept of love which avoids many moral objections has little to say about problems which arise from human love in certain contexts. Examples of these problems must now be considered.

Love found in intimate human relationships often gives rise to moral perplexity. When such situations occur, what has Christianity to say? In a moral perplexity the question I ask myself is, 'What ought I to do?' I have no clear-cut choice between right and wrong. I have conflicting obligations. No reference to a categorical law or immovable principles seems to help. But is not this what Christianity does? Does it not take a strange view of such problems by ignoring their complexity and by treating them as problems of casuistry? Is Christianity any more than 'thou shalt' and 'thou shalt not'?

But of course it is. There is a distinction between the general will of God and the special will of God. The general will of God refers to anything it makes sense to call the will of God. The special will of God is what God wants me to do here and now in this situation. But not only moral principles clash, divine precepts clash too, leaving the believer praying to know the will of God. There is religious perplexity as well as moral perplexity.

But there is a difference. Even when I do not know the will of God for me, I can rule out certain answers because *they could not* be the will of God. The known will of God is 'the given' in terms of which the problem must be solved. If I believe, I must start 'here' and bring all else into relation with 'the here'. In moral perplexity I do not start anywhere in that sense. Certain difficulties arise which call for some kind of an answer. My answer need not conform to any pre-established code, however. The question is, 'What can I do?' (This is not a question about logical possibilities!) 'What can I do and still live with myself as a person?' No one outside the dilemma can answer the question.

What does Christianity say in face of such situations? Simone Weil herself has some strange things to say. She is suspicious of most forms of human attachment. She claims that this attachment can arise from two motives—namely, from a recognition of good in the loved one or from a need for the loved one. Simone Weil holds the view that there is evil involved in love which arises solely from need. She even compares it with drunkenness and avarice: 'that which was at first a search for some desired good is transformed into a need by the mere passage of time'.[28] When this happens between persons, 'When the attachment of one being to another is made up of need and nothing else', then, according to Simone Weil, 'it is a fearful thing. Few things in this world can reach such a degree of ugliness and horror.' [29]

But if we think of examples of human love where the need for the loved ones has destroyed the people involved, would we feel happy about talking in this way? Consider Tolstoy's *Anna Karenina* or Hardy's *Jude the Obscure*. We might call what happened to Anna and Vronsky or to

Sue and Jude tragic, but surely not ugly or horrible! Simone Weil seems far too concerned with the preservation of the autonomy of the people involved in such relationships. In order to preserve this autonomy she advocates what she calls 'transforming affection into friendship'.[30] 'Do not allow yourself to be imprisoned by any affection. Keep your solitude.' [31] This may have some point where friendship is concerned, but it seems out of place in relationships such as those between husband and wife, lover and loved one, or parents and children. Here, one is often involved through mutual need in precisely the kind of way which Simone Weil deplores. Apart from advocating detachment, she has nothing positive to say about the problems which arise from the nature of such love. We are still faced with such problems as those portrayed by Tolstoy and Hardy.

Consider the situation in *Jude the Obscure*. Sue and Jude are both unhappily married. They love each other and want to live with each other. They regard marriage as sacred, but on the other hand Jude was tricked into marriage, while Sue married out of a 'love of being loved'. Eventually, Sue goes to live with Jude, but her conflict is not resolved; indeed, it is just beginning. She has a choice: she can either stay with Jude or return to the husband she does not love. She knows that if she leaves Jude it will break him, and yet, in the end, this is what she does. We may feel uneasy about her choice. We might have chosen differently, but then it would have been our problem and not Sue's. In dilemmas such as this, if one asks the person involved who is to decide what he ought to do, the appropriate answer is, 'I am.'

Tolstoy's Anna decides differently. She stays with her lover, though she realizes that the social death to which the relationship has condemned her is slowly destroying her as a person. She ends it all in suicide. What would Christians say about these decisions? That Sue did the will of God, I suppose. But did she have obligations to Jude? What is one to say to Anna? Repent and return to God?

I am not denying that prayer and the kind of contemplation Simone Weil advocates can help in the case of some problems. For example, a marriage may look like breaking up. The husband and wife think at first that parting is the only answer. On the other hand, if the husband and wife pray about their difficulties, they may, through prayer, find a way of going on which preserves some integrity in their relationship. It may not be the life they dreamed of when they started their married life, but it is something, nevertheless, which gives their marriage a meaning. In the very act of praying, and the kind of reflection on one's life this involves, the possibility of a new way through difficulty is seen.

On the other hand, prayer and reflection seem out of place in other situations, such as those described by Tolstoy and Hardy. This is partly because although waiting on God may bring new insight to a perplexity, the insight must be in accordance with the known will of God. Any answer is not permissible. Most Christians, I take it, would say that it cannot be the will of God for Anna to stay with Vronsky or for Sue to remain with Jude. This is the difficulty. What morality allows to be considered as a serious possibility, religion dismisses. Such dismissal ignores the complexity of such situations. It will not do simply to call these tragedies horrible or ugly. Neither will it do to say, as many Christians tend to, that had it not been for sin these situations would not have occurred. In the novels mentioned, Christians might say, 'But for the sin of adultery the tragedies would not have occurred.' Even so, now that sin *has* occurred, what does Christianity say about obligations created in sinning? Or can there be no obligation as the result of sin?

In any case, sin will not explain all tragedies. In Faulkner's *Pantaloon in Black* the Negro whose young wife dies gets drunk and kills a workmate who had made a habit of tormenting him. The story illustrates what Simone Weil says about such relationships: 'When the degree of necessity is extreme, deprivation leads to death. This is the case when all the vital energy of one being is bound up with another by some attachment.' [32]

What ought he not to have done in order to avoid ending his life in tragedy? The answer, I presume, is: loved his wife so much. But how odd to say, as Simone Weil does, that what such people ought to do is 'to transform affection into friendship', or to say with Kierkegaard, 'you must not love in such a way that the loss of the beloved would reveal the fact that you were desperate . . .'.[33] In the relationships we have considered, how could the death or deprivation of the loved one reveal anything else?

As I said at the outset, there is no one answer to the jungle of problems arising from the Christian concept of love. This chapter simply tries to show that these problems are more complex than we often suppose, and that there are more problems than we care to think, to which God alone has the answers.

NOTES

1. Kierkegaard, *Works of Love,* O.U.P., 1946, 34.
2. *Ibid.,* 50.
3. Weil, Simone, *Gravity and Grace,* Routledge, 1952, 56.
4. *Works of Love.*
5. Kierkegaard, *Fear and Trembling,* O.U.P., 1939, 34.
6. The concept of 'understanding' actions is of central importance for moral philosophy, and requires far more attention than the passing reference I give it above. To pursue the concept, however, would take the argument too far from the track I want to follow.
7. Anderson, John, 'Art and Morality', *Australasian Journal of Psychology and Philosophy,* December 1941, 255-6.
8. I owe this observation on the psychology of persecution to Professor G. P. Henderson.

9. *The Rebel,* Peregrine ed., 24.
10. *Fundamental Principles of the Metaphysic of Ethics,* trans. Abbott, 1949 ed., 52.
11. *Waiting on God,* Fontana Ed., 98-9.
12. *Ibid.,* 102.
13. *Ibid.,* 100.
14. *Ibid.*
15. *Ibid.,* 101.
16. See p. 222.
17. *Waiting on God,* 104.
18. *Ibid.,* 122.
19. *Tractatus,* 6.44.
20. *Waiting on God,* 105.
21. *Ibid.,* 136.
22. *Letter to a Priest,* Routledge, 1953, 10 and 11.
23. *Waiting on God,* 137.
24. *The Brothers Karamazov,* Bk. V, ch. v.
27. *Waiting on God,* 101.
26. *Ibid.*
27. *Ibid.*
28. *Ibid.,* 155.
29. *Ibid.*
30. *Ibid.;* see p. 158.
31. *Gravity and Grace,* 60.
32. *Ibid.,* 155.
33. See p. 221.

SEX

Sexual Perversion

Thomas Nagel

There is something to be learned about sex from the fact that we possess a concept of sexual perversion. I wish to examine the concept, defending it against the charge of unintelligibility and trying to say exactly what about human sexuality qualifies it to admit of perversions. Let me make some preliminary comments about the problem before embarking on its solution.

From *Journal of Philosophy,* Vol. LXI, No. 1 (January 16, 1969), pp. 5-17. Reprinted by permission of the author and the editor.

My research was supported in part by the National Science Foundation.

Some people do not believe that the notion of sexual perversion makes sense, and even those who do disagree over its application. Nevertheless I think it will be widely conceded that, if the concept is viable at all, it must meet certain general conditions. First, if there are any sexual perversions, they will have to be sexual desires or practices that can be plausibly described as in some sense unnatural, though the explanation of this natural/unnatural distinction is of course the main problem. Second, certain practices will be perversions if anything is, such as shoe fetishism, bestiality, and sadism; other practices, such as unadorned sexual intercourse, will not be; about still others there is controversy. Third, if there are perversions, they will be unnatural sexual *inclinations* rather than merely unnatural practices adopted not from inclination but for other reasons. I realize that this is at variance with the view, maintained by some Roman Catholics, that contraception is a sexual perversion. But although contraception may qualify as a deliberate perversion of the sexual and reproductive functions, it cannot be significantly described as a *sexual* perversion. A sexual perversion must reveal itself in conduct that expresses an unnatural *sexual* preference. And although there might be a form of fetishism focused on the employment of contraceptive devices, that is not the usual explanation for their use.

I wish to declare at the outset my belief that the connection between sex and reproduction has no bearing on sexual perversion. The latter is a concept of psychological, not physiological interest, and it is a concept that we do not apply to the lower animals, let alone to plants, all of which have reproductive functions that can go astray in various ways. (Think of seedless oranges.) Insofar as we are prepared to regard higher animals as perverted, it is because of their psychological, not their anatomical similarity to humans. Furthermore, we do not regard as a perversion every deviation from the reproductive function of sex in humans: sterility, miscarriage, contraception, abortion.

Another matter that I believe has no bearing on the concept of sexual perversion is social disapprobation or custom. Anyone inclined to think that in each society the perversions are those sexual practices of which the community disapproves, should consider all the societies that have frowned upon adultery and fornication. These have not been regarded as unnatural practices, but have been thought objectionable in other ways. What is regarded as unnatural admittedly varies from culture to culture, but the classification is not a pure expression of disapproval or distaste. In fact it is often regarded as a *ground* for disapproval, and that suggests that the classification has an independent content.

I am going to attempt a psychological account of sexual perversion, which will depend on a specific psychological theory of sexual desire and human sexual interactions. To approach this solution I wish first to consider a contrary position, one which provides a basis for skepticism about the existence of any sexual perversions at all, and perhaps about the very significance of the term. The skeptical argument runs as follows:

"Sexual desire is simply one of the appetites, like hunger and thirst. As such it may have various objects, some more common than others perhaps, but none in any sense 'natural.' An appetite is identified as sexual by means of the organs and erogenous zones in which its satisfaction can be to some extent localized, and the special sensory pleasures which form the core of that satisfaction. This enables us to recognize widely divergent goals, activities, and desires as sexual, since it is conceivable in principle that anything should produce sexual pleasure and that a nondeliberate, sexually charged desire for it should arise (as a result of conditioning, if nothing else). We may fail to empathize with some of these desires, and some of them, like sadism, may be objectionable on extraneous grounds, but once we have observed that they meet the criteria for being sexual, there is nothing more to be said on *that* score. Either they are sexual or they are not: sexuality does not admit of imperfection, or perversion, or any other such qualification—it is not that sort of affection."

This is probably the received radical position. It suggests that the cost of defending a psychological account may be to deny that sexual desire is an appetite. But insofar as that line of defense is plausible, it should make us suspicious of the simple picture of appetites on which the skepticism depends. Perhaps the standard appetites, like hunger, cannot be classed as pure appetites in that sense either, at least in their human versions.

Let us approach the matter by asking whether we can imagine anything that would qualify as a gastronomical perversion. Hunger and eating are importantly like sex in that they serve a biological function and also play a significant role in our inner lives. It is noteworthy that there is little temptation to describe as perverted an appetite for substances that are not nourishing. We should probably not consider someone's appetites as *perverted* if he liked to eat paper, sand, wood, or cotton. Those are merely rather odd and very unhealthy tastes: they lack the psychological complexity that we expect of perversions. (Coprophilia, being already a sexual perversion, may be disregarded.) If on the other hand someone liked to eat cookbooks, or magazines with pictures of food in them, and preferred these to ordinary food—or if when hungry he sought satisfaction by fondling a napkin or ashtray from his favorite restaurant—then the concept of perversion might seem appropriate (in fact it would be natural to describe this as a case of gastronomical fetishism). It would be natural to describe as gastronomically perverted someone who could eat only by having food forced down his throat through a funnel, or only if the meal were a living animal. What helps in such cases is the peculiarity of the desire itself, rather than the inappropriateness of its object to the biological function that the desire serves. Even an appetite, it would seem, can have perversions if in addition to its biological function it has a significant psychological structure.

In the case of hunger, psychological complexity is provided by the activities that give it expression. Hunger is not merely a disturbing sensation that can be quelled by eating; it is an attitude toward edible portions of the external world, a desire to relate to them in rather special ways. The method of ingestion: chewing, savoring, swallowing, appreciating the texture and smell, all are important components of the relation, as is the passivity and controllability of the food (the only animals we eat live are helpless mollusks). Our relation to food depends also on our size: we do not live upon it or burrow into it like aphids or worms. Some of these features are more central than others, but any adequate phenomenology of eating would have to treat it as a relation to the external world and a way of appropriating bits of that world, with characteristic affection. Displacements or serious restrictions of the desire to eat could then be described as perversions, if they undermined that direct relation between man and food which is the natural expression of hunger. This explains why it is easy to imagine gastronomical fetishism, voyeurism, exhibitionism, or even gastronomical sadism and masochism. Indeed some of these perversions are fairly common.

If we can imagine perversions of an appetite like hunger, it should be possible to make sense of the concept of sexual perversion. I do not wish to imply that sexual desire is an appetite—only that being an appetite is no bar to admitting of perversions. Like hunger, sexual desire has as its characteristic object a certain relation with something in the external world; only in this case it is usually a person rather than an omelet, and the relation is considerably more complicated. This added complication allows scope for correspondingly complicated perversions.

The fact that sexual desire is a feeling about other persons may tempt us to take a pious view of its psychological content. There are those who believe that sexual desire is properly the expression of some other attitude, like love, and that when it occurs by itself it is incomplete and unhealthy—or at any rate subhuman. (The extreme Platonic version of such a view is that sexual practices are all vain attempts to express something they cannot in principle achieve: this makes them all perversions, in a sense.) I do not believe that any such view is correct. Sexual desire is complicated enough without having to be linked to anything else as a condition for phenomenological analysis. It cannot be denied that sex may serve various functions—economic, social, altruistic—but it also has its own content as a relation between persons, and it is only by analyzing that relation that we can understand the conditions of sexual perversion.

I believe it is very important that the object of sexual attraction is a particular individual, who transcends the properties that make him attractive. When different persons are attracted to a single person for different reasons: eyes, hair, figure, laugh, intelligence—we feel that the object of their desire is nevertheless the same, namely that person. There is even an inclination to feel that this is so if the lovers have different sexual aims, if they include both men and women, for example. Different specific attractive characteristics seem to provide enabling conditions for the operation of a single basic feeling, and the different aims all provide expressions of it. We approach the sexual attitude toward the person through the features that we find attractive, but these features are not the objects of that attitude.

This is very different from the case of an omelet. Various people may desire it for different reasons, one for its fluffiness, another for its mushrooms, another for its unique combination of aroma and visual aspect; yet we do not enshrine the transcendental omelet as the true common object of their affections. Instead we might say that several desires have accidentally converged on the same object: any omelet with the crucial characteristics would do as well. It is not similarly true that any person with the same flesh distribution and way of smoking can be substituted as object for a particular sexual desire that has been elicited by those characteristics. It may be that they will arouse attraction whenever they recur, but it will be a new sexual attraction with a new particular object, not merely a transfer of the old desire to someone else. (I believe this is true even in cases where the new object is unconsciously identified with a former one.)

The importance of this point will emerge when we see how complex a psychological interchange constitutes the natural development of sexual attraction. This would be incomprehensible if its object were not a particular person, but rather a person of a certain *kind*. Attraction is only the beginning, and fulfillment does not consist merely of behavior and contact expressing this attraction, but involves much more.

The best discussion of these matters that I have seen appears in part III of Sartre's *Being and Nothingness*.[1] Since it has influenced my own views, I shall say a few things about it now. Sartre's treatment of sexual desire and of love, hate, sadism, masochism, and further attitudes toward others, depends on a general theory of consciousness and the body which we can neither expound nor assume here. He does not discuss perversion, and this is partly because he regards sexual desire as one form of the perpetual attempt of an embodied consciousness to come to terms with the existence of others, an attempt that is as doomed to fail in this form as it is in any of the others, which include sadism and masochism (if not certain of the more impersonal deviations) as well as several nonsexual attitudes. According to Sartre, all attempts to incorporate the other into my world as another subject, i.e., to apprehend him at once as an object for me and as a subject for which I am an object, are unstable and doomed to collapse into one or other of the two aspects. Either I reduce him entirely to an object, in which case his subjectivity escapes the possession or appropriation I can extend to that object; or I become merely an object for him, in which case I am no longer in a position to appropriate his subjectivity. Moreover, neither of these aspects is stable; each is continually in danger of giving way to the other. This has the consequence that there can be no such thing as a successful sexual relation, since the deep aim of sexual desire cannot in principle be accomplished. It seems likely, therefore, that the view will not permit a basic distinction between successful or complete and unsuccessful or incomplete sex, and therefore cannot admit the concept of perversion.

I do not adopt this aspect of the theory, nor many of its metaphysical underpinnings. What interests me is Sartre's picture of the attempt. He says that the type of possession that is the object of sexual desire is carried out by "a double reciprocal incarnation" and that this is accomplished, typically in the form of a caress, in the following way: "I make myself flesh in order to impel the Other to realize *for herself* and *for me* her own flesh, and my caresses cause my flesh to be born for me in so far as it is for the Other *flesh causing her to be born as flesh*" (391; italics Sartre's). The incarnation in question is described variously as a clogging or troubling of consciousness, which is inundated by the flesh in which it is embodied.

The view I am going to suggest, I hope in less obscure language, is related to this one, but it differs from Sartre's in allowing sexuality to achieve its goal on occasion and thus in providing the concept of perversion with a foothold.

Sexual desire involves a kind of perception, but not merely a single perception of its object, for in the paradigm case of mutual desire there is a complex system of superimposed mutual perceptions—not only perceptions of the sexual object, but perceptions of oneself. Moreover, sexual awareness of another involves considerable self-awareness to begin with—more than is involved in ordinary sensory perception. The experience is felt as an assault on oneself by the view (or touch, or whatever) of the sexual object.

Let us consider a case in which the elements can be separated. For clarity we will restrict ourselves initially to the somewhat artificial case of desire at a distance. Suppose a man and a woman, whom we may call Romeo and Juliet, are at opposite ends of a cocktail lounge, with many mirrors on the walls which permit unobserved observation, and even mutual unobserved observation. Each of them is sipping a martini and studying other people in the mirrors. At some point Romeo notices Juliet. He is moved, somehow, by the softness of her hair and the diffidence with which she sips her martini, and this arouses him sexually. Let us say that *X senses Y* whenever X regards Y with sexual desire. (Y need not be a person, and X's apprehension of Y can be visual, tactile, olfactory, etc., or purely imaginary; in the present example we shall concentrate on vision.) So Romeo senses Juliet, rather than merely noticing her. At this stage he is aroused by an unaroused object, so he is more in the sexual grip of his body than she of hers.

Let us suppose, however, that Juliet now senses Romeo in another mirror on the opposite wall, though neither of them yet knows that he is seen by the other (the mirror angles provide three-quarter views). Romeo then begins to notice in Juliet the subtle signs of sexual arousal: heavy-lidded stare, dilating pupils, faint flush, et cetera. This of course renders her much more bodily, and he not only notices but senses this as well.

His arousal is nevertheless still solitary. But now, cleverly calculating the line of her stare without actually looking her in the eyes, he realizes that it is directed at him through the mirror on the opposite wall. That is, he notices, and moreover senses, Juliet sensing him. This is definitely a new development, for it gives him a sense of embodiment not only through his own reactions but through the eyes and reactions of another. Moreover, it is separable from the initial sensing of Juliet; for sexual arousal might begin with a person's sensing that he is sensed and being assailed by the perception of the other person's desire rather than merely by the perception of the person.

But there is a further step. Let us suppose that Juliet, who is a little slower than Romeo, now senses that he senses her. This puts Romeo in a position to notice, and be aroused by, her arousal at being sensed by him. He senses that she senses that he senses her. This is still another level of arousal, for he becomes conscious of his sexuality through his awareness of its effect on her and of her awareness that this effect is due to him. Once she takes the same step and senses that he senses her sensing him, it becomes difficult to state, let alone imagine, further iterations, though they may be logically distinct. If both are alone, they will presumably turn to look at each other directly, and the proceedings will continue on another plane. Physical contact and intercourse are perfectly natural extensions of this complicated visual exchange, and mutual touch can involve all the complexities of awareness present in the visual case, but with a far greater range of subtlety and acuteness.

Ordinarily, of course, things happen in a less orderly fashion—sometimes in a great rush—but I believe that some version of this overlapping system of distinct sexual perceptions and interactions is the basic framework of any full-fledged sexual relation and that relations involving only part of the complex are significantly incomplete. The account is only schematic, as it must be to achieve generality. Every real sexual act will be psychologically far more specific and detailed, in ways that depend not only on the physical techniques employed and on anatomical details, but also on countless features of the participants' conceptions of themselves and of each other, which become embodied in the act. (It is a familiar enough fact, for example, that people often take their social roles and the social roles of their partners to bed with them.)

The general schema is important, however, and the proliferation of levels of mutual awareness it involves is an example of a type of complexity that typifies human interactions. Consider aggression, for example. If I am angry with someone, I want to make him feel it, either to produce self-reproach by getting him to see himself through the eyes of my anger, and to dislike what he sees—or else to produce reciprocal anger or fear, by getting him to perceive my anger as a threat or attack. What I want will depend on the details of my anger, but in either case it will involve a desire that the object of that anger be aroused. This accomplishment constitutes the fulfillment of my emotion, through domination of the object's feelings.

Another example of such reflexive mutual recognition is to be found in the phenomenon of meaning, which appears to involve an intention to produce a belief or other effect in another by bringing about his recognition of one's intention to produce that effect. (That result is due to H. P. Grice,[2] whose position I shall not attempt to reproduce in detail.) Sex has a related structure: it involves a desire that one's partner be aroused by the recognition of one's desire that he or she be aroused.

It is not easy to define the basic types of awareness and arousal of which these complexes are composed, and that remains a lacuna in this discussion. I believe that the object of awareness is the same in one's own case as it is in one's sexual awareness of another, although the two awarenesses will not be the same, the difference being as great as that between feeling angry and experiencing the anger of another. All stages of sexual perception are varieties of identification of a person with his body. What is perceived is one's own or another's *subjection* to or *immersion* in his body, a phenomenon which has been recognized with loathing by St. Paul and St. Augustine, both of whom regarded "the law of sin which is in my members" as a grave threat to the dominion of the holy will.[3] In sexual desire and its expression the blending of involuntary response with deliberate control is extremely important. For Augustine, the revolution launched against him by his body is symbolized by erection and the other involuntary physical components of arousal. Sartre too stresses the fact that the penis is not a prehensile organ. But mere involuntariness characterizes other bodily processes as well. In sexual desire the involuntary responses are combined with submission to spontaneous impulses: not only one's pulse and secretions but one's actions are taken over by the body; ideally, deliberate control is needed only to guide the expression of those impulses. This is to some extent also true of an appetite like hunger, but the takeover there is more localized, less pervasive, less extreme. One's whole body does not become saturated with hunger as it can with desire. But the most characteristic feature of a specifically sexual immersion in the body is its ability to fit into the complex of mutual perceptions that we have described. Hunger leads to spontaneous interactions with food; sexual desire leads to spontaneous interactions with other persons, whose bodies are asserting their sovereignty in the same way, producing involuntary reactions and spontaneous impulses in *them*. These reactions are perceived, and the perception of them is perceived, and that perception is in turn perceived; at each step the domination of the person by his body is reinforced, and the sexual partner becomes more possessible by physical contact, penetration, and envelopment.

Desire is therefore not merely the perception of a preexisting embodiment of the other, but ideally a contribution to his further embodiment which in turn enhances the original subject's sense of himself. This explains why it is important that the partner be aroused, and not merely aroused, but aroused by the awareness of one's desire. It also explains the sense in which desire has unity and possession as its object: physical possession must eventuate in creation of the sexual object in the image of one's desire, and not merely in the object's recognition of that desire, or in his or her own private arousal. (This may reveal a male bias: I shall say something about that later.)   shattered - cut - off

To return, finally, to the topic of perversion: I believe that various familiar deviations constitute truncated or incomplete versions of the complete configuration, and may therefore be regarded as perversions of the central impulse.

In particular, narcissistic practices and intercourse with animals, infants, and inanimate objects seem to be stuck at some primitive version of the first stage. If the object is not alive, the experience is reduced entirely to an awareness of one's own sexual embodiment. Small children and animals permit awareness of the embodiment of the other, but present obstacles to reciprocity, to the recognition by the sexual object of the subject's desire as the source of his (the object's) sexual self-awareness.

Sadism concentrates on the evocation of passive self-awareness in others, but the sadist's engagement is itself active and requires a retention of deliberate control which impedes awareness of himself as a bodily subject of passion in the required sense. The victim must recognize him as the source of his own sexual passivity, but only as the active source. De Sade claimed that the object of sexual desire was to evoke involuntary responses from one's partner, especially audible ones. The infliction of pain is no doubt the most efficient way to accomplish this, but it requires a certain abrogation of one's own exposed spontaneity. All this, incidentally, helps to explain why it is tempting to regard as sadistic an excessive preoccupation with sexual technique, which does not permit one to abandon the role of agent at any stage of the sexual act. Ideally one should be able to surmount one's technique at some point.

A masochist on the other hand imposes the same disability on his partner as the sadist imposes on himself. The masochist cannot find a satisfactory embodiment as the object of another's sexual desire, but only as the object of his control. He is passive not in relation to his partner's passion but in relation to his nonpassive agency. In addition, the subjection to one's body characteristic of pain and physical restraint is of a very different kind from that of sexual excitement: pain causes people to contract rather than dissolve.

Both of these disorders have to do with the second stage, which involves the awareness of oneself as an object of desire. In straightforward sadism and masochism other attentions are substituted for desire as a source of the object's self-awareness. But it is also possible for nothing of that sort to be substituted, as in the case of a masochist who is satisfied with self-inflicted pain or of a sadist who does not insist on playing a role in the suffering that arouses him. Greater difficulties of classification are presented by three other categories of sexual activity: elaborations of the sexual act; intercourse of more than two persons; and homosexuality.

If we apply our model to the various forms that may be taken by two-

Re [Reach]

party heterosexual intercourse, none of them seem clearly to qualify as perversions. Hardly anyone can be found these days to inveigh against oral-genital contact, and the merits of buggery are urged by such respectable figures as D. H. Lawrence and Norman Mailer. There may be something vaguely sadistic about the latter technique (in Mailer's writings it seems to be a method of introducing an element of rape), but it is not obvious that this has to be so. In general, it would appear that any bodily contact between a man and a woman that gives them sexual pleasure, is a possible vehicle for the system of multi-level interpersonal awareness that I have claimed is the basic psychological content of sexual interaction. Thus a liberal platitude about sex is upheld.

About multiple combinations, the least that can be said is that they are bound to be complicated. If one considers how difficult it is to carry on two conversations simultaneously, one may appreciate the problems of multiple simultaneous interpersonal perception that can arise in even a small-scale orgy. It may be inevitable that some of the component relations should degenerate into mutual epidermal stimulation by participants otherwise isolated from each other. There may also be a tendency toward voyeurism and exhibitionism, both of which are incomplete relations. The exhibitionist wishes to display his desire without needing to be desired in return; he may even fear the sexual attention of others. A voyeur, on the other hand, need not require any recognition by his object at all: certainly not a recognition of the voyeur's arousal.

It is not clear whether homosexuality is a perversion if that is measured by the standard of the described configuration, but it seems unlikely. For such a classification would have to depend on the possibility of extracting from the system a distinction between male and female sexuality; and much that has been said so far applies equally to men and women. Moreover, it would have to be maintained that there was a natural tie between the type of sexuality and the sex of the body, and also that two sexualities of the same type could not interact properly.

Certainly there is much support for an aggressive-passive distinction between male and female sexuality. In our culture the male's arousal tends to initiate the perceptual exchange, he usually makes the sexual approach, largely controls the course of the act, and of course penetrates whereas the woman receives. When two men or two women engage in intercourse they cannot both adhere to these sexual roles. The question is how essential the roles are to an adequate sexual relation. One relevant observation is that a good deal of deviation from these roles occurs in heterosexual intercourse. Women can be sexually aggressive and men passive, and temporary reversals of role are not uncommon in heterosexual exchanges of reasonable length. If such conditions are set aside, it may be urged that there is something irreducibly perverted in attraction to a body anatomically like one's own. But alarming as some people in our culture may find such attraction, it remains psychologically unilluminating to class it as perverted. Certainly if homosexuality is a perversion, it is so in a very different sense from that in which shoe-fetishism is

a perversion, for some version of the full range of interpersonal perceptions seems perfectly possible between two persons of the same sex.

In any case, even if the proposed model is correct, it remains implausible to describe as perverted every deviation from it. For example, if the
partners in heterosexual intercourse indulge in private heterosexual fantasies, that obscures the recognition of the real partner and so, on the
theory, constitutes a defective sexual relation. It is not, however, generally regarded as a perversion. Such examples suggest that a simple dichot-
omy between perverted and unperverted sex is too crude to organize the
phenomena adequately.

I should like to close with some remarks about the relation of perversion to good, bad, and morality. The concept of perversion can hardly
fail to be evaluative in some sense, for it appears to involve the notion
of an ideal or at least adequate sexuality which the perversions in some
way fail to achieve. So, if the concept is viable, the judgment that a person or practice or desire is perverted will constitute a sexual evaluation,
implying that better sex, or a better specimen of sex, is possible. This in
itself is a very weak claim, since the evaluation might be in a dimension
that is of little interest to us. (Though, if my account is correct, that will
not be true.)

Whether it is a moral evaluation, however, is another question entirely
—one whose answer would require more understanding of both morality
and perversion than can be deployed here. Moral evaluation of acts and
of persons is a rather special and very complicated matter, and by no
means all our evaluations of persons and their activities are moral evaluations. We make judgments about people's beauty or health or intelligence which are evaluative without being moral. Assessments of their
sexuality may be similar in that respect.

Futhermore, moral issues aside, it is not clear that unperverted sex is
necessarily *preferable* to the perversions. It may be that sex which receives the highest marks for perfection *as sex* is less enjoyable than certain perversions; and if enjoyment is considered very important, that
might outweigh considerations of sexual perfection in determining rational preference.

That raises the question of the relation between the evaluative content
of judgments of perversion and the rather common *general* distinction
between good and bad sex. The latter distinction is usually confined to
sexual acts, and it would seem, within limits, to cut across the other:
even someone who believed, for example, that homosexuality was a perversion could admit a distinction between better and worse homosexual
sex, and might even allow that good homosexual sex could be better *sex*
than not very good unperverted sex. If this is correct, it supports the
position that, if judgments of perversion are viable at all, they represent
only one aspect of the possible evaluation of sex, even *qua sex*. Moreover
it is not the only important aspect: certainly sexual deficiencies that evidently do not constitute perversions can be the object of great concern.

Finally, even if perverted sex is to that extent not so good as it might be, bad sex is generally better than none at all. This should not be controversial: it seems to hold for other important matters, like food, music, literature, and society. In the end, one must choose from among the available alternatives, whether their availability depends on the environment or on one's own constitution. And the alternatives have to be fairly grim before it becomes rational to opt for nothing.

NOTES

1. Translated by Hazel E. Barnes (New York: Philosophical Library: 1956).
2. "Meaning," *Philosophical Review*, LXVI, 3 (July 1957): 377-388.
3. See Romans, VII, 23; and the *Confessions,* Book 8, v.

Better Sex

Sara Ruddick

It might be argued that there is no specifically sexual morality.[1] We have, of course, become accustomed to speaking of sexual morality, but the "morality" of which we speak has a good deal to do with property, the division of labor, and male power, and little to do with our sexual lives. Sexual experiences, like experiences in driving automobiles, render us liable to specific moral situations. As drivers we must guard against infantile desires for revenge and excitement. As lovers we must guard against cruelty and betrayal, for we know sexual experiences provide special opportunities for each. We drive soberly because, before we get into a car, we believe that it is wrong to be careless of life. We resist temptations to adultery because we believe it wrong to betray trust, whether it be a parent, a sexual partner, or a political colleague who is betrayed. As lovers and drivers we act on principles that are particular applications of general moral principles. Moreover, given the superstitions from which sexual experience has suffered, it is wise to free ourselves, as lovers, from any moral concerns, other than those we have

From Robert Baker and Frederick Elliston, eds., *Philosophy and Sex* (Buffalo: Prometheus Books, 1975), pp. 83-104. Reprinted by permission of the author and the publisher.

as human beings. There is no specifically sexual morality, and none should be invented. Or so it might be argued.

When we examine our moral "intuitions," however, the analogy with driving fails us. Unburdened of *sexual* morality, we do not find it easy to apply general moral principles to our sexual lives. "Morally average lovers can be cruel, violate trusts, and neglect social duties with less opprobrium precisely *because* they are lovers. Only political passions and psychological or physical deprivation serve as well as sexual desire to excuse what would otherwise be seriously and clearly immoral acts. (Occasionally, sexual desire is itself conceived of as a deprivation, an involuntary lust. And there is, of course, a tradition that sees sexual morality as a way of controlling those unable to be sexless: "It is better to marry than to burn.") Often, in our sexual lives, we neither flout nor simply apply general moral principles. Rather, the values of sexual experience themselves figure in the construction of moral dilemmas. The conflict between better sex (more complete, natural, and pleasurable sex acts) and, say, social duty is not seen as a conflict between the immoral and compulsive, on one hand, and the morally good, on the other, but as a conflict between alternative moral acts.

Our intuitions vary but at least they suggest we can use "good" sex as a positive weight on some moral balance. What is that weight? Why do we put it there? How do we, in the first place, evaluate sexual experiences? On reflection, should we endorse these evaluations? These are the questions whose answers should constitute a specifically sexual morality.

In answering them, I will first consider three characteristics that have been used to distinguish some sex acts as better than others—greater pleasure, completeness, and naturalness. Other characteristics may be relevant to evaluating sex acts, but these three are central. If they have *moral* significance, then the sex acts characterized by them will be better than others not so characterized.

After considering those characteristics in virtue of which some sex acts are allegedly better than others, I will ask whether the presence of those characteristics renders the acts *morally* superior. I will not consider here the unclear and overused distinction between the moral and the amoral, nor the illegitimate but familiar distinction between the moral and the prudent. I hope it is sufficient to set out dogmatically and schematically the moral notions I will use. I am confident that better sex is morally preferable to other sex, but I am not at all happy with my characterization of its moral significance. Ultimately, sexual morality cannot be considered apart from a "prudential" morality in which it is shown that what is good is good for us and what is good for us makes us good. In such a morality, not only sex, but art, fantasy, love, and a host of other intellectual and emotional enterprises will regain old moral significances and acquire new ones. My remarks here, then, are partial and provisional.

A characteristic renders a sex act morally preferable to one without that characteristic if it gives, increases, or is instrumental in increasing the "benefit" of the act for the person engaging in it. Benefits can be classified as peremptory or optional. Peremptory benefits are experiences, relations, or objects that anyone who is neither irrational nor anhedonic will want so long as s/he wants anything at all. Optional benefits are experiences, relations, or objects that anyone, neither irrational nor anhedonic, will want so long as s/he will not thereby lose a peremptory benefit. There is widespread disagreement about which benefits are peremptory. Self-respect, love, and health are common examples of peremptory benefits. Arms, legs, and hands are probably optional benefits. A person still wanting a great deal might give up limbs, just as s/he would give up life, when mutilation or death is required by self-respect. As adults we are largely responsible for procuring our own benefits and greatly dependent on good fortune for success in doing so. However, the moral significance of benefits is most clearly seen not from the standpoint of the person procuring and enjoying them but from the standpoint of another *caring* person, for example, a lover, parent, or political leader responsible for procuring benefits for specific others. A benefit may then be described as an experience, relation, or object that anyone who properly cares for another is obliged to attempt to secure for him/her. Criteria for the virtue of care and for benefit are reciprocally determined, the virtue consisting in part in recognizing and attempting to secure benefits for the person cared for, the identification of benefit depending on its recognition by those already seen to be properly caring.

In talking of benefits I shall be looking at our sexual lives from the vantage point of hope, not of fear. The principal interlocutor may be considered to be a child asking what s/he should rightly and reasonably hope for in living, rather than a potential criminal questioning conventional restraints. The specific question the child may be imagined to ask can now be put: In what way is better sex beneficial or conducive to experiences or relations or objects that are beneficial?

A characteristic renders a sex act morally preferable to one without that characteristic if either the act is thereby more just or the act is thereby likely to make the person engaging in it more just. Justice includes giving others what is due them, taking no more than what is one's own, and giving and taking according to prevailing principles of fairness.

A characteristic renders a sex act morally preferable to one without that characteristic if because of the characteristic the act is more virtuous or more likely to lead to virtue. A virtue is a disposition to attempt, and an ability to succeed in, good acts—acts of justice, acts that express or produce excellence, and acts that yield benefits to oneself or others.

SEXUAL PLEASURE

Sensual experiences give rise to sensations and experiences that are paradigms of what is pleasant. Hedonism, in both its psychological and ethical forms, has blinded us to the nature and to the benefits of sensual pleasure by overextending the word "pleasure" to cover anything enjoyable or even agreeable.[2] The paradigmatic type of pleasure is sensual. Pleasure is a temporally extended, more or less intense quality of particular experiences. Pleasure is enjoyable independent of any function pleasurable activity fulfills. The infant who continues to suck well after s/he is nourished, expressing evident pleasure in doing so, gives us a demonstration of the nature of pleasure.[3]

As we learn more about pleasant experiences we not only apply but also extend and attenuate the primary notion of "pleasure." But if pleasure is to have any nonsophistical psychological or moral interest, it must retain its connections with those paradigm instances of sensual pleasure that give rise to it. We may, for example, extend the notion of pleasure so that particular episodes in the care of children give great pleasure; but the long-term caring for children, however intrinsically rewarding, is not an experience of pleasure or unpleasure.

Sexual pleasure is a species of sensual pleasure with its own conditions of arousal and satisfaction. Sexual acts vary considerably in pleasure, the limiting case being a sexual act where no one experiences pleasure even though someone may experience affection or "relief of tension" through orgasm. Sexual pleasure can be considered either in a context of deprivation and its relief or in a context of satisfaction. Psychological theories have tended to emphasize the frustrated state of sexual desire and to construe sexual pleasure as a relief from that state. There are, however, alternative accounts of sexual pleasure that correspond more closely with our experience. Sexual pleasure is "a primary distinctively poignant pleasure experience that manifests itself from early infancy on. . . . Once experienced it continues to be savored. . . ."[4] Sexual desire is not experienced as frustration but as part of sexual pleasure. Normally, sexual desire transforms itself gradually into the pleasure that appears, misleadingly, to be an aim extrinsic to it. The natural structure of desire, not an inherent quality of frustration, accounts for the pain of an aroused but unsatisfied desire.

Sexual desire, like addictive pleasure generally, does not, except very temporarily, result in satiety. Rather, it increases the demand for more of the same while sharply limiting the possibility of substitutes. The experience of sensual pleasures, and particularly of sexual pleasures, has a pervasive effect on our perceptions of the world. We find bodies inviting, social encounters alluring, smells, tastes, and sights resonant because our perception of them includes their sexual significance. Merleau-Ponty has written of a patient for whom "perception had lost its erotic structure, both temporally and physically."[5] As the result of a brain injury the patient's capacity for sexual desire and pleasure (though not his capacity for performing sexual acts) was impaired. He no longer sought sexual intercourse of his own accord, was left indifferent by the sights and smells of available bodies, and if in the midst of sexual intercourse his partner turned away, he showed no signs of displeasure. The capacity for sexual pleasure, upon which the erotic structure of perception depends, can be accidentally damaged. The question that this case raises is whether it would be desirable to interfere with this capacity in a more systematic way than we now do. With greater biochemical and psychiatric knowledge we shall presumably be able to manipulate it at will.[6] And if that becomes possible, toward what end should we interfere? I shall return to this question after describing the other two characteristics of better sex—completeness and naturalness.

COMPLETE SEX ACTS

The completeness of a sexual act depends upon the *relation* of the participants to their own and each other's *desire*. A sex act is complete if each partner allows him/herself to be "taken over" by an active desire, which is desire not merely for the other's body but also for his/her active desire. Completeness is hard to characterize, though complete sex acts are at least as natural as any others—especially, it seems, among those people who take them casually and for granted. The notion of "completeness" (as I shall call it) has figured under various guises in the work of Sartre, Merleau-Ponty, and more recently Thomas Nagel. "The being which desires is consciousness making itself body." [7] "What we try to possess, then, is not just a body, but a body brought to life by consciousness." [8] "It is important that the partner be aroused, and not merely aroused, but aroused by the awareness of one's desire." [9]

The precondition of complete sex acts is the "embodiment" of the participants. Each participant submits to sexual desires that take over consciousness and direct action. It is sexual desire and not a separable satisfaction of it (for example, orgasm) that is important here. Indeed, Sartre finds pleasure external to the essence of desire, and Nagel gives an example of embodiment in which the partners do not touch each other. Desire is pervasive and "overwhelming," but it does not make its subject its involuntary victim (as it did the Boston Strangler, we are told), nor does it, except at its climax, alter capacities for ordinary perceptions, memories, and inferences. Nagel's embodied partners can presumably get themselves from bar stools to bed while their consciousness is "clogged" with desire. With what, then, is embodiment contrasted?

Philosophers make statements that when intended literally are evidence of pathology: "Human beings are automata"; "I never really see physical objects"; "I can never know what another person is feeling." The clearest statement of disembodiment that I know of is W. T. Stace's claim: "I become aware of my body in the end chiefly because it insists on accompanying me wherever I go." [10] What "just accompanies me" can also stay away. "When my body leaves me/I'm lonesome for it./ . . . body/goes away I don't know where/ and it's lonesome to drift/above the space it/fills when it's here." [11] If "the body is felt more as one object among other objects in the world than as the core of the individual's own being," [12] then what appears to be bodily can be dissociated from the "real self." Both a generalized separation of "self" from body and particular disembodied experiences have had their advocates. The attempt at disembodiment has also been seen as conceptually confused and psychologically disastrous.

We may often experience ourselves as relatively disembodied, observing or "using" our bodies to fulfill our intentions. On some occasions, however, such as in physical combat, sport, physical suffering, or danger, we "become" our bodies; our consciousness becomes bodily experience of bodily activity.[13] Sexual acts are occasions for such embodiment; they may, however, fail for a variety of reasons, for example, because of pretense or an excessive need for self-control. If someone is embodied by sexual desire, s/he submits to its direction. Spontaneous impulses of desire become his/her movements—some involuntary, like gestures of "courting behavior" or physical expressions of intense pleasure, and some deliberate. His/Her consciousness, or "mind," is taken over by desire and the pursuit of its object, in the way that at other times it may be taken over by an intellectual problem or by obsessive fantasies. But unlike the latter takeovers, this one is bodily. A desiring consciousness is flooded with specifically sexual feelings that eroticize all perception and movement. Consciousness "becomes flesh."

Granted the precondition of embodiment, complete sex acts occur when each partner's embodying desire is active and actively responsive to the other's. This second aspect of complete sex constitutes a "reflexive mutual recognition" of desire by desire.[14]

The partner *actively* desires another person's desire. Active desiring includes more than embodiment, which might be achieved in objectless masturbation. It is more, also, than merely being aroused by and then taken over by desire, though it may come about as a result of deliberate arousal. It commits the actively desiring person to his/her desire and requires him/her to identify with it—that is, to recognize herself as a sexual agent as well as respondent. (Active desiring is less encouraged in women, and probably more women than men feel threatened by it.)

The other recognizes and responds to the partner's desire. Merely to recognize the desire as desire, not to reduce it to an itch or to depersonalize it as a "demand," may be threatening. Imperviousness to desire is the deepest defense against it. We have learned from research on families whose members tend to become schizophrenic that such imperviousness, the refusal to recognize a feeling for what it is, can force a vulnerable person to deny or to obscure the real nature of his/her feelings. Imperviousness tends to deprive even a relatively invulnerable person of his efficacy. The demand that our feelings elicit a response appropriate to them is part of a general demand that *we* be recognized, that our feelings be allowed to make a difference.

There are many ways in which sexual desire may be recognized, countless forms of submission and resistance. In complete sex, desire is recognized by a responding and active desire that commits the other, as it committed the partner. Given responding desire, both people identify themselves as sexually desiring the other. They are neither seducer nor seduced, neither suppliant nor benefactress, neither sadist nor victim, but sexual agents acting sexually out of their recognized desire. Indeed, in complete sex one not only welcomes and recognizes active desire, one desires it. Returned and endorsed desire becomes one of the features of an erotically structured perception. Desiring becomes desirable. (Men are less encouraged to desire the other's active and demanding desire, and such desiring is probably threatening to more men than women.)

In sum, in complete sex two persons embodied by sexual desire actively desire and respond to each other's active desire. Although it is difficult to write of complete sex without suggesting that one of the partners is the initiator, while the other responds, complete sex is reciprocal sex. The partners, whatever the circumstances of their coming together, are equal in activity and responsiveness of desire.

Sexual acts can be partly incomplete. A necrophiliac may be taken over by desire, and a "frigid" woman may respond to her lover's desire without being embodied by her own. Partners whose sexual activities are accompanied by private fantasies engage in an incomplete sex act. Consciousness is used by desire but remains apart from it, providing it with stimulants and controls. Neither partner responds to the other's desire, though each may appear to. Sartre's "dishonest masturbator," for whom masturbation is the sex act of choice, engages in a paradigmatically incomplete sex act: "He asks only to be slightly distanced from his own body, only for there to be a light coating of otherness over his flesh and over his thoughts. His personae are melting sweets. . . . The masturbator is enchanted at never being able to feel himself sufficiently another, and at producing for himself alone the diabolic appearance of a couple that fades away when one touches it. . . . Masturbation is the derealisation of the world and of the masturbator himself." [15]

Completeness is more difficult to describe than incompleteness, for it turns on precise but subtle ways of responding to a particular person's desire with specific expressions of impulse that are both spontaneous and responsive.

There are many possible sex acts that are pleasurable but not complete. Sartre, Nagel, and Merleau-Ponty each suggest that the desire for the responsive desire of one's partner is the "central impulse" of sexual desire.[16] The desire for a sleeping woman, for example, is possible only "in so far as this sleep appears on the ground of consciousness." [17] This seems much too strong. Some lovers desire that their partners resist, others like them coolly controlled, others prefer them asleep. We would not say that there was anything abnormal or less fully sexual about desire. Whether or not complete sex is preferable to incomplete sex (the question to which I shall turn shortly), incompleteness does not disqualify a sex act from being fully sexual.

The final characteristic of allegedly better sex acts is that they are "natural" rather than "perverted." The ground for classifying sexual acts as either natural or unnatural is that the former type serve or could serve the evolutionary and biological function of sexuality—namely, reproduction. "Natural" sexual desire has as its "object" living persons of the opposite sex, and in particular their postpubertal genitals. The "aim" of natural sexual desire—that is, the act that "naturally" completes it—is genital intercourse. Perverse sex acts are deviations from the natural object (for example, homosexuality, fetishism) or from the standard aim (for example, voyeurism, sadism). Among the variety of objects and aims of sexual desire, I can see no other ground for selecting some as natural, except that they are of the type that can lead to reproduction.[18]

The connection of sexual desire with reproduction gives us the criterion but not the motive of the classification. The concept of perversion depends on a disjointedness between our experience of sexual desire from infancy on and the function of sexual desire—reproduction. In our collective experience of sexuality, perverse desires are as natural as nonperverse ones. The sexual desire of the polymorphously perverse child has many objects—for example, breasts, anus, mouth, genitals—and many aims—for example, autoerotic or other-directed looking, smelling, touching, hurting. From the social and developmental point of view, natural sex is an achievement, partly biological, partly conventional, consisting in a dominant organization of sexual desires in which perverted aims or objects are subordinate to natural ones. The concept of perversion reflects the vulnerability as much as the evolutionary warrant of this organization.

The connection of sexual desire with reproduction is not sufficient to yield the concept of perversion, but it is surely necessary. Nagel, however, thinks otherwise. There are, he points out, many sexual acts that do not lead to reproduction but that we are not even inclined to call perverse—for example, sexual acts between partners who are sterile. Perversion, according to him, is a psychological concept while reproduction is (only?) a physiological one. (Incidentally, this view of reproduction seems to me the clearest instance of male bias in Nagel's paper.)

Nagel is right about our judgments of particular acts, but he draws the wrong conclusions from those judgments. The perversity of sex acts does not depend upon whether they are intended to achieve reproduction. "Natural" sexual desire is for heterosexual genital activity, not for reproduction. The ground for classifying that desire as natural is that it is so organized that it *could* lead to reproduction in normal physiological circumstances. The reproductive organization of sexual desires gives us a *criterion* of naturalness, but the *virtue* of which it is a criterion is the "naturalness" itself, not reproduction. Our vacillating attitude toward the apparently perverse acts of animals reflects our shifting from criterion to virtue. If, when confronted with a perverse act of animals, we withdraw the label "perverted" from our similar acts rather than extend it to theirs, we are relinquishing the reproductive criterion of naturalness, while retaining the virtue. Animals cannot be "unnatural." If, on the other hand, we "discover" that animals can be perverts too, we are maintaining our criterion, but giving a somewhat altered sense to the "naturalness" of which it is a criterion.

Nagel's alternative attempt to classify acts as natural or perverted on the basis of their completeness fails. "Perverted" and "complete" are evaluations of an entirely different order. The completeness of a sex act depends upon qualities of the participants' experience and upon qualities of their relation—qualities of which they are the best judge. To say a sex act is perverted is to pass a conventional judgment about characteristics of the act, which could be evident to any observer. As one can pretend to be angry but not to shout, one can pretend to a complete, but not to a natural, sex act (though one may, of course, conceal desires for perverse sex acts or shout in order to mask one's feelings). As Nagel himself sees, judgments about particular sex acts clearly differentiate between perversion and completeness. Unadorned heterosexual intercourse where each partner has private fantasies is clearly "natural" and clearly "incomplete," but there is nothing prima facie incomplete about exclusive oral-genital intercourse or homosexual acts. If many perverse acts are incomplete, as Nagel claims, this is an important fact *about* perversion, but it is not the basis upon which we judge its occurrence.

IS BETTER SEX REALLY BETTER?

Some sex acts are, allegedly, better than others insofar as they are more pleasurable, complete, and natural. What is the moral significance of this evaluation? In answering this question, official sexual morality sometimes appeals to the social consequences of particular types of better sex acts. For example, since dominantly perverse organizations of sexual impulses limit reproduction, the merits of perversion depend upon the need to limit or increase population. Experience of sexual pleasure may be desirable if it promotes relaxation and communication in an acquisitive society, undesirable if it limits the desire to work or, in armies, to kill. The social consequences of complete sex have not received particular attention, because the quality of sexual experience has been of little interest to moralists. It might be found that those who had complete sexual relations were more cooperative, less amenable to political revolt. If so, complete sexual acts would be desirable in just and peaceable societies, undesirable in unjust societies requiring revolution.

The social desirability of types of sexual acts depends on particular social conditions and independent criteria of social desirability. It may be interesting and important to assess particular claims about the social desirability of sex acts, but this is not my concern. What is my concern is the extent to which we will allow our judgments of sexual worth to be influenced by social considerations. But this issue cannot even be raised until we have a better sense of sexual worth.

THE BENEFIT OF SEXUAL PLEASURE

To say that an experience is pleasant is to give a self-evident, terminal reason for seeking it. We can sometimes "see" that an experience is pleasant. When, for example, we observe someone's sensual delight in eating, his/her behavior can expressively characterize pleasure. We can only question the benefit of such an experience by referring to other goods with which it might conflict. Though sensual pleasures may not be sufficient to warrant giving birth or to deter suicide, so long as we live they are self-evidently benefits to us.

The most eloquent detractors of sexual experience have admitted that it provides sensual pleasures so poignant that once experienced they are repeatedly, almost addictively, sought. Yet, unlike other appetites, such as hunger, sexual desire can be permanently resisted, and resistance has been advocated. How can the prima facie benefits of sexual pleasure appear deceptive?

There are several grounds for complaint. Sexual pleasure is ineradicably mixed, frustration being part of every sexual life. The capacity for sexual pleasure is unevenly distributed, cannot be voluntarily acquired, and diminishes through no fault of its subject. If such a pleasure were an intrinsic benefit, benefit would in this case be independent of moral effort. Then again, sexual pleasures are not serious. Enjoyment of them is one of life's greatest recreations, but none of its business. And finally, sexual desire has the defects of its strengths. Before satisfaction, it is, at the least, distracting; in satisfaction, it "makes one little roome, an everywhere." Like psychosis, sexual desire turns us from "reality"— whether the real be God, social justice, children, or intellectual endeavor. This turning away is more than a social consequence of desire, though it is that. Lovers themselves feel that their sexual desires are separate from their "real" political, domestic, ambitious, social selves.

If the plaintiff is taken to argue that sensual pleasures are not peremptory benefits, s/he is probably right. We can still want a good deal and forego sexual pleasures. We often forego pleasure just because we want something incompatible with it, for example, a good marriage. We must distinguish between giving up some occasions for sexual pleasure and giving up sexual pleasure itself. When all circumstances of sexual pleasure seem to threaten a peremptory benefit, such as self-respect, then the hope and the possibility of sexual pleasure may be relinquished. Since sexual pleasure is such a great, though optional, benefit, its loss is a sad one.

In emphasizing the unsocial, private nature of sexual experiences, the plaintiff is emphasizing a morally important characteristic of them. But the case against desire, as I have sketched it, is surely overstated. The mixed, partly frustrated character of any desire is not particularly pronounced for sexual desire, which is in fact especially plastic, or adaptable to changes (provided perverse sex acts have not been ruled out). Inhibition, social deprivation, or disease make our sexual lives unpleasant, but that is because they interfere with sexual desire, not because the desire is by its nature frustrating. More than other well-known desires (for example, desire for knowledge, success, or power), sexual desire is simply and completely satisfied upon attaining its object. Partly for this reason, even if we are overtaken by desire during sexual experience, our sexual experiences do not overtake us. Lovers turn away from the world while loving, but return—sometimes all too easily—when loving is done. The moralist rightly perceives sexual pleasure as a recreation, and those who upon realizing its benefits make a business of its pursuit appear ludicrous. The capacity for recreation, however, is surely a benefit that any human being rightly hopes for who hopes for anything. Indeed, in present social and economic conditions we are more likely to lay waste our powers in work than in play. Thus, though priest, revolutionary, and parent are alike in fearing sexual pleasure, this fear should inspire us to psychological and sociological investigation of the fearing rather than to moral doubt about the benefit of sexual pleasure.

THE MORAL SIGNIFICANCE OF PERVERSION

What is the moral significance of the perversity of a sexual act? Next to none, so far as I can see. Though perverted sex may be "unnatural" both from an evolutionary and developmental perspective, there is no connection, inverse or correlative, between what is natural and what is good. Perverted sex is sometimes said to be less pleasurable than natural sex. We have little reason to believe that this claim is true and no clear idea of the kind of evidence on which it would be based. In any case, to condemn perverse acts for lack of pleasure is to recognize the worth of pleasure, not of naturalness.

There are many other claims about the nature and consequences of perversion. Some merely restate "scientific" facts in morally tinged terminology. Perverse acts are, by definition and according to psychiatric theory, "immature" and "abnormal," since natural sex acts are selected by criteria of "normal" sexual function and "normal" and "mature" psychological development. But there is no greater connection of virtue with maturity and normality than there is of virtue with nature. The elimination of a village by an invading army would be no less evil if it were the expression of controlled, normal, natural, and mature aggression.

Nagel claims that many perverted sex acts are incomplete, and in making his point, gives the most specific arguments that I have read for the inferiority of perverted sex. But as he points out, there is no reason to think an act consisting solely of oral-genital intercourse is incomplete; it is doubtful whether homosexual acts and acts of buggery are especially liable to be incomplete; and the incompleteness of sexual intercourse with animals is a relative matter depending upon their limited consciousness. And again, the alleged inferiority is not a consequence of perversion but of incompleteness, which can afflict natural sex as well.

Perverted acts might be thought to be inferior because they cannot result in children. Whatever the benefits and moral significance of the procreation and care of children (and I believe they are extensive and complicated), the virtue of proper care for children neither requires nor follows from biological parenthood. Even if it did, only a sexual life consisting solely of perverse acts rules out conception.

If perverted sex acts did rule out normal sex acts, if one were *either* perverted *or* natural, then certain kinds of sexual relations would be denied some perverts—relations that are benefits to those who enjoy them. It seems that sexual relations with the living and the human would be of greater benefit than those with the dead or with animals. But there is no reason to think that heterosexual relations are of greater benefit than homosexual ones. It might be that children can only be raised by heterosexual couples who perform an abundance of natural sex acts. If so (though it seems unlikely), perverts will be denied the happiness of parenthood. This would be an *indirect* consequence of perverted sex and might yield a moral dilemma: How is one to choose between the benefits of children and the benefits of more pleasurable, more complete sex acts?

Some perversions are immoral on independent grounds. Sadism is the obvious example, though sadism practiced with a consenting masochist is far less evil than other, more familiar forms of aggression. Voyeurism may seem immoral because, since it must be secret to be satisfying, it violates others' rights to privacy.[19] Various kinds of rape can constitute perversion if rape, rather than genital intercourse, is the aim of desire. Rape is seriously immoral, a vivid violation of respect for persons. Sometimes doubly perverse rape is doubly evil (the rape of a child), but in other cases (the rape of a pig) its evil is halved. In any case, though rape is always wrong, it is only perverse when raping becomes the aim and not the means of desire.

Someone can be dissuaded from acting on his perverse desires either from moral qualms or from social fears. Although there may be ample basis for the latter, I can find none for the former except the possible indirect loss of the benefits of child care. I am puzzled about this since reflective people who do not usually attempt to legislate the preferences of others think differently. There is no doubt that beliefs in these matters involve deep emotions that should be respected. But for those who do in fact have perverted desires, the first concern will be to satisfy them, not to divert or to understand them. For sexual pleasure is intrinsically a benefit, and complete sex acts, which depend upon expressing the desires one in fact has, are both beneficial and conducive to virtue. Therefore, barring extrinsic moral or social considerations, perverted

Better Sex 255

sex acts are preferable to natural ones if the latter are less pleasurable or less complete.

THE MORAL SIGNIFICANCE OF COMPLETENESS

Complete sex consists in mutually embodied, mutually active, responsive desire. Embodiment, activity, and mutual responsiveness are instrumentally beneficial because they are conducive to our psychological well-being, which is an intrinsic benefit. The alleged pathological consequences of disembodiment are more specific and better documented than those of perversity.[20] To dissociate oneself from one's actual body, either by creating a delusory body or by rejecting the bodily, is to court a variety of ill effects, ranging from self-disgust to diseases of the will, to faulty mental development, to the destruction of a recognizable "self," and finally to madness. It is difficult to assess psychiatric claims outside their theoretical contexts, but in this case I believe that they are justified. Relative embodiment is a stable, *normal* condition that is not confined to cases of complete embodiment. But psychiatrists tell us that exceptional physical occasions of embodiment seem to be required in order to balance tendencies to reject or to falsify the body. Sexual acts are not the only such occasions, but they do provide an immersion of consciousness in the bodily, which is pleasurable and especially conducive to correcting experiences of shame and disgust that work toward disembodiment.

The mutual responsiveness of complete sex is also instrumentally beneficial. It satisfies a general desire to be recognized as a particular "real" person and to make a difference to other particular "real" people. The satisfaction of this desire in sexual experience is especially rewarding, its thwarting especially cruel. Vulnerability is increased in complete sex by the active desiring of the partners. When betrayal, or for that matter, tenderness or ecstasy, ensues, one cannot dissociate oneself from the desire with which one identified and out of which one acted. The psychic danger is real, as people who attempt to achieve a distance from their desires could tell us. But the cost of distance is as evident as its gains. Passivity in respect to one's own sexual desire not only limits sexual pleasure but, more seriously, limits the extent to which the experience of sexual pleasure can be included as an experience of a coherent person. With passivity comes a kind of irresponsibility in which one can hide from one's desire, even from one's pleasure, "playing" seducer or victim, tease or savior. Active sexual desiring in complete sex acts affords an especially threatening but also especially happy occasion to relinquish these and similar roles. To the extent that the roles confuse and confound our intimate relations, the benefit from relinquishing them in our sexual acts, or the loss from adhering to them then, is especially poignant.

In addition to being beneficial, complete sex acts are morally superior for three reasons. They tend to resolve tensions fundamental to moral life; they are conducive to emotions that, if they become stable and dominant, are in turn conducive to the virtue of loving; and they involve a preeminently moral virtue—respect for persons.

In one of its aspects, morality is opposed to the private and untamed. Morality is "civilization," social and regulating; desire is "discontent" resisting the regulation. Obligation, rather than benefit, is the notion central to morality so conceived, and the virtues required of a moral person are directed to preserving right relations and social order. Both the insistence on natural sex and the encouragement of complete sex can be looked upon as attempts to make sexual desire more amenable to regulation. But whereas the regulation of perverted desires is extrinsic to them, those of completeness modify the desires themselves. The desiring sensual body that in our social lives we may laugh away or disown becomes our "self" and enters into a social relation. Narcissism and altruism are satisfied in complete sex acts in which one gives what one receives by receiving it. Social and private "selves" are unified in an act in which impersonal, spontaneous impulses govern an action that is responsive to a particular person. For this to be true we must surmount our social "roles" as well as our sexual "techniques," though we incorporate rather than surmount our social selves. We must also surmount regulations imposed in the name of naturalness if our desires are to be spontaneously expressed. Honestly spontaneous first love gives us back our private desiring selves while allowing us to see the desiring self of another. Mutually responding partners confirm each others' desires and declare them good. Such occasions, when we are "moral" without cost, help reconcile us to our moral being and to the usual mutual exclusion between our social and private lives.

The connection between sex and certain emotions—particularly love, jealousy, fear, and anger—is as evident as it is obscure. Complete sex acts seem more likely than incomplete pleasurable ones to lead toward affection and away from fear and anger, since any guilt and shame will be extrinsic to the act and meliorated by it. It is clear that we need not feel for someone any affection beyond that required (if any is) simply to participate with him/her in a complete sex act. However, it is equally clear that sexual pleasure, especially as experienced in complete sex acts, is conducive to many feelings—gratitude, tenderness, pride, appreciation, dependency, and others. These feelings magnify their object who occasioned them. When these magnifying feelings become stable and habitual they are conducive to love—not universal love, of course, but love of a particular sexual partner. However, even "selfish" love is a virtue, a disposition to care for someone as her interests and demands would dictate. Neither the best sex nor the best love require each other, but they go together more often than reason would expect—often enough to count the virtue of loving as one of the rewards of the capacity for sexual pleasure exercised in complete sex acts.

It might be argued that the coincidence of sex acts and several valued emotions is a cultural matter. It is notoriously difficult to make judgments about the emotional and, particularly, the sexual lives of others, especially culturally alien others. There is, however, some anthropological evidence that at first glance relativizes the connection between good sex and valued emotion. For example, among the Manus of New Guinea, it seems that relations of affection and love are encouraged primarily among brother and sister, while easy familiarity, joking, and superficial sexual play is expected only between cross-cousins. Sexual intercourse is, however, forbidden between siblings and cross-cousins but required of married men and women, who are as apt to hate as to care for each other and often seem to consider each other strangers. It seems, however, that the Manus do not value or experience complete or even pleasurable sex. Both men and women are described as puritanical, and the sexual life of women seems blantantly unrewarding. Moreover, their emotional life is generally impoverished. This impoverishment, in conjunction with an unappreciated and unrewarding sexual life dissociated from love or affection, would argue for a connection between better sex and valued emotions. If, as Peter Winch suggests, cultures provide their members with particular possibilities of making sense of their lives, and thereby with possibilities of good and evil, the Manus might be said to deny themselves one possibility both of sense and of good—namely the coincidence of good sex and of affection and love. Other cultures, including our own, allow this possibility, whose realization is encouraged in varying degrees by particular groups and members of the culture.[21]

Finally, as Sartre has suggested, complete sex acts preserve a respect for persons. Each person remains conscious and responsible, a "subject" rather than a depersonalized, will-less, or manipulated "object." Each actively desires that the other likewise remain a "subject." Respect for persons is a central virtue when matters of justice and obligation are at issue. Insofar as we can speak of respect for persons in complete sex acts, there are different, often contrary requirements of respect. Respect for persons, typically and in sex acts, requires that *actual present* partners participate, partners whose desires are recognized and endorsed. Respect for persons typically requires taking a distance from both one's own demands and those of others. But in sex acts the demands of desire take over, and equal distance is replaced by mutual responsiveness. Respect typically requires refusing to treat another person merely as a means to fulfilling demands. In sex acts, another person is so clearly a means to satisfaction that s/he is always on the verge of becoming merely a means ("intercourse counterfeits masturbation"). In complete sex acts, instrumentality vanishes only because it is mutual and mutually desired. Respect requires encouraging, or at least protecting, the autonomy of another. In complete sex, autonomy of will is recruited by desire, and freedom from others is replaced by frank dependence on another person's desire. Again the respect consists in the reciprocity of desiring dependence, which bypasses rather than violates autonomy.

Despite the radical differences between respect for persons in the usual moral contexts and respect for persons in sex acts, it is not, I think, a mere play on words to talk of respect in the latter case. When, in any sort of intercourse, persons are respected, their desires are not only, in fair measure, fulfilled. In addition, their desires are active and determine, in fair measure, the form of intercourse and the manner and condition of desire's satisfaction. These conditions are not only met in sexual intercourse when it is characterized by completeness; they come close to defining completeness.

Sartre is not alone in believing that just because the condition of completeness involves respect for persons, complete sex is impossible. Completeness is surely threatened by pervasive tendencies to fantasy, to possessiveness, and to varieties of a sadomaochistic desire. But a complete sex act, as I see it, does not involve an heroic restraint on our sexual interpulses. Rather, a complete sex act is a normal mode of sexual activity expressing the natural structure and impulses of sexual desire.

While complete sex is morally superior because it involves respect for persons, incomplete sex acts do not necessarily involve immoral disrespect for persons. They may, depending upon the desires and expectations of the partners; but they may involve neither respect nor disrespect. Masturbation, for example, allows only the limited completeness of embodiment and often fails of that. But masturbation only rarely involves disrespect to anyone. Even the respect of the allegedly desirable sleeping woman may not be violated if she is unknowingly involved in a sex act. Disrespect, though likely, may be obviated by her sensibilities and expectations that she has previously expressed and her partner has understood. Sex acts provide one context in which respect for persons can be expressed. That context is important both because our sexual lives are of such importance to us and because they are so liable to injury because of the experience and the fear of the experience of disrespect. But many complete sex acts in which respect is maintained make other casual and incomplete sex acts unthreatening. In this case a goodly number of swallows can make a summer.

In sum, then, complete sex acts are superior to incomplete ones. First, they are, whatever their effects, better than various kinds of incomplete sex acts because they involve a kind of "respect for persons" in acts that are otherwise prone to violation of respect for, and often to violence to, persons. Second, complete sex acts are good because they are good for us. They are conducive to some fairly clearly defined kinds of psychological well-being that are beneficial. They are conducive to moral well-being because they relieve tensions that arise in our attempts to be moral and because they encourage the development of particular virtues.

To say that complete sex acts are preferable to incomplete ones is not to court a new puritanism. There are many kinds and degrees of incompleteness. Incomplete sex acts may not involve a disrespect for persons. Complete sex acts only *tend* to be good for us, and the realization of these tendencies depends upon individual lives and circumstances of sexual activity. The proper object of sexual desire is sexual pleasure. It would be a foolish ambition indeed to limit one's sexual acts to those in which completeness was likely. Any sexual act that is pleasurable is prima facie good, though the more incomplete it is—the more private, essentially autoerotic, unresponsive, unembodied, passive, or imposed—the more likely it is to be harmful to someone.

ON SEXUAL MORALITY: CONCLUDING REMARKS

There are many questions we have neglected to consider because we have not been sufficiently attentive to the quality of sexual lives. For example, we know little about the ways of achieving better sex. When we must choose between inferior sex and abstinence, how and when will our choice of inferior sex damage our capacity for better sex? Does, for example, the repeated experience of controlled sexual disembodiment ("desire which takes over will take you too far") that we urge (or used to urge) on adolescents damage their capacity for complete sex? The answers to this and similar questions are not obvious, though unfounded opinions are always ready at hand.

Some of the traditional sexual vices might be condemned on the ground that they are inimical to better sex. Obscenity, or repeated public exposure to sexual acts, might impair our capacity for pleasure or for response to desire. Promiscuity might undercut the tendency of complete sex acts to promote emotions that magnify their object. Other of the traditional sexual vices are neither inimical nor conducive to better sex, but are condemned because of conflicting nonsexual benefits and obligations. For example, infidelity qua infidelity neither secures nor prevents better sex. The obligations of fidelity have many sources, one of which may be a past history of shared complete sex acts, a history that included promises of exclusive intimacy. Such past promises are as apt to conflict with as to accord with a current demand for better sex. I have said nothing about how such a conflict would be settled. I hope I have shown that where the possibility of better sex conflicts with obligations and other benefits, we have a *moral dilemma*, not just an occasion for moral self-discipline.

The pursuit of more pleasurable and more complete sex acts is, among many moral activities, distinguished not for its exigencies but for its rewards. Since our sexual lives are so important to us, and since, whatever our history and our hopes, we are sexual beings, this pursuit rightly engages our moral reflection. It should not be relegated to the immoral, nor to the "merely" prudent.

NOTES

1. An earlier version of this paper was published in *Moral Problems,* edited by James Rachels (New York: Harper & Row, 1971). I am grateful to many friends and students for their comments on the earlier version, especially to Bernard Gert, Evelyn Fox Keller, and James Rachels.

2. This may be a consequence of the tepidness of the English "pleasant." It would be better to speak of lust and its satisfaction if our suspicion of pleasure had not been written into that part of our language.

3. The example is from Sigmund Freud, *Three Essays on Sexuality,* standard ed., vol. 7 (London: Hogarth, 1963), p. 182. The concept of pleasure I urge here is narrower but also, I think, more useful than the popular one. It is a concept that, to paraphrase Wittgenstein, we (could) learn when we learn the language. The idea of paradigmatic uses and subsequent more-or-less-divergent, more-or-less "normal" uses also is derived from Wittgenstein.

4. George Klein, "Freud's Two Theories of Sexuality," in L. Berger, ed., *Clinical-Cognitive Psychology: Models and Integrations* (Englewood Cliffs, N.J.: Prentice-Hall, 1969), pp. 131-81. This essay gives a clear idea of alternative psychological accounts of sexual pleasure.

5. Maurice Merleau-Ponty, *Phenomenology of Perception,* trans. Colin Smith (London: Routledge & Kegan Paul, 1962), p. 156.

6. See Kurt Vonnegut, Jr., "Welcome to the Monkey House," in *Welcome to the Monkey House* (New York: Dell, 1968), which concerns both the manipulation and the benefit of sexual pleasure.

7. Jean-Paul Sartre, *Being and Nothingness,* trans. Hazel E. Barnes (New York: Philosophical Library, 1956), p. 389.

8. Merleau-Ponty, *Phenomenology of Perception,* p. 167.

9. Thomas Nagel, "Sexual Perversion," *The Journal of Philosophy* 66, no. 1 (January 16, 1969): 13; herein, pp. 255-56. My original discussion of completeness was both greatly indebted to and confused by Nagel's. I have tried here to dispel some of the confusion.

10. W. T. Stace, "Solipsism," from *The Theory of Knowledge and Existence;* reprinted in Tillman, Berofsky, and O'Connor, eds., *Introductory Philosophy* (New York: Harper & Row, 1967), p. 113.

11. Denise Levertov, "Gone Away," in *O Taste and See* (New York: New Directions, 1962), p. 59. Copyright by Denise Levertov Goodman, New Directions Publishing Corporation, New York.

12. R. D. Laing, *The Divided Self* (Baltimore: Pelican Books, 1965), p. 69.

13. We need not become our bodies on such occasions. Pains, muscular feelings, and emotions can be reduced to mere "sensations" that may impinge on "me" but that I attempt to keep at a distance. Laing describes the case of a man who when beaten up felt that any damage to his body could not really hurt *him.* See *The Divided Self,* p. 68.

14. Nagel, "Sexual Perversion," p. 254.

15. Jean-Paul Sartre, *Saint Genet* (New York: Braziller, 1963), p. 398; cited and translated by R. D. Laing, *Self and Others* (New York: Pantheon, 1969), pp. 39-40.

16. Ibid., p. 13.

17. Sartre, *Being and Nothingness,* p. 386.

18. See, in support of this point, Sigmund Freud, *Introductory Lectures on Psychoanalysis,* standard ed., vol. 26 (London: Hogarth, 1963), chaps. 20, 21.

19. I am indebted to Dr. Leo Goldberger for this example.

20. See, for example, R. D. Laing, *The Divided Self;* D. W. Winnicott, "Transitional Objects and Transitional Phenomena," *International Journal of Psychoanalysis* 34 (1953): 89-97; Paul Federn, *Ego Psychology and the Psychoses* (New York: Basic Books, 1952); Phyllis Greenacre, *Trauma, Growth, and Personality* (New York: International Universities Press, 1969); Paul Schilder, *The Image and Appearance of the Human Body* (New York: Inter-

national Universities Press, 1950); Moses Laufer, "Body Image and Masturbation in Adolescence," *The Psychoanalytic Study of the Child* 23 (1968):
114-46. Laing's work is most specific about both the nature and consequences
of disembodiment, but the works cited, and others similar to them, give the
clinical evidence upon which much of Laing's work depends.
21. The evidence about the life of the Manus comes from Margaret Mead,
Growing Up in New Guinea (Harmondsworth, Eng.: Penguin Books, 1942).
Peter Winch's discussion can be found in his "Understanding a Primitive
Society," *American Philosophical Quarterly* 1 (1964): 307-34.

Plain Sex

Alan Goldman

I

Several recent articles on sex herald its acceptance as a legitimate topic
for analytic philosophers (although it has been a topic in philosophy
since Plato). One might have thought conceptual analysis unnecessary in
this area; despite the notorious struggles of judges and legislators to
define pornography suitably, we all might be expected to know what
sex is and to be able to identify at least paradigm sexual desires and activities without much difficulty. Philosophy is nevertheless of relevance
here if for no other reason than that the concept of sex remains at the
center of moral and social consciousness in our, and perhaps any, society.
Before we can get a sensible view of the relation of sex to morality, perversion, social regulation, and marriage, we require a sensible analysis
of the concept itself; one which neither understates its animal pleasure
nor overstates its importance within a theory or system of value. I say
"before," but the order is not quite so clear, for questions in this area,
as elsewhere in moral philosophy, are both conceptual and normative at
the same time. Our concept of sex will partially determine our moral
view of it, but as philosophers we should formulate a concept that will
accord with its proper moral status. What we require here, as elsewhere,
is "reflective equilibrium," a goal not achieved by traditional and recent
analyses together with their moral implications. Because sexual activity,
like other natural functions such as eating or exercising, has become imbedded in layers of cultural, moral, and superstitious superstructure, it

is hard to conceive it in its simplest terms. But partially for this reason, it is only by thinking about plain sex that we can begin to achieve this conceptual equilibrium.

I shall suggest here that sex continues to be misrepresented in recent writings, at least in philosophical writings, and I shall criticize the predominant form of analysis which I term "means-end analysis." Such conceptions attribute a necessary external goal or purpose of sexual activity, whether it be reproduction, the expression of love, simple communication, or interpersonal awareness. They analyze sexual activity as a means to one of these ends, implying that sexual desire is a desire to reproduce, to love or be loved, or to communicate with others. All definitions of this type suggest false views of the relation of sex to perversion and morality by implying that sex which does not fit one of these models or fulfill one of these functions is in some way deviant or incomplete.

The alternative, simpler analysis with which I will begin is that sexual desire is desire for contact with another person's body and for the pleasure which such contact produces; sexual activity is activity which tends to fulfill such desire of the agent. Whereas Aristotle and Butler were correct in holding that pleasure is normally a byproduct rather than a goal of purposeful action, in the case of sex this is not so clear. The desire for another's body is, principally among other things, the desire for the pleasure that physical contact brings. On the other hand, it is not a desire for a particular sensation detachable from its causal context, a sensation which can be derived in other ways. This definition in terms of the general goal of sexual desire appears preferable to an attempt to more explicitly list or define specific sexual activities, for many activities such as kissing, embracing, massaging, or holding hands may or may not be sexual, depending upon the context and more specifically upon the purposes, needs, or desires into which such activities fit. The generality of the definition also represents a refusal (common in recent psychological texts) to overemphasize orgasm as the goal of sexual desire or genital sex as the only norm of sexual activity (this will be hedged slightly in the discussion of perversion below).

Central to the definition is the fact that the goal of sexual desire and activity is the physical contact itself, rather than something else which this contact might express. By contrast, what I term "means-end analyses" posit ends which I take to be extraneous to plain sex, and they view sex as a means to these ends. Their fault lies not in defining sex in terms of its general goal, but in seeing plain sex as merely a means to other separable ends. I term these "means-end analyses" for convenience, although "means-separable-end analyses," while too cumbersome, might be more fully explanatory. The desire for physical contact with another person is a minimal criterion for (normal) sexual desire, but is both necessary and sufficient to qualify normal desire as sexual. Of course, we may want to express other feelings through sexual acts in various contexts; but without the desire for the physical contact in and for itself, or when it is sought for other reasons, activities in which contact is involved are not predominantly sexual. Furthermore, the desire for physical contact in itself, without the wish to express affection or other feelings through it, is sufficient to render sexual the activity of the agent which fulfills it. Various activities with this goal alone, such as kissing and caressing in certain contexts, qualify as sexual even without the presence of genital symptoms of sexual excitement. The latter are not therefore necessary criteria for sexual activity.

This initial analysis may seem to some either over- or underinclusive. It might seem too broad in leading us to interpret physical contact as sexual desire in activities such as football and other contact sports. In these cases, however, the desire is not for contact with another body per se, it is not directed toward a particular person for that purpose, and it is not the goal of the activity—the goal is winning or exercising or knocking someone down or displaying one's prowess. If the desire is purely for contact with another specific person's body, then to interpret it as sexual does not seem an exaggeration. A slightly more difficult case is that of a baby's desire to be cuddled and our natural response in wanting to cuddle it. In the case of the baby, the desire may be simply for the physical contact, for the pleasure of the caresses. If so, we may characterize this desire, especially in keeping with Freudian theory, as sexual or protosexual. It will differ nevertheless from full-fledged sexual desire in being more amorphous, not directed outward toward another specific person's body. It may also be that what the infant unconsciously desires is not physical contact per se but signs of affection, tenderness, or security, in which case we have further reason for hesitating to characterize its wants as clearly sexual. The intent of our response to the baby is often the showing of affection, not the pure physical contact, so that our definition in terms of action which fulfills sexual desire *on the part of the agent* does not capture such actions, whatever we say of the baby. (If it is intuitive to characterize our response as sexual as well, there is clearly no problem here for my analysis.) The same can be said of signs of affection (or in some cultures polite greeting) among men or women: these certainly need not be homosexual when the intent is only to show friendship, something extrinsic to plain sex although valuable when added to it.

Our definition of sex in terms of the desire for physical contact may appear too narrow in that a person's personality, not merely her or his body, may be sexually attractive to another, and in that looking or conversing in a certain way can be sexual in a given context without bodily contact. Nevertheless, it is not the contents of one's thoughts per se that are sexually appealing, but one's personality as embodied in certain manners of behavior. Furthermore, if a person is sexually attracted by another 's personality, he or she will desire not just further conversation, but actual sexual contact. While looking at or conversing with someone can be interpreted as sexual in given contexts it is so when intended as preliminary to, and hence parasitic upon, elemental sexual interest. Voyeurism or viewing a pornographic movie qualifies as a sexual activity, but only as an imaginative substitute for the real thing (otherwise a deviation from the norm as expressed in our definition). The same is true of masturbation as a sexual activity without a partner.

That the initial definition indicates at least an ingredient of sexual desire and activity is too obvious to argue. We all know what sex is, at least in obvious cases, and do not need philosophers to tell us. My preliminary analysis is meant to serve as a contrast to what sex is not, at least for another's body, and I take as central the immersion in the physical aspect of one's own existence and attention to the physical embodiment of the other. One may derive pleasure in a sex act from expressing certain feelings to one's partner or from awareness of the attitude of one's partner, but sexual desire is essentially desire for physical contact itself: it is a bodily desire for the body of another that dominates our mental life for more or less brief periods. Traditional writings were correct to emphasize the purely physical or animal aspect of sex; they were wrong only in condemning it. This characterization of sex as an intensely pleasurable physical activity and acute physical desire may seem to some to capture only its barest level. But it is worth distinguishing and focusing upon the least common denominator in order to avoid the false views of sexual morality and perversion which emerge from thinking that sex is essentially something else.

II

We may turn then to what sex is not, to the arguments regarding supposed conceptual connections between sex and other activities which it is necessary to conceptually distinguish. The most comprehensible attempt to build an extraneous purpose into the sex act identifies that purpose as reproduction, its primary biological function. While this may be "nature's" purpose, it certainly need not be ours (the analogy with eating, while sometimes overworked, is pertinent here). While this identification may once have had a rational basis which also grounded the identification of the value and morality of sex with that applicable to reproduction and childrearing, the development of contraception rendered the connection weak. Methods of contraception are by now so familiar and so widely used that it is not necessary to dwell upon the changes wrought by these developments in the concept of sex itself and in a rational sexual ethic dependent upon that concept. In the past, the ever present possibility of children rendered the concepts of sex and sexual morality different from those required at present. There may be good reasons, if the presence and care of both mother and father are beneficial to children, for restricting reproduction to marriage. Insofar as society has a legitimate role in protecting children's interests, it may be justified in giving marriage a legal status, although this question is complicated by the fact (among others) that children born to single mothers deserve no penalties. In any case, the point here is simply that these questions are irrelevant at the present time to those regarding the morality of sex and its potential social regulation. (Further connections with marriage will be discussed below.)

It is obvious that the desire for sex is not necessarily a desire to reproduce, that the psychological manifestation has become, if it were not always, distinct from its biological roots. There are many parallels, as previously mentioned, with other natural functions. The pleasures of eating and exercising are to a large extent independent of their roles in nourishment or health (as the junk-food industry discovered with a vengeance). Despite the obvious parallel with sex, there is still a tendency for many to think that sex acts which can be reproductive are, if not more moral or less immoral, at least more natural. These categories of morality and "naturalness," or normality, are not to be identified with each other, as will be argued below, and neither is applicable to sex by virtue of its connection to reproduction. The tendency to identify reproduction as the conceptually connected end of sex is most prevalent now in the pronouncements of the Catholic church. There the assumed analysis is clearly tied to a restrictive sexual morality according to which acts become immoral and unnatural when they are not oriented towards reproduction, a morality which has independent roots in the Christian sexual ethic as it derives from Paul. However, the means-end analysis fails to generate a consistent sexual ethic: homosexual and oral-genital sex is condemned while kissing or caressing, acts equally unlikely to lead in themselves to fertilization, even when properly characterized as sexual according to our definition, are not.

III

Before discussing further relations of means-end analyses to false or inconsistent sexual ethics and concepts of perversion, I turn to other examples of these analyses. One common position views sex as essentially an expression of love or affection between the partners. It is generally recognized that there are other types of love besides sexual, but sex itself is taken as an expression of one type, sometimes termed "romantic" love.[1] Various factors again ought to weaken this identification. First, there are other types of love besides that which it is appropriate to express sexually, and "romantic" love itself can be expressed in many other ways. I am not denying that sex can take on heightened value and meaning when it becomes a vehicle for the expression of feelings of love or tenderness, but so can many other usually mundane activities such as getting up early to make breakfast on Sunday, cleaning the house, and so on. Second, sex itself can be used to communicate many other emotions besides love, and, as I will argue below, can communicate nothing in particular and still be good sex.

On a deeper level, an internal tension is bound to result from an identification of sex, which I have described as a physical-psychological desire, with love as a long-term, deep emotional relationship between two individuals. As this type of relationshp, love is permanent, at least in intent, and more or less exclusive. A normal person cannot deeply love more than a few individuals even in a lifetime. We may be suspicious that those who attempt or claim to love many love them weakly if at all. Yet, fleeting sexual desire can arise in relation to a variety of other individuals one finds sexually attractive. It may even be, as some have claimed, that sexual desire in humans naturally seeks variety, while this is obviously false of love. For this reason, monogamous sex, even if justified, almost always represents a sacrifice or the exercise of self-control on the part of the spouses, while monogamous love generally does not. There is no such thing as casual love in the sense in which I intend the term "love." It may occasionally happen that a spouse falls deeply in love with someone else (especially when sex is conceived in terms of love), but this is relatively rare in comparison to passing sexual desires for others; and while the former often indicates a weakness or fault in the marriage relation, the latter does not.

If love is indeed more exclusive in its objects than is sexual desire, this explains why those who view sex as essentially an expression of love would again tend to hold a repressive or restrictive sexual ethic. As in the case of reproduction, there may be good reasons for reserving the total commitment of deep love to the context of marriage and family—the normal personality may not withstand additional divisions of ultimate commitment and allegiance. There is no question that marriage itself is best sustained by a deep relation of love and affection; and even if love is not naturally monogamous, the benefits of family units to children provide additional reason to avoid serious commitments elsewhere which weaken family ties. It can be argued similarly that monogamous sex strengthens families by restricting and at the same time guaranteeing an outlet for sexual desire in marriage. But there is more force to the argument that recognition of a clear distinction between sex and love in society would help avoid disastrous marriages which result from adolescent confusion of the two when sexual desire is mistaken for permanent love, and would weaken damaging jealousies which arise in marriages in relation to passing sexual desires. The love and affection of a sound marriage certainly differs from the adolescent romantic variety, which is often a mere substitute for sex in the context of a repressive sexual ethic.

In fact, the restrictive sexual ethic tied to the means-end analysis in terms of love again has failed to be consistent. At least, it has not been applied consistently, but forms part of the double standard which has curtailed the freedom of women. It is predictable in light of this history that some women would now advocate using sex as another kind of means, as a political weapon or as a way to increase unjustly denied power and freedom. The inconsistency in the sexual ethic typically attached to the sex-love analysis, according to which it has generally been taken with a grain of salt when applied to men, is simply another example of the impossibility of tailoring a plausible moral theory in this area to a conception of sex which builds in conceptually extraneous factors.

I am not suggesting here that sex ought never to be connected with love or that it is not a more significant and valuable activity when it is. Nor am I denying that individuals need love as much as sex and perhaps emotionally need at least one complete relationship which encompasses both. Just as sex can express love and take on heightened significance when it does, so love is often naturally accompanied by an intermittent desire for sex. But again love is accompanied appropriately by desires for other shared activities as well. What makes the desire for sex seem more intimately connected with love is the intimacy which is seen to be a natural feature of mutual sex acts. Like love, sex is held to lay one bare psychologically as well as physically. Sex is unquestionably intimate, but beyond that the psychological toll often attached may be a function of the restrictive sexual ethic itself, rather than a legitimate apology for it. The intimacy involved in love is psychologically consuming in a generally healthy way, while the psychological tolls of sexual relations, often including embarrassment as a correlate of intimacy, are too often the result of artificial sexual ethics and taboos. The intimacy involved in both love and sex is insufficient in any case in light of previous points to render a means-end analysis in these terms appropriate.

IV

In recent articles, Thomas Nagel and Robert Solomon, who recognize that sex is not merely a means to communicate love, nevertheless retain the form of this analysis while broadening it. For Solomon, sex remains a means of communicating (he explicitly uses the metaphor of body language), although the feelings that can be communicated now include, in addition to love and tenderness, domination, dependence, anger, trust, and so on.[2] Nagel does not refer explicitly to communication, but his analysis is similar in that he views sex as a complex form of interpersonal awareness in which desire itself is consciously communicated on several different levels. In sex, according to his analysis, two people are aroused by each other, aware of the other's arousal, and further aroused by this awareness.[3] Such multileveled conscious awareness of one's own and the other's desire is taken as the norm of a sexual relation, and this model is therefore close to that which views sex as a means of interpersonal communication.

Solomon's analysis is beset by the same difficulties as those pointed out in relation to the narrower sex-love concept. Just as love can be communicated by many activities other than sex, which do not therefore become properly analyzed as essentially vehicles of communication (making breakfast, cleaning the house, and so on), the same is true of the other feelings mentioned by Solomon. Domination can be communicated through economic manipulation, trust by a joint savings account. Driving a car can be simultaneously expressing anger, pride, joy, and so on. We may, in fact, communicate or express feelings in anything we do, but this does not make everything we do into language. Driving a car is not to be defined as an automotive means of communication, although with a little ingenuity we might work out an automotive vocabulary (tailgating as an expression of aggression or impatience; beating another car away from a stoplight as expressing domination) to match the vocabulary of "body language." That one can communicate various feelings during sex acts does not make these acts merely or primarily a means of communicating.

More importantly, to analyze sex as a means of communication is to overlook the intrinsic nature and value of the act itself. Sex is not a gesture or series of gestures, in fact not necessarily a means to any other end, but a physical activity intensely pleasurable in itself. When a language is used, the symbols normally have no importance in themselves; they function merely as vehicles for what can be communicated by them. Furthermore skill in the use of language is a technical achievement that must be carefully learned; if better sex is more successful communication by means of a more skillful use of body language, then we had all better be well schooled in the vocabulary and grammar. Solomon's analysis, which uses the language metaphor, suggests the appropriateness of a sex-manual approach, the substitution of a bit of technological prowess for the natural pleasure of the unforced surrender to feeling and desire.

It may be that Solomon's position could be improved by using the analogy of music rather than that of language, as an aesthetic form of communication. Music might be thought of as a form of aesthetic communicating, in which the experience of the "phonemes" themselves is generally pleasing. And listening to music is perhaps more of a sexual experience than having someone talk to you. Yet, it seems to me that insofar as music is aesthetic and pleasing in itself, it is not best conceived as primarily a means for communicating specific feelings. Such an analysis does injustice to aesthetic experience in much the same way as the sex-communication analysis debases sexual experience itself.[4]

For Solomon, sex that is not a totally self-conscious communicative art tends toward vulgarity,[5] whereas I would have thought it the other way around. This is another illustration of the tendency of means-end analyses to condemn what appears perfectly natural or normal sex on my account. Both Solomon and Nagel use their definitions, however, not primarily to stipulate moral norms for sex, as we saw in earlier analyses, but to define norms against which to measure perversion. Once again, neither is capable of generating consistency or reflective equilibrium with our firm intuitions as to what counts as subnormal sex, the problem being that both build factors into their norms which are extraneous to an unromanticized view of normal sexual desire and activity. If perversion represents a breakdown in communication, as Solomon maintains, then any unsuccessful or misunderstood advance should count as perverted. Furthermore, sex between husband and wife married for several years, or between any partners already familiar with each other, would be, if not perverted, nevertheless subnormal or trite and dull, in that the communicative content would be minimal in lacking all novelty. In fact the pleasures of sex need not wear off with familiarity, as they would if dependent upon the communicative content of the feelings. Finally, rather than a release or relief from physical desire through a substitute imaginative outlet, masturbation would become a way of practicing or rehearsing one's technique or vocabulary on oneself, or simply a way of talking to oneself, as Solomon himself says.[6]

Nagel fares no better in the implications of his overintellectualized norm. Spontaneous and heated sex between two familiar partners may well lack the complex conscious multileveled interpersonal awareness of which he speaks without being in the least perverted. The egotistical desire that one's partner be aroused by one's own desire does not seem a primary element of the sexual urge, and during sex acts one may like one's partner to be sometimes active and aroused, sometimes more passive. Just as sex can be more significant when love is communicated, so it can sometimes be heightened by an awareness of the other's desire. But at other times this awareness of an avid desire of one's partner can be merely distracting. The conscious awareness to which Nagel refers may actually impede the immersion in the physical of which I spoke above, just as may concentration upon one's "vocabulary" or technique. Sex is a way of relating to another, but primarily a physical rather than intellectual way. For Nagel, the ultimate in degeneration or perversion would have to be what he calls "mutual epidermal stimulation" [7] without mutual awareness of each other's state of mind. But this sounds like normal, if not ideal, sex to me (perhaps only a minimal description of it). His model certainly seems more appropriate to a sophisticated seduction scene than to the sex act itself,[8] which according to the model would often have to count as a subnormal anticlimax to the intellectual foreplay. While Nagel's account resembles Solomon's means-end analysis of sex, here the sex act itself does not even qualify as a preferred or central means to the end of interpersonal communication.

V

I have now criticized various types of analyses sharing or suggesting a common means-end form. I have suggested that analyses of this form relate to attempts to limit moral or natural sex to that which fulfills some purpose or function extraneous to basic sexual desire. The attempts to brand forms of sex outside the idealized models as immoral or perverted fail to achieve consistency with intuitions that they themselves do not directly question. The reproductive model brands oral-genital sex a deviation, but cannot account for kissing or holding hands; the communication account holds voyeurism to be perverted but cannot accommodate sex acts without much conscious thought or seductive nonphysical foreplay; the sex-love model makes most sexual desire seem degrading or base. The first and last condemn extramarital sex on the sound but irrelevant grounds that reproduction and deep commitment are best confined to family contexts. The romanticization of sex and the confusion of sexual desire with love operate in both directions: sex outside the context of romantic love is repressed; once it is repressed, partners become more difficult to find and sex becomes romanticized further, out of proportion to its real value for the individual.

What all these analyses share in addition to a common form is accordance with and perhaps derivation from the Platonic-Christian moral tradition, according to which the animal or purely physical element of humans is the source of immorality, and plain sex in the sense I defined it is an expression of this element, hence in itself to be condemned. All the analyses examined seem to seek a distance from sexual desire itself in attempting to extend it conceptually beyond the physical. The love and communication analyses seek refinement or intellectualization of the desire; plain physical sex becomes vulgar, and too straightforward sexual encounters without an aura of respectable cerebral communicative content are to be avoided. Solomon explicitly argues that sex cannot be a "mere" appetite, his argument being that if it were, subway exhibitionism and other vulgar forms would be pleasing.[9] This fails to recognize that sexual desire can be focused or selective at the same time as being physical. Lower animals are not attracted by every other member of their species, either. Rancid food forced down one's throat is not pleasing, but that certainly fails to show that hunger is not a physical appetite. Sexual desire lets us know that we are physical beings and, indeed, animals; this is why traditional Platonic morality is so thorough in its condemnation. Means-end analyses continue to reflect this tradition, sometimes unwittingly. They show that in conceptualizing sex it is still difficult, despite years of so-called revolution in this area, to free ourselves from the lingering suspicion that plain sex as physical desire is an expression of our "lower selves," that yielding to our animal natures is subhuman or vulgar.

VI

Having criticized these analyses for the sexual ethics and concepts of perversion they imply, it remains to contrast my account along these lines. To the question of what morality might be implied by my analysis, the answer is that there are no moral implications whatever. Any analysis of sex which imputes a moral character to sex acts in themselves is wrong for that reason. There is no morality intrinsic to sex, although general moral rules apply to the treatment of others in sex acts as they apply to all human relations. We can speak of a sexual ethic as we can speak of a business ethic, without implying that business in itself is either moral or immoral or that special rules are required to judge business practices which are not derived from rules that apply elsewhere as well. Sex is not in itself a moral category, although like business it invariably places us into relations with others in which moral rules apply. It gives us opportunity to do what is otherwise recognized as wrong, to harm others, deceive them or manipulate them against their wills. Just as the fact that an act is sexual in itself never renders it wrong or adds to its wrongness if it is wrong on other grounds (sexual acts towards minors are wrong on other grounds, as will be argued below), so no wrong act is to be excused because done from a sexual motive. If a "crime of passion" is to be excused, it would have to be on grounds of temporary insanity rather than sexual context (whether insanity does, constitute a legitimate excuse for certain actions is too big a topic to argue here). Sexual motives are among others which may become deranged, and the fact that they are sexual has no bearing in itself on the moral character, whether negative or exculpatory, of the actions deriving from them. Whatever might be true of war, it is certainly not the case that all's fair in love or sex.

Our first conclusion regarding morality and sex is therefore that no conduct otherwise immoral should be excused because it is sexual conduct, and nothing in sex is immoral unless condemned by rules which apply elsewhere as well. The last clause requires further clarification. Sexual conduct can be governed by particular rules relating only to sex itself. But these precepts must be implied by general moral rules when these are applied to specific sexual relations or types of conduct. The same is true of rules of fair business, ethical medicine, or courtesy in driving a car. In the latter case, particular acts on the road may be reprehensible, such as tailgating or passing on the right, which seem to bear no resemblance as actions to any outside the context of highway safety. Nevertheless their immorality derives from the fact that they place others in danger, a circumstance which, when avoidable, is to be condemned in any context. This structure of general and specifically applicable rules describes a reasonable sexual ethic as well. To take an extreme case, rape is always a sexual act and it is always immoral. A rule against rape can therefore be considered an obvious part of sexual morality which has no bearing on nonsexual conduct. But the immorality of rape derives from its being an extreme violation of a person's body, of the right not to be humiliated, and of the general moral prohibition against using other persons against their wills, not from the fact that it is a sexual act.

The application elsewhere of general moral rules to sexual conduct is further complicated by the fact that it will be relative to the particular desires and preferences of one's partner (these may be influenced by and hence in some sense include misguided beliefs about sexual morality itself). This means that there will be fewer specific rules in the area of sexual ethics than in other areas of conduct, such as driving cars, where the relativity of preference is irrelevant to the prohibition of objectively dangerous conduct. More reliance will have to be placed upon the general moral rule, which in this area holds simply that the preferences, desires, and interests of one's partner or potential partner ought to be taken into account. This rule is certainly not specifically formulated to govern sexual relations; it is a form of the central principle of morality itself. But when applied to sex, it prohibits certain actions, such as molestation of children, which cannot be categorized as violations of the rule without at the same time being classified as sexual. I believe this last case is the closest we can come to an action which is wrong *because* it is sexual, but even here its wrongness is better characterized as deriving from the detrimental effects such behavior can have on the future emotional and sexual life of the naive victims, and from the fact that such behavior therefore involves manipulation of innocent persons without regard for their interests. Hence, this case also involves violation of a general moral rule which applies elsewhere as well.

Aside from faulty conceptual analyses of sex and the influence of the Platonic moral tradition, there are two more plausible reasons for thinking that there are moral dimensions intrinsic to sex acts per se. The first is that such acts are normally intensely pleasurable. According to a hedonistic, utilitarian moral theory they therefore should be at least prima facie morally right, rather than morally neutral in themselves. To me this seems incorrect and reflects unfavorably on the ethical theory in question. The pleasure intrinsic to sex acts is a good, but not, it seems to me, a good with much positive moral significance. Certainly I can have no duty to pursue such pleasure myself, and while it may be nice to give pleasure of any form to others, there is no ethical requirement to do so, given my right over my own body. The exception relates to the context of sex acts themselves, when one partner derives pleasure from the other and ought to return the favor. This duty to reciprocate takes us out of the domain of hedonistic utilitarianism, however, and into a Kantian moral framework, the central principles of which call for just such reciprocity in human relations. Since independent moral judgments regarding sexual activities constitute one area in which ethical theories are to be tested, these observations indicate here, as I believe others indicate elsewhere, the fertility of the Kantian, as opposed to the utilitarian, principle in reconstructing reasoned moral consciousness.

It may appear from this alternative Kantian viewpoint that sexual acts must be at least prima facie wrong in themselves. This is because they invariably involve at different stages the manipulation of one's partner for one's own pleasure, which might appear to be prohibited on the formulation of Kant's principle which holds that one ought not to treat another as a means to such private ends. A more realistic rendering of this formulation, however, one which recognizes its intended equivalence to the first universalizability principle, admits no such absolute prohibition. Many human relations, most economic transactions for example, involve using other individuals for personal benefit. These relations are immoral only when they are one-sided, when the benefits are not mutual, or when the transactions are not freely and rationally endorsed by all parties. The same holds true of sexual acts. The central principle governing them is the Kantian demand for reciprocity in sexual relations. In order to comply with the second formulation of the categorical imperative, one must recognize the subjectivity of one's partner (not merely by being aroused by her or his desire, as Nagel describes). Even in an act which by its nature "objectifies" the other, one recognizes a partner as a subject with demands and desires by yielding to those desires, by allowing oneself to be a sexual object as well, by giving pleasure or ensuring that the pleasures of the acts are mutual. It is this kind of reciprocity which forms the basis for morality in sex, which distinguishes right acts from wrong in this area as in others. (Of course, prior to sex acts one must gauge their effects upon potential partners and take these longer range interests into account.)

VII

I suggested earlier that in addition to generating confusion regarding the rightness or wrongness of sex acts, false conceptual analyses of the means-end form cause confusion about the value of sex to the individual. My account recognizes the satisfaction of desire and the pleasure this brings as the central psychological function of the sex act for the individual. Sex affords us a paradigm of pleasure, but not a cornerstone of value. For most of us it is not only a needed outlet for desire but also the most enjoyable form of recreation we know. Its value is nevertheless easily mistaken by being confused with that of love, when it is taken as essentially an expression of that emotion. Although intense, the pleasures of sex are brief and repetitive rather than cumulative. They give value to the specific acts which generate them, but not the lasting kind of value which enhances one's whole life. The briefness of these pleasures contributes to their intensity (or perhaps their intensity makes them necessarily brief), but it also relegates them to the periphery of most rational plans for the good life.

By contrast, love typically develops over a long term relation; while its pleasures may be less intense and physical, they are of more cumulative value. The importance of love to the individual may well be central in a rational system of value. And it has perhaps an even deeper moral significance relating to the identification with the interests of another person, which broadens one's possible relationships with others as well. Marriage is again important in preserving this relation between adults and children, which seems as important to the adults as it is to the children in broadening concerns which have a tendency to become selfish. Sexual desire, by contrast, is desire for another which is nevertheless essentially self-regarding. Sexual pleasure is certainly a good for the individual, and for many it may be necessary in order for them to function in a reasonably cheerful way. But it bears little relation to those other values just discussed, to which some analyses falsely suggest a conceptual connection.

VIII

While my initial analysis lacks moral implications in itself, as it should, it does suggest by contrast a concept of sexual perversion. Since the concept of perversion is itself a sexual concept, it will always be defined relative to some definition of normal sex; and any conception of the norm will imply a contrary notion of perverse forms. The concept suggested by my account again differs sharply from those implied by the means-end analyses examined above. Perversion does not represent a deviation from the reproductive function (or kissing would be perverted), from a loving relationship (or most sexual desire and many heterosexual acts would be perverted), or from efficiency in communicating (or unsuccessful seduction attempts would be perverted). It is a deviation from a norm, but the norm in question is merely statistical. Of course, not all sexual acts that are statistically unusual are perverted—a three-hour continuous sexual act would be unusual but not necessarily abnormal in the requisite sense. The abnormality in question must relate to the *form of the desire* itself in order to constitute sexual perversion; for example, desire, not for contact with another, but for merely looking, for harming or being harmed, for contact with items of clothing. This concept of sexual abnormality is that suggested by my definition of normal sex in terms of its typical desire. However not all unusual desires qualify either, only those with the typical physical sexual effects upon the individual who satisfies them. These effects, such as erection in males, were not built into the original definition of sex in terms of sexual desire, for they do not always occur in activities that are properly characterized as sexual, say, kissing for the pleasure of it. But they do seem to bear a closer relation to the definition of activities as perverted. (For those who consider only genital sex sexual, we could build such symptoms into a narrower definition, then speaking of sex in a broad sense as well as "proper" sex.)

Solomon and Nagel disagree with this statistical notion of perversion. For them the concept is evaluative rather than statistical. I do not deny that the term "perverted" is often used evaluatively (and purely emotively for that matter), or that it has a negative connotation for the average speaker. I do deny that we can find a norm, other than that of statistically usual desire, against which all and only activities that properly count as sexual perversions can be contrasted. Perverted sex is simply abnormal sex, and if the norm is not to be an idealized or romanticized extraneous end or purpose, it must express the way human sexual desires usually manifest themselves. Of course not all norms in other areas of discourse need be statistical in this way. Physical health is an example of a relatively clear norm which does not seem to depend upon the numbers of healthy people. But the concept in this case achieves its clarity through the connection of physical health with other clearly desirable physical functions and characteristics, for example, living longer. In the case of sex, that which is statistically abnormal is not necessarily incapacitating in other ways, and yet these abnormal desires with sexual effects upon their subject do count as perverted to the degree to which their objects deviate from usual ones. The connotations of the concept of perversion beyond those connected with abnormality or statistical deviation derive more from the attitudes of those likely to call certain acts perverted than from specifiable features of the acts themselves. These connotations add to the concept of abnormality that of *sub*normality, but there is no norm against which the latter can be measured intelligibly in accord with all and only acts intuitively called perverted.

The only proper evaluative norms relating to sex involve degrees of pleasure in the acts and moral norms, but neither of these scales coincides with statistical degrees of abnormality, according to which perversion is to be measured. The three parameters operate independently (this was implied for the first two when it was held above that the pleasure of sex is a good, but not necessarily a moral good). Perverted sex may be more or less enjoyable to particular individuals than normal sex, and more or less moral, depending upon the particular relations involved. Raping a sheep may be more perverted than raping a woman, but certainly not more condemnable morally.[10] It is nevertheless true that the evaluative connotations attaching to the term "perverted" derive partly from the fact that most people consider perverted sex highly immoral. Many such acts are forbidden by long standing taboos, and it is sometimes difficult to distinguish what is forbidden from what is immoral. Others, such as sadistic acts, are genuinely immoral, but again not at all because of their connection with sex or abnormality. The principles which condemn these acts would condemn them equally if they were common and non-sexual. It is not true that we properly could continue to consider acts perverted which were found to be very common practice across societies. Such acts, if harmful, might continue to be condemned properly as immoral, but it was just shown that the immorality of an act does not vary with its degree of perversion. If not harmful, common acts previously considered abnormal might continue to be called perverted for a time by the moralistic minority; but the term when applied to such cases would retain only its emotive negative connotation without consistent logical criteria for application. It would represent merely prejudiced moral judgments.

To adequately explain why there is a tendency to so deeply condemn perverted acts would require a treatise in psychology beyond the scope of this paper. Part of the reason undoubtedly relates to the tradition of repressive sexual ethics and false conceptions of sex; another part to the fact that all abnormality seems to disturb and fascinate us at the same time. The former explains why sexual perversion is more abhorrent to many than other forms of abnormality; the latter indicates why we tend to have an emotive and evaluative reaction to perversion in the first place. It may be, as has been suggested according to a Freudian line,[11] that our uneasiness derives from latent desires we are loathe to admit, but this thesis takes us into psychological issues I am not competent to judge. Whatever the psychological explanation, it suffices to point out here that the conceptual connection between perversion and genuine or consistent moral evaluation is spurious and again suggested by misleading means-end idealizations of the concept of sex.

The position I have taken in this paper against those concepts is not totally new. Something similar to it is found in Freud's view of sex, which of course was genuinely revolutionary, and in the body of writings deriving from Freud to the present time. But in his revolt against romanticized and repressive conceptions, Freud went too far—from a refusal to view sex as merely a means to a view of it as the end of all human behavior, although sometimes an elaborately disguised end. This pansexualism led to the thesis (among others) that repression was indeed an inevitable and necessary part of the social regulation of any form, a strange consequence of a position that began by opposing the repressive aspects of the means-end view. Perhaps the time finally has arrived when we can achieve a reasonable middle ground in this area, at least in philosophy if not in society.

NOTES

1. Even Bertrand Russell, whose writing in this area was a model of rationality, at least for its period, tends to make this identification and to condemn plain sex in the absence of love: "sex intercourse apart from love has little value, and is to be regarded primarily as experimentation with a view to love." *Marriage and Morals* (New York: Bantam, 1959), p. 87.
2. Robert Solomon, "Sex and Perversion," *Philosophy and Sex*, ed. R. Baker and F. Elliston (Buffalo: Prometheus, 1975).
3. Thomas Nagel, "Sexual Perversion," *The Journal of Philosophy* 66, no. 1 (16 January 1969).
4. Sex might be considered (at least partially) as communication in a very broad sense in the same way as performing ensemble music, in the sense that there is in both ideally a communion or perfectly shared experience with another. This is, however, one possible ideal view whose central feature is not necessary to sexual acts or desire per se. And in emphasizing the communication of specific feelings by means of body language, the analysis under consideration narrows the end to one clearly extrinsic to plain and even good sex.
5. Solomon, pp. 284-285.
6. Ibid., p. 283. One is reminded of Woody Allen's rejoinder to praise of his technique: "I practice a lot when I'm alone."
7. Nagel, p. 15.
8. Janice Moulton made the same point in a paper at the Pacific APA meeting, March 1976.
9. Solomon, p. 285.
10. The example is like one from Sara Ruddick, "Better Sex," *Philosophy and Sex*, p. 96.
11. See Michael Slote, "Inapplicable Concepts and Sexual Perversion," *Philosophy and Sex*.

MARRIAGE

Monogamy: A Critique

John McMurtry

"Remove away that black'ning church
Remove away that marriage hearse
Remove away that man of blood
You'll quite remove the ancient curse."

William Blake

I

Almost all of us have entered or will one day enter a specifically standardized form of monogamous marriage. This cultural requirement is
so very basic to our existence that we accept it for most part as a kind
of intractable given: dictated by the laws of God, Nature, Government
and Good Sense all at once. Though it is perhaps unusual for a social
practice to be so promiscuously underwritten, we generally find comfort
rather than curiosity in this fact and seldom wonder how something
could be divinely inspired, biologically determined, coerced and reasoned out all at the same time. We simply take for granted.

Those in society who are officially charged with the thinking function
with regard to such matters are no less responsible for this uncritical
acceptance than the man on the street. The psychoanalyst traditionally
regards our form of marriage as a necessary restraint on the anarchic id
and no more to be queried than civilization itself. The lawyer is as
undisposed to questioning the practice as he is to criticizing the principle of private property (this is appropriate, as I shall later point out).
The churchman formally perceives the relationship between man and
wife to be as inviolable and insusceptible to question as the relationship
between the institution he works for and the Christ. The sociologist
standardly accepts the formalized bonding of heterosexual pairs as the
indispensable basis of social order and perhaps a societal universal. The
politician is as incapable of challenging it as he is in the virtue of his
own continued holding of office. And the philosopher (at least the

Reprinted from *The Monist*, Vol. 56, No. 4, with the permission of the author and the
publisher.

English-speaking philosopher), as with most issues of socially controversial or sexual dimensions, ignores the question almost altogether.

Even those irreverent adulterers and unmarried couples who would seem to be challenging the institution in the most basic possible way, in practice, tend merely to mimic its basic structure in unofficial form. The coverings of sanctity, taboo and cultural habit continue to hold them with the grip of public clothes.

II

"Monogamy" means, literally, "one marriage." But it would be wrong to suppose that this phrase tells us much about our particular species of official wedlock. The greatest obstacle to the adequate understanding of our monogamy institution has been the failure to identify clearly and systematically the full complex of principles it involves. There are four such principles, each carrying enormous restrictive force and together constituting a massive social control mechanism that has never, so far as I know, been fully schematized.

To come straight to the point, the four principles in question are as follows:

1. *The partners are required to enter a formal contractual relation:* (a) whose establishment demands a specific official participant, certain conditions of the contractors (legal age, no blood ties, etc.) and a standard set of procedures; (b) whose governing terms are uniform for all and exactly prescribed by law; and (c) whose dissolution may only be legally effected by the decision of state representatives.

The ways in which this elaborate principle of contractual requirement are importantly restrictive are obvious. One may not enter into a marriage union without entering into a contract presided over by a state-investured official.[1] One may not set any of the terms of the contractual relationship by which one is bound for life. And one cannot dissolve the contract without legal action and costs, court proceedings and in many places actual legislation. (The one and only contract in all English-speaking law that is not dissoluble by the consent of the contracting parties.) The extent of control here—over the most intimate and putatively "loving" relationships in all social intercourse—is so great as to be difficult to catalogue without exciting in oneself a sense of disbelief.

Lest it be thought there is always the real option of entering a common law relationship free of such encumbrances, it should be noted that: (a) these relationships themselves are subject to state regulation, though of a less imposing sort; and (much more important) (b) there are very formidable selective pressures against common law partnerships such as employment and job discrimination, exclusion from housing and lodging facilities, special legal disablements,[2] loss of social and moral status (consider such phrases as "living in sin," "make her an honest woman," etc.), family shame and embarrassment, and so on.

2. *The number of partners involved in the marriage must be two and only two* (as opposed to three, four, five or any of the almost countless other possibilities of intimate union).

This second principle of our specific form of monogamy (the concept of "one marriage," it should be pointed out, is consistent with any number of participating partners) is perhaps the most important and restrictive of the four principles we are considering. Not only does it confine us to just *one* possibility out of an enormous range, but it confines us to that single possibility which involves the *least* number of people, two. It is difficult to conceive of a more thoroughgoing mechanism for limiting extended social union and intimacy. The fact that this monolithic restriction seems so "natural" to us (if it were truly "natural" of course, there would be no need for its rigorous cultural prescription by everything from severe criminal law[3] to ubiquitous housing regulations) simply indicates the extent to which its hold is implanted in our social structure. It is the institutional basis of what I will call the "binary frame of sexual consciousness," a frame through which all our heterosexual relationships are typically viewed ("two's company, three's a crowd") and in light of which all larger circles of intimacy seem almost inconceivable.[4]

3. *No person may participate in more than one marriage at a time or during a lifetime* (unless the previous marriage has been officially dissolved by, normally, one partner's death or successful divorce).

Violation of this principle is, of course, a criminal offence (bigamy) which is punishable by a considerable term in prison. Of various general regulations of our marriage institution it has experienced the most significant modification: not indeed in principle, but in the extent of flexibility of its "escape hatch" of divorce. The case with which this escape hatch is open has increased considerably in the past few years (the grounds for divorce being more permissive than previously) and it is in this regard most of all that the principles of our marriage institution have undergone formal alteration. That is, in plumbing rather than substance.

4. *No married person may engage in any sexual relationship with any person whatever other than the marriage partner.*

Although a consummated sexual act with another person alone constitutes an act of adultery, lesser forms of sexual and erotic relationships[5] may also constitute grounds for divorce (i.e., cruelty) and are generally proscribed as well by informal social convention and taboo. In other words, the fourth and final principle of our marriage institution involves not only a prohibition of sexual intercourse per se outside one's wedlock (this term deserves pause) but a prohibition of all one's erotic relations whatever outside this bond. The penalties for violation here are as various as they are severe, ranging from permanent loss of spouse, children, chattel, and income to job dismissal and social ostracism. In this way, possibly the most compelling natural force towards expanded intimate relations with others [6] is strictly confined within the narrowest possible circle for (barring delinquency) the whole of adult life. The sheer weight and totality of this restriction is surely one of the great wonders of all historical institutional control.

III

With all established institutions, apologetics for perpetuation are never wanting. Thus it is with our form of monogamous marriage.

Perhaps the most celebrated justification over the years has proceeded from a belief in a Supreme Deity who secretly utters sexual and other commands to privileged human representatives. Almost as well known a line of defence has issued from a conviction, similarly confident, that the need for some social regulation of sexuality demonstrates the need for our specific type of two-person wedlock. Although these have been important justifications in the sense of being very widely supported, they are not—having other grounds than reasons—susceptible to treatment here.

If we put aside such arguments, we are left I think with two major claims. The first is that our form of monogamous marriage promotes a profound affection between the partners which is not only of great worth in itself but invaluable as a sanctuary from the pressures of outside society. Since, however, there are no secure grounds whatever for supposing that such "profound affection" is not at least as easily achievable by any number of *other* marriage forms (i.e., forms which differ in one or more of the four principles), this justification conspicuously fails to perform the task required of it.

The second major claim for the defence is that monogamy provides a specially loving context for child upbringing. However here again there are no grounds at all for concluding that it does so as, or any more, effectively than other possible forms of marriage (the only alternative type of upbringing to which it has apparently been shown to be superior is nonfamily institutional upbringing, which of course is not relevant to the present discussion). Furthermore, the fact that at least half the span of a normal monogamous marriage *involves no child-upbringing at all* is disastrously overlooked here, as is the reinforcing fact that there is no reference to or mention of the quality of child-upbringing in any of the prescriptions connected with it.

In brief, the second major justification of our particular type of wedlock scents somewhat too strongly of red herring to pursue further.

There is, it seems, little to recommend the view that monogamy specially promotes "profound affection" between the partners or a "loving context" for child-upbringing. Such claims are simply without force. On the other hand, there are several aspects to the logic and operation of the four principles of this institution which suggest that it actually *inhibits* the achievement of these desiderata. Far from uniquely abetting the latter, it militates against them. In these ways:

(1) Centralized official control of marriage (which the Church gradually achieved through the mechanism of Canon Law after the Fall of the Roman Empire [7] in one of the greatest seizures of social power in history) necessarily alienates the partners from full responsibility for and freedom in their relationship. "Profound closeness" between the partners—or least an area of it—is thereby expropriated rather than promoted, and "sanctuary" from the pressures of outside society prohibited rather than fostered.

(2) Limitation of the marriage bond to two people necessarily restricts, in perhaps the most unilateral possible way consistent with offspring survival, the number of adult sources of affection, interest, material support and instruction for the young. The "loving context for child-upbringing" is thereby dessicated rather than nourished: providing the structural conditions for such notorious and far-reaching problems as (a) sibling rivalry for scarce adult attention,[8] and (b) parental oppression through exclusive monopoly of the child's means of life.[9]

(3) Formal exclusion of all others from erotic contact with the marriage partner systematically promotes conjugal insecurity, jealousy and alienation by:

(a) Officially underwriting a literally totalitarian expectation of sexual confinement on the part of one's husband or wife: which expectation is, *ceteris paribus,* inevitably more subject to anxiety and disappointment than one less extreme in its demand and/or cultural-juridical backing; [10]

(b) Requiring so complete a sexual isolation of the marriage partners that should one violate the fidelity code the other is left alone and susceptible to a sense of fundamental deprivation and resentment;

(c) Stipulating such a strict restraint of sexual energies that there are habitual violations of the regulation: which violations *qua* violations are frequently if not always attended by (i) willful deception and reciprocal suspicion about the occurrence or quality of the extramarital relationship, (ii) anxiety and fear on both sides of permanent estrangement from partner and family, and/or (iii) overt and covert antagonism over the prohibited act in both offender (who feels "trapped") and offended (who feels "betrayed").

The disadvantages of the four principles of monogamous marriage do not, however, end with inhibiting the very effects they are said to promote. There are further shortcomings:

(1) The restriction of marriage union to two partners necessarily prevents the strengths of larger groupings. Such advantages as the following are thereby usually ruled out.

(a) The security, range and power of larger socioeconomic units;

(b) The epistemological and emotional substance, variety and scope of more pluralist interactions;

(c) The possibility of extra-domestic freedom founded on more adult providers and upbringers as well as more broadly based circles of intimacy.

(2) The sexual containment and isolation which the four principles together require variously stimulates such social malaises as:

(*a*) Destructive aggression (which notoriously results from sexual frustration);

(*b*) Apathy, frustration and dependence within the marriage bond;

(*c*) Lack of spontaneity, bad faith and distance in relationships without the marriage bond;

(*d*) Sexual phantasizing, perversion, fetishism, prostitution and pornography in the adult population as a whole.[11]

Taking such things into consideration, it seems difficult to lend credence to the view that the four principles of our form of monogamous marriage constitute a structure beneficial either to the marriage partners themselves or to their offspring (or indeed to anyone else). One is moved to seek for some other ground of the institution, some ground that lurks beneath the reach of our conventional apprehensions.

IV

The ground of our marriage institution, the essential principle that underwrites all four restrictions, is this: *the maintenance by one man or woman of the effective right to exclude indefinitely all others from erotic access to the conjugal partner.*

The first restriction creates, elaborates on, and provides for the enforcement of this right to exclude. And the second, third and fourth restrictions together ensure that the said right to exclude is—respectively —not cooperative, not simultaneously or sequentially distributed, and not permissive of even casual exception.

In other words, the four restrictions of our form of monogamous marriage together constitute a state-regulated, indefinite and exclusive ownership by two individuals of one another's sexual powers. Marriage is simply a form of private property.[12]

That our form of monogamous marriage is when the confusing layers of sanctity, apologetic and taboo are cleared away another species of private property should not surprise us.[13] The history of the institution is so full of suggestive indicators—dowries, inheritance, property alliances, daughter sales (of which women's wedding rings are a carry-over) bride exchanges, legitimacy and illegitimacy—that it is difficult not to see some intimate connections between marital and ownership ties. We are better able still to apprehend the ownership essence of our marriage institution, when in addition we consider:

(*a*) That until recently almost the only way to secure official dissolution of consummated marriage was to be able to demonstrate violation of one or both partner's sexual ownership (i.e., adultery);

(*b*) That the imperative of premarital chastity is tantamount to a demand for retrospective sexual ownership by the eventual marriage partner;

(*c*) That successful sexual involvement with a married person is prosecutable as an expropriation of ownership—"alienation of affections"—which is restituted by cash payment;

(*d*) That the incest taboo is an iron mechanism which protects the conjugal ownership of sexual properties: both the husband's and wife's from the access of affectionate offspring and the offsprings' (who themselves are future marriage partners) from access of siblings and parents; [14]

(*e*) That the language of the marriage ceremony is the language of exclusive possession ("take," "to have and to hold," "forsaking all others and keeping you only unto him/her," etc.), not to mention the proprietary locutions associated with the marital relationship (e.g., "he's mine," "she belongs to him," "keep to your own husband," "wife stealer," "possessive husband," etc.).

V

Of course, it would be remarkable if marriage in our society was not a relationship akin to private property. In our socioeconomic system we relate to virtually everything of value by individual ownership: by, that is, the effective right to exclude others from the thing concerned.[15] That we do so as well with perhaps the most highly valued thing of all —the sexual partners' sexuality—is only to be expected. Indeed it would probably be an intolerable strain on our entire social structure if we did otherwise.

This line of thought deserves pursuit. The real secret of our form of monogamous marriage is not that it functionally provides for the needs of adults who love one another or the children they give birth to, but that it serves the maintenance of our present social system. It is an institution which is indispensable to the persistence of the capitalist order,[16] in the following ways:

(1) A basic principle of current social relations is that some people legally acquire the use of other people's personal powers from which they may exclude other members of society. This system operates in the workplace (owners and hirers of all types contractually acquire for their exclusive use workers' regular labour powers) and in the family (husbands and wives contractually acquire for their exclusive use their partner's sexual properties). A conflict between the structures of these primary relations—as would obtain were there a suspension of the restrictions governing our form of monogamous marriage—might well undermine the systemic coherence of present social intercourse.

(2) The fundamental relation between individuals and things which satisfy their needs is, in our present society, that each individual has or does not have the effective right to exclude other people from the thing in question.[17] A rudimentary need is that for sexual relationship(s). Therefore the object of this need must be related to the one who needs it as owner or not owner (i.e., via marriage or not-marriage, or approximations

thereto) if people's present relationship to what they need is to retain—again—systemic coherence.

(3) A necessary condition for the continued existence of the present social formation is that its members feel powerful motivation to gain favorable positions in it. But such social ambition is heavily dependent on the preservation of exclusive monogamy in that:

(*a*) The latter confines the discharge of primordial sexual energies to a single unalterable partner and thus typically compels the said energies to seek alternative outlet, such as business or professional success; [18]

(*b*) The exclusive marriage necessarily reduces the sexual relationships available to any one person to absolute (nonzero) minimum, a unilateral promotion of sexual shortage which in practice renders hierarchial achievement essential as an economic and "display" means for securing scarce partners.[19]

(4) Because the exclusive marriage necessarily and dramatically reduces the possibilities of sexual-love relationships, it thereby promotes the existing economic system by:

(*a*) Rendering extreme economic self-interest—the motivational basis of the capitalistic process—less vulnerable to altruistic subversion;

(*b*) Disciplining society's members into the habitual repression of natural impulse required for long-term performance of repetitive and arduous work tasks;

(*c*) Developing a complex of suppressed sexual desires to which sales techniques may effectively apply in creating those new consumer wants which provide indispensable outlets for ever-increasing capital funds.

(5) The present form of marriage is of fundamental importance to:

(*a*) The continued relative powerlessness of the individual family: which, with larger numbers would constitute a correspondingly increased command of social power;

(*b*) The continued high demand for homes, commodities and services: which, with the considerable economies of scale that extended unions would permit, would otherwise falter;

(*c*) The continued strict necessity for adult males to sell their labour power and adult women to remain at home (or vice versa): which strict necessity would diminish as the economic base of the family unit extended;

(*d*) The continued immense pool of unsatisfied sexual desires and energies in the population at large: without which powerful interests and institutions would lose much of their conventional appeal and force; [20]

(*e*) The continued profitable involvement of lawyers, priests and state officials in the jurisdictions of marriage and divorce and the myriad official practices and proceedings connected thereto.[21]

VI

If our marriage institution is a linchpin of our present social structure, then a breakdown in this institution would seem to indicate a breakdown in our social structure. On the face of it, the marriage institution is breaking down—enormously increased divorce rates, nonmarital sexual relationships, wife-swapping, the Playboy philosophy, and communes. Therefore one might be led by the appearance of things to anticipate a profound alteration in the social system.

But it would be a mistake to underestimate the tenacity of an established order or to overestimate the extent of change in our marriage institution. Increased divorce rates merely indicate the widening of a traditional escape hatch. Nonmarital relationships imitate and culminate in the marital mold. Wife-swapping presupposes ownership, as the phrase suggests. The Playboy philosophy is merely the view that if one has the money one has the right to be titillated, the commercial call to more fully exploit a dynamic sector of capital investment. And communes—the most hopeful phenomenon—almost nowhere offer a *praxis* challenge to private property in sexuality. It may be changing. But history, as the old man puts it, weighs like a nightmare on the brains of the living.

NOTES

1. Any person who presides over a marriage and is not authorized by law to do so is guilty of a criminal offense and is subject to several years imprisonment (e.g., Canadian Criminal Code, Sec. 258).
2. For example, offspring are illegitimate, neither wife nor children are legal heirs, and husband has no right of access or custody should separation occur.
3. "Any kind of conjugal union with more than one person at the same time, whether or not it is by law recognized as a binding form of marriage—is guilty of an indictable offence and is liable to imprisonment for five years" (Canadian Criminal Code, Sec. 257, [1][a][ii]). Part 2 of the same section adds: "Where an accused is charged with an offence under this section, no averment or proof of the method by which the alleged relationship was entered into, agreed to or consented to is necessary in the indictment or upon the trial of the accused, nor is it necessary upon the trial to prove that the persons who are alleged to have entered into the relationship had or intended to have sexual intercourse."

   (Here and elsewhere, I draw examples from Canadian criminal law. There is no reason to suspect the Canadian code is eccentric in these instances.)
4. Even the sexual revolutionary Wilhelm Reich seems constrained within the limits of this "binary frame." Thus he says (my emphasis): "Nobody has the right to prohibit his or her partner from entering a temporary or lasting sexual relationship with someone else. He has only the right *either to withdraw or to win the partner back."* (Wilhelm Reich, *The Sexual Revolution,* trans. by T. P. Wolfe [New York: Farrar, Strauss & Giroux, 1970], p. 28.) The possibility of sexual partners extending their union to include the other loved party as opposed to one partner having either to "win" against this third party or to "withdraw" altogether,) does not seem even to occur to Reich.
5. I will be using "sexual" and "erotic" interchangeably throughout the paper.

6. It is worth noting here that: (a) man has by nature the most "open" sexual instinct—year-round operativeness and variety of stimuli—of all the species (except perhaps the dolphin); and (b) it is a principle of human needs in general that maximum satisfaction involves regular variation in the form of the need-object.

7. "Roman Law had no power of intervening in the formation of marriages and there was no legal form of marriage. . . . Marriage was a matter of simple private agreement and divorce was a private transaction" (Havelock Ellis, *Studies in the Psychology of Sex* [New York: Random House, 1963], Vol. II, Part 3, p. 429).

8. The dramatic reduction of sibling rivalry through an increased number of adults in the house is a phenomenon which is well known in contemporary domestic communes.

9. One of the few other historical social relationships I can think of in which persons hold thoroughly exclusive monopoly over other persons' means of life is slavery. Thus, as with another's slave, it is a criminal offence "to receive" or "harbour" another's child without "right of possession" (Canadian Criminal Code, Sec. 250).

10. Certain cultures, for example, permit extramarital sexuality by married persons with friends, guests, or in-laws with no reported consequences of jealousy. From such evidence, one is led to speculate that the intensity and extent of jealousy at a partner's extramarital sexual involvement is in direct proportion to the severity of the accepted cultural regulations against such involvements. In short such regulations do not prevent jealousy so much as effectively engender it.

11. It should not be forgotten that at the same time marriage excludes marital partners from sexual contact with others, it necessarily excludes those others from sexual contact with marital partners. Walls face two ways.

12. Those aspects of marriage law which seem to fall outside the pale of sexual property holding—for example, provisions for divorce if the husband fails to provide or is convicted of a felony or is an alcoholic—may themselves be seen as simply prescriptive characterizations of the sort of sexual property which the marriage partner must remain to retain satisfactory conjugal status: a kind of permanent warranty of the "good working order" of the sexual possession.

    What constitutes the "good working order" of the conjugal possession is, of course, different in the case of the husband and in the case of the wife: an *asymmetry* within the marriage institution which, I gather, women's liberation movements are anxious to eradicate.

13. I think it is instructive to think of even the nonlegal aspects of marriage, for example, its sentiments as essentially private property structured. Thus the preoccupation of those experiencing conjugal sentiments with expressing how much "my very own," "my precious," the other is: with expressing, that is, how valuable and inviolable the ownership is and will remain.

14. I think the secret to the long mysterious incest taboo may well be the fact that in all its forms it protects sexual property: not only conjugal (as indicated above) but paternal and tribal as well. This crucial line of thought, however, requires extended separate treatment.

15. Sometimes—as with political patronage, criminal possession, *de facto* privileges and so forth—a *power* to exclude others exists with no corresponding "right" (just as sometimes a right to exclude exists with no corresponding power). Properly speaking, thus, I should here use the phrase "power to

exclude," which covers "effective right to exclude" as well as all nonjuridical enablements of this sort.

16. It is no doubt indispensable as well—in some form or other—to any private property order. Probably (if we take the history of Western society as our data base) the more thoroughgoing and developed the private property formation is, the more total the sexual ownership prescribed by the marriage institution.

17. Things in unlimited supply—like, presently, oxygen—are not of course related to people in this way.

18. This is, of course, a Freudian or quasi-Freudian claim. "Observation of daily life shows us," says Freud, "that most persons direct a very tangible part of their sexual motive powers to their professional or business activities" (Sigmund Freud, *Dictionary of Psychoanalysis*, ed. by Nandor Fodor and Frank Gaynor [New York: Fawcett Publications, Premier Paperbook, 1966], p. 139).

19. It might be argued that exclusive marriage also protects those physically less attractive persons who—in an "open" situation—might be unable to secure any sexual partnership at all. The force of this claim depends, I think, on improperly continuing to posit the very principle of exclusiveness which the "open" situation rules out (e.g., in the latter situation, *x* might be less attractive to *y* than *z* is and yet *z* not be rejected, any more than at present an intimate friend is rejected who is less talented than another intimate friend).

20. The sexual undercurrents of corporate advertisements, religious systems, racial propaganda and so on is too familiar to dwell on here.

21. It is also possible that exclusive marriage protects the adult youth power structure in the manner outlined on p. 281.

Marriage, Love, and Procreation

Michael D. Bayles

The current era is one of that vulgar form of hedonism rejected by philosophical hedonists such as Epicurus and John Stuart Mill.[1] Apologists thinly disguise the tawdriness of a hedonism of biological pleasures by appeals to individual rights and autonomy. Far too frequently these appeals merely mask a refusal to accept responsibility. This failure to accept personal responsibility is periodically atoned for by ritualistic and ill-conceived attempts to help the poor and underprivileged people of the world.

One of the central focuses of the current vulgar hedonism has been sexual liberation. Premarital intercourse, gay liberation, no-fault divorce, open marriage (read, "open adultery"), polygamy, and orgies all have their advocates. About the only forms of sexual behavior yet to have strong advocates are pedophilia and bestiality. Any day now one may expect grade-school children to assert their right to happiness through pedophilia and animal lovers to argue that disapproval of bestiality is unfair to little lambs.

The result, especially in Western society, is an emphasis on sex that is out of all proportion to its significance for a eudaemonistic life—that is, a life worth living, including elements besides pleasure. The only ultimate test for the value of a life is whether at its end it is found to have been worth living. It is difficult to conceive of a person's thinking his life significant because it was a second-rate approximation to the sexual achievements of the notorious rabbit. However, many people seem to think such a life offers the highest ideal of a "truly human" existence, forgetting Aristotle's insight that reproduction is characteristic of all living things, not just humans.[2] Consequently, the institution of marriage has been attacked for hindering the achievement of this vulgar hedonistic ideal.

ATTACKS ON MARRIAGE

Not all attacks on the institution of marriage have been based solely on the vulgar hedonistic ideal. A more broad ranging, although no more plausible, attack has recently been made by John McMurtry. His attack is directed not against marriage per se but against that form of it found in Western society—monogamy. McMurtry does not merely find that monogamous marriage hinders the achievement of the vulgar hedonistic ideal. He also claims it is at least one of the causes of the following social ills: (1) Central official control of marriage *"necessarily* alienates the partners from full responsibility for and freedom in their relationship."[3] (2) Monogamy restricts the sources of adult affection and support available to children.[4] (3) It "systematically promotes conjugal insecurity, jealousy, and alienation. . . ."[5] (4) It "prevents the strengths of larger groupings."[6] (5) It stimulates aggression, apathy, frustration, lack of spontaneity, perversion, fetishism, prostitution, and pornography.[7] (6) It serves to maintain the status quo and capitalism.[8] (7) It supports the powerlessness of the individual family by keeping it small.[9] (8) By promoting many small families it creates a high demand for homes and consumer goods and services.[10] (9) It makes it necessary for many more males to sell their labor than would be necessary if monogamy were not practiced.[11] (10) By limiting opportunities for sexual satisfaction it channels unsatisfied desire into support for various institutions and interests.[12] (11) Finally, it promotes financial profit for lawyers, priests, and so forth, in marriage and divorce proceedings.[13] Such a catalog of evils omits only a few social problems such as political corruption and environmental deterioration, although even they are hinted at in numbers 8 and 11.

Many people have hoped that the simple-mindedness that attributes all or most or even many of society's ills to a single factor would disappear. At one time private ownership of the means of production was the *bête noir* of society.[14] Recently it has been replaced in that role by unlimited population growth.[15] Both of these beasts have been slain by the St. George of reasonableness.[16] McMurtry has called forth yet another single-factor beast. There is no reason to suppose this one to be any more powerful than its predecessors.

No attempt will be made in this essay to examine in detail McMurtry's criticisms of monogamous marriage. In general they are characterized by a lack of historical and sociological perspective. It is unclear whether he is attacking the ideal of monogamous marriage as it perhaps existed a hundred years ago or as it exists today. Yet this difference is crucial. A century ago divorce was not widely recognized or accepted; today that is not true. When divorce was not recognized, concubinage and prostitution were quite prevalent, as was simply abandoning one's family. Such practices certainly mitigated the effect of the strict social rules that McMurtry discusses. Also, he criticizes monogamy for limiting the access of children to adult affection and support, since they must rely upon their parents alone for care. But in the extended family, which existed until the urbanization of society, that limitation was considerably less common than it may be at present.

McMurtry seems to be unaware of the social realities of modern society. He emphasizes the law as it is written rather than the law in action. It is generally recognized that despite the wording of statutes, marriages can in practice now be dissolved by mutual consent.[17] Nor is adultery usually prosecuted in those states in which it is still a crime. Nor does McMurtry present any sociological evidence for the various effects that he claims monogamous marriage has. Sometimes the evidence may well be against him. For example, he claims that monogamy supports the high demand for homes. Yet, for a century in Ireland monogamy coincided with a low demand for new homes. Couples simply postponed marriage until the male inherited the home of his parents, and those who did not inherit often did not marry.[18]

Underlying McMurtry's view of monogamous marriage is the Kantian conception of the marriage contract. According to Kant, marriage "is the Union of two Persons of different sex for life-long reciprocal possession of their sexual faculties." [19] McMurtry takes the following principle to be the essential ground of monogamous marriage: "the maintenance by one man or woman of the effective right to exclude indefinitely all others from erotic access to the conjugal partner." [20] Since by "possession" Kant meant legal ownership and the consequent right to exclude others, these two views come to the same thing. They both view marriage as chiefly concerned with private ownership of the means to sexual gratification, thus combining capitalism with vulgar hedonism (although Kant was not a hedonist).

Such a view of marriage is pure nonsense. However, it has more plausibility in today's era of vulgar hedonism than it did in Kant's time.

Historically, the official aims of marriage, according to the Catholic Church—which was the only church during the period of the establishment of monogamous marriage in Western society—were procreation and companionship. There was also a tendency to view it as a legitimate outlet for man's sinful nature.[21] It is this latter element that Kant and McMurtry have taken as the chief one.

In addition to the avowed purposes of marriage there were the actual social functions that it performed. The family unit was the basic social unit, not only for the education of children (that is, socialization, not formal schooling—which has only become widespread during the past century), but also for the production of necessities, including food and clothing, and for recreation. These historical functions of the extended-family unit based on monogamous marriage have been undermined by the development of industrial, urban society.[22] Consequently, the moral and legal status and functions of marriage require reexamination in the light of current social conditions.

Before undertaking such a reexamination it is necessary to distinguish between rules of marriage and attendant social rules. They are mixed together in the traditional social institution of monogamous marriage, but there is no necessity for this mix and it is probably unjustified. In particular one must distinguish between penal laws prohibiting various forms of sexual union—homosexual, premarital, adulterous—and private arranging laws granting legal recognition to the marital relationship.[23] Private arranging laws do not prescribe punishment for offenses; instead, they enable people to carry out their desires. People are not punished for improperly made marriages; instead, the marriages are invalid and unenforceable. Laws against fornication, prostitution, cohabitation, and homosexuality are almost always penal. Objections to them cannot be transferred directly to the marriage relationship. All of these penal laws could be abolished and monogamous marriage could still be retained.

It may be claimed that despite their nonpenal form, marriage laws do in fact penalize those who prefer other forms of relationship. If homosexual and polygamous relationships are not legally recognized as "marriages," then persons desiring these forms of relationship are being deprived of some degree of freedom. When considering freedom one must be clear about what one is or is not free to do. Consider, for example, the case of gambling. One must distinguish between laws that forbid gambling and the absence of laws that recognize gambling debts. The latter does not deprive people of the freedom to contract gambling debts; it simply does not allow the use of legal enforcement to collect them. Similarly, the absence of laws recognizing polygamous and homosexual marriages does not deprive people of the freedom to enter polygamous and homosexual unions. Instead, it merely fails to provide legal recourse to enforce the agreements of the parties to such unions. The absence of laws recognizing such marriages does not deprive people of a freedom they previously had, for they were never able to have such agreements legally enforced. Nor have people been deprived of a freedom they would have if there were no legal system, for in the absence of a legal system no agreements can be legally enforced. If there is a ground for complaint, then, it must be one of inequality—that one type of relationship is legally recognized but others are not. However, a charge of inequality is warranted only if there are no relevant reasonable grounds for distinguishing between relationships. To settle that issue one must be clear about the state's or society's interests in marriage.

The rest of this essay is concerned with the purposes or functions of the marriage relationship in which society has a legitimate interest. It is not possible here to set out and to justify the purposes for which governments may legislate. It is assumed that the state may act to facilitate citizens' engaging in activities that they find desirable and to protect the welfare and equality of all citizens, including future ones. Government has an especially strong responsibility for the welfare of children. Of course, these legitimate governmental or social interests and responsibilities must be balanced against other interests and values of citizens, including those of privacy and freedom from interference.

There is no attempt or intention to justify penal laws prohibiting forms of relationship other than monogamous marriage. Indeed, it is generally assumed that they ought not be prohibited and that more people will enter into them than has been the case. In such a context, monogamous marriage would become a more specialized form of relationship, entered into by a smaller proportion of the population than previously. Underlying this assumption are the general beliefs that many people are unqualified or unfit for a marital relationship and ought never to enter one and that many people marry for the wrong reasons. If true, these beliefs may explain why both marriage and divorce rates have been steadily rising in most Western countries during this century.[24]

PROMOTING INTERPERSONAL RELATIONSHIPS

Alienation from others and loss of community are perceived by many to be among the most serious ills of modern, mass society. In such a situation it seems unlikely that many would deny the need for intimate interpersonal relationships of affection. The importance of such relationships for a good or *eudaemonistic* life have been recognized by philosophers as diverse as Aristotle and G. E. Moore.[25] In considering such interpersonal relationships to be among the most valuable elements of a good life, one must distinguish between the value of a good and the strength of the desire for it. Many people have a stronger desire for life than for such interpersonal relationships, but they may still recognize such relationships as more valuable than mere life. Life itself is of little value, but it is a necessary condition for most other things of value.

Among the most valuable forms of interpersonal relationship are love, friendship, and trust. These relationships are limited with respect to the number of persons with whom one can have them. Classically, there has been a distinction between agapeic and erotic love. Agapeic love is the love of all mankind—general benevolence. The concept of erotic love is more limited. In today's world erotic love is apt to be confused with sexual desire and intercourse. But there can be and always has been sex without love and love without sex. Personal love is more restricted than either agapeic love or sexual desire. It implies a concern for another that is greater than that for most people. Hence, it cannot be had for an unlimited number of other people.[26] Similar distinctions must be drawn between friendship and acquaintance, trust of a political candidate and that of a friend.

Such interpersonal relationships require intimacy. Intimacy involves a sharing of information about one another that is not shared with others. Moreover, it often involves seclusion from others—being in private where others cannot observe.[27] In some societies where physical privacy is not possible, psychological privacy—shutting out the awareness of the presence of others—substitutes. Consequently, these valuable interpersonal relationships require intimacy and usually physical privacy from others, and at the very least nonintrusion upon the relationship.

Moreover, these forms of interpersonal relationship require acts expressing the concern felt for the other person. In most societies acts of sexual intercourse have been such expressions of love and concern. It is not physically or psychologically necessary that sexual intercourse have this quasi-symbolic function, but it is a natural function of sexual intercourse. All that is here meant by "natural" is that in most societies sexual intercourse has this function, for which there is some psychological basis even though it is not contrary to scientific laws for it to be otherwise. Intercourse usually involves an element of giving of oneself, and one's sexual identity is frequently a central element of one's self-image. It is not, however, sexual intercourse that is intrinsically valuable but the feelings and attitudes, the underlying interpersonal relationship, that it expresses. Nonsexual acts also currently express such relationships, but sexual intercourse is still one of the most important ways of doing so. If sexual intercourse ceases to have this function in society, some other act will undoubtedly replace it in this function. Moreover, sexual intercourse will have lost much of its value.

If these interpersonal relationships of personal love and trust are of major value, it is reasonable for the state to seek to protect and foster them by according legal recognition to them in marriage. The specific forms of this recognition cannot be fully discussed. However, there is some basis for treating the partners to a marriage as one person. Historically, of course, the doctrine that the parties to a marriage are one person has supported the subjugation of women in all sorts of ways, for example, in their disability from owning property. But there is an underlying rationale for joint responsibility. Two people who, without a special reason such as taxes, keep separate accounts of income and expenditures do not have the love and trust of a couple who find such an accounting unnecessary. Moreover, in such a joint economic venture there is no point to allowing one party to sue the other. Only the advent of insurance, whereby neither spouse, but a third party, pays, makes such suits seem profitable. Another recognition of these relationships—albeit one not frequently invoked—is that one is not forced to testify against his or her spouse. More important is that neither party is encouraged to violate the trust and intimacy of the relationship, for example, by encouraging one to inform authorities about bedroom comments of his or her spouse.[28]

The character of these valuable forms of interpersonal relationship provides an argument against according marriages of definite duration legal recognition equal to that accorded those that are intentionally of indefinite duration. For it to be "intentionally of indefinite duration," neither partner may, when entering the marriage, intend it to be for a specific period of time, for example, five years, nor may the marriage contract specify such a period. The following argument is not to show that marriages for a definite duration should not be recognized, but merely to show that they should not have equal standing with those intentionally of indefinite duration. The basic reason for unequal recognition is that interpersonal relationships that are not intentionally of indefinite duration are less valuable than those that are.

Suppose one were to form a friendship with a colleague, but the two mutually agree to be friends for only three years, with an option to renew the friendship at that time. Such an agreement would indicate a misunderstanding of friendship. Such agreements make sense for what Aristotle called friendships of utility, but in the modern world these friendships are business partnerships.[29] While there is nothing wrong with business friendships, they do not have the intrinsic value of personal friendships. In becoming close personal friends with someone, one establishes a concern and trust that would be seriously weakened or destroyed by setting a time limit to the friendship. It is sometimes claimed that time limits may be set because people will only be together for a while. But one need not see a person every day or even every year to remain friends. However, extended separation usually brings about a withering away of the friendship.

Similarly, the personal relationship of love and trust in marriage is of lesser value if it is intentionally for only a definite period of time. Moreover, the entering into a relationship that is intentionally of indefinite duration and legally recognized symbolizes a strength of commitment not found in other types of relationships. While two unmarried people may claim that there is no definite limit to their mutual commitment, their commitment is always questionable. Entering into a marital relationship assures the commitment more than does a mere verbal avowal.

There are two common objections to this argument. First, it is sometimes said that there may be special reasons for making marriages of short, definite duration, for example, if one partner will only live in the area for a while. But a personal love that is not strong enough to overcome difficulties of moving to another area and possible sacrifices of employment is not as close and strong as a love that can. Many married couples make such compromises and sacrifices. Second, it is sometimes claimed that commitment is in fact stronger when not legally reinforced, when one does not need the law to support the relationship. However, this claim overlooks the fact that when a married couple's relationship rests substantially upon their legal obligations, their relationship has already begun to deteriorate. The strength of commitment is established by the willingness to enter into a legal relationship that cannot be broken simply, without any difficulties. A person who is not willing to undertake the risk of the legal involvement in divorce should he desire to terminate the relationship is probably unsure of his commitment. Moreover, the legal relationship provides security against a sudden and unexpected change in one's life—the breakup of the social aspects will take some time, giving one a chance to prepare for a new style of life. Even then the change is often very difficult.

Hence, if marriage is for the purpose of providing legal recognition of some of the most valuable interpersonal relationships, it should grant more protection and recognition to those intentionally of indefinite duration than to others. Such a conclusion does not imply that divorce should be impossible or exceedingly difficult. Friendships frequently do not last forever despite their not being intended for a limited period of time. The same may happen to a marital relationship. So while this argument supports not according legal recognition to relationships intended to be of definite duration equal to that accorded those intended to be of indefinite duration, it does not support restrictions on divorce in the latter case. Moreover, the average length of time of marriages has increased considerably since the seventeenth century. When a couple married then, one of them was likely to die within twenty years. With today's increased life expectancy, both parties may live close to fifty years after they marry.[30] Obviously, with such an increased possible length of marriage, there is a greater chance for marital breakdown and divorce. One may expect more divorces in marriages that have lasted twenty to twenty-five years simply because there are more such marriages. Nevertheless, such marriages are intentionally of indefinite duration—for life.

PROTECTING THE WELFARE OF CHILDREN

Another area of pervasive social interest that has historically centered in marriage concerns the procreation and raising of children. Society has an interest not only in the number of children born but their quality of life. This fact is in deep conflict with the current emphasis on the freedom of individuals to make reproductive decisions unfettered by social rules and restrictions. Moreover, it is an area in which social control has traditionally been weak. Child abuse is widespread, and efforts to prevent it are mediocre at best. There are few general legal qualifications or tests for becoming a parent. Yet parenthood is one of the most potentially dangerous relationships that one person can have with another. If one is a poor college teacher, then at worst a few students do not receive a bit of education they might have. But as a parent one potentially can ruin completely the lives of one's children. At the least, they may develop into psychological misfits incapable of leading responsible and rewarding lives.

Essentially, there are three areas of social interest and responsibility with respect to procreation and the raising of children. First, there is a social interest in the sheer number of children born. The current emphasis on population control makes this interest abundantly clear.[31] Second, there is a social interest in the potentialities of children. This area includes concern for genetic and congenital birth defects and abnormalities. Over 5 percent of all children born have a genetic defect. The possibility of genetic control of those who are born will soon take on major significance. Already, approximately sixty genetic diseases as well as almost all chromosomal abnormalities can be detected *in utero*, and adult carriers of about eighty genetic defects can be identified.[32] Given the possibility of genetic control, society can no longer risk having genetically disadvantaged children by leaving the decision of whether to have children to the unregulated judgment of individual couples. Some social regulations with respect to genetic screening and, perhaps, eugenic sterilization are needed. While potential parents have interests of privacy and freedom in reproductive decisions, the social interests in preventing the suffering and inequality of possibly defective children may outweigh them in certain types of cases.

Third, the care and development of those who are born is a social interest and responsiblity. This interest has been recognized for some time in the form of children's homes and compulsory education. However, increasing knowledge about childhood development extends the area in which social interests and responsibility may be reasonably involved. To give an example at the most elementary level, the nutritional diet of children during their first three years is crucial for their future development. So also is their psychological support. The welfare of future generations is not a private but a social matter. It is a proper task of society, acting through its government, to ensure that the members of the next generation are not physical or psychological cripples due to the ignorance, negligence, or even indifference of parents.

Historically, society has attempted to control procreation through the institution of marriage. Society's means were primarily to stigmatize children born out of wedlock and to encourage the having of many children. It is now recognized that no useful purpose is served by stigmatizing children born out of wedlock as illegitimate. (However, some useful purpose may be served by not according children born out of wedlock all the rights of those born in wedlock, for example, inheritance without parental recognition.) The emphasis on having as many children as one can has also disappeared. It is not this historical concern with procreation that is misplaced in modern society but the forms that the concern has taken.

If society has the responsibility to protect the welfare of children, then some social regulation and control of human reproduction and development is justified. Such regulation and control need not be effected by penal laws. For example, social concern has traditionally been expressed in adoptions through regulations to ensure that those who adopt children are fit to care for them. That some regulations have been inappropriate and not reasonably related to the welfare of children is not in question. Rather, the point is that there has been regulation without penal laws, or at least without resorting primarily to penal laws. Nor can social regulation and control be solely by legislation. Legislation alone is usually ineffective; it must be supported by informal social rules and expectations.

Not only has modern biomedicine made sex possible without procreation; it has also made procreation possible without sex. The techniques of artificial insemination and fertilization, embryo transfer, ova donation, ectogenesis, and cloning now, or soon will, make it possible for people to reproduce without sexual intercourse.[33] Hence, not only may one have sex for pleasure, but one may reproduce for pleasure without sexual intercourse. Not only may people reproduce outside marriage; they are not even biologically required to have intercourse. Thus, sex and marriage may become dissociated from reproduction.

However, there are strong reasons for restricting procreation primarily to marriages of indefinite duration, which does not imply that such marriages should be restricted to procreation. Marriage has traditionally been the central social institution concerned with procreation. Consequently, if society is to exercise some control over procreation in the future, it would involve the least change in conditions to do so through marriage. Moreover, there is considerable evidence that the disruption of family life contributes to juvenile delinquency. Whether divorce or marital breakdown (with or without divorce) is a prime cause of such delinquency does not matter. The point is that the disruption of home life does seriously affect the development of children.[34] The chance of such disruption outside of a marriage that is intentionally of indefinite duration is higher than for that within. Moreover, there is some reason to believe that the presence of both mother and father is instrumental in the psychological development of children. In any case, the presence of two people rather than one provides the security that there will be someone to care for the children should one of the parents die. Generally, children are better off being with one parent than in a state orphanage, but better off still with both parents. Hence, for the welfare of children it seems best that procreation and child rearing primarily occur within the context of marriages intentially of indefinite duration.

While society has a responsibility for the care and development of children, this general responsibility is best carried out if specific adults have obligations to care for specific children. In the past, the biological parent-child relation has reinforced the allocation of responsibility for specific children and has been a major factor in monogamy.[35] The separation of reproduction and sexual intercourse threatens disruption of this assignment. For example, if gestation occurs in an artificial womb in a laboratory, there may be no "parents," only a specific research group. More realistically, if a woman has an embryo from ova and sperm donors transferred to her uterus, it is unclear who are the child's parents. However, if there is to be optimal care for children, specific adults must have obligations for specific children. It cannot be left to somebody in general, for then nobody in particular is likely to do it. "Let George do it" is too prevalent and careless an attitude to allow with regard to children.

McMurtry's contention that monogamy restricts the care for children is not well founded.[36] First, if there are no specific adults responsible for children, they may become "lost" in large groups and victims of the "it's not my job" syndrome. Second, monogamy per se does not cut children off from the support and care of others. One must distinguish the marital relationship from living arrangements. It is the isolated situation of the family that deprives children of such support. In many married-student housing complexes children have access to other adults. Even in general-residential neighborhoods with separate family housing units, such support is available if there is a sense of community in the neighborhood.

Given the social interests in and responsibility for the procreation and development of children, some more effective controls of parenthood appear desirable. If the primary locus of reproduction is to be within marriages of intentionally indefinite duration, then the easiest way to institute controls is to add requirements for people to enter such marriages. A few requirements such as blood tests are already generally prevalent. Alternatively, one might have a separate licensing procedure for procreation. Nonmarried couples and single people might also qualify for such licenses. Moreover, couples who want to marry but not have children would not have to meet requirements. However, the only requirements suggested below that might bar marriages are almost as important for those couples who do not have children as for those who do. If the requirements were tied to marriage they would be easier to administer. The only drawback is that unmarried people would not have to meet them. However, such requirements can and should be part of the medical practice of the "artificial" techniques of reproduction—artificial insemination and embryo transfer. And there are few if any effective methods, except generally accepted social rules, to control procreation outside of marriage.

One obvious requirement would be genetic screening. With modern medical techniques genetic problems do not imply that couples cannot become married, but they might be expected not to have children who are their genetic offspring. Artificial insemination and embryo transfer make it possible for almost everyone to have children, even though the children might not be genetically theirs. A general distinction between biological and social parenthood should be made, with legal emphasis on the latter.

More important, perhaps, is some general expectation of psychological fitness for family life and the raising of children. The difficulty with such an expectation is the absence of any clear criteria for fitness and reliable methods for determining who meets them. Perhaps, however, some formal instruction in family relations and child rearing would be appropriate. The Commission on Population Growth and the American Future has already called for an expansion of education for parenthood.[37] It is only a bit further to require some sort of minimal family education for marriage. Probably the easiest method for ensuring such education would be to make it a required subject in secondary schools. If that were done, few people would have difficulty meeting this requirement for marriage.

There should not be any financial or property qualifications for marriage.[38] Society's interest in and responsibility for the welfare of the population in general is such that governments should ensure an adequate standard of living for all persons. Were that to be done there would be no reason to impose any financial restrictions on marriage. Nonetheless, prospective parents should have more concern for their financial situation than is now frequently the case. The adequate care of children is an expensive task, financially as well as psychologically and temporally.

CONCLUSION

It may be objected that neither the argument from interpersonal relations nor that from the welfare of children specifically supports monogamous marriage. While loving relationships cannot extend to an indefinite number of people, they can extend to more than one other person. Also, a polygamous union may provide a reasonable environment for procreation. Hence, neither of the arguments supports monogamous marriage per se.

Logically, the objection is quite correct. But it is a misunderstanding of social philosophy to expect arguments showing that a certain arrangement is always best under all circumstances. The most that can be shown is that usually, or as a rule, one social arrangement is preferable to another. Practically, polygamous marriage patterns will probably never be prevalent.[39] For centuries they have been gradually disappearing throughout the world. If a disproportionate sex distribution of the population occurs in some areas or age groups (such as the elderly), then they may increase in significance. Unless that occurs, most people will probably continue to prefer marital monogamy.

More important, the burden of this paper has not been to defend the traditional ideal of marital union or even the current practice. Many of the traditional rules of marriage have been unjust, for example, the inequality between the sexes, both legally and in terms of social roles. Instead, it has been to defend social recognition of marriage of intentionally indefinite duration as a unique and socially valuable institution that society has interests in promoting and regulating. In particular, society has interests in and responsibility for promoting a certain form of valuable interpersonal relationship and protecting the welfare of children. Both of these purposes can be well served by monogamous marriage.

The image, then, is of a society with various forms of living together, but one in which marriage of intentionally indefinite duration would have a distinctive though lessened role as a special kind of socially and legally recognized relationship. There would not be laws prohibiting non-marital forms of cohabitation. Divorce would be based on factual marital breakdown or mutual consent, with due regard for the welfare of children. Monogamous marriage would recognize a special form of personal relationship in which reproduction and child rearing primarily occur. Given the social interest in decreasing procreation, many people might marry but not have children, and others might not marry at all. Details of the legal marital relationship have not been specified, nor could they be in this brief essay except with respect to the main social interests. Questions of inheritance, legal residence and name, social-security benefits, and so on, have not been specified. Changes in laws with respect to many of these matters can be made without affecting the arguments for the value of, social responsibility for, and interests in marriage. Above all, it is an image in which sexual intercourse plays a much smaller role in the conception of marriage and the good life in general, a society in which vulgar hedonism has at least been replaced by a broader-based *eudaemonism.*

NOTES

1. Epicurus, "Letter to Menoeceus," in *The Stoic and Epicurean Philosophers,* ed. Whitney J. Oates (New York: Modern Library, 1957), p. 31. Epicurus even wrote, "Sexual intercourse has never done a man good, and he is lucky if it has not harmed him" (Fragment 8 in *The Stoic and Epicurean Philosophers*). John Stuart Mill, *Utilitarianism,* chap. 2, especially paragraphs 1-9.
2. *De Anima* 2. 4.
3. Monogamy: A Critique," *The Monist* 56 (1972); reprinted herein, pp. 277-287. This quote appears on page 281 of this volume (italics added). Subsequent references to McMurtry's essay are to pages in this volume.
4. Ibid., p. 281.
5. Ibid.
6. Ibid.
7. Ibid., p. 282.
8. Ibid., p. 283.
9. Ibid., p. 284.
10. Ibid.
11. Ibid.
12. Ibid., p. 284.
13. Ibid., p. 284.
14. Karl Marx and Friedrich Engels, "Manifesto of the Communist Party," in *Basic Writings on Politics and Philosophy,* ed. Lewis S. Feuer (Garden City, N.Y.: Doubleday, Anchor Books, 1959), especially p. 24.

15. Paul R. Ehrlich, *The Population Bomb* (New York: Ballantine Books, 1968).
16. Even new Marxists perceive other sources of problems. See Milovan Djilas, *The New Class* (New York: Praeger, 1964); and, more generally, Richard T. De George, *The New Marxism* (New York: Pegasus, 1968), chap. 2. The importance of population for pollution, with which it is most frequently connected, has been contested by Barry Commoner, *The Closing Circle* (New York: Knopf, 1971), pp. 133-35. Ehrlich now clearly recognizes that various causal factors are important, although he still disagrees with Commoner on the importance of population growth; see Paul R. Ehrlich et al., *Human Ecology* (San Francisco: W. H. Freeman and Company, 1973), chap. 7, esp. pp. 206, 213-15, 221.
17. Max Rheinstein, *Marriage Stability, Divorce, and the Law* (Chicago: University of Chicago Press, 1972), p. 251.
18. Edwin D. Driver, "Population Policies of State Governments in the United States: Some Preliminary Observations," *Villanova Law Review* 15 (1970): 846-47.
19. Immanuel Kant, *The Philosophy of Law*, trans. W. Hastie (Edinburgh: T. & T. Clark, 1887), p. 110.
20. McMurtry, "Monogamy," p. 282; italics in original omitted.
21. See John T. Noonan, Jr., *Contraception* (Cambridge, Mass.: Harvard University Press, 1966), pp. 312-14.
22. Keith G. McWalter, "Marriage as Contract: Towards a Functional Redefinition of the Marital Status," *Columbia Journal of Law and Social Problems* 9 (1973): 615.
23. Robert S. Summers, "The Technique Element of Law," *California Law Review* 59 (1971): 736-37, 741-45.
24. Burton M. Leiser, *Liberty, Justice and Morals* (New York: Macmillan Co., (1973), p. 126; R[oland] Pressat, *Population*, trans. Robert and Danielle Atkinson (Baltimore: Penguin Books, 1970), pp. 84, 86; U.S. Commission on Population Growth and the American Future, *Population and the American Future* (New York: Signet, New American Library, 1972), pp. 102-03.
25. Aristotle, *Nicomachean Ethics* 9, 9-12; George Edward Moore, *Principia Ethica* (Cambridge: At the University Press, 1903), p. 188, 203-05.
26. It is thus misleading for McMurtry to write of monogamous marriage excluding "almost *countless* other possibilities of *intimate* union" with any number of persons (p. 279; my italics). On the limited nature of personal love or friendship see also Aristotle, *Nicomachean Ethics* 9. 10.
27. For a discussion of these relationships and the need for privacy, see Charles Fried, "Privacy," in *Law, Reason, and Justice*, ed. Graham Hughes (New York: New York University Press, 1969), pp. 45-69.
28. See the discussion (in another context) of such a case in Nazi Germany by H. L. A. Hart, "Positivism and the Separation of Law and Morals," *Harvard Law Review* 71 (1958): 618-20; and Lon L. Fuller, "Positivism and Fidelity to Law—A Reply to Professor Hart," *Harvard Law Review* 71 (1958): 652-55.
29. *Nicomachean Ethics* 8. 3. The vulgar hedonists treat marriage as a form of friendship for pleasure, but that is not the highest form of friendship.
30. Pressat, *Population*, p. 52.
31. For a more complete discussion see my "Limits to a Right to Procreate," in *Ethics and Population*, ed. Michael D. Bayles (Cambridge, Mass.: Schenkman Publishing Company, 1975).

32. Daniel Callahan, *The Tyranny of Survival* (New York: Macmillan Co., 1973), p. 219.
33. For a good general survey of these techniques and some suggestions for social controls, see George A. Hudock, "Gene Therapy and Genetic Engineering: Frankenstein Is Still a Myth, But It Should Be Reread Periodically," *Indiana Law Journal* 48 (1973): 533-58. Various ethical issues are discussed in Joseph Fletcher, *The Ethics of Genetic Control* (Garden City, N.Y.: Doubleday, Anchor Books, 1974). Successful human embryo implantation and growth to term after *in vitro* fertilization has been reported in Britain (see *Time,* July 29, 1974, p. 58-59; and *Newsweek,* July 29, 1974, p. 70).
34. President's Commission on Law Enforcement and Administration of Justice, *The Challenge of Crime in a Free Society* (New York: Avon Books, 1968), pp. 184-89.
35. Daniel Callahan, "New Beginnings in Life: A Philosopher's Response," in *The New Genetics and the Future of Man,* ed. Michael P. Hamilton (Grand Rapids, Mich.: William B. Eerdmans Publishing Company, 1972), pp. 102-03.
36. "Monogamy," p. 281.
37. *Population and the American Future,* pp. 126-33, esp. 133.
38. For some suggested financial requirements as well as others, see Jack Parsons, *Population versus Liberty* (Buffalo, N.Y.: Prometheus Books, 1971), p. 349.
39. Even McMurtry appears to recognize this fact; see "Monogamy," p. 278.

Is Adultery Immoral?

Richard Wasserstrom

Many discussions of the enforcement of morality by the law take as illustrative of the problem under consideration the regulation of various types of sexual behavior by the criminal law. It was, for example, the Wolfenden Report's recommendations concerning homosexuality and prostitution that led Lord Devlin to compose his now famous lecture, "The Enforcement of Morals." And that lecture in turn provoked important philosophical responses from H. L. A. Hart, Ronald Dworkin, and others.

Much, if not all, of the recent philosophical literature on the enforcement of morals appears to take for granted the immorality of the sexual behavior in question. The focus of discussion, at least, is whether such

From *Today's Moral Problems,* ed. Richard Wasserstrom (New York: Macmillan, 1975), pp. 240-51. Reprinted by permission of the author and the publisher.

things as homosexuality, prostitution, and adultery ought to be made illegal even if they are immoral, and not whether they are immoral.

I propose in this paper to think about the latter, more neglected topic, that of sexual morality, and to do so in the following fashion. I shall consider just one kind of behavior that is often taken to be a case of sexual immorality—adultery. I am interested in pursuing at least two questions. First, I want to explore the question of in what respects adulterous behavior falls within the domain of morality at all: For this surely is one of the puzzles one encounters when considering the topic of sexual morality. It is often hard to see on what grounds much of the behavior is deemed to be either moral or immoral, for example, private homosexual behavior between consenting adults. I have purposely selected adultery because it seems a more plausible candidate for moral assessment than many other kinds of sexual behavior.

The second question I want to examine is that of what is to be said about adultery, without being especially concerned to stay within the area of morality. I shall endeavor, in other words, to identify and to assess a number of the major arguments that might be advanced against adultery. I believe that they are the chief arguments that would be given in support of the view that adultery is immoral, but I think they are worth considering even if some of them turn out to be nonmoral arguments and considerations.

A number of the issues involved seem to me to be complicated and difficult. In a number of places I have at best indicated where further philosophical exploration is required without having successfully conducted the exploration myself. The paper may very well be more useful as an illustration of how one might begin to think about the subject of sexual morality than as an elucidation of important truths about the topic.

Before I turn to the arguments themselves there are two preliminary points that require some clarification. Throughout the paper I shall refer to the immorality of such things as breaking a promise, deceiving someone, etc. In a very rough way, I mean by this that there is something morally wrong that is done in doing the action in question. I mean that the action is, in a strong sense of *"prima facie,"* *prima facie* wrong or unjustified. I do not mean that it may never be right or justifiable to do the action; just that the fact that it is an action of this description always does count against the rightness of the action. I leave entirely open the question of what it is that makes actions of this kind immoral in this sense of "immoral."

The second preliminary point concerns what is meant or implied by the concept of adultery. I mean by "adultery" any case of extramarital sex, and I want to explore the arguments for and against extramarital sex, undertaken in a variety of morally relevant situations. Someone might claim that the concept of adultery is conceptually connected with the concept of immorality, and that to characterize behavior as adulterous is already to characterize it as immoral or unjustified in the sense described above. There may be something to this. Hence the importance of making it clear that I want to talk about extramarital sexual relations. If they are always immoral, this is something that must be shown by argument. If the concept of adultery does in some sense entail or imply immorality, I want to ask whether that connection is a rationally based one. If not all cases of extramarital sex are immoral (again, in the sense described above), then the concept of adultery should either be weakened accordingly or restricted to those classes of extramarital sex for which the predication of immorality is warranted.

One argument for the immorality of adultery might go something like this: what makes adultery immoral is that it involves the breaking of a promise, and what makes adultery seriously wrong is that it involves the breaking of an important promise. For, so the argument might continue, one of the things the two parties promise each other when they get married is that they will abstain from sexual relationships with third persons. Because of this promise both spouses quite reasonably entertain the expectation that the other will behave in conformity with it. Hence, when one of the parties has sexual intercourse with a third person he or she breaks that promise about sexual relationships which was made when the marriage was entered into, and defeats the reasonable expectations of exclusivity entertained by the spouse.

In many cases the immorality involved in breaching the promise relating to extramarital sex may be a good deal more serious than that involved in the breach of other promises. This is so because adherence to this promise may be of much greater importance to the parties than is adherence to many of the other promises given or received by them in their lifetime. The breaking of this promise may be much more hurtful and painful than is typically the case.

Why is this so? To begin with, it may have been difficult for the non-adulterous spouse to have kept the promise. Hence that spouse may feel the unfairness of having restrained himself or herself in the absence of reciprocal restraint having been exercised by the adulterous spouse. In addition, the spouse may perceive the breaking of the promise as an indication of a kind of indifference on the part of the adulterous spouse. If you really cared about me and my feelings—the spouse might say—you would not have done this to me. And third, and related to the above, the spouse may see the act of sexual intercourse with another as a sign of affection for the other person and as an additional rejection of the non-adulterous spouse as the one who is loved by the adulterous spouse. It is not just that the adulterous spouse does not take the feelings of the spouse sufficiently into account, the adulterous spouse also indicates through the act of adultery affection for someone other than the spouse. I will return to these points later. For the present, it is sufficient to note that a set of arguments can be developed in support of the proposition that certain kinds of adultery are wrong just because they involve the breach of a

serious promise which, among other things, leads to the intentional infliction of substantial pain by one spouse upon the other.

Another argument for the immorality of adultery focuses not on the
existence of a promise of sexual exclusivity but on the connection between adultery and deception. According to this argument, adultery involves deception. And because deception is wrong, so is adultery.

Although it is certainly not obviously so, I shall simply assume in this
paper that deception is always immoral. Thus the crucial issue for my
purposes is the asserted connection between extramarital sex and deception. Is it plausible to maintain, as this argument does, that adultery
always does involve deception and is on that basis to be condemned?

The most obvious person on whom deceptions might be practiced is
the nonparticipating spouse; and the most obvious thing about which the
nonparticipating spouse can be deceived is the existence of the adulterous
act. One clear case of deception is that of lying. Instead of saying that the
afternoon was spent in bed with A, the adulterous spouse asserts that it
was spent in the library with B, or on the golf course with C.

There can also be deception even when no lies are told. Suppose, for
instance, that a person has sexual intercourse with someone other than his
or her spouse and just does not tell the spouse about it. Is that deception?
It may not be a case of lying if, for example, the spouse is never asked by
the other about the situation. Still, we might say, it is surely deceptive because of the promises that were exchanged at marriage. As we saw earlier,
these promises provide a foundation for the reasonable belief that neither
spouse will engage in sexual relationships with any other persons. Hence
the failure to bring the fact of extramarital sex to the attention of the
other spouse deceives that spouse about the present state of the marital
relationship.

Adultery, in other words, can involve both active and passive deception. An adulterous spouse may just keep silent or, as is often the fact,
the spouse may engage in an increasingly complex way of life devoted to
the concealment of the facts from the nonparticipating spouse. Lies, half-
truths, clandestine meetings, and the like may become a central feature
of the adulterous spouse's existence. These are things that can and do
happen, and when they do they make the case against adultery an easy
one. Still, neither active nor passive deception is inevitably a feature of
an extramarital relationship.

It is possible, though, that a more subtle but pervasive kind of decep-
tiveness is a feature of adultery. It comes about because of the connection
in our culture between sexual intimacy and certain feelings of love and
affection. The point can be made indirectly at first by seeing that one way
in which we can, in our culture, mark off our close friends from our mere
acquaintances is through the kinds of intimacies that we are prepared to
share with them. I may, for instance, be willing to reveal my very private
thoughts and emotions to my closest friends or to my wife, but to no one
else. My sharing of these intimate facts about myself is from one perspec-

tive a way of making a gift to those who mean the most to me. Revealing these things and sharing them with those who mean the most to me is one means by which I create, maintain, and confirm those interpersonal relationships that are of most importance to me.

Now in our culture, it might be claimed, sexual intimacy is one of the chief currencies through which gifts of this sort are exchanged. One way to tell someone—particularly someone of the opposite sex—that you have feelings of affection and love for them is by allowing to them or sharing with them sexual behaviors that one doesn't share with the rest of the world. This way of measuring affection was certainly very much a part of the culture in which I matured. It worked something like this. If you were a girl, you showed how much you liked someone by the degree of sexual intimacy you would allow. If you liked a boy only a little, you never did more than kiss—and even the kiss was not very passionate. If you liked the boy a lot and if your feeling was reciprocated, necking, and possibly petting, was permissible. If the attachment was still stronger and you thought it might even become a permanent relationship, the sexual activity was correspondingly more intense and more intimate, although whether it would ever lead to sexual intercourse depended on whether the parties (and particularly the girl) accepted fully the prohibition on nonmarital sex. The situation for the boy was related, but not exactly the same. The assumption was that males did not naturally link sex with affection in the way in which females did. However, since women did, males had to take this into account. That is to say, because a woman would permit sexual intimacies only if she had feelings of affection for the male and only if those feelings were reciprocated, the male had to have and express those feelings, too, before sexual intimacies of any sort would occur.

The result was that the importance of a correlation between sexual intimacy and feelings of love and affection was taught by the culture and assimilated by those growing up in the culture. The scale of possible positive feelings toward persons of the other sex ran from casual liking at the one end to the love that was deemed essential to and characteristic of marriage at the other. The scale of possible sexual behavior ran from brief, passionless kissing or hand-holding at the one end to sexual intercourse at the other. And the correlation between the two scales was quite precise. As a result, any act of sexual intimacy carried substantial meaning with it, and no act of sexual intimacy was simply a pleasurable set of bodily sensations. Many such acts were, of course, more pleasurable to the participants because they were a way of saying what the participants feelings were. And sometimes they were less pleasurable for the same reason. The point is, however, that in any event sexual activity was much more than mere bodily enjoyment. It was not like eating a good meal, listening to good music, lying in the sun, or getting a pleasant back rub. It was behavior that meant a great deal concerning one's feelings for persons of the opposite sex in whom one was most interested and with whom

[handwritten marginal note: morality has a cultural base]

one was most involved. It was among the most authoritative ways in which one could communicate to another the nature and degree of one's affection.

If this sketch is even roughly right, then several things become somewhat clearer. To begin with, a possible rationale for many of the rules of conventional sexual morality can be developed. If, for example, sexual intercourse is associated with the kind of affection and commitment to another that is regarded as characteristic of the marriage relationship, then it is natural that sexual intercourse should be thought properly to take place between persons who are married to each other. And if it is thought that this kind of affection and commitment is only to be found within the marriage relationship, then it is not surprising that sexual intercourse should only be thought to be proper within marriage.

Related to what has just been said is the idea that sexual intercourse ought to be restricted to those who are married to each other as a means by which to confirm the very special feelings that the spouses have for each other. Because the culture teaches that sexual intercourse means that the strongest of all feelings for each other are shared by the lovers, it is natural that persons who are married to each other should be able to say this to each other in this way. Revealing and confirming verbally that these feelings are present is one thing that helps to sustain the relationship; engaging in sexual intercourse is another.

In addition, this account would help to provide a framework within which to make sense of the notion that some sex is better than other sex. As I indicated earlier, the fact that sexual intimacy can be meaningful in the sense described tends to make it also the case that sexual intercourse can sometimes be more enjoyable than at other times. On this view, sexual intercourse will typically be more enjoyable where the strong feelings of affection are present than it will be where it is merely "mechanical." This is so in part because people enjoy being loved, especially by those whom they love. Just as we like to hear words of affection, so we like to receive affectionate behavior. And the meaning enhances the independently pleasurable behavior.

More to the point, moreover, an additional rationale for the prohibition on extramarital sex can now be developed. For given this way of viewing the sexual world, extramarital sex will almost always involve deception of a deeper sort. If the adulterous spouse does not in fact have the appropriate feelings of affection for the extramarital partner, then the adulterous spouse is deceiving that person about the presence of such feelings. If, on the other hand, the adulterous spouse does have the corresponding feelings for the extramarital partner but not toward the nonparticipating spouse, the adulterous spouse is very probably deceiving the nonparticipating spouse about the presence of such feelings toward that spouse. Indeed, it might be argued, whenever there is no longer love between the two persons who are married to each other, there is deception just because being married implies both to the participants and to the world that such a bond exists. Deception is inevitable, the argument might conclude, because the feelings of affection that ought to accompany any act of sexual intercourse can only be held toward one other person at any given time in one's life. And if this is so, then the adulterous spouse always deceives either the partner in adultery or the nonparticipating spouse about the existence of such feelings. Thus extramarital sex involves deception of this sort and is for this reason immoral even if no deception vis-à-vis the occurrence of the act of adultery takes place.

What might be said in response to the foregoing arguments? The first thing that might be said is that the account of the connection between sexual intimacy and feelings of affection is inaccurate. Not inaccurate in the sense that no one thinks of things that way, but in the sense that there is substantially more divergence of opinion than that account suggests. For example, the view I have delineated may describe reasonably accurately the concepts of the sexual world in which I grew up, but it does not capture the sexual *weltanschauung* of today's youth at all. Thus, whether or not adultery implies deception in respect to feelings depends very much on the persons who are involved and the way they look at the "meaning" of sexual intimacy.

Second, the argument leaves to be answered the question of whether it is desirable for sexual intimacy to carry the sorts of messages described above. For those persons for whom sex does have these implications, there are special feelings and sensibilities that must be taken into account. But it is another question entirely whether any valuable end—moral or otherwise—is served by investing sexual behavior with such significance. That is something that must be shown and not just assumed. It might, for instance, be the case that substantially more good than harm would come from a kind of demystification of sexual behavior: one that would encourage the enjoyment of sex more for its own sake and one that would reject the centrality both of the association of sex with love and of love with only one other person.

I regard these as two of the more difficult, unresolved issues that our culture faces today in respect to thinking sensibly about the attitudes toward sex and love that we should try to develop in ourselves and in our children. Much of the contemporary literature that advocates sexual liberation of one sort or another embraces one or the other of two different views about the relationship between sex and love.

One view holds that sex should be separated from love and affection. To be sure sex is probably better when the partners genuinely like and enjoy each other. But sex is basically an intensive, exciting sensuous activity that can be enjoyed in a variety of suitable settings with a variety of suitable partners. The situation in respect to sexual pleasure is no different from that of the person who knows and appreciates fine food and who can have a very satisfying meal in any number of good restaurants with any number of congenial companions. One question that must be settled here is whether sex can be so demystified; another, more important question is whether it would be desirable to do so. What would we gain and what might we lose if we all lived in a world in which an act of sexual intercourse was no more or less significant or enjoyable than having a delicious meal in a nice setting with a good friend? The answer to this question lies beyond the scope of this paper.

The second view seeks to drive the wedge in a different place. It is not the link between sex and love that needs to be broken; rather, on this view, it is the connection between love and exclusivity that ought to be severed. For a number of the reasons already given, it is desirable, so this argument goes, that sexual intimacy continue to be reserved to and shared with only those for whom one has very great affection. The mistake lies in thinking that any "normal" adult will only have those feeling toward one other adult during his or her lifetime—or even at any time in his or her life. It is the concept of adult, not ideas about sex, that, on this view, needs demystification. What are thought to be both unrealistic and unfortunate are the notions of exclusivity and possessiveness that attach to the dominant conception of love between adults in our and other cultures. Parents of four, five, six, or even ten children can certainly claim and sometimes claim correctly that they love all of their children, that they love them all equally, and that it is simply untrue to their feelings to insist that the numbers involved diminish either the quantity or the quality of their love. If this is an idea that is readily understandable in the case of parents and children, there is no necessary reason why it is an impossible or undesirable ideal in the case of adults. To be sure, there is probably a limit to the number of intimate, "primary" relationships that any person can maintain at any given time without the quality of the relationship being affected. But one adult ought surely be able to love two, three, or even six other adults at any one time without that love being different in kind or degree from that of the traditional, monogamous, lifetime marriage. And as between the individuals in these relationships, whether within a marriage or without, sexual intimacy is fitting and good.

The issues raised by a position such as this one are also surely worth exploring in detail and with care. Is there something to be called "sexual love" which is different from parental love or the nonsexual love of close friends? Is there something about love in general that links it naturally and appropriately with feelings of exclusivity and possession? Or is there something about sexual love, whatever that may be, that makes these feelings especially fitting here? Once again the issues are conceptual, empirical, and normative all at once: What is love? How could it be different? Would it be a good thing or a bad thing if it were different?

Suppose, though, that having delineated these problems we were now to pass them by. Suppose, moreover, we were to be persuaded of the possibility and the desirability of weakening substantially either the links between sex and love or the links between sexual love and exclusivity. Would it not then be the case that adultery could be free from all of the morally objectionable features described so far? To be more specific, let us imagine that a husband and wife have what is today sometimes characterized as an "open marriage." Suppose, that is, that they have agreed in advance that extramarital sex is—under certain circumstances—acceptable behavior for each to engage in. Suppose, that as a result there is no impulse to deceive each other about the occurrence or nature of any such relationships, and that no deception in fact occurs. Suppose, too, that there is no deception in respect to the feelings involved between the adulterous spouse and the extramarital partner. And suppose, finally, that one or the other or both of the spouses then has sexual intercourse in circumstances consistent with these understandings. Under this description, so the agreement might conclude, adultery is simply not immoral. At a minimum, adultery cannot very plausibly be condemned either on the ground that it involves deception or on the ground that it requires the breaking of a promise.

At least two responses are worth considering. One calls attention to the connection between marriage and adultery; the other looks to more instrumental arguments for the immorality of adultery. Both issues deserve further exploration.

One way to deal with the case of the "open marriage" is to question whether the two persons involved are still properly to be described as being married to each other. Part of the meaning of what it is for two persons to be married to each other, so this argument would go, is to have committed oneself to have sexual relationships only with one's spouse. Of course, it would be added, we know that that commitment is not always honored. We know that persons who are married to each other often do commit adultery. But there is a difference between being willing to make a commitment to marital fidelity, even though one may fail to honor that commitment, and not making the commitment at all. Whatever the relationship may be between the two individuals in the case described above, the absence of any commitment to sexual exclusivity requires the conclusion that their relationship is not a marital one. For a commitment to sexual exclusivity is a necessary although not a sufficient condition for the existence of a marriage.

Although there may be something to this suggestion, as it is stated it is too strong to be acceptable. To begin with, I think it is very doubtful that there are many, if any, *necessary* conditions for marriage; but even if there are, a commitment to sexual exclusivity is not such a condition.

To see that this is so, consider what might be taken to be some of the essential characteristics of a marriage. We might be tempted to propose that the concept of marriage requires the following: a formal ceremony of some sort in which mutual obligations are undertaken between two persons of the opposite sex; the capacity on the part of the persons involved to have sexual intercourse with each other; the willingness to have sexual intercourse only with each other; and feelings of love and affection between the two persons. The problem is that we can imagine relationships that are clearly marital and yet lack one or more of these features. For example, in our own society, it is possible for two persons to be married without going through a formal ceremony, as in the common-law marriages recognized in some jurisdictions. It is also possible for two persons to get married even though one or both lacks the capacity to engage in sexual intercourse. Thus, two very elderly persons who have neither the desire nor the ability to have intercourse can, nonetheless, get married, as can persons whose sexual organs have been injured so that intercourse is not possible. And we certainly know of marriages in which love was not present at the time of the marriage, as, for instance, in marriages of state and marriages of convenience.

Counterexamples not satisfying the condition relating to the abstention from extramarital sex are even more easily produced. We certainly know of societies and cultures in which polygamy and polyandry are practiced, and we have no difficulty in recognizing these relationships as cases of marriages. It might be objected, though, that these are not counterexamples because they are plural marriages rather than marriages in which sex is permitted with someone other than with one of the persons to whom one is married. But we also know of societies in which it is permissible for married persons to have sexual relationships with persons to whom they were not married, for example, temple prostitutes, concubines, and homosexual lovers. And even if we knew of no such societies, the conceptual claim would still, I submit, not be well taken. For suppose all of the other indicia of marriage were present: suppose the two persons were of the opposite sex. Suppose they had the capacity and desire to have intercourse with each other, suppose they participated in a formal ceremony in which they understood themselves voluntarily to be entering into a relationship with each other in which substantial mutual commitments were assumed. If all these conditions were satisfied, we would not be in any doubt about whether or not the two persons were married even though they had not taken on a commitment of sexual exclusivity and even though they had expressly agreed that extramarital sexual intercourse was a permissible behavior for each to engage in.

A commitment to sexual exclusivity is neither a necessary nor a sufficient condition for the existence of a marriage. It does, nonetheless, have this much to do with the nature of marriage: like the other indicia enumerated above, its presence tends to establish the existence of a marriage. Thus, in the absence of a formal ceremony of any sort, an explicit commitment to sexual exclusivity would count in favor of regarding the two persons as married. The conceptual role of the commitment to sexual exclusivity can, perhaps, be brought out through the following example. Suppose we found a tribe which had a practice in which all the other indicia of marriage were present but in which the two parties were *prohibited* ever from having sexual intercourse with each other. Moreover, suppose that sexual intercourse with others was clearly permitted. In such a case we would, I think, reject the idea that the two were married to each other and we would describe their relationship in other terms, for example, as some kind of formalized, special friendship relation—a kind of heterosexual "blood-brother" bond.

Compare that case with the following. Suppose again that the tribe had a practice in which all of the other indicia of marriage were present, but instead of a prohibition on sexual intercourse between the persons in the relationship there was no rule at all. Sexual intercourse was permissible with the person with whom one had this ceremonial relationship, but it was no more or less permissible than with a number of other persons to whom one was not so related (for instance, all consenting adults of the opposite sex). Although we might be in doubt as to whether we ought to describe the persons as married to each other, we would probably conclude that they were married and that they simply were members of a tribe whose views about sex were quite different from our own.

What all of this shows is that *a prohibition* on sexual intercourse between the two persons involved in a relationship is conceptually incompatible with the claim that the two of them are married. The *permissibility* of intramarital sex is a necessary part of the idea of marriage. But such incompatibility follows simply from the added permissibility of extramarital sex.

These arguments do not, of course, exhaust the arguments for the prohibition on extramarital sexual relations. The remaining argument that I wish to consider—as I indicated earlier—is a more instrumental one. It seeks to justify the prohibition by virtue of the role that it plays in the development and maintenance of nuclear families. The argument, or set of arguments, might, I believe, go something like this.

Consider first a farfetched nonsexual example. Suppose a society were organized so that after some suitable age—say, 18, 19, or 20—persons were forbidden to eat anything but bread and water with anyone but their spouse. Persons might still choose in such a society not to get married. Good food just might not be very important to them because they have underdeveloped taste buds. Or good food might be bad for them because there is something wrong with their digestive system. Or good food might be important to them, but they might decide that the enjoyment of good food would get in the way of attainment of other things that were more important. But most persons would, I think, be led to favor marriage in part because they preferred a richer, more varied, diet to one of bread and water. And they might remain married because the family was the only legitimate setting within which good food was obtainable. If it is important to have society organized so that persons will both get married and stay married, such an arrangement would be well suited to the preservation of the family, and the prohibitions relating to food consumption could be understood as fulfilling that function.

It is obvious that one of the more powerful human desires is the desire for sexual gratification. The desire is a natural one, like hunger and thirst, in the sense that it need not be learned in order to be present within us and operative upon us. But there is in addition much that we do learn about what the act of sexual intercourse is like. Once we experience sexual intercourse ourselves—and in particular once we experience orgasm—we discover that it is among the most intensive, short-term pleasures of the body.

Because this is so, it is easy to see how the prohibition upon extramarital sex helps to hold marriage together. At least during that period of life when the enjoyment of sexual intercourse is one of the desirable bodily pleasures, persons will wish to enjoy those pleasures. If one consequence of being married is that one is prohibited from having sexual intercourse with anyone but one's spouse, then the spouses in a marriage are in a position to provide an important source of pleasure for each other that is unavailable to them elsewhere in the society.

The point emerges still more clearly if this rule of sexual morality is seen as of a piece with the other rules of sexual morality. When this prohibition is coupled, for example, with the prohibition on nonmarital sexual intercourse, we are presented with the inducement both to get married and to stay married. For if sexual intercourse is only legitimate within marriage, then persons seeking that gratification which is a feature of sexual intercourse are furnished explicit social directions for its attainment; namely marriage.

Nor, to continue the argument, is it necessary to focus exclusively on the bodily enjoyment that is involved. Orgasm may be a significant part of what there is to sexual intercourse, but it is not the whole of it. We need only recall the earlier discussion of the meaning that sexual intimacy has in our own culture to begin to see some of the more intricate ways in which sexual exclusivity may be connected with the establishment and maintenance of marriage as the primary heterosexual, love relationship. Adultery is wrong, in other words, because a prohibition on extramarital sex is a way to help maintain the institutions of marriage and the nuclear family.

Now I am frankly not sure what we are to say about an argument such as this one. What I am convinced of is that, like the arguments discussed earlier, this one also reveals something of the difficulty and complexity of the issues that are involved. So, what I want now to do—in the brief and final portion of this paper—is to try to delineate with reasonable precision what I take several of the fundamental, unresolved issues to be.

The first is whether this last argument is an argument for the *immorality* of extramarital sexual intercourse. What does seem clear is that there are differences between this argument and the ones considered earlier. The earlier arguments condemned adulterous behavior because it was behavior that involved breaking of a promise, taking unfair advantage, or deceiving another. To the degree to which the prohibition on extramarital sex can be supported by arguments which invoke considerations such as these, there is little question but that violations of the prohibition are properly regarded as immoral. And such a claim could be defended on one or both of two distinct grounds. The first is that things like promise-breaking and deception are just wrong. The second is that adultery involving promise-breaking or deception is wrong because it involves the straightforward infliction of harm on another human being—typically the nonadulterous spouse—who has a strong claim not to have that harm so inflicted.

The argument that connects the prohibition on extramarital sex with the maintenance and preservation of the institution of marriage is an argument for the instrumental value of the prohibition. To some degree this counts, I think, against regarding all violations of the prohibition as obvious cases of immorality. This is so partly because hypothetical imperatives are less clearly within the domain of morality than are categorical ones, and even more because instrumental prohibitions are within the domain of morality only if the end they serve or the way they serve it is itself within the domain of morality.

What this should help us see, I think, is the fact that the argument that connects the prohibition on adultery with the preservation of marriage is at best seriously incomplete. Before we ought to be convinced by it, we ought to have reasons for believing that marriage is a morally desirable and just social institution. And this is not quite as easy or obvious a task as it may seem to be. For the concept of marriage is, as we have seen, both a loosely structured and a complicated one. There may be all sorts of intimate, interpersonal relationships which will resemble but not be identical with the typical marriage relationship presupposed by the traditional sexual morality. There may be a number of distinguishable sexual and loving arrangements which can all legitimately claim to be called *marriages*. The prohibitions of the traditional sexual morality may be effective ways to maintain some marriages and ineffective ways to promote and preserve others. The prohibitions of the traditional sexual morality may make good psychological sense if certain psychological theories are true, and they may be purveyors of immense psychological mischief if other psychological theories are true. The prohibitions of the traditional sexual morality may seem obviously correct if sexual intimacy carries the meaning that the dominant culture has often ascribed to it, and they may seem equally bizarre when sex is viewed through the perspective of the counterculture. Irrespective of whether instrumental arguments of this sort are properly deemed moral arguments, they ought not to fully convince anyone until questions like these are answered.

5

PHILOSOPHY
and the CLAIMS
OF RELIGION

Socrates is in many ways the paradigm philosopher, not least in his reputation as a dangerous religious heretic. One of the charges that led to his trial and execution was that he did not believe in the traditional gods of his city-state (*Apology* 24b-c). Seeing the way Socrates mercilessly quizzed the fundamentalist religious beliefs of the self-satisfied Euthyphro, one can begin to understand why the good citizens of Athens thought the philosopher lacked proper reverence in theological matters. The popular mind's connection of philosophy and religious heresy has not been broken in the intervening centuries; in fact, it has been strengthened. Many people assume that a commitment to philosophical investigation is necessarily antithetical to faith; that a true philosopher *must* be a skeptic about the claims of religion.

Why should philosophy seem necessarily heretical or atheistic? Part of the reason is a misunderstanding of the nature of Socratic philosophy. It is tempting to believe that philosophy is only a body of doctrine, tempting to assume that a philosopher holds particular substantive beliefs about the nature of reality. On this model, philosophy is an *ideology*—a world-view—of a sort, and as such, it competes with other ideologies. It can seem inevitable that philosophy and Christianity, for example, should conflict with one another. After all, they're both world-views, aren't they? They can't *both* be right, can they?

This conception misconstrues the nature of philosophy. Based on the Socratic model, philosophy is an *activity*, not a body of doctrine. It is not an ideology, so it cannot compete with ideologies. Socratic philosophy is the activity of rational clarification, the search for structures of justification for beliefs, attitudes, and actions, and as such it is not necessarily the enemy of religious commitment. Consider, for example, orthodox Christianity. Philosophical investigation *might* show its beliefs, attitudes, and actions to possess the appropriate structures of justification —to be the *correct* beliefs, attitudes, and injunctions. Socratic philosophy is thus not *inevitably* inconsistent with religious belief.

On the other hand, there is undoubtedly a tension present in the relationship of philosophy to religious belief—a legitimate tension not to be removed by calling attention to philosophy as an activity. This tension is produced by the *kind* of activity Socratic philosophy is. Philosophy insists upon unbiased, open, critical investigation of every claim. It takes nothing for granted; it recognizes no authority outside the self-critical powers of the mind itself. Religious systems, however, present themselves as the fully-present *truth*; they are *proclaimed*, not offered for investigation and cool judgment. The claims of religion deal with ultimate matters: the nature of transcendent reality, the fate of the person after death, the way of virtue. These matters are fundamentally important to us, for we fear death and we want to know virtue and the real. Religion claims to have answers for our deepest questions; it preaches these answers as the only truths and demands our unwavering acceptance of them.

Is it any wonder, then, that philosophy and religion are so often at odds? We hunger for truth, virtue, and immortality. Religion says, "Here they are; take them now, or lose them forever." Philosophy says, "Go slowly, Religion. What are the justifications for your claims? Let us see your arguments." Socrates says to Euthyphro, to Athens, "How do you know? What do you mean?" Is it any wonder that they grew tired of the gadfly's bite?

This tension, the tension between the hungers of our soul and the scruples of our intellect, cannot be removed, and it *ought* not, for it is one of the marks of our humanity. Once the Socratic intellect has awakened, it is fatal to try to lull it back to sleep. The philosopher cannot be a simple believer; he or she cannot fail to pay attention to argument, evidence, and the difference between sense and nonsense. In the same manner, the philosopher examining religion cannot be a mere thinking machine; he or she must pay attention to the promptings of spirit as well as intellect. To do both at once is very difficult; it is no wonder that many of us fail to live with the resultant tension, lapsing into an unthinking (perhaps enthusiastic) fundamentalism or into an arid and dogmatic skepticism. It seems that neither alternative commends itself to a fully realized human being.

Is there another alternative? Can religious belief be compatible with the requirements of Socratic philosophy? In this section we have arranged readings to pose that very question. The reader encounters philosophers' attempts to grasp the essence of religion as a cultural phenomenon and to understand the function and value of religious ideas in social life. We have included philosophers' arguments for the existence of God, as well as arguments that those philosophers fail. Included are accounts of religious experience, along with philosophical reflections on what, if anything, those experiences demonstrate. The problem of evil is explored, as are the objections to religion from the biological and physical sciences. Finally, reflections on the relationship of reason to religious faith are discussed.

Encountering the claims of religion gives us another important occasion for philosophy. It is, to be sure, an occasion fraught with special tension, inevitable since the passions, hopes, and fears of religious faith seem so hopelessly out of joint with the cool and careful scrutiny demanded of the philosopher. Still, neither religion nor philosophy seems about to disappear. Beliefs about the existence of gods, the fate of the soul, and the conquest of evil have been a part of most of human history; in the West, at least, the questioning, Socratic intellect has become a fundamental ideal of our culture. In this context philosophy plays a crucial role. It can, through its techniques of self-critical reflection, help us to balance the proper claims of the passionate soul and the rational mind.

WHAT IS RELIGION?

Religion as a Cultural System

Clifford Geertz

As we are to deal with meaning, let us begin with a paradigm: viz. that sacred symbols function to synthesize a people's ethos—the tone, character, and quality of their life, its moral and aesthetic style and mood—and their world-view—the picture they have of the way things in sheer actuality are, their most comprehensive ideas of order (Geertz, 1958). In religious belief and practice a group's ethos is rendered intellectually reasonable by being shown to represent a way of life ideally adapted to the actual state of affairs the world-view describes, while the

From *Anthropological Approaches to the Study of Religion*, ed. Michael Banton (London: Tavistock Publications, 1965), pp. 3-28, 35-40, 42-46. Reprinted by permission of the publisher.

world-view is rendered emotionally convincing by being presented as an image of an actual state of affairs peculiarly well arranged to accommodate such a way of life. This confrontation and mutual confirmation has two fundamental effects. On the one hand, it objectivizes moral and aesthetic preferences by depicting them as the imposed conditions of life implicit in a world with a particular structure, as mere common sense given the unalterable shape of reality. On the other, it supports these received beliefs about the world's body by invoking deeply felt moral and aesthetic sentiments as experiential evidence for their truth. Religious symbols formulate a basic congruence between a particular style of life and a specific (if, most often, implicit) metaphysic, and in so doing sustain each with the borrowed authority of the other.

Phrasing aside, this much may perhaps be granted. The notion that religion tunes human actions to an envisaged cosmic order and projects images of cosmic order onto the plane of human experience is hardly novel. But it is hardly investigated either, so that we have very little idea of how, in empirical terms, this particular miracle is accomplished. We just know that it is done, annually, weekly, daily, for some people almost hourly; and we have an enormous ethnographic literature to demonstrate it. But the theoretical framework which would enable us to provide an analytic account of it, an account of the sort we can provide for lineage segmentation, political succession, labor exchange, or the socialization of the child, does not exist.

Let us, therefore, reduce our paradigm to a definition, for, although it is notorious that definitions establish nothing in themselves, they do, if they are carefully enough constructed, provide a useful orientation, or reorientation, of thought, such that an extended unpacking of them can be an effective way of developing and controlling a novel line of inquiry. They have the useful virtue of explicitness: they commit themselves in a way discursive prose, which in this field especially, is always liable to substitute rhetoric for argument, does not. Without further ado, then, a *religion* is:

(1) a system of symbols which acts to
(2) establish powerful, pervasive, and long-lasting moods and motivations in men by
(3) formulating conceptions of a general order of existence and
(4) clothing these conceptions with such an aura of factuality that
(5) the moods and motivations seem uniquely realistic.

1. a system of symbols which acts to . . .

Such a tremendous weight is being put on the term 'symbol' here that our first move must be to decide with some precision what we are going to mean by it. This is no easy task, for, rather like 'culture', 'symbol' has been used to refer to a great variety of things, often a number of them at the same time. In some hands it is used for anything which signifies something else to someone: dark clouds are the symbolic precursors of an oncoming rain. In others it is used only for explicitly conventional signs of one sort or another: a red flag is a symbol of danger, a white of surrender. In others it is confined to something which expresses in an oblique and figurative manner that which cannot be stated in a direct and literal one, so that there are symbols in poetry but not in science, and symbolic logic is misnamed. In yet others, however (Langer, 1953, 1960, 1962), it is used for any object, act, event, quality, or relation which serves as a vehicle for a conception—the conception is the symbol's 'meaning'—and that is the approach I shall follow here. The number 6, written, imagined, laid out as a row of stones, or even punched into the program tapes of a computer is a symbol. But so also is the Cross, talked about, visualized, shaped worriedly in air or fondly fingered at the neck, the expanse of painted canvas called 'Guernica' or the bit of painted stone called a churinga, the word 'reality', or even the morpheme '-ing.' They are all symbols, or at least symbolic elements, because they are tangible formulations of notions, abstractions from experience fixed in perceptible forms, concrete embodiments of ideas, attitudes, judgments, longings, or beliefs. To undertake the study of cultural activity—activity in which symbolism forms the positive content—is thus not to abandon social analysis for a Platonic cave of shadows, to enter into a mentalistic world of introspective psychology or, worse, speculative philosophy, and wander there forever in a haze of 'Cognitions', 'Affections', 'Conations', and other elusive entities. Cultural acts, the construction, apprehension, and utilization of symbolic forms, are social events like any other; they are as public as marriage and as observable as agriculture.

They are not, however, exactly the same thing; or, more precisely, the symbolic dimension of social events is, like the psychological, itself theoretically abstractable from those events as empirical totalities. There is still, to paraphrase a remark of Kenneth Burke's (1941, p. 9), a difference between building a house and drawing up a plan for building a house, and reading a poem about having children by marriage is not quite the same thing as having children by marriage. Even though the building of the house may proceed under the guidance of the plan or—a less likely occurrence—the having of children may be motivated by a reading of the poem, there is something to be said for not confusing our traffic with symbols with our traffic with objects or human beings, for these latter are not in themselves symbols, however often they may function as such.[1] No matter how deeply interfused the cultural, the social, and the psychological may be in the everyday life of houses, farms, poems, and marriages, it is useful to distinguish them in analysis, and, so doing, to isolate the generic traits of each against the normalized background of the other two (Parsons & Shils, 1951).

So far as culture patterns, i.e. systems or complexes of symbols, are concerned, the generic trait which is of first importance for us here is that they are extrinsic sources of information (Geertz, 1964a). By 'extrinsic', I mean only that—unlike genes, for example—they lie outside the boundaries of the individual organism as such in that intersubjective world of common understandings into which all human individuals are born, in which they pursue their separate careers, and which they leave persisting behind them after they die (Schutz, 1962). By 'sources of information', I mean only that—like genes—they provide a blueprint or template in terms of which processes external to themselves can be given a definite form (Horowitz, 1956). As the order of bases in a strand of DNA forms a coded program, a set of instructions, or a recipe, for the synthesization of the structurally complex proteins which shape organic functioning, so culture patterns provide such programs for the institution of the social and psychological processes which shape public behavior. Though the sort of information and the mode of its transmission are vastly different in the two cases, this comparison of gene and symbol is more than a strained analogy of the familiar 'social heredity' sort. It is actually a substantial relationship, for it is precisely the fact that genetically programmed processes are so highly generalized in men, as compared with lower animals, that culturally programmed ones are so important, only because human behavior is so loosely determined by intrinsic sources of information that extrinsic sources are so vital (Geertz, 1962). To build a dam a beaver needs only an appropriate site and the proper materials—his mode of procedure is shaped by his physiology. But man, whose genes are silent on the building trades, needs also a conception of what it is to build a dam, a conception he can get only from some symbolic source—a blueprint, a textbook, or a string of speech by someone who already knows how dams are built, or of course, from manipulating graphic or linguistic elements in such a way as to attain for himself a conception of what dams are and how they are built.

This point is sometimes put in the form of an argument that cultural patterns are 'models', that they are sets of symbols whose relations to one another 'model' relations among entities, processes or what-have-you in physical, organic, social, or psychological systems by 'paralleling', 'imitating', or 'simulating' them (Craik, 1952). The term 'model' has, however, two senses—an 'of' and a 'for' sense—and though these are but aspects of the same basic concept they are very much worth distinguishing for analytic purposes. In the first, what is stressed is the manipulation of symbol structures so as to bring them, more or less closely, into parallel with the pre-established non-symbolic system, as when we grasp how dams work by developing a theory of hydraulics or constructing a flow chart. The theory or chart models physical relationships in such a way—i.e. by expressing their structure in synoptic form—as to render them apprehensible: it is a model *of* 'reality'. In the second, what is stressed is the manipulation of the non-symbolic systems in terms of the relationships expressed in the symbolic, as when we construct a dam according to the specifications implied in an hydraulic theory or the conclusions drawn from a flow chart. Here, the theory is a model under whose guidance physical relationships are organized: it is a model *for* 'reality'. For psychological and social systems, and for cultural models that we would not ordinarily refer to as 'theories', but rather as 'doctrines', 'melodies', or 'rites', the case is in no way different. Unlike genes, and other non-symbolic information sources, which are only models *for,* not models *of,* culture patterns have an intrinsic double aspect: they give meaning, i.e. objective conceptual form, to social and psychological reality both by shaping themselves to it and by shaping it to themselves.

It is, in fact, this double aspect which sets true symbols off from other sorts of significative forms. Models *for* are found, as the gene example suggests, through the whole order of nature, for wherever there is a communication of pattern such programs are, in simple logic, required. Among animals, imprint learning is perhaps the most striking example, because what such learning involves is the automatic presentation of an appropriate sequence of behavior by a model animal in the presence of a learning animal which serves, equally automatically, to call out and stabilize a certain set of responses genetically built into the learning animal (Lorenz, 1952). The communicative dance of two bees, one of which has found nectar and the other of which seeks it, is another, somewhat different, more complexly coded, example (von Frisch, 1962). Craik (1952) has even suggested that the thin trickle of water which first finds its way down from a mountain spring to the sea and smooths a little channel for the greater volume of water that follows after it plays a sort of model *for* function. But models *of*— linguistic, graphic, mechanical, natural, etc. processes which function not to provide sources of information in terms of which other processes can be patterned, but to represent those patterned processes as such, to express their structure in an alternative medium—are much rarer and may perhaps be confined, among living animals, to man. The perception of the structural congruence between one set of processes, activities, relations, entities, etc. and another set for which it acts as a program, so that the program can be taken as a representation, or conception—a symbol—of the programmed, is the essence of human thought. The inter-transposability of models *for* and models *of* which symbolic formulation makes possible is the distinctive characteristic of our mentality.

2.   . . . to establish powerful, pervasive, and long-lasting moods and motivations in men by . . .

So far as religious symbols and symbol systems are concerned this inter-transposability is clear. The endurance, courage, independence, perseverance, and passionate willfulness in which the vision quest practices the Plains Indian are the same flamboyant virtues by which he attempts to live: while achieving a sense of revelation he stabilizes a sense of direction (Lowie, 1924). The consciousness of defaulted obligation, secreted guilt, and, when a confession is obtained, public shame in which Manus' seance rehearses him are the same sentiments that underlie the sort of duty ethic by which his property-conscious society is maintained: the gaining of an absolution involves the forging of a conscience (Fortune, 1935). And the same self-discipline which rewards a Javanese mystic staring fixedly into the flame of a lamp with what he takes to be an intimation of divinity drills him in that rigorous control of emotional expression which is necessary to a man who would follow a quietistic style of life (Geertz, 1960). Whether one sees the conception of a personal guardian spirit, a family tutelary or an immanent God as synoptic formulations of the character of reality or as templates for producing reality with such a character seems largely arbitrary, a matter of which aspect, the model *of* or model *for*, one wants for the moment to bring into focus. The concrete symbols involved—one or another mythological figure materializing in the wilderness, the skull of the deceased household head hanging censoriously in the rafters, or a disembodied 'voice in the stillness' soundlessly chanting enigmatic classical poetry—point in either direction. They both express the world's climate and shape it.

They shape it by inducing in the worshipper a certain distinctive set of dispositions (tendencies, capacities, propensities, skills, habits, liabilities, pronenesses) which lend a chronic character to the flow of his activity and the quality of his experience. A disposition describes not an activity or an occurrence but a probability of an activity being performed or an occurrence occurring in certain circumstances: 'When a cow is said to be a ruminant, or a man is said to be a cigarette-smoker, it is not being said that the cow is ruminating now or that the man is smoking a cigarette now. To be a ruminant is to tend to ruminate from time to time, and to be a cigarette-smoker is to be in the habit of smoking cigarettes' (Ryle, 1949, p. 117). Similarly, to be pious is not to be performing something we would call an act of piety, but to be liable to perform such acts. So, too, with the Plains Indian's bravura, the Manus' compunctiousness, or the Javanese's quietism which, in their contexts, form the substance of piety. The virtue of this sort of view of what are usually called 'mental traits' or, if the Cartesianism is unavowed, 'psychological forces' (both unobjectionable enough terms in themselves) is that it gets them out of any dim and inaccessible realm of private sensation into that same well-lit world of observables in which reside the brittleness of glass, the inflammability of paper, and, to return to the metaphor, the dampness of England.

So far as religious activities are concerned (and learning a myth by heart is as much a religious activity as detaching one's finger at the knuckle), two somewhat different sorts of disposition are induced by them: moods and motivations.

A motivation is a persisting tendency, a chronic inclination to perform certain sorts of act and experience certain sorts of feeling in certain sorts of situation, the 'sorts' being commonly very heterogenous and rather ill-defined classes in all three cases:

'. . . on hearing that a man is vain [i.e. motivated by vanity] we expect him to behave in certain ways, namely to talk a lot about himself, to cleave to the society of the eminent, to reject criticisms, to seek the footlights and to disengage himself from conversations about the merits of others. We expect him to indulge in roseate daydreams about his own successes, to avoid recalling past failures and to plan for his own advancement. To be vain is to tend to act in these and innumerable other kindred ways. Certainly we also expect the vain man to feel certain pangs and flutters in certain situations; we expect him to have an acute sinking feeling when an eminent person forgets his name, and to feel buoyant of heart and light of toe on hearing of the misfortunes of his rivals. But feelings of pique and buoyancy are not more directly indicative of vanity than are public acts of boasting or private acts of daydreaming. . . .' (Ryle, 1949, p. 86).

Similarly for any motivations. As a motive, 'flamboyant courage' consists in such enduring propensities as to fast in the wilderness, to conduct solitary raids on enemy camps, and to thrill to the thought of counting coup. 'Moral circumspection' consists in such ingrained tendencies as to honor onerous promises, to confess secret sins in the face of severe public disapproval, and to feel guilty when vague and generalized accusations are made at seances. And 'dispassionate tranquility' consists in such persistent inclinations as to maintain one's poise come hell or high water, to experience distaste in the presence of even moderate emotional displays, and to indulge in contentless contemplations of featureless objects. Motives are thus neither acts (i.e. intentional behaviors) nor feelings, but liabilities to perform particular classes of act or have particular classes of feeling. And when we say that a man is religious, i.e. motivated by religion, this is at least part—though only part—of what we mean.

Another part of what we mean is that he has, when properly stimulated, a susceptibility to fall into certain moods, moods we sometimes lump together under such covering terms as 'reverential', 'solemn', or 'worshipful'. Such generalized rubrics actually conceal, however, the enormous empirical variousness of the dispositions involved, and, in fact, tend to assimilate them to the unusually grave tone of most of our own religious life. The moods that sacred symbols induce, at different times and in different places, range from exultation to melancholy, from self-confidence to self-pity, from an incorrigible playfulness to a bland listlessness—to say nothing of the erogenous power of so many of the world's myths and rituals. No more than there is a single sort of motivation one can call piety is there a single sort of mood one can call worshipful.

The major difference between moods and motivations is that where the latter are, so to speak, vectorial qualities, the former are merely scalar. Motives have a directional cast, they describe a certain overall course, gravitate toward certain, usually temporary, consummations. But moods vary only as to intensity: they go nowhere. They spring from certain circumstances but they are responsive to no ends. Like fogs, they just settle and lift; like scents, suffuse and evaporate. When present they are totalistic: if one is sad everything and everybody seems dreary; if one is gay, everything and everybody seems splendid. Thus, though a man can be vain, brave, willful and independent at the same time, he can't very well be playful and listless, or exultant and melancholy, at the same time (Ryle, 1949, p. 99). Further, where motives persist for more or less extended periods of time, moods merely recur with greater or lesser frequency, coming and going for what are often quite unfathomable reasons. But perhaps the most important difference, so far as we are concerned, between moods and motivations is that motivations are 'made meaningful' with reference to the ends toward which they are conceived to conduce, whereas moods are 'made meaningful' with reference to the conditions from which they are conceived to spring. We interpret motives in terms of their consummations, but we interpret moods in terms of their sources. We say that a person is industrious because he wishes to succeed, we say that a person is worried because he is conscious of the hanging threat of nuclear holocaust. And this is no less the case when the interpretations invoked are ultimate. Charity becomes Christian charity when it is enclosed in a conception of God's purposes; optimism is Christian optimism when it is grounded in a particular conception of God's nature. The assiduity of the Navaho finds its rationale in a belief that, since 'reality' operates mechanically, it is coercible; their chronic fearfulness finds its rationale in a conviction that, however 'reality' operates, it is both enormously powerful and terribly dangerous (Kluckhohn, 1949).

3. . . . by formulating conceptions of a general order of existence and . . .

That the symbols or symbol systems which induce and define dispositions we set off as religious and those which place those dispositions in a cosmic framework are the same symbols ought to occasion no surprise. For what else do we mean by saying that a particular mood of awe is religious and not secular except that it springs from entertaining a conception of all-pervading vitality like mana ?nd not from a visit to the Grand Canyon? Or that a particular case of asceticism is an example of a religious motivation except that it is directed toward the achievement of an unconditioned end like nirvana and not a conditioned one like weight-reduction? If sacred symbols did not at one and the same time induce dispositions in human beings and formulate, however obliquely, inarticulately, or unsystematically, general ideas of order, then the empirical differentia of religious activity or religious experience would not exist. A man can indeed be said to be 'religious' about golf, but not merely if he pursues it with passion and plays it on Sundays: he must also see it as symbolic of some transcendent truths. And the pubescent boy gazing soulfully into the eyes of the pubescent girl in a William Steig cartoon and murmering, 'There is something about you, Ethel, which gives me a sort of religious feeling', is, like most adolescents, confused. What any particular religion affirms about the fundamental nature of reality may be obscure, shallow, or, all too often, perverse, but it must, if it is not to consist of the mere collection of received practices and conventional sentiments we usually refer to as moralism, affirm something. If one were to essay a minimal definition of religion today it would perhaps not be Tylor's famous 'belief in spiritual beings', to which Goody (1961), wearied of theoretical subtleties, has lately urged us to return, but rather what Salvador de Madariaga has called 'the relatively modest dogma that God is not mad'.

Usually, of course, religions affirm very much more than this: we believe, as James (1904, Vol. 2, p. 299) remarked, all that we can and would believe everything if we only could. The thing we seem least able to tolerate is a threat to our powers of conception, a suggestion that our ability to create, grasp, and use symbols may fail us, for were this to happen we would be more helpless, as I have already pointed out, than the beavers. The extreme generality, diffuseness, and variability of man's innate (i.e. genetically programmed) response capacities means that without the assistance of cultural patterns he would be functionally incomplete, not merely a talented ape who had, like some under-privileged child, unfortunately been prevented from realizing his full potentialities, but a kind of formless monster with neither sense of direction nor power of self-control, a chaos of spasmodic impulses and vague emotions (Geertz, 1962). Man depends upon symbols and symbol systems with a dependence so great as to be decisive for his creatural viability and, as a result, his sensitivity to even the remotest indication that they may prove unable to cope with one or another aspect of experience raises within him the gravest sort of anxiety:

> '[Man] can adapt himself somehow to anything his imagination can cope with; but he cannot deal with Chaos. Because his characteristic function and highest asset is conception, his greatest fright is to meet what he cannot construe—the "uncanny", as it is popularly called. It need not be a new object; we do meet new things, and "understand" them promptly, if tentatively, by the nearest analogy, when our minds are functioning freely; but under mental stress even perfectly familiar things may become suddenly disorganized and give us the horrors. Therefore our most important assets are always the symbols of our general *orientation* in nature, on the earth, in society, and in what we are doing: the symbols of our *Weltanschauung* and *Lebensanschauung*. Consequently, in a primitive society, a daily ritual is incorporated in common activities, in eating, washing, fire-making, etc., as well as in pure ceremonial; because the need of reasserting the tribal morale and recognizing its cosmic conditions is constantly felt. In Christian Europe the Church brought men daily (in some orders even hourly) to their knees, to enact if not to contemplate their assent to the ultimate concepts' (Langer, 1960, p. 287, italics original).

There are at least three points where chaos—a tumult of events which lack not just interpretation but *interpretability*—threatens to break in upon man: at the limits of his analytic capacities, at the limits of his powers of endurance, and at the limits of his moral insight. Bafflement, suffering, and a sense of intractable ethical paradox are all, if they become intense enough or are sustained long enough, radical challenges to the proposition that life is comprehensible and that we can, by taking thought, orient ourselves effectively within it—challenges with which any religion, however 'primitive', which hopes to persist must attempt somehow to cope.

Of the three issues, it is the first which has been least investigated by modern social anthropologists (though Evans-Pritchard's (1937) classic discussion of why granaries fall on some Azande and not on others, is a notable exception). Even to consider people's religious beliefs as attempts to bring anomalous events or experiences—death, dreams, mental fugues, volcanic eruptions, or marital infidelity—within the circle of the at least potentially explicable seems to smack of Tyloreanism or worse. But it does appear to be a fact that at least some men—in all probability, most men—are unable to leave unclarified problems of analysis merely unclarified, just to look at the stranger features of the world's landscape in dumb astonishment or bland apathy without trying to develop, however fantastic, inconsistent, or simple-minded, some notions as to how such features might be reconciled with the more ordinary deliverances of experience. Any chronic failure of one's explanatory apparatus, the complex of received culture patterns (common sense, science, philosophical speculation, myth) one has for mapping the empirical world, to explain things which cry out for explanation tends to lead to a deep disquiet—a tendency rather more widespread and a disquiet rather deeper than we have sometimes supposed since the pseudo-science view of religious belief was, quite rightfully, deposed. After all, even that high priest of heroic atheism, Lord Russell, once remarked that although the problem of the existence of God had never bothered him, the ambiguity of certain mathematical axioms had threatened to unhinge his mind. And Einstein's profound dissatisfaction with quantum mechanics was based on a—surely religious—inability to believe that, as he put it, God plays dice with the universe.

But this quest for lucidity and the rush of metaphysical anxiety that occurs when empirical phenomena threaten to remain intransigently opaque is found on much humbler intellectual levels. Certainly, I was struck in my own work, much more than I had at all expected to be, by the degree to which my more animistically inclined informants behaved like true Tyloreans. They seemed to be constantly using their beliefs to 'explain' phenomena: or, more accurately, to convince themselves that the phenomena were explainable within the accepted scheme of things, for they commonly had only a minimal attachment to the particular soul possession, emotional disequilibrium, taboo infringement, or bewitchment hypothesis they advanced and were all too ready to abandon it for some other, in the same genre, which struck them as more plausible given the facts of the case. What they were *not* ready to do was abandon it for no other hypothesis at all; to leave events to themselves.

And what is more, they adopted this nervous cognitive stance with respect to phenomena which had no immediate practical bearing on their own lives, or for that matter on anyone's. When a peculiarly shaped, rather large toadstool grew up in a carpenter's house in the short space of a few days (or, some said, a few hours), people came from miles around to see it, and everyone had some sort of explanation—some animist, some animatist, some not quite either—for it. Yet it would be hard to argue that the toadstool had any social value in Radcliffe-Brown's (1952) sense, or was connected in any way with anything which did and for which it could have been standing proxy, like the Andaman cicada. Toadstools play about the same role in Javanese life as they do in ours and in the ordinary course of things Javanese have about as much interest in them as we do. It was just that this one was 'odd', 'strange', 'uncanny'—*aneh*. And the odd, strange, and uncanny simply must be accounted for—or, again, the conviction that it *could be accounted* for sustained. One does not shrug off a toadstool which grows five times as fast as a toadstool has any right to grow. In the broadest sense the 'strange' toadstool did have implications, and critical ones, for those who heard about it. It threatened their most general ability to understand the world, raised the uncomfortable question of whether the beliefs which they held about nature were workable, the standards of truth they used valid.

Nor is this to argue that it is only, or even mainly, sudden eruptions of extraordinary events which engender in man the disquieting sense that his cognitive resources may prove unavailing or that this intuition appears only in its acute form. More commonly it is a persistent, constantly re-experienced difficulty in grasping certain aspects of nature, self, and society, in bringing certain elusive phenomena within the sphere of culturally formulatable fact, which renders man chronically uneasy and toward which a more equable flow of diagnostic symbols is consequently directed. It is what lies beyond a relatively fixed frontier of accredited knowledge that, looming as a constant background to the daily round of practical life, sets ordinary human experience in a permanent context of metaphysical concern and raises the dim, back-of-the-mind suspicion that one may be adrift in an absurd world:

'Another subject which is matter for this characteristic intellectual enquiry [among the Iatmul] is the nature of ripples and waves on the surface of water. It is said secretly that men, pigs, trees, grass—all the objects in the world—are only patterns of waves. Indeed there seems to be some agreement about this, although it perhaps conflicts with the theory of reincarnation, according to which the ghost of the dead is blown as a mist by the East Wind up the river and into the womb of the deceased's son's wife. Be that as it may—there is still the question of how ripples and waves are caused. The clan which claims the East Wind as a totem is clear enough about this: the Wind with her mosquito fan causes the waves. But other clans have personified the waves and say that they are a person (Kontum-mali) independent of the wind. Other clans, again, have other theories. On one occasion I took some Iatmul natives down to the coast and found one of them sitting by himself gazing with rapt attention at the sea. It was a windless day, but a slow swell was breaking on the beach. Among the totemic ancestors of his clan he counted a personified slit gong who had floated down the river to the sea and who was believed to cause the waves. He was gazing at the waves which were heaving and breaking when no wind was blowing, demonstrating the truth of his clan myth' (Bateson, 1958, pp. 130-131).[2]

The second experiential challenge in whose face the meaningfulness of a particular pattern of life threatens to dissolve into a chaos of thingless names and nameless things—the problem of suffering—has been rather more investigated, or at least described, mainly because of the great amount of attention given in works on tribal religion to what are perhaps its two main loci: illness and mourning. Yet for all the fascinated interest in the emotional aura that surrounds these extreme situations, there has been, with a few exceptions such as Lienhardt's recent (1961, pp. 151ff) discussion of Dinka divining, little conceptual advance over the sort of crude confidence-type theory set forth by Malinowski: viz. that religion helps one to endure 'situations of emotional stress' by 'open[ing] up escapes from such situations and such impasses as offer no empirical way out except by ritual and belief into the domain of the supernatural' (1948, p. 67). The inadequacy of this 'theology of optimism', as Nadel (1957) rather drily called it, is, of course, radical. Over its career religion has probably disturbed men as much as it has cheered them; forced them into a head-on, unblinking confrontation of the fact that they are born to trouble as often as it has enabled them to avoid such a confrontation by projecting them into sort of infantile fairy-tale world where—Malinowski again (1948, p. 67)—'hope cannot fail nor desire deceive'. With the possible exception of Christian Science, there are few if any religious traditions, 'great' or 'little', in which the proposition that life hurts is not strenuously affirmed and in some it is virtually glorified:

'She was an old [Ba-Ila] woman of a family with a long genealogy. Leza, "the Besetting-One", stretched out his hand against the family. He slew her mother and father while she was yet a child, and in the course of years all connected with her perished. She said to herself, "Surely I shall keep those who sit on my thighs." But no, even they, the children of her children, were taken from her. . . . Then came into her heart a desperate resolution to find God and to ask the meaning of it all. . . . So she began to travel, going through country after country, always with the thought in her mind: "I shall come to where the earth ends and there I shall find a road to God and I shall ask him: "What have I done to thee that thou afflictist me in this manner?" She never found where the earth ends, but though disappointed, she did not give up her search, and as she passed through the different countries they asked her, "What have you come for, old woman?" And the answer would be, "I am seeking Leza." "Seeking Leza! For what?" "My brothers, you ask me! Here in the nations is there one who suffers as I have suffered?" And they would ask again, "How have you suffered?" "In this way. I am alone. As you see me, a solitary old woman; that is how I am!" And they answered, "Yes, we see. That is how you are! Bereaved of friends and husband? In what do you differ from others? The Besetting-One sits on the back of every one of us and we cannot shake him off." She never obtained her desire: she died of a broken heart' (Smith & Dale, 1920, II, pp. 197ff; quoted in Radin, 1957, pp. 100-101).

As a religious problem, the problem of suffering is, paradoxically, not how to avoid suffering but how to suffer, how to make of physical pain, personal loss, worldly defeat, or the helpless contemplation of others' agony something bearable, supportable—something, as we say, sufferable. It was in this effort that the Ba-Ila woman—perhaps necesrily, perhaps not—failed and, literally not knowing how to feel about what had happened to her, how to suffer, perished in confusion and despair. Where the more intellective aspects of what Weber called the Problem of Meaning are a matter of affirming the ultimate explicability of experience, the more affective aspects are a matter of affirming its ultimate sufferableness. As religion on one side anchors the power of our symbolic resources for formulating analytic ideas in an authoritative conception of the overall shape of reality, so on another side it anchors the power of our, also symbolic, resources for expressing emotions—moods, sentiments, passions, affections, feelings—in a similar conception of its pervasive tenor, its inherent tone and temper. For those able to embrace them, and for so long as they are able to embrace them, religious symbols provide a cosmic guarantee not only for their ability to comprehend the world, but also, comprehending it, to give a precision to their feeling, a definition to their emotions which enables them, morosely or joyfuly, grimly or cavalierly, to endure it.

Consider in this light the well-known Navaho curing rites usually referred to as 'sings' (Kluckhohn & Leighton, 1946; Reichard, 1950). A sing—the Navaho have about sixty different ones for different purposes, but virtually all of them are dedicated to removing some sort of physical or mental illness—is a kind of religious psychodrama in which there are three main actors: the 'singer' or curer, the patient, and, as a kind of antiphonal chorus, the patient's family and friends. The structure of all the sings, the drama's plot, is quite similar. There are three main acts: a purification of the patient and audience; a statement, by means of repetitive chants and ritual manipulations, of the wish to restore well-being ('harmony') in the patient; an identification of the patient with the Holy People and his consequent 'cure'. The purification rites involved forced sweating, induced vomiting, etc. to expel the sickness from the patient physically. The chants, which are numberless, consist mainly of simple optative phrases ('may the patient be well', 'I am getting better all over', etc.). And, finally, the identification of the patient with the Holy People, and thus with cosmic order generally, is accomplished through the agency of a sand painting depicting the Holy People in one or another appropriate mythic setting. The singer places the patient on the painting, touching the feet, hands, knees, shoulders, breast, back, and head of the divine figures and then the corresponding parts of the patient, performing thus what is essentially a communion rite between the patient and the Holy People, a bodily identification of the human and the divine (Reichard, 1950). This is the climax of the sing: the whole curing process may be likened, Reichard says, to a spiritual osmosis in which the illness in man and the power of the deity penetrate the ceremonial membrane in both directions, the former being neutralized by the latter. Sickness seeps out in the sweat, vomit, and other purification rites; health seeps in as the Navaho patient touches, through the medium of the singer, the sacred sand painting. Clearly, the symbolism of the sing focuses upon the problem of human suffering and attempts to cope with it by placing it in a meaningful context, providing a mode of action through which it can be expressed, being expressed understood, and being understood, endured. The sustaining effect of the sing (and since the commonest disease is tuberculosis, it can in most cases be only sustaining), rest ultimately on its ability to give the stricken person a vocabulary in terms of which to grasp the nature of his distress and relate it to the wider world. Like a calvary, a recitation of Buddha's emergence from his father's palace or a performance of *Oedipus Tyrannos* in other religious traditions, a sing is mainly concerned with the presentation of a specific and concrete image of truly human, and so endurable, suffering powerful enough to resist the challenge of emotional meaninglessness raised by the existence of intense and unremovable brute pain.

The problem of suffering passes easily into the problem of evil, for if suffering is severe enough it usually, though not always, seems morally undeserved as well, at least to the sufferer. But they are not, however, exactly the same thing—a fact I think Weber, too influenced by the biases of a monotheistic tradition in which, as the various aspects of human experience must be conceived to proceed from a single, voluntaristic source, man's pain reflects directly on God's goodness, did not fully recognize in his generalization of the dilemmas of Christian theodicy Eastward. For where the problem of suffering is concerned with threats to our ability to put our 'undisciplined squads of emotion' into some sort of soldierly order, the problem of evil is concerned with threats to our ability to make sound moral judgments. What is involved in the problem of evil is not the adequacy of our symbolic resources to govern our affective life, but the adequacy of those resources to provide a workable set of ethical criteria, normative guides to govern our action. The vexation here is the gap between things as they are and as they ought to be if our conceptions of right and wrong make sense, the gap between what we deem various individuals deserve and what we see that they get—a phenomenon summed up in that profound quatrain:

> The rain falls on the just
> And on the unjust fella;
> But mainly upon the just,
> Because the unjust has the just's umbrella.

Or if this seems too flippant an expression of an issue that, in some-what different form, animates the Book of Job and the *Baghavad Gita,* the following classical Javanese poem, known, sung, and repeatedly quoted in Java by virtually everyone over the age of six, puts the point —the discrepancy between moral prescriptions and material rewards, the seeming inconsistency of 'is' and 'ought'—rather more elegantly:

> We have lived to see a time without order
> In which everyone is confused in his mind.
> One cannot bear to join in the madness,
> But if he does not do so
> He will not share in the spoils,
> And will starve as a result.
> Yes, God; wrong is wrong:
> Happy are those who forget,
> Happier yet those who remember and have deep insight.

Nor is it necessary to be theologically self-conscious to be religiously sophisticated. The concern with intractable ethical paradox, the disquiet-ing sense that one's moral insight is inadequate to one's moral expe-rience, is as alive on the level of so-called 'primitive' religion as it is on that of the so-called 'civilized'. The set of notions about 'division in the world' that Lienhardt describes (1961, pp. 28-55) for the Dinka is a useful case in point. Like so many peoples, the Dinka believe that the sky, where 'Divinity' is located, and earth, where man dwells, were at one time con-tiguous, the sky lying just above the earth and being connected to it by a rope, so that men could move at will between the two realms. There was no death and the first man and woman were permitted but a single grain of millet a day, which was all that they at that time required. One day, the woman—of course—decided, out of greed, to plant more than the permitted grain of millet and in her avid haste and industry ac-cidentally struck Divinity with the handle of the hoe. Offended, he se-vered the rope, withdrew into the distant sky of today, and left man to labor for his food, to suffer sickness and death, and to experience sepa-ration from the source of his being, his Creator. Yet the meaning of this strangely familiar story to the Dinka is, as indeed is Genesis to Jews and Christians, not homiletic but descriptive:

> 'Those [Dinka] who have commented on these stories have sometimes made it clear that their sympathies lie with Man in his plight, and draw attention to the smallness of the fault for which Divinity withdrew the benefits of his closeness. The image of striking Divinity with a hoe . . . often evokes a certain amusement, almost as though the story were in-

dulgently being treated as too childish to explain the consequences attributed to the event. But it is clear that the point of the story of Divinity's withdrawal from men is not to suggest an improving moral judgement on human behaviour. It is to represent a total situation known to the Dinka today. Men now are—as the first man and woman then became—active, self-assertive, inquiring, acquisitive. Yet they are also subject to suffering and death, ineffective, ignorant and poor. Life is insecure; human calculations often prove erroneous, and men must often learn by experience that the consequences of their acts are quite other than they may have anticipated or consider equitable. Divinity's withdrawal from Man as the result of a comparatively trifling offence, by human standards, presents the contrast between equitable human judgements and the action of the Power which are held ultimately to control what happens in Dinka life. . . . To the Dinka, the moral order is ultimately constituted according to principles which often elude men, which experience and tradition in part reveal, and which human action cannot change . . . The myth of Divinity's withdrawal then reflects the facts of existence as they are known. The Dinka are in a universe which is largely beyond their control, and where events may contradict the most reasonable human expectations' (Lienhardt, 1961, p. 53-54).

Thus the problem of evil, or perhaps one should say the problem *about* evil, is in essence the same sort of problem of or about bafflement and the problem of or about suffering. The strange opacity of certain empirical events, the dumb senselessness of intense or inexorable pain, and the enigmatic unaccountability of gross iniquity all raise the uncomfortable suspicion that perhaps the world, and hence man's life in the world, has no genuine order at all—no empirical regularity, no emotional form, no moral coherence. And the religious response to this suspicion is in each case the same: the formulation, by means of symbols, of an image of such a genuine order of the world which will account for, and even celebrate, the perceived ambiguities, puzzles, and paradoxes in human experience. The effort is not to deny the undeniable—that there are unexplained events, that life hurts, or that rain falls upon the just—but to deny that there are inexplicable events, that life is unendurable, and that justice is a mirage. The principles which constitute the moral order may indeed often elude men, as Lienhardt puts it, in the same way as fully satisfactory explanations of anomalous events or effective forms for the expression of feeling often elude them. What is important, to a religious man at least, is that this elusiveness be accounted for, that it be not the result of the fact that there are no such principles, explanations, or forms, that life is absurd and the attempt to make moral, intellectual or emotional sense out of experience is bootless. The Dinka can admit, in fact insist upon, the moral ambiguities and contradictions of life as they live it because these ambiguities and contradictions are seen not as ultimate, but as the 'rational', 'natural', 'logical' (one may choose one's own adjective here, for none of them is truly adequate) outcome of the moral structure of reality which the myth of the withdrawn 'Divinity' depicts, or as Lienhardt says, 'images'.

The Problem of Meaning in each of its intergrading aspects (how these aspects in fact intergrade in each particular case, what sort of interplay there is between the sense of analytic, emotional, and moral impotence, seems to me one of the outstanding, and except for Weber untouched, problems for comparative research in this whole field) is a matter of affirming, or at least recognizing, the inescapability of ignorance, pain, and injustice on the human plane while simultaneously denying that these irrationalities are characteristic of the world as a whole. And it is in terms of religious symbolism, a symbolism relating man's sphere of existence to a wider sphere within which it is conceived to rest, that both the affirmation and the denial are made.[3]

4. . . . and clothing those conceptions with such an aura of factuality that . . .

There arises here, however, a profounder question: how is it that this denial comes to be believed? how is it that the religious man moves from a troubled perception of experienced disorder to a more or less settled conviction of fundamental order? just what does 'belief' mean in a religious context? Of all the problems surrounding attempts to conduct anthropological analysis of religion this is the one that has perhaps been most troublesome and therefore the most often avoided, usually by relegating it to psychology, that raffish outcast discipline to which social anthropologists are forever consigning phenomena they are unable to deal with within the framework of a denatured Durkheimianism. But the problem will not go away, it is not 'merely' psychological (nothing social is), and no anthropological theory of religion which fails to attack it is worthy of the name. We have been trying to stage Hamlet without the Prince quite long enough.

It seems to me that it is best to begin any approach to this issue with frank recognition that religious belief involves not a Baconian induction from everyday experience—for then we should all be agnostics—but rather a prior acceptance of authority which transforms that experience. The existence of bafflement, pain, and moral paradox—of The Problem of Meaning—is one of the things that drive men toward belief in gods, devils, spirits, totemic principles, or the spiritual efficacy of cannibalism (an enfolding sense of beauty or a dazzling perception of power are others), but it is not the basis upon which those beliefs rest, but rather their most important field of application:

'We point to the state of the world as illustrative of doctrine, but never as evidence for it. So Belsen illustrates a world of original sin, but original sin is not an hypothesis to account for happenings like Belsen. We justify a particular religious belief by showing its place in the total religious conception; we justify a religious belief as a whole by referring to authority. We accept authority because we discover it at some point in the world at which we worship, at which we accept the lordship of something not ourselves. We do not worship authority, but we accept authority as defining the worshipful. So someone may discover the possibility of worship in the life of the Reformed Churches and accept the Bible as authoritative; or in the Roman Church and accept papal authority' (Mac-Intyre, 1957, pp. 201-202).

This is, of course, a Christian statement of the matter; but it is not to be despised on that account. In tribal religions authority lies in the persuasive power of traditional imagery; in mystical ones in the apodictic force of supersensible experience; in charismatic ones in the hypnotic attraction of an extraordinary personality. But the priority of the acceptance of an authoritative criterion in religious matters over the revelation which is conceived to flow from that acceptance is not less complete than in scriptural or hieratic ones. The basic axiom underlying what we may perhaps call 'the religious perspective' is everywhere the same: he who would know must first believe.

But to speak of 'the religious perspective' is, by implication, to speak of one perspective among others. A perspective is a mode of seeing, in that extended sense of 'see' in which it means 'discern', 'apprehend', 'understand', or 'grasp'. It is a particular way of looking at life, a particular manner of construing the world, as when we speak of an historical perspective, a scientific perspective, an aesthetic perspective, a common-sense perspective, or even the bizarre perspective embodied in dreams and in hallucinations.[4] The question then comes down to, first, what is 'the religious perspective' generically considered, as differentiated from other perspectives; and second, how do men come to adopt it.

If we place the religious perspective against the background of three of the other major perspectives in terms of which men construe the world —the common-sensical, the scientific, and the aesthetic—its special character emerges more sharply. What distinguishes common sense as a mode of 'seeing' is, as Schutz (1962) has pointed out, a simple acceptance of the world, its objects, and its processes as being just what they seem to be—what is sometimes called naïve realism—and the pragmatic motive, the wish to act upon that world so as to bend it to one's practical purposes, to master it, or so far as that proves impossible, to adjust to it. The world of everyday life, itself, of course, a cultural product, for it is framed in terms of the symbolic conceptions of 'stubborn fact' handed down from generation to generation, is the established scene and given object of our actions. Like Mt. Everest it is just there and the thing to do with it, if one feels the need to do anything with it at all, is to climb it. In the scientific perspective it is precisely this givenness which disappears (Schutz, 1962). Deliberate doubt and systematic inquiry, the suspension of the pragmatic motive in favor of disinterested observation, the attempt to analyze the world in terms of formal concepts whose relationship to the informal conceptions of common sense become increasingly problematic—these are the hallmarks of the attempts to grasp the world scientifically. And as for the aesthetic perspective, which under the rubric of 'the aesthetic attitude' has been perhaps most exquisitely examined, it involves a different sort of suspension of naïve realism and practical interest, in that instead of questioning the credentials of everyday experience that experience is merely ignored in favor of an eager dwelling upon appearances, an engrossment in surfaces, an absorption in things, as we say, 'in themselves': 'The function of artistic illusion is not "make-believe" . . . but the very opposite, disengagement from belief—the contemplation of sensory qualities without their usual meanings of "here's that chair", "That's my telephone" . . . etc. The knowledge that what is before us has no practical significance in the world is what enables us to give attention to its appearance as such' (Langer, 1957, p. 49). And like the common-sensical and the scientific (or the historical, the philosophical, and the autistic), this perspective, this 'way of seeing' is not the product of some mysterious Cartesian chemistry, but is induced, mediated, and in fact created by means of symbols. It is the artist's skill which can produce those curious quasi-objects—poems, dramas, sculptures, symphonies—which, dissociating themselves from the solid world of common sense, take on the special sort of eloquence only sheer appearances can achieve.

The religious perspective differs from the common-sensical in that, as already pointed out, it moves beyond the realities of everyday life to wider ones which correct and complete them, and its defining concern is not action upon those wider realities but acceptance of them, faith in them. It differs from the scientific perspective in that it questions the realities of everyday life not out of an institutionalized scepticism which dissolves the world's givenness into a swirl of probabilistic hypotheses, but in terms of what it takes to be wider, nonhypothetical truths. Rather than detachment, its watchword is commitment; rather than analysis, encounter. And it differs from art in that instead of effecting a disengagement from the whole question of factuality, deliberately manufacturing an air of semblance and illusion, it deepens the concern with fact and seeks to create an aura of utter actuality. It is this sense of the 'really real' upon which the religious perspective rests and which the symbolic activities of religion as a cultural system are devoted to producing, intensifying, and, so far as possible, rendering inviolable by the discordant revelations of secular experience. It is, again, the imbuing of a certain specific complex of symbols—of the metaphysic they formulate and the style of life they recommend—with a persuasive authority which, from an analytic point of view is the essence of religious action.

Which brings us, at length, to ritual. For it is in ritual—i.e. consecrated behavior—that this conviction that religious conceptions are veridical and that religious directives are sound is somehow generated. It is in some sort of ceremonial form—even if that form be hardly more than the recitation of a myth, the consultation of an oracle, or the decoration of a grave—that the moods and motivations which sacred symbols induce in men and the general conceptions of the order of existence which they formulate for men meet and reinforce one another. In a ritual, the world as lived and the world as imagined, fused under the agency of a single set of symbolic forms, turn out to be the same world, producing thus that idiosyncratic transformation in one's sense of reality to which Santayana refers in my epigraph.* Whatever role divine intervention may or may not play in the creation of faith—and it is not the business of the scientist to pronounce upon such matters one way or the other—it is, primarily at least, out of the context of concrete acts of religious observance that religious conviction emerges on the human plane.

5. . . . that the moods and motivations seem uniquely realistic

But no one, not even a saint, lives in the world religious symbols formulate all of the time, and the majority of men live in it only at moments. The everyday world of common-sense objects and practical acts is, as Schutz (1962, pp. 226ff.) says, the paramount reality in human experience—paramount in the sense that it is the world in which we are most solidly rooted, whose inherent actuality we can hardly question (however much we may question certain portions of it), and from whose pressures and requirements we can least escape. A man, even large groups of men, may be aesthetically insensitive, religiously unconcerned, and unequipped to pursue formal scientific analysis, but he cannot be completely lacking in common sense and survive. The dispositions which religious rituals induce thus have their most important impact—from a human point of view—outside the boundaries of the ritual itself as they reflect back to color the individual's conception of the established world of bare fact. The peculiar tone that marks the Plains vision quest, the Manus confession, or the Javanese mystical exercise pervades areas of the life of these peoples far beyond the immediately religious, impressing upon them a distinctive style in the sense both of a dominant mood and a characteristic movement. The interweaving of the malignant and the comic, which the Rangda-Barong combat depicts, animates a very wide range of everyday Balinese behavior, much of which, like the ritual itself, has an air of candid fear narrowly contained by obsessive playfulness. Religion is sociologically interesting not because, as vulgar positivism would have it (Leach, 1954, pp. 10ff.), it describes the social order (which, in so far as it does, it does not only very obliquely but very incompletely), but because, like environment, political power, wealth, jural obligation, personal affection, and a sense of beauty, it shapes it.

The movement back and forth between the religious perspective and the common-sense perspective is actually one of the more obvious empirical occurrences on the social scene, though, again, one of the most neglected by social anthropologists, virtually all of whom have seen it happen countless times. Religious belief has usually been presented as an homogeneous characteristic of an individual, like his place of resi-

---

* Any attempt to speak without speaking any particular language is not more hopeless than the attempt to have a religion that shall be no religion in particular. . . . Thus every living and healthy religion has a marked idiosyncrasy, its power consists in its special and surprising message and in the bias which that revelation gives to life. The vistas it opens and the mysteries it propounds are another world to live in; and another world to live in—whether we expect ever to pass wholly over into it or no—is what we mean by having a religion. Santayana: *Reason in Religion* (1906)

dence, his occupational role, his kinship position, and so on. But religious belief in the midst of ritual, where it engulfs the total person, transporting him, so far as he is concerned, into another mode of existence, and religious belief as the pale, remembered reflection of that experience in the midst of everyday life are not precisely the same thing, and the failure to realize this has led to some confusion, most especially in connection with the so-called 'primitive mentality' problem. Much of the difficulty between Lévy-Bruhl (1926) and Malinowski (1948) on the nature of 'native thought', for example, arises from a lack of full recognition of this distinction; for where the French philosopher was concerned with the view of reality savages adopted when taking a specifically religious perspective, the Polish-English ethnographer was concerned with that which they adopted when taking a strictly common-sense one. Both perhaps vaguely sensed that they were not talking about exactly the same thing, but where they went astray was in failing to give a specific accounting of the way in which these two forms of 'thought'— or, as I would rather say, these two modes of symbolic formulation— interacted, so that where Lévy-Bruhl's savages tended to live, despite his postludial disclaimers, in a world composed entirely of mystical encounters, Malinowski's tended to live, despite his stress on the functional importance of religion, in a world composed entirely of practical actions. They became reductionists (an idealist is as much of a reductionist as a materialist) in spite of themselves because they failed to see man as moving more or less easily, and very frequently, between radically contrasting ways of looking at the world, ways which are not continuous with one another but separated by cultural gaps across which Kierkegaardian leaps must be made in both directions:

> 'There are as many innumerable kinds of different shock experiences as there are different finite provinces of meaning upon which I may bestow the accent of reality. Some instances are: the shock of falling asleep as the leap into the world of dreams; the inner transformation we endure if the curtain in the theatre rises as the transition to the world of the stageplay; the radical change in our attitude if, before a painting, we permit our visual field to be limited by what is within the frame as the passage into the pictorial world; our quandary relaxing into laughter, if, in listening to a joke, we are for a short time ready to accept the fictitious world of the jest as a reality in relation to which the world of our daily life takes on the character of foolishness; the child's turning toward his toy as the transition into the play-world; and so on. But also the religious experiences in all their varieties—for instance, Kierkegaard's experience of the "instant" as the leap into the religious sphere—are examples of such a shock, as well as the decision of the scientist to replace all passionate participation in the affairs of "this world" by a disinterested [analytical] attitude' (Schutz, 1962, p. 231).

The recognition and exploration of the qualitative difference—an empirical, not a transcendental difference—between religion pure and religion applied, between an encounter with the supposedly 'really real' and a viewing of ordinary experience in light of what that encounter seems to reveal, will, therefore, take us further toward an understanding of what a Bororo means when he says 'I am a parakeet', or a Christian when he says 'I am a sinner', than either a theory of primitive mysticism in which the commonplace world disappears into a cloud of curious ideas or of a primitive pragmatism in which religion disintegrates into a collection of useful fictions. The parakeet example, which I take from Percy (1961), is a good one. For, as he points out, it is unsatisfactory to say either that the Bororo thinks he is literally a parakeet (for he does not try to mate with other parakeets), that his statement is false or nonsense (for, clearly, he is not offering—or at least not only offering—the sort of class-membership argument which can be confirmed or refuted as, say, 'I am a Bororo' can be confirmed or refuted), or yet again that it is false scientifically but true mythically (because that leads immediately to the pragmatic fiction notion which, as it denies the accolade of truth to 'myth' in the very act of bestowing it, is internally self-contradictory). More coherently it would seem to be necessary to see the sentence as having a different sense in the context of the 'finite province of meaning' which makes up the religious perspective and of that which makes up the common-sensical. In the religious, our Bororo is 'really' a 'parakeet', and given the proper ritual context might well 'mate' with other 'parakeets'— with metaphysical ones like himself not commonplace ones such as those which fly bodily about in ordinary trees. In the common-sensical perspective he is a parakeet in the sense—I assume—that he belongs to a clan whose members regard the parakeet as their totem, a membership from which, given the fundamental nature of reality as the religious perspective reveals it, certain moral and practical consequences flow. A man who says he is a parakeet is, if he says it in normal conversation, saying that, as myth and ritual demonstrate, he is shot through with parakeet-ness and that this religious fact has some crucial social implications—we parakeets must stick together, not marry one another, not eat mundane parakeets, and so on, for to do otherwise is to act against the grain of the whole universe. It is this placing of proximate acts in ultimate contexts that makes religion, frequently at least, socially so powerful. It alters, often radically, the whole landscape presented to common sense, alters it in such a way that the moods and motivations induced by religious practice seem themselves supremely practical, the only sensible ones to adopt given the way things 'really' are.

Having ritually 'leapt' (the image is perhaps a bit too athletic for the actual facts—'slipped' might be more accurate) into the framework of meaning which religious conceptions define and, the ritual ended, returned again to the common-sense world, a man is—unless, as sometimes happens, the experience fails to register—changed. And as he is changed so also is the common-sense world, for it is now seen as but the partial form of a wider reality which corrects and completes it. But this correction and completion is not, as some students of 'comparative religion' (e.g. Campbell, 1949, pp. 236-237) would have it, everywhere the same in content. The nature of the bias religion gives to ordinary life varies with the religion involved, with the particular dispositions induced in the believer by the specific conceptions of cosmic order he has come to accept. On the level of the 'great' religions, organic distinctiveness is usually recognized, at times insisted upon to the point of zealotry. But even at its simplest folk and tribal levels—where the individuality of religious traditions has so often been dissolved into such desiccated types as 'animism', 'animatism', 'totemism', 'shamanism', 'ancestor worship', and all the other insipid categories by means of which ethnographers of religion devitalize their data—the idiosyncratic character of how various groups of men behave because of what they believe they have experienced is clear. A tranquil Javanese would be no more at home in guilt-ridden Manus than an activist Crow would be in passionless Java. And for all the witches and ritual clowns in the world, Rangda and Barong are not generalized but thoroughly singular figurations of fear and gaiety. What men believe is as various as what they are—a proposition that holds with equal force when it is inverted.

It is this particularity of the impact of religious systems upon social systems (and upon personality systems) which renders general assessments of the value of religion in either moral or functional terms impossible. The sorts of moods and motivations which characterize a man who has just come from an Aztec human sacrifice are rather different from those of one who has just put off his Kachina mask. Even within the same society, what one 'learns' about the essential pattern of life from a sorcery rite and from a commensal meal will have rather diverse effects on social and psychological functioning. One of the main methodological problems in writing about religion scientifically is to put aside at once the tone of the village atheist and that of the village preacher, as well as their more sophisticated equivalents, so that the social and psychological implications of particular religious beliefs can emerge in a clear and neutral light. And when that is done, overall questions about whether religion is 'good' or 'bad', 'functional' or 'dysfunctional', 'ego strengthening' or 'anxiety producing' disappear like the chimeras they are, and one is left with particular evaluations, assessments, and diagnoses in particular cases. There remain, of course, the hardly unimportant questions of whether this or that religious assertion is true, this or that religious experience genuine, or whether true religious assertions and genuine religious experiences are possible at all. But such questions cannot even be asked, much less answered, within the self-imposed limitations of the scientific perspective.

NOTES

1. The reverse mistake, especially common among neo-Kantians such as Cassirer (1953–57), of taking symbols to be identical with, or 'constitutive of', their referents is equally pernicious. 'One can point to the moon with one's finger,' some, probably well-invented, Zen Master is supposed to have said, 'but to take one's finger for the moon is to be a fool.'

2. That the chronic and acute forms of this sort of cognitive concern are closely interrelated, and that responses to the more unusual occasions of it are patterned on responses established in coping with the more usual is also clear from Bateson's description, however, as he goes on to say: 'On another occasion I invited one of my informants to witness the development of photographic plates. I first desensitised the plates and then developed them in an open dish in moderate light, so that my informant was able to see the gradual appearance of the images. He was much interested, and some days later made me promise never to show this process to members of other clans. Kontum-mali was one of his ancestors, and he saw in the process of photographic development the actual embodiment of ripples into images, and regarded this as a demonstration of the clan's secret' (Bateson, 1958).

3. This is *not*, however, to say that everyone in every society does this; for as the immortal Don Marquis once remarked, you don't have to have a soul unless you really want one The oft-heard generalization (e.g. Kluckhohn, 1953) that religion is a human universal embodies a confusion between the probably true (though on present evidence unprovable) proposition that there is no human society in which cultural patterns that we can, under the present definition or one like it, call religious are totally lacking, and the surely untrue proposition that all men in all societies are, in any meaningful sense of the term, religious. But if the anthropological study of religious commitment is underdeveloped, the anthropological study of religious non-commitment is non-existent. The anthropology of religion will have come of age when some more subtle Malinowski writes a book called 'Belief and Unbelief (or even "Faith and Hypocrisy") in a Savage Society'.

4. The term 'attitude' as in 'aesthetic attitude' (Bell, 1914) or 'natural attitude' (Schutz, 1962; the phrase is originally Husserl's) is another, perhaps more common term for what I have here called 'perspective'. But I have avoided it because of its strong subjectivist connotations, its tendency to place the stress upon a supposed inner state of an actor rather than on a certain sort of relation—a symbolically mediated one—between an actor and a situation. This is not to say, of course, that a phenomenological analysis of religious experience, if cast in inter-subjective, non-transcendental, genuinely scientific terms (see Percy, 1958) is not essential to a full understanding of religious belief, but merely that that is not the focus of my concern here. 'Outlook', 'frame of reference', 'frame of mind', 'orientation', 'stance', 'mental set', etc. are other terms sometimes employed, depending upon whether the analyst wishes to stress the social, psychological, or cultural aspects of the matter.

REFERENCES

BATESON, G., 1958. *Naven*. Stanford: Stanford University Press, 2nd ed.

BATESON, G. & MEAD, M. 1942. *Balinese Character*. New York: N.Y. Academy of Sciences.

BELL, C. 1914. *Art*. London: Chatto & Windus.

BELO, J. 1949. *Bali: Rangda and Barong*. New York: J. J. Augustin.

——— 1960. *Trance in Bali*. New York: Columbia University Press.

BURKE, K. 1941. *The Philosophy of Literary Form*. n.p.: Louisiana State University Press.

CAMPBELL, J. 1949. *The Here with a Thousand Faces*. New York: Pantheon.

CASSIRIR, E. 1953-57. *The Philosophy of Symbolic Forms* (trans. R. Mannheim). New Haven: Yale University Press. 3 vols.

COVARRUBIAS, M. 1937. *The Island of Bali*. New York: Knopf.

CRAIK, K. 1952. *The Nature of Explanation*. Cambridge: Cambridge University Press.

EVANS-PRITCHARD, E. E. 1937. *Witchcraft, Oracles and Magic Among the Azande*. Oxford: Clarendon Press.

FIRTH, R. 1951. *Elements of Social Organization*. London: Watts; New York: Philosophical Library.

FORTUNE, R. F. 1935. *Manus Religion*. Philadelphia: American Philosophical Society.

VON FRISCH, K. 1962. Dialects in the Language of the Bees. *Scientific American*, August.

GEERTZ, C. 1958. Ethos, World-View and the Analysis of Sacred Symbols. *Antioch Review*, Winter (1957-58): 421-437.

———— 1960. *The Religion of Java*. Glencoe, Ill.: The Free Press.

———— 1962. The Growth of Culture and the Evolution of Mind. In J. Scher (ed.), *Theories of the Mind*. New York: The Free Press, pp. 713-740.

———— 1964a. Ideology as a Cultural System. In D. Apter (ed.), *Ideology of Discontent*. New York: The Free Press.

———— 1964b. 'Internal Conversion' in Contemporary Bali. In J. Bastin & R. Roolvink (eds.), *Malayan and Indonesian Studies*, Oxford: Oxford University Press, pp. 282-302.

GOODY, J. 1961. Religion and Ritual: The Definition Problem. *British Journal of Sociology* 12: 143-164.

HOROWITZ, N. H. 1956. The Gene. *Scientific American*, February.

JAMES, WILLIAM. 1904. *The Principles of Psychology*. New York: Henry Holt, 2 vols.

JANOWITZ, M. 1963. Anthropology and the Social Sciences. *Current Anthropology* 4: 139, 146-154.

KLUCKHOHN, C. 1949. The Philosophy of the Navaho Indians. In F. S. C. Northrop (ed.), *Ideological Differences and World Order*. New Haven: Yale University Press, pp. 356-384.

———— 1953. Universal Categories of Culture. In A. L. Kroeber (ed.), *Anthropology Today*. Chicago: University of Chicago Press, pp. 507-523.

KLUCKHOHN, C. & LEIGHTON, D. 1946. *The Navaho*. Cambridge, Mass.: Harvard University Press.

LANGER, S. 1953. *Feeling and Form*. New York: Scribner's.

———— 1960. *Philosophy in a New Key*. Fourth Edition. Cambridge, Mass.: Harvard University Press.

———— 1962. *Philosophical Sketches*. Baltimore: Johns Hopkins.

LEACH, E. R. 1954. *Political Systems of Highland Burma*. London: Bell; Cambridge, Mass.: Harvard University Press.

LÉVY-BRUHL, L. 1926. *How Natives Think*. New York: Knopf.

LIENHARDT, G. 1961. *Divinity and Experience*. Oxford: Clarendon Press.

LORENZ, K. 1952. *King Solomon's Ring*. London: Methuen.

LOWIE, R. H. 1924. *Primitive Religion*. New York: Boni and Liveright.

MACINTYRE, A. 1957. The Logical Status of Religious Belief. In A. MacIntyre (ed.), *Metaphysical Beliefs*. London: SCM Press, pp. 167-211.

MALINOWSKI, B. 1948. *Magic, Science and Religion*. Boston: Beacon Press.

NADEL, S. F. 1957. Malinowski on Magic and Religion. In R. Firth (ed.), *Man and Culture*. London: Routledge & Kegan Paul, pp. 189-208.

PARSONS, T. & SHILS, E. 1951. *Toward a General Theory of Action*. Cambridge, Mass.: Harvard University Press.

PERCY, W. 1958. Symbol, Consciousness and Intersubjectivity. *Journal of Philosophy* 15: 631-641.

———— 1961. The Symbolic Structure of Interpersonal Process. *Psychiatry* 24: 39-52.

RADCLIFFE-BROWN, A. R. 1952. *Structure and Function in Primitive Society*. Glencoe, Ill.: Free Press.

RADIN, P. 1957. *Primitive Man as a Philosopher*. New York: Dover.

REICHARD, G. 1950. *Navaho Religion*. New York: Pantheon, 2 vols.

RYLE, G. 1949. *The Concept of Mind*. London: Hutchinson; New York: Barnes & Noble.

SANTAYANA, G. 1905-1906. *Reason in Religion*. Vol. 2 of *The Life of Reason, or The Phases of Human Progress*. London: Constable; New York: Scribner's.

SCHUTZ, A. 1962. *The Problem of Social Reality* (vol. I. of *Collected Papers*). The Hague: Martinus Nijhoff.

SINGER, M. 1955. The Cultural Pattern of Indian Civilization. *Far Eastern Quarterly* 15: 23-36.

———— 1958. The Great Tradition in a Metropolitan Center: Madras. In M. Singer (ed.), *Traditional India*. Philadelphia: American Folklore Society, pp. 140-82.

SMITH, C. W. & DALE, A. M. 1920. *The Ila-Speaking Peoples of Northern Rhodesia*. London: Macmillan.

DE ZOETE, B. & SPIES, W. 1938. *Dance and Drama in Bali*. London: Faber & Faber.

Religion Versus the Religious

John Dewey

Never before in history has mankind been so much of two minds, so divided into two camps, as it is today. Religions have traditionally been allied with ideas of the supernatural, and often have been based upon explicit beliefs about it. Today there are many who hold that nothing worthy of being called religious is possible apart from the supernatural. Those who hold this belief differ in many respects. They range from those who accept the dogmas and sacraments of the Greek and Roman Catholic church as the only sure means of access to the supernatural to the theist or mild deist. Between them are the many Protestant denominations who think the Scriptures, aided by a pure conscience, are adequate avenues to supernatural truth and power. But they agree in one point: the necessity for a Supernatural Being and for an immortality that is beyond the power of nature.

The opposed group consists of those who think the advance of culture and science has completely discredited the supernatural and with it all religions that are allied with belief in it. But they go beyond this point. The extremists in this group believe that with elimination of the supernatural not only must historic religions be dismissed but with them everything of a religious nature. When historical knowledge has discredited the claims made for the supernatural character of the persons said to have founded historic religions; when the supernatural inspiration attributed to the literatures held sacred has been riddled, and when anthropological and psychological knowledge has disclosed the all-too-human source from which religious beliefs and practices have sprung, everything religious must, they say, also go.

There is one idea held in common by these two opposite groups: identification of the religious with the supernatural. The question I shall raise in these chapters concerns the ground for and the consequences of this identification: its reasons and its value. In the discussion I shall develop another conception of the nature of the religious phase of experience, one that separates it from the supernatural and the things that have grown up about it. I shall try to show that these derivations are encumbrances and that what is genuinely religious will undergo an emancipation when it is relieved from them; that then, for the first time, the religious aspect of experience will be free to develop freely on its own account.

From *A Common Faith* (New Haven: Yale University Press, 1934), pp. 2-28. Reprinted by permission of the publisher.

This view is exposed to attack from both the other camps. It goes contrary to traditional religions, including those that have the greatest hold upon the religiously minded today. The view announced will seem to them to cut the vital nerve of the religious element itself in taking away the basis upon which traditional religions and institutions have been founded. From the other side, the position I am taking seems like a timid halfway position, a concession and compromise unworthy of thought that is thoroughgoing. It is regarded as a view entertained from mere tendermindedness, as an emotional hangover from childhood indoctrination, or even as a manifestation of a desire to avoid disapproval and curry favor.

The heart of my point, as far as I shall develop it in this first section, is that there is a difference between religion, *a* religion, and the religious; between anything that may be denoted by a noun substantive and the quality of experience that is designated by an adjective. It is not easy to find a definition of religion in the substantive sense that wins general acceptance. However, in the *Oxford Dictionary* I find the following: "Recognition on the part of man of some unseen higher power as having control of his destiny and as being entitled to obedience, reverence and worship."

This particular definition is less explicit in assertion of the supernatural character of the higher unseen power than are others that might be cited. It is, however, surcharged with implications having their source in ideas connected with the belief in the supernatural, characteristic of historic religions. Let us suppose that one familiar with the history of religions, including those called primitive, compares the definition with the variety of known facts and by means of the comparison sets out to determine just what the definition means. I think he will be struck by three facts that reduce the terms of the definition to such a low common denominator that little meaning is left.

He will note that the "unseen powers" referred to have been conceived in a multitude of incompatible ways. Eliminating the differences, nothing is left beyond the bare reference to something unseen and powerful. This has been conceived as the vague and undefined Mana of the Melanesians; the Kami of primitive Shintoism; the fetish of the Africans; spirits, having some human properties, that pervade natural places and animate natural forces; the ultimate and impersonal principle of Buddhism; the unmoved mover of Greek thought; the gods and semidivine heroes of the Greek and Roman Pantheons; the personal and loving Providence of Christianity, omnipotent, and limited by a corresponding evil power; the arbitrary Will of Moslemism; the supreme legislator and judge of deism. And these are but a few of the outstanding varieties of ways in which the invisible power has been conceived.

There is no greater similarity in the ways in which obedience and reverence have been expressed. There has been worship of animals, of ghosts, of ancestors, phallic worship, as well as of a Being of dread power and of love and wisdom. Reverence has been expressed in the human sacrifices of the Peruvians and Aztecs; the sexual orgies of some Oriental religions; exorcisms and ablutions; the offering of the humble and contrite mind of the Hebrew prophet, the elaborate rituals of the Greek and Roman Churches. Not even sacrifice has been uniform; it is highly sublimated in Protestant denominations and in Moslemism. Where it has existed it has taken all kinds of forms and been directed to a great variety of powers and spirits. It has been used for expiation, for propitiation and for buying special favors. There is no conceivable purpose for which rites have not been employed.

Finally, there is no discernible unity in the moral motivations appealed to and utilized. They have been as far apart as fear of lasting torture, hope of enduring bliss in which sexual enjoyment has sometimes been a conspicuous element; mortification of the flesh and extreme asceticism; prostitution and chastity; wars to extirpate the unbeliever, and philanthropic zeal; servile acceptance of imposed dogma, along with brotherly love and aspiration for a reign of justice among men.

I have, of course, mentioned only a sparse number of the facts which fill volumes in any well-stocked library. It may be asked by those who do not like to look upon the darker side of the history of religions why the darker facts should be brought up. We all know that civilized man has a background of bestiality and superstition and that these elements are still with us. Indeed, have not some religions, including the most influential forms of Christianity, taught that the heart of man is totally corrupt? How could the course of religion in its entire sweep not be marked by practices that are shameful in their cruelty and lustfulness, and by beliefs that are degraded and intellectually incredible? What else than what we find could be expected, in the case of people having little knowledge and no secure method of knowing; with primitive institutions, and with so little control of natural forces that they lived in a constant state of fear?

I gladly admit that historic religions have been relative to the conditions of social culture in which peoples lived. Indeed, what I am concerned with is to press home the logic of this method of disposal of outgrown traits of past religions. Beliefs and practices in a religion that now prevails are by this logic relative to the present state of culture. If so much flexibility has obtained in the past regarding an unseen power, the way it affects human destiny, and the attitudes we are to take toward it, why should it be assumed that change in conception and action has now come to an end? The logic involved in getting rid of inconvenient aspects of past religions compels us to inquire how much in religions now accepted are survivals from outgrown cultures. It compels us to ask what conception of unseen powers and our relations to them would be consonant with the best achievements and aspirations of the present. It demands that in imagination we wipe the slate clean and start afresh by asking what would be the idea of the unseen, of the manner of its control over us and the ways in which reverence and obedience would be manifested, if whatever is basically religious in experience had the opportunity to express itself free from all historic encumbrances.

So we return to the elements of the definition that has been given. What boots it to accept, in defense of the universality of religion, a definition that applies equally to the most savage and degraded beliefs and practices that have related to unseen powers and to noble ideals of a religion having the greatest share of moral content? There are two points involved. One of them is that there is nothing left worth preserving in the notions of unseen powers, controlling human destiny to which obedience, reverence and worship are due, if we glide silently over the nature that has been attributed to the powers, the radically diverse ways in which they have been supposed to control human destiny, and in which submission and awe have been manifested. The other point is that when we begin to select, to choose, and say that some present ways of thinking about the unseen powers are better than others; that the reverence shown by a free and self-respecting human being is better than the servile obedience rendered to an arbitrary power by frightened men; that we should believe that control of human destiny is exercised by a wise and loving spirit rather than by madcap ghosts or sheer force—when I say, we begin to choose, we have entered upon a road that has not yet come to an end. We have reached a point that invites us to proceed farther.

For we are forced to acknowledge that concretely there is no such thing as religion in the singular. There is only a multitude of religions. "Religion" is a strictly collective term and the collection it stands for is not even of the kind illustrated in textbooks of logic. It has not the unity of a regiment or assembly but that of any miscellaneous aggregate. Attempts to prove the universality prove too much or too little. It is probable that religions have been universal in the sense that all the peoples we know anything about have had *a* religion. But the differences among them are so great and so shocking that any common element that can be extracted is meaningless. The idea that religion is universal proves too little in that the older apologists for Christianity seem to have been better advised than some modern ones in condemning every religion but one as an impostor, as at bottom some kind of demon worship or at any rate a superstitious figment. Choice among religions is imperative, and the necessity for choice leaves nothing of any force in the argument from universality. Moreover, when once we enter upon the road of choice, there is at once presented a possibility not yet generally realized.

For the historic increase of the ethical and ideal content of religions suggests that the process of purification may be carried further. It indicates that further choice is imminent in which certain values and functions in experience may be selected. This possibility is what I had in mind in speaking of the difference between the religious and a religion. I am not proposing a religion, but rather the emancipation of elements and outlooks that may be called religious. For the moment we have a religion, whether that of the Sioux Indian or of Judaism or of Christianity, that moment the ideal factors in experience that may be called religious take on a load that is not inherent in them, a load of current beliefs and of institutional practices that are irrelevant to them.

I can illustrate what I mean by a common phenomenon in contemporary life. It is widely supposed that a person who does not accept any religion is thereby shown to be a non-religious person. Yet it is conceivable that the present depression in religion is closely connected with the fact that religions now prevent, because of their weight of historic encumbrances, the religious quality of experience from coming to consciousness and finding the expression that is appropriate to present conditions, intellectual and moral. I believe that such is the case. I believe that many persons are so repelled from what exists as a religion by its intellectual and moral implications, that they are not even aware of attitudes in themselves that if they came to fruition would be genuinely religious. I hope that this remark may help make clear what I mean by the distinction between "religion" as a noun substantive and "religious" as adjectival.

To be somewhat more explicit, a religion (and as I have just said there is no such thing as religion in general) always signifies a special body of beliefs and practices having some kind of institutional organization, loose or tight. In contrast, the adjective "religious" denotes nothing in the way of a specifiable entity, either institutional or as a system of beliefs. It does not denote anything to which one can specifically point as one can point to this and that historic religion or existing church. For it does not denote anything that can exist by itself or that can be organized into a particular and distinctive form of existence. It denotes attitudes that may be taken toward every object and every proposed end or ideal.

Before, however, I develop my suggestion that realization of the distinction just made would operate to emancipate the religious quality from encumbrances that now smother or limit it, I must refer to a position that in some respects is similar in words to the position I have taken, but that in fact is a whole world removed from it. I have several times used the phrase "religious elements of experience." Now at present there is much talk, especially in liberal circles, of religious experience as vouching for the authenticity of certain beliefs and the desirability of certain practices, such as particular forms of prayer and worship. It is even asserted that religious experience is the ultimate basis of religion itself. The gulf between this position and that which I have taken is what I am now concerned to point out.

Those who hold to the notion that there is a definite kind of experience which is itself religious, by that very fact make out of it something specific, as a kind of experience that is marked off from experience as aesthetic, scientific, moral, political; from experience as companionship and friendship. But "religious" as a quality of experience signifies something that may belong to all these experiences. It is the polar opposite of some type of experience that can exist by itself. The distinction comes out clearly when it is noted that the concept of this distinct kind of experience is used to validate a belief in some special kind of object and also to justify some special kind of practice.

For there are many religionists who are now dissatisfied with the older "proofs" of the existence of God, those that go by the name of onto-logical, cosmological and teleological. The cause of the dissatisfaction is perhaps not so much the arguments that Kant used to show the in-sufficiency of these alleged proofs, as it is the growing feeling that they are too formal to offer any support to religion in action. Anyway, the dissatisfaction exists. Moreover, these religionists are moved by the rise of the experimental method in other fields. What is more natural and proper, accordingly, than that they should affirm they are just as good empiricists as anybody else—indeed, as good as the scientists themselves? As the latter rely upon certain kinds of experience to prove the existence of certain kinds of objects, so the religionists rely upon a certain kind of experience to prove the existence of the object of religion, especially the supreme object, God.

The discussion may be made more definite by introducing, at this point, a particular illustration of this type of reasoning. A writer says: "I broke down from overwork and soon came to the verge of nervous prostration. One morning after a long and sleepless night . . . I re-solved to stop drawing upon myself so continuously and begin drawing upon God. I determined to set apart a quiet time every day in which I could relate my life to its ultimate source, regain the consciousness that in God I live, move and have my being. That was thirty years ago. Since then I have had literally not one hour of darkness or despair."

This an impressive record. I do not doubt its authenticity nor that of the experience related. It illustrates a religious aspect of experience. But it illustrates also the use of that quality to carry a superimposed load of a particular religion. For having been brought up in the Christian religion, its subject interprets it in the terms of the personal God characteristic of that religion. Taoists, Buddhists, Moslems, persons of no religion including those who reject all supernatural influence and power, have had experiences similar in their effect. Yet another author commenting upon the passage says: "The religious expert can be more sure that this God exists than he can of either the cosmological God of speculative surmise or the Christlike God involved in the validity of moral optimism," and goes on to add that such experiences "mean that God the savior, the power that gives victory over sin on certain condi-tions that man can fulfill, is an existent, accessible and scientifically knowable reality." It should be clear that this inference is sound only if the conditions, of whatever sort, that produce the effect are called "God." But most readers will take the inference to mean that the existence of a particular Being, of the type called "God" in the Chris-tian religion, is proved by a method akin to that of experimental science.

In reality, the only thing that can be said to be "proved" is the existence of some complex of conditions that have operated to effect an adjustment in life, an orientation, that brings with it a sense of security and peace. The particular interpretation given to this complex of conditions is not inherent in the experience itself. It is derived from the culture with which a particular person has been imbued. A fatalist will give one name to it; a Christian Scientist another, and the one who rejects all supernatural being still another. The determining factor in the interpretation of the experience is the particular doctrinal apparatus into which a person has been inducted. The emotional deposit connected with prior teaching floods the whole situation. It may readily confer upon the experience such a peculiarly sacred preciousness that all inquiry into its causation is barred. The stable outcome is so invaluable that the cause to which it is referred is usually nothing but a reduplication of the thing that has occurred, plus some name that has acquired a deeply emotional quality.

The intent of this discussion is not to deny the genuineness of the result nor its importance in life. It is not, save incidentally, to point out the possibility of a purely naturalistic explanation of the event. My purpose is to indicate what happens when religious experience is already set aside as something *sui generis*. The actual religious quality in the experience described is the *effect* produced, the better adjustment in life and its conditions, not the manner and cause of its production. The way in which the experience operated, its function, determines its religious value. If the reorientation actually occurs, it, and the sense of security and stability accompanying it, are forces on their own account. It takes place in different persons in a multitude of ways. It is sometimes brought about by devotion to a cause; sometimes by a passage of poetry that opens a new perspective; sometimes as was the case with Spinoza—deemed an atheist in his day—through philosophical reflection.

The difference between an experience having a religious force because of what it does in and to the processes of living and religious experience as a separate kind of thing gives me occasion to refer to a previous remark. If this function were rescued through emancipation from dependence upon specific types of beliefs and practices, from those elements that constitute a religion, many individuals would find that experiences having the force of bringing about a better, deeper and enduring adjustment in life are not so rare and infrequent as they are commonly supposed to be. They occur frequently in connection with many significant moments of living. The idea of invisible powers would take on the meaning of all the conditions of nature and human association that support and deepen the sense of values which carry one through periods of darkness and despair to such an extent that they lose their usual depressive character.

I do not suppose for many minds the dislocation of the religious from a religion is easy to effect. Tradition and custom, especially when emotionally charged, are a part of the habits that have become one with our very being. But the possibility of the transfer is demonstrated by its actuality. Let us then for the moment drop the term "religious," and ask what are the attitudes that lend deep and enduring support to the processes of living. I have, for example, used the words "adjustment" and "orientation." What do they signify?

While the words "accommodation," "adaptation," and "adjustment" are frequently employed as synonyms, attitudes exist that are so different that for the sake of clear thought they should be discriminated. There are conditions we meet that cannot be changed. If they are particular and limited, we modify our own particular attitudes in accordance with them. Thus we accommodate ourselves to changes in weather, to alterations in income when we have no other recourse. When the external conditions are lasting we become inured, habituated, or, as the process is now often called, conditioned. The two main traits of this attitude, which I should like to call accommodation, are that it affects *particular* modes of conduct, not the entire self, and that the process is mainly *passive*. It may, however, become general and then it becomes fatalistic resignation or submission. There are other attitudes toward the environment that are also particular but that are more active. We re-act against conditions and endeavor to change them to meet our wants and demands. Plays in a foreign language are "adapted" to meet the needs of an American audience. A house is rebuilt to suit changed conditions of the household; the telephone is invented to serve the demand for speedy communication at a distance; dry soils are irrigated so that they may bear abundant crops. Instead of accommodating ourselves to conditions, we modify conditions so that they will be accommodated to our wants and purposes. This process may be called adaptation.

Now both of these processes are often called by the more general name of adjustment. But there are also changes in ourselves in relation to the world in which we live that are much more inclusive and deep seated. They relate not to this and that want in relation to this and that condition of our surroundings, but pertain to our being in its entirety. Because of their scope, this modification of ourselves is enduring. It lasts through any amount of vicissitude of circumstances, internal and external. There is a composing and harmonizing of the various elements of our being such that, in spite of changes in the special conditions that surround us, these conditions are also arranged, settled, in relation to us. This attitude includes a note of submission. But it is voluntary, not externally imposed; and as voluntary it is something more than a mere Stoical resolution to endure unperturbed throughout the buffetings of fortune. It is more outgoing, more ready and glad, than the latter attitude, and it is more active than the former. And in calling it voluntary, it is not meant that it depends upon a particular resolve or volition. It is a change *of* will conceived as the organic plenitude of our being, rather than any special change *in* will.

It is the claim of religions that they effect this generic and enduring change in attitude. I should like to turn the statement around and say that whenever this change takes place there is a definitely religious attitude. It is not *a* religion that brings it about, but when it occurs, from whatever cause and by whatever means, there is a religious outlook and function. As I have said before, the doctrinal or intellectual apparatus and the institutional accretions that grow up are, in a strict sense, adventitious to the intrinsic quality of such experiences. For they are affairs of the traditions of the culture with which individuals are inoculated. Mr. Santayana has connected the religious quality of experience with the imaginative, as that is expressed in poetry. "Religion and poetry," he says, "are identical in essence, and differ merely in the way in which they are attached to practical affairs. Poetry is called religion when it intervenes in life, and religion, when it merely supervenes upon life, is seen to be nothing but poetry." The difference between intervening *in* and supervening *upon* is as important as is the identity set forth. Imagination may play upon life or it may enter profoundly into it. As Mr. Santayana puts it, "poetry has a universal and a moral function," for "its highest power lies in it relevance to the ideals and purposes of life." Except as it intervenes, "all observation is observation of brute fact, all discipline is mere repression, until these facts digested and this discipline embodied in humane impulses become the starting point for a creative movement of the imagination, the firm basis for ideal constructions in society, religion, and art."

If I may make a comment upon this penetrating insight of Mr. Santayana, I would say that the difference between imagination that only supervenes and imagination that intervenes is the difference between one that completely interpenetrates all the elements of our being and one that is interwoven with only special and partial factors. There actually occurs extremely little observation of brute facts merely for the sake of the facts, just as there is little discipline that is repression and nothing but repression. Facts are usually observed with reference to some practical end and purpose, and that end is presented only imaginatively. The most repressive discipline has some end in view to which there is at least imputed an ideal quality; otherwise it is purely sadistic. But in such cases of observation and discipline imagination is limited and partial. It does not extend far; it does not permeate deeply and widely.

The connection between imagination and the harmonizing of the self is closer than is usually thought. The idea of a whole, whether of the whole personal being or of the world, is an imaginative, not a literal, idea. The limited world of our observation and reflection becomes the Universe only through imaginative extension. It cannot be apprehended in knowledge nor realized in reflection. Neither observation, thought, nor practical activity can attain that complete unification of the self which is called a whole. The *whole* self is an ideal, an imaginative projection. Hence the idea of a thoroughgoing and deep-seated harmonizing of the self with the Universe (as a name for the totality of conditions with which the self is connected) operates only through imagination—which is one reason why this composing of the self is not voluntary in the sense of an act of special volition or resolution. An "adjustment" possesses the will rather than is its express product. Religionists have been right in thinking of it as an influx from sources beyond conscious deliberation and purpose—a fact that helps explain, psychologically, why it has so generally been attributed to a supernatural source and that, perhaps, throws some light upon the reference of it by William James to unconscious factors. And it is pertinent to note that the unification of the self throughout the ceaseless flux of what it does, suffers, and achieves, cannot be attained in terms of itself. The self is always directed toward something beyond itself and so its own unification depends upon the idea of the integration of the shifting scenes of the world into that imaginative totality we call the Universe.

The intimate connection of imagination with ideal elements in experience is generally recognized. Such is not the case with respect to its connection with faith. The latter has been regarded as a substitute for knowledge, for sight. It is defined, in the Christian religion, as *evidence* of things not seen. The implication is that faith is a kind of anticipatory vision of things that are now invisible because of the limitations of our finite and erring nature. Because it is a substitute for knowledge, its material and object are intellectual in quality. As John Locke summed up the matter, faith is "assent to a proposition . . . on the credit of its proposer." Religious faith is then given to a body of propositions as true on the credit of their supernatural author, reason coming in to demonstrate the reasonableness of giving such credit. Of necessity there results the development of theologies, or bodies of systematic propositions, to make explicit in organized form the content of the propositions to which belief is attached and assent given. Given the point of view, those who hold that religion necessarily implies a theology are correct.

But belief or faith has also a moral and practical import. Even devils, according to the older theologians, believe—and tremble. A distinction was made, therefore, between "speculative" or intellectual belief and an act called "justifying" faith. Apart from any theological context, there is a difference between belief that is a conviction that some end should be supreme over conduct, and belief that some object or being exists as a truth for the intellect. Conviction in the moral sense signifies being conquered, vanquished, in our active nature by an ideal end; it signifies acknowledgment of its rightful claim over our desires and purposes. Such acknowledgment is practical, not primarily intellectual. It goes beyond evidence that can be presented to *any* possible observer. Reflection, often long and arduous, may be involved in arriving at the conviction, but the import of thought is not exhausted in discovery of evidence that can justify intellectual assent. The authority of an ideal over choice and conduct is the authority of an ideal, not of a fact, of a truth guaranteed to intellect, not of the status of the one who propounds the truth.

Such moral faith is not easy. It was questioned of old whether the

Son of Man should find faith on the earth in his coming. Moral faith has been bolstered by all sorts of arguments intended to prove that its object is not ideal and that its claim upon us is not primarily moral or practical, since the ideal in question is already embedded in the existent frame of things. It is argued that the ideal is already the final reality at the heart of things that exist, and that only our senses or the corruption of our natures prevent us from apprehending its prior existential being. Starting, say, from such an idea as that justice is more than a moral ideal because it is embedded in the very make-up of the actually existent world, men have gone on to build up vast intellectual schemes, philosophies, and theologies, to prove that ideals are real not as ideals but as antecedently existing actualities. They have failed to see that in converting moral realities into matters of intellectual assent they have evinced lack of *moral* faith. Faith that something should be in existence as far as lies in our power is changed into the intellectual belief that it is already in existence. When physical existence does not bear out the assertion, the physical is subtly changed into the metaphysical. In this way, moral faith has been inextricably tied up with intellectual beliefs about the supernatural.

The tendency to convert ends of moral faith and action into articles of an intellectual creed has been furthered by a tendency of which psychologists are well aware. What we ardently desire to have thus and so, we tend to believe is already so. Desire has a powerful influence upon intellectual beliefs. Moreover, when conditions are adverse to realization of the objects of our desire—and in the case of significant ideals they are extremely adverse—it is an easy way out to assume that after all they are already embodied in the ultimate structure of what is, and that appearances to the contrary are *merely* appearances. Imagination then merely supervenes and is freed from the responsibility for intervening. Weak natures take to reverie as a refuge as strong ones do to fanaticism. Those who dissent are mourned over by the first class and converted through the use of force by the second.

What has been said does not imply that all moral faith in ideal ends is by virtue of that fact religious in quality. The religious is "morality touched by emotion" only when the ends of moral conviction arouse emotions that are not only intense but are actuated and supported by ends so inclusive that they unify the self. The inclusiveness of the end in relation to both self and the "universe" to which an inclusive self is related is indispensable. According to the best authorities, "religion" comes from a root that means being bound or tied. Originally, it meant being bound by vows to a particular way of life—as *les religieux* were monks and nuns who had assumed certain vows. The religious attitude signifies something that is bound through imagination to a *general* attitude. This comprehensive attitude, moreover, is much broader than anything indicated by "moral" in its usual sense. The quality of attitude is displayed in art, science and good citizenship.

If we apply the conception set forth to the terms of the definition earlier quoted, these terms take on a new significance. An unseen power controlling our destiny becomes the power of an ideal. All possibilities, as possibilities, are ideal in character. The artist, scientist, citizen, parent, as far as they are actuated by the spirit of their callings, are controlled by the unseen. For all endeavor for the better is moved by faith in what is possible, not by adherence to the actual. Nor does this faith depend for its moving power upon intellectual assurance or belief that the things worked for must surely prevail and come into embodied existence. For the authority of the object to determine our attitude and conduct, the right that is given it to claim our allegiance and devotion is based on the intrinsic nature of the ideal. The outcome, given our best endeavor, is not with us. The inherent vice of all intellectual schemes of idealism is that they convert the idealism of action into a system of beliefs about antecedent reality. The character assigned this reality is so different from that which observation and reflection lead to and support that these schemes inevitably glide into alliance with the supernatural.

All religions, marked by elevated ideal quality, have dwelt upon the power of religion to introduce perspective into the piecemeal and shifting episodes of existence. Here too we need to reverse the ordinary statement and say that whatever introduces genuine perspective is religious, not that religion is something that introduces it. There can be no doubt (referring to the second element of the definition) of our dependence upon forces beyond our control. Primitive man was so impotent in the face of these forces that, especially in an unfavorable natural environment, fear became a dominant attitude, and, as the old saying goes, fear created the gods.

With increase of mechanisms of control, the element of fear has, relatively speaking, subsided. Some optimistic souls have even concluded that the forces about us are on the whole essentially benign. But every crisis, whether of the individual or of the community, reminds man of the precarious and partial nature of the control he exercises. When man, individually and collectively, has done his uttermost, conditions that at different times and places have given rise to the ideas of Fate and Fortune, of Chance and Providence, remain. It is the part of manliness to insist upon the capacity of mankind to strive to direct natural and social forces to humane ends. But unqualified absolutistic statements about the omnipotence of such endeavors reflect egoism rather than intelligent courage.

The fact that human destiny is so interwoven with forces beyond human control renders it unnecessary to suppose that dependence and the humility that accompanies it have to find the particular channel that is prescribed by traditional doctrines. What is especially significant is rather the form which the sense of dependence takes. Fear never gave stable perspective in the life of anyone. It is dispersive and withdrawing. Most religions have in fact added rites of communion to those of expiation and propitiation. For our dependence is manifested in those relations to the environment that support our undertakings and aspirations as much as it is in the defeats inflicted upon us. The essentially unreligious attitude is that which attributes human achievement and purpose to man in isolation from the world of physical nature and his fellows. Our successes are dependent upon the cooperation of nature. The sense of the dignity of human nature is as religious as is the sense of awe and reverence when it rests upon a sense of human nature as a coöperating part of a larger whole. Natural piety is not of necessity either a fatalistic acquiescence in natural happenings or a romantic idealization of the world. It may rest upon a just sense of nature as the whole of which we are parts, while it also recognizes that we are parts that are marked by intelligence and purpose, having the capacity to strive by their aid to bring conditions into greater consonance with what is humanly desirable. Such piety is an inherent constituent of a just perspective in life.

Understanding and knowledge also enter into a perspective that is religious in quality. Faith in the continued disclosing of truth through directed cooperative human endeavor is more religious in quality than is any faith in a completed revelation. It is of course now usual to hold that revelation is not completed in the sense of being ended. But religions hold that the essential framework is settled in its significant moral features at least, and that new elements that are offered must be judged by conformity to this framework. Some fixed doctrinal apparatus is necessary for *a* religion. But faith in the possibilities of continued and rigorous inquiry does not limit access to truth to any channel or scheme of things. It does not first say that truth is universal and then add there is but one road to it. It does not depend for assurance upon subjection to any dogma or item of doctrine. It trusts that the natural interactions between man and his environment will breed more intelligence and generate more knowledge provided the scientific methods that define intelligence in operation are pushed further into the mysteries of the world, being themselves promoted and improved in the operation. There is such a thing as faith in intelligence becoming religious in quality—a fact that perhaps explains the efforts of some religionists to disparage the possibilities of intelligence as a force. They properly feel such faith to be a dangerous rival.

Lives that are consciously inspired by loyalty to such ideals as have been mentioned are still comparatively infrequent to the extent of that comprehensiveness and intensity which arouse an ardor religious in function. But before we infer the incompetency of such ideals and of the actions they inspire, we should at least ask ourselves how much of the existing situation is due to the fact that the religious factors of experience have been drafted into supernatural channels and thereby loaded with irrelevant encumbrances. A body of beliefs and practices that are apart from the common and natural relations of mankind must, in the degree in which it is influential, weaken and sap the force of the possibilities inherent in such relations. Here lies one aspect of the emancipation of the religious from religion.

Any activity pursued in behalf of an ideal end against obstacles and in spite of threats of personal loss because of conviction of its general and enduring value is religious in quality. Many a person, inquirer, artist, philanthropist, citizen, men and women in the humblest walks of life, have achieved, without presumption and without display, such unification of themselves and of their relations to the conditions of existence. It remains to extend their spirit and inspiration to ever wider numbers. If I have said anything about religions and religion that seems harsh, I have said those things because of a firm belief that the claim on the part of religions to possess a monopoly of ideals and of the supernatural means by which alone, it is alleged, they can be furthered, stands in the way of the realization of distinctively religious values inherent in natural experience. For that reason, if for no other, I should be sorry if any were misled by the frequency with which I have employed the adjective "religious" to conceive of what I have said as a disguised apology for what have passed as religions. The opposition between religious values as I conceive them and religions is not to be bridged. Just because the release of the values is so important, their identification with the creeds and cults of religions must be dissolved.

RELIGIOUS EPISTEMOLOGY: REASON

The Ontological Argument

St. Anselm

CHAPTER II

Truly there is a God, although the fool hath said in his heart, There is no God.

And so, Lord, do thou, who dost give understanding to faith, give me, so far as thou knowest it to be profitable, to understand that thou art as we believe; and that thou art that which we believe. And, indeed, we believe that thou art a being than which nothing greater can be conceived. Or is there no such nature, since the fool hath said in his heart, there is

Reprinted from *Basic Writings* by St. Anselm, by permission of The Open Court Publishing Company, La Salle, Illinois. Copyright © 1910.

no God (Psalms xiv. 1). But, at any rate, this very fool, when he hears of this being of which I speak—a being than which nothing greater can be conceived—understands what he hears, and what he understands is in his understanding; although he does not understand it to exist.

For, it is one thing for an object to be in the understanding, and another to understand that the object exists. When a painter first conceives of what he will afterwards perform, he has it in his understanding, but he does not yet understand it to be, because he has not yet performed it. But after he has made the painting, he both has it in his understanding, and he understands that it exists, because he has made it.

Hence, even the fool is convinced that something exists in the understanding, at least, than which nothing greater can be conceived. For, when he hears of this, he understands it. And whatever is understood, exists in the understanding. And assuredly that, than which nothing greater can be conceived, cannot exist in the understanding alone. For, suppose it exists in the understanding alone: then it can be conceived to exist in reality; which is greater.

Therefore, if that, than which nothing greater can be conceived, exists in the understanding alone, the very being, than which nothing greater can be conceived, is one, than which a greater can be conceived. But obviously this is impossible. Hence, there is no doubt that there exists a being, than which nothing greater can be conceived, and it exists both in the understanding and in reality.

CHAPTER III

God cannot be conceived not to exist.—God is that, than which nothing greater can be conceived.—That which can be conceived not to exist is not God.

And it assuredly exists so truly, that it cannot be conceived not to exist. For, it is possible to conceive of a being which cannot be conceived not to exist; and this is greater than one which can be conceived not to exist. Hence, if that, than which nothing greater can be conceived, can be conceived not to exist, it is not that, than which nothing greater can be conceived. But this is an irreconcilable contradiction. There is, then, so truly a being than which nothing greater can be conceived to exist, that it cannot even be conceived not to exist; and this being thou art, O Lord, our God.

So truly, therefore, dost thou exist, O Lord, my God, that thou canst not be conceived not to exist; and rightly. For, if a mind could conceive of a being better than thee, the creature would rise above the Creator; and this is most absurd. And, indeed, whatever else there is, except thee alone, can be conceived not to exist. To thee alone, therefore, it belongs to exist more truly than all other beings, and hence in a higher degree than all others. For, whatever else exists does not exist so truly, and hence in a less degree it belongs to it to exist. Why, then, has the fool said in his heart, there is no God (Psalms xiv. i), since it is so evident, to a rational mind, that thou dost exist in the highest degree of all? Why, except that he is dull and a fool?

CHAPTER IV

How the fool has said in his heart what cannot be conceived.—A thing may be conceived in two ways: (1) when the word signifying it is conceived; (2) when the thing itself is understood. As far as the word goes, God can be conceived not to exist; in reality he cannot.

But how has the fool said in his heart what he could not conceive; or how is it that he could not conceive what he said in his heart? since it is the same to say in the heart, and to conceive.

But, if really, nay, since really, he both conceived, because he said in his heart; and did not say in his heart, because he could not conceive; there is more than one way in which a thing is said in the heart or conceived. For, in one sense, an object is conceived, when the word signifying it is conceived; and in another, when the very entity, which the object is, is understood.

In the former sense, then, God can be conceived not to exist; but in the latter, not at all. For no one who understands what fire and water are can conceive fire to be water, in accordance with the nature of the facts themselves, although this is possible according to the words. So, then, no one who understands what God is can conceive that God does not exist; although he says these words in his heart, either without any or with some foreign, signification. For, God is that than which a greater cannot be conceived. And he who thoroughly understands this, assuredly understands that this being so truly exists, that not even in concept can it be non-existent. Therefore, he who understands that God so exists, cannot conceive that he does not exist.

I thank thee, gracious Lord, I thank thee; because what I formerly believed by thy bounty, I now so understand by thine illumination, that if I were unwilling to believe that thou dost exist, I should not be able not to understand this to be true.

The Five Ways

St. Thomas Aquinas

The existence of God can be proved in five ways.

The first and more manifest way is the argument from motion. It is certain, and evident to our senses, that in the world some things are in motion. Now whatever is moved is moved by another, for nothing can be moved except it is in potentiality to that towards which it is moved; whereas a thing moves inasmuch as it is in act. For motion is nothing else than the reduction of something from potentiality to actuality. But nothing can be reduced from potentiality to actuality, except by something in a state of actuality. Thus that which is actually hot, as fire, makes wood, which is potentially hot, to be actually hot, and thereby moves and changes it. Now it is not possible that the same thing should be at once in actuality and potentiality in the same respect, but only in different respects. For what is actually hot cannot simultaneously be potentially hot; but it is simultaneously potentially cold. It is therefore impossible that in the same respect and in the same way a thing should be both mover and moved, i.e., that it should move itself. Therefore, whatever is moved must be moved by another. If that by which it is moved be itself moved, then this also must needs be moved by another, and that by another again. But this cannot go on to infinity, because then there would be no first mover, and, consequently, no other mover, seeing that subsequent movers move only inasmuch as they are moved by the first mover; as the staff moves only because it is moved by the hand. Therefore it is necessary to arrive at a first mover, moved by no other; and this everyone understands to be God.

The second way is from the nature of efficient cause. In the world of sensible things we find there is an order of efficient causes. There is no case known (neither is it, indeed, possible) in which a thing is found to be the efficient cause of itself; for so it would be prior to itself, which is impossible. Now in efficient causes it is not possible to go on to infinity, because in all efficient causes following in order, the first is the cause of the intermediate cause, and the intermediate is the cause of the ultimate cause, whether the intermediate cause be several, or one only. Now to take away the cause is to take away the effect. Therefore, if there be no

From Anton C. Pegis, ed., *Introduction to St. Thomas Aquinas* (New York: The Modern Library, 1948), pp. 25-27. Reprinted by permission of the editor.

first cause among efficient causes, there will be no ultimate, nor any intermediate, cause. But if in efficient causes it is possible to go on to infinity, there will be no first efficient cause, neither will there be an ultimate effect, nor any intermediate efficient causes; all of which is plainly false. Therefore it is necessary to admit a first efficient cause, to which everyone gives the name of God.

The third way is taken from possibility and necessity, and runs thus. We find in nature things that are possible to be and not to be, since they are found to be generated, and to be corrupted, and consequently, it is possible for them to be and not to be. But it is impossible for these always to exist, for that which can not-be at some time is not. Therefore, if everything can not-be, then at one time there was nothing in existence. Now if this were true, even now there would be nothing in existence, because that which does not exist begins to exist only through something already existing. Therefore, if at one time nothing was in existence, it would have been impossible for anything to have begun to exist; and thus even now nothing would be in existence—which is absurd. Therefore, not all beings are merely possible, but there must exist something the existence of which is necessary. But every necessary thing either has its necessity caused by another, or not. Now it is impossible to go on to infinity in necessary things which have their necessity caused by another, as has been already proved in regard to efficient causes. Therefore we cannot but admit the existence of some being having of itself its own necessity, and not receiving it from another, but rather causing in others their necessity. This all men speak of as God.

The fourth way is taken from the gradation to be found in things. Among beings there are some more and some less good, true, noble, and the like. But *more* and *less* are predicted of different things according as they resemble in their different ways something which is the maximum, as a thing is said to be hotter according as it more nearly resembles that which is hottest; so that there is something which is truest, something best, something noblest, and, consequently, something which is most being, for those things that are greatest in truth are greatest in being, as it is written in *Metaph.* ii.[1] Now the maximum in any genus is the cause of all in that genus, as fire, which is the maximum of heat, is the cause of all hot things, as is said in the same book.[2] Therefore there must also be something which is to all beings the cause of their being, goodness, and every other perfection; and this we call God.

The fifth way is taken from the governance of the world. We see that things which lack knowledge, such as natural bodies, act for an end, and this is evident from their acting always, or nearly always, in the same way, so as to obtain the best result. Hence it is plain that they achieve their end, not fortuitously, but designedly. Now whatever lacks knowledge cannot move towards an end, unless it be directed by some being endowed with knowledge and intelligence; as the arrow is directed by the archer. Therefore some intelligent being exists by whom all natural things are directed to their end; and this being we call God.

NOTES

1. *Metaph.* Ia, i (993b 30).
2. *Ibid.* (993b 25).

Is the World Intelligently Designed?

David Hume

Not to lose any time in circumlocutions, said Cleanthes, addressing himself to Demea, much less in replying to the pious declamations of Philo, I shall briefly explain how I conceive this matter. Look round the world: Contemplate the whole and every part of it. You will find it to be nothing but one great machine, subdivided into an infinite number of lesser machines, which again admit of subdivisions to a degree beyond what human senses and faculties can trace and explain. All these various machines, and even their most minute parts, are adjusted to each other with an accuracy which ravishes into admiration all men who have ever contemplated them. The curious adapting of means to ends, throughout all nature, resembles exactly, though it much exceeds, the productions of human contrivance—of human design, thought, wisdom, and intelligence. Since therefore the effects resemble each other, we are led to infer, by all the rules of analogy, that the causes also resemble, and that the Author of Nature is somewhat similar to the mind of man, though possessed of much larger faculties, proportioned to the grandeur of the work which he has executed. By this argument *a posteriori*, and by this argument alone, do we prove at once the existence of a Deity and his similarity to human mind and intelligence.

I shall be so free, Cleanthes, said Demea, as to tell you that from the beginning I could not approve of your conclusion concerning the similarity of the Deity to men, still less can I approve of the mediums by which you endeavor to establish it. What! No demonstration of the Being of God! No abstract arguments! No proofs *a priori*! Are these which have hitherto been so much insisted on by philosophers all fallacy, all sophism? Can we reach no farther in this subject than experience and probability? I will say not that this is betraying the cause of a Deity; but surely, by this affected candor, you give advantages to atheists

From *Dialogues Concerning Natural Religion,* ed. Nelson Pike (Indianapolis: Bobbs-Merrill, 1970), pp. 22-24, 53, 68-74. Reprinted by permission of the publisher.

which they never could obtain by the mere dint of argument and reasoning.

What I chiefly scruple in this subject, said Philo, is not so much that all religious arrangements are by Cleanthes reduced to experience, as that they appear not to be even the most certain and irrefragable of that inferior kind. That a stone will fall, that fire will burn, that the earth has solidity, we have observed a thousand and a thousand times; and when any new instance of this nature is presented, we draw without hesitation the accustomed inference. The exact similarity of the cases gives us a perfect assurance of a similar event, and a stronger evidence is never desired nor sought after. But wherever you depart, in the least, from the similarity of the cases, you diminish proportionably the evidence; and may at last bring it to a very weak *analogy,* which is confessedly liable to error and uncertainty. After having experienced the circulation of the blood in human creatures, we make no doubt that it takes place in Titius and Maevius; but from its circulation in frogs and fishes it is only a presumption, though a strong one, from analogy that it takes place in men and other animals. The analogical reasoning is much weaker when we infer the circulation of the sap in vegetables from our experience that the blood circulates in animals; and those who hastily followed that imperfect analogy are found, by more accurate experiments, to have been mistaken.

If we see a house, Cleanthes, we conclude, with the greatest certainty, that it had an architect or builder because this is precisely that species of effect which we have experienced to proceed from that species of cause. But surely you will not affirm that the universe bears such a resemblance to a house that we can with the same certainty infer a similar cause, or that the analogy is here entire and perfect. The dissimilitude is so striking that the utmost you can here pretend to is a guess, a conjecture, a presumption concerning a similar cause; and how that pretension will be received in the world, I leave you to consider.

PART V

But to show you still more inconveniences, continued Philo, in your anthropomorphism, please to take a new survey of your principles. *Like effects prove like causes.* This is the experimental argument; and this, you say too, is the sole theological argument. Now it is certain that the liker the effects are which are seen and the liker the causes which are inferred, the stronger is the argument. Every departure on either side diminishes the probability and renders the experiment less conclusive. You cannot doubt of the principle; neither ought you to reject its consequences.

In a word, Cleanthes, a man who follows your hypothesis is able, perhaps, to assert or conjecture that the universe sometime arose from something like design; but beyond that position he cannot ascertain one single circumstance, and is left afterwards to fix every point of his theology by the utmost license of fancy and hypothesis. This world, for aught he knows, is very faulty and imperfect, compared to a superior standard; and was only the first rude essay of some infant deity who afterwards abandoned it, ashamed of his lame performance; it is the work only of some dependent, inferior deity, and is the object of derision to his super-iors; it is the production of old age and dotage in some superannuated deity; and ever since his death has run on at adventures, from the first impulse and active force which it received from him. You justly give signs of horror, Demea, at these strange suppositions; but these, and a thousand more of the same kind, are Cleanthes' suppositions, not mine. From the moment the attributes of the Deity are supposed finite, all these have place. And I cannot, for my part, think that so wild and unsettled a system of theology is, in any respect, preferable to none at all.

These suppositions I absolutely disown, cried Cleanthes; they strike me, however, with no horror, especially when proposed in that rambling way in which they drop from you. On the contrary, they give me plea-sure when I see that, by the utmost indulgence of your imagination, you never get rid of the hypothesis of design in the universe, but are obliged at every turn to have recourse to it. To this concession I adhere steadily; and this I regard as a sufficient foundation for religion.

PART VIII

Without any great effort of thought, I believe that I could, [continued Philo] in an instant, propose other systems of cosmogony which would have some faint appearance of truth; though it is a thousand, a million to one if either yours or any one of mine be the true system.

For instance, what if I should revive the old Epicurean hypothesis? This is commonly, and I believe justly, esteemed the most absurd system that has yet been proposed; yet I know not whether, with a few altera-tions, it might not be brought to bear a faint appearance of probability. Instead of supposing matter infinite, as Epicurus did, let us suppose it finite. A finite number of particles is only susceptible of finite trans-positions; and it must happen, in an eternal duration, that every possible order or position must be tried an infinite number of times. This world, therefore, with all its events, even the most minute, has before been produced and destroyed, and will again be produced and destroyed, with-out any bounds and limitations. No one who has a conception of the powers of infinite, in comparison of finite, will ever scruple this de-termination.

But this supposes, said Demea, that matter can acquire motion without any voluntary agent or first mover.

And where is the difficulty, replied Philo, of that supposition? Every event, before experience, is equally difficult and incomprehensible; and every event, after experience, is equally easy and intelligible. Motion, in many instances, from gravity, from elasticity, from electricity, begins in matter, without any known voluntary agent; and to suppose always, in these cases, an unknown voluntary agent is mere hypothesis—and hypothesis attended with no advantages. The beginning of motion in matter itself is as conceivable *a priori* as its communication from mind and intelligence.

Besides, why may not motion have been propagated by impulse through all eternity, and the same stock of it, or nearly the same, be still upheld in the universe? As much as is lost by the composition of motion, as much is gained by its resolution. And whatever the causes are, the fact is certain that matter is and always has been in continual agitation, as far as human experience or tradition reaches. There is not probably, at present, in the whole universe, one particle of matter at absolute rest.

And this very consideration, too, continued Philo, which we have stumbled on in the course of the argument suggests a new hypothesis of cosmogony that is not absolutely absurd and improbable. Is there a system, an order, an economy of things, by which matter can preserve that perpetual agitation which seems essential to it, and yet maintain a constancy in the forms which it produces? There certainly is such an economy, for this is actually the case with the present world. The continual motion of matter, therefore, in less than infinite transpositions, must produce this economy or order; and, by its very nature, that order, when once established, supports itself for many ages if not to eternity. But wherever matter is so poised, arranged, and adjusted, as to continue in perpetual motion, and yet preserve a constancy in the forms, its situation must, of necessity, have all the same appearance of art and contrivance which we observe at present. All the parts of each form must have a relation to each other and to the whole; and the whole itself must have a relation to the other parts of the universe, to the element in which the form subsists, to the materials with which it repairs its waste and decay, and to every other form which is hostile or friendly. A defect in any of these particulars destroys the form; and the matter of which it is composed is again set loose, and is thrown into irregular motions and fermentations till it unite itself to some other regular form. If no such form be prepared to receive it, and if there be a great quantity of this corrupted matter in the universe, the universe itself is entirely disordered, whether it be the feeble embryo of a world in its first beginnings that is thus destroyed or the rotten carcass of one languishing in old age and infirmity. In either case, a chaos ensues till finite though innumerable revolutions produce, at last, some forms whose parts and organs are so adjusted as to support the forms amidst a continued succession of matter.

Suppose (for we shall endeavor to vary the expression) that matter were thrown into any position by a blind, unguided force; it is evident that this first position must, in all probability, be the most confused and most disorderly imaginable, without any resemblance to those works of human contrivance which, along with a symmetry of parts, discover an adjustment of means to ends and a tendency to self-preservation. If the actuating force cease after this operation, matter must remain forever in disorder, and continue an immense chaos, without any proportion or activity. But suppose that the actuating force, whatever it be, still continues in matter, this first position will immediately give place to a second which will likewise, in all probability, be as disorderly as the first, and so on through many sucessions of changes and revolutions. No particular order or position ever continues a moment unaltered. The original force, still remaining in activity, gives a perpetual restlessness to matter. Every possible situation is produced, and instantly destroyed. If a glimpse or dawn of order appears for a moment, it is instantly hurried away and confounded by that never-ceasing force which actuates every part of matter.

Thus the universe goes on for many ages in a continued succession of chaos and disorder. But is it not possible that it may settle at last, so as not to lose its motion and active force (for that we have supposed inherent in it), yet so as to preserve a uniformity of appearance, amidst the continual motion and fluctuation of its parts? This we find to be the case with the universe at present. Every individual is perpetually changing, and every part of every individual; and yet the whole remains, in appearance, the same. May we not hope for such a position or rather be assured of it from the eternal revolutions of unguided matter; and may not this account for all the appearing wisdom and contrivance which is in the universe? Let us contemplate the subject a little, and we shall find that this adjustment if attained by matter of a seeming stability in the forms, with a real and perpetual revolution or motion of parts, affords a plausible, if not a true, solution of the difficulty.

It is in vain, therefore, to insist upon the uses of the parts in animals or vegetables, and their curious adjustment to each other. I would fain know how an animal could subsist unless its parts were so adjusted? Do we not find that it immediately perishes whenever this adjustment ceases, and that its matter, corrupting, tries some new form? It happens indeed that the parts of the world are so well adjusted that some regular form immediately lays claim to this corrupted matter; and if it were not so, could the world subsist? Must it not dissolve, as well as the animal, and pass through new positions and situations till in great but finite succession it fall, at last, into the present or some such order?

It is well, replied Cleanthes, you told us that this hypothesis was suggested on a sudden, in the course of the argument. Had you had leisure to examine it, you would soon have perceived the insuperable objections to which it is exposed. No form, you say, can subsist unless it possess those powers and organs requisite for its subsistence; some new order or economy must be tried, and so on, without intermission, till at last some order which can support and maintain itself is fallen upon. But according to this hypothesis, whence arise the many conveniences and advantages which men and all animals possess? Two eyes, two ears are not absolutely necessary for the subsistence of the species. Human race might have been propagated and preserved without horses, dogs, cows, sheep, and those innumerable fruits and products which serve to our satisfaction and enjoyment. If no camels had been created for the use of man in the sandy deserts of Africa and Arabia, would the world have been dissolved? If no loadstone had been framed to give that wonderful and useful direction to the needle, would human society and the human kind have been immediately extinguished? Though the maxims of nature be in general very frugal, yet instances of this kind are far from being rare; and any one of them is a sufficient proof of design—and of a benevolent design—which gave rise to the order and arrangement of the universe.

At least, you may safely infer, said Philo, that the foregoing hypothesis is so far incomplete and imperfect, which I shall not scruple to allow. But can we ever reasonably expect greater success in any attempts of this nature? Or can we ever hope to erect a system of cosmogony that will be liable to no exceptions, and will contain no circumstance repugnant to our limited and imperfect experience of the analogy of nature? Your theory itself cannot surely pretend to any such advantage; even though you have run into *anthropomorphism,* the better to preserve a conformity to common experience. Let us once more put it to trial. In all instances which we have ever seen, ideas are copied from real objects, and are ectypal, not archetypal, to express myself in learned terms. You reverse this order and give thought the precedence. In all instances which we have ever seen, thought has no influence upon matter except where that matter is so conjoined with it as to have an equal reciprocal influence upon it. No animal can move immediately anything but the members of its own body; and, indeed, the equality of action and reaction seems to be an universal law of nature; but your theory implies a contradiction to this experience. These instances, with many more which it were easy to collect (particularly the supposition of a mind or system of thought that is eternal or, in other words, an animal ingenerable and immortal)—these instances, I say, may teach all of us sobriety in condemning each other, and let us see that as no system of this kind ought ever to be received from a slight analogy, so neither ought any to be rejected on account of a small incongruity. For that is an inconvenience from which we can justly pronounce no one to be exempted.

All religious systems, it is confessed, are subject to great and insuperable difficulties. Each disputant triumphs in his turn, while he carries on an offensive war, and exposes the absurdities, barbarities, and pernicious tenets of his antagonist. But all of them, on the whole, prepare a complete triumph for the *sceptic,* who tells them that no system ought ever to be embraced with regard to such subjects; for this plain reason, that no absurdity ought ever to be assented to with regard to any subject. A total suspense of judgment is here our only reasonable recourse. And if every attack, as is commonly observed, and no defence among theologians is successful, how complete must be *his* victory who remains always, with all mankind, on the offensive, and has himself no fixed station or abiding city which he is ever, on any occasion, obliged to defend?

RELIGIOUS EPISTEMOLOGY: EXPERIENCE

The Ascent to Mount Carmel

St. John of the Cross

The main theme and final goal: the soul's union with God.

This treatise deals with the manner in which a soul may prepare itself to attain to union with God. It gives useful advice and instruction, both to beginners and to those more advanced in the spiritual life, so that they may learn how to free themselves from all that is temporal and not weigh themselves down with the spiritual, and remain in that complete nakedness and freedom of the spirit which are necessary for union with God.

The entire doctrine which I intend to discuss in the Ascent to Mount Carmel is contained in the following stanzas, and they describe also the manner of ascending to the peak of the mountain, that is, that high state of perfection which we here designate as the union of the soul with God. The poem reads as follows:

1

In a dark night,
My longing heart aglow with love,
—Oh, blessed lot!—
I went forth unseen
From my house that was at last in deepest rest.

2

Secure and protected by darkness,
I climbed the secret ladder, in disguise,
—Oh, blessed lot!—
In darkness, veiled and concealed I went
Leaving behind my house in deepest rest.

From St. John of the Cross, *The Dark Night of the Soul*, trans., by Kurt F. Reinhardt (New York: Frederick Ungar Publishing Co., 1957), pp. 1-3, 32-44, 51-53. Reprinted by permission of the publisher.

3

Oh, blissful night!
Oh, secret night, when I remained unseeing and unseen,
When the flame burning in my heart
Was my only light and guide.

4

This inward light,
A safer guide than noonday's brightness,
Showed me the place where He awaited me
—My soul's Beloved—
A place of solitude.

5

Oh, night that guided me!
Oh, night more lovely than the rosy dawn!
Oh, night whose darkness guided me
To that sweet union,
In which the lover and Beloved are made one.

6

Upon the flower of my breast,
Kept undefiled for Him alone,
He fell asleep,
While I was waking,
Caressing Him with gentle cedars' breeze.

7

And when Aurora's breath
Began to spread His curled hair,
His gentle hand
He placed upon my neck,
And all my senses were in bliss suspended.

8

Forgetful of myself,
My head reclined on my Beloved,
The world was gone
And all my cares at rest,
Forgotten all my grief among the lilies.

CHAPTER IV

To be guided by faith, the soul must be in darkness.

It seems to be appropriate at this juncture to describe in greater detail the darkness that must be in the soul if it wishes to enter into this abyss of faith. If a soul aspires to supernatural transformation, it is clear that it must be far removed from all that is contained in its sensual and rational nature. For we call supernatural that which transcends nature, so that the natural is left behind. The soul must completely and by its own will empty itself of everything that can be contained in it with respect to affection and volition, in such a way that, regardless of how many supernatural gifts it may receive, it will remain detached from them and in darkness. It must be like a blind man, finding its only support in dark faith, taking it as its guide and light, and leaning upon none of the things which it understands, enjoys, feels, and imagines. And if the soul does not make itself blind in this manner, remaining in total darkness, it will not attain to those greater things which are taught by faith.

When St. Paul said: "He who would come into the presence of God, must first believe that God exists" (Heb. 11:6), he meant by this that he who aspires to being joined with God in perfect union must not walk by the way of understanding, nor lean on either joyful sensations, or inner feelings, or imagination, but he must believe in God's Being, which is hidden as much from the understanding as from desire, imagination and any other sensory apperception, nor can it be known at all in this life in its essential nature. Even the highest concerning God that can be felt and perceived in this life is infinitely remote from Him and from the pure possession of Him. The goal which the soul pursues is thus beyond even the highest things that can be known or perceived. And the soul must therefore pass beyond everything to a state of unknowing.

The soul which attains to this state makes no longer use of any particular ways or methods—whether they relate to understanding, apperception, or feeling—although it bears within itself all possible ways, after the manner of one who owns nothing, yet possesses all things.

On this road, then, the soul, by becoming blind in its faculties, will see the light, as Our Saviour says in the Gospel: "I have come into this world for judgment, that those who are blind should see, and those who see should become blind" (John 9:39). This saying evidently applies to this spiritual road, where the soul which has entered into darkness and has become blind in all its natural lights, will learn to see supernaturally.

And in order that we may proceed from here on with less confusion, it appears necessary to describe in the following chapter what we mean when we speak of the union of the soul with God. For, once this is clearly understood, what we shall have to say in subsequent chapters will become a great deal more intelligible.

CHAPTER V

The union of the soul with God is a union of love and of likeness, not division of substance.

To understand, then, the nature of this union, it must be known that God dwells or is present substantially [*per essentiam*] in every soul, even in the soul of the greatest sinner. This kind of union between God and all His creatures is never lacking, since it is in and by this union that He sustains their being; and if it were ever lacking, these creatures would immediately cease to be and would fall back into nothingness. Thus, if we here speak of the union of the soul with God, we do not have in mind this ever-present substantial union, but we do mean that union of the soul with God which is consummated in the soul's transformation in God—a union which can come about only when the soul attains to a likeness with God by virtue of love. We shall therefore call this the union of likeness, to distinguish it from the union of substance or essence. The former is supernatural, the latter natural. And the supernatural union comes about when the two wills—that of the soul and that of God—are conformed in one, so that there is nothing in the one that is repugnant to the other. Thus, when the soul rids itself totally of that which is repugnant to and not in conformity with the Divine will, it is transformed in God through love.

This applies not only to whatever is repugnant to God in human action, but also in habit, so that the soul must not only desist from all voluntary acts of imperfection but must also completely overcome the acquired habits of these imperfections. And since no creature nor the actions or capabilities of any creature can ever measure up or attain to that which is God, the soul must be stripped of all creaturely attachments as well as of its own activities and capabilities—that is to say, of its understanding, its likings, and its feelings—so that, when all that which is unlike God and unconformed to Him is cast out, the soul may then receive the likeness of God.

Supernatural being is communicated only by love and grace. Not all souls, however, abide in God's love and grace, and those who do abide in them do not possess them in the same degree; for some attain higher degrees of love than others. And thus, God communicates Himself most to that soul which has progressed farthest in love and has most conformed its will to God's will. And that soul which has attained to a total conformity and likeness of its will and God's will is totally united with Him and supernaturally transformed in Him.

Let me clarify [the nature of this union] by a simile. Picture a ray of sunlight that is striking a window. Now if the window is coated with stains or vapors, the ray will be unable to illumine it and transform it into its own light; this it could do only if the window were stainless and pure. And the greater or lesser degree of illumination will be strictly in proportion to the window's greater or lesser purity; and this will be so, not because of the ray of sunlight but because of the condition of the window. Thus, if the window were entirely clean and pure, the ray would transform and illumine it in such a way that it would become almost undistinguishable from the brightness of the ray and would diffuse the same light as the ray. And yet, however much the window may resemble the ray of sunlight, it actually retains its own distinct nature. But this does not prevent us from saying that this window is luminous as a ray of the sun or is sunlight by participation. Now the soul is like this window: the Divine light of the Being of God is unceasingly beating upon it, or, to use a better expression, the Divine light is ever dwelling in it.

When the soul thus allows God to work in it, it will soon be transformed and transfigured in God, and God will communicate to it His supernatural Being in such a way that the soul appears to be God Himself, and it will indeed be God by participation. Yet it remains true nevertheless that the soul's natural being—notwithstanding the soul's supernatural transformation—remains as distinct from the Being of God as it was before, even as the window has and retains a nature of its own, distinct from the nature of the ray, although it owes its luminosity to the light of the sun.

This consideration should make it clearer why a soul can not dispose itself for this union by either understanding, or sensory apperception, or inner feelings and imaginings, or by any other experiences relating either to God or to anything else, but only by purity and love, that is, by perfect resignation and total detachment from all things for the sake of God alone. And as there can be no perfect transformation unless there be perfect purity, the soul will not be perfect unless it be totally cleansed and wholly pure.

Those souls [who attain to Divine union] do so according to their greater or smaller capacity and thus not in the same degree; and the degree of union depends also on what the Lord wishes to grant to each soul. And it is similar in the beatific vision: though some souls will have a more perfect vision of God in Heaven than others, they all see God, and all are content, since their capacity is satisfied. And in this life, too, all souls [who have attained to the state of perfection] will be equally satisfied, each one according to its knowledge of God and thus according to its capacity. A soul, on the other hand, that does not attain to a degree of purity corresponding to its capacity, will never find true peace and contentment.

CHAPTER VI

The three theological virtues perfect the three faculties of the soul.

We shall now endeavor to show how the three faculties of the soul—understanding, memory, and will—are brought into this spiritual night, which is the means leading to the end of Divine union. To do this, it is necessary first of all to explain in this chapter how the three theological virtues—faith, hope, and love [*caritas*]—by means of which the soul is united with God according to its faculties, produce an identical emptiness and darkness, each one with respect to its corresponding faculty. Thus, faith produces darkness in the understanding; hope, in the memory; love, in the will. Subsequently, we shall describe how the understanding is perfected in the darkness of faith, and memory in the emptiness of hope; and we shall then show how the will must be voided and stripped of all affection in order to move toward God. For, as we have pointed out, the soul is united with God in this life not through the understanding, nor through joyous feelings, nor through imagination, nor through any other sensory experience; but only through faith, which perfects the understanding; through hope, which prefects the memory; and through love, which perfects the will.

Faith, then, tells us what cannot be comprehended with the [natural] *understanding.* According to St. Paul, "Faith is the substance of our hopes; it convinces us of things we cannot see" (Heb. 11:1). Although the understanding may give its consent with a firm and perfect assurance, the things of faith are not revealed to the understanding; for, if they were revealed to it, there would be no need for faith. Wherefore, though faith gives certainty to the understanding, it does not illumine it, but leaves it in darkness.

As to *hope*, there is no doubt that it in its turn plunges the *memory* into emptiness and darkness with respect to both things here below and things above. For hope has always to do with that which is not yet in our possession, since, if we already possessed it, there would no longer be room for hope. This is what St. Paul means when he says: "Hope would no longer be hope if its object were in plain view; for how could a man still hope for something that is fully seen [that is, fully possessed]?" (Rom. 8:24).

And, similarly, *love* empties the *will* of all things, since it obliges us to love God above them all; this, however, we cannot do unless we detach our affection from all of them in order to attach it wholly to God. Wherefore, Christ tells us through the mouth of St. Luke: "No one can be My disciple who does not detach himself from all that he [wilfully] possesses." (Luke, 14:33). All three of these virtues, then, plunge the soul into darkness and emptiness with respect to all things.

This, then, is the spiritual night which we have called *active;* for all the soul is able to do to enter into this night, it does by its own power. And as, when we were speaking of the night of sense, we described a method of emptying the faculties of sense of all the objects of sense— so that the soul might advance from its point of departure to the intermediate state of faith—so also, in this spiritual night, we shall, with Divine aid, describe a method whereby the spiritual faculties are emptied and purified of all that is not God. As a result, the spiritual faculties will then be placed in the darkness of the three [theological] virtues, which, as we have seen, are the means that dispose the soul for its union with God. And it should be noted that I am now speaking in particular to those who have begun to enter the state of contemplation.

CHAPTER VII

The narrow road; detachment of the understanding; spiritual poverty.

Speaking of the road [that leads to eternal life], Our Saviour said: "How small is the gate and how narrow the road that leads to Life; and there are few who find it" (Matt. 7:14). Now what Christ says of the small gate, we may understand in relation to the sensual part of man; and what He says of the narrow road, may be understood in relation to the spiritual or rational part. And the reason for His saying that "there are few who find it" is that there are few who know how to enter and who actually desire to enter into this total nakedness and emptiness of the spirit. For this path that leads to the high mountain of perfection is steep and narrow and therefore requires travellers who are not weighed down and encumbered by any cares for either the lower things of sense or the higher things of the spirit. Since this is an undertaking in which the prize of our search is God alone, He alone must be the object of our striving and our victory.

Hence we can see clearly that the soul which travels on this road must not only be free from all creaturely attachments but must also be spiritually poor and as dead to its own self. This is why Our Lord taught us through the mouth of St. Mark that priceless doctrine which, because of its great importance and because it specifically applies to our purpose, I shall quote here in full and then explain in its true spiritual meaning.

Our Lord says: "If any man wishes to go My way, let him deny his own self, and take up his cross, and follow Me. He who tries to save his life will lose it; but he who loses his life for My sake will save it" (Mark 8:34–35).

I wish someone would properly teach us how to understand, practise, and inwardly grasp the true meaning and significance of this counsel, so that spiritual persons would see how different is the method they should employ on this road from what many of them regard as proper. While some believe that any kind of withdrawal from the world and any external reform suffice, others are content with practising the virtues and continuing in prayer and penance; but neither attain to that nakedness, self-denial, and spiritual poverty which the Lord here commends to us; for they prefer feeding and clothing their natural selves with spiritual feelings and consolations to emptying themselves of all things and renouncing their natural selves for God's sake. Or they think that it suffices to strip their natural selves of worldly things, without purifying themselves by the total renunciation also of spiritual attachments. Thus, when they get a glimpse of this concrete and perfect life of the spirit—which manifests itself in the complete absence of all sweetness, in aridity, distaste, and in the many trials that are the true spiritual cross—they flee from it as from death. What they seek in their communion with God is sweet and delectable feelings; but this is a sort of spiritual gluttony rather than self-denial and spiritual poverty. As far as their spirituality is concerned, they become enemies of Christ. They seek themselves in God, which is the very opposite of love; for to seek oneself in God is to seek the favors and refreshing delights of God, whereas to seek God in oneself is to incline oneself to choose, for Christ's sake, all that is most distasteful; and this is love of God.

And when Our Lord said that he who tries to save his life will lose it, He meant that he who desires to possess anything for himself will lose it; whereas he who for Christ's sake renounces all that his will can desire and enjoy, and chooses that which is most like to the Cross, will save his life. This is precisely what His Majesty taught to those two disciples [the sons of Zebedee] who asked that they be allowed a place on His right and on His left. He answered their request for such glory by offering them the cup of which He had to drink, as a thing more precious and more secure on this earth than any joy of possession.

To drink of this cup, however, is to die to the natural self by detachment and self-annihilation, so that the soul may be able to travel by this narrow path unimpeded, since there remains to it nothing but self-denial and the Cross. And this Cross is the pilgrim's staff on which the soul may lean on its way to God and which greatly eases its burden and travail. Wherefore Our Lord said through the mouth of St. Matthew: "My yoke is easy, and My burden is light" (Matt. 11:30). For if a man resolves to carry this cross willingly, that is, if he is truly determined to undergo and bear hardships and trials for God's sake, he will find in them great solace and sweetness. If, on the other hand, he desires to possess anything or remains attached to anything whatsover, his self is not totally stripped and emptied of all things, and he will not be able to continue his upward journey on this narrow path. For progress [in the spiritual life] can be made only by imitating Christ, Who is the Way, the Truth, and the Life; and no one can come to the Father, except through Christ (cf. John 14:6).

Christ, then, is the Way, and this way is death to the natural self in both sense and spirit. And I shall now try to explain how we must die [to our natural selves], following the example of Christ, Who is our guiding light.

First, it is certain that, as far as the senses are concerned, He died (spiritually) in His life and (naturally) in His death. For, as He said, He had not in His life where to lay His head, and in His death He had even less.

Second, it is equally certain that in the hour of His death He felt annihilated and abandoned also in His soul, deprived of all consolation and help, since His Father left His humanity in a state of such complete aridity that the cry "My God, My God, why hast Thou forsaken Me?" (Matt. 27:46) forced itself upon His lips. This was, with respect to His sensory nature, the greatest desolation He had suffered in His life. And yet, it was then that he wrought the greatest work of His entire life, greater than any of His miracles and other mighty deeds—the reconciliation and union of the human race with God, through grace.

The words of David, "I was reduced to nothingness and unknowing," (Ps. 72:22), point to the mystery of the small gate and the narrow way, so that the truly spiritual man may learn to understand the way of Christ, the way of union with God. He will learn from these words that the more he becomes as nothing, the more intimately he is united with God and the greater is the work that he accomplishes. This union, then, consists not in delights, consolations, and sweet spiritual feelings, but in a living sensual and spiritual, internal and external, death of the cross.

Mysticism

William James

Over and over again in these lectures I have raised points and left
them open and unfinished until we should have come to the subject
of Mysticism. Some of you, I fear, may have smiled as you noted my
reiterated postponements. But now the hour has come when mysticism
must be faced in good earnest, and those broken threads wound up
together. One may say truly, I think, that personal religious experience
has its root and centre in mystical states of consciousness; so for us,
who in these lectures are treating personal experience as the exclusive
subject of our study, such states of consciousness ought to form the
vital chapter from which the other chapters get their light. Whether
my treatment of mystical states will shed more light or darkness, I do
not know, for my own constitution shuts me out from their enjoyment
almost entirely, and I can speak of them only at second hand. But though
forced to look upon the subject so externally, I will be as objective and
receptive as I can; and I think I shall at least succeed in convincing
you of the reality of the states in question, and of the paramount importance of their function.

First of all, then I ask, What does the expression "mystical states of
consciousness" mean? How do we part off mystical states from other
states?

The words "mysticism" and "mystical" are often used as terms of
mere reproach, to throw at any opinion which we regard as vague and
vast and sentimental, and without a base in either facts or logic. For
some writers a "mystic" is any person who believes in thought-transfer-
ence, or spirit-return. Employed in this way the word has little value:
there are too many less ambiguous synonyms. So, to keep it useful by
restricting it, I will do what I did in the case of the word "religion,"
and simply propose to you four marks which, when an experience has
them, may justify us in calling it mystical for the purpose of the present
lectures. In this way we shall save verbal disputation, and the recrimi-
nations that generally go therewith.

1. *Ineffability.*—The handiest of the marks by which I classify a state
of mind as mystical is negative. The subject of it immediately says that
it defies expression, that no adequate report of its contents can be given
in words. It follows from this that its quality must be directly experienced; it cannot be imparted or transferred to others. In this peculiarity

From *The Varieties of Religious Experience* by William James. Reprinted by permission of the David McKay Company, Inc.

mystical states are more like states of feeling than like states of intellect. No one can make clear to another who has never had a certain feeling, in what the quality or worth of it consists. One must have musical ears to know the value of a symphony; one must have been in love one's self to understand a lover's state of mind. Lacking the heart or ear, we cannot interpret the musician or the lover justly, and are even likely to consider him weak minded or absurd. The mystic finds that most of us accord to his experiences an equally incompetent treatment.

2. *Noetic quality.*—Although so similar to states of feeling, mystical states seem to those who experience them to be also states of knowledge. They are states of insight into depths of truth unplumbed by the discursive intellect. They are illuminations, revelations, full of significance and importance, all inarticulate though they remain; and as a rule they carry with them a curious sense of authority for aftertime.

These two characters will entitle any state to be called mystical, in the sense in which I use the word. Two other qualities are less sharply marked, but are usually found. These are:—

3. *Transiency.*—Mystical states cannot be sustained for long. Except in rare instances, half an hour, or at most an hour or two, seems to be the limit beyond which they fade into the light of common day. Often, when faded, their quality can but imperfectly be reproduced in memory; but when they recur it is recognized; and from one recurrence to another it is susceptible of continuous development in what is felt as inner richness and importance.

4. *Passivity.*—Although the oncoming of mystical states may be facilitated by preliminary voluntary operations, as by fixing the attention, or going through certain bodily performances, or in other ways which manuals of mysticism prescribe; yet when the characteristic sort of consciousness once has set in, the mystic feels as if his own will were in abeyance, and indeed sometimes as if he were grasped and held by a superior power. This latter peculiarity connects mystical states with certain definite phenomena of secondary or alternative personality, such as prophetic speech, automatic writing, or the mediumistic trance. When these latter conditions are well pronounced, however, there may be no recollection whatever of the phenomenon, and it may have no significance for the subject's usual inner life, to which, as it were, it makes a mere interruption. Mystical states, strictly so-called, are never merely interruptive. Some memory of their content always remains, and a profound sense of their importance. They modify the inner life of the subject between the times of their recurrence. Sharp divisions in this region are, however, difficult to make, and we find all sorts of gradations and mixtures.

These four characteristics are sufficient to mark out a group of states of consciousness peculiar enough to deserve a special name and to call for careful study. Let it then be called the mystical group.

Our next step should be to gain acquaintance with some typical examples. Professional mystics at the height of their development have often elaborately organized experiences and a philosophy based thereupon. But you remember what I said in my first lecture: phenomena are best understood when placed within their series, studied in their germ and in their over-ripe decay, and compared with their exaggerated and degenerated kindred. The range of mystical experience is very wide, much too wide for us to cover in the time at our disposal. Yet the method of serial study is so essential for interpretation that if we really wish to reach conclusions we must use it. I will begin, therefore, with phenomena which claim no special religious significance, and end with those of which the religious pretensions are extreme.

The simplest rudiment of mystical experience would seem to be that deepened sense of the significance of a maxim or formula which occasionally sweeps over one. "I've heard that said all my life," we exclaim, "but I never realized its full meaning until now." "When a fellow-monk," said Luther, "one day repeated the words of the Creed: 'I believe in the forgiveness of sins,' I saw the Scripture in an entirely new light; and straightway I felt as if I were born anew. It was as if I had found the door of paradise thrown wide open." [1] This sense of deeper significance is not confined to rational propositions. Single words,[2] and conjunctions of words, effects of light on land and sea, odors and musical sounds, all bring it when the mind is tuned aright. Most of us can remember the strangely moving power of passages in certain poems read when we were young, irrational doorways as they were through which the mystery of fact, the wildness and the pang of life, stole into our hearts and thrilled them. The words have now perhaps become mere polished surfaces for us; but lyric poetry and music are alive and significant only in proportion as they fetch these vague vistas of a life continuous with our own, beckoning and inviting, yet ever eluding our pursuit. We are alive or dead to the eternal inner message of the arts according as we have kept or lost this mystical susceptibility.

A more pronounced step forward on the mystical ladder is found in an extremely frequent phenomenon, that sudden feeling, namely, which sometimes sweeps over us, of having "been here before," as if at some indefinite past time, in just this place, with just these people, we were already saying just these things. As Tennyson writes:

> "Moreover, something is or seems
> That touches me with mystic gleams,
> Like glimpses of forgotten dreams—
>
> "Of something felt, like something here;
> Of something done, I know not where;
> Such as no language may declare." [3]

Sir James Crichton-Browne has given the technical name of "dreamy states" to these sudden invasions of vaguely reminiscent consciousness.[4] They bring a sense of mystery and of the metaphysical duality of things, and the feeling of an enlargement of perception which seems imminent but which never completes itself. In Dr. Crichton-Browne's opinion they connect themselves with the perplexed and scared disturbances of self-consciousness which occasionally precede epileptic attacks. I think that this learned alienist takes a rather absurdly alarmist view of an intrinsically insignificant phenomenon. He follows it along the downward ladder, to insanity; our path pursues the upward ladder chiefly. The divergence shows how important it is to neglect no part of a phenomenon's connections, for we make it appear admirable or dreadful according to the context by which we set it off.

The next step into mystical states carries us into a realm that public opinion and ethical philosophy have long since branded as pathological, though private practice and certain lyric strains of poetry seem still to bear witness to its ideality. I refer to the consciousness produced by intoxicants and anaesthetics, especially by alcohol. The sway of alcohol over mankind is unquestionably due to its power to stimulate the mystical faculties of human nature, usually crushed to earth by the cold facts and dry criticisms of the sober hour. Sobriety diminishes, discriminates, and says no; drunkenness expands, unites, and says yes. It is in fact the great exciter of the *Yes* function in man. It brings its votary from the chill periphery of things to the radiant core. It makes him for the moment one with truth. Not through mere perversity do men run after it. To the poor and the unlettered it stands in the place of symphony concerts and of literature; and it is part of the deeper mystery and tragedy of life that whiffs and gleams of something that we immediately recognize as excellent should be vouchsafed to so many of us only in the fleeting earlier phases of what in its totality is so degrading a poisoning. The drunken consciousness is one bit of the mystic consciousness, and our total opinion of it must find its place in our opinion of that larger whole.

Nitrous oxide and ether, especially nitrous oxide, when sufficiently diluted with air, stimulate the mystical consciousness in an extraordinary degree. Depth beyond depth of truth seems revealed to the inhaler. This truth fades out, however, or escapes, at the moment of coming to; and if any words remain over in which it seemed to clothe itself, they prove to be the veriest nonsense. Nevertheless, the sense of a profound meaning having been there persists; and I know more than one person who is persuaded that in the nitrous oxide trance we have a genuine metaphysical revelation.

Some years ago I myself made some observations on this aspect of nitrous oxide intoxication, and reported them in print. One conclusion was forced upon my mind at that time, and my impression of its truth has ever since remained unshaken. It is that our normal waking consciousness, rational consciousness as we call it, is but one special type of consciousness, whilst all about it, parted from it by the filmiest of screens, there lie potential forms of consciousness entirely different. We may go through life without suspecting their existence; but apply the requisite stimulus, and at a touch they are there in all their completeness, definite types of mentality which probably somewhere have their field of application and adaptation. No account of the universe in its totality can be final which leaves these other forms of consciousness quite disregarded. How to regard them is the question—for they are so discontinuous with ordinary consciousness. Yet they may determine attitudes though they cannot furnish formulas, and open a region though they fail to give a map. At any rate, they forbid a premature closing of our accounts with reality. Looking back on my own experiences, they all converge towards a kind of insight to which I cannot help ascribing some metaphysical significance. The keynote of it is invariably a reconciliation. It is as if the opposites of the world, whose contradictoriness and conflict make all our difficulties and troubles, were melted into unity. Not only do they, as contrasted species, belong to one and the same genus, but *one of the species,* the nobler and better one, *is itself the genus, and so soaks up and absorbs its opposite into itself.* This is a dark saying, I know, when thus expressed in terms of common logic, but I cannot wholly escape from its authority. I feel as if it must mean something, something like what the hegelian philosophy means, if one could only lay hold of it more clearly. Those who have ears to hear, let them hear; to me the living sense of its reality only comes in the artificial mystic state of mind.[5]

Certain aspects of nature seem to have a peculiar power of awakening such mystical moods. Most of the striking cases which I have collected have occurred out of doors. Literature has commemorated this fact in many passages of great beauty—this extract, for example, from Amiel's Journal Intime:—

> "Shall I ever again have any of those prodigious reveries which sometimes came to me in former days? One day, in youth, at sunrise, sitting in the ruins of the castle of Faucigny; and again in the mountains, under the noonday sun, above Lavey, lying at the foot of a tree and visited by three butterflies; once more at night upon the shingly shore of the Northern Ocean, my back upon the sand and my vision ranging through the milky way;—such grand and spacious, immortal, cosmogonic reveries, when one reaches to the stars, when one owns the infinite! Moments divine, ecstatic hours; in which our thought flies from world to world, pierces the great enigma, breathes with a respiration broad, tranquil, and deep as the respiration of the ocean, serene and limitless as the blue firmament; . . . instants of irresistible intuition in which one feels one's self great as the universe, and calm as a god. . . . What hours, what memories! The vestiges they leave behind are enough to fill us with belief and enthusiasm, as if they were visits of the Holy Ghost."

Even the least mystical of you must by this time be convinced of the existence of mystical moments as states of consciousness of an entirely specific quality, and of the deep impression which they make on those who have them. A Canadian psychiatrist, Dr. R. M. Bucke, gives to the more distinctly characterized of these phenomena the name of cosmic consciousness. "Cosmic consciousness in its more striking instances is not," Dr. Bucke says, "simply an expansion or extension of the self-conscious mind with which we are all familiar, but the superaddition of a function as distinct from any possessed by the average man as *self-consciousness* is distinct from any function possessed by one of the higher animals."

> "The prime characteristic of cosmic consciousness is a consciousness of the cosmos, that is, of the life and order of the universe. Along with the consciousness of the cosmos there occurs an intellectual enlightenment which alone would place the individual on a new plane of existence—would make him almost a member of a new species. To this is added a state of moral exaltation, an indescribable feeling of elevation, elation, and joyousness, and a quickening of the moral sense, which is fully as striking, and more important than is the enhanced intellectual power. With these come what may be called a sense of immortality, a consciousness of eternal life, not a conviction that he shall have this, but the consciousness that he has it already." [6]

We have now seen enough of this cosmic or mystic consciousness, as it comes sporadically. We must next pass to its methodical cultivation as an element of the religious life. Hindus, Buddhists, Mohammedans, and Christians all have cultivated it methodically.

In India, training in mystical insight has been known from time immemorial under the name of yoga. Yoga means the experimental union of the individual with the divine. It is based on persevering exercise; and the diet, posture, breathing, intellectual concentration, and moral discipline vary slightly in the different systems which teach it. The yogi, or disciple, who has by these means overcome the obscurations of his lower nature sufficiently, enters into the condition termed *samâdhi,* "and comes face to face with facts which no instinct or reason can ever know." He learns—

> "That the mind itself has a higher state of existence, beyond reason, a superconscious state, and that when the mind gets to that higher state, then this knowledge beyond reasoning comes. . . . All the different steps in yoga are intended to bring us scientifically to the superconscious state or Samâdhi. . . . Just as unconscious work is beneath consciousness, so there is another work which is above consciousness, and which, also, is not accompanied with the feeling of egoism. . . . There is no feeling of *I,* and yet the mind works, desireless, free from restlessness, objectless, bodiless. Then the Truth shines in its full effulgence, and we know ourselves—for Samâdhi lies potential in us all—for what we truly are, free, immortal, omnipotent, loosed from the finite, and its contrasts of good and evil altogether, and identical with the Atman or Universal Soul." [7]

The Vedantists say that one may stumble into superconsciousness sporadically, without the previous discipline, but it is then impure. Their test of its purity, like our test of religion's value, is empirical: its fruits must be good for life. When a man comes out of Samâdhi, they assure us that he remains "enlightened, a sage, a prophet, a saint, his whole character changed, his life changed, illumined." [8]

The Buddhists used the word "samâdhi" as well as the Hindus; but "dhyâna" is their special word for higher states of contemplation. There seem to be four stages recognized in dhyâna. The first stage comes through concentration of the mind upon one point. It excludes desire, but not discernment or judgment: it is still intellectual. In the second stage the intellectual functions drop off, and the satisfied sense of unity remains. In the third stage the satisfaction departs, and indifference begins, along with memory and self-consciousness. In the fourth stage the indifference, memory, and self-consciousness are perfected. [Just what "memory" and "self-consciousness" mean in this connection is doubtful. They cannot be the faculties familiar to us in the lower life.] Higher stages still of contemplation are mentioned—a region where there exists nothing, and where the mediator says: "There exists absolutely nothing," and stops. Then he reaches another region where he says: "There are neither ideas nor absence of ideas," and stops again. Then another region where, "having reached the end of both idea and perception, he stops finally." This would seem to be, not yet Nirvâna, but as close an approach to it as this life affords.[9]

In the Mohammedan world the Sufi sect and various dervish bodies are the possessors of the mystical tradition. The Sufis have existed in Persia from the earliest times, and as their pantheism is so at variance with the hot and rigid monotheism of the Arab mind, it has been suggested that Sufism must have been inoculated into Islam by Hindu influences. We Christians know little of Sufism, for its secrets are disclosed only to those initiated. To give its existence a certain liveliness in your minds, I will quote a Moslem document, and pass away from the subject.

Al-Ghazzali, a Persian philosopher and theologian, who flourished in the eleventh century, and ranks as one of the greatest doctors of the Moslem church, has left us one of the few autobiographies to be found outside of Christian literature. Strange that a species of book so abundant among ourselves should be so little represented elsewhere—the absence of strictly personal confessions is the chief difficulty to the purely literary student who would like to become acquainted with the inwardness of religions other than the Christian.

M. Schmölders has translated a part of Al-Ghazzali's autobiography into French: [10]—

> "The Science of the Sufis," says the Moslem author, "aims at detaching the heart from all that is not God, and at giving to it for sole occupation the meditation of the divine being. Theory being more easy for me than practice, I read [certain books] until I understood all that can be learned by study and hearsay. Then I recognized that what pertains most exclusively to their method is just what no study can grasp, but only transport, ecstasy, and the transformation of the soul. How great, for example, is the difference between knowing the definitions of health, of

satiety, with their causes and conditions, and being really healthy or filled. How different to know in what drunkenness consists—as being a state occasioned by a vapor that rises from the stomach—and *being* drunk effectively. Without doubt, the drunken man knows neither the definition of drunkenness nor what makes it interesting for science. Being drunk, he knows nothing; whilst the physician, although not drunk, knows well in what drunkenness consists, and what are its predisposing conditions. Similarly there is a difference between knowing that nature of abstinence, and *being* abstinent or having one's soul detached from the world.—Thus I had learned what words could teach of Sufism, but what was left could be learned neither by study nor through the ears, but solely by giving one's self up to ecstasy and leading a pious life.

"Reflecting on my situation, I found myself tied down by a multitude of bonds—temptations on every side. Considering my teaching, I found it was impure before God. I saw myself struggling with all my might to achieve glory and to spread my name. [Here follows an account of his six months' hesitation to break away from the conditions of his life at Bagdad, at the end of which he fell ill with a paralysis of the tongue.] Then, feeling my own weakness, and having entirely given up my own will, I repaired to God like a man in distress who has no more resources. He answered, as he answers the wretch who invokes him. My heart no longer felt any difficulty in renouncing glory, wealth, and my children. So I quitted Bagdad, and reserving from my fortune only what was indispensable for my subsistence, I distributed the rest. I went to Syria, where I remained about two years, with no other occupation than living in retreat and solitude, conquering my desires, combating my passions, training myself to purify my soul, to make my character perfect, to prepare my heart for meditating on God—all according to the methods of the Sufis, as I had read of them.

"This retreat only increased my desire to live in solitude, and to complete the purification of my heart and fit it for meditation. But the vicissitudes of the times, the affairs of the family, the need of subsistence, changed in some respects my primitive resolve, and interfered with my plans for a purely solitary life. I had never yet found myself completely in ecstasy, save in a few single hours; nevertheless, I kept the hope of attaining this state. Every time that the accidents led me astray, I sought to return; and in this situation I spent ten years. During this solitary state things were revealed to me which it is impossible either to describe or to point out. I recognized for certain that the Sufis are assuredly walking in the path of God. Both in their acts and in their inaction, whether internal or external, they are illumined by the light which proceeds from the prophetic source. The first condition for a Sufi is to purge his heart entirely of all that is not God. The next key of the contemplative life consists in the humble prayers which escape from the fervent soul, and in the meditations on God in which the heart is swallowed up entirely. But in reality this is only the beginning of the Sufi life, the end of Sufism being total absorption in God. The intuitions and all that precede are, so to speak, only the threshold for those who enter. From the beginning, revelations take place in so flagrant a shape that the Sufis see before them, whilst wide awake, the angels and the souls of the prophets. They hear their voices and obtain their favors. Then the transport rises from the perception of forms and figures to a degree which escapes all expression, and which no man may seek to give an account of without his words involving sin.

"Whosoever has had no experience of the transport knows of the true nature of prophetism nothing but the name. He may meanwhile be sure of its existence, both by experience and by what he hears the Sufis say. As there are men endowed only with the sensitive faculty who reject what is offered them in the way of objects of the pure understanding, so there are intellectual men who reject and avoid the things perceived by the prophetic faculty. A blind man can understand nothing of colors save what he has learned by narration and hearsay. Yet God has brought prophetism near to men in giving them all a state analogous to it in its principal characters. This state is sleep. If you were to tell a man who was himself without experience of such a phenomenon that there are people who at times swoon away so as to resemble dead men, and who [in dreams] yet perceive things that are hidden, he would deny it [and give his reasons]. Nevertheless, his arguments would be refuted by actual experience. Wherefore, just as the understanding is a stage of human life in which an eye opens to discern various intellectual objects uncomprehended by sensation; just so in the prophetic the sight is illumined by a light which uncovers hidden things and objects which the intellect fails to reach. The chief properties of prophetism are perceptible only during the transport, by those who embrace the Sufi life. The prophet is endowed with qualities to which you possess nothing analogous, and which consequently you cannot possibly understand. How should you know their true nature, since one knows only what one can comprehend? But the transport which one attains by the method of the Sufis is like an immediate perception, as if one touched the objects with one's hand." [11]

This incommunicableness of the transport is the keynote of all mysticism. Mystical truth exists for the individual who has the transport, but for no one else. In this, as I have said, it resembles the knowledge given to us in sensations more than that given by conceptual thought. Thought, with its remoteness and abstractness, has often enough in the history of philosophy been contrasted unfavorably with sensation. It is a commonplace of metaphysics that God's knowledge cannot be discursive but must be intuitive, that is, must be constructed more after the pattern of what in ourselves is called immediate feeling, than after that of proposition and judgment. But *our* immediate feelings have no content but what the five senses supply; and we have seen and shall see again that mystics may emphatically deny that the senses play any part in the very highest type of knowledge which their transports yield.

In the Christian church there have always been mystics. Although many of them have been viewed with suspicion some have gained favor in the eyes of the authorities. The experiences of these have been treated as precedents, and a codified system of mystical theology has been based upon them, in which everything legitimate finds its place.[12] The basis of the system is "orison" or meditation, the methodical elevation of the soul towards God. Through the practice of orison the higher levels of mystical experience may be attained. It is odd that Protestantism, especially evangelical Protestantism, should seemingly have abandoned everything methodical in this line. Apart from what prayer may lead to, Protestant mystical experience appears to have been almost exclusively sporadic. It has been left to our mind-curers to reintroduce methodical meditation into our religious life.

The first thing to be aimed at in orison is the mind's detachment from outer sensations, for these interfere with its concentration upon ideal things. Such manuals as Saint Ignatius's Spiritual Exercises recommend the disciple to expel sensation by a graduated series of efforts to imagine holy scenes. The acme of this kind of discipline would be a semi-hallucinatory mono-ideism—an imaginary figure of Christ, for example, coming fully to occupy the mind. Sensorial images of this sort, whether literal or symbolic, play an enormous part in mysticism.[13] But in certain cases imagery may fall away entirely, and in the very highest raptures it tends to do so. The state of consciousness becomes then insusceptible of any verbal description. Mystical teachers are unanimous as to this. Saint John of the Cross, for instance, one of the best of them, thus describes the condition called the "union of love," which, he says, is reached by "dark contemplation." In this the Deity compenetrates the soul, but in such a hidden way that the soul—

"finds no terms, no means, no comparison whereby to render the sublimity of the wisdom and the delicacy of the spiritual feeling with which she is filled. . . . We receive this mystical knowledge of God clothed in none of the kinds of images, in none of the sensible representations, which our mind makes use of in other circumstances. Accordingly in this knowledge, since the senses and the imagination are not employed, we get neither form nor impression, nor can we give any account or furnish any likeness, although the mysterious and sweet-tasting wisdom comes home so clearly to the inmost parts of our soul. Fancy a man seeing a certain kind of thing for the first time in his life. He can understand it, use and enjoy it, but he cannot apply a name to it, nor communicate any idea of it, even though all the while it be a mere thing of sense. How much greater will be his powerlessness when it goes beyond the senses! This is the peculiarity of the divine language. The more infused, intimate, spiritual, and supersensible it is, the more does it exceed the senses, both inner and outer, and impose silence upon them. . . . The soul then feels as if placed in a vast and profound solitude, to which no created thing has access, in an immense and boundless desert, desert the more delicious the more solitary it is. There, in this abyss of wisdom, the soul grows by what it drinks in from the well-springs of the comprehension of love, . . . and recognizes, however sublime and learned may be the terms we employ, how utterly vile, insignificant, and improper they are when we seek to discourse of divine things by their means." [14]

I cannot pretend to detail to you the sundry stages of the Christian mystical life.[15] Our time would not suffice, for one thing; and moreover; I confess that the subdivisions and names which we find in the Catholic books seem to me to represent nothing objectively distinct. So many men, so many minds: I imagine that these experiences can be as infinitely varied as are the idiosyncrasies of individuals.

To the medical mind these ecstasies signify nothing but suggested and imitated hypnoid states, on an intellectual basis of superstition, and a corporeal one of degeneration and hysteria. Undoubtedly these pathological conditions have existed in many and possibly in all the cases, but that fact tells us nothing about the value for knowledge of the consciousness which they induce. To pass a spiritual judgment upon these states, we must not content ourselves with superficial medical talk, but inquire into their fruits for life.

Their fruits appear to have been various. Stupefaction, for one thing, seems not to have been altogether absent as a result. You may remember the helplessness in the kitchen and schoolroom of poor Margaret Mary Alacoque. Many other ecstatics would have perished but for the care taken of them by admiring followers. The "other-worldliness" encouraged by the mystical consciousness makes this over-abstraction from practical life peculiarly liable to befall mystics in whom the character is naturally passive and the intellect feeble; but in natively strong minds and characters we find quite opposite results. The great Spanish mystics, who carried the habit of ecstasy as far as it has often been carried, appear for the most part to have shown indomitable spirit and energy, and all the more so for the trances in which they indulged.

Saint Ignatius was a mystic, but his mysticism made him assuredly one of the most powerfully practical human engines that ever lived. Saint John of the Cross, writing of the intuitions and "touches" by which God reaches the substance of the soul, tells us that—

> "They enrich it marvelously. A single one of them may be sufficient to abolish at a stroke certain imperfections of which the soul during its whole life had vainly tried to rid itself, and to leave it adorned with virtues and loaded with supernatural gifts. A single one of these intoxicating consolations may reward it for all the labors undergone in its life—even were they numberless. Invested with an invincible courage, filled with an impassioned desire to suffer for its God, the soul then is seized with a strange torment—that of not being allowed to suffer enough." [16]

Saint Teresa is as emphatic, and much more detailed. You may perhaps remember a passage I quoted from her in my first lecture.[17] There are many similar pages in her autobiography. Where in literature is a more evidently veracious account of the formation of a new centre of spiritual energy, than is given in her description of the effects of certain ecstasies which in departing leave the soul upon a higher level of emotional excitement?

> "Often, infirm and wrought upon with dreadful pains before the ecstasy, the soul emerges from it full of health and admirably disposed for action . . . as if God had willed that the body itself, already obedi-

ent to the soul's desires, should share in the soul's happiness. . . . The soul after such a favor is animated with a degree of courage so great that if at that moment its body should be torn to pieces for the cause of God, it would feel nothing but the liveliest comfort. Then it is that promises and heroic resolutions spring up in profusion in us, soaring desires, horror of the world, and the clear perception of our proper nothingness. . . . What empire is comparable to that of a soul who, from this sublime summit to which God has raised her, sees all the things of earth beneath her feet, and is captivated by no one of them? How ashamed she is of her former attachments! How amazed at her blindness! What lively pity she feels for those whom she recognizes still shrouded in the darkness! . . . She groans at having ever been sensitive to points of honor, at the illusion that made her ever see as honor what the world calls by that name. Now she sees in this name nothing more than an immense lie of which the world remains a victim. She discovers, in the new light from above, that in genuine honor there is nothing spurious, that to be faithful to this honor is to give our respect to what deserves to be respected really, and to consider as nothing, or as less than nothing, whatsoever perishes and is not agreeable to God. . . . She laughs when she sees grave persons, persons of orison, caring for points of honor for which she now feels profoundest contempt. It is suitable to the dignity of their rank to act thus, they pretend, and it makes them more useful to others. But she knows that in despising the dignity of their rank for the pure love of God they would do more good in a single day than they would effect in ten years by preserving it. . . . She laughs at herself that there should ever have been a time in her life when she made any case of money, when she ever desired it. . . . Oh! if human beings might only agree together to regard it as so much useless mud, what harmony would then reign in the world! With what friendship we would all treat each other if our interest in honor and in money could not disappear from earth! For my own part, I feel as if it would be a remedy for all our ills." [18]

Mystical conditions may, therefore, render the soul more energetic in the lines which their inspiration favors. But this could be reckoned an advantage only in case the inspiration were a true one. If the inspiration were erroneous, the energy would be all the more mistaken and misbegotten. So we stand once more before that problem of truth which confronted us at the end of the lectures on saintliness. You will remember that we turned to mysticism precisely to get some light on truth. Do mystical states establish the truth of those theological affections in which the saintly life has its root?

In spite of their repudiation of articulate self-description, mystical states in general assert a pretty distinct theoretic drift. It is possible to give the outcome of the majority of them in terms that point in definite philosophical directions. One of these directions is optimism, and the other is monism. We pass into mystical states from out of ordinary consciousness as from a less into a more, as from a smallness into a vastness, and at the same time as from an unrest to a rest. We feel them as reconciling, unifying states. They appeal to the yes-function more than to the no-function in us. In them the unlimited absorbs the limits and peacefully closes the account. Their very denial of every adjective you may propose as applicable to the ultimate truth—He, the Self, the Atman, is to be described by "No! no!" only, say the Upanishads [19]—though it seems on the surface to be a no-function, is a denial made on behalf of a deeper yes. Whoso calls the Absolute anything in particular, or says that it is *this,* seems implicitly to shut it off from being *that*—it is as if he lessened it. So we deny the "this," negating the negation which it seems to us to imply, in the interests of the higher affirmative attitude by which we are possessed. The fountain-head of Christian mysticism is Dionysius the Areopagite. He describes the absolute truth by negatives exclusively.

> "The cause of all things is neither soul nor intellect; nor has it imagination, opinion, or reason, or intelligence; nor is it reason or intelligence; nor is it spoken or thought. It is neither number, nor order, nor magnitude, nor littleness, nor equality, nor inequality, nor similarity, nor dissimilarity. It neither stands, nor moves, nor rests. . . . It is neither essence, nor eternity, nor time. Even intellectual contact does not belong to it. It is neither science nor truth. It is not even royalty or wisdom; not one; not unity; not divinity or goodness; nor even spirit as we know it," etc., *ad libitum.*[20]

But these qualifications are denied by Dionysius, not because the truth falls short of them, but because it so infinitely excels them. It is above them. It is *super*-lucent, *super*-splendent, *super*-essential, *super*-sublime, *super everything* that can be named. Like Hegel in his logic, mystics journey towards the positive pole of truth only by the "Methode der Absoluten Negativität." [21]

This overcoming of all the usual barriers between the individual and the Absolute is the great mystic achievement. In mystic states we both become one with the Absolute and we become aware of our oneness. This is the everlasting and triumphant mystical tradition, hardly altered by differences of clime or creed. In Hinduism, in Neoplatonism, in Sufism, in Christian mysticism, in Whitmanism, we find the same recurring note, so that there is about mystical utterances an eternal unanimity which ought to make a critic stop and think, and which brings it about that the mystical classics have, as has been said, neither birthday nor native land. Perpetually telling of the unity of man with God, their speech antedates languages, and they do not grow old.[22]

I have now sketched with extreme brevity and insufficiency, but as fairly as I am able in the time allowed, the general traits of the mystic range of consciousness. *It is on the whole pantheistic and optimistic, or at least the opposite of pessimistic. It is anti-naturalistic, and harmonizes best with twice-bornness and so-called other-worldly states of mind.*

My next task is to inquire whether we can invoke it as authoritative. Does it furnish any *warrant for the truth* of the twice-bornness and supernaturality and pantheism which it favors? I must give my answer to this question as concisely as I can.

In brief my answer is this—and I will divide it into three parts:—

(1) Mystical states, when well developed, usually are, and have the right to be, absolutely authoritative over the individuals to whom they come.

(2) No authority emanates from them which should make it a duty for those who stand outside of them to accept their revelations uncritically.

(3) They break down the authority of the non-mystical or rationalistic consciousness, based upon the understanding and the senses alone. They show it to be only one kind of consciousness. They open out the possibility of other orders of truth, in which, so far as anything in us vitally responds to them, we may freely continue to have faith.

I will take up these points one by one.

1

As a matter of psychological fact, mystical states of a well-pronounced and emphatic sort *are* usually authoritative over those who have them.[23] They have been "there," and know. It is vain for rationalism to grumble about this. If the mystical truth that comes to a man proves to be a force that he can live by, what mandate have we of the majority to order him to live in another way? We can throw him into a prison or a madhouse, but we cannot change his mind—we commonly attach it only the more stubbornly to its beliefs.[24] It mocks our utmost efforts, as a matter of fact, and in point of logic it absolutely escapes our jurisdiction. Our own more "rational" beliefs are based on evidence exactly similar in nature to that which mystics quote for theirs. Our senses, namely, have assured us of certain states of fact; but mystical experiences are as direct perceptions of fact for those who have them as any sensations ever were for us. The records show that even though the five senses be in abeyance in them, they are absolutely sensational in their epistemological quality, if I may be pardoned the barbarous expression—that is, they are face to face presentations of what seems immediately to exist.

The mystic is, in short, *invulnerable,* and must be left whether we relish it or not, in undisturbed enjoyment of his creed. Faith, says Tolstoy, is that by which men live. And faith-state and mystic state are practically convertible terms.

2

But I now proceed to add that mystics have no right to claim that we ought to accept the deliverance of their peculiar experiences, if we are ourselves outsiders and feel no private call thereto. The utmost they can ever ask of us in this life is to admit that they establish a presumption. They form a consensus and have an unequivocal outcome; and it would be odd, mystics might say, if such a unanimous type of experience should prove to be altogether wrong. At bottom, however, this would only be an appeal to numbers like the appeal of rationalism the other way; and the appeal to numbers has no logical force. If we acknowledge it, it is for "suggestive," not for logical reasons: we follow the majority because to do so suits our life.

But even this presumption from the unanimity of mystics is far from being strong. In characterizing mystic states as pantheistic, optimistic, etc., I am afraid I over-simplified the truth. I did so for expository reasons, and to keep the closer to the classic mystical tradition. The classic religious mysticism, it now must be confessed, is only a "privileged case." It is an *extract,* kept true to type by the selection of the fittest specimens and their preservation in "schools." It is carved out from a much larger mass; and if we take the larger mass as seriously as religious mysticism has historically taken itself, we find that the supposed unanimity largely disappears. To begin with, even religious mysticism itself, the kind that accumulates traditions and makes schools, is much less unanimous than I have allowed. It has been both ascetic and antinomianly self-indulgent within the Christian church.[25] It is dualistic in Sankhya, and monistic in Vedanta philosophy. I called it pantheistic; but the great Spanish mystics are anything but pantheists. They are with few exceptions non-metaphysical minds, for whom "the category of personality" is absolute. The "union" of man with God is for them much more like an occasional miracle than like an original identity.[26] How different again, apart from the happiness common to all, is the mysticism of Walt Whitman, Edward Carpenter, Richard Jefferies, and other naturalistic pantheists, from the more distinctively Christian sort.[27] The fact is that the mystical feeling of enlargement, union, and emancipation has no specific intellectual content whatever of its own. It is capable of forming matrimonial alliances with material furnished by the most diverse philosophies and theologies, provided only they can find a place in their framework for its peculiar emotional mood. We have no right, therefore, to invoke its prestige as distinctively in favor of any special belief, such as that in absolute idealism, or in the absolute monistic identity, or in the absolute goodness of the world. It is only relatively in favor of all these things—it passes out of common human consciousness in the direction in which they lie.

So much for religious mysticism proper. But more remains to be told, for religious mysticism is only one half of mysticism. The other half has no accumulated traditions except those which the text-books on insanity supply. Open any one of these, and you will find abundant cases in which "mystical ideas" are cited as characteristic symptoms of enfeebled or deluded states of mind. In delusional insanity, paranoia, as they sometimes call it, we may have a *diabolical* mysticism, a sort of religious mysticism turned upside down. The same sense of ineffable importance in the smallest events, the same texts and words coming with new meanings, the same voices and visions and leadings and missions, the same controlling by extraneous powers; only this time the emotion is pessimistic: instead of consolations we have desolations; the meanings are dreadful; and the powers are enemies to life. It is evident that from the point of view of their psychological mechanism, the classic mysticism and these lower mysticisms spring from the same mental level, from that great subliminal or transmarginal region of which science is beginning to admit the existence, but of which so little is really known. That region contains every kind of matter: "seraph and snake" abide there side by side. To come from thence is no infallible credential. What comes must be sifted and tested, and run the gauntlet of confrontation with the total context of experience, just like what comes from the outer world of sense. Its value must be ascertained by empirical methods, so long as we are not mystics ourselves.

Once more, then, I repeat that non-mystics are under no obligation to acknowledge in mystical states a superior authority conferred on them by their intrinsic nature.[28]

3

Yet, I repeat once more, the existence of mystical states absolutely overthrows the pretension of non-mystical states to be the sole and ultimate dictators of what we may believe. As a rule, mystical states merely add a supersensuous meaning to the ordinary outward data of consciousness. They are excitements like the emotions of love or ambition, gifts to our spirit by means of which facts already objectively before us fall into a new expressiveness and make a new connection with our active life. They do not contradict these facts as such, or deny anything that our senses have immediately seized.[29] It is the rationalistic critic rather who plays the part of denier in the controversy, and his denials have no strength, for there never can be a state of facts to which new meaning may not truthfully be added, provided the mind ascend to a more enveloping point of view. It must always remain an open question whether mystical states may not possibly be such superior points of view, windows through which the mind looks out upon a more extensive and inclusive world. The difference of the views seen from the different mystical windows need not prevent us from entertaining this supposition. The wider world would in that case prove to have a mixed constitution like that of this world, that is all. It would have its celestial and its infernal regions, its tempting and its saving moments, its valid experiences and its counterfeit ones, just as our world has them; but it would be a wider world all the same. We should have to use its experiences by selecting and subordinating and substituting just as is our custom in this ordinary naturalistic world; we should be liable to error just as we are now; yet the counting in of that wider world of meanings, and the serious dealing with it, might, in spite of all the perplexity, be indispensable stages in our approach to the final fullness of the truth.

In this shape, I think, we have to leave the subject. Mystical states indeed wield no authority due simply to their being mystical states. But the higher ones among them point in directions to which the religious sentiments even of non-mystical men incline. They tell of the supremacy of the ideal, of vastness, of union, of safety, and of rest. They offer us *hypotheses,* hypotheses which we may voluntarily ignore, but which as thinkers we cannot possibly upset. The supernaturalism and optimism to which they would persuade us may, interpreted in one way or another, be after all the truest of insights into the meaning of this life.

"Oh, the little more, and how much it is; and the little less, and what worlds away!" It may be that possibility and permission of this sort are all that our religious consciousness requires to live on. In my last lecture I shall have to try to persuade you that this is the case. Meanwhile, however, I am sure that for many of my readers this diet is too slender. If supernaturalism and inner union with the divine are true, you think, then not so much permission, as compulsion to believe, ought to be found. Philosophy has always professed to prove religious truth by coercive argument; and the construction of philosophies of this kind has always been one favorite function of the religious life, if we use this term in the large historic sense. But religious philosophy is an enormous subject, and in my next lecture I can only give that brief glance at it which my limits will allow.

NOTES

1. Newman's *Securus judicat orbis terrarum* is another instance.
2. "Mesopotamia" is the stock comic instance.—An excellent old German lady, who had done some traveling in her day, used to describe to me her *Sehnsucht* that she might yet visit "Philadelphia," whose wondrous name had always haunted her imagination. Of John Foster it is said that "single words (as *chalcedony*), or the names of ancient heroes, had a mighty fascination over him. 'At any time the word *hermit* was enough to transport him.' The words *woods* and *forests* would produce the most powerful emotion." Foster's Life, by Ryland, New York, 1846, p. 3.
3. The Two Voices. In a letter to Mr. B. P. Blood, Tennyson reports of himself as follows:—

"I have never had any revelations through anaesthetics, but a kind of waking trance—this for lack of a better word—I have frequently had, quite up from boyhood, when I have been all alone. This has come upon me through repeating my own name to myself silently, till all at once, as it were out of the intensity of the consciousness of individuality, individuality itself seemed to dissolve and fade away into boundless being, and this not a confused state but the clearest, the surest of the surest, utterly beyond words—where death was an almost laughable impossibility—the loss of personality (if so it were) seeming no extinction, but the only true life. I am ashamed of my feeble description. Have I not said the state is utterly beyond words?"

Professor Tyndall, in a letter, recalls Tennyson saying of this condition:

"By God Almighty! there is no delusion in the matter! It is no nebulous ecstasy, but a state of transcendent wonder, associated with absolute clearness of mind." Memoirs of Alfred Tennyson, ii. 473.

4. The Lancet, July 6 and 13, 1895, reprinted as the Cavendish Lecture, on Dreamy Mental States, London, Baillière, 1895. They have been a good deal discussed of late by psychologists. See, for example, Bernard-Leroy: L'Illusion de Fausse Reconnaissance, Paris, 1898.

5. What reader of Hegel can doubt that that sense of a perfected Being with all its otherness soaked up into itself, which dominates his whole philosophy, must have come from the prominence in his consciousness of mystical moods like this, in most persons kept subliminal? The notion is thoroughly characteristic of the mystical level, and the *Aufgabe* of making it articulate was surely set to Hegel's intellect by mystical feeling.

6. Cosmic Consciousness: a study in the evolution of the human Mind, Philadelphia, 1901, p. 2.

7. My quotations are from Vivekananda, Raja Yoga, London, 1896. The completest source of information on Yoga is the work translated by Vhiari Lala Mitra: Yoga Vasishta Maha Ramayana, 4 vols. Calcutta, 1891–99.

8. A European witness, after carefully comparing the results of Yoga with those of the hypnotic or dreamy states artificially producible by us, says: "It makes of its true disciples good, healthy, and happy men. . . . Through the mastery which the yogi attains over his thoughts and his body, he grows into a 'character.' By the subjection of his impulses and propensities to his will, and the fixing of the latter upon the ideal of goodness, he becomes a 'personality' hard to influence by others, and thus almost the opposite of what we usually imagine a 'medium' so-called, or 'psychic subject' to be." Karl Kellner: Yoga: Eine Skizze, München, 1896, p. 21.

9. I follow the account in C. F. Koeppen: Die Religion des Buddha, Berlin, 1857, i, 585ff.

10. For a full account of him, see D. B. MacDonald: The Life of Al-Ghazzali, in the Journal of the American Oriental Society, 1899, vol. ix, p. 71.

11. A. Schmölders: Essai sur les écoles philosophiques chez les Arabes, Paris, 1842, pp. 54-68, abridged.

12. Görres's Christliche Mystik gives a full account of the facts. So does Ribet's Mystique Divine, 2 vols., Paris, 1890. A still more methodical modern work is the Mystica Theologia of Vallcornera, 2 vols., Turin, 1890.

13. M. Récéjac, in a recent volume, makes them essential. Mysticism he defines as "the tendency to draw near to the Absolute morally, *and by the aid of Symbols.*" See his Fondements de la Connaissance mystique, Paris, 1897, p. 66. But there are unquestionably mystical conditions in which sensible symbols play no part.

14. Saint John of the Cross: The Dark Night of the Soul, book ii, ch. xvii, in Vie et Œuvres, 3me édition, Paris, 1893, iii, 428-432. Chapter xi, of book ii, of Saint John's Ascent of Carmel is devoted to showing the harmfulness for the mystical life of the use of sensible imagery.

15. In particular I omit mention of visual and auditory hallucinations, verbal and graphic automatisms, and such marvels as "levitation," stigmatization, and the healing of disease. These phenomena, which mystics have often presented (or are believed to have presented), have no essential mystical significance, for they occur with no consciousness of illumination whatever, when they occur, as they often do, in persons of non-mystical mind. Consciousness of illumination is for us the essential mark of "mystical" states.

16. Œuvres, ii, 320.
17. Ibid., p. 22.
18. Autobiography, pp. 229, 200, 231-233, 243.
19. Müller's translation, part ii, p. 180.
20. T. Davidson's translation, in Journal of Speculative Philosophy, 1893, vol. xxii, p. 399.
21. "Deus propter excellentiam non immerito Nihil vocatur." Scotus Erigena, quoted by Andrew Seth: Two Lectures on Theism, New York, 1897, p. 55.
22. Compare M. Maeterlinck: L'Ornement des Noces spirituelles de Ruysbroeck, Bruxelles, 1891, Introduction, p. xix.
23. I abstract from weaker states, and from those cases of which the books are full, where the director (but usually not the subject) remains in doubt whether the experience may not have proceeded from the demon.
24. Example: Mr. John Nelson writes of his imprisonment for preaching Methodism: "My soul was as a watered garden, and I could sing praises to God all day long; for he turned my captivity into joy, and gave me to rest as well on the boards, as if I had been on a bed of down. Now could I say, 'God's service is perfect freedom,' and I was carried out much in prayer that my enemies might drink of the same river of peace which my God gave so largely to me." Journal, London, no date, p. 172.
25. Ruysbroeck, in the work which Maeterlinck has translated, has a chapter against the antinomianism of disciples. H. Delacroix's book (Essai sur le mysticisme spéculatif en Allemagne au XIVme Siècle, Paris, 1900) is full of antinomian material. Compare also A. Jundt: Les Amis de Dieu au XIV Siècle, Thèse de Strasbourg, 1879.
26. Compare Paul Rousselot: Les Mystiques Espagnols, Paris, 1869, ch. xii.
27. See Carpenter's Towards Democracy, especially the latter parts, and Jefferies's wonderful and splendid mystic rhapsody, The Story of my Heart.
28. In chapter i of book ii, of his work Degeneration, "Max Nordau" seeks to undermine all mysticism by exposing the weakness of the lower kinds. Mysticism for him means any sudden perception of hidden significance in things. He explains such perception by the abundant uncompleted associations which experiences may arouse in a degenerate brain. These give to him who has the experience a vague and vast sense of its leading further, yet they awaken no definite or useful consequent in his thought. The explanation is a plausible one for certain sorts of feeling of significance; and other alienists (Wernicke, for example, in his Grundriss der Psychiatrie, Theil ii, Leipzig, 1896) have explained "paranoiac" conditions by a laming of the association organ. But the higher mystical flights, with their positiveness and abruptness, are surely products of no such merely negative condition. It seems far more reasonable to ascribe them to inroads from the subconscious life, of the cerebral activity correlative to which we as yet know nothing.
29. They sometimes add subjective audita et visa to the facts, but as these are usually interpreted as transmundane, they oblige no alteration in the facts of sense.

The Argument from Religious Experience

C.D. Broad

I shall confine myself in this article to specifically religious experience and the argument for the existence of God which has been based on it.

This argument differs in the following important respect from the other two empirical types of argument. The Argument from Design and the arguments from ethical premises start from facts which are common to every one. But some people seem to be almost wholly devoid of any specifically religious experience; and among those who have it the differences of kind and degree are enormous. Founders of religions and saints, e.g., often claim to have been in direct contact with God, to have seen and spoken with Him, and so on. An ordinary religious man would certainly not make any such claim, though he might say that he had had experiences which assured him of the existence and presence of God. So the first thing that we have to notice is that capacity for religious experience is in certain respects like an ear for music. There are a few people who are unable to recognize and distinguish the simplest tune. But they are in a minority, like the people who have absolutely no kind of religious experience. Most people have some light appreciation of music. But the differences of degree in this respect are enormous, and those who have not much gift for music have to take the statements of accomplished musicians very largely on trust. Let us, then, compare tone-deaf persons to those who have no recognizable religious experience at all; the ordinary followers of a religion to men who have some taste for music but can neither appreciate the more difficult kinds nor compose; highly religious men and saints to persons with an exceptionally fine ear for music who may yet be unable to compose it; and the founders of religions to great musical composers, such as Bach and Beethoven.

This analogy is, of course, incomplete in certain important respects. Religious experience raises three problems, which are different though closely interconnected. (i) What is the *psychological analysis* of religious experience? Does it contain factors which are present also in certain experiences which are not religious? Does it contain any factor which never occurs in any other kind of experience? If it contains no such factor, but is a blend of elements each of which can occur separately

From C. D. Broad, *Religion, Philosophy and Psychical Research* (London: Routledge and Kegan Paul, Ltd., 1953), pp. 190-201. Reprinted by permission of the publisher.

or in non-religious experiences, its psychological peculiarity must consist in the characteristic way in which these elements are blended in it. Can this peculiar structural feature of religious experience be indicated and described? (ii) What are the *genetic and causal conditions* of the existence of religious experience? Can we trace the origin and development of the disposition to have religious experiences (*a*) in the human race, and (*b*) in each individual? Granted that the disposition is present in nearly all individuals at the present time, can we discover and state the variable conditions which call it into activity on certain occasions and leave it in abeyance on others? (iii) Part of the content of religious experience is alleged knowledge or well-founded belief about the nature of reality, e.g., that we are dependent on a being who loves us and whom we ought to worship, that values are somehow conserved in spite of the chances and changes of the material world at the mercy of which they seem *prima facie* to be, and so on. Therefore there is a third problem. Granted that religious experience exists, that it has such-and-such a history and conditions, that it seems vitally important to those who have it, and that it produces all kinds of effects which would not otherwise happen, is it *veridical?* Are the claims to knowledge or well-founded belief about the nature of reality, which are an integral part of the experience, *true or probable?* Now, in the case of musical experience, there are analogies to the psychological problem and to the genetic or causal problem, but there is no analogy to the epistemological problem of validity. For, so far as I am aware, no part of the content of musical experience is alleged knowledge about the nature of reality; and therefore no question of its being veridical or delusive can arise.

Premise — Since both musical experience and religious experience certainly exist, any theory of the universe which was incompatible with their existence would be false, and any theory which failed to show the connexion between their existence and the other facts about reality would be inadequate. So far the two kinds of experience are in exactly the same position. But a theory which answers to the condition that it allows of the *existence* of religious experience and indicates the *connexion* between its existence and other facts about reality may leave the question as to its *validity* quite unanswered. Or, alternatively, it may throw grave doubt on its cognitive claims, or else it may tend to support them. Suppose, e.g., that it could be shown that religious experience contains no elements which are not factors in other kinds of experience. Suppose further it could be shown that this particular combination of factors tends to originate and to be activated only under certain conditions which are known to be very commonly productive of false beliefs held with strong conviction. Then a satisfactory answer to the questions of psychological analysis and causal antecedents would have tended to answer the epistemological question of validity in the negative. On the other hand, it might be that the only theory which would satisfactorily account for the origin of the religious disposition and for the occurrence of actual religious experiences under certain conditions was a theory which allowed some of the cognitive claims made by religious experience to be true or probable. Thus the three problems, though entirely distinct from each other, may be very closely connected; and it is the existence of the third problem in connexion with religious experience which puts it, for the present purpose, in a different category from musical experience.

In spite of this essential difference the analogy is not to be despised, for it brings out at least one important point. If a man who had no ear for music were to give himself airs on that account, and were to talk *de haut en bas* about those who can appreciate music and think it highly important, we should regard him, not as an advanced thinker, but as a self-satisfied Philistine. And, even if he did not do this but only propounded theories about the nature and causation of musical experience, we might think it reasonable to feel very doubtful whether his theories would be adequate or correct. In the same way, when persons without religious experience regard themselves as being *on that ground* superior to those who have it, their attitude must be treated as merely silly and offensive. Similarly, any theories about religious experience constructed by persons who have little or none of their own should be regarded with grave suspicion. (For that reason it would be unwise to attach very much weight to anything that the present writer may say on this subject.)

On the other hand, we must remember that the possession of a great capacity for religious experience, like the possession of a great capacity for musical appreciation and composition, is no guarantee of high general intelligence. A man may be a saint or a magnificent musician and yet have very little common sense, very little power of accurate introspection or of seeing causal connexions, and scarcely any capacity for logical criticism. He may also be almost as ignorant about other aspects of reality as the non-musical or non-religious man is about musical or religious experience. If such a man starts to theorize about music or religion, his theories may be quite as absurd, though in a different way, as those made by persons who are devoid of musical or religious experience. Fortunately it happens that some religious mystics of a high order have been extremely good at introspecting and describing their own experiences. And some highly religious persons have had very great critical and philosophical abilities. St. Teresa is an example of the first, and St. Thomas Aquinas of the second.

Now I think it must be admitted that, if we compare and contrast the statements made by religious mystics of various times, races, and religions, we find a common nucleus combined with very great differences of detail. Of course the interpretations which they have put on their experiences are much more varied than the experiences themselves. It it obvious that the interpretations will depend in a large measure on the traditional religious beliefs in which various mystics have been brought up. I think that such traditions probably act in two different ways.

(i) The tradition no doubt affects the theoretical interpretation of experiences which would have taken place even if the mystic had been brought up in a different tradition. A feeling of unity with the rest of the universe will be interpreted very differently by a Christian who has been brought up to believe in a personal God and by a Hindu mystic who has been trained in a quite different metaphysical tradition.

(ii) The traditional beliefs, on the other hand, probably determine many of the details of the experience itself. A Roman Catholic mystic may have visions of the Virgin and the saints, whilst a Protestant mystic pretty certainly will not.

Thus the relations between the experiences and the traditional beliefs are highly complex. Presumably the outlines of the belief are determined by the experience. Then the details of the belief are fixed for a certain place and period by the special peculiarities of the experiences had by the founder of a certain religion. These beliefs then become traditional in that religion. Thenceforth they in part determine the details of the experiences had by subsequent mystics of that religion, and still more do they determine the interpretations which these mystics will put upon their experiences. Therefore, when a set of religious beliefs has once been established, it no doubt tends to produce experiences which can plausibly be taken as evidence for it. If it is a tradition in a certain religion that one can communicate with saints, mystics of that religion will seem to see and to talk with saints in their mystical visions; and this fact will be taken as further evidence for the belief that one can communicate with saints.

Much the same double process of causation takes place in sense-perception. On the one hand, the beliefs and expectations which we have at any moment largely determine what *interpretation* we shall put on a certain sensation which we should in any case have had then. On the other hand, our beliefs and expectations do to some extent determine and modify some of the sensible characteristics of the *sensa themselves*. When I am thinking only of diagrams a certain visual stimulus may produce a sensation of a sensibly flat sensum; but a precisely similar stimulus may produce a sensation of a sensibly solid sensum when I am thinking of solid objects.

Such explanations, however, plainly do not account for the first origin of religious beliefs, or for the features which are common to the religious experiences of persons of widely different times, races, and traditions.

Now, when we find that there are certain experiences which, though never very frequent in a high degree of intensity, have happened in a high degree among a few men at all times and places; and when we find that, in spite of differences in detail which we can explain, they involve certain fundamental conditions which are common and peculiar to them; two alternatives are open to us. (i) We may suppose that these men are in contact with an aspect of reality which is not revealed to ordinary persons in their everyday experience. And we may suppose that the characteristics which they agree in ascribing to reality on the basis of these experiences probably do belong to it. Or (ii) we may suppose that they are all subject to a delusion from which other men are free. In order to illustrate these alternatives it will be useful to consider three partly analogous cases, two of which are real and the third imaginary.

(a) Most of the detailed facts which biologists tell us about the minute structure and changes in cells can be perceived only by persons who have had a long training in the use of the microscope. In this case we believe that the agreement among trained microscopists really does correspond to facts which untrained persons cannot perceive. (b) Persons of all races who habitually drink alcohol to excess eventually have perceptual experiences in which they seem to themselves to see snakes or rats crawling about their rooms or beds. In this case we believe that this agreement among drunkards is merely a uniform hallucination. (c) Let us now imagine a race of beings who can walk about and touch things but cannot see. Suppose that eventually a few of them developed the power of sight. All that they might tell their still blind friends about colour would be wholly unintelligible to and unverifiable by the latter. But they would also be able to tell their blind friends a great deal about what the latter would feel if they were to walk in certain directions. These statements would be verified. This would not, of course, *prove* to the blind ones that the unintelligible statements about colour correspond to certain aspects of the world which they cannot perceive. But it would show that the seeing persons had a source of additional information about matters which the blind ones could understand and test for themselves. It would not be unreasonable then for the blind ones to believe that probably the seeing ones are also able to perceive other aspects of reality which they are describing correctly when they make their unintelligible statements containing colour-names. The question then is whether it is reasonable to regard the agreement between the experiences of religious mystics as more like the agreement among trained microscopists about the minute structure of cells, or as more like the agreement among habitual drunkards about the infestation of their rooms by pink rats or snakes, or as more like the agreement about colours which the seeing men would express in their statements to the blind men.

Why do we commonly believe that habitual excess of alcohol is a cause of a uniform delusion and not a source of additional information? The main reason is as follows. The things which drunkards claim to perceive are not fundamentally different in kind from the things that other people perceive. We have all seen rats and snakes, though the rats have generally been grey or brown and not pink. Moreover the drunkard claims that the rats and snakes which he sees are literally present in his room and on his bed, in the same sense in which his bed is in his room and his quilt is on his bed. Now we may fairly argue as follows. Since these are the sort of things which we could see if they were there, the fact that we cannot see them makes it highly probable that they are not there. Again, we know what kinds of perceptible effect would generally follow from the presence in a room of such things as rats or snakes. We should expect fox-terriers or mongooses to show traces of excitement, cheese to be nibbled, corn to disappear from bins, and so on. We find that no such effects are observed in the bedrooms of persons suffering from *delirium tremens*. It therefore seems reasonable to conclude that the agreement among drunkards is a sign, not of a revelation, but of a delusion.

Now the assertions in which religious mystics agree are not such that they conflict with what we can perceive with our senses. They are about the structure and organization of the world as a whole and about the relations of men to the rest of it. And they have so little in common with the facts of daily life that there is not much chance of direct collision. I think that there is only one important point on which there is conflict. Nearly all mystics seem to be agreed that time and change and unchanging duration are unreal or extremely superficial, whilst these seem to plain men to be the most fundamental features of the world. But we must admit, on the one hand, that these temporal characteristics present very great philosophical difficulties and puzzles when we reflect upon them. On the other hand, we may well suppose that the mystic finds it impossible to state clearly in ordinary language what it is that he experiences about the facts which underlie the appearance of time and change and duration. Therefore it is not difficult to allow that what we experience as the temporal aspect of reality corresponds in some sense to certain facts, and yet that these facts appear to us in so distorted a form in our ordinary experience that a person who sees them more accurately and directly might refuse to apply temporal names to them.

Let us next consider why we feel fairly certain that the agreement among trained microscopists about the minute structure of cells expresses an objective fact, although we cannot get similar experiences. One reason is that we have learned enough, from simpler cases of visual perception, about the laws of optics to know that the arrangement of lenses in a microscope is such that it will reveal minute structure, which is otherwise invisible, and will not simply create optical delusions. Another reason is that we know of other cases in which trained persons can detect things which untrained people will overlook, and that in many cases the existence of these things can be verified by indirect methods. Probably most of us have experienced such results of training in our own lives.

Now religious experience is not in nearly such a strong position as this. We do not know much about the laws which govern its occurrence and determine its variations. No doubt there are certain standard methods of training and meditation which tend to produce mystical experiences. These have been elaborated to some extent by certain Western mystics and to a very much greater extent by Eastern Yogis. But I do not think that we can see here, as we can in the case of microscopes and the training which is required to make the best use of them, any conclusive reason why these methods should produce veridical rather than delusive experiences. Uniform methods of training and meditation would be likely to produce more or less similar experiences, whether these experiences were largely veridical or wholly delusive.

Is there any analogy between the facts about religious experience and the fable about the blind men some of whom gained the power of sight? It might be said that many ideals of conduct and ways of life, which we can all recognize now to be good and useful, have been introduced into human history by the founders of religions. These persons have made actual ethical discoveries which others can afterwards recognize to be true. It might be said that this is at least roughly analogous to the case of the seeing men telling the still blind men of facts which the latter could and did verify for themselves. And it might be said that this makes it reasonable for us to attach some weight to what founders of religions tell us about things which we cannot understand or verify for ourselves; just as it would have been reasonable for the blind men to attach some weight to the unintelligible statements which the seeing men made to them about colours.

I think that this argument deserves a certain amount of respect, though I should find it hard to estimate how much weight to attach to it. I should be inclined to sum up as follows. When there is a nucleus of agreement between the experiences of men in different places, times, and traditions, and when they all tend to put much the same kind of interpretation on the cognitive content of these experiences, it is reasonable to ascribe this agreement to their all being in contact with a certain objective aspect of reality *unless* there be some positive reason to think otherwise. The practical postulate which we go upon everywhere else is to treat cognitive claims as veridical unless there be some positive reason to think them delusive. This, after all, is our only guarantee for believing that ordinary sense-perception is veridical. We cannot *prove* that what people agree in perceiving really exists independently of them; but we do always assume that ordinary waking sense-perception is veridical unless we can produce some positive ground for thinking that it is delusive in any given case. I think it would be inconsistent to treat the experiences of religious mystics on different principles. So far as they agree they should be provisionally accepted as veridical unless there be some positive ground for thinking that they are not. So the next question is whether there is any positive ground for holding that they are delusive.

There are two circumstances which have been commonly held to cast doubt on the cognitive claims of religious and mystical experience. (i) It is alleged that founders of religions and saints have nearly always had certain neuropathic symptoms or certain bodily weaknesses, and that these would be likely to produce delusions. Even if we accept the premises, I do not think that this is a very strong argument. (*a*) It is equally true that many founders of religions and saints have exhibited great endurance and great power of organization and business capacity which would have made them extremely successful and competent in secular affairs. There are very few offices in the cabinet or in the highest branches of the civil service which St. Thomas Aquinas could not have held with conspicuous success. I do not, of course, regard this as a positive reason *for* accepting the metaphysical doctrines which saints and founders of religions have based on their experiences; but it is relevant as a *rebuttal* of the argument which we are considering. (*b*) Probably very few people of extreme genius in science or art are perfectly normal mentally or physically, and some of them are very crazy and eccentric indeed. Therefore it would be rather surprising if persons of religious genius were completely normal, whether their experiences be veridical or delusive. (*c*) Suppose, for the sake of argument, that there is an aspect of the world which remains altogether outside the ken of ordinary persons in their daily life. Then it seems very likely that some degree of mental and physical abnormality would be a necessary condition for getting sufficiently loosened from the objects of ordinary sense-perception to come into cognitive contact with this aspect of reality. Therefore the fact that those persons who claim to have this peculiar kind of cognition generally exhibit certain mental and physical abnormalities is rather what might be anticipated if their claims were true. One might need to be slightly 'cracked' in order to have some peep-holes into the super-sensible world. (*d*) If mystical experience were veridical, it seems quite likely that it would *produce* abnormalities of behaviour in those who had it strongly. Let us suppose, for the sake of argument, that those who have religious experience are in frequent contact with an aspect of reality of which most men get only rare and faint glimpses. Then such persons are, as it were, living in two worlds, while the ordinary man is living in only one of them. Or, again, they might be compared to a man who has to conduct his life with one ordinary eye and another of a telescopic kind. Their behaviour may be appropriate to the aspect of reality which they alone perceive and think all-important; but, for that very reason, it may be inappropriate to those other aspects of reality which are all that most men perceive or judge to be important and on which all our social institutions and conventions are built.

(ii) A second reason which is commonly alleged for doubt about the claims of religious experience is the following. It is said that such experience always originates from and remains mixed with certain other factors, e.g., sexual emotion, which are such that experiences and beliefs that arise from them are very likely to be delusive. I think that there are a good many confusions on this point, and it will be worth while to begin by indicating some of them.

When people say that B 'originated from' A, they are liable to confuse at least three different kinds of connexion between A and B. (i) It might be that A is a necessary but insufficient condition of the existence of B. (ii) It might be that A is a necessary and sufficient condition of the existence of B. Or (iii) it might be that B simply *is* A in a more complex and disguised form. Now, when there is in fact evidence only for the first kind of connexion, people are very liable to jump to the conclusion that there is the third kind of connexion. It may well be the case, e.g., that no one who was incapable of strong sexual desires and emotions could have anything worth calling religious experience. But it is plain that the possession of a strong capacity for sexual experience is not a *sufficient* condition of having religious experience; for we know that the former quite often exists in persons who show hardly any trace of the latter. But, even if it could be shown that a strong capacity for sexual desire and emotion is *both* necessary and sufficient to produce religious experience, it would not follow that the latter is just the former in disguise. In the first place, it is not at all easy to discover the exact meaning of this metaphorical phrase when it is applied to psychological topics. And, if we make use of physical analogies, we are not much helped. A mixture of oxygen and hydrogen in presence of a spark is necessary and sufficient to produce water accompanied by an explosion. But water accompanied by an explosion is not a mixture of oxygen and hydrogen and a spark 'in a disguised form', whatever that may mean.

Now I think that the present rather vaguely formulated objection to the validity of the claims of religious experience might be stated somewhat as follows. 'In the individual, religious experience originates from, and always remains mixed with, sexual desires and emotions. The other generative factor of it is the religious tradition of the society in which he lives, the teachings of his parents, nurses, schoolmasters, etc. In the race religious experience originated from a mixture of false beliefs about nature and man, irrational fears, sexual and other impulses, and so on. Thus the religious tradition arose from beliefs which we now recognize to have been false and from emotions which we now recognize to have been irrelevant and misleading. It is now drilled into children by those who are in authority over them at a time of life when they are intellectually and emotionally at much the same stage as the primitive savages among whom it originated. It is, therefore, readily accepted, and it determines beliefs and emotional dispositions which persist long after the child has grown up and acquired more adequate knowledge of nature and of himself.'

Persons who use this argument might admit that it does not definitely *prove* that religious beliefs are false and groundless. False beliefs and irrational fears in our remote ancestors *might* conceivably be the origin of true beliefs and of an appropriate feeling of awe and reverence in ourselves. And, if sexual desires and emotions be an essential condition and constituent of religious experience, the experience *may* nevertheless be veridical in important respects. We might merely have to rewrite one of the beatitudes and say 'Blessed are the *im*pure in heart, for they shall see God'. But, although it is logically possible that such causes should produce such effects, it would be said that they are most unlikely to do so. They seem much more likely to produce false beliefs and misplaced emotions.

It is plain that this argument has considerable plausibility. But it is worth while to remember that modern science has almost as humble an ancestry as contemporary religion. If the primitive witch-smeller is the spiritual progenitor of the Archbishop of Canterbury, the primitive rain-maker is equally the spiritual progenitor of the Cavendish Professor of Physics. There has obviously been a gradual refinement and purification of religious beliefs and concepts in the course of history, just as there has been in the beliefs and concepts of science. Certain persons of religious genius, such as some of the Hebrew prophets and the founders of Christianity and of Buddhism, do seem to have introduced new ethico-religious concepts and beliefs which have won wide acceptance, just as certain men of scientific genius, such as Galileo, Newton, and Einstein, have done in the sphere of science. It seems somewhat arbitrary to count this process as a continual approximation to true knowledge of the material aspect of the world in the case of science, and to refuse to regard it as at all similar in the case of religion. Lastly, we must remember that all of us have accepted the current common-sense and scientific view of the material world on the authority of our parents, nurses, masters, and companions at a time when we had neither the power nor the inclination to criticize it. And most of us accept, without even understanding, the more recondite doctrines of contemporary physics simply on the authority of those whom we have been taught to regard as experts.

On the whole, then, I do not think that what we know of the conditions under which religious beliefs and emotions have arisen in the life of the individual and the race makes it reasonable to think that they are *specially* likely to be delusive or misdirected. At any rate any argument which starts from that basis and claims to reach such a conclusion will need to be very carefully handled if its destructive effects are to be confined within the range contemplated by its users. It is reasonable to think that the concepts and beliefs of even the most perfect religions known to us are extremely inadequate to the facts which they express; that they are highly confused and are mixed up with a great deal of positive error and sheer nonsense; and that, if the human race goes on and continues to have religious experiences and to reflect on them, they will be altered and improved almost out of recognition. But all this could be said, *mutatis mutandis*, of scientific concepts and theories. The claim of any particular religion or sect to have complete or final truth on these subjects seems to me to be too ridiculous to be worth a moment's consideration. But the opposite extreme of holding that the whole religious experience of mankind is a gigantic system of pure delusion seems to me to be almost (though not quite) as far-fetched.

RELIGIOUS EPISTEMOLOGY: FAITH

Reason and Revelation

St. Thomas Aquinas

CHAPTER 3

On the Way in Which Divine Truth is to Be Made Known

[1]   The way of making truth known is not always the same, and, as the Philosopher has very well said, "it belongs to an educated man to seek such certitude in each thing as the nature of that thing allows." [1] The remark is also introduced by Boethius.[2] But, since such is the case, we must first show what way is open to us in order that we may make known the truth which is our object.

[2]   There is a twofold mode of truth in what we profess about God. Some truths about God exceed all the ability of the human reason. Such is the truth that God is triune. But there are some truths which the natural reason also is able to reach. Such are that God exists, that He is one, and the like. In fact, such truths about God have been proved demonstratively by the philosophers, guided by the light of the natural reason.

[3]   That there are certain truths about God that totally surpass man's ability appears with the greatest evidence. Since, indeed, the principle of all knowledge that the reason perceives about some thing is the understanding of the very substance of that being (for according to Aristotle "what a thing is" is the principle of demonstration),[3] it is necessary that the way in which we understand the substance of a thing determines the way in which we know what belongs to it. Hence, if the human intellect comprehends the substance of some thing, for example, that of a stone or of a triangle, no intelligible characteristic belonging to that thing surpasses the grasp of the human reason. But this does not happen to us in the case of God. For the human intellect is not able to reach a comprehension of the divine substance through its natural power. For, according to its manner of knowing in the present life, the

From St. Thomas Aquinas, *On The Truth of the Catholic Faith*, Summa Contra Gentiles, Book I, trans. by Anton Pegis. Copyright © 1955 by Doubleday and Co., Inc. Reprinted by permission of Doubleday and Co., Inc.

intellect depends on the sense for the origin of knowledge; and so those things that do not fall under the senses cannot be grasped by the human intellect except in so far as the knowledge of them is gathered from sensible things. Now, sensible things cannot lead the human intellect to the point of seeing in them the nature of the divine substance; for sensible things are effects that fall short of the power of their cause. Yet, beginning with sensible things, our intellect is led to the point of knowing about God that He exists, and other such characteristics that must be attributed to the First Principle. There are, consequently, some intelligible truths about God that are open to the human reason; but there are others that absolutely surpass its power.

[4]   We may easily see the same point from the gradation of intellects. Consider the case of two persons of whom one has a more penetrating grasp of a thing by his intellect than does the other. He who has the superior intellect understands many things that the other cannot grasp at all. Such is the case with a very simple person who cannot at all grasp the subtle speculations of philosophy. But the intellect of an angel surpasses the human intellect much more than the intellect of the greatest philosopher surpasses the intellect of the most uncultivated simple person; for the distance between the best philosopher and a simple person is contained within the limits of the human species, which the angelic intellect surpasses. For the angel knows God on the basis of a more noble effect than does man; and this by as much as the substance of an angel, through which the angel in his natural knowledge is led to the knowledge of God, is nobler than sensible things and even than the soul itself, through which the human intellect mounts to the knowledge of God. The divine intellect surpasses the angelic intellect much more than the angelic surpasses the human. For the divine intellect is in its capacity equal to its substance, and therefore it understands fully what it is, including all its intelligible attributes. But by his natural knowledge the angel does not know what God is, since the substance itself of the angel, through which he is led to the knowledge of God, is an effect that is not equal to the power of its cause. Hence, the angel is not able, by means of his natural knowledge, to grasp all the things that God understands in Himself; nor is the human reason sufficient to grasp all the things that the angel understands through his own natural power. Just as, therefore, it would be the height of folly for a simple person to assert that what a philosopher proposes is false on the ground that he himself cannot understand it, so (and even more so) it is the acme of stupidity for a man to suspect as false what is divinely revealed through the ministry of the angels simply because it cannot be investigated by reason.

[5]   The same thing, moreover, appears quite clearly from the defect that we experience every day in our knowledge of things. We do not know a great many of the properties of sensible things, and in most cases we are not able to discover fully the natures of those properties that we

apprehend by the sense. Much more is it the case, therefore, that the human reason is not equal to the task of investigating all the intelligible characteristics of that most excellent substance.

[6] The remark of Aristotle likewise agrees with this conclusion. He says that "our intellect is related to the prime beings, which are most evident in their nature, as the eye of an owl is related to the sun." [4]

[7] Sacred Scripture also gives testimony to this truth. We read in Job: "Peradventure thou wilt comprehend the steps of God, and wilt find out the Almighty perfectly?" (11:7). And again: "Behold, God is great, exceeding our knowledge" (Job 36:26). And St. Paul: "We know in part" (I Cor. 13:9).

[8] We should not, therefore, immediately reject as false, following the opinion of the Manicheans and many unbelievers, everything that is said about God even though it cannot be investigated by reason. — *good point* —

But we cannot say it is true either

CHAPTER 4

That the Truth About God to Which the Natural Reason Reaches Is Fittingly Proposed to Men for Belief

[1] Since, therefore, there exists a twofold truth concerning the divine being, one to which the inquiry of the reason can reach, the other which surpasses the whole ability of the human reason, it is fitting that both of these truths be proposed to man divinely for belief. This point must first be shown concerning the truth that is open to the inquiry of the reason; otherwise, it might perhaps seem to someone that, since such a truth can be known by the reason, it was uselessly given to men through a supernatural inspiration as an object of belief.

[2] Yet, if this truth were left solely as a matter of inquiry for the human reason, three awkward consequences would follow.

[3] The first is that few men would possess the knowledge of God. For there are three reasons why most men are cut off from the fruit of diligent inquiry which is the discovery of truth. Some do not have the physical disposition for such work. As a result, there are many who are naturally not fitted to pursue knowledge; and so, however much they tried, they would be unable to reach the highest level of human knowledge which consists in knowing God. Others are cut off from pursuing this truth by the necessities imposed upon them by their daily lives. For some men must devote themselves to taking care of temporal matters. Such men would not be able to give so much time to the leisure of contemplative inquiry as to reach the highest peak at which human investigation can arrive, namely, the knowledge of God. Finally, there are some who are cut off by indolence. In order to know the things that the reason can investigate concerning God, a knowledge of many things

must already be possessed. For almost all of philosophy is directed towards the knowledge of God, and that is why metaphysics, which deals with divine things, is the last part of philosophy to be learned. This means that we are able to arrive at the inquiry concerning the aforementioned truth only on the basis of a great deal of labor spent in study. Now, those who wish to undergo such a labor for the mere love of knowledge are few, even though God has inserted into the minds of men a natural appetite for knowledge.

[4] The second awkward effect is that those who would come to discover the abovementioned truth would barely reach it after a great deal of time. The reasons are several. There is the profundity of this truth, which the human intellect is made capable of grasping by natural inquiry only after a long training. Then, there are many things that must be presupposed, as we have said. There is also the fact that, in youth, when the soul is swayed by the various movements of the passions, it is not in a suitable state for the knowledge of such lofty truth. On the contrary, "one becomes wise and knowing in repose," as it is said in the *Physics*.[5] The result is this. If the only way open to us for the knowledge of God were solely that of the reason, the human race would remain in the blackest shadows of ignorance. For then the knowledge of God, which especially renders men perfect and good, would come to be possessed only by a few, and these few would require a great deal of time in order to reach it.

[5] The third awkward effect is this. The investigation of the human reason for the most part has falsity present within it, and this is due partly to the weakness of our intellect in judgment, and partly to the admixture of images. The result is that many, remaining ignorant of the power of demonstration, would hold in doubt those things that have been most truly demonstrated. This would be particularly the case since they see that, among those who are reputed to be wise men, each one teaches his own brand of doctrine. Furthermore, with the many truths that are demonstrated, there sometimes is mingled something that is false, which is not demonstrated but rather asserted on the basis of some probable or sophistical argument, which yet has the credit of being a demonstration. That is why it was necessary that the unshakeable certitude and pure truth concerning divine things should be presented to men by way of faith.

[6] Beneficially, therefore, did the divine Mercy provide that it should instruct us to hold by faith even those truths that the human reason is able to investigate. In this way, all men would easily be able to have a share in the knowledge of God, and this without uncertainty and error.

[7] Hence it is written: "Henceforward you walk not as also the Gentiles walk in the vanity of their mind, having their understanding dark-

ened" (Eph. 4:17–18). And again: "All thy children shall be taught of the Lord" (Isa. 54:13).

CHAPTER 5

That the Truths the Human Reason Is Not Able to Investigate are Fittingly Proposed to Men for Belief

[1] Now, perhaps some will think that men should not be asked to believe what the reason is not adequate to investigate, since the divine Wisdom provides in the case of each thing according to the mode of its nature. We must therefore prove that it is necessary for man to receive from God as objects of belief even those truths that are above the human reason.

[2] No one tends with desire and zeal towards something that is not already known to him. But, as we shall examine later on in this work, men are ordained by the divine Providence towards a higher good than human fragility can experience in the present life.[6] That is why it was necessary for the human mind to be called to something higher than the human reason here and now can reach, so that it would thus learn to desire something and with zeal tend towards something that surpasses the whole state of the present life. This belongs especially to the Christian religion, which in a unique way promises spiritual and eternal goods. And so there are many things proposed to men in it that transcend human sense. The Old Law, on the other hand, whose promises were of a temporal character, contained very few proposals that transcended the inquiry of the human reason. Following this same direction, the philosophers themselves, in order that they might lead men from the pleasure of sensible things to virtue, were concerned to show that there were in existence other goods of a higher nature than these things of sense, and that those who gave themselves to the active or contemplative virtues would find much sweeter enjoyment in the taste of these higher goods.

[3] It is also necessary that such truth be proposed to men for belief so that they may have a truer knowledge of God. For then only do we know God truly when we believe Him to be above everything that it is possible for man to think about Him; for, as we have shown,[7] the divine substance surpasses the natural knowledge of which man is capable. Hence, by the fact that some things about God are proposed to man that surpass his reason, there is strengthened in man the view that God is something above what he can think.

[4] Another benefit that comes from the revelation to men of truths that exceed the reason is the curbing of presumption, which is the mother of error. For there are some who have such a presumptuous opinion of their own ability that they deem themselves able to measure

the nature of everything; I mean to say that, in their estimation, everything is true that seems to them so, and everything is false that does not. So that the human mind, therefore, might be freed from this presumption and come to a humble inquiry after truth, it was necessary that some things should be proposed to man by God that would completely surpass his intellect.

[5]   A still further benefit may also be seen in what Aristotle says in the *Ethics*.[8] There was a certain Simonides who exhorted people to put aside the knowledge of divine things and to apply their talents to human occupations. He said that "he who is a man should know human things, and he who is mortal, things that are mortal." Against Simonides Aristotle says that "man should draw himself towards what is immortal and divine as much as he can." And so he says in the *De animalibus* that, although what we know of the higher substances is very little, yet that little is loved and desired more than all the knowledge that we have about less noble substances.[9] He also says in the *De caelo et mundo* that when questions about the heavenly bodies can be given even a modest and merely plausible solution, he who hears this experiences intense joy.[10] From all these considerations it is clear that even the most imperfect knowledge about the most noble realities brings the greatest perfection to the soul. Therefore, although the human reason cannot grasp fully the truths that are above it, yet, if it somehow holds these truths at least by faith, it acquires great perfection for itself.

[6]   Therefore it is written: "For many things are shown to thee above the understanding of men" (Ecclus. 3:25). Again: "So the things that are of God no man knoweth but the Spirit of God. But to us God hath revealed them by His Spirit" (I Cor. 2:11, 10).

CHAPTER 6

That to Give Assent to the Truths of Faith Is Not Foolishness Even Though They are Above Reason

[1]   Those who place their faith in this truth, however, "for which the human reason offers no experimental evidence,"[11] do not believe foolishly, as though "following artificial fables" (II Peter 1:16). For these "secrets of divine Wisdom" (Job 11:6) the divine Wisdom itself, which knows all things to the full, has deigned to reveal to men. It reveals its own presence, as well as the truth of its teaching and inspiration, by fitting arguments; and in order to confirm those truths that exceed natural knowledge, it gives visible manifestation to works that surpass the ability of all nature. Thus, there are the wonderful cures of illnesses, there is the raising of the dead, and the wonderful immutation in the heavenly bodies; and what is more wonderful, there is the inspiration given to human minds, so that simple and untutored persons, filled with the gift of the Holy Spirit, come to possess instantaneously the highest wisdom

and the readiest eloquence. When these arguments were examined, through the efficacy of the abovementioned proof, and not the violent assault of arms or the promise of pleasures, and (what is most wonderful of all) in the midst of the tyranny of the persecutors, an innumerable throng of people, both simple and most learned, flocked to the Christian faith. In this faith there are truths preached that surpass every human intellect; the pleasures of the flesh are curbed; it is taught that the things of the world should be spurned. Now, for the minds of mortal men to assent to these things is the greatest of miracles, just as it is a manifest work of divine inspiration that, spurning visible things, men should seek only what is invisible. Now, that this has happened neither without preparation nor by chance, but as a result of the disposition of God, is clear from the fact that through many pronouncements of the ancient prophets God had foretold that He would do this. The books of these prophets are held in veneration among us Christians, since they give witness to our faith.

[2] The manner of this confirmation is touched on by St. Paul: "Which," that is, human salvation, "having begun to be declared by the Lord, was confirmed unto us by them that hear Him: God also bearing them witness of signs, and wonders, and divers miracles, and distributions of the Holy Ghost" (Heb. 2:3–4).

[3] This wonderful conversion of the world to the Christian faith is the clearest witness of the signs given in the past; so that it is not necessary that they should be further repeated, since they appear most clearly in their effect. For it would be truly more wonderful than all signs if the world had been led by simple and humble men to believe such lofty truths, to accomplish such difficult actions, and to have such high hopes. Yet it is also a fact that, even in our own time, God does not cease to work miracles through His saints for the confirmation of the faith.

[4] On the other hand, those who founded sects committed to erroneous doctrines proceeded in a way that is opposite to this. The point is clear in the case of Mohammed. He seduced the people by promises of carnal pleasure to which the concupiscence of the flesh goads us. His teaching also contained precepts that were in conformity with his promises, and he gave free rein to carnal pleasure. In all this, as is not unexpected, he was obeyed by carnal men. As for proofs of the truth of his doctrine, he brought forward only such as could be grasped by the natural ability of anyone with a very modest wisdom. Indeed, the truths that he taught he mingled with many fables and with doctrines of the greatest falsity. He did not bring forth any signs produced in a supernatural way, which alone fittingly gives witness to divine inspiration; for a visible action that can be only divine reveals an invisibly inspired teacher of truth. On the contrary, Mohammed said that he was sent in the power of his arms— which are signs not lacking even to robbers and tyrants. What is more, no wise men, men trained in things divine and human, believed in him

from the beginning. Those who believed in him were brutal men and desert wanderers, utterly ignorant of all divine teaching, through whose numbers Mohammed forced others to become his followers by the violence of his arms. Nor do divine pronouncements on the part of preceding prophets offer him any witness. On the contrary, he perverts almost all the testimonies of the Old and New Testaments by making them into fabrications of his own, as can be seen by anyone who examines his law. It was, therefore, a shrewd decision on his part to forbid his followers to read the Old and New Testaments, lest these books convict him of falsity. It is thus clear that those who place any faith in his words believe foolishly.

CHAPTER 7

That the Truth of Reason Is Not Opposed to the Truth of the Christian Faith

[1]   Now, although the truth of the Christian faith which we have discussed surpasses the capacity of the reason, nevertheless that truth that the human reason is naturally endowed to know cannot be opposed to the truth of the Christian faith. For that with which the human reason is naturally endowed is clearly most true; so much so, that it is impossible for us to think of such truths as false. Nor is it permissible to believe as false that which we hold by faith, since this is confirmed in a way that is so clearly divine. Since, therefore, only the false is opposed to the true, as is clearly evident from an examination of their definitions, it is impossible that the truth of faith should be opposed to those principles that the human reason knows naturally.

[2]   Furthermore, that which is introduced into the soul of the student by the teacher is contained in the knowledge of the teacher—unless his teaching is fictitious, which it is improper to say of God. Now, the knowledge of the principles that are known to us naturally has been implanted in us by God; for God is the Author of our nature. These principles, therefore, are also contained by the divine Wisdom. Hence, whatever is opposed to them is opposed to the divine Wisdom, and, therefore, cannot come from God. That which we hold by faith as divinely revealed, therefore, cannot be contrary to our natural knowledge.

[3]   Again. In the presence of contrary arguments our intellect is chained, so that it cannot proceed to the knowledge of the truth. If, therefore, contrary knowledges were implanted in us by God, our intellect would be hindered from knowing truth by this very fact. Now, such an effect cannot come from God.

[4]   And again. What is natural cannot change as long as nature does not. Now, it is impossible that contrary opinions should exist in the same knowing subject at the same time. No opinion or belief, therefore, is implanted in man by God which is contrary to man's natural knowledge.

[5]   Therefore, the Apostle says: "The word is nigh thee, even in thy mouth and in thy heart. This is the word of faith, which we preach" (Rom. 10:8). But because it overcomes reason, there are some who think that it is opposed to it: which is impossible.

[6]   The authority of St. Augustine also agrees with this. He writes as follows: "That which truth will reveal cannot in any way be opposed to the sacred books of the Old and the New Testament." [12]

[7]   From this we evidently gather the following conclusion: whatever arguments are brought forward against the doctrines of faith are conclusions incorrectly derived from the first and self-evident principles imbedded in nature. Such conclusions do not have the force of demonstration; they are arguments that are either probable or sophistical. And so, there exists the possibility to answer them.

CHAPTER 8

How the Human Reason Is Related to the Truth of Faith

[1]   There is also a further consideration. Sensible things, from which the human reason takes the origin of its knowledge, retain within themselves some sort of trace of a likeness to God. This is so imperfect, however, that it is absolutely inadequate to manifest the substance of God. For effects bear within themselves, in their own way, the likeness of their causes, since an agent produces its like; yet an effect does not always reach to the full likeness of its cause. Now, the human reason is related to the knowledge of the truth of faith (a truth which can be most evident only to those who see the divine substance) in such a way that it can gather certain likenesses of it, which are yet not sufficient so that the truth of faith may be comprehended as being understood demonstratively or through itself. Yet it is useful for the human reason to exercise itself in such arguments, however weak they may be, provided only that there be present no presumption to comprehend or to demonstrate. For to be able to see something of the loftiest realities, however thin and weak the sight may be, is, as our previous remarks indicate, a cause of the greatest joy.

[2]   The testimony of Hilary agrees with this. Speaking of this same truth, he writes as follows in his *De Trinitate:* "Enter these truths by believing, press forward, persevere. And though I may know that you will not arrive at an end, yet I will congratulate you in your progress. For, though he who pursues the infinite with reverence will never finally reach the end, yet he will always progress by pressing onward. But do not intrude yourself into the divine secret, do not, presuming to comprehend the sum total of intelligence, plunge yourself into the mystery of the unending nativity; rather, understand that these things are incomprehensible." [13]

NOTES

1. Aristotle, *Nicomachean Ethics*, I, 3 (1094b 24).
2. Boethius, *De Trinitate*, II (*PL*, 64, col. 1250).
3. Aristotle, *Posterior Analytics*, II, 3 (90b 31).
4. Aristotle, *Metaphysics*, Iα, 1 (993b 9).
5. Aristotle, *Physics*, VII, 3 (247b 9).
6. *SCG*, III, ch. 48.
7. Ibid., ch. 3.
8. Aristotle, *Nicomachean Ethics*, X, 7 (1177b 31).
9. Aristotle, *De partibus animalium*, I, 5 (644b 32).
10. Aristotle, *De caelo et mundo*, II, 12 (291b 26).
11. St. Gregory, *Homiliae in evangelia*, II, hom. 26, i (*PL.*, 76, col. 1197).
12. St. Augustine, *De genesi ad litteram*, II, c. 18 (*PL*, 34, col. 280).
13. St. Hilary, *De Trinitate*, II, 10, ii (*PL*, 10, coll. 58-59).

Truth as Subjectivity

Soren Kierkegaard

All essential knowledge relates to existence, or only such knowledge as has an essential relationship to existence is essential knowledge. All knowledge which does not inwardly relate itself to existence, in the reflection of inwardness, is, essentially viewed, accidental knowledge; its degree and scope is essentially indifferent. That essential knowledge is essentially related to existence does not mean the above-mentioned identity which abstract thought postulates between thought and being; nor does it signify objectively, that knowledge corresponds to some thing existent as its object. But it means that knowledge has a relationship to the knower, who is essentially an existing individual, and that for this reason all essential knowledge is essentially related to existence. Only ethical and ethico-religious knowledge has an essential relationship to the existence of the knower.

Mediation is a mirage, like the I-am-I. From the abstract point of view everything is and nothing comes into being. Mediation can therefore have no place in abstract thought, because it presupposes *movement*. Objec-

From "The Subjective Truth, Inwardness; Truth is Subjectivity," in Sören Kierkegaard, *Concluding Unscientific Postscript*, transl. by David F. Swenson and Walter Lowrie (copyright 1941 © 1969 by Princeton University Press; Princeton Paperback, 1968), pp. 176-188. Reprinted by permission of Princeton University Press and the American Scandinavian Foundation.

tive knowledge may indeed have the existent for its object; but since the knowing subject is an existing individual, and through the fact of his existence in process of becoming, philosophy must first explain how a particular existing subject is related to a knowledge of mediation. It must explain what he is in such a moment, if not pretty nearly *distrait;* where he is, if not in the moon? There is constant talk of mediation and mediation; is mediation then a man, as Peter Deacon believes that *Imprimatur* is a man? How does a human being manage to become something of this kind? Is this dignity, this great *philosophicum,* the fruit of study, or does the magistrate give it away, like the office of deacon or grave-digger? Try merely to enter into these and other such plain questions of a plain man, who would gladly become mediation if it could be done in some lawful and honest manner, and not either by saying *ein zwei drei kokolorum,* or by forgetting that he is himself an existing human being, for whom existence is therefore something essential, and an ethico-religious existence a suitable *quantum satis.* A speculative philosopher may perhaps find it in bad taste to ask such questions. But it is important not to direct the polemic to the wrong point, and hence not to begin in a fantastic objective manner to discuss *pro* and *contra* whether there is a mediation or not, but to hold fast what it means to be a human being.

In an attempt to make clear the difference of way that exists between an objective and a subjective reflection, I shall now proceed to show how a subjective reflection makes its way inwardly in inwardness. Inwardness in an existing subject culminates in passion; corresponding to passion in the subject the truth becomes a paradox; and the fact that the truth becomes a paradox is rooted precisely in its having a relationship to an existing subject. Thus the one corresponds to the other. By forgetting that one is an existing subject, passion goes by the board and the truth is no longer a paradox; the knowing subject becomes a fantastic entity rather than a human being, and the truth becomes a fantastic object for the knowledge of this fantastic entity.

When the question of truth is raised in an objective manner, reflection is directed objectively to the truth, as an object to which the knower is related. Reflection is not focussed upon the relationship, however, but upon the question of whether it is the truth to which the knower is related. If only the object to which he is related is the truth, the subject is accounted to be in the truth. When the question of the truth is raised subjectively, reflection is directed subjectively to the nature of the individual's relationship; if only the mode of this relationship is in the truth, the individual is in the truth even if he should happen to be thus related to what is not true.[1] Let us take as an example the knowledge of God. Objectively, reflection is directed to the problem of whether this object is the true God; subjectively, reflection is directed to the question whether the individual is related to a something *in such a manner* that his relationship is in truth a God-relationship. On which side is the truth now to be found? Ah, may we not here resort to a mediation, and say: It is on neither side, but in the mediation of both? Excellently well said, provided we might have it explained how an existing individual manages to be in a state of mediation. For to be in a state of mediation is to be finished, while to exist is to become. Nor can an existing individual be in two places at the same time—he cannot be an identity of subject and object. When he is nearest to being in two places at the same time he is in passion; but passion is momentary, and passion is also the highest expression of subjectivity.

The existing individual who chooses to pursue the objective way enters upon the entire approximation-process by which it is proposed to bring God to light objectively. But this is in all eternity impossible, because God is a subject, and therefore exists only for subjectivity in inwardness. The existing individual who chooses the subjective way apprehends instantly the entire dialectical difficulty involved in having to use some time, perhaps a long time, in finding God objectively; and he feels this dialectical difficulty in all its painfulness, because every moment is wasted in which he does not have God.[2] That very instant he has God, not by virtue of any objective deliberation, but by virtue of the infinite passion of inwardness. The objective inquirer, on the other hand, is not embarrassed by such dialectical difficulties as are involved in devoting an entire period of investigation to finding God—since it is possible that the inquirer may die tomorrow; and if he lives he can scarcely regard God as something to be taken along if convenient, since God is precisely that which one takes *a tout prix,* which in the understanding of passion constitutes the true inward relationship to God.

It is at this point, so difficult dialectically, that the way swings off for everyone who knows what it means to think, and to think existentially; which is something very different from sitting at a desk and writing about what one has never done, something very different from writing *de omnibus dubitandum* and at the same time being as credulous existentially as the most sensuous of men. Here is where the way swings off, and the change is marked by the fact that while objective knowledge rambles comfortably on by way of the long road of approximation without being impelled by the urge of passion, subjective knowledge counts every delay a deadly peril, and the decision so infinitely important and so instantly pressing that it is as if the opportunity had already passed.

Now when the problem is to reckon up on which side there is most truth, whether on the side of one who seeks the true God objectively, and pursues the approximate truth of the God-idea; or on the side of one who, driven by the infinite passion of his need of God, feels an infinite concern for his own relationship to God in truth (and to be at one and the same time on both sides equally, is as we have noted not possible for an existing individual, but is merely the happy delusion of an imaginary I-am-I): the answer cannot be in doubt for anyone who has not been demoralized with the aid of science. If one who lives in the midst of Christendom goes up to the house of God, the house of the true God, with the true conception of God in his knowledge, and prays, but prays in a false spirit; and one who lives in an idolatrous community prays with the entire passion of the infinite, although his eyes rest upon the image of an idol: where is there most truth? The one prays in truth to God though he worships in idol; the other prays falsely to the true God, and hence worships in fact an idol.

When one man investigates objectively the problem of immortality, and another embraces an uncertainty with the passion of the infinite: where is there most truth, and who has the greater certainty? The one has entered upon a never-ending approximation, for the certainty of immortality lies precisely in the subjectivity of the individual; the other is immortal, and fights for his immortality by struggling with the uncertainty. Let us consider Socrates. Nowadays everyone dabbles in a few proofs; some have several such proofs, others fewer. But Socrates! He puts the question objectively in a problematic manner: *if* there is an immortality. He must therefore be accounted a doubter in comparison with one of our modern thinkers with the three proofs? By no means. On this "if" he risks his entire life, he has the courage to meet death, and he has with the passion of the infinite so determined the pattern of his life that it must be found acceptable—*if* there is an immortality. Is any better proof capable of being given for the immortality of the soul? But those who have the three proofs do not at all determine their lives in conformity therewith; if there is an immortality it must feel disgust over their manner of life: can any better refutation be given of the three proofs? The bit of uncertainty that Socrates had, helped him because he himself contributed the passion of the infinite; the three proofs that the others have do not profit them at all, because they are dead to spirit and enthusiasm, and their three proofs, in lieu of proving anything else, prove just this. A young girl may enjoy all the sweetness of love on the basis of what is merely a weak hope that she is beloved, because she rests everything on this weak hope; but many a wedded matron more than once subjected to the strongest expressions of love, has in so far indeed had proofs, but strangely enough has not enjoyed *quod erat demonstrandum.* The Socratic ignorance, which Socrates held fast with the entire passion of his inwardness, was thus an expression for the principle that the eternal truth is related to an existing individual, and that this truth must therefore be a paradox for him as long as he exists; and yet it is possible that there was more truth in the Socratic ignorance as it was in him, than in the entire objective truth of the System, which flirts what the times demand and accommodates itself to *Privatdocents.*

The objective accent falls on WHAT is said, the subjective accent on HOW it is said. This distinction holds even in the aesthetic realm, and receives definite expression in the principle that what is in itself true may in the mouth of such and such a person become untrue. In these times this distinction is particularly worthy of notice, for if we wish to express in a single sentence the difference between ancient times and our own, we should doubtless have to say: "In ancient times only an individual here and there knew the truth; now all know it, except that the inwardness of its appropriation stands in an inverse relationship to the extent of its dissemination."[3] Aesthetically the contradiction that truth becomes untruth in this or that person's mouth, is best construed comically: In the ethico-religious sphere, accent is again on the "how." But this is not to be understood as referring to demeanor, expression, or the like; rather it refers to the relationship sustained by the existing individual, in his own existence, to the content of his utterance. Objectively the interest is focussed merely on the thought-content, subjectively on the inwardness. At its maximum this inward "how" is the passion of the infinite, and the passion of the infinite is the truth. But the passion of the infinite is precisely subjectivity, and thus subjectivity becomes the truth. Objectively there is no infinite decisiveness, and hence it is objectively in order to annul the difference between good and evil, together with the principle of contradiction, and therewith also the infinite difference between the true and the false. Only in subjectivity is there decisiveness, to seek objectivity is to be in error. It is the passion of the infinite that is the decisive factor and not its content, for its content is precisely itself. In this manner subjectivity and the subjective "how" constitute the truth.

But the "how" which is thus subjectively accentuated precisely because the subject is an existing individual, is also subject to a dialectic with respect to time. In the passionate moment of decision, where the road swings away from objective knowledge, it seems as if the infinite decision were thereby realized. But in the same moment the existing individual finds himself in the temporal order, and the subjective "how" is transformed into a striving, a striving which receives indeed its impulse and a repeated renewal from the decisive passion of the infinite, but is nevertheless a striving.

When subjectivity is the truth, the conceptual determination of the truth must include an expression for the antithesis to objectivity, a memento of the fork in the road where the way swings off; this expression will at the same time serve as an indication of the tension of the subjective inwardness. Here is such a definition of truth: *An objective uncertainty held fast in an appropriation-process of the most passionate inwardness is the truth,* the highest truth attainable for an *existing* individual. At the point where the way swings off (and where this is cannot be specified objectively, since it is a matter of subjectivity), there objective knowledge is placed in abeyance. Thus the subject merely has, objectively, the uncertainty; but it is this which precisely increases the tension of that infinite passion which constitutes his inwardness. The truth is precisely the venture which chooses an objective uncertainty with the passion of the infinite. I contemplate the order of nature in the hope of finding God, and I see omnipotence and wisdom; but I also see much else that disturbs my mind and excites anxiety. The sum of all this is an objective uncertainty. But it is for this very reason that the inwardness becomes as intense as it is, for it embraces this objective uncertainty with the entire passion of the infinite. In the case of a mathematical proposition the objectivity is given, but for this reason the truth of such a proposition is also an indifferent truth.

But the above definition of truth is an equivalent expression for faith. Without risk there is no faith. Faith is precisely the contradiction between the infinite passion of the individual's inwardness and the objective uncertainty. If I am capable of grasping God objectively, I do not believe, but precisely because I cannot do this I must believe. If I wish to preserve myself in faith I must constantly be intent upon holding fast the objective uncertainty, so as to remain out upon the deep, over seventy thousand fathoms of water, still preserving my faith.

In the principle that subjectivity, inwardness, is the truth, there is comprehended the Socratic wisdom, whose everlasting merit it was to have become aware of the essential significance of existence, of the fact that the knower is an existing individual. For this reason Socrates was in the truth by virtue of his ignorance, in the highest sense in which this was possible within paganism. To attain to an understanding of this, to comprehend that the misfortune of speculative philosophy is again and again to have forgotten that the knower is an existing individual, is in our objective age difficult enough. But to have made an advance upon Socrates without even having understood what he understood, is at any rate not "Socratic." Compare the "Moral" of the *Fragments*.

Let us now start from this point, and as was attempted in the *Fragments,* seek a determination of thought which will really carry us further. I have nothing here to do with the question of whether this proposed thought-determination is true or not, since I am merely experimenting; but it must at any rate be clearly manifest that the Socratic thought is understood within the new proposal, so that a least I do not come out behind Socrates.

When subjectivity, inwardness, is the truth, the truth becomes objectively a paradox; and the fact that the truth is objectively a paradox shows in its turn that subjectivity is the truth. For the objective situation is repellent; and the expression for the objective repulsion constitutes the tension and the measure of the corresponding inwardness. The paradoxical character of the truth is its objective uncertainty; this uncertainty is an expression for the passionate inwardness, and this passion is precisely the truth. So far the Socratic principle. The eternal and essential truth, the truth which has an essential relationship to an existing individual because it pertains essentially to existence (all other knowledge being from the Socratic point of view accidental, its scope and degree a matter of indifference), is a paradox. But the eternal essential truth is by no means in itself a paradox; but it becomes paradoxical by virtue of its relationship to an existing individual. The Socratic ignorance gives expression to the objective uncertainty attaching to the truth, while his inwardness in existing is the truth. To anticipate here what will be developed later, let me make the following remark. The Socratic ignorance is an analogue to the category of the absurd, only that there is still less of objective certainty in the absurd, and in the repellent effect that the absurd exercises. It is certain only that it is absurd, and precisely on that account it incites to an infinitely greater tension in the corresponding inwardness. The Socratic inwardness in existing is an analogue to faith; only that the inwardness of faith, corresponding as it does, not to the repulsion of the Socratic ignorance, but to the repulsion exerted by the absurd, is infinitely more profound.

Socratically the eternal essential truth is by no means in its own nature paradoxical, but only in its relationship to an existing individual. This finds expression in another Socratic proposition, namely, that all knowledge is recollection. This proposition is not for Socrates a cue to the speculative enterprise, and hence he does not follow it up; essentially it becomes a Platonic principle. Here the way swings off; Socrates concentrates essentially upon accentuating existence, while Plato forgets this and loses himself in speculation. Socrates' infinite merit is to have been an *existing* thinker, not a speculative philosopher who forgets what it means to exist. For Socrates therefore the principle that all knowledge is recollection has at the moment of his leave-taking and as the constantly rejected possibility of engaging in speculation, the following two-fold significance: (1) that the knower is essentially *integer,* and that with respect to the knowledge of the eternal truth he is confronted with no other difficulty than the circumstances that he exists; which difficulty, however, is so essential and decisive for him that it means that existing, the process of transformation to inwardness in and by existing, is the truth; (2) that existence in time does not have any decisive significance, because the possibility of taking oneself back into eternity through recollection is always there, though this possibility is constantly nullified by utilizing the time, not for speculation, but for the transformation to inwardness in existing.[4]

The infinite merit of the Socratic position was precisely to accentuate the fact that the knower is an existing individual, and that the task of existing is his essential task. Making an advance upon Socrates by failing to understand this, is quite a mediocre achievement. This Socratic principle we must therefore bear in mind, and then inquire whether the formula may not be so altered as really to make an advance beyond the Socratic position.

Subjectivity, inwardness, has been posited as the truth; can any expression for the truth be found which has a still higher degree of inwardness? Aye, there is such an expression, provided the principle that subjectivity or inwardness is the truth begins by positing the opposite principle: that subjectivity is untruth. Let us not at this point succumb to such haste as to fail in making the necessary distinctions. Speculative philosophy also says that subjectivity is untruth, but says it in order to stimulate a movement in precisely the opposite direction, namely, in the direction of the principle that objectivity is the truth. Speculative philosophy determines subjectivity negatively as tending toward objectivity. This second determination of ours, however, places a hindrance in its own way while proposing to begin, which has the effect of making the inwardness far more intensive. Socratically speaking, subjectivity is untruth if it refuses to understand that subjectivity is truth, but, for example, desires to become objective. Here, on the other hand, subjectivity in beginning upon the task of becoming the truth through a subjectifying process, is in the difficulty that it is already untruth. Thus, the labor of the task is thrust backward, backward, that is, in inwardness. So far is it from being the case that the way tends in the direction of objectivity, that the beginning merely lies still deeper in subjectivity.

But the subject cannot be untruth eternally, or eternally be presupposed as having been untruth; it must have been brought to this condition in time, or here become untruth in time. The Socratic paradox consisted in the fact that the eternal was related to an existing individual, but now existence has stamped itself upon the existing individual a second time. There has taken place so essential an alteration in him that he cannot now possibly take himself back into the eternal by way of recollection. To do this is to speculate; to be able to do this, but to reject the possibility by apprehending the task of life as a realization of inwardness in existing, is the Socratic position. But now the difficulty is that what followed Socrates on his way as a rejected possibility, has become an impossibility. If engaging in speculation was a dubious merit even from the point of view of the Socratic, it is now neither more nor less than confusion.

The paradox emerges when the eternal truth and existence are placed in juxtaposition with one another; each time the stamp of existence is brought to bear, the paradox becomes more clearly evident. Viewed Socratically the knower was simply an existing individual, but now the existing individual bears the stamp of having been essentially altered by existence.

Let us now call the untruth of the individual *Sin*. Viewed eternally he cannot be sin, nor can he be eternally presupposed as having been in sin. By coming into existence therefore (for the beginning was that subjectivity is untruth), he becomes a sinner. He is not born as a sinner in the sense that he is presupposed as being a sinner before he is born, but he is born in sin and as a sinner. This we might call *Original Sin*. But if existence has in this manner acquired a power over him, he is prevented from taking himself back into the eternal by way of recollection. If it was paradoxical to posit the eternal truth in relationship to an existing individual, it is now absolutely paradoxical to posit it in relationship to such an individual as we have here defined. But the more difficult it is made for him to take himself out of existence by way of recollection, the more profound is the inwardness that his existence may have in existence; and when it is made impossible for him, when he is held so fast in existence that the back door of recollection is forever closed to him, then his inwardness will be the most profound possible. But let us never forget that the Socratic merit was to stress the fact that the knower is an existing individual; for the more difficult the matter becomes, the greater the temptation to hasten along the easy road of speculation, away from fearful dangers and crucial decisions, to the winning of renown and honors and property, and so forth. If even Socrates understood the dubiety of taking himself speculatively out of existence back into the eternal, although no other difficulty confronted the existing individual except that he existed, and that existing was his essential task, now it is impossible. Forward he must, backward he cannot go.

Subjectivity is the truth. By virtue of the relationship subsisting between the eternal truth and the existing individual, the paradox came into being. Let us now go further, let us suppose that the eternal essential truth is itself a paradox. How does the paradox come into being? By putting the eternal essential truth into juxtaposition with existence. Hence when we posit such a conjunction within the truth itself, the truth becomes a paradox. The eternal truth has come into being in time: this is the paradox. If in accordance with the determinations just posited, the subject is prevented by sin from taking himself back into the eternal, now he need not trouble himself about this; for now the eternal essential truth is not behind him but in front of him, through its being in existence or having existed, so that if the individual does not existentially and in existence lay hold of the truth, he will never lay hold of it.

Existence can never be more sharply accentuated than by means of these determinations. The evasion by which speculative philosophy attempts to recollect itself out of existence has been made impossible. With reference to this, there is nothing for speculation to do except to arrive at an understanding of this impossibility; every speculative attempt which insists on being speculative shows *eo ipso* that it has not understood it. The individual may thrust all this away from him, and take refuge in speculation; but it is impossible first to accept it, and then to revoke it by means of speculation, since it is definitely calculated to prevent speculation.

When the eternal truth is related to an existing individual it becomes a paradox. The paradox repels in the inwardness of the existing individual, through the objective uncertainty and the corresponding Socratic ignorance. But since the paradox is not in the first instance itself paradoxical (but only in its relationship to the existing individual), it does not repel with a sufficient intensive inwardness. For without risk there is no faith, and the greater the risk the greater the faith; the more objective security the less inwardness (for inwardness is precisely subjectivity), and the less objective security the more profound the possible inwardness. When the paradox is paradoxical in itself, it repels the individual by virtue of its absurdity, and the corresponding passion of inwardness is faith. But subjectivity, inwardness, is the truth; for otherwise we have forgotten what the merit of the Socratic position is. But there can be no stronger expression for inwardness than when the retreat out of existence into the eternal by way of recollection is impossible; and when, with truth confronting the individual as a paradox, gripped in the anguish and pain of sin, facing the tremendous risk of the objective insecurity, the individual believes. But without risk no faith, not even the Socratic form of faith, much less the form of which we here speak.

When Socrates believed that there was a God, he held fast to the objective uncertainty with the whole passion of his inwardness, and it is precisely in this contradiction and in this risk, that faith is rooted. Now it is otherwise. Instead of the objective uncertainty, there is here a certainty, namely, that objectively it is absurd; and this absurdity, held fast in the passion of inwardness, is faith. The Socratic ignorance is as a witty jest in comparison with the earnestness of facing the absurd; and the Socratic existential inwardness is as Greek light-mindedness in comparison with the grave strenuosity of faith.

What now is the absurd? The absurd is—that the eternal truth has come into being in time, that God has come into being, has been born, has grown up, and so forth, precisely like any other individual human being, quite indistinguishable from other individuals.

NOTES

1. The reader will observe that the question here is about essential truth or about the truth which is essentially related to existence, and that it is precisely for the sake of clarifying it as inwardness or as subjectivity that this contrast is drawn.
2. In this manner God certainly becomes a postulate, but not in the otiose manner in which this word is commonly understood. It becomes clear rather that the only way in which an existing individual comes into relation with God, is when the dialectical contradiction brings his passion to the point of despair, and helps him to embrace God with the "category of despair" (faith). Then the postulate is so far from being arbitrary that it is precisely a life-necessity. It is then not so much that God is a postulate, as that the existing individual's postulation of God is a necessity.
3. *Stages on Life's Way*. Though ordinarily not wishing an expression of opinion on the part of reviewers, I might at this point almost desire it, provided such opinions, so far from flattering me, amounted to an assertion of the daring truth that what I say is something that everybody knows, even every child, and that the cultured know infinitely much better. If it only stands fast that everyone knows it, my standpoint is in order, and I shall doubtless make shift to manage with the unity of the comic and the tragic. If there were anyone who did not know it I might perhaps be in danger of being dislodged from my position of equilibrium by the thought that I might be in a position to communicate to someone the needful preliminary knowledge. It is just this which engages my interest so much, this that the cultured are accustomed to say: that everyone knows what the highest is. This was not the case in paganism, nor in Judaism, nor in the seventeen centuries of Christianity. Hail to the nineteenth century! Everyone knows it. What progress has been made since the time when only a few knew it. To make up for this, perhaps, we must assume that no one nowadays does it.
4. This will perhaps be the proper place to offer an explanation with respect to a difficulty in the plan of the *Fragments*, which had its ground in the fact that I did not wish at once to make the case as difficult dialectically as it is, because in our age terminologies and the like are turned so topsy-turvy that it is al-

most impossible to secure oneself against confusion. In order if possible clearly to exhibit the difference between the Socratic position (which was supposed to be the philosophical, the pagan-philosophical position) and the experimentally evoked thought-determination which really makes an advance beyond the Socratic, I carried the Socratic back to the principle that all knowledge is recollection. This is, in a way, commonly assumed, and only one who with a specialized interest concerns himself with the Socratic, returning again and again to the sources, only for him would it be of importance on this point to distinguish between Socrates and Plato. The proposition does indeed belong to both, only that Socrates is always departing from it, in order to exist. By holding Socrates down to the proposition that all knowledge is recollection, he becomes a speculative philosopher instead of an existential thinker, for whom existence is the essential thing. The recollection-principle belongs to speculative philosophy, and recollection is immanence, and speculatively and eternally there is no paradox. But the difficulty is that no human being is speculative philosophy; the speculative philosopher himself is an existing individual, subject to the claims that existence makes upon him. There is no merit in forgetting this, but a great merit in holding it fast, and this is precisely what Socrates did. To accentuate existence, which also involves the qualification of inwardness, is the Socratic position; the Platonic tendency, on the other hand, is to pursue the lure of recollections and immanence. This puts Socrates fundamentally in advance of speculative philosophy; he does not have a fantastic beginning, in which the speculative philosopher first disguises himself, and then goes on and on to speculate, forgetting the most important thing of all, which is to exist. But precisely because Socrates is thus in advance of speculation, he presents, when properly delineated, a certain analogous resemblance to that which the experiment described as in truth going beyond the Socratic. The truth as paradox in the Socratic sense becomes analogous to the paradox *sensu eminentiori,* the passion of inwardness in existing becomes an analogue to faith *sensu eminentiori.* That the difference is none the less infinite, that the characterization which the *Fragments* made of that which in truth goes beyond the Socratic remains unchanged, it will be easy to show; but by using at once apparently the same determinations, or at any rate the same words, about these two different things, I feared to cause a misunderstanding. Now I think there can be no objection to speaking of the paradoxical and of faith in reference to Socrates, since it is quite correct to do so when properly understood. Besides, the old Greeks also used the word *pistis,* though not by any means in the sense of the experiment; and they used it in such a manner that, especially with reference to a work of Aristotle where the term is employed, it would be possible to set forth some very enlightening considerations bearing upon its difference from faith *sensu eminentiori.*

IMPEDIMENTS to RELIGIOUS BELIEF: INTERNAL

God and Evil

H.J. McCloskey

A. THE PROBLEM STATED

Evil is a problem for the theist in that a contradiction is involved in
the fact of evil on the one hand, and the belief in the omnipotence
and perfection of God on the other. God cannot be both all-powerful
and perfectly good if evil is real. This contradiction is well set out in
its detail by Mackie in his discussion of the problem.[1] In his discussion
Mackie seeks to show that this contradiction cannot be resolved in
terms of man's free will. In arguing in this way Mackie neglects a large
number of important points, and concedes far too much to the theist.
He implicitly allows that whilst physical evil creates a problem, this
problem is reducible to the problem of moral evil and that therefore
the satisfactoriness of solutions of the problem of evil turns on the
compatibility of free will and absolute goodness. In fact physical evils
create a number of distinct problems which are not reducible to the
problem of moral evil. Further, the proposed solution of the problem
of moral evil in terms of free will renders the attempt to account for
physical evil in terms of moral good, and the attempt thereby to reduce
the problem of evil to the problem of moral evil, completely untenable.
Moreover, the account of moral evil in terms of free will breaks down
on more obvious and less disputable grounds than those indicated by
Mackie. Moral evil can be shown to remain a problem whether or not
free will is compatible with absolute goodness. I therefore propose in this
paper to reopen the discussion of "the problem of evil", by approaching
it from a more general standpoint, examining a wider variety of solutions than those considered by Mackie and his critics.

The fact of evil creates a problem for the theist; but there are a
number of simple solutions available to a theist who is content seriously
to modify his theism. He can either admit a limit to God's power, or
he can deny God's moral perfection. He can assert either (1) that God
is not powerful enough to make a world that does not contain evil, or

From *The Philosophical Quarterly*, Vol. 10 (1960), pp. 97-114. Reprinted by permission of the author and the editor.

(2) that God created only the good in the universe and that some other power created the evil, or (3) that God is all-powerful but morally imperfect, and chose to create an imperfect universe. Few Christians accept these solutions, and this is no doubt partly because such 'solutions' ignore the real inspiration of religious beliefs, and partly because they introduce embarrassing complications for the theist in his attempts to deal with other serious problems. However, if any one of these 'solutions' is accepted, then the problem of evil is avoided, and a weakened version of theism is made secure from attacks based upon the fact of the occurrence of evil.

For more orthodox theism, according to which God is both omnipotent and perfectly good, evil creates a real problem; and this problem is well-stated by the Jesuit, Father G. H. Joyce. Joyce writes:

> "The existence of evil in the world must at all times be the greatest of all problems which the mind encounters when it reflects on God and His relation to the world. If He is, indeed, all-good and all-powerful, how has evil any place in the world which He has made? Whence came it? Why is it here? If He is all-good why did He allow it to arise? If all-powerful why does He not deliver us from the burden? Alike in the physical and moral order creation seems so grievously marred that we find it hard to understand how it can derive in its entirety from God." [2]

The facts which give rise to the problem are of two general kinds, and give rise to two distinct types of problem. These two general kinds of evil are usually referred to as 'physical' and as 'moral' evil. These terms are by no means apt—suffering for instance is not strictly physical evil—and they conceal significant differences. However, this terminology is too widely-accepted, and too convenient to be dispensed with here, the more especially as the various kinds of evil, whilst important as distinct kinds, need not for our purposes be designated by separate names.

Physical evil and moral evil then are the two general forms of evil which independently and jointly constitute conclusive grounds for denying the existence of God in the sense defined, namely as an all-powerful, perfect Being. The acuteness of these two general problems is evident when we consider the nature and extent of the evils of which account must be given. To take physical evils, looking first at the less important of these.

(a) *Physical evils:* Physical evils are involved in the very constitution of the earth and animal kingdom. There are deserts and icebound areas; there are dangerous animals of prey, as well as creatures such as scorpions and snakes. There are also pests such as flies and fleas and the hosts of other insect pests, as well as the multitude of lower parasites such as tapeworms, hookworms and the like. Secondly, there are the various natural calamities and the immense human suffering that follows in their wake—fires, floods, tempests, tidal-waves, volcanoes, earthquakes, droughts and famines. Thirdly, there are the vast numbers of diseases that torment and ravage man. Diseases such as leprosy, cancer, polio-myelitis, appear *prima facie* not to be creations which are to be ex-pected of a benevolent Creator. Fourthly, there are the evils with which so many are born—the various physical deformities and defects such as misshapen limbs, blindness, deafness, dumbness, mental deficiency and insanity. Most of these evils contribute towards increasing human pain and suffering; but not all physical evils are reducible simply to pain. Many of these evils are evils whether or not they result in pain. This is important, for it means that, unless there is one solution to such diverse evils, it is both inaccurate and positively misleading to speak of *the* problem of physical evil. Shortly I shall be arguing that no one 'solution' covers all these evils, so we shall have to conclude that physical evils create not one problem but a number of distinct problems for the theist.

The nature of the various difficulties referred to by the theist as the problem of physical evil is indicated by Joyce in a way not untypical among the more honest, philosophical theists, as follows:

> "The actual amount of suffering which the human race endures is im-mense. Disease has store and to spare of torments for the body: and dis-ease and death are the lot to which we must all look forward. At all times, too, great numbers of the race are pinched by want. Nor is the world ever free for very long from the terrible sufferings which follow in the track of war. If we concentrate our attention on human woes, to the exclusion of the joys of life, we gain an appalling picture of the ills to which the flesh is heir. So too if we fasten our attention on the sterner side of nature, on the pains which men endure from natural forces—on the storms which wreck their ships, the cold which freezes them to death, the fire which consumes them—if we contemplate this aspect of nature alone we may be led to wonder how God came to deal so harshly with His Creatures as to provide them with such a home."

Many such statements of the problem proceed by suggesting, if not by stating, that the problem arises at least in part by concentrating one's attention too exclusively on one aspect of the world. This is quite con-trary to the facts. The problem is not one that results from looking at only one aspect of the universe. It may be the case that over-all pleasure predominates over pain, and that physical goods in general predominate over physical evils, but the opposite may equally well be the case. It is both practically impossible and logically impossible for this question to be resolved. However, it is not an unreasonable presumption, with the large bulk of mankind inadequately fed and housed and without adequate medical and health services, to suppose that physical evils at present predominate over physical goods. In the light of the facts at our disposal, this would seem to be a much more reasonable conclusion than the conclusion hinted at by Joyce and openly advanced by less cautious theists, namely, that physical goods in fact outweigh physical evils in the world.

However, the question is not, Which predominates, physical good or physical evil? The problem of physical evil remains a problem whether the balance in the universe is on the side of physical good or not, because the problem is that of accounting for the fact that physical evil occurs at all.

(*b*) *Moral evil:* Physical evils create one of the groups of problems referred to by the theist as 'the problem of evil'. Moral evil creates quite a distinct problem. Moral evil is simply immorality—evils such as selfishness, envy, greed, deceit, cruelty, callousness, cowardice and the larger scale evils such as wars and the atrocities they involve.

Moral evil is commonly regarded as constituting an even more serious problem than physical evil. Joyce so regards it, observing:

> "The man who sins thereby offends God. . . . We are called on to explain how God came to create an order of things in which rebellion and even final rejection have such a place. Since a choice from among an infinite number of possible worlds lay open to God, how came He to choose one in which these occur? Is not such a choice in flagrant opposition to the Divine Goodness?"

Some theists seek a solution by denying the reality of evil or by describing it as a 'privation' or absence of good. They hope thereby to explain it away as not needing a solution. This, in the case of most of the evils which require explanation, seems to amount to little more than an attempt to sidestep the problem simply by changing the name of that which has to be explained. It can be exposed for what it is simply by describing some of the evils which have to be explained. That is why a survey of the data to be accounted for is a most important part of the discussion of the problem of evil.

In *The Brothers Karamazov*, Dostoievsky introduces a discussion of the problem of evil by reference to some then recently committed atrocities. Ivan states the problem:

> " 'By the way, a Bulgarian I met lately in Moscow', Ivan went on . . . 'told me about the crimes committed by Turks in all parts of Bulgaria through fear of a general rising of the Slavs. They burn villages, murder, outrage women and children, and nail their prisoners by the ears to the fences, leave them till morning, and in the morning hang them—all sorts of things you can't imagine. People talk sometimes of bestial cruelty, but that's a great injustice and insult to the beasts; a beast can never be so cruel as a man, so artistically cruel. The tiger only tears and gnaws and that's all he can do. He would never think of nailing people by the ears, even if he were able to do it. These Turks took a pleasure in torturing children too; cutting the unborn child from the mother's womb, and tossing babies up in the air and catching them on the points of their bayonets

before their mothers' eyes. Doing it before the mother's eyes was what gave zest to the amusement. Here is another scene that I thought very interesting. Imagine a trembling mother with her baby in her arms, a circle of invading Turks around her. They've planned a diversion: they pet the baby to make it laugh. They succeed; the baby laughs. At that moment, a Turk points a pistol four inches from the baby's face. The baby laughs with glee, holds out its little hands to the pistol, and he pulls the trigger in the baby's face and blows out its brains. Artistic, wasn't it?' " [3]

Ivan's statement of the problem was based on historical events. Such happenings did not cease in the nineteenth century. *The Scourge of the Swastika* by Lord Russell of Liverpool contains little else than descriptions of such atrocities; and it is simply one of a host of writings giving documented lists of instances of evils, both physical and moral.

Thus the problem of evil is both real and acute. There is a clear *prima facie* case that evil and God are incompatible—both cannot exist. Most theists admit this, and that the onus is on them to show that the conflict is not fatal to theism; but a consequence is that a host of proposed solutions are advanced.

The mere fact of such a multiplicity of proposed solutions, and the widespread repudiation of each other's solutions by theists, in itself suggests that the fact of evil is an insuperable obstacle to theism as defined here. It also makes it impossible to treat of all proposed solutions, and all that can be attempted here is an examination of those proposed solutions which are most commonly invoked and most generally thought to be important by theists.

Some theists admit the reality of the problem of evil, and then seek to sidestep it, declaring it to be a great mystery which we poor humans cannot hope to comprehend. Other theists adopt a rational approach and advance rational arguments to show that evil, properly understood, is compatible with, and even a consequence of God's goodness. The arguments to be advanced in this paper are directed against the arguments of the latter theists; but in so far as these arguments are successful against the rational theists, to that extent they are also effective in showing that the non-rational approach in terms of great mysteries is positively irrational.

B. PROPOSED SOLUTIONS TO THE PROBLEM OF PHYSICAL EVIL

Of the large variety of arguments advanced by theists as solutions to the problem of physical evil, five popularly used and philosophically significant solutions will be examined. They are, in brief: (i) Physical good (pleasure) requires physical evil (pain) to exist at all; (ii) Physical evil is God's punishment of sinners; (iii) Physical evil is God's warning and reminder to man; (iv) Physical evil is the result of the natural laws, the operations of which are on the whole good; (v) Physical evil increases the total good.

(i) *Physical good is impossible without physical evil:* Pleasure is possible only by way of contrast with pain. Here the analogy of colour is used. If everything were blue we should, it is argued, understand neither what colour is nor what blue is. So with pleasure and pain.

The most obvious defect of such an argument is that it does not cover all physical goods and evils. It is an argument commonly invoked by those who think of physical evil as creating only one problem, namely the problem of human pain. However, the problems of physical evils are not reducible to the one problem, the problem of pain; hence the argument is simply irrelevant to much physical evil. Disease and insanity are evils, but health and sanity are possible in the total absence of disease and insanity. Further, if the argument were in any way valid even in respect of pain, it would imply the existence of only a speck of pain, and not the immense amount of pain in the universe. A speck of yellow is all that is needed for an appreciation of blueness and of colour generally. The argument is therefore seen to be seriously defective on two counts even if its underlying principle is left unquestioned. If its underlying principle is questioned, the argument is seen to be essentially invalid. Can it seriously be maintained that if an individual were born crippled and deformed and never in his life experienced pleasure, that he could not experience pain, not even if he were severely injured? It is clear that pain is possible in the absence of pleasure. It is true that it might not be distinguished by a special name and called 'pain', but the state we now describe as a painful state would nonetheless be possible in the total absence of pleasure. So too the converse would seem to apply. Plato brings this out very clearly in Book 9 of the *Republic* in respect of the pleasures of taste and smell. These pleasures seem not to depend for their existence on any prior experience of pain. Thus the argument is unsound in respect of its main contention; and in being unsound in this respect, it is at the same time ascribing a serious limitation to God's power. It maintains that God cannot create pleasure without creating pain, although as we have seen, pleasure and pain are not correlatives.

(ii) *Physical evil is God's punishment for sin:* This kind of explanation was advanced to explain the terrible Lisbon earthquake in the 18th century, in which 40,000 people were killed. There are many replies to this argument, for instance Voltaire's. Voltaire asked: "Did God in this earthquake select the 40,000 least virtuous of the Portuguese citizens?" The distribution of disease and pain is in no obvious way related to the virtue of the persons afflicted, and popular saying has it that the distribution is slanted in the opposite direction. The only way of meeting the fact that evils are not distributed proportionately to the evil of the sufferer is by suggesting that all human beings, including children, are such miserable sinners, that our offences are of such enormity, that God would be justified in punishing all of us as severely as it is possible for humans to be punished; but even then, God's apparent caprice in the selection of His victims requires explanation. In any case it is by no means clear that young children who very often suffer severely are guilty of sin of such an enormity as would be necessary to justify their sufferings as punishment.

Further, many physical evils are simultaneous with birth—insanity, mental defectiveness, blindness, deformities, as well as much disease. No crime or sin of *the child* can explain and justify these physical evils as punishment; and, for a parent's sin to be punished in the child is injustice or evil of another kind.

Similarly, the sufferings of animals cannot be accounted for as punishment. For these various reasons, therefore, this argument must be rejected. In fact it has dropped out of favour in philosophical and theological circles, but it continues to be invoked at the popular level.

(iii) *Physical evil is God's warning to men:* It is argued, for instance of physical calamities, that "they serve a moral end which compensates the physical evil which they cause. The awful nature of these phenomena, the overwhelming power of the forces at work, and man's utter helplessness before them, rouse him from the religious indifference to which he is so prone. They inspire a reverential awe of the Creator who made them, and controls them, and a salutary fear of violating the laws which He has imposed" (Joyce). This is where immortality is often alluded to as justifying evil.

This argument proceeds from a proposition that is plainly false; and that the proposition from which it proceeds is false is conceded implicitly by most theologians. Natural calamities do not necessarily turn people to God, but rather present the problem of evil in an acute form; and the problem of evil is said to account for more defections from religion than any other cause. Thus if God's object in bringing about natural calamities is to inspire reverence and awe, He is a bungler. There are many more reliable methods of achieving this end. Equally important, the use of physical evil to achieve this object is hardly the course one would expect a benevolent God to adopt when other, more effective, less evil methods are available to Him, for example, miracles, special revelation, etc.

(iv) *Evils are the results of the operation of laws of nature:* This fourth argument relates to most physical evil, but it is more usually used to account for animal suffering and physical calamities. These evils are said to result from the operation of the natural laws which govern these objects, the relevant natural laws being the various causal laws, the law of pleasure-pain as a law governing sentient beings, etc. The theist argues that the non-occurrence of these evils would involve either the constant intervention by God in a miraculous way, and contrary to his own natural laws, or else the construction of a universe with different components subject to different laws of nature; for God, in creating a certain kind of being, must create it subject to its appropriate law; He cannot create it and subject it to any law of His own choosing. Hence He creates a world which has components and laws good in their total effect, although calamitous in some particular effects.

Against this argument three objections are to be urged. First, it does not cover all physical evil. Clearly not all disease can be accounted for along these lines. Secondly, it is not to give a reason against God's miraculous intervention simply to assert that it would be unreasonable for Him constantly to intervene in the operation of His own laws. Yet this is the only reason that theists seem to offer here. If, by intervening in respect to the operation of His laws, God could thereby eliminate an evil, it would seem to be unreasonable and evil of Him not to do so. Some theists seek a way out of this difficulty by denying that God has the power miraculously to intervene; but this is to ascribe a severe limitation to His power. It amounts to asserting that when His Creation has been effected, God can do nothing else except contemplate it. The third objection is related to this, and is to the effect that it is already to ascribe a serious limitation to God's omnipotence to suggest that He could not make sentient beings which did not experience pain, nor sentient beings without deformities and deficiencies, nor natural phenomena with different laws of nature governing them. There is no reason why better laws of nature governing the existing objects are not possible on the divine hypothesis. Surely, if God is all-powerful, He could have made a better universe in the first place, or one with better laws of nature governing it, so that the operation of its laws did not produce calamities and pain. To maintain this is not to suggest that an omnipotent God should be capable of achieving what is logically impossible. All that has been indicated here is logically possible, and therefore not beyond the powers of a being Who is really omnipotent.

This fourth argument seeks to exonerate God by explaining that He created a universe sound on the whole, but such that He had no direct control over the laws governing His creations, and had control only in His selection of His creations. The previous two arguments attribute the detailed results of the operations of these laws directly to God's will. Theists commonly use all three arguments. It is not without significance that they betray such uncertainty as to whether God is to be *commended* or *exonerated*.

(v) *The universe is better with evil in it:* This is the important argument. One version of it runs:

> "Just as the human artist has in view the beauty of his composition as a whole, not making it his aim to give to each several part the highest degree of brilliancy, but that measure of adornment which most contributes to the combined effect, so it is with God" (Joyce).

Another version of this general type of argument explains evil not so much as *a component* of a good whole, seen out of its context as a mere component, but rather as *a means* to a greater good. Different as these versions are, they may be treated here as one general type of argument, for the same criticisms are fatal to both versions.

This kind of argument if valid simply shows that some evil may enrich the universe; it tells us nothing about *how much* evil will enrich this particular universe, and how much will be too much. So, even if valid in principle—and shortly I shall argue that it is not valid—such an argument does not in itself provide a justification for the evil in the universe. It shows amply that the evil which occurs might have a justification. In view of the immense amount of evil the probabilities are against it.

This is the main point made by Wisdom in his discussion of this argument. Wisdom sums up his criticism as follows:

> "It remains to add that, unless there are independent arguments in favour of this world's being the best logically possible world, it is probable that some of the evils in it are not logically necessary to a compensating good; it is probable because there are so many evils." [4]

Wisdom's reply brings out that the person who relies upon this argument as a conclusive and complete argument is seriously mistaken. The argument, if valid, justifies only some evil. A belief that it justifies all the evil that occurs in the world is mistaken, for a second argument, by way of a supplement to it, is needed. This supplementary argument would take the form of a proof that all the evil that occurs is *in fact* valuable and necessary as a means to greater good. Such a supplementary proof is in principle impossible; so, at best, this fifth argument can be taken to show only that some evil *may be* necessary for the production of good, and that the evil in the world may perhaps have a justification on this account. This is not to justify a physical evil, but simply to suggest that physical evil might nonetheless have a justification, although we may never come to know this justification.

Thus the argument even if it is valid as a general form of reasoning is unsatisfactory because inconclusive. It is, however, also unsatisfactory in that it follows on the principle of the argument that, just as it is possible that evil in the total context contributes to increasing the total ultimate good, so equally, it will hold that good in the total context may increase the ultimate evil. Thus if the principle of the argument were sound, we could never know whether evil is really evil, or good really good. (Aesthetic analogies may be used to illustrate this point.) By implication it follows that it would be dangerous to eliminate evil because we may thereby introduce a discordant element into the divine symphony of the universe; and, conversely, it may be wrong to condemn the elimination of what is good, because the latter may result in the production of more, higher goods.

So it follows that, even if the general principle of the argument is not questioned, it is still seen to be a defective argument. On the one hand, it proves too little—it justifies only some evil and not necessarily all the evil in the universe; on the other hand it proves too much because it creates doubts about the goodness of apparent goods. These criticisms in themselves are fatal to the argument as a solution to the problem of physical evil. However, because this is one of the most popular and plausible accounts of physical evil, it is worthwhile considering whether it can properly be claimed to establish even the very weak conclusion indicated above.

Why, and in what way, is it supposed that physical evils such as pain and misery, disease and deformity, will heighten the total effect and add to the value of the moral whole? The answer given is that physical evil enriches the whole by giving rise to moral goodness. Disease, insanity, physical suffering and the like are said to bring into being the noble moral virtues—courage, endurance, benevolence, sympathy and the like. This is what the talk about the enriched whole comes to. W. D. Niven makes this explicit in his version of the argument:

> "Physical evil has been the goad which has impelled men to most of those achievements which made the history of man so wonderful. Hardship is a stern but fecund parent of invention. Where life is easy because physical ills are at a minimum we find man degenerating in body, mind, and character."

And Niven concludes by asking:

> "Which is preferable—a grim fight with the possibility of splendid triumph; or no battle at all?" [5]

The argument is: Physical evil brings moral good into being, and in fact is an essential precondition for the existence of some moral goods. Further, it is sometimes argued in this context that those moral goods which are possible in the total absence of physical evils are more valuable in themselves if they are achieved as a result of a struggle. Hence physical evil is said to be justified on the grounds that moral good plus physical evil is better than the absence of physical evil.

A common reply, and an obvious one, is that urged by Mackie.[6] Mackie argues that whilst it is true that moral good plus physical evil together are better than physical good alone, the issue is not as simple as that, for physical evil also gives rise to and makes possible many moral evils that would not or could not occur in the absence of physical evil. It is then urged that it is not clear that physical evils (for example, disease and pain) plus some moral goods (for example, courage) plus some moral evil (for example, brutality) are better than physical good and those moral goods which are possible and which would occur in the absence of physical evil.

This sort of reply, however, is not completely satisfactory. The objection it raises is a sound one, but it proceeds by conceding too much to the theist, and by overlooking two more basic defects of the argument. It allows implicitly that the problem of physical evil may be reduced to the problem of moral evil; and it neglects the two objections which show that the problem of physical evil cannot be so reduced.

The theist therefore happily accepts this kind of reply, and argues that, if he can give a satisfactory account of moral evil he will then have accounted for both physical and moral evil. He then goes on to account for moral evil in terms of the value of free will and/or its goods. This general argument is deceptively plausible. It breaks down for the two reasons indicated here, but it breaks down at another point as well. If free will alone is used to justify moral evil, then even if no moral good occurred, moral evil would still be said to be justified; but physical evil would have no justification. Physical evil is not essential to free will; it is only justified if moral good actually occurs, and if the moral good which results from physical evils outweighs the moral evils. This means that the argument from free will cannot alone justify physical evil along these lines; and it means that the argument from free will and its goods does not justify physical evil, because such an argument is incomplete, and necessarily incomplete. It needs to be supplemented by factual evidence that it is logically and practically impossible to obtain.

The correct reply, therefore, is first that the argument is irrelevant to many instances of physical evil, and secondly that it is not true that physical evil plus the moral good it produces is better than physical good and its moral goods. Much pain and suffering, in fact much physical evil generally, for example in children who die in infancy, animals and the insane passes unnoticed; it therefore has no morally uplifting effects upon others, and cannot by virtue of the examples chosen have such effects on the sufferers. Further, there are physical evils such as insanity and much disease to which the argument is inapplicable. So there is a large group of significant cases not covered by the argument. And where the argument is relevant, its premise is plainly false. It can be shown to be false by exposing its implications in the following way.

We either have obligations to lessen physical evil or we have not. If we have obligations to lessen physical evil then we are thereby reducing the total good in the universe. If, on the other hand, our obligation is to increase the total good in the universe it is our duty to prevent the reduction of physical evil and possibly even to increase the total amount of physical evil. Theists usually hold that we are obliged to reduce the physical evil in the universe; but in maintaining this, the theist is, in terms of this account of physical evil, maintaining that it is his duty to reduce the total amount of real good in the universe, and thereby to make the universe worse. Conversely, if by eliminating the physical evil he is not making the universe worse, then that amount of evil which he eliminates was unnecessary and in need of justification. It is relevant to notice here that evil is not always eliminated for morally praiseworthy reasons. Some discoveries have been due to positively unworthy motives, and many other discoveries which have resulted in a lessening of the sufferings of mankind have been due to no higher a motive than a scientist's desire to earn a reasonable living wage.

This reply to the theist's argument brings out its untenability. The theist's argument is seen to imply that war plus courage plus the many other moral virtues war brings into play are better than peace and its virtues; that famine and its moral virtues are better than plenty; that disease and its moral virtues are better than health. Some Christians in the past, in consistency with this mode of reasoning, opposed the use of anaesthetics to leave scope for the virtues of endurance and courage, and they opposed state aid to the sick and needy to leave scope for the virtues of charity and sympathy. Some have even contended that war is a good in disguise, again in consistency with this argument. Similarly the theist should, in terms of this fifth argument, in his heart if not aloud regret the discovery of the Salk polio vaccine because Dr. Salk has in one blow destroyed infinite possibilities of moral good.

There are three important points that need to be made concerning this kind of account of physical evil. (*a*) We are told, as by Niven, Joyce and others, that pain is a goad to action and that part of its justification lies in this fact. This claim is empirically false as a generalization about all people and all pain. Much pain frustrates action and wrecks people and personalities. On the other hand many men work and work well without being goaded by pain or discomfort. Further, to assert that men need goading is to ascribe another evil to God, for it is to claim that God made men naturally lazy. There is no reason why God should not have made men naturally industrious; the one is no more incompatible with free will than the other. Thus the argument from physical evil being a goad to man breaks down on three distinct counts. Pain often frustrates human endeavour, pain is not essential as a goad with many men, and where pain is a goad to higher endeavours, it is clear that less evil means to this same end are available to an omnipotent God. (*b*) The real fallacy in the argument is in the assumption that all or the highest moral excellence results from physical evil. As we have already seen, this assumption is completely false. Neither all moral goodness nor the highest moral goodness is triumph in the face of adversity or benevolence towards others in suffering. Christ Himself stressed this when He observed that the two great commandments were commandments to love. Love does not depend for its possibility on the existence and conquest of evil. (*c*) The 'negative' moral virtues which are brought into play by the various evils—courage, endurance, charity, sympathy and the like—besides not representing the highest forms of moral virtue, are in fact commonly supposed by the theist and atheist alike not to have the value this fifth argument ascribes to them. We—theists and atheists alike—reveal our comparative valuations of these virtues and of physical evil when we insist on state aid for the needy; when we strive for peace, for plenty, and for harmony within the state.

In brief, the good man, the morally admirable man, is he who loves what is good knowing that it is good and preferring it because it is good. He does not need to be torn by suffering or by the spectacle of another's sufferings to be morally admirable. Fortitude in his own sufferings, and sympathetic kindness in others' may reveal to us his goodness; but his goodness is not necessarily increased by such things.

Five arguments concerning physical evil have now been examined. We have seen that the problem of physical evil is a problem in its own right, and one that cannot be reduced to the problem of moral evil; and further, we have seen that physical evil creates not one but a number of problems to which no one nor any combination of the arguments examined offers a solution.

C. PROPOSED SOLUTIONS TO THE PROBLEM OF MORAL EVIL

The problem of moral evil is commonly regarded as being the greater of the problems concerning evil. As we shall see, it does create what appear to be insuperable difficulties for the theist; but so too, apparently, do physical evils.

For the theist moral evil must be interpreted as a breach of God's law and as a rejection of God Himself. It may involve the eternal damnation of the sinner, and in many of its forms it involves the infliction of suffering on other persons. Thus it aggravates the problem of physical evil, but its own peculiar character consists in the fact of sin. How could a morally perfect, all-powerful God create a universe in which occur such moral evils as cruelty, cowardice and hatred, the more especially as these evils constitute a rejection of God Himself by His creations, and as such involve them in eternal damnation?

The two main solutions advanced relate to free will and to the fact that moral evil is a consequence of free will. There is a third kind of solution more often invoked implicitly than as an explicit and serious argument, which need not be examined here as its weaknesses are plainly evident. This third solution is to the effect that moral evils and even the most brutal atrocities have their justification in the moral goodness they make possible or bring into being.

(i) *Free will alone provides a justification for moral evil:* This is perhaps the more popular of the serious attempts to explain moral evil. The argument in brief runs: men have free will; moral evil is a consequence of free will; a universe in which men exercise free will even with lapses into moral evil is better than a universe in which men become *automata* doing good always because predestined to do so. Thus on this argument it is the mere fact of the supreme value of free will itself that is taken to provide a justification for its corollary moral evil.

(ii) *The goods made possible by free will provide a basis for accounting for moral evil:* According to this second argument, it is not the mere fact of free will that is claimed to be of such value as to provide a justification of moral evil, but the fact that free will makes certain goods possible. Some indicate the various moral virtues as the goods that free will makes possible, whilst others point to beatitude, and others again to beatitude achieved by man's own efforts or the virtues achieved as a result of one's own efforts. What all these have in common is the claim that the good consequences of free will provide a justification of the bad consequences of free will, namely moral evil.

Each of these two proposed solutions encounters two specific criticisms, which are fatal to their claims to be real solutions.

(i) To consider first the difficulties to which the former proposed solution is exposed. (*a*) A difficulty for the first argument—that it is free will alone that provides a justification for moral evil—lies in the fact that the theist who argues in this way has to allow that it is logically possible on the free will hypothesis that all men should always will what is evil, and that even so, a universe of completely evil men possessing free will is better than one in which men are predestined to virtuous living. It has to be contended that the value of free will itself is so immense that it more than outweighs the total moral evil, the eternal punishment of the wicked, and the sufferings inflicted on others by the sinners in their evilness. It is this paradox that leads to the formulation of the second argument; and it is to be noted that the explanation of moral evil switches to the second argument or to a combination of the first and second argument, immediately the theist refuses to face the logical possibility of complete wickedness, and insists instead that in fact men do not always choose what is evil.

(*b*) The second difficulty encountered by the first argument relates to the possibility that free will is compatible with less evil, and even with no evil, that is, with absolute goodness. If it could be shown that free will is compatible with absolute goodness, or even with less moral evil than actually occurs, then all or at least some evil will be left unexplained by free will alone.

Mackie, in his recent paper, and Joyce, in his discussion of this argument, both contend that free will is compatible with absolute goodness. Mackie argues that if it is not possible for God to confer free will on men and at the same time ensure that no moral evil is committed He cannot really be omnipotent. Joyce directs his argument rather to fellow-theists, and it is more of an *ad hominem* argument addressed to them. He writes:

> "Free will need not (as is often assumed) involve the power to choose wrong. Our ability to misuse the gift is due to the conditions under which it is exercised here. In our present state we are able to reject what is truly good, and exercise our power of preference in favour of some baser attraction. Yet it is not necessary that it should be so. And all who accept Christian revelation admit that those who attain their final beatitude exercise freedom of will, and yet cannot choose aught but what is truly good. They possess the knowledge of Essential Goodness; and to it, not simply to good in general, they refer every choice. Moreover, even in our present condition it is open to omnipotence so to order our circumstances and to confer on the will such instinctive impulses that we should in every election adopt the right course and not the wrong one."

To this objection, that free will is compatible with absolute goodness and that therefore a benevolent, omnipotent God would have given man free will and ensured his absolute virtue, it is replied that God is being required to perform what is logically impossible. It is logically impossible, so it is argued, for free will and absolute goodness to be combined, and hence, if God lacks omnipotence only in this respect, He cannot be claimed to lack omnipotence in any sense in which serious theists have ascribed it to Him.

Quite clearly, if free will and absolute goodness are logically incompatible, then God, in not being able to confer both on man does not lack omnipotence in any important sense of the term. However, it is not clear that free will and absolute goodness are logically opposed; and Joyce does point to considerations which suggest that they are not logical incompatibles. For my own part I am uncertain on this point; but my uncertainty is not a factual one but one concerning a point of usage. It is clear that an omnipotent God could create rational agents predestined always to make virtuous 'decisions'; what is not clear is whether we should describe such agents as having free will. The considerations to which Joyce points have something of the status of test cases, and they would suggest that we should describe such agents as having free will. However, no matter how we resolve the linguistic point, the question remains—Which is more desirable, free will and moral evil and the physical evil to which free will gives rise, or this special free will or pseudo-free will which goes with absolute goodness? I suggest that the latter is clearly preferable. Later I shall endeavour to defend this conclusion; for the moment I am content to indicate the nature of the value judgment on which the question turns at this point.

The second objection to the proposed solution of the problem of moral evil in terms of free will alone, is related to the contention that free will is compatible with less moral evil than occurs, and possibly with no moral evil. We have seen what is involved in the latter contention. We may now consider what is involved in the former. It may be argued that free will is compatible with less moral evil than in fact occurs on various grounds. 1. God, if He were all-powerful, could miraculously intervene to prevent some or perhaps all moral evil; and He is said to do so on occasions in answer to prayers (for example, to prevent wars) or of His own initiative (for instance, by producing calamities which serve as warnings, or by working miracles, etc.).

2. God has made man with a certain nature. This nature is often interpreted by theologians as having a bias to evil. Clearly God could have created man with a strong bias to good, whilst still leaving scope for a decision to act evilly. Such a bias to good would be compatible with freedom of the will. 3. An omnipotent God could so have ordered the world that it was less conducive to the practice of evil.

These are all considerations advanced by Joyce, and separately and jointly, they establish that God could have conferred free will upon us, and at least very considerably *reduced* the amount of moral evil that would have resulted from the exercise of free will. This is sufficient to show that *not all* the moral evil that exists can be justified by reference to free will alone. This conclusion is fatal to the account of moral evil in terms of free will alone. The more extreme conclusion that Mackie seeks to establish—that absolute goodness is compatible with free will— is not essential as a basis for refuting the free will argument. The difficulty is as fatal to the claims of theism whether all moral evil or only some moral evil is unaccountable. However, whether Mackie's contentions are sound is still a matter of logical interest, although not of any real moment in the context of the case against theism, once the fact that less moral evil is compatible with free will has been established.

(ii) The second free will argument arises out of an attempt to circumvent these objections. It is not free will, but the value of the goods achieved through free will that is said to be so great as to provide a justification for moral evil.

(a) This second argument meets a difficulty in that it is now necessary for it to be supplemented by a proof that the number of people who practise moral virtue or who attain beatitude or who attain beatitude and/or virtue after a struggle is sufficient to outweigh the evilness of moral evil, the evilness of their eternal damnation and the physical evil they cause to others. This is a serious defect in the argument, because it means that the argument can at best show that moral evil *may have* a justification, and not that it has a justification. It is both logically and practically impossible to supplement and complete the argument. It is necessarily incomplete and inconclusive even if its general principle is sound.

(b) This second argument is designed also to avoid the other difficulty of the first argument—that free will may be compatible with no evil and certainly with less evil. It is argued that even if free will is compatible with absolute goodness it is still better that virtue and beatitude be attained after a genuine personal struggle; and this, it is said, would not occur if God in conferring free will nonetheless prevented moral evil or reduced the risk of it. Joyce argues in this way:

> "To receive our final beatitude as the fruit of our labours, and as the recompense of a hard-worn victory, is an incomparably higher destiny than to receive it without any effort on our part. And since God in His wisdom has seen fit to give us such a lot as this, it was inevitable that man should have the power to choose wrong. We could not be called to merit the reward due to victory without being exposed to the possibility of defeat."

There are various objections which may be urged here. First, this argument implies that the more intense the struggle, the greater is the triumph and resultant good, and the better the world; hence we should apparently, on this argument, court temptation and moral struggles to attain greater virtue and to be more worthy of our reward. Secondly, it may be argued that God is being said to be demanding too high a price for the goods produced. He is omniscient. He knows that many will sin and not attain the goods or the Good free will is said to make possible. He creates men with free will, with the natures men have, in the world as it is constituted, knowing that in His doing so He is committing many to moral evil and eternal damnation. He could avoid all this evil by creating men with rational wills predestined to virtue, or He could eliminate much of it by making men's natures and the conditions in the world more conducive to the practice of virtue. He is said not to choose to do this. Instead, at the cost of the sacrifice of the many, He is said to have ordered things so as to allow fewer men to attain this higher virtue and higher beatitude that result from the more intense struggle.

In attributing such behaviour to God, and in attempting to account for moral evil along these lines, theists are, I suggest, attributing to God immoral behaviour of a serious kind—of a kind we should all unhesitatingly condemn in a fellow human being.

We do not commend people for putting temptation in the way of others. On the contrary, anyone who today advocated, or even allowed where he could prevent it, the occurrence of evil and the sacrifice of the many—even as a result of their own freely chosen actions—for the sake of the higher virtue of the few, would be condemned as an immoralist. To put severe temptation in the way of the many, knowing that many and perhaps even most will succumb to the temptation, for the sake of the higher virtue of the few, would be blatant immorality; and it would be immoral whether or not those who yielded to the temptation possessed free will. This point can be brought out by considering how a conscientious moral agent would answer the question: Which should I choose for other people, a world in which there are intense moral struggles and the possibility of magnificent triumphs and the certainty of many defeats, or a world in which there are less intense struggles, less magnificent triumphs but more triumphs and fewer defeats, or a world in which there are no struggles, no triumphs and no defeats? We are constantly answering less easy questions than this in a way that conflicts with the theist's contentions. If by modifying our own behaviour we can save someone else from an intense moral struggle and almost certain moral evil, for example if by refraining from gambling or excessive drinking ourselves we can help a weaker person not to become a confirmed gambler or an alcoholic, or if by locking our car and not leaving it unlocked and with the key in it we can prevent people yielding to the temptation to become car thieves, we feel obliged to act accordingly, even though the persons concerned would freely choose the evil course of conduct. How much clearer is the decision with which God is said to be faced—the choice between the higher virtue of some and the evil of others, or the higher but less high virtue of many more, and the evil of many fewer. Neither alternative denies free will to men.

These various difficulties dispose of each of the main arguments relating to moral evil. There are in addition to these difficulties two other objections that might be urged.

If it could be shown that man has not free will both arguments collapse; and even if it could be shown that God's omniscience is incompatible with free will they would still break down. The issues raised here are too great to be pursued in this paper; and they can simply be noted as possible additional grounds from which criticisms of the main proposed solutions of the problem of moral evil may be advanced.

The other general objection is by way of a follow up to points made in objections (*b*) to both arguments (i) and (ii). It concerns the relative value of free will and its goods and evils and the value of the best of the alternatives to free will and its goods. Are free will and its goods so much more valuable than the next best alternatives that their superior value can really justify the immense amount of evil that is introduced into the world by free will?

Theologians who discuss this issue ask, Which is better—men with free will striving to work out their own destinies, or automata-machine-like creatures, who never make mistakes because they never make decisions? When put in this form we naturally doubt whether free will plus moral evil plus the possibility of the eternal damnation of the many and the physical evil of untold billions are quite so unjustified after all; but the fact of the matter is that the question has not been fairly put. The real alternative is, on the one hand, rational agents with free wills making many bad and some good decisions on rational and non-rational grounds, and 'rational' agents predestined always 'to choose' the right things for the right reasons—that is, if the language of automata must be used, rational automata. Predestination does not imply the absence of rationality in all senses of that term. God, were He omnipotent, could preordain the decisions and the reasons upon which they were based; and such a mode of existence would seem to be in itself a worthy mode of existence, and one preferable to an existence with free will, irrationality and evil.

D. CONCLUSION

In this paper it has been maintained that God, were He all powerful and perfectly good, would have created a world in which there was no unnecessary evil. It has not been argued that God ought to have created a perfect world, nor that He should have made one that is in any way logically impossible. It has simply been argued that a benevolent God could, and would, have created a world devoid of superfluous evil. It has been contended that there is evil in this world—unnecessary evil—and that the more popular and philosophically more significant of the many attempts to explain this evil are completely unsatisfactory. Hence we must conclude from the existence of evil that there cannot be an omnipotent, benevolent God.

NOTES

1. "Evil and Omnipotence," *Mind,* 1955.
2. Joyce: *Principles of Natural Theology,* ch. XVII. All subsequent quotations from Joyce in this paper are from this chapter of this work.

3. 244, Garnett translation, Heinemann.
4. *Mind,* 1931.
5. W. D. Niven, *Encyclopedia of Religion and Ethics.*

Joyce's corresponding argument runs:

"Pain is the great stimulant to action. Man no less than animals is impelled to work by the sense of hunger. Experience shows that, were it not for this motive the majority of men would be content to live in indolent ease. Man must earn his bread.

"One reason plainly why God permits suffering is that man may rise to a height of heroism which would otherwise have been beyond his scope. Nor are these the only benefits which it confers. That sympathy for others which is one of the most precious parts of our experience, and one of the most fruitful sources of well-doing, has its origin in the fellow-feeling engendered by endurance of similar trials. Furthermore, were it not for these trials, man would think little enough of a future existence, and of the need of striving after his last end. He would be perfectly content with his existence, and would seek little of any higher good. These considerations here briefly advanced suffice at least to show how important is the office filled by pain in human life, and with what little reason it is asserted that the existence of so much suffering is irreconcilable with the wisdom of the Creator."

And:

"It may be asked whether the Creator could not have brought man to perfection without the use of suffering. Most certainly He could have conferred upon him a similar degree of virtue without requiring any effort on his part. Yet it is easy to see that there is a special value attaching to a conquest of difficulties such as man's actual demands, and that in God's eyes this may well be an adequate reason for assigning this life to us in preference to another. . . . Pain has value in respect to the next life, but also in respect to this. The advance of scientific discovery, the gradual improvement of the organization of the community, the growth of material civilization are due in no small degree to the stimulus afforded by pain."

6. Mackie, "Evil and Omnipotence," *Mind,* 1955.

Evil and the Final Harmony

Feodor Dostoyevsky

A well-educated, cultured gentleman and his wife beat their own child with a birch-rod, a girl of seven. I have an exact account of it. The papa was glad that the birch was covered with twigs. 'It stings more,' said he, and so he began stinging his daughter. I know for a fact

From Fyodor Dostoyevsky, *The Brothers Karamazov,* trans. by Constance Garnett, Random House, Inc.

there are people who at every blow are worked up to sensuality, to literal sensuality, which increases progressively at every blow they inflict. They beat for a minute, for five minutes, for ten minutes, more often and more savagely. The child screams. At last the child cannot scream, it gasps, 'Daddy! daddy!' By some diabolical unseemly chance the case was brought into court. A counsel is engaged. The Russian people have long called a barrister 'a conscience for hire.' The counsel protests in his client's defence. 'It's such a simple thing,' he says, 'an everyday domestic event. A father corrects the child. To our shame be it said, it is brought into court.' The jury, convinced by him, give a favourable verdict. The public roars with delight that the torturer is acquitted. Ah, pity I wasn't there! I would have proposed to raise a subscription in his honour! . . . Charming pictures.

"But I've still better things about children. I've collected a great, great deal about Russian children, Alyosha. There was a little girl of five who was hated by her father and mother, 'most worthy and respectable people, of good education and breeding.' You see, I must repeat again, it is a peculiar characteristic of many people, this love of torturing children, and children only. To all other types of humanity these torturers behave mildly and benevolently, like cultivated and humane Europeans; but they are very fond of tormenting children, even fond of children themselves in that sense. It's just their defencelessness that tempts the tormentor, just the angelic confidence of the child who has no refuge and no appeal, that sets his vile blood on fire. In every man, of course, a demon lies hidden—the demon of rage, the demon of lustful heat at the screams of the tortured victim, the demon of lawlessness let off the chain, the demon of diseases that follow on vice, gout, kidney disease, and so on.

"This poor child of five was subjected to every possible torture by those cultivated parents. They beat her, thrashed her, kicked her for no reason till her body was one bruise. Then, they went to greater refinements of cruelty—shut her up all night in the cold and frost in a privy, and because she didn't ask to be taken up at night (as though a child of five sleeping its angelic, sound sleep could be trained to wake and ask), they smeared her face and filled her mouth with excrement, and it was her mother, her mother did this. And that mother could sleep, hearing the poor child's groans! Can you understand why a little creature, who can't even understand what's done to her, should beat her little aching heart with her tiny fist in the dark and the cold, and weep her meek unresentful tears to dear, kind God to protect her? Do you understand that, friend and brother, you pious and humble novice? Do you understand why this infamy must be and is permitted? Without it, I am told, man could not have existed on earth, for he could not have known good and evil. Why should he know that diabolical good and evil when it costs so much? Why, the whole world of knowledge is not worth that child's prayer to 'dear, kind God'! I say nothing of the sufferings of grown-up people, they have eaten the apple, damn them, and the devil take them all!" But these little ones! I am making you suffer, Alyosha, you are not yourself. I'll leave off if you like."

"Never mind, I want to suffer too," muttered Alyosha.

"One picture, only one more, because it's so curious, so characteristic, and I have only just read it in some collection of Russian antiquities. I've forgotten the name. I must look it up. It was in the darkest days of serfdom at the beginning of the century, and long live the Liberator of the People! There was in those days a general of aristocratic connections, the owner of great estates, one of those men—somewhat exceptional, I believe, even then—who, retiring from the service into a life of leisure, are convinced that they've earned absolute power over the lives of their subjects. There were such men then. So our general, settled on his property of two thousand souls, lives in pomp, and domineers over his poor neighbours as though they were dependents and buffoons. He has kennels of hundreds of hounds and nearly a hundred dog-boys—all mounted, and in uniform. One day a serf boy, a little child of eight, threw a stone in play and hurt the paw of the general's favourite hound. 'Why is my favourite dog lame?' He is told that the boy threw a stone that hurt the dog's paw. 'So you did it.' The general looked the child up and down. 'Take him.' He was taken—taken from his mother and kept shut up all night. Early that morning the general comes out on horseback, with the hounds, his dependents, dog-boys, and huntsmen, all mounted around him in full hunting parade. The servants are summoned for their edification, and in front of them all stands the mother of the child. The child is brought from the lock-up. It's a gloomy cold, foggy autumn day, a capital day for hunting. The general orders the child to be undressed; the child is stripped naked. He shivers, numb with terror, not daring to cry. . . . 'Make him run,' commands the general. 'Run! run!' shout the dog-boys. The boy runs. . . . 'At him!' yells the general, and he sets the whole pack of hounds on the child. The hounds catch him, and tear him to pieces before his mother's eyes! . . . I believe the general was afterwards declared incapable of administering his estates. Well—what did he deserve? To be shot? To be shot for the satisfaction of our moral feelings? Speak, Alyosha!"

"To be shot," murmured Alyosha, lifting his eyes to Ivan with a pale, twisted smile.

"Bravo!" cried Ivan delighted. "If even you say so . . . You're a pretty monk! So there is a little devil sitting in your heart, Aloysha Karamazov!"

"What I said was absurd, but——"

"That's just the point, that 'but'!" cried Ivan. "Let me tell you, novice, that the absurd is only too necessary on earth. The world stands on absurdities, and perhaps nothing would have come to pass in it without them. We know what we know!"

"What do you know?"

"I understand nothing," Ivan went on, as though in delirium. "I don't want to understand anything now. I want to stick to the fact. I made up my mind long ago not to understand. If I try to understand any-thing, I shall be false to the fact and I have determined to stick to the fact."

"Why are you trying me?" Alyosha cried, with sudden distress. "Will you say what you mean at last?"

"Of course, I will; that's what I've been leading up to. You are dear to me, I don't want to let you go, and I won't give you up to your Zossima."

Ivan for a minute was silent, his face became all at once very sad.

"Listen! I took the case of children only to make my case clearer. Of the other tears of humanity with which the earth is soaked from its crust to its centre, I will say nothing. I have narrowed my subject on purpose. I am a bug, and I recognise in all humility that I cannot un-derstand why the world is arranged as it is. Men are themselves to blame, I suppose; they were given paradise, they wanted freedom, and stole fire from heaven, though they knew they would become unhappy, so there is no need to pity them. With my pitiful, earthly, Euclidian un-derstanding, all I know is that there is suffering and that there are none guilty; that cause follows effect, simply and directly; that everything flows and finds its level—but that's only Euclidian nonsense, I know that, and I can't consent to live by it! What comfort is to me that there are none guilty and that cause follows effect simply and directly, and that I know it—I must have justice, or I will destroy myself. And not justice in some remote infinite time and space, but here on earth, and that I could see myself. I have believed in it. I want to see it, and if I am dead by then, let me rise again, for if it all happens without me, it will be too unfair. Surely I haven't suffered, simply that I, my crimes and my sufferings, may manure the soil of the future harmony for some-body else. I want to see with my own eyes the hind lie down with the lion and the victim rise up and embrace his murderer. I want to be there when every one suddenly understands what it has all been for. All the religions of the world are built on this longing, and I am a believer. But then there are the children, and what am I to do about them? That's a question I can't answer. For the hundredth time I re-peat, there are numbers of questions, but I've only taken the children, because in their case what I mean is so unanswerably clear. Listen! If all must suffer to pay for the eternal harmony, what have children to do with it, tell me, please? It's beyond all comprehension why they should suffer, and why they should pay for the harmony. Why should they, too, furnish material to enrich the soil for the harmony of the future? I understand solidarity in sin among men. I understand soli-darity in retribution, too; but there can be no such solidarity with chil-dren. And if it is really true that they must share responsibility for all their fathers' crimes, such a truth is not of this world and is beyond my comprehension. Some jester will say, perhaps, that the child would have grown up and have sinned, but you see he didn't grow up, he was torn to pieces by the dogs, at eight years old. Oh, Alyosha, I am not blaspheming! I understand, of course, what an upheaval of the universe it will be, when everything in heaven and earth blends in one hymn of praise and everything that lives and has lived cries aloud: 'Thou art just, O Lord, for Thy ways are revealed.' When the mother embraces the fiend who threw her child to the dogs, and all three cry aloud with tears, 'Thou art just, O Lord!' then, of course, the crown of knowledge will be reached and all will be made clear. But what pulls me up here is that I can't accept that harmony. And while I am on earth, I make haste to take my own measures. You see, Alyosha, perhaps it really may happen that if I live to that moment, or rise again to see it, I, too, perhaps, may cry aloud with the rest, looking at the mother embracing the child's torturer, 'Thou art just, O Lord!' but I don't want to cry aloud then. While there is still time, I hasten to protect myself and so I renounce the higher harmony altogether. It's not worth the tears of that one tortured child who beat itself on the breast with its little fist and prayed in its stinking outhouse, with its unexpiated tears to 'dear, kind God'! It's not worth it, because those tears are unatoned for. They must be atoned for, or there can be no harmony. But how? How are you going to atone for them? Is it possible? By their being avenged? But what do I care for avenging them? What do I care for a hell for oppressors? What good can hell do, since those children have already been tortured? And what becomes of harmony, if there is hell? I want to forgive. I want to embrace. I don't want more suffering. And if the sufferings of children go to swell the sum of sufferings which was necessary to pay for truth, then I protest that the truth is not worth such a price. I don't want the mother to embrace the oppressor who threw her son to the dogs! She dare not forgive him! Let her forgive him for herself, if she will, let her forgive the torturer for the immeasurable suffering of her mother's heart. But the sufferings of her tortured child she has no right to forgive; she dare not forgive the torturer, even if the child were to forgive him! And if that is so, if they dare not forgive, what becomes of harmony? Is there in the whole world a being who would have the right to forgive and could forgive? I don't want harmony. From love for humanity I don't want it. I would rather be left with the unavenged suffering. I would rather remain with my unavenged suffering and unsatisfied indignation, *even if I were wrong.* Besides, too high a price is asked for harmony; it's beyond our means to pay so much to enter on it. And so I hasten to give back my entrance ticket, and if I am an honest man I am bound to give it back as soon as possible. And that I am doing. It's not God that I don't accept, Alyosha, only I most respectfully return Him the ticket."

"That's rebellion," murmured Alyosha, looking down.

"Rebellion? I am sorry you call it that," said Ivan earnestly. "One can hardly live in rebellion, and I want to live. Tell me yourself, I challenge you—answer. Imagine that you are creating a fabric of human destiny with the object of making men happy in the end, giving them peace and rest at last, but that it was essential and inevitable to torture to death only one tiny creature—that baby beating its breast with its fist, for instance—and to found that edifice on its unavenged tears, would you consent to be the architect on those conditions? Tell me, and tell the truth."

"No, I wouldn't consent," said Alyosha softly.

"And can you admit the idea that men for whom you are building it would agree to accept their happiness on the foundation of the unexpiated blood of a little victim? And accepting it would remain happy for ever?"

IMPEDIMENTS to RELIGIOUS BELIEF: EXTERNAL

Intellectual Impediments to Religious Belief

H.J. Paton

1. DIFFERENT TYPES OF IMPEDIMENT

There are many impediments to religion. Among these human wickedness—or human sinfulness, if we use the language of theology—is the most formidable, but it is by no means the only one; and under this head we ought not to include the sin of thinking about religion, as is sometimes done by those who are guilty of the sin of thinking too little. Another obstacle is to be found in the aberrations of religion itself and in the unworthiness of its professed followers. These impediments are patent enough from the religious point of view. We must now take a more detached standpoint and consider some of the alleged incompatibilities between religious belief and the rest of our knowledge. This ungrateful task may be described as a study of the *intellectual* impediments to religion. The views with which we have to deal are commonplace among thinkers, and are dimly apprehended even by the unthinking masses, so that it would be foolish, and indeed wrong, to pass them over in silence or to pretend that they are not serious.

From *The Modern Predicament* by H. J. Paton, George Allen and Unwin, Ltd., pps. 103-115. Reprinted by permission of the publisher.

2. RELIGION AND SCIENCE

Intellectual impediments to religion are made possible by the intellectual element in religion itself. Every religion, and certainly every developed religion, offers us a doctrine of man, a doctrine of history, a doctrine of the universe, and a doctrine of God. The exact status of such doctrines may be difficult to determine, and obsession with theory may be one of the major religious aberrations. Nevertheless religion cannot get on without some sort of doctrine, even if this be reduced to the barest minimum.

Doctrine necessarily claims to be true, and this means that it enters into competition with other doctrines also claiming to be true. We may hold that one doctrine is true from one point of view and another from another; but ultimately there can be only one truth, or one comprehensive system of truths, in which divergent points of view are reconciled. We may not be able to effect this reconciliation, but to abandon the belief that such a reconciliation is possible is to abandon reason altogether and to have no defence against lunacy.

What are the doctrines with which religion, so far as it is doctrinal, may, and does, come into conflict? They can all be summed up in one word—science. But this bald statement is in need of some further elucidation.

In the first place, science has to be interpreted widely. It includes, not only the natural sciences, but also the mental and social sciences, such as psychology and anthropology. It covers also the modern methods of historical and literary criticism. The development of all these disciplines in the last four hundred years has brought religion face to face with a situation very different from any that existed before.

In the second place, it may be objected that there is no such thing as science—there are only sciences in the plural—and that all this talk about a conflict between religion and science is too vague to be profitable.

In such an objection there is some truth, and we ought always to be chary of those who are in the habit of telling us that Science (with a capital S) teaches us this or that and admits of no further argument. Assertions of this kind often spring, not directly from science, but from semi-popular philosophy, and some of the impediments to religion may fall under this description. Nevertheless we are blind if we fail to see that in method, in outlook, and in what can be described as atmosphere, science—all science—may be opposed to religion. Even if scientific knowledge is ultimately compatible with religion, it does not appear to be so at first sight; and indeed it seems to contradict a great deal formerly considered by theologians to be necessary for a saving faith. Furthermore, whatever may be true as regards logical compatibility, there is at least a psychological opposition between the scientific and the religious attitude. The gradual spread of the scientific outlook—and we are all affected by it even if the scientists say we are not nearly as much affected as we ought to be—has tended, not so much to refute religious belief,

447

but rather to make it fade and wither. To quote Professor Price: 'it has led to that inner emptiness and lack of faith . . . which is our fundamental and, as it seems, incurable disease'.

It may be replied that all this is very much out of date—a mere survival of Victorian rationalism long ago abandoned. Those who comfort themselves thus are, I am afraid, deceived. It is true that science today—apart from the followers of Karl Marx, who was more of a prophet than a scientist—is not so cocksure as it once was about the finality of its teaching and is more prepared for revolutionary discoveries. It is also true that the note of hostility to religion is often, though by no means always, less strident than it was in the past. All this is to the good, but the main reason for the lesser stridency is that the modern rationalist no longer considers himself to be battling for victory: he supposes that the victory is already won. The greater amiability of present-day discussions is no doubt a straw that can help to show which way the tide is running; but those who clutch at that straw may only give the impression that they are drowning men.

3. RELIGION AND PHYSICS

The tide of science which threatens to submerge religion began to flow when Copernicus discovered that the earth was not the centre of the physical universe, but only one of the planets revolving round the sun. This tidal movement became more perceptible when Galileo confirmed his discovery and began to develop the modern methods of observation and measurement which have led to such astonishing triumphs. As if aware of the impending danger, the Church reacted violently, and condemned these doctrines as incompatible with Holy Scripture. Yet in spite of its utmost endeavours the tide has flowed relentlessly for more than four hundred years. Its rise has continuously accelerated and is certain—unless there is a world catastrophe—to accelerate more and more. During the whole of this period—if we may change the metaphor—religion has been fighting a rearguard action, abandoning one position after another till it is uncertain how much is left.

Why is it that the amazing achievements of modern physics and astronomy have seemed so inimical to religion? It is not merely that they overthrow primitive Biblical speculations about the physical universe—although, when a book has been regarded as divinely inspired throughout, to contradict the least part of it may seem to destroy the authority of the whole. Nor is it merely that man is seen as the creature of a day, clinging precariously to a whirling planet in a solar system which is itself utterly insignificant amid the vast reaches of interstellar space and astronomical time. These and many other considerations all play their part; but perhaps the main impediments to religion arise from two things—from the character of scientific method and from the conception of the world as governed throughout by unvarying law.

On scientific method little need here be said, although psychologically it may be the strongest influence of all. A scientific training makes it difficult or impossible to accept statements on authority, to be satisfied with second- or third-hand evidence, to believe in marvels which cannot be experimentally repeated, or to adopt theories which cannot be verified by empirical observation. There may be exceptions to this rule; for some scientists seem to lose their critical power once they stray beyond the narrow limits of their own subject. But there can be no doubt that in this respect the influence of science is both powerful and pervasive, and that it is unfavourable to much that passes for religion. How far that influence may in its turn lead to error or extravagance it is not here necessary to enquire. For our present purpose it is enough to recognize that the whole attitude, not merely of scientists, but of thoughtful men brought up in a scientific age, towards all the problems of life, whether secular or sacred, has been affected to an extent which it is almost impossible to exaggerate. Here may be found perhaps the greatest impediment to the unquestioning acceptance of any simple and traditional religious faith.

It is more difficult to gauge the effects which follow from conceiving the physical universe as subject to laws which admit of no exceptions. As late as the eighteenth century many thinkers regarded the discovery of physical laws as a revelation of the divine plan by which the universe is governed; and the very simplicity and comprehensiveness of the plan was taken to be a proof of divine benevolence and wisdom. Yet at least as early as Descartes it was already realized that physical laws were independent of, if not opposed to, the idea of purpose in the universe. It is this second interpretation which has prevailed. When Laplace, speaking of the existence of God, said 'I have no need of that hypothesis,' he meant that the conception of God's activity or purpose played no part in his formulation of scientific law, as it had done in the work of other thinkers, including the great Isaac Newton himself. In that specific sense the dictum of Laplace is the universal assumption of science to-day.

If modern physics is unfavourable to belief in a divine purpose or plan, it is still more unfavourable to belief in miracles. So far as these are considered to be breaches of physical laws, they cannot be accepted without rejecting the most fundamental presuppositions of science. Hence it is not surprising that they have become somewhat of an embarrassment to religion. At one time they were invoked to guarantee the truth of revelation. Now, if they are defended at all, it is revelation that is invoked to guarantee the truth of miracles, and their occurrence is explained as the manifestation of some higher law.

So far as physics is incompatible with miracles and has no use for a divine purpose in the universe, it is hard to see how we can retain the idea of providence in general and of special providences in particular. But this is not the worst. The character of scientific law appears to require a universal determinism which applies to the movements of human bodies as much as to the movement of the smallest electron or the remotest star. This cuts at the roots of all morality and so of religion as well.

There are some who seek to escape from this gloomy situation by reminding us that the old-fashioned mechanical views of physics are now abandoned. The concepts of mechanical cause and effect have been given up, and in place of causal laws we are left only with statistical averages. Physics itself even recognizes a principle of indeterminacy and so leaves at least a chink for human freedom. Hence perhaps the future before religion is not quite so black as it has been painted.

Without any wish to be dogmatic on these difficult subjects we must still ask ourselves whether those who find comfort in such considerations may not also be clutching at straws. To abandon the old-fashioned view of causation is by no means to give up the universality of law: all it amounts to is that the laws have a different character. The microscopic space left open by the principle of indeterminacy is far too small for the exercise of human freedom—if indeed we can conceive human freedom at all as manifested only in the apparent chinks and interstices of the physical universe. The late Professor Susan Stebbing was right when she said 'It cannot be maintained that all that is required for human freedom is some amount of uncertainty in the domain of microphysics'. And if we wish to argue that the new physics is less unfavourable to religion than the old, we must take into our reckoning what is called the second law of thermodynamics, according to which the universe is steadily running down. It is hard to see how this can offer any ground either for moral optimism or for religious faith.

The general effect of the modern scientific outlook is summed up in the eloquent, and by now familiar, words of Mr. Bertrand Russell. 'That man is the product of causes which had no prevision of the end they were achieving; that his origin, his growth, his hopes and fears, his loves and beliefs, are but the outcome of accidental collocations of atoms; that no fire, no heroism, no intensity of thought and feeling, can preserve an individual life beyond the grave; that all the labours of the ages, all the inspiration, all the noon-day brightness of human genius, are destined to extinction in the vast death of the solar system, and that the whole temple of man's achievement must inevitably be buried beneath the débris of a universe in ruins—all these things, if not quite beyond dispute, are yet so nearly certain, that no philosophy which rejects them can hope to stand. Only within the scaffolding of these truths, only on the firm foundations of unyielding despair, can the soul's habitation henceforth be safely built'.

If Mr. Russell's views be regarded as suspect, let us listen to the less eloquent, but hardly less despairing, words of a deeply religious thinker—Dr. Albert Schweitzer. 'My solution of the problem', he says, 'is that we must make up our minds to renounce completely the optimistic-ethical interpretation of the world. If we take the world as it is, it is impossible to attribute to it a meaning in which the aims and objects of mankind and of individual men have a meaning also.'

4. RELIGION AND BIOLOGY

If the first great wave that threatened to engulf religion came from physics, the second came from biology. The Darwinian theory of evolution overthrew the belief that each species was the object of a special creation and possessed a fixed and unchanging character. This served to upset the authority alike of Aristotle and of the book of Genesis. But still worse than this, the process of evolution appeared to be mechanical rather than purposive, blind rather than intelligent, and so to render nugatory the argument from design, which was commonly regarded as the most cogent proof for the existence of God. Furthermore, from a human point of view evolution in its working seemed wasteful and even cruel, and the main qualities making for survival appeared to be lust and violence and deceit. It gave less than no support to belief in the wisdom and benevolence of the Creator or to the view that the end of creation was the furtherance of virtue. But perhaps the greatest shock of all came from the discovery that man, far from having been specially created in the image of God, was himself the product of this unintelligent process of evolution and must look back to a long line of ape-like ancestors. Nowadays we take all this calmly in our stride, partly perhaps through lack of imagination. We may even feel in a curious way that it unites us more intimately with the world of nature of which we form a part. But it should not cause us surprise if to our Victorian grandfathers it seemed that

'The pillard'd firmament is rott'nness,
And earths base built on stubble.'

In comparison with this the other shocks from biology may seem unimportant, but we have to remember that the effect of scientific discoveries is cumulative. Of these further shocks we need mention only one.

It has always been recognized that the soul is in some ways dependent on the body; and we all know from ordinary experience how a minor indisposition, or even fatigue, may dull our mind and blunt our emotions and weaken our will. But the development of physiology began to show in ever minuter detail how close is the connexion between mind and body, and how utterly we depend on the structure of our brain and nervous system. The very existence of the soul began to be questioned. Why should we postulate a soul instead of recognizing that mental functions are completely dependent on bodily functions? Above all, why should we suppose, against all the empirical evidence, that the soul could exist as a separate entity after the death of the body? The belief in immortality, one of the strongholds of religion, or at least of many religions, was being steadily undermined. Conclusions based on these detailed discoveries were supported further by the general theory of evolution, which abolished the sharp separation of man from the other animals, as also by the general theory that physical laws govern the movements of all bodies, not excluding the organic bodies of plants and animals and men. Some philosophers and scientists hold it out as a possibility, and indeed as an ideal, that the laws of biology, and even of psychology, may one day be reduced to laws of physics.

One general result emerges from all this. Man displays his intelligence in discovering laws of nature and then awakes, perhaps with horror, to the fact that these laws apply to himself: for science he is only one object among many others and has to be understood in the same way as the rest. Thus man is finally entangled in the meshes of the net that he himself has woven; and when we say this, we must add that it is true, not merely of his body, but of his soul. Science is, as it were, a machine constructed by man in order to master the universe; but the machine has turned against its maker and seeks to master him as well.

RELIGION AND PSYCHOLOGY

The third great wave threatening religion comes from psychology, which is, at least etymologically, the science of the soul. This is a more recent wave; and as we disappear gasping under its onrush, we are hardly yet in a position to study its shape. Indeed its shape is perhaps not yet definitely formed. Its exponents at times contradict one another with a freedom ordinarily reserved for philosophers; and some of them indulge in a boldness of speculation from which a respectable philosopher would shrink. We are offered a choice between different schools of thought.

Thus there is a Behaviouristic school, which, as a further expansion of physiology, makes still more formidable the impediments already considered. The Behaviourists ignore in practice, if they do not also deny in theory, the mental phenomena formerly considered open to introspection—our thoughts, our emotions, our volitions, and so on: they are content to study only the bodily behaviour of human and other animals, and so to blur still further the dividing line between man and the brutes. A very different method is adopted by the schools of psychoanalysis which originate from Freud, both by those which seek to carry further the work of the master and by those which attempt to modify and improve it. All of them start from an examination of human consciousness, especially of human dreams; and they claim on this basis to bring under scientific investigation the vast and obscure domain of the unconscious, whose existence had been merely suspected and whose character had not been seriously explored. According to them the human mind is like an iceberg, by far the greater part of which is under water and not amenable to direct observation. By means of inference they attempt to describe in detail these murky nether regions; and they have been able, as it were, to draw up from the ocean's depths many strange, and on the whole unpleasing, objects for our contemplation and instruction.

The schools which consider human consciousness to be worthy of scientific attention take up different attitudes to religion. As we have seen, they may regard it as a harmful illusion or as a healing and even 'real' illusion, whatever that may be. But, broadly speaking, even at the best they offer cold comfort to religion, and the attitude of Freud himself is conspicuously hostile. Besides, they exhibit the general tendency to assume determinism in mental processes; they encourage the view that reason has little or no part to play in human behaviour; and even if they regard mind as a possible object of study, it is for them only one object among others and requires no special principles for its understanding. All psychology is an example of what I meant when I said that the soul is entangled in the meshes of the scientific net which man has devised for the better understanding of the physical world. And many psychologists believe that religious experience can be explained—or explained away—in accordance with the ordinary laws that have been found to account for other mental phenomena.

This third wave is perhaps logically less intimidating to religion than the other two, if only because psychology is not yet fully developed as a science. Psycho-analysis has called attention to mental phenomena hitherto neglected; it has thrown light on dark places; and it has done mental healing a service for which the world must be grateful. Whatever be its defects, it has opened up the way for fresh advances, but has it already advanced so far that even its fundamental concepts are firmly established? Sometimes it may seem not to have got much beyond a stage like that in chemistry when the phenomena of combustion were explained by postulating a hypothetical substance, now forgotten, which was known as 'phlogiston'; or at least—if this is too depreciatory—not beyond the comparatively recent stage in physics when 'ether' had to be postulated as an elastic substance permeating all space and forming a medium through which rays of light were propagated. It may be heretical to say so, but it seems to me rather improbable that our old friends, the Ego, the Super-Ego, and the Id, will occupy permanent niches in the scientific pantheon.

Nevertheless, even if this third wave may not yet be so very imposing logically, psychologically—partly perhaps by its very vagueness—it is to-day almost the most formidable of the three, at least as far as popular or semi-popular thinking is concerned. In spite of attempts to make use of it in the interests of religion, it produces an emotional and intellectual background so different from that of religious tradition that the combination of the two becomes very difficult. What is sometimes said of philosophers is even more true of religious beliefs—they are usually not refuted, but merely abandoned. When the spiritual climate has altered, they may simply fade away; and we seem to be witnessing something rather like this at the present crisis of our civilization.

6. RELIGION AND HISTORY

There are other human sciences besides psychology, and their influence has also tended to be psychologically, if not logically, unfavourable to religion. Anthropology, for example, tends on the whole to blur sharp distinctions between the primitive and the developed, and among heathen superstitions it finds parallels even for the most sacred mysteries of the higher religions. It suggests that religion is a survival of something primitive in the experience of the race, just as psychology suggests it is a survival of something primitive in the experience of the child. Even economics takes a hand in the unholy assault. The classical economists may have been tempted at times to suppose that the 'economic man' was, not a mere useful abstraction, but the only kind of man there is; and this tendency has been hardened into a dogma by the Marxists. They tell us that our bourgeois religion, like our bourgeois morality, is only an ideology—that is, an illusory 'rationalization' of purely economic factors—and one of the main impediments to human progress. All these human sciences, among which sociology also may be included, have the common characteristic of treating man as one object among other objects: they tend to explain his thoughts, his actions, and his emotions as the effect of forces outside himself—forces whose influence can be determined, and even controlled, in accordance with ascertainable scientific laws.

Here then we have a whole series of little wavelets, not perhaps very impressive in isolation and colliding at times with one another, yet all driving inexorably in the same general direction. But belonging to the same series there is one special wave so menacing that we may be inclined to call it the fourth great wave—the wave of historical method and historical criticism.

The modern development of the historical method is particularly menacing to Christianity, since of all the great religions Christianity has laid most stress on history—the history of the Jews, the history of the Founder, and the history of the Church. Modern criticism has undermined first the authority of the Old Testament and then the authority of the New in such a way that the traditional belief in an infallible Book, written down by God's penmen at His dictation, can no longer be accepted by any intelligent man of independent judgement who has given serious consideration to the subject. We have instead a most fallible human record compiled by mortal men, who, even if they were gifted with a special religious insight, were unacquainted with the canons of historical evidence and unfamiliar with the ideals of historical accuracy. Christian thinkers have made great and creditable efforts to adjust themselves to this new situation—the other world religions are probably not even yet fully awake to their danger. The methods of modern scholarship may be able to sort out what is reasonably certain from what is at least doubtful as well as from what is in all probability fictitious. On these points there are, and are bound to be, differences among scholars, and it is only experts who can profitably form an opinion. Hence it is always possible, and it may often be justifiable, to dismiss the arguments of laymen in these subjects as ignorant or exaggerated. Nevertheless the plain man used to be faced with a plain situation which he could understand. He was told that every historical statement in the Bible, or at least in the New Testament, was true. He has now to be told that while the religious teaching in the Bible retains its unique value, some of its historical statements are true, while some are untrue, and others have been traditionally misunderstood. Even if he is sensible enough not to hold that if anything goes, the whole thing goes, he yet feels that he does not know where he stands, and that he is ill-equipped to come to a decision in matters about which the doctors differ. This is a new impediment to the simplicity of religious faith.

To the thoughtful man all this opens up questions which are philosophical rather than historical. He has been told, in traditional language, that religious faith is necessary for salvation, and the question he asks himself is this. Granted that religious faith is very much more than an intellectual belief in historical facts, can a belief in historical facts be necessary for salvation, and so for religious faith, when only the most expert scholarship is competent to decide whether these alleged facts are historical or not? If he answers in the negative, if indeed he comes to the conclusion that no belief in historical facts and no skill in historical scholarship can be necessary for what he calls salvation, his view of what is essential to religion has undergone a revolution, and he has entered a new path, not knowing where it may lead.

7. RELIGION AND PHILOSOPHY

I have not mentioned philosophy as one of the waves with which religion has to struggle. Philosophers do not speak with one voice, and the best of them are more anxious that men should think for themselves than that they should accept any doctrine dogmatically. But if we may speak of general trends, the movement of philosophy in this country has been, on the whole, away from religion. The Oxford Idealism which prevailed at the end of the Victorian age did at least have religious sympathies. The Realism which tended to replace it later, if it was not always sympathetic, was seldom other than neutral. The more modern school of Logical Positivism, which owes its rise to the great influence of Mr. Bertrand Russell, is often openly hostile or indifferent. We have moved far from the days when philosophy was the handmaid of theology. Like other handmaids at the present time, she now considers herself to be not only as good as her mistress but—if the colloquialism may be pardoned—a damn' sight better; and if she were inclined to enter again into domestic service, it would be as the handmaid, not of theology, but of science.

So far as Logical Positivism places a linguistic ban on theology and even on ethics, it has already been examined briefly; but it would be a mistake to regard the doctrine that all statements about God are nonsense as the central feature of the modern linguistic movement as a whole. There is already a marked tendency to get beyond the earlier dogmatism, and even to display an interest in religion as well as in other problems more akin to those which have occupied philosophy in the past. As originally expounded Logical Positivism sweeps so much away into one comprehensive rubbish heap that it is difficult not to feel there must be something wrong with it; but its boundaries are becoming so blurred that it is almost time the name was dropped. All I wish to point out here is that a modern philosophy which had—and may still have—a very great following, especially among the younger intellectuals, is, perhaps I should not say hostile, but politely contemptuous, towards everything in the nature of religious belief. In this respect, as in others, it would seem to be a faithful mirror of an attitude widely prevalent at the present time.

8. THE PREDICAMENT OF RELIGION

I have no wish to pretend that the contentions I have put forward are conclusive or that they are all equally sound. Like Logical Positivism itself, they sweep so much away along with religion that we may begin to doubt their validity. What I have stated is the case which is widely accepted and has got to be answered. Nevertheless it is folly not to see that the case is very strong and that, although in certain respects it may be specially menacing to Christianity, it is a threat, not to a particular religion, but to all religion as such.

There are doubtless many other reasons, some of them less creditable, for the growing indifference to religion; but reasons of the type I have described are worthy of special consideration since they spring, not from human wickedness and folly, but from the highest achievements of human thought. They affect, not only the intellectuals, but also, through them, the immense mass of men who take their opinions at second and third and fourth hand. The whole spiritual atmosphere is altered, and even the ordinary religious man speaks to-day in a different tone about special providences and the hope of immortality, if he speaks of them at all.

In such circumstances it is unconvincing to tell us that the conflict of religion and science is now happily out-moded, that so and so has put forward new theories about scientific methodology and somebody else has confirmed some statement in the Biblical record from a newly-discovered papyrus or from some archaeological remains. This is mere tinkering with the subject; and we should not be surprised if those who have been brought up in the new atmosphere and have little or no experience of religion are apt to dismiss the easy optimism of some religious teachers as springing from blindness or ignorance, if not from hypocrisy. Nor can it be denied that they sometimes have ample excuse. The situation to be faced is one unknown to St. Paul and St. Augustine, to Aquinas and Duns Scotus, to Luther and Calvin; and it can be met, if it is to be met at all, only by a new effort of thinking at least as great as any of theirs. So long as this is lacking, the modern world is bound to suffer from a divided mind and from a conflict between the heart and the head. If religion has to satisfy the whole man, its demand is that the men who follow it must be whole-minded as well as whole-hearted. The very wholeness at which religion aims is impossible unless the spiritual disease caused by the fatal rift between science and religion can receive its own specific intellectual cure.

6

DEATH
and the
MEANING of LIFE

BUCKDANCER'S CHOICE

So I would hear out those lungs,
The air split into nine levels,
Some gift of tongues of the whistler

In the invalid's bed: my mother,
Warbling all day to herself
The thousand variations of one song;

It is called Buckdancer's Choice.
For years, they have all been dying
Out, the classic buck-and-wing men

Of traveling minstrel shows;
With them also an old woman
Was dying of breathless angina,

Yet still found breath enough
To whistle up in my head
A sight like a one-man band,

Freed black, with cymbals at heel,
An ex-slave who thrivingly danced
To the ring of his own clashing light

Through the thousand variations of one song
All day to my mother's prone music,
The invalid's warbler's note,

While I crept close to the wall
Sock-footed, to hear the sounds alter,
Her tongue like a mockingbird's break

Through stratum after stratum of a tone
Proclaiming what choices there are
For the last dancers of their kind,

For ill women and for all slaves
Of death, and children enchanted at walls
With a brass-beating glow underfoot,

Not dancing but nearly risen
Through barnlike, theatrelike houses
On the wings of the buck and wing.

James Dickey

In James Dickey's splendid poem, most of us can readily identify with the child, now grown up to be the poem's narrator. We too have known people about to die, "slaves of death" like the invalid mother and the black buckdancers; and, like the child, we have sometimes been mystified that these dying persons are able to go on doing such normal, everyday things—whistling, earning a living—while they wait for their end. How can they? Shouldn't they be doing something *extraordinary*, making preparations, at least *raging* against their doom? How could one give over one's last hours to "warbling . . . all day the thousand variations of one song"?

A moment's thought reveals the self-indulgence and myopia of such an attitude; for we too, all of us without exception, are the slaves of death. Dickey's child, standing in stocking-feet, is just as much death's prisoner as is his bedridden mother. He too will surely die, perhaps without the grace of a warning. As I write, and as you read, our own deaths approach, inexorably; yet we whistle on—reading philosophy, making love, making money, making children—"the thousand variations of one song."

How can we do it? Ordinarily, of course, we camouflage the reality to make it bearable. We make ourselves forget how fragile we are, how powerless we are to alter the natural laws which have dominion over us and which are blind to our cherished desires.

Our personality is entirely dependent upon external circumstances which have unlimited power to crush it. But we would rather die than admit this. From our point of view the equilibrium of the world is a combination of circumstances so ordered that our personality remains intact and seems to belong to us. All the circumstances of the past that have wounded our personality appear to us to be disturbances of balance which should in-

fallibly be made up for one day or another by phenomena having a contrary effect. The near approach of death is horrible chiefly because it forces
the knowledge upon us that these compensations will never come.[1]

In addition, we make ourselves forget how trivial and temporary are
the activities which consume the greatest part of our energies. Over
some of these routines—eating and sleeping, for instance—we have no
real control; they are rooted in our physiology. What of the routines we
have chosen? How do they look to us—what sense do they have—face-
to-face with death? For a single sort of example, consider all our enormously powerful desires to "succeed": we want so much to be popular,
to be rich, to be a member of Phi Beta Kappa, to be loved. Think of
the hours we devote to such pursuits. What's the point? Even if—as is
not likely—all our dreams come true, what do we have? Money, a few
pleasant hours, a few initials after our name. There are, as the proverb
says, no pockets in a shroud—and no place to hang a ϕBK key either.
Viewed from the grave, all is vanity.

What happens to our lives when this reality is acknowledged? Many
people, some philosophers among them, have argued that once we clearly
see that we are death's permanent slaves, once we *feel* this as well as
assent to it intellectually, then our daily routines necessarily lose their
sense and become insupportable. In his *Confession*, Tolstoy tells of the
despair and anger which can paralyze the person who has perceived
death's threat to his life's meaning.

> I could give no reasonable meaning to any single action or to my whole life.
> I was only surprised that I could have avoided understanding this from the
> very beginning—it has been so long known to all. Today or tomorrow sick-
> ness and death will come (they had come already) to those I love or to me;
> nothing will remain but stench and worms. Sooner or later my affairs, what-
> ever they be, will be forgotten, and I shall not exist. Then why go on mak-
> ing any effort? . . . How can man fail to see this? And how go on living?
> . . . One can only live while one is intoxicated with life; as soon as one is
> sober it is impossible not to see that it is all a mere fraud and a stupid
> fraud. That is precisely what is is: there is nothing either amusing or witty
> about it, it is simply cruel and stupid.[2]

Is Tolstoy's an extreme reaction? The facts are not, it seems, in dispute: we *will* all die, we *will* all be forgotten, any effort to which we
set our hands *will* someday go to dust. Do these putative facts necessarily
rob life of its ordinary meaning? If they do, could there be some extraordinary meaning to a person's life which even annihilation cannot
menace? In this section we have arranged several responses to these
fundamental philosophical questions, ranging from the Christian denial
of death's finality to Tom Nagel's attempt to draw the venom from the
recognition of life's absurdity.

NOTES

1. Simone Weil, *Waiting for God* (New York: Harper and Row, 1973), p. 224.
2. Leo Tolstoy, *A Confession*, trans. Aylmer Maude (London: Oxford University Press, 1974), pp. 19-20.

STATEMENT of the PROBLEM

My Confession

Leo Tolstoy

CHAPTER I

I was christened and educated in the Orthodox Christian Faith; I was taught it in my childhood, and in my boyhood and youth. Nevertheless, when, at eighteen years of age, I left the university in the second year, I had discarded all belief in anything I had been taught.

To judge by what I can now remember, I never had a serious belief; I merely trusted in what my elders made their profession of faith, but even this trust was very precarious.

I remember once in my twelfth year, a boy, now long since dead, Volodinka M———, a pupil in the gymnasium, spent a Sunday with us, and brought us the news of the last discovery in the gymnasium. This discovery was that there was no God, and that all we were taught on the subject was a mere invention (this was in 1838). I remember well how interested my elder brothers were in this news; I was admitted to their deliberations, and we all eagerly accepted the theory as something particularly attractive and possibly quite true.

I remember, also, that when my elder brother, Dmitri, then at the university, with the impulsiveness natural to his character, gave himself up to a passionate faith, began to attend the church services regularly, to fast, and to lead a pure and moral life, we all of us, and some older than ourselves, never ceased to hold him up to ridicule, and for some incomprehensible reason gave him the nickname of Noah. I remember

From *The Works of Leo N. Tolstoy* (New York: T. Y. Crowell, 1917).

that Musin-Pushkin, then curator of the University of Kazan, having invited us to a ball, tried to persuade my brother, who had refused the invitation, by the jeering argument that even David danced before the Ark.

I sympathized then with these jokes of my elders, and drew from them this conclusion,—that I was bound to learn my catechism, and go to church, but that it was not necessary to take all this too seriously.

I also remember that I read Voltaire when I was very young, and that his tone of mockery amused without disgusting me.

This estrangement from all belief went on in me, as it does now, and always has done, in those of the same social position and culture. This falling off, as it seems to me, for the most part goes on thus: people live as others live, and their lives are guided, not by the principles of the faith that is taught them, but by their very opposite; belief has no influence on life, nor on the relations among men—it is relegated to some other sphere apart from life and independent of it; if the two ever come into contact at all, belief is only one of the outward phenomena, and not one of the constituent parts of life.

By a man's life, by his acts, it was then, as it is now, impossible to know whether he was a believer or not. If there be a difference between one who openly professes the doctrines of the Orthodox Church, and one who denies them, the difference is to the advantage of the former. Then, as now, the open profession of the Orthodox doctrines was found mostly among dull, stern, immoral men, and those who think much of their own importance. Intellect, honor, frankness, good nature, and morality are oftener met with among those who call themselves disbelievers.

The school-boy is taught his catechism and sent to church; chinovniks, or functionaries, are required to show a certificate of having taken the holy communion. But the man belonging to our class, who is done with school and does not enter the public service, may now live a dozen years —still more was this the case formerly—without being once reminded of the fact that he lives among Christians, and is reckoned as a member of the Orthodox Christian Church.

Thus it happens that now, as formerly, the influence of early religious teaching, accepted merely on trust and upheld by authority, gradually fades away under the knowledge and practical experience of life, which is opposed to all its principles, and that a man often believes for years that his early faith is still intact, while all the time not a trace of it remains in him.

A certain S————, a clever and veracious man, once related to me how he came to give up his belief.

Twenty-six years ago, while he was off on a hunting expedition, he knelt down to pray before he lay down to rest, according to a habit of his from childhood. His elder brother, who was of the party, lay on some straw and watched him. When S———— had finished, and was preparing to lie down, his brother said to him:—

"Ah, so you still keep that up?"

Nothing more passed between them, but from that day S——— ceased to pray and to go to church. For thirty years S——— has not said a prayer, has not taken the communion, has not been in a church,—not because he shared the convictions of his brother, or even knew them,—not because he had come to any conclusions of his own,—but because his brother's words were like the push of a finger against a wall ready to tumble over with its own weight; they proved to him that what he had taken for belief was an empty form, and that consequently every word he uttered, every sign of the cross he made, every time he bowed his head during his prayers, his act was unmeaning. When he once admitted to himself that such acts had no meaning in them, he could not continue them.

Thus it has been, and is, I believe, with the large majority of men. I am speaking of men of our class, I am speaking of men who are true to themselves, and not of those who make of religion a means of obtaining some temporal advantage. (These men are truly absolute unbelievers; for if faith be to them a means of obtaining any worldly end, it is most certainly no faith at all.) Such men of our own class are in this position: the light of knowledge and life has melted the artificially constructed edifice of belief within, and they have either observed that and cleared away the superincumbent ruins, or they have remained unconscious of it.

The belief instilled from childhood in me, as in so many others, gradually disappeared, but with this difference; that as from fifteen years of age I had begun to read philosophical works, I became very early conscious of my own disbelief. From the age of sixteen I ceased to pray, and ceased, from conviction, to attend the services of the church and to fast. I no longer accepted the faith of my childhood, but I believed in something, though I could not exactly explain in what. I believed in a God,—or rather, I did not deny the existence of a God,—but what kind of God I could not have told; I denied neither Christ nor His teaching, but in what that teaching consisted I could not have said.

Now, when I think over that time, I see clearly that all the faith I had, the only belief which, apart from mere animal instinct, swayed my life, was a belief in the possibility of perfection, though what it was in itself, or what would be its results, I could not have said.

I tried to reach intellectual perfection; my studies were extended in every direction of which my life afforded me a chance; I strove to strengthen my will, forming for myself rules which I forced myself to follow; I did my best to develop my physical powers by every exercise calculated to give strength and agility, and by way of accustoming myself to patient endurance; I subjected myself to many voluntary hardships and trials of privation. All this I looked on as necessary to obtain the perfection at which I aimed.

At first, of course, moral perfection seemed to me the main end, but I soon found myself contemplating in its stead an ideal of general perfectibility; in other words, I wished to be better, not in my own eyes nor in God's, but in the sight of other men. And very soon this striving to be better in the sight of men feeling again changed into another,— the desire to have more power than others, to secure for myself a greater share of fame, of social distinction, and of wealth.

CHAPTER II

At some future time I may relate the story of my life, and dwell in detail on the pathetic and instructive incidents of my youth. I think that many and many have had the same experiences as I did. I desired with all my soul to be good; but I was young, I had passions, and I was alone, wholly alone, in my search after goodness. Every time I tried to express the longings of my heart to be morally good, I was met with contempt and ridicule, but as soon as I gave way to low passions, I was praised and encouraged.

Ambition, love of power, love of gain, lechery, pride, anger, vengeance, were held in high esteem.

As I gave way to these passions, I became like my elders and I felt that they were satisfied with me. A kind-hearted aunt of mine, a really good woman with whom I lived, used to say to me that there was one thing above all others which she wished for me—an intrigue with a married woman: *"Rien ne forme un jeune homme, comme une liaison avec une femme comme il faut."* Another of her wishes for my happiness was that I should become an adjutant, and, if possible, to the Emperor; the greatest piece of good fortune of all she thought would be that I should find a very wealthy bride, who would bring me as her dowry as many slaves as could be.

I cannot now recall those years without a painful feeling of horror and loathing.

I put men to death in war. I fought duels to slay others, I lost at cards, wasted my substance wrung from the sweat of peasants, punished the latter cruelly, rioted with loose women, and deceived men. Lying, robbery, adultery of all kinds, drunkenness, violence, murder. There was not one crime which I did not commit, and yet I was not the less considered by my equals a comparatively moral man.

Such was my life during ten years.

During that time I began to write, out of vanity, love of gain, and pride. I followed as a writer the same path which I had chosen as a man. In order to obtain the fame and the money for which I wrote, I was obliged to hide what was good and to say what was evil. Thus I did. How often while writing have I cudgeled my brains to conceal under the mask of indifference or pleasantry those yearnings for something better which formed the real thought of my life. I succeeded in this also, and was praised.

At twenty-six years of age, on the close of the war, I came to Petersburg and made the acquaintance of the authors of the day. I met with a healthy reception and much flattery.

Before I had time to look around, the prejudices and views of life common to the writers of the class with which I associated became my own, and completely put an end to all my former struggles after a better life. These views, under the influence of the dissipation of my life, supplied a theory which justified it.

The view of life taken by these my fellow-writers was that life is a development, and the principal part in that development is played by ourselves, the thinkers, while among the thinkers the chief influence is again due to us, the artists, the poets. Our vocation is to teach men.

In order to avoid answering the very natural question, "What do I know, and what can I teach?" the theory in question is made to contain the formula that it is not necessary to know this, but that the artist and the poet teach unconsciously.

I was myself considered a marvelous artist and poet, and I therefore very naturally adopted this theory. I, an artist and poet, wrote and taught I knew not what. For doing this I received money; I kept a splendid table, had excellent lodgings, women, society; I had fame. Naturally what I taught was very good.

The faith in poetry and the development of life was a true faith, and I was one of its priests. To be one of its priests was very advantageous and agreeable. I long remained in this belief, and never once doubted its truth.

But in the second, and especially in the third year of this way of life, I began to doubt the infallibility of the doctrine, and to examine it more closely. What first led me to doubt was the fact that I began to notice the priests of this belief did not agree among themselves. Some said:—

"We are the best and most useful teachers; we teach what is needful, and all others teach wrong."

They disputed, quarreled, abused, deceived, and cheated one another. Moreover, there were many among us who, quite indifferent to the question who was right or who was wrong, advanced only their own private interests by the aid of our activity. All this forced on me doubts as to the truth of our belief.

Again, having begun to doubt the truth of our literary faith, I began to study its priests more closely, and became convinced that almost all the priests of this faith were immoral men, most of them worthless and insignificant, and beneath the moral level of those with whom I associated during my former dissipated and military career; but conceited and self-satisfied as only those can be who are wholly saints, or those who know not what holiness is.

I grew disgusted with mankind and with myself, and I understood that this belief was a delusion. The strangest thing in all this was that, though I soon saw the falseness of this belief and renounced it, I did not renounce the rank given me by these men,—the rank of artist, poet, teacher. I was simple enough to imagine that I was a poet and artist, and could teach all men without knowing what I was teaching. But so I did.

By my companionship with these men I had gained a new vice,—a pride developed to a morbid extreme, and an insane self-confidence in teaching men what I myself did not know.

When I now think over that time, and remember my own state of mind and that of these men (a state of mind common enough among thousands still), it seems to me pitiful, terrible, and ridiculous; it excites the feelings which overcome us as we pass through a madhouse.

We were all then convinced that it behooved us to speak, to write, and to print as fast as we could, as much as we could, and that on this depended the welfare of the human race. And thousands of us wrote, printed, and taught, and all the while confuted and abused one another. Quite unconscious that we ourselves knew nothing, that to the simplest of all problems in life—what is right and what is wrong—we had no answer, we all went on talking together without one to listen, at times abetting and praising one another on condition that we were abetted and praised in turn, and again turning upon one another in wrath— in short, we reproduced the scenes in a madhouse.

Thousands of laborers worked day and night, to the limit of their strength, setting up the type and printing millions of words to be spread by the post all over Russia, and still we continued to teach, unable to teach enough, angrily complaining the while that we were not much listened to.

A strange state of things indeed, but now it is comprehensible to me. The real motive that inspired all our reasoning was the desire for money and praise, to obtain which we knew of no other means than writing books and newspapers, and so we did. But in order to hold fast to the conviction that while thus uselessly employed we were very important men, it was necessary to justify our occupation to ourselves by another theory, and the following was the one we adopted:—

Whatever is, is right; everything that is, is due to development; development comes from civilization; the measure of civilization is the diffusion of books and newspapers; we are paid and honored for the books and newspapers which we write, and we are therefore the most useful and best of men!

This reasoning might have been conclusive had we all been agreed; but, as for every opinion expressed by one of us there instantly appeared from another one diametrically opposite, we had to hesitate before accepting it. But we did not notice this; we received money, and were praised by those of our party, consequently we—each one of us—considered that we were in the right.

It is now clear to me that between ourselves and the inhabitants of a madhouse there was no difference: at the time I only vaguely suspected this, and, like all madmen, thought all were mad except myself.

CHAPTER III

I lived in this senseless manner another six years, up to the time of my marriage. During this time I went abroad. My life in Europe, and my acquaintance with many eminent and learned foreigners, confirmed my belief in the doctrine of general perfectibility, as I found the same theory prevailed among them. This belief took the form which is common among most of the cultivated men of our day. This belief was expressed in the word "progress." It then appeared to me this word had a real meaning. I did not as yet understand that, tormented like every other man by the question, "How was I to live better?" when I answered that I must live for progress, I was only repeating the answer of a man carried away in a boat by the waves and the wind, who to the one important question for him, "Where are we to steer?" should answer, "We are being carried somewhere."

I did not see this then; only at rare intervals my feelings, and not my reason, were roused against the common superstition of our age, which leads men to ignore their own ignorance of life.

Thus, during my stay in Paris, the sight of a public execution revealed to me the weakness of my superstitious belief in progress. When I saw the head divided from the body, and heard the sound with which they fell separately into the box, I understood, not with my reason, but with my whole being, that no theory of the wisdom of all established things, nor of progress, could justify such an act; and that if all the men in the world from the day of creation, by whatever theory, had found this thing necessary, I knew it was not necessary, it was a bad thing, and that therefore I must judge of what was right and necessary, not by what men said and did, not by progress, but what I felt to be true in my heart.

Another instance of the insufficiency of this superstition of progress as a rule for life was the death of my brother. He fell ill while still young, suffered much during a whole year, and died in great pain. He was a man of good abilities, of a kind heart, and of a serious temper, but he died without understanding why he had lived, and still less what his death meant for him. No theories could give an answer to these questions, either to him or to me, during the whole period of his long and painful lingering.

But these occasions for doubt were few and far between; on the whole, I continued to live in the profession of the faith of progress. "Everything develops, and I myself am developing; and why this is so will one day be apparent," was the formula I was obliged to adopt.

On my return from abroad I settled in the country, and occupied myself with the organization of schools for the peasantry. This occupation was especially dear to my heart, because it was free from the spirit of falseness so evident to me in the career of a literary teacher.

Here again I acted in the name of progress, but this time I brought a spirit of critical inquiry to the system on which the progress rested. I said to myself that progress was often attempted in an irrational manner, and that it was necessary to leave a primitive people and the children of peasants perfectly free to choose the way of progress which they thought best. In reality I was still bent on the solution of the same impossible problem,—how to teach without knowing what I had to teach. In the highest spheres of literature I had understood that it was impossible to do this because I had seen that each taught differently, and that the teachers quarreled among themselves, and scarcely succeeded in concealing their ignorance from one another. Having now to deal with peasants' children, I thought that I could get over this difficulty by allowing the children to learn what they liked. It seems now absurd when I remember the expedients by which I carried out this whim of mine to teach, though I knew in my heart that I could teach nothing useful, because I myself did not know what was necessary.[1]

After a year spent in this employment with the school I again went abroad, for the purpose of finding out how I was to teach without knowing anything.

I believed that I had found a solution abroad, and, armed with all that essence of wisdom, I returned to Russia, the same year in which the peasants were freed from serfdom; and, accepting the office of arbitrator,[2] I began to teach the uneducated people in the schools, and the educated classes in the journal which I began to publish. Things seemed to be going on well, but I felt that my mind was not in a normal state and that a change was near. I might even then, perhaps, have come to that state of despair to which I was brought fifteen years later, if it had not been for a new experience in life which promised me safety—family life.

For a year I was occupied with arbitration, with the schools and with my newspaper, and got so involved that I was harassed to death; the struggle over the arbitration was so hard for me, my activity in the schools was so dubious to me, my shuffling in the newspaper became so repugnant to me, consisting as it did in forever the same thing,—in the desire to teach all people and to hide the fact that I did not know how or what to teach,—that I fell ill, more with a mental than physical sickness, gave up everything, and started for the steppes to the Bashkirs to breathe a fresher air, to drink kumiss, and live an animal life.

After I returned I married. The new circumstances of a happy family life completely led me away from the search after the meaning of life as a whole. My life was concentrated at this time in my family, my wife and children, and consequently in the care for increasing the means of life. The effort to effect my own individual perfection, already replaced by the striving after general progress, was again changed into an effort to secure the particular happiness of my family.

In this way fifteen years passed.

Notwithstanding that during these fifteen years I looked upon the craft of authorship as a very trifling thing, I continued all the time to write. I had experienced the seductions of authorship, the temptations of an enormous pecuniary reward and of great applause for valueless work, and gave myself up to it as a means of improving my material position, and of stifling in my soul all questions regarding my own life and life in general. In my writings I taught what for me was the only truth,—that the object of life should be our highest happiness and that of our family.

Thus I lived; but, five years ago, a strange state of mind began to grow upon me: I had moments of perplexity, of a stoppage, as it were, of life, as if I did not know how I was to live, what I was to do, and I began to wander, and was a victim to low spirits. But this passed, and I continued to live as before. Later, these periods of perplexity began to return more and more frequently, and invariably took the same form. These stoppages of life always presented themselves to me with the same questions: "Why?" and "What after?"

At first it seemed to me that these were aimless, unmeaning questions; it seemed to me that all they asked about was well known, and that if at any time when I wished to find answers to them I could do so without much trouble—that just at that time I could not be bothered with this, but whenever I should stop to think them over I should find an answer. But these questions presented themselves to my mind with ever increasing frequency, demanding an answer with still greater and greater persistence, and like dots grouped themselves into one black spot.

It was with me as it happens in the case of every mortal internal ailment—at first appear the insignificant symptoms of indisposition, disregarded by the patient; then these symptoms are repeated more and more frequently, till they merge in uninterrupted suffering. The sufferings increase, and the patient, before he has time to look around, is confronted with the fact that what he took for a mere indisposition has become more important to him than anything else on earth, that it is death!

This is exactly what happened to me. I became aware that this was not a chance indisposition, but something very serious, and that if all these questions continued to recur, I should have to find an answer to them. And I tried to answer them. The questions seemed so foolish, so simple, so childish; but no sooner had I taken hold of them and attempted to decide them than I was convinced, first, that they were neither childish nor silly, but were concerned with the deepest problems of life; and, in the second place, that I could not decide them—could not decide them, however I put my mind upon them.

Before occupying myself with my Samara estate, with the education of my son, with the writing of books, I was bound to know why I did these things. As long as I do not know the reason "why" I cannot do anything. I cannot live. While thinking about the management of my household and estate, which in these days occupied much of my time, suddenly this question came into my head:—

"Well and good, I have now six thousand desyatins in the government of Samara, and three hundred horses—what then?"

I was perfectly disconcerted, and knew not what to think. Another time, dwelling on the thought of how I should educate my children, I asked myself, *"Why?"* Again, when considering by what means the well-being of the people might best be promoted, I suddenly exclaimed, "But what concern have I with it?" When I thought of the fame which my works were gaining me, I said to myself:—

"Well, what if I should be more famous than Gogol, Pushkin, Shakespear, Molière—than all the writers of the world—well, and what then?"

I could find no reply. Such questions will not wait; they demand an immediate answer; without one it is impossible to live; but answer there was none.

I felt that the ground on which I stood was crumbling, that there was nothing for me to stand on, that what I had been living for was nothing, that I had no reason for living.

CHAPTER IV

My life had come to a stop. I was able to breathe, to eat, to drink, to sleep, and I could not help breathing, eating, drinking, sleeping; but there was no real life in me because I had not a single desire, the fulfilment of which I could feel to be reasonable. If I wished for anything, I knew beforehand that, were I to satisfy the wish, or were I not to satisfy it, nothing would come of it. Had a fairy appeared and offered me all I desired, I should not have known what to say. If I had, in moments of excitement, I will not say wishes, but the habits of former wishes, at calmer moments I knew that it was a delusion, that I really wished for nothing. I could not even wish to know the truth, because I guessed in what it consisted.

The truth was, that life was meaningless. Every day of life, every step in it, brought me, as it were, nearer the precipice, and I saw clearly that before me there was nothing but ruin. And to stop was impossible; to go back was impossible; and it was impossible to shut my eyes so as not to see that there was nothing before me but suffering and actual death, absolute annihilation.

Thus I, a healthy and a happy man, was brought to feel that I could live no longer,—some irresistible force was dragging me onward to escape from life. I do not mean that I wanted to kill myself.

The force that drew me away from life was stronger, fuller, and more universal than any wish; it was a force like that of my previous attachment to life, only in a contrary direction. With all my force I struggled away from life. The idea of suicide came as naturally to me as formerly that of bettering my life. This thought was so attractive to me that I was compelled to practise upon myself a species of self-deception in order to avoid carrying it out too hastily. I was unwilling to act hastily, only because I wanted to employ all my powers in clearing away the confusion of my thoughts; if I should not clear them away, I could at any time kill myself. And here was I, a man fortunately situated, hiding away a cord, to avoid being tempted to hang myself by it to the transom between the closets of my room, where I undressed alone every evening; and I ceased to go hunting with a gun because it offered too easy a way of getting rid of life. I knew not what I wanted; I was afraid of life; I struggled to get away from it, and yet there *was* something I hoped for from it.

Such was the condition I had to come to, at a time when all the circumstances of my life were preeminently happy ones, and when I had not reached my fiftieth year. I had a good, loving, and beloved wife, good children, and a large estate, which, without much trouble on my part, was growing and increasing; I was more than ever respected by my friends and acquaintances; I was praised by strangers, and could lay claim to having made my name famous without much self-deception. Moreover, I was not mad or in an unhealthy mental state; on the contrary, I enjoyed a mental and physical strength which I have seldom found in men of my class and pursuits; I could keep up with a peasant in mowing, and could continue mental labor for eight or ten hours at a stretch, without any evil consequences. And in this state of things it came to this,—that I could not live, and as I feared death I was obliged to employ ruses against myself so as not to put an end to my life.

The mental state in which I then was seemed to me summed up in the following: My life was a foolish and wicked joke played on me by some one. Notwithstanding that fact that I did not recognize a "Some one," who may have created me, this conclusion that some one had wickedly and foolishly made a joke of me in bringing me into the world seemed to me the most natural of all conclusions.

I could not help reasoning that *there*, somewhere, is some one who is now diverting himself at my expense, as he watches me, as after from thirty to forty years of a life of study and development, of mental and bodily growth with all my powers matured and having reached that summit of life from which it is seen in its completeness, I stand like a fool on this height, understanding clearly that there is nothing in life, that there never was anything, and never will be. To him it must seem ridiculous.

But whether there is, or is not, such a being, in either case it did not help me. I could not attribute a reasonable motive to any single act in my whole life. I was only astonished that I could not have realized this at the very beginning. All this had so long been known to me! Illness and death would come (indeed, they had come), if not to-day, then tomorrow, to those whom I loved, to myself, and nothing remains but stench and worms. All my acts, whatever I did, would sooner or later be forgotten, and I myself be nowhere. Why, then, busy one's self with anything? How could men fail to see this, and live? How wonderful this is! It is possible to live only as long as life intoxicates us; as soon as we are sober again we see that it is all a delusion, and a stupid delusion! In this, indeed, there is nothing either ludicrous or amusing; it is only cruel and stupid!

There is an old Eastern fable about a traveler in the steppes who is attacked by a furious wild beast. To save himself the traveler gets into a waterless well; but at the bottom of it he sees a dragon with its jaws wide open to devour him. The unhappy man dares not get out for fear of the wild beast, and dares not descend for fear of the dragon, so he catches hold of the branch of a wild plant growing in a crevice of the well. His arms grow tired, and he feels that he must soon perish, death awaiting him on either side, but he still holds on; and he sees two mice, one black and one white, gradually making their way round the stem of the wild plant on which he is hanging, nibbling it through. The plant will soon give way and break off, and he will fall into the jaws of the dragon. The traveler sees this, and knows that he must inevitably perish; but, while still hanging, he looks around him, and, finding some drops of honey on the leaves of the wild plant, he stretches out his tongue and licks them.

Thus do I cling to the branch of life, knowing that the dragon of death inevitably awaits me, ready to tear me to pieces, and I cannot understand why such tortures have fallen to my lot. I also strive to suck the honey which once comforted me, but this honey no longer rejoices me, while the white mouse and the black, day and night, gnaw through the branch to which I cling. I see the dragon plainly, and the honey is no longer sweet. I see the dragon, from which there is no escape, and the mice, and I cannot turn my eyes away from them. It is no fable, but a living, undeniable truth, to be understood of all men.

The former delusion of happiness in life which hid from me the horror of the dragon no longer deceives me. However I may reason with myself that I cannot understand the meaning of life, that I must live without thinking, I cannot do this, because I have done so too long already. Now I cannot help seeing the days and nights hurrying by and bringing me nearer to death. I can see but this, because this alone is true—all the rest is a lie. The two drops of honey, which more than anything else drew my eyes away from the cruel truth, my love for my family and for my writings, to which later I gave the name of art, were no longer sweet to me.

"My family," I said to myself; "but a family—a wife and children—are also human beings, and subject to the same conditions as I myself; they must either be living in a lie, or they must see the terrible truth. Why should they live? Why should I love them, care for them, bring them up, and watch over them? To bring them to the despair which fills myself, or to make dolts of them? As I love them, I cannot conceal from them the truth—every step they take in knowledge leads them to it, and that truth is death."

"Art, poetry?" . . . .

Under the influence of success, and flattered by praise, I had long been persuading myself that this was a work which must be done notwithstanding the approach of death, which would destroy everything—my writings, and the memory of them; but I soon saw that this was only another delusion, I saw clearly that art is only the ornament and charm of life. Life having lost its charm for me, how could I make others see a charm in it? While I was not living my own life, but one that was external to me was bearing me away on its billows, while I believed that life had a meaning, though I could not say what it was, the reflections of life of every kind in poetry and art gave me delight, it was pleasant to me to look at life in the mirror of art; but when I tried to discover the meaning of life, when I felt the necessity of living myself, the mirror became either unnecessary, superfluous, and ridiculous, or painful. I could no longer take comfort from what I saw in the mirror—that my position was stupid and desperate.

It was a genuine cause of rejoicing when in the depths of my soul I believed that my life had a meaning. Then this play of lights, the comic, the tragic, the pathetic, the beautiful, and the terrible in life, amused me. But when I knew that life was meaningless and terrible, the play in the mirror could no longer entertain me. No sweetness could be sweet to me when I saw the dragon, and the mice nibbling away my support.

Nor was that all. Had I simply come to know that life has no meaning, I might have quietly accepted it, might have known that was my allotted portion. But I could not rest calmly on this. Had I been like a man living in a forest, out of which he knows that there is no issue, I could have lived on; but I was like a man lost in a forest, and who, terrified by the thought that he is lost, rushes about trying to find a way out, and, though he knows each step leads him still farther astray, cannot help rushing about.

It was this that was terrible! And to get free from this horror, I was ready to kill myself. I felt a horror of what awaited me; I knew that this horror was more horrible than the position itself, but I could not patiently await the end. However persuasive the argument might be that all the same a blood-vessel in the heart would be ruptured or something would burst and all be over, still I could not patiently await the end. The horror of the darkness was too great to bear, and I longed to free myself from it as speedily as possible by a rope or a pistol ball. This was the feeling that, above all, drew me to think of suicide.

NOTES

1. See "School Scenes from Yasnaya Polyana," Vol. XV.
2. *Posrednik,* sometimes translated Justice of the Peace.

Death

Thomas Nagel

"The syllogism he had learnt from Kiesewetter's logic: 'Caius is a man, men are mortal, therefore Caius is mortal,' had always seem to him correct as applied to Caius, but certainly not as applied to himself. . . . What did Caius know of the smell of that striped leather ball Vanya had been so fond of?"

Tolstoy, The Death of Ivan Ilyich

If, as many people believe, death is the unequivocal and permanent end of our existence, the question arises whether it is a bad thing to die. There is conspicuous disagreement about the matter: some people think death is dreadful; others have no objection to death *per se*, though they hope their own will be neither premature nor painful.

Those in the former category tend to think those in the latter are blind to the obvious, while the latter suppose the former to be prey to some sort of confusion. On the one hand it can be said that life is all one has, and the loss of it is the greatest loss one can sustain. On the other hand it may be objected that death deprives this supposed loss of its subject, and that if one realizes that death is not an unimaginable condition of the persisting person, but a mere blank, one will see that it can have no value whatever, positive or negative.

Since I want to leave aside the question whether we are, or might be, immortal in some form, I shall simply use the word "death" and its cognates in this discussion to mean *permanent* death, unsupplemented by any form of conscious survival. I wish to consider whether death is in itself an evil, and how great an evil, and of what kind, it might be. This question should be of interest even to those who believe that we do not die permanently, for one's attitude toward immortality must depend in part on one's attitude toward death.

Clearly if death is an evil at all, it cannot be because of its positive features, but only because of what it deprives us of. I shall try to deal with the difficulties surrounding the natural view that death is an evil because it brings to an end all the goods that life contains.[1] An account of these goods need not occupy us here, except to observe that some of them, like perception, desire, activity, and thought, are so general as to be constitutive of human life. They are widely regarded as formidable benefits in themselves, despite the fact that they are conditions of misery

From NOUS, Vol. 4, No. 1 (1970), pp. 73-80. Reprinted by permission of publisher and author.

as well as of happiness, and that a sufficient quantity of more particular evils can perhaps outweigh them. That is what is meant, I think, by the allegation that it is good simply to be alive, even if one is undergoing terrible experiences. The situation is roughly this: There are elements which, if added to one's experience, make life better; there are other elements which, if added to one's experience, make life worse. But what remains when these are set aside is not merely *neutral*: it is emphatically positive. Therefore life is worth living even when the bad elements of experience are plentiful, and the good ones too meager to outweigh the bad ones on their own. The additional positive weight is supplied by experience itself, rather than by any of its contents.

I shall not discuss the value that one person's life or death may have for others, or its objective value, but only the value it has for the person who is its subject. That seems to me the primary case, and the case which presents the greatest difficulties. Let me add only two observations. First, the value of life and its contents does not attach to mere organic survival: almost everyone would be indifferent (other things equal) between immediate death and immediate coma followed by death twenty years later without reawakening. And second, like most goods, this can be multiplied by time: more is better than less. The added quantities need not be temporarily continuous (though continuity has its social advantages). People are attracted to the possibility of long-term suspended animation or freezing, followed by the resumption of conscious life, because they can regard it from within simply as a *continuation* of their present life. If these techniques are ever perfected, what from outside appeared as a dormant interval of three hundred years could be experienced by the subject as nothing more than a sharp discontinuity in the character of his experiences. I do not deny, of course, that this has its own disadvantages. Family and friends may have died in the meantime; the language may have changed; the comforts of social, geographical, and cultural familiarity would be lacking. Nevertheless these inconveniences would not obliterate the basic advantage of continued, though discontinuous, existence.

If we turn from what is good about life to what is bad about death, the case is completely different. Essentially, though there may be problems about their specification, what we find desirable in life are certain states, conditions, or types of activity. It is *being* alive, *doing* certain things, having certain experiences, that we consider good. But if death is an evil, it is the *loss of life*, rather than the state of being dead, or nonexistent, or unconscious, that is objectionable.[2] This asymmetry is important. If it is good to be alive, that advantage can be attributed to a person at each point of his life. It is a good of which Bach had more than Schubert, simply because he lived longer. Death, however, is not an evil of which Shakespeare has so far received a larger portion than Proust. If death is a disadvantage, it is not easy to say when a man suffers it.

There are two other indications that we do not object to death merely because it involves long periods of nonexistence. First, as has been mentioned, most of us would not regard the *temporary* suspension of life, even for substantial intervals, as in itself a misfortune. If it develops that people can be frozen without reduction of the conscious lifespan, it will be inappropriate to pity those who are temporarily out of circulation. Second, none of us existed before we were born (or conceived), but few regard that as a misfortune. I shall have more to say about this later.

The point that death is not regarded as an unfortunate state enables us to refute a curious but very common suggestion about the origin of the fear of death. It is often said that those who object to death have made the mistake of trying to imagine what it is like to *be* dead. It is alleged that the failure to realize that this task is logically impossible (for the banal reason that there is nothing to imagine) leads to the conviction that death is a mysterious and therefore terrifying prospective state. But this diagnosis is evidently false, for it is just as impossible to imagine being totally unconscious as to imagine being dead (though it is easy enough to imagine oneself, from the outside, in either of those conditions). Yet people who are averse to death are not usually averse to unconsciousness (so long as it does not entail a substantial cut in the total duration of waking life).

If we are to make sense of the view that to die is bad, it must be on the ground that life is a good and death is the corresponding deprivation or loss, bad not because of any positive features but because of the desirability of what it removes. We must now turn to the serious difficulties which this hypothesis raises, difficulties about loss and privation in general, and about death in particular.

Essentially, there are three types of problem. First, doubt may be raised whether *anything* can be bad for a man without being positively unpleasant to him: specifically, it may be doubted that there are any evils which consist merely in the deprivation or absence of possible goods, and which do not depend on someone's *minding* that deprivation. Second, there are special difficulties, in the case of death, about how the supposed misfortune is to be assigned to a subject at all. There is doubt both as to who its subject is, and as to *when* he undergoes it. So long as a person exists, he has not yet died, and once he has died, he no longer exists; so there seems to be no time when death, if it is a misfortune, can be ascribed to its unfortunate subject. The third type of difficulty concerns the asymmetry, mentioned above, between our attitudes to posthumous and prenatal nonexistence. How can the former be bad if the latter is not?

It should be recognized that if these are valid objections to counting death as an evil, they will apply to many other supposed evils as well. The first type of objection is expressed in general form by the common remark that what you don't know can't hurt you. It means that even if a man is betrayed by his friends, ridiculed behind his back, and despised by people who treat him politely to his face, none of it can be counted as a misfortune for him so long as he does not suffer as a result. It means that a man is not injured if his wishes are ignored by the executor of his will, or if, after his death, the belief becomes current that all the literary works on which his fame rests were really written by his brother, who died in Mexico at the age of 28. It seems to me worth asking what assumptions about good and evil lead to these drastic restrictions.

All the questions have something to do with time. There certainly are goods and evils of a simple kind (including some pleasures and pains) which a person possesses at a given time simply in virtue of his condition at that time. But this is not true of all the things we regard as good or bad for a man. Often we need to know his history to tell whether something is a misfortune or not; this applies to ills like deterioration, deprivation, and damage. Sometimes his experimental state is relatively unimportant—as in the case of a man who wastes his life in the cheerful pursuit of a method of communicating with asparagus plants. Someone who holds that all goods and evils must be temporarily assignable states of the person may of course try to bring difficult cases into line by pointing to the pleasure or pain that more complicated goods and evils cause. Loss, betrayal, deception, and ridicule are on this view bad because people suffer when they learn of them. But it should be asked how our ideas of human value would have to be constituted to accommodate these cases directly instead. One advantage of such an account might be that it would enable us to explain why the discovery of these misfortunes causes suffering—in a way that makes it reasonable. For the natural view is that the discovery of betrayal makes us unhappy because it is bad to be betrayed—not that betrayal is bad because its discovery makes us unhappy.

It therefore seems to me worth exploring the position that most good and ill fortune has as its subject a person identified by his history and his possibilities, rather than merely by his categorical state of the moment—and that while this subject can be exactly located in a sequence of places and times, the same is not necessarily true of the goods and ills that befall him.[3]

These ideas can be illustrated by an example of deprivation whose severity approaches that of death. Suppose an intelligent person receives a brain injury that reduces him to the mental condition of a contented infant, and that such desires as remain to him can be satisfied by a custodian, so that he is free from care. Such a development would be widely regarded as a severe misfortune, not only for his friends and relations, or for society, but also, and primarily, for the person himself. This does not mean that a contented infant is unfortunate. The intelligent adult who has been *reduced* to this condition is the subject of the misfortune. He is the one we pity, though of course he does not mind his condition —there is some doubt, in fact, whether he can be said to exist any longer.

The view that such a man has suffered a misfortune is open to the same objections which have been raised in regard to death. He does not mind his condition. It is in fact the same condition he was in at the age of three months, except that he is bigger. If we did not pity him then, why pity him now; in any case, who is there to pity? The intelligent adult has disappeared, and for a creature like the one before us, happiness consists in a full stomach and a dry diaper.

If these objections are invalid, it must be because they rest on a mistaken assumption about the temporal relation between the subject of a misfortune and the circumstances which constitute it. If, instead of concentrating exclusively on the oversized baby before us, we consider the person he was, and the person he *could* be now, then his reduction to this state and the cancellation of his natural adult development constitute a perfectly intelligible catastrophe.

This case should convince us that it is arbitrary to restrict the goods and evils that can befall a man to nonrelational properties ascribable to him at particular times. As it stands, that restriction excludes not only such cases of gross degeneration, but also a good deal of what is important about success and failure, and other features of a life that have the character of processes. I believe we can go further, however. There are goods and evils which are irreducibly relational; they are features of the relations between a person, with spatial and temporal boundaries of the usual sort, and circumstances which may not coincide with him either in space or in time. A man's life includes much that does not take place within the boundaries of his body and his mind, and what happens to him can include much that does not take place within the boundaries of his life. These boundaries are commonly crossed by the misfortunes of being deceived, or despised, or betrayed. (If this is correct, there is a simple account of what is wrong with breaking a deathbed promise. It is an injury to the dead man. For certain purposes it is possible to regard time as just another type of distance.) The case of mental degeneration shows us an evil that depends on a contrast between the reality and the possible alternatives. A man is the subject of good and evil as much because he has hopes which may or may not be fulfilled, or possibilities which may or may not be realized, as because of his capacity to suffer and enjoy. If death is an evil, it must be accounted for in these terms, and the impossibility of locating it within life should not trouble us.

When a man dies we are left with his corpse, and while a corpse can suffer the kind of mishap that may occur to an article of furniture, it is not a suitable object for pity. The man, however, is. He has lost his life, and if he had not died, he would have continued to live it, and to possess whatever good there is in living. If we apply to death the account suggested for the case of dementia, we shall say that although the spatial and temporal locations of the individual who suffered the loss are clear enough, the misfortune itself cannot be so easily located. One must be content just to state that his life is over and there will never be any more of it. That *fact*, rather than his past or present condition, constitutes his misfortune, if it is one. Nevertheless if there is a loss, someone must suffer it, and *he* must have existence and specific spatial and temporal location even if the loss itself does not. The fact that Beethoven had no children may have been a cause of regret to him, or a sad thing for the world, but it cannot be described as a misfortune for the children that he never had. All of us, I believe, are fortunate to have been born. But unless good and ill can be assigned to an embryo, or even to an unconnected pair of gametes, it cannot be said that not to be born is a misfortune. (That is a factor to be considered in deciding whether abortion and contraception are akin to murder.)

This approach also provides a solution to the problem of temporal asymmetry, pointed out by Lucretius. He observed that no one finds it disturbing to contemplate the eternity preceding his own birth, and he took this to show that it must be irrational to fear death, since death is simply the mirror image of the prior abyss. That is not true, however, and the difference between the two explains why it is reasonable to regard them differently. It is true that both the time before a man's birth and the time after his death are times when he does not exist. But the time after his death is time of which his death deprives him. It is time in which, had he not died then, he would be alive. Therefore any death entails the loss of some life that its victim would have led had he not died at that or any earlier point. We know perfectly well what it would be for him to have had it instead of losing it, and there is no difficulty in identifying the loser.

But we cannot say that the time prior to a man's birth is time in which he would have lived had he been born not then but earlier. For aside from the brief margin permitted by premature labor, he *could* not have been born earlier: anyone born substantially earlier than he was would have been someone else. Therefore the time prior to his birth is not time in which his subsequent birth prevents him from living. His birth, when it occurs, does not entail the loss to him of any life whatever.

The direction of time is crucial in assigning possibilities to people or other individuals. Distinct possible lives of a single person can diverge from a common beginning, but they cannot converge to a common conclusion from diverse beginnings. (The latter would represent not a set of different possible lives of one individual, but a set of distinct possible individuals, whose lives have identical conclusions.) Given an identifiable individual, countless possibilities for his continued existence are imaginable, and we can clearly conceive of what it would be for him to go on existing indefinitely. However inevitable it is that this will not come about, its possibility is still that of the continuation of a good for him, if life is the good we take it to be.[4]

We are left, therefore, with the question whether the nonrealization of this possibility is in every case a misfortune, or whether it depends on what can naturally be hoped for. This seems to me the most serious difficulty with the view that death is always an evil. Even if we can dispose of the objections against admitting misfortune that is not experienced, or cannot be assigned to a definite time in the person's life, we still have to set some limits on *how* possible a possibility must be for its nonrealization to be a misfortune (or good fortune, should the possibility be a bad one). The death of Keats at 24 is generally regarded as tragic; that of Tolstoy at 82 is not. Although they will both be dead forever, Keats's death deprived him of many years of life which were allowed to Tolstoy; so in a clear sense Keats's loss was greater (though not in the sense standardly employed in mathematical comparison between infinite quantities). However, this does not prove that Tolstoy's loss was insignificant. Perhaps we record an objection only to evils which are gratuitously added to the inevitable; the fact that it is worse to die at 24 than at 82 does not imply that it is not a terrible thing to die at 82, or even at 806. The question is whether we can regard as a misfortune any limitation, like mortality, that is normal to the species. Blindness or near-blindness is not a misfortune for a mole, nor would it be for a man, if that were the natural condition of the human race.

The trouble is that life familiarizes us with the goods of which death deprives us. We are already able to appreciate them, as a mole is not able to appreciate vision. If we put aside doubts about their status as goods and grant that their quantity is in part a function of their duration, the question remains whether death, no matter when it occurs, can be said to deprive its victim of what is in the relevant sense a possible continuation of life.

The situation is an ambiguous one. Observed from without, human beings obviously have a natural lifespan and cannot live much longer than a hundred years. A man's sense of his own experience, on the other hand, does not embody this idea of a natural limit. His existence defines for him an essentially open-ended possible future, containing the usual mixture of goods and evils that he has found so tolerable in the past. Having been gratuitously introduced to the world by a collection of natural, historical, and social accidents, he finds himself the subject of a *life*, with an indeterminate and not essentially limited future. Viewed in this way, death, no matter how inevitable, is an abrupt cancellation of indefinitely extensive possible goods. Normality seems to have nothing to do with it, for the fact that we will all inevitably die in a few score years cannot by itself imply that it would not be good to live longer. Suppose that we were all inevitably going to die in *agony*— physical agony lasting six months. Would inevitability make *that* prospect any less unpleasant? And why should it be different for a deprivation? If the normal lifespan were a thousand years, death at 80 would be a tragedy. As things are, it may just be a more widespread tragedy. If there is no limit to the amount of life that it would be good to have, then it may be that a bad end is in store for us all.

NOTES

1. As we shall see, this does not mean that it brings to an end all the goods that a man can possess.
2. It is sometimes suggested that what we really mind is the process of *dying*. But I should not really object to dying if it were not followed by death.

3. It is certainly not true in general of the things that can be said of him. For example, Abraham Lincoln was taller than Louis XIV. But when?

4. I confess to being troubled by the above argument, on the ground that it is too sophisticated to explain the simple difference between our attitudes to prenatal and posthumous nonexistence. For this reason I suspect that something essential is omitted from the account of the badness of death by an analysis which treats it as a deprivation of possibilities. My suspicion is supported by the following suggestion of Robert Nozick. We could imagine discovering that people developed from individual spores that had existed indefinitely far in advance of their birth. In this fantasy, birth never occurs naturally more than 100 years before the permanent end of the spore's existence. But then we discover a way to trigger the premature hatching of these spores, and people born who have thousands of years of active life before them. Given such a situation, it would be possible to imagine *oneself* having come into existence thousands of years previously. If we put aside the question whether this would really be the same person, even given the identity of the spore, then the consequence appears to be that a person's birth at a given time could deprive him of many earlier years of possible life. Now while it would be cause for regret that one had been deprived of all those possible years of life by being born too late, the feeling would differ from that which many people have about death. I conclude that something about the future prospect of permanent nothingness is not captured by the analysis in terms of denied possibilities. If so, then Lucretius's argument still awaits an answer.

THE "AESTHETIC" RESPONSE

The Rotation Method

Soren Kierkegaard

> Chremylos: You get too much at last of everything.
>   Of love,
> Karion: of bread,
> Chremylos: of music,
> Karion: and of sweetmeats.
> Chremylos: Of honor,
> Karion: cakes,

"The Rotation Method," in Sören Kierkegaard, *Either/Or*, Vol. I trans. by David F. Swenson and Lillian Marvin Swenson (copyright 1944 © 1959 by Princeton University Press; Princeton Paperback, 1971), pp. 281-296. Reprinted by permission of Princeton University Press.

Chremylos:		of courage,	
Karion:			and of figs.
Chremylos:	Ambition,		
Karion:		barley-cakes,	
Chremylos:		high office,	
Karion:			lentils.

(Aristophanes' Plutus, v. 189ff.)

Starting from a principle is affirmed by people of experience to be a very reasonable procedure; I am willing to humor them, and so begin with the principle that all men are bores. Surely no one will prove himself so great a bore as to contradict me in this. This principle possesses the quality of being in the highest degree repellent, an essential requirement in the case of negative principles, which are in the last analysis the principles of all motion. It is not merely repellent, but infinitely forbidding; and whoever has this principle back of him cannot but receive an infinite impetus forward, to help him make new discoveries. For if my principle is true, one need only consider how ruinous boredom is for humanity, and by properly adjusting the intensity of one's concentration upon this fundamental truth, attain any desired degree of momentum. Should one wish to attain the maximum momentum, even to the point of almost endangering the driving power, one need only say to oneself: Boredom is the root of all evil. Strange that boredom, in itself so staid and stolid, should have such power to set in motion. The influence it exerts is altogether magical, except that it is not the influence of attraction, but of repulsion.

In the case of children, the ruinous character of boredom is universally acknowledged. Children are always well-behaved as long as they are enjoying themselves. This is true in the strictest sense; for if they sometimes become unruly in their play, it is because they are already beginning to be bored—boredom is already approaching, though from a different direction. In choosing a governess one, therefore, takes into account not only her sobriety, her faithfulness, and her competence, but also her aesthetic qualifications for amusing the children; and there would be no hesitancy in dismissing a governess who was lacking in this respect, even if she had all the other desirable virtues. Here, then, the principle is clearly acknowledged; but so strange is the way of the world, so pervasive the influence of habit and boredom, that this is practically the only case in which the science of aesthetics receives its just dues. If one were to ask for a divorce because his wife was tiresome, or demand the abdication of a king because he was boring to look at, or the banishment of a preacher because he was tiresome to listen to, or the dismissal of a prime minister, or the execution of a journalist, because he was terribly tiresome, one would find it impossible to force it through. What wonder, then, that the world goes from bad to worse, and that its evils increase more and more, as boredom increases, and boredom is the root of all evil.

The history of this can be traced from the very beginning of the world. The gods were bored, and so they created man. Adam was bored because he was alone, and so Eve was created. Thus boredom entered the world, and increased in proportion to the increase of population. Adam was bored alone; then Adam and Eve were bored together; then Adam and Eve and Cain and Abel were bored *en famille*; then the population of the world increased, and the peoples were bored *en masse*. To divert themselves they conceived the idea of constructing a tower high enough to reach the heavens. This idea is itself as boring as the tower was high, and constitutes a terrible proof of how boredom gained the upper hand. The nations were scattered over the earth, just as people now travel abroad, but they continued to be bored. Consider the consequences of this boredom. Humanity fell from its lofty height, first because of Eve, and then from the Tower of Babel. What was it, on the other hand, that delayed the fall of Rome, was it not *panis* and *circenses*? And is anything being done now? Is anyone concerned about planning some means of diversion? Quite the contrary, the impending ruin is being accelerated. It is proposed to call a constitutional assembly. Can anything more tiresome be imagined, both for the participants themselves, and for those who have to hear and read about it? It is proposed to improve the financial condition of the state by practicing economy. What could be more tiresome? Instead of increasing the national debt, it is proposed to pay it off. As I understand the political situation, it would be an easy matter for Denmark to negotiate a loan of fifteen million dollars. Why not consider this plan? Every once in a while we hear of a man who is a genius, and therefore neglects to pay his debts—why should not a nation do the same, if we were all agreed? Let us then borrow fifteen millions, and let us use the proceeds, not to pay our debts, but for public entertainment. Let us celebrate the millennium in a riot of merriment. Let us place boxes everywhere, not, as at present, for the deposit of money, but for the free distribution of money. Everything would become gratis; theaters gratis, women of easy virtue gratis, one would drive to the park gratis, be buried gratis, one's eulogy would be gratis; I say gratis, for when one always has money at hand, everything is in a certain sense free. No one should be permitted to own any property. Only in my own case would there be an exception. I reserve to myself securities in the Bank of London to the value of one hundred dollars a day, partly because I cannot do with less, partly because the idea is mine, and finally because I may not be able to hit upon a new idea when the fifteen millions are gone.

What would be the consequences of all this prosperity? Everything great would gravitate toward Copenhagen, the greatest artists, the greatest dancers, the greatest actors. Copenhagen would become a second Athens. What then? All rich men would establish their homes in this city. Among others would come the Shah of Persia, and the King of England would also come. Here is my second idea. Let us kidnap the Shah of Persia. Perhaps you say an insurrection might take place in

Persia and a new ruler be placed on the throne, as has often happened before, the consequence being a fall in price for the old Shah. Very well then, I propose that we sell him to the Turks; they will doubtless know how to turn him into money. Then there is another circumstance which our politicians seem entirely to have overlooked. Denmark holds the balance of power in Europe. It is impossible to imagine a more fortunate lot. I know that from my own experience; I once held the balance of power in a family and could do as I pleased; the blame never fell on me, but always on the others. O that my words might reach your ears, all you who sit in high places to advise and rule, you king's men and men of the people, wise and understanding citizens of all classes! Consider the crisis! Old Denmark is on the brink of ruin; what a calamity! It will be destroyed by boredom. Of all calamities the most calamitous! In ancient times they made him king who extolled most beautifully the praises of the deceased king; in our times we ought to make him king who utters the best witticism, and make him crown prince who gives occasion for the utterance of the best witticism.

O beautiful, emotional sentimentality, how you carry me away! Should I trouble to speak to my contemporaries, to initiate them into my wisdom? By no means. My wisdom is not exactly *zum Gebrauch für Jedermann*,[1] and it is always more prudent to keep one's maxims of prudence to oneself. I desire no disciples; but if there happened to be someone present at my deathbed, and I was sure that the end had come, then I might in an attack of philanthropic delirium, whisper my theory in his ear, uncertain whether I had done him a service or not. People talk so much about man being a social animal; at bottom, he is a beast of prey, and the evidence for this is not confined to the shape of his teeth. All this talk about society and the social is partly inherited hypocrisy, partly calculated cunning.

All men are bores. The word itself suggests the possibility of a subdivision. It may just as well indicate a man who bores others as one who bores himself. Those who bore others are the mob, the crowd, the infinite multitude of men in general. Those who bore themselves are the elect, the aristocracy; and it is a curious fact that those who do not bore themselves usually bore others, while those who bore themselves entertain others. Those who do not bore themselves are generally people who, in one way or another, keep themselves extremely busy; these people are precisely on this account the most tiresome, the most utterly unendurable. This species of animal life is surely not the fruit of man's desire and woman's lust. Like all lower forms of life, it is marked by a high degree of fertility, and multiplies endlessly. It is inconceivable that nature should require nine months to produce such beings; they ought rather to be turned out by the score. The second class, the aristocrats, are those who bore themselves. As noted above, they generally entertain others—in a certain external sense sometimes the mob, in a deeper sense only their fellow initiates. The more profoundly they bore themselves, the more powerfully do they serve to divert these latter, even when their boredom reaches its zenith, as when they either die of boredom (the passive form) or shoot themselves out of curiosity (the active form).

It is usual to say that idleness is a root of all evil. To prevent this evil one is advised to work. However, it is easy to see, both from the nature of the evil that is feared and the remedy proposed, that this entire view is of a very plebeian extraction. Idleness is by no means as such a root of evil; on the contrary, it is a truly divine life, provided one is not himself bored. Idleness may indeed cause the loss of one's fortune, and so on, but the high-minded man does not fear such dangers; he fears only boredom. The Olympian gods were not bored, they lived happily in happy idleness. A beautiful woman, who neither sews nor spins nor bakes nor reads nor plays the piano, is happy in her idleness, for she is not bored. So far from idleness being the root of all evil, it is rather the only true good. Boredom is the root of all evil, and it is this which must be kept at a distance. Idleness is not an evil; indeed one may say that every human being who lacks a sense for idleness proves that his consciousness has not yet been elevated to the level of the humane. There is a restless activity which excludes a man from the world of the spirit, setting him in a class with the brutes, whose instincts impel them always to be on the move. There are men who have an extraordinary talent for transforming everything into a matter of business, whose whole life is business, who fall in love, marry, listen to a joke, and admire a picture with the same industrious zeal with which they labor during business hours. The Latin proverb, *otium est pulvinar diaboli*,[2] is true enough, but the devil gets no time to lay his head on this pillow when one is not bored. But since some people believe that the end and aim of life is work, the disjunction, idleness-work, is quite correct. I assume that it is the end and aim of every man to enjoy himself, and hence my disjunction is no less correct.

Boredom is the daemonic side of pantheism. If we remain in boredom as such, it becomes the evil principle; if we annul it, we posit it in its truth; but we can only annul boredom by enjoying ourselves—*ergo*, it is our duty to enjoy ourselves. To say that boredom is annulled by work betrays a confusion of thought; for idleness can certainly be annulled by work, since it is its opposite, but not boredom, and experience shows that the busiest workers, whose constant buzzing most resembles an insect's hum, are the most tiresome of creatures; if they do not bore themselves, it is because they have no true conception of what boredom is; but then it can scarcely be said that they have overcome boredom.

Boredom is partly an inborn talent, partly an acquired immediacy. The English are in general the paradigmatic nation. A true talent for indolence is very rare; it is never met with in nature, but belongs to the world of the spirit. Occasionally, however, you meet a traveling Englishman who is, as it were, the incarnation of this talent—a heavy, immovable animal, whose entire language exhausts its riches in a single word of one syllable, an interjection by which he signifies his deepest admiration and his supreme indifference, admiration and indifference having been neutralized in the unity of boredom. No other nation produces such miracles of nature; every other national will always show himself a little more vivacious, not so absolutely still-born. The only analogy I know of is the apostle of the empty enthusiasm, who also makes his way through life on an interjection. This is the man who everywhere makes a profession of enthusiasm, who cries Ah! or Oh! whether the event be significant or insignificant, the difference having been lost for him in the emptiness of a blind and noisy enthusiasm. The second form of boredom is usually the result of a mistaken effort to find diversion. The fact that the remedy against boredom may also serve to produce boredom, might appear to be a suspicious circumstance; but it has this effect only in so far as it is incorrectly employed. A misdirected search for diversion, one which is eccentric in its direction, conceals boredom within its own depths and gradually works it out toward the surface, thus revealing itself as that which it immediately is. In the case of horses, we distinguish between blind staggers and sleepy staggers, but call both staggers; and so we can also make a distinction between two kinds of boredom, though uniting both under the common designation of being tiresome.

Pantheism is, in general, characterized by fullness; in the case of boredom we find the precise opposite, since it is characterized by emptiness; but it is just this which makes boredom a pantheistic conception. Boredom depends on the nothingness which pervades reality; it causes a dizziness like that produced by looking down into a yawning chasm, and this dizziness is infinite. The eccentric form of diversion noted above sounds forth without producing an echo, which proves it to be based on boredom; for in nothingness not even an echo can be produced.

Now since boredom as shown above is the root of all evil, what can be more natural than the effort to overcome it? Here, as everywhere, however, it is necessary to give the problem calm consideration; otherwise one may find oneself driven by the daemonic spirit of boredom deeper and deeper into the mire in the very effort to escape. Everyone who feels bored cries out for change. With this demand I am in complete sympathy, but it is necessary to act in accordance with some settled principle.

My own dissent from the ordinary view is sufficiently expressed in the use I make of the word, "rotation." This word might seem to conceal an ambiguity, and if I wished to use it so as to find room in it for the ordinary method, I should have to define it as a change of field. But the farmer does not use the word in this sense. I shall, however, adopt this meaning for a moment, in order to speak of the rotation which depends on change in its boundless infinity, its extensive dimension, so to speak.

This is the vulgar and inartistic method, and needs to be supported by illusion. One tires of living in the country, and moves to the city; one tires of one's native land, and travels abroad; one is *europamüde*,[3] and goes to America, and so on; finally one indulges in a sentimental hope of endless journeyings from star to star. Or the movement is different but still extensive. One tires of porcelain dishes and eats on silver; one tires of silver and turns to gold; one burns half of Rome to get an idea of the burning of Troy. This method defeats itself; it is plain endlessness. And what did Nero gain by it? Antonine was wiser; he says: "It is in your power to review your life, to look at things you saw before, from another point of view."

My method does not consist in change of field, but resembles the true rotation method in changing the crop and the mode of cultivation. Here we have at once the principle of limitation, the only saving principle in the world. The more you limit yourself, the more fertile you become in invention. A prisoner in solitary confinement for life becomes very inventive, and a spider may furnish him with much entertainment. One need only hark back to one's schooldays. We were at an age when aesthetic considerations were ignored in the choice of one's instructors, most of whom were for that reason very tiresome; how fertile in invention one then proved to be! How entertaining to catch a fly and hold it imprisoned under a nut shell and to watch how it pushed the shell around; what pleasure from cutting a hole in the desk, putting a fly in it, and then peeping down at it through a piece of paper! How entertaining sometimes to listen to the monotonous drip of water from the roof! How close an observer one becomes under such circumstances, when not the least noise nor movement escapes one's attention! Here we have the extreme application of the method which seeks to achieve results intensively, not extensively.

The more resourceful in changing the mode of cultivation one can be, the better; but every particular change will always come under the general categories of *remembering* and *forgetting*. Life in its entirety moves in these two currents, and hence it is essential to have them under control. It is impossible to live artistically before one has made up one's mind to abandon hope; for hope precludes self-limitation. It is a very beautiful sight to see a man put out to sea with the fair wind of hope, and one may even use the opportunity to be taken in tow; but one should never permit hope to be taken aboard one's own ship, least of all as a pilot; for hope is a faithless shipmaster. Hope was one of the dubious gifts of Prometheus; instead of giving men the foreknowledge of the immortals, he gave them hope.

To forget—all men wish to forget, and when something unpleasant happens, they always say: Oh, that one might forget! But forgetting is an art that must be practiced beforehand. The ability to forget is conditioned upon the method of remembering, but this again depends upon the mode of experiencing reality. Whoever plunges into his experiences with the momentum of hope will remember in such wise that he is unable to forget. *Nil admirari* is therefore the real philosophy.[4] No moment must be permitted so great a significance that it cannot be forgotten when convenient; each moment ought, however, to have so much significance that it can be recollected at will. Childhood, which is the age which remembers best, is at the same time most forgetful. The more poetically one remembers, the more easily one forgets; for remembering poetically is really only another expression for forgetting. In a poetic memory the experience has undergone a transformation, by which it has lost all its painful aspects. To remember in this manner, one must be careful how one lives, how one enjoys. Enjoying an experience to its full intensity to the last minute will make it impossible either to remember or to forget. For there is then nothing to remember except a certain satiety, which one desires to forget, but which now comes back to plague the mind with an involuntary remembrance. Hence, when you begin to notice that a certain pleasure or experience is acquiring too strong a hold upon the mind, you stop a moment for the purpose of remembering. No other method can better create a distaste for continuing the experience too long. From the beginning one should keep the enjoyment under control, never spreading every sail to the wind in any resolve; one ought to devote oneself to pleasure with a certain suspicion, a certain wariness, if one desires to give the lie to the proverb which says that no one can have his cake and eat it too. The carrying of concealed weapons is usually forbidden, but no weapon is so dangerous as the art of remembering. It gives one a very peculiar feeling in the midst of one's enjoyment to look back upon it for the purpose of remembering it.

One who has perfected himself in the twin arts of remembering and forgetting is in a position to play at battledore and shuttlecock with the whole of existence.

The extent of one's power to forget is the final measure of one's elasticity of spirit. If a man cannot forget he will never amount to much. Whether there be somewhere a Lethe gushing forth, I do not know; but this I know, that the art of forgetting can be developed. However, this art does not consist in permitting the impressions to vanish completely; forgetfulness is one thing, and the art of forgetting is something quite different. It is easy to see that most people have a very meager understanding of this art, for they ordinarily wish to forget only what is unpleasant, not what is pleasant. This betrays a complete one-sidedness. Forgetting is the true expression for an ideal process of assimilation by which the experience is reduced to a sounding-board for the soul's own music. Nature is great because it has forgotten that it was chaos; but this thought is subject to revival at any time. As a result of attempting to forget only what is unpleasant, most people have a conception of oblivion as an untamable force which drowns out the past. But forgetting is really a tranquil and quiet occupation, and one which should be exercised quite as much in connection with the pleasant as with the unpleasant. A pleasant experience has as past something unpleasant about it, by which it stirs a sense of privation; this unpleasantness is taken away by an act of forgetfulness. The unpleasant has a sting, as all admit. This, too, can be removed by the art of forgetting. But if one attempts to dismiss the unpleasant absolutely from mind, as many do who dabble in the art of forgetting, one soon learns how little that helps. In an unguarded moment it pays a surprise visit, and it is then invested with all the forcibleness of the unexpected. This is absolutely contrary to every orderly arrangement in a reasonable mind. No misfortune or difficulty is so devoid of affability, so deaf to all appeals, but that it may be flattered a little; even Cerberus accepted bribes of honey-cakes, and it is not only the lassies who are beguiled. The art in dealing with such experiences consists in talking them over, thereby depriving them of their bitterness; not forgetting them absolutely, but forgetting them for the sake of remembering them. Even in the case of memories such that one might suppose an eternal oblivion to be the only safe-guard, one need permit oneself only a little trickery, and the deception will succeed for the skillful. Forgetting is the shears with which you cut away what you cannot use, doing it under the supreme direction of memory. Forgetting and remembering are thus identical arts, and the artistic achievement of this identity is the Archimedean point from which one lifts the whole world. When we say that we *consign* something to oblivion, we suggest simultaneously that it is to be forgotten and yet also remembered.

The art of remembering and forgetting will also insure against sticking fast in some relationship of life, and make possible the realization of a complete freedom.

One must guard against *friendship*. How is a friend defined? He is not what philosophy calls the necessary other, but the superfluous third. What are friendship's ceremonies? You drink each other's health, you open an artery and mingle your blood with that of the friend. It is difficult to say when the proper moment for this arrives, but it announces itself mysteriously; you feel some way that you can no longer address one another formally. When once you have had this feeling, then it can never appear that you have made a mistake, like Geert Vestphaler, who discovered that he had been drinking to friendship with the public hangman. What are the infallible marks of friendship? Let antiquity answer: *idem velle, idem nolle, ea demum firma amicitia,*[5] and also extremely tiresome. What are the infallible marks of friendship? Mutual assistance in word and deed. Two friends form a close association in order to be everything to one another, and that although it is impossible for one human being to be anything to another human being except to be in his way. To be sure one may help him with money, assist him in and out of his coat, be his humble servant, and tender him congratulations on New Year's Day, on the day of his wedding, on the birth of a child, on the occasion of a funeral.

But because you abstain from friendship it does not follow that you abstain from social contacts. On the contrary, these social relationships may at times be permitted to take on a deeper character, provided you always have so much more momentum in yourself that you can sheer off at will, in spite of sharing for a time in the momentum of the common movement. It is believed that such conduct leaves unpleasant memories, the unpleasantness being due to the fact that a relationship which has meant something now vanishes and becomes as nothing. But this is a misunderstanding. The unpleasant is merely a piquant ingredient in the sullenness of life. Besides, it is possible for the same relationship again to play a significant role, though in another manner. The essential thing is never to stick fast, and for this it is necessary to have oblivion back of one. The experienced farmer lets his land lie fallow now and then, and the theory of social prudence recommends the same. Everything will doubtless return, though in a different form; that which has once been present in the rotation will remain in it, but the mode of cultivation will be varied. You therefore quite consciously hope to meet your friends and acquaintances in a better world, but you do not share the fear of the crowd that they will be altered so that you cannot recognize them; your fear is rather lest they be wholly unaltered. It is remarkable how much significance even the most insignificant person can gain from a rational mode of cultivation.

One must never enter into the relation of *marriage*. Husband and wife promise to love one another for eternity. This is all very fine, but it does not mean very much; for if their love comes to an end in time, it will surely be ended in eternity. If, instead of promising forever, the parties would say: until Easter, or until May-day comes, there might be some meaning in what they say; for then they would have said something definite, and also something that they might be able to keep. And how does a marriage usually work out? In a little while one party begins to perceive that there is something wrong, then the other party complains, and cries to heaven: faithless! faithless! A little later the second party reaches the same standpoint, and a neutrality is established in which the mutual faithlessness is mutually canceled, to the satisfaction and contentment of both parties. But it is now too late, for there are great difficulties connected with divorce.

Such being the case with marriage, it is not surprising that the attempt should be made in so many ways to bolster it up with moral supports. When a man seeks separation from his wife, the cry is at once raised that he is depraved, a scoundrel, etc. How silly, and what an indirect attack upon marriage! If marriage has reality, then he is sufficiently punished by forfeiting this happiness; if it has no reality, it is absurd to abuse him because he is wiser than the rest. When a man grows tired of his money and throws it out of the window, we do not call him a scoundrel; for either money has reality, and so he is sufficiently punished by depriving himself of it, or it has none, and then he is, of course, a wise man.

One must always take care not to enter into any relationship in which there is a possibility of many members. For this reason friendship is dangerous, to say nothing of marriage. Husband and wife are indeed said to become one, but this is a very dark and mystic saying. When you are one of several, then you have lost your freedom; you cannot send for your traveling boots whenever you wish, you cannot move aimlessly about in the world. If you have a wife it is difficult; if you have a wife and perhaps a child, it is troublesome; if you have a wife and children, it is impossible. True, it has happened that a gypsy woman has carried her husband through life on her back, but for one thing this is very rare, and for another, it is likely to be tiresome in the long run—for the husband. Marriage brings one into fatal connection with custom and tradition, and traditions and customs are like the wind and weather, altogether incalculable. In Japan, I have been told, it is the custom for husbands to lie in childbed. Who knows but the time will come when the customs of foreign countries will obtain a foothold in Europe?

Friendship is dangerous, marriage still more so; for woman is and ever will be the ruin of a man, as soon as he contracts a permanent relation with her. Take a young man who is fiery as an Arabian courser, let him marry, he is lost. Woman is first proud, then is she weak, then she swoons, then he swoons, then the whole family swoons. A woman's love is nothing but dissimulation and weakness.

But because a man does not marry, it does not follow that his life need be wholly deprived of the erotic element. And the erotic ought also to have infinitude; but poetic infinitude, which can just as well be limited to an hour as to a month. When two beings fall in love with one another and begin to suspect that they were made for each other, it is time to have the courage to break it off; for by going on they have everything to lose and nothing to gain. This seems a paradox, and it is so for the feeling, but not for the understanding. In this sphere it is particularly necessary that one should make use of one's moods; through them one may realize an inexhaustible variety of combinations.

One should never accept appointment to an official position. If you do, you will become a mere Richard Roe, a tiny little cog in the machinery of the body politic; you even cease to be master of your own conduct, and in that case your theories are of little help. You receive a title, and this brings in its train every sin and evil. The law under which you have become a slave is equally tiresome, whether your advancement is fast or slow. A title can never be got rid of except by the commission of some crime which draws down on you a public whipping; even then you are not certain, for you may have it restored to you by royal pardon.

Even if one abstains from involvement in official business, one ought not to be inactive, but should pursue such occupations as are compatible with a sort of leisure; one should engage in all sorts of breadless arts. In this connection the self-development should be intensive rather than extensive, and one should, in spite of mature years, be able to prove the truth of the proverb that children are pleased with a rattle and tickled with a straw.

If one now, according to the theory of social jurisprudence, varies the soil—for if he had contact with one person only, the rotation method would fail as badly as if a farmer had only one acre of land, which would make it impossible for him to fallow, something which is of extreme importance—then one must also constantly vary himself, and this is the essential secret. For this purpose one must necessarily have control over one's moods. To control them in the sense of producing them at will is impossible, but prudence teaches how to utilize the moment. As an experienced sailor always looks out over the water and sees a squall coming from far away, so one ought always to see the mood a little in advance. One should know how the mood affects one's own mind and the mind of others, before putting it on. You first strike a note or two to evoke pure tones, and see what there is in a man; the intermediate tones follow later. The more experience you have, the more readily you will be convinced that there is often much in a man which is not suspected. When sentimental people, who as such are extremely tiresome, become angry, they are often very entertaining. Badgering a man is a particularly effective method of exploration.

The whole secret lies in arbitrariness. People usually think it easy to be arbitrary, but it requires much study to succeed in being arbitrary so as not to lose oneself in it, but so as to derive satisfaction from it. One does not enjoy the immediate but something quite different which he arbitrarily imports into it. You go to see the middle of a play, you read the third part of a book. By this means you insure yourself a very different kind of enjoyment from that which the author has been so kind as to plan for you. You enjoy something entirely accidental; you consider the whole of existence from this standpoint; let its reality be stranded thereon. I will cite an example. There was a man whose chatter certain circumstances made it necessary for me to listen to. At every opportunity he was ready with a little philosophical lecture, a very tiresome harangue. Almost in despair, I suddenly discovered that he perspired copiously when talking. I saw the pearls of sweat gather on his brow, unite to form a stream, glide down his nose, and hang at the extreme point of his nose in a drop-shaped body. From the moment of making this discovery, all was changed. I even took pleasure in inciting him to begin his philosophical instruction, merely to observe the perspiration on his brow and at the end of his nose.

The poet Baggesen says somewhere of someone that he was doubtless a good man, but that there was one insuperable objection against him, that there was no word that rhymed with his name. It is extremely wholesome thus to let the realities of life split upon an arbitrary interest. You transform something accidental into the absolute, and, as such, into the object of your admiration. This has an excellent effect, especially when one is excited. This method is an excellent stimulus for many persons. You look at everything in life from the standpoint of a wager, and so forth. The more rigidly consistent you are in holding fast to your arbitrariness, the more amusing the ensuing combinations will be. The degree of consistency shows whether you are an artist or a bungler; for to a certain extent all men do the same. The eye with which you look at reality must constantly be changed. The Neo-Platonists assumed that human beings who had been less perfect on earth became after death more or less perfect animals, all according to their deserts. For example, those who had exercised the civic virtues on a lower scale (retail dealers) were transformed into busy animals, like bees. Such a view of life, which here in this world sees all men transformed into animals or plants (Plotinus also thought that some would become plants), suggests rich and varied possibilities. The painter Tischbein sought to idealize every human being into an animal. His method has the fault of being too serious, in that it endeavors to discover a real resemblance.

The arbitrariness in oneself corresponds to the accidental in the external world. One should therefore always have an eye open for the accidental, always be *expeditus*,[6] if anything should offer. The so-called social pleasures for which we prepare a week or two in advance amount to so little; on the other hand, even the most insignificant thing may accidentally offer rich material for amusement. It is impossible here to go into detail, for no theory can adequately embrace the concrete. Even the most completely developed theory is poverty-stricken compared with the fullness which the man of genius easily discovers in his ubiquity.

NOTES

1. For use of everyone.
2. Idleness is Devil's pillow.
3. Tired of Europe.
4. To wonder at nothing.
5. To want the same thing and not to want the same thing, this finally is a firm friendship.
6. Ready to go.

THE CHRISTIAN RESPONSE

The Christian View
of Death

John Calvin

But, most strange to say, many who boast of being Christians, instead of thus longing for death, are so afraid of it that they tremble at the very mention of it as a thing ominous and dreadful. We cannot wonder, indeed, that our natural feelings should be somewhat shocked at the mention of our dissolution. But it is altogether intolerable that the light of piety should not be so powerful in a Christian breast as with greater consolation to overcome and suppress that fear. For if we reflect that this our tabernacle, unstable, defective, corruptible, fading, pining, and putrid, is dissolved, in order that it may forthwith be renewed in sure, perfect, incorruptible, in fine, in heavenly glory, will not faith compel us eagerly to desire what nature dreads? If we reflect that by death we are recalled from exile to inhabit our native country, a heavenly country, shall this give us no comfort? But everything longs for permanent existence. I admit this, and therefore contend that we ought to look to future immortality, where we may obtain that fixed condition which nowhere appears on the earth. For Paul admirably enjoins believers to hasten cheerfully to death, not because they "would be unclothed, but clothed upon" (2 Cor. v. 2). Shall the lower animals, and inanimate creatures themselves, even wood and stone, as conscious of their present vanity, long for the final resurrection, that they may with the sons of God be delivered from vanity (Rom. viii. 19); and shall we, endued with the light of intellect, and more than intellect, enlightened by the Spirit of God, when our essence is in question, rise no higher than the corruption of this earth? But it is not my purpose, nor is this the place, to plead against this great perverseness. At the outset, I declared that I had no wish to engage in a diffuse discussion of common-places. My advice to those whose minds are thus timid is to read the short treatise of Cyprian De Mortalitate, unless it be more accordant with their deserts to send them to the philosophers, that by inspecting what they say on the contempt of death, they may begin to

From *Christian Religion*, "The Christian View of Death," by John Calvin (London: James Clarke and Co., Ltd., 1957). Reprinted by permission of the publisher.

blush. This, however, let us hold as fixed, that no man has made much progress in the school of Christ who does not look forward with joy to the day of death and final resurrection (2 Tim. iv. 18; Tit. ii. 13); for Paul distinguishes all believers by this mark; and the usual course of Scripture is to direct us thither whenever it would furnish us with an argument for substantial joy. "Look up," says our Lord, "and lift up your heads: for your redemption draweth nigh" (Luke xxi. 28). It is reasonable, I ask, that what he intended to have a powerful effect in stirring us up to alacrity and exultation should produce nothing but sadness and consternation? If it is so, why do we still glory in him as our Master? Therefore, let us come to a sounder mind, and how repugnant so ever the blind and stupid longing of the flesh may be, let us doubt not to desire the advent of the Lord not in wish only, but with earnest sighs, as the most propitious of all events. He will come as a Redeemer to deliver us from an immense abyss of evil and misery, and lead us to the blessed inheritance of his life and glory.

Thus, indeed, it is; the whole body of the faithful, so long as they live on the earth, must be like sheep for the slaughter, in order that they may be conformed to Christ their head (Rom. viii. 36). Most deplorable, therefore, would their situation be did they not, by raising their mind to heaven, become superior to all that is in the world, and rise above the present aspect of affairs (1 Cor. xv. 19). On the other hand, when once they have raised their head above all earthly objects, though they see the wicked flourishing in wealth and honour, and enjoying profound peace, indulging in luxury and splendour, and revelling in all kinds of delights, though they should moreover be wickedly assailed by them, suffer insult from their pride, be robbed by their avarice or assailed by any other passion, they will have no difficulty in bearing up under these evils. They will turn their eye to that day (Isaiah xxv. 8: Rev. vii. 17) on which the Lord will receive his faithful servants, wipe away all tears from their eyes, clothe them in a robe of glory and joy, feed them with the ineffable sweetness of his pleasures, exalt them to share with him in his greatness; in fine, admit them to a participation in his happiness. But the wicked who may have flourished on the earth, he will cast forth in extreme ignominy, will change their delights into torments, their laughter and joy into wailing and gnashing of teeth, their peace into the gnawing of conscience, and punish their luxury with unquenchable fire. He will also place their necks under the feet of the godly, whose patience they abused. For, as Paul declares, "it is a righteous thing with God to recompense tribulation to them that trouble you; and to you who are troubled rest with us, when the Lord Jesus shall be revealed from heaven" (2 Thess. i. 6, 7). This, indeed, is our consolation; deprived of it, we must either give way to despondency, or resort to our destruction to the vain solace of the world. The Psalmist confesses, "My feet were almost gone, my steps had well nigh slipt: for I was envious at the foolish when I saw the prosperity of the wicked" (Psalm lxxiii. 3, 4); and he found no resting-place until he entered the sanctuary, and considered the latter end of the righteous and the wicked. To conclude in one word, the cross of Christ then only triumphs in the breasts of believers over the devil and the flesh, sin and sinners, when their eyes are directed to the power of his resurrection.

CHAPTER XXV

Of the Last Resurrection

1. Although Christ, the Sun of righteousness, shining upon us through the gospel, hath, as Paul declares, after conquering death, given us the light of life; and hence on believing we are said to have passed from "death unto life," being no longer strangers and pilgrims, but fellow-citizens with the saints, and of the household of God, who has made us sit with his only begotten Son in heavenly places, so that nothing is wanting to our complete felicity; yet, lest we should feel it grievous to be exercised under a hard warfare, as if the victory obtained by Christ had produced no fruit, we must attend to what is elsewhere taught concerning the nature of hope. For since we hope for what we see not, and faith, as is said in another passage, is "the evidence of things not seen," so long as we are imprisoned in the body we are absent from the Lord. For which reason Paul says, "Ye are dead, and your life is hid with Christ in God. When Christ, who is our life, shall appear, then shall ye also appear with him in glory." Our present condition, therefore, requires us to "live soberly, righteously, and godly;" "looking for that blessed hope, and the glorious appearing of the great God and our Saviour Jesus Christ." Here there is no need of no ordinary patience, lest, worn out with fatigue, we either turn backwards or abandon our post. Wherefore, all that has hitherto been said of our salvation calls upon us to raise our minds towards heaven, that, as Peter exhorts, though we now see not Christ, "yet believing," we may "rejoice with joy unspeakable and full of glory," receiving the end of our faith, even the salvation of our souls.[1] For this reason Paul says, that the faith and charity of the saints have respect to the faith and hope which is laid up for them in heaven (Col. i. 5). When we thus keep our eyes fixed upon Christ in heaven, and nothing on earth prevents us from directing them to the promised blessedness, there is a true fulfilment of the saying, "where your treasure is, there will your heart be also" (Matth. vi. 21). Hence the reason why faith is so rare in the world; nothing being more difficult for our sluggishness than to surmount innumerable obstacles in striving for the prize of our high calling. To the immense load of miseries which almost overwhelm us, are added the jeers of profane men, who assail us for our simplicity, when spontaneously renouncing the allurements of the present life we seem, in seeking a happiness which lies hid from us, to catch at a fleeting shadow. In short, we are beset above and below, behind and before, with violent

temptations, which our minds would be altogether unable to withstand, were they not set free from earthly objects, and devoted to the heavenly life, though apparently remote from us. Wherefore, he alone has made solid progress in the gospel who has acquired the habit of meditating continually on a blessed resurrection.

2. In ancient times philosophers discoursed, and even debated with each other, concerning the chief good: none however, except Plato, acknowledged that it consisted in union with God. He could not, however, form even an imperfect idea of its true nature; nor is this strange, as he had learned nothing of the sacred bond of that union. We even in this our earthly pilgrimage know wherein our perfect and only felicity consists,—a felicity which, while we long for it, daily inflames our hearts more and more, until we attain to full fruition. Therefore I said, that none participate in the benefits of Christ save those who raise their minds to the resurrection. This, accordingly, is the mark which Paul sets before believers, and at which he says they are to aim, forgetting everything until they reach it (Phil. iii. 8). The more strenuously, therefore, must we contend for it, lest if the world engross us we be severely punished for our sloth.[2] Accordingly, he in another passage distinguishes believers by this mark, that their conversation is in heaven, from whence they look for the Saviour (Phil. iii. 20). And that they may not faint in their course, he associates all the other creatures with them. As shapeless ruins are everywhere seen, he says, that all things in heaven and earth struggle for renovation. For since Adam by his fall destroyed the proper order of nature, the creatures groan under the servitude to which they have been subjected through his sin; not that they are at all endued with sense, but that they naturally long for the state of perfection from which they have fallen. Paul therefore describes them as groaning and travailing in pain (Rom. viii. 19); so that we who have received the first-fruits of the Spirit may be ashamed to grovel in our corruption, instead of at least imitating the inanimate elements which are bearing the punishment of another's sin. And in order that he may stimulate us the more powerfully, he terms the final advent of Christ *our redemption*. It is true, indeed, that all the parts of our redemption are already accomplished; but as Christ was once offered for sins (Heb. ix. 28), so he shall again appear without sin unto salvation. Whatever, then, be the afflictions by which we are pressed, let this redemption sustain us until its final accomplishment.

3. The very importance of the subject ought to increase our ardour. Paul justly contends, that if Christ rise not the whole gospel is delusive and vain (1 Cor. xv. 13–17); for our condition would be more miserable than that of other mortals, because we are exposed to much hatred and insult, and incur danger every hour; nay, are like sheep destined for slaughter; and hence the authority of the gospel would fail, not in one part merely, but in its very essence, including both our adoption and the accomplishment of our salvation. Let us, therefore,

give heed to a matter of all others the most serious, so that no length of time may produce weariness. I have deferred the brief consideration to be given of it to this place, that my readers may learn, when they have received Christ, the author of perfect salvation, to rise higher, and know that he is clothed with heavenly immortality and glory, in order that the whole body may be rendered conformable to the Head. For thus the Holy Spirit is ever setting before us in his person an example of the resurrection. It is difficult to believe that after our bodies have been consumed with rottenness, they will rise again at their appointed time. And hence, while many of the philosophers maintained the immortality of the soul, few of them assented to the resurrection of the body. Although in this they were inexcusable, we are thereby reminded that the subject is too difficult for human apprehension to reach it. To enable faith to surmount the great difficulty, Scripture furnishes two auxiliary proofs, the one the likeness of Christ's resurrection, and the other the omnipotence of God. Therefore, whenever the subject of the resurrection is considered, let us think of the case of our Saviour, who, having completed his mortal course in our nature which he had assumed, obtained immortality, and is now the pledge of our future resurrection. For in the miseries by which we are beset, we always bear "about in the body the dying of the Lord Jesus, that the life also of Jesus might be made manifest in our mortal flesh" (2 Cor. iv. 10). It is not lawful, it is not even possible, to separate him from us, without dividing him. Hence Paul's argument, "If there be no resurrection of the dead, then is Christ not risen" (1 Cor. xv. 13); for he assumes it as an acknowledged principle, that when Christ was subjected to death, and by rising gained a victory over death, it was not on his own account, but in the Head was begun what must necessarily be fulfilled in all the members, according to the degree and order of each. For it would not be proper to be made equal to him in all respects. It is said in the psalm, "Neither wilt thou suffer thine Holy One to see corruption" (Ps. xvi. 10). Although a portion of this confidence appertain to us according to the measure bestowed on us, yet the full effect appeared only in Christ, who, free from all corruption, resumed a spotless body. Then, that there may be no doubt as to our fellowship with Christ in a blessed resurrection, and that we may be contented with this pledge, Paul distinctly affirms that he sits in the heavens, and will come as a judge on the last day for the express purpose of changing our vile body, "that it may be fashioned like unto his glorious body" (Phil. iii. 21). For he elsewhere says that God did not raise up his Son from death to give an isolated specimen of his mighty power, but that the Spirit exerts the same efficacy in regard to them that believe; and accordingly he says, that the Spirit when he dwells in us is life, because the end for which he was given is to quicken our mortal body (Rom. viii. 10, 11; Col. iii. 4). I briefly glance at subjects which might be treated more copiously, and deserve to be adorned more splendidly, and yet in the little I have said I trust pious readers will find sufficient materials for building up their faith. Christ rose again, that he might have us as partakers with him of future life. He was raised up by the Father, inasmuch as he was the Head of the Church, from which he cannot possibly be dissevered. He was raised up by the power of the Spirit, who also in us performs the office of quickening. In fine, he was raised up to be the resurrection and the life. But as we have said, that in this mirror we behold a living image of the resurrection, so it furnishes a sure evidence to support our minds, provided we faint not, nor grow weary at the long delay, because it is not ours to measure the periods of time at our own pleasure; but to rest patiently till God in his own time renew his kingdom. To this Paul refers when he says, "But every man in his own order: Christ the first-fruits; afterward they that are Christ's at his coming" (1 Cor. xv. 23).

But lest any question should be raised as to the resurrection of Christ on which ours is founded, we see how often and in what various ways he has borne testimony to it. Scoffing men will deride the narrative which is given by the Evangelist as a childish fable. For what importance will they attach to a message which timid women bring, and the disciples, almost dead with fear, afterwards confirm? Why does not Christ rather place the illustrious trophies of his victory in the midst of the temple and the forum? Why does he not come forth, and in the presence of Pilate strike terror? Why does he not show himself alive again to the priests and all Jerusalem? Profane men will scarcely admit that the witnesses whom he selects are well qualified. I answer, that though at the commencement their infirmity was contemptible, yet the whole was directed by the admirable providence of God, so that partly from love to Christ and religious zeal, partly from incredulity, those who were lately overcome with fear now hurry to the sepulchre, not only that they might be eyewitnesses of the fact, but that they might hear angels announce what they actually saw. How can we question the veracity of those who regarded what the women told them as a fable, until they saw the reality? It is not strange that the whole people and also the governor, after they were furnished with sufficient evidence for conviction, were not allowed to see Christ or the other signs (Matth. xxvii. 66; xxviii. 11). The sepulchre is sealed, sentinels keep watch, on the third day the body is not found. The soldiers are bribed to spread the report that his disciples had stolen the body. As if they had had the means of deforcing a band of soldiers, or been supplied with weapons, or been trained so as to make such a daring attempt. But if the soldiers had not courage enough to repel them, why did they not follow and apprehend some of them by the aid of the populace? Pilate, therefore, in fact, put his signet to the resurrection of Christ, and the guards who were placed at the sepulchre by their silence or falsehood also became heralds of his resurrection. Meanwhile, the voice of angels was heard, "He is not here, but is risen" (Luke xxiv. 6). The celestial splendour plainly shows that they were not men but angels. Afterwards, if any doubt still remained, Christ himself removed it. The disciples saw him frequently; they even touched his hands and his feet, and their unbelief is of no little avail in confirming our faith. He discoursed to them of the mysteries of the kingdom of God, and at length, while they beheld, ascended to heaven. This spectacle was exhibited not to eleven apostles only, but was seen by more than five hundred brethren at once (1 Cor. xv. 6). Then by sending the Holy Spirit he gave a proof not only of life but also of supreme power, as he had foretold, "It is expedient for you that I go away: for if I go not away, the Comforter will not come unto you" (John xvi. 7). Paul was not thrown down on the way by the power of a dead man, but felt that he whom he was opposing was possessed of sovereign authority. To Stephen he appeared for another purpose—viz. that he might overcome the fear of death by the certainty of life. To refuse assent to these numerous and authentic proofs is not diffidence, but depraved and therefore infatuated obstinacy.

But a more difficult question here arises, How can the resurrection, which is a special benefit of Christ, be common to the ungodly, who are lying under the curse of God? We know that in Adam all died. Christ has come to be the resurrection and the life (John xi. 25). Is it to revive the whole human race indiscriminately? But what more incongruous than that the ungodly in their obstinate blindness should obtain what the pious worshippers of God receive by faith only? It is certain, therefore, that there will be one resurrection to judgment, and another to life, and that Christ will come to separate the kids from the goats (Matth. xxv. 32). I observe, that this ought not to seem very strange, seeing something resembling it occurs every day. We know that in Adam we were deprived of the inheritance of the whole world, and that the same reason which excludes us from eating of the tree of life, excludes us also from common food. How comes it, then, that God not only makes his sun to rise on the evil and on the good, but that, in regard to the uses of the present life, his inestimable liberality is constantly flowing forth in rich abundance? Hence we certainly perceive, that things which are proper to Christ and his members, abound to the wicked also: not that their possession is legitimate, but that they may thus be rendered more inexcusable. Thus the wicked often experience the beneficence of God, not in ordinary measures, but such as sometimes throw all the blessings of the godly into the shade, though they eventually lead to greater damnation. Should it be objected, that the resurrection is not properly compared to fading and earthly blessings, I again answer, that when the devils were first alienated from God, the fountain of life, they deserved to be utterly destroyed; yet, by the admirable counsel of God, an intermediate state was prepared, where without life they might live in death. It ought not to seem in any respect more absurd that there is to be an adventitious resurrection of the ungodly which will drag them against their will before the tribunal of Christ, whom they now refuse to receive as their master and teacher. To be consumed by death would be a light punishment were they not, in order to the punishment of their rebellion, to be sisted before the Judge whom they have provoked to a vengeance without measure and without end. But although we are to hold, as already observed, and as is contained in the celebrated confession of Paul to Felix, "That there shall be a resurrection of the dead, both of the just and unjust" (Acts xxiv. 15); yet Scripture more frequently sets forth the resurrection as intended, along with celestial glory, for the children of God only: because, properly speaking, Christ comes not for the destruction, but for the salvation of the world; and, therefore, in the Creed the life of blessedness only is mentioned.

10. But since the prophecy, that death shall be swallowed up in victory (Hosea xiii. 14), will then only be completed, let us always remember that the end of the resurrection is eternal happiness, of whose excellence scarcely the minutest part can be described by all that human tongues can say. For though we are truly told that the kingdom of God will be full of light, and gladness, and felicity, and glory, yet the things meant by these words remain most remote from sense, and as it were involved in enigma, until the day arrive on which he will manifest his glory to us face to face (1 Cor. xv. 54). "Now," says John, "are we the sons of God; and it doth not yet appear what we shall be: but we know that, when he shall appear, we shall be like him; for we shall see him as he is" (1 John iii. 2). Hence, as the prophets were unable to give a verbal description of that spiritual blessedness, they usually delineated it by corporeal objects. On the other hand, because the fervour of desire must be kindled in us by some taste of its sweetness, let us specially dwell upon this thought, If God contains in himself as an inexhaustible fountain all fulness of blessing, those who aspire to the supreme good and perfect happiness must not long for anything beyond him. This we are taught in several passages, "Fear not, Abraham; I am thy shield, and thy exceeding great reward" (Gen. xv. 1). With this accords David's sentiment, "The Lord is the portion of mine inheritance, and of my cup; thou maintainest my lot. The lines are fallen unto me in pleasant places" (Ps. xvi. 5, 6). Again, "I shall be satisfied when I awake with thy likeness" (Ps. xvii. 15). Peter declares that the purpose for which believers are called is, that they may be "partakers of the divine nature" (2 Pet. i. 4). How so? Because "he shall come to be glorified in his saints, and to be admired in all them that believe" (2 Thess. i. 10). If our Lord will share his glory, power, and righteousness with the elect, nay, will give himself to be enjoyed by them; and what is better still, will, in a manner, become one with them, let us remember that every kind of happiness is herein included. But when we have made great progress in thus meditating, let us understand that if the conceptions of our minds be contrasted with the sublimity of the mystery, we are still halting at the very entrance.[3] The more necessary is it for us to cultivate sobriety in this matter, lest, unmindful of our feeble capacity, we presume to take too lofty a flight, and be overwhelmed by the brightness of the celestial glory. We feel how much we are stimulated by an excessive desire of knowing more than is given us to know, and hence

frivolous and noxious questions are ever and anon springing forth: by frivolous, I mean questions from which no advantage can be extracted. But there is a second class which is worse than frivolous; because those who indulge in them involve themselves in hurtful speculations. Hence I call them noxious. The doctrine of Scripture on the subject ought not to be made the ground of any controversy, and it is that as God, in the varied distribution of gifts to his saints in this world, gives them unequal degrees of light, so when he shall crown his gifts, their degrees of glory in heaven will also be unequal. When Paul says, "Ye are our glory and our joy" (2 Thess. ii. 19), his words do not apply indiscriminately to all; nor do those of our Saviour to his apostles, "Ye also shall sit on twelve thrones judging the twelve tribes of Israel" (Matth. xix. 28). But Paul, who knew that as God enriches the saints with spiritual gifts in this world, he will in like manner adorn them with glory in heaven, hesitates not to say, that a special crown is laid up for him in proportion to his labours. Our Saviour, also, to commend the dignity of the office which he had conferred on the apostles, reminds them that the fruit of it is laid up in heaven. This, too, Daniel says, "They that be wise shall shine as the brightness of the firmament; and they that turn many to righteousness as the stars for ever and ever" (Dan. xii. 3). Any one who attentively considers the Scriptures will see not only that they promise eternal life to believers, but a special reward to each. Hence the expression of Paul, "The Lord grant unto him that he may find mercy of the Lord in that day" (2 Tim. i. 18; iv. 14). This is confirmed by our Saviour's promise, that they "shall receive an hundredfold, and shall inherit everlasting life" (Matth. xix. 29). In short, as Christ, by the manifold variety of his gifts, begins the glory of his body in this world, and gradually increases it, so he will complete it in heaven.

11. While all the godly with one consent will admit this, because it is sufficiently attested by the word of God, they will, on the other hand, avoid perplexing questions which they feel to be a hinderance in their way, and thus keep within the prescribed limits. In regard to myself, I not only individually refrain from a superfluous investigation of useless matters, but also think myself bound to take care that I do not encourage the levity of others by answering them. Men puffed up with vain science are often inquiring how great the difference will be between prophets and apostles, and again, between apostles and martyrs; by how many degrees virgins will surpass those who are married; in short, they leave not a corner of heaven untouched by their speculations. Next it occurs to them to inquire to what end the world is to be repaired, since the children of God will not be in want of any part of this great and incomparable abundance, but will be like the angels, whose abstinence from food is a symbol of eternal blessedness. I answer, that independent of use, there will be so much pleasantness in the very sight, so much delight in the very knowledge, that this happiness will far surpass all the means of enjoyment which are now afforded. Let us suppose ourselves placed in the richest quarter of the

globe, where no kind of pleasure is wanting, who is there that is not ever and anon hindered and excluded by disease from enjoying the gifts of God? who does not oftentimes interrupt the course of enjoyment by intemperance? Hence it follows, that fruition, pure and free from all defect, though it be of no use to a corruptible life, is the summit of happiness. Others go further, and ask whether dross and other impurities in metals will have no existence at the restitution, and are inconsistent with it. Though I should go so far as concede this to them, yet I expect with Paul a reparation of those defects which first began with sin, and on account of which the whole creation groaneth and travaileth with pain (Rom. viii. 22). Others go a step further, and ask, What better condition can await the human race, since the blessing of offspring shall then have an end? The solution of this difficulty also is easy. When Scripture so highly extols the blessing of offspring, it refers to the progress by which God is constantly urging nature forward to its goal; in perfection itself we know that the case is different. But as such alluring speculations instantly captivate the unwary, who are afterwards led farther into the labyrinth, until at length, every one becoming pleased with his own view, there is no limit to disputation, the best and shortest course for us will be to rest contented with seeing through a glass darkly until we shall see face to face. Few out of the vast multitude of mankind feel concerned how they are to get to heaven; all would fain know before the time what is done in heaven. Almost all, while slow and sluggish in entering upon the contest, are already depicting to themselves imaginary triumphs.

12. Moreover, as language cannot describe the severity of the divine vengeance on the reprobate, their pains and torments are figured to us by corporeal things, such as darkness, wailing and gnashing of teeth, unextinguishable fire, the ever-gnawing worm (Matth. viii. 12; xxii. 13; Mark ix. 43; Isa. lxvi. 21). It is certain that by such modes of expression the Holy Spirit designed to impress all our senses with dread, as when it is said, "Tophet is ordained of old; yea, for the king it is prepared: he hath made it deep and large; the pile thereof is fire and much wood; the breath of the Lord, like a stream of brimstone, doth kindle it" (Isa. xxx. 33). As we thus require to be assisted to conceive the miserable doom of the reprobate, so the consideration on which we ought chiefly to dwell is the fearful consequence of being estranged from all fellowship with God, and not only so, but of feeling that his majesty is adverse to us, while we cannot possibly escape from it. For, first, his indignation is like a raging fire, by whose touch all things are devoured and annihilated. Next, all the creatures are the instruments of his judgment, so that those to whom the Lord will thus publicly manifest his anger will feel that heaven, and earth, and sea, all beings, animate and inanimate, are, as it were, inflamed with dire indignation against them, and armed for their destruction. Wherefore, the Apostle made no trivial declaration, when he said that unbelievers shall be "punished with everlasting destruction from the presence of the Lord, and from

the glory of his power" (2 Thess. i. 9). And whenever the prophets strike terror by means of corporeal figures, although in respect of our dull understanding there is no extravagance in their language, yet they give preludes of the future judgment in the sun and the moon, and the whole fabric of the world. Hence unhappy consciences find no rest, but are vexed and driven about by a dire whirlwind, feeling as if torn by an angry God, pierced through with deadly darts, terrified by his thunderbolt, and crushed by the weight of his hand; so that it were easier to plunge into abysses and whirlpools than endure these terrors for a moment. How fearful, then, must it be to be thus beset throughout eternity! On this subject there is a memorable passage in the ninetieth Psalm: Although God by a mere look scatters all mortals, and brings them to nought, yet as his worshippers are more timid in this world, he urges them the more, that he may stimulate them, while burdened with the cross, to press onward until he himself shall be all in all.

NOTES

1. 2 Tim. i. 10; John v. 24; Eph. ii. 6, 19; Rom. viii. 16-18; Heb. xi. 1; 2 Cor. v. 6; Col. iii. 8; Titus ii. 12.
2. French, "nous receovions un povre salaire de nostre lascheté et paresse;"—we receive a poor salary for our carelessness and sloth.
3. French, Et encore quand nons aurons bien profité en cette mediation, si nous faut il entendre que nous sommes encore tout au bas et à la premiere entree, et que jamais nous n'approcherons durant cette vie à la hautesse de ce mystere."—And still, when we shall have profited much by thus meditating, we must understand that we are still far beneath it, and at the very threshold, and that never during this life shall we approach the height of this mystery.

Immortality

Peter Geach

Everybody knows that men die, and though most of us have read the advertisement 'Millions now living will never die', it is commonly believed that every man born will some day die; yet historically many men have believed that there is a life after death, and indeed that this

From Peter Geach, *God and the Soul* (London: Routledge and Kegan Paul, 1969), pp. 17-29. Reprinted by permission of the author and the publisher.

after-life will never end. That is: there has been a common belief both in *survival* of bodily death and in *immortality*. Now a philosopher might interest himself specially in immortality, as opposed to survival; conceding survival for the sake of argument, he might raise and examine conceptual difficulties about *endless* survival. But the question of immortality cannot even arise unless men do survive bodily death; and, as we shall see, there are formidable difficulties even about survival. It is these difficulties I shall be discussing, not the special ones about endless survival.

There are various views as to the character of the after-life. One view is that man has a subtle, ordinarily invisible, body which survives the death of the ordinary gross body. This view has a long history, and seems to be quite popular in England at the moment. So far as I can see, the view is open to no philosophical objection, but likewise wholly devoid of philosophical interest; the mind-body problem must after all be just the same for an ethereal body as for a gross one. There could clearly be no philosophical reasons for belief in such subtle bodies, but only empirical ones; such reasons are in fact alleged, and we are urged to study the evidence.

Philosophy can at this point say something: about what sort of evidence would be required. The existence of subtle bodies is a matter within the purview of physical science; evidence for it should satisfy such criteria of existence as physicists use, and should refer not only to what people say they have seen, heard, and felt, but also to effects produced by subtle bodies on physicists' apparatus. The believer in 'subtle bodies' must, I think, accept the physicist's criteria of existence; there would surely be a conceptual muddle in speaking of 'bodies' but saying they might be incapable of affecting any physical apparatus. For what distinguishes real physical objects from hallucinations, even collective hallucinations, is that physical objects act on one another, and do so in just the same way whether they are being observed or not; this is the point, I think, at which a phenomenalist account of physical objects breaks down. If, therefore, 'subtle bodies' produce no physical effects, they are not bodies at all.

How is it, then, that 'subtle bodies' have never forced themselves upon the attention of physicists, as X-rays did, by spontaneous interference with physical apparatus? There are supposed to be a lot of 'subtle bodies' around, and physicists have a lot of delicate apparatus; yet physicists not engaged in psychical research are never bothered by the interference of 'subtle bodies'. In the circumstances I think it wholly irrational to believe in 'subtle bodies'. Moreover, when I who am no physicist am invited to study the evidence for 'subtle bodies', I find that very fact suspicious. The discoveries of X-rays and electrons did not appeal to the lay public, but to physicists, to study the evidence; and so long as physicists (at least in general) refuse to take 'subtle bodies' seriously, a study of evidence for them by a layman like myself would be a waste of time.

When *philosophers* talk of life after death, what they mostly have in mind is a doctrine that may be called Platonic—it is found in its essentials in the *Phaedo*. It may be briefly stated thus: 'Each man's make-up includes a wholly immaterial thing, his mind and soul. It is the mind that sees and hears and feels and thinks and chooses—in a word, is conscious. The mind is the person; the body is extrinsic to the person, like a suit of clothes. Though body and mind affect one another, the mind's existence is quite independent of the body's; and there is thus no reason why the mind should not go on being conscious indefinitely after the death of the body, and even if it never again has with any body that sort of connexion which it now has.

This Platonic doctrine has a strong appeal, and there are plausible arguments in its favour. It appears a clearly intelligible supposition that I should go on after death having the same sorts of experience as I now have, even if I then have no body at all. For although these experiences are connected with processes in the body—sight, for example, with processes in the eyes, optic nerves, and brain—nevertheless there is no necessity of thought about the connexion—it is easy to conceive of someone who has no eyes having the experience called sight. He would be having the same experience as I who have eyes do, and I know what sort of experience that is because I have the experience.

Let us now examine these arguments. When a word can be used to stand for a private experience, like the words 'seeing' or 'pain', it is certainly tempting to suppose that the giving these words a meaning is itself a private experience—indeed that they get their meaning just from the experiences they stand for. But this is really nonsense: if a sentence I hear or utter contains the word 'pain', do I help myself to grasp its sense by giving myself a pain? Might not this be, on the contrary, rather distracting? As Wittgenstein said, to think you get the concept of pain by having a pain is like thinking you get the concept of a minus qualtity by running up an overdraft. Our concepts of seeing, hearing, pain, anger, etc., apply in the first instance to human beings; we willingly extend them (say) to cats, dogs, and horses, but we rightly feel uncomfortable about extending them to very alien creatures and speaking of a slug's hearing or an angry ant. Do we know at all what it would be to apply such concepts to an immaterial being? I think not.

One may indeed be tempted to evade difficulties by saying: 'An immaterial spirit is angry or in pain if it feels *the same way* as I do when I am angry or in pain'. But, as Wittgenstein remarked, this is just like saying: 'Of course I know what it is for the time on the Sun to be five o'clock: it's five o'clock on the Sun at the very moment when it's five o'clock here!'—which plainly gets us no forrader. If there is a difficulty in passing from 'I am in pain' or 'Smith is in pain' to 'an immaterial spirit is in pain', there is equally a difficulty in passing from 'Smith feels the same way as I do' to 'an immaterial spirit feels the same way as I do'.

In fact, the question is, whether a private experience does suffice, as is here supposed, to give a meaning to a psychological verb like 'to see'. I am not trying to throw doubt on there being private experiences; of course men have thoughts they do not utter and pains they do not show; of course I may see something without any behaviour to show I see it; nor do I mean to emasculate these propositions with neo-behaviourist dialectics. But it is not a question of whether seeing is (sometimes) a private experience, but whether one can attach meaning to the verb 'to see' by a private uncheckable performance; and this is what I maintain one cannot do to any word at all.

One way to show that a word's being given a meaning cannot be a private uncheckable performance is the following: We can take a man's word for it that a linguistic expression has given him some private experience—e.g. has revived a painful memory, evoked a visual image, or given him a thrill in the pit of the stomach. But we cannot take his word for it that he attached a sense to the expression, even if we accept his *bona fides*; for later events may convince us that in fact he attached no sense to the expression. Attaching sense to an expression is thus not to be identified with any private experience that accompanies the expression; and I have argued this, not by attacking the idea of private experiences, but by contrasting the attaching of sense to an expression with some typical private experiences that may be connected with the expression.

We give words a sense—whether they are psychological words like 'seeing' and 'pain', or other words—by getting into a way of using them; and though a man can invent for himself a way of using a word, it must be a way that other people *could* follow—otherwise we are back to the idea of conferring meaning by a private uncheckable performance. Well, how do we eventually use such words as 'see', 'hear', 'feel', when we have got into the way of using them? We do not exercise these concepts only so as to pick our cases of seeing and the rest in our separate worlds of sense-experience; on the contrary, these concepts are used in association with a host of other concepts relating, e.g., to the physical characteristics of what is seen and the behaviour of those who do see. In saying this I am not putting forward a theory, but just reminding you of very familiar features in the everyday use of the verb 'to see' and related expressions; our ordinary talk about seeing would cease to be intelligible if there were cut out of it such expressions as 'I can't see, it's too far off', 'I caught his eye', 'Don't look round', etc. Do not let the bogy of behaviourism scare you off observing these features; I am not asking you to believe that 'to see' is itself a word for a kind of behaviour. But the concept of seeing can be maintained only because it has threads of connexion with these other non-psychological concepts; break enough threads, and the concept of seeing collapses.

We can now see the sort of difficulties that arise if we try to apply concepts like *seeing* and *feeling* to disembodied spirits. Let me give an actual case of a psychological concept's collapsing when its connexions were broken. Certain hysterics claimed to have a magnetic sense; it was discovered, however, that their claim to be having magnetic sensations did not go with the actual presence of a magnet in their environment, but only with their belief that a magnet was present. Psychologists did not now take the line: We may take the patients' word for it that they have peculiar sensations—only the term 'magnetic sensations' has proved inappropriate, as having been based on a wrong causal hypothesis. On the contrary, patients' reports of magnetic sensations were thenceforward written off as being among the odd things that hysterical patients sometimes say. Now far fewer of the ordinary connexions of a sensation-concept were broken here than would be broken if we tried to apply a sensation-concept like seeing to a disembodied spirit.

If we conclude that the ascription of sensations and feelings to a disembodied spirit does not make sense, it does not obviously follow, as you might think, that we must deny the possibility of disembodied spirits altogether. Aquinas for example was convinced that there are disembodied spirits but ones that cannot see or hear or feel pain or fear or anger; he allowed them no mental operations except those of thought and will. Damned spirits would suffer from frustration of their evil will, but not from aches and pains or foul odours or the like. It would take me too far to discuss whether his reasons for thinking this were good; I want to show what follows from this view. In our human life thinking and choosing are intricately bound up with a play of sensations and mental images and emotions; if after a lifetime of thinking and choosing in this human way there is left only a disembodied mind whose thought is wholly non-sensuous and whose rational choices are unaccompanied by any human feelings—can we still say there remains the same person? Surely not: such a soul is not the person who died but a mere remnant of him. And this is just what Aquinas says (in his commentary on I Corinthians 15): *anima mea non est ego*, my soul is not I; and if only souls are saved, *I* am not saved, nor is any man. If some time after Peter Geach's death there is again a man identifiable as Peter Geach, then Peter Geach again, or still, lives: otherwise not.

Though a surviving mental remnant of a person, preserving some sort of physical continuity with the man you knew, would not be Peter Geach, this does not show that such a measure of survival is not possible; but its possibility does raise serious difficulties, even if such dehumanized thinking and willing is really conceivable at all. For *whose* thinking would this be? Could we tell whether *one* or *many* disembodied spirits thought the thoughts in question? We touch here on the old problem: what constitutes there being two disembodied minds (at the same time, that is)? Well, what constitutes there being two pennies? It may happen that one penny is bent and corroded while another is in mint condition; but such differences cannot be what make the two pennies to be two—the two pennies could not have these varied fortunes if they were not already distinct. In the same way, differences of memories or of aims could not constitute the difference between two disembodied minds, but could only supervene upon a difference already existing. What does constitute the difference between two disembodied human minds? If we could find no ground of differentiation, then not only would that which survived be a mere remnant of a person—there would not even be a surviving individuality.

Could we say that souls are different because in the first instance they were souls of different bodies, and then remain different on that account when they are no longer embodied? I do not think this solution would do at all if differentiation by reference to different bodies were merely retrospective. It might be otherwise if we held, with Aquinas, that the relation to a body was not merely retrospective—that each disembodied human soul permanently retained a capacity for reunion to such a body as would reconstitute a man identifiable with the man who died. This might satisfactorily account for the individuation of disembodied human souls; they would differ by being fitted for reunion to different bodies; but it would entail that the possibility of disembodied human souls stood or fell with the *possibility* of a dead man's living again *as a man*.

Some Scholastics held that just as two pennies or two cats differ by being different bits of matter, so human souls differ by containing different 'spiritual matter'. Aquinas regarded this idea as self-contradictory; it is at any rate much too obscure to count as establishing a possibility of distinct disembodied souls. Now this recourse to 'spiritual matter' might well strike us merely as the filling of a conceptual lacuna with a non-sensical piece of jargon. But it is not only Scholastic philosophers who assimilate mental processes to physical ones, only thinking of mental processes as taking place in an *immaterial* medium; and many people think it easy to conceive of distinct disembodied souls because they are illegitimately ascribing to souls a sort of differentiation—say, by existing *side by side*—that can be significantly ascribed only to bodies. The same goes for people who talk about souls as being 'fused' or 'merged' in a Great Soul; they are imagining some such change in the world of souls as occurs to a drop of water falling into a pool or to a small lump of wax that is rubbed into a big one. Now if only people *talked* about 'spiritual matter', instead of just thinking in terms of it unawares, their muddle could be more easily detected and treated.

To sum up what I have said so far: The possibility of life after death for Peter Geach appears to stand or fall with the possibility of there being once again a man identifiable as Peter Geach. The existence of a disembodied soul would not be a survival of the person Peter Geach; and even in such a truncated form, individual existence seems to require at least a persistent possibility of the soul's again entering into the make-up of a man who is identifiably Peter Geach.

This suggests a form of belief in survival that seems to have become quite popular of late in the West—at any rate as a half-belief—namely, the belief in reincarnation. Could it in fact have a clear sense to say that a baby born in Oxford this year is Hitler living again?

How could it be shown that the Oxford baby was Hitler? Presumably by memories and similarities of character. I maintain that no amount of such evidence would make it reasonable to identify the baby as Hitler. Similarities of character are of themselves obviously insufficient. As regards memories: If on growing up the Oxford baby reveals knowledge of what we should ordinarily say only Hitler can have known, does this establish a presumption that the child is Hitler? Not at all. In normal circumstances we know when to say 'only he can have known that'; when queer things start happening, we have no right to stick to our ordinary assumptions as to what can be known. And suppose that for some time the child 'is' Hitler by our criteria, and later on 'is' Goering? or might not several children simultaneously satisfy the criteria for 'being' Hitler?

These are not merely captious theoretical objections. Spirit-mediums, we are told, will in trance convincingly enact the part of various people: sometimes of fictitious characters, like Martians, or Red Indians ignorant of Red Indian languages, or the departed 'spirits' of Johnny Walker and John Jamieson; there are even stories of mediums' giving convincing 'messages' from people who were alive and normally conscious at the time of the 'message'. Now a medium giving messages from the dead is not said to be the dead man, but rather to be controlled by his spirit. What then can show whether the Oxford child 'is' Hitler or is merely 'controlled' by Hitler's spirit? For all these reasons the appearance that there might be good evidence for reincarnation dissolves on a closer view.[1]

Nor do I see, for that matter, how the mental phenomena of mediumship could ever make it reasonable to believe that a human soul survived and communicated. For someone to carry on in a dramatic way quite out of his normal character is a common hysterical symptom; so if a medium does this in a trance, it is no evidence of anything except an abnormal condition of the medium's own mind. As for the medium's telling us things that 'only the dead can have known', I repeat that in these queer cases we have no right to stick to our ordinary assumptions about what can be known. Moreover, as I said, there are cases, as well-authenticated as any, in which the medium convincingly enacted the part of X and told things that 'Only X could have known' when X was in fact alive and normally conscious, so that his soul was certainly not trying to communicate by way of the medium! Even if we accept all the queer stories of spirit-messages, the result is only to open up a vast field of queer possibilities—not in the least to force us to say that mediums were possessed by such-and-such souls. This was argued by Bradley long ago in his essay 'The Evidences of Spiritualism', and he has never been answered.

How could a living man be rightly identifiable with a man who previously died? Let us first consider our normal criteria of personal identity. When we say an old man is the same person as the baby born seventy years before, we believe that the old man has material continuity with the baby. Of course this is not a criterion in the sense of being what we judge identity by; for the old man will not have been watched for seventy years continuously, even by rota! But something we regarded as disproving the material continuity (e.g. absence of a birthmark, different fingerprints) would disprove personal identity. Further, we believe that material continuity establishes a one–one relation: one baby grows up into one old man, and one old man has grown out of one baby. (Otherwise there would have to be at some stage a drastic change, a fusion or fission, which we should regard as destroying personal identity.) Moreover, the baby-body never coexists with the aged body, but develops into it.

Now it seems to me that we cannot rightly identify a man living 'again' with a man who died unless *material* conditions of identity are fulfilled. There must be some one–one relation of material continuity between the old body and the new. I am not saying that the new body need be even in part materially *identical* with the old; this, unlike material continuity, is not required for personal identity, for the old man need not have kept even a grain of matter from the baby of seventy years ago.

We must here notice an important fallacy. I was indicating just now that I favour Aquinas's doctrine that two coexisting souls differ by being related to two different bodies and that two coexisting human bodies, like two pennies or two cats, differ by being different bits of matter. Well, if it is difference of matter that makes two bodies different, it may seem to follow that a body can maintain its identity only if at least some identifiable matter remains in it all the time; otherwise it is no more the same body than the wine in a cask that is continuously emptied and refilled is the same wine. But just this is the fallacy: it does not follow, if difference in a certain respect at a certain time suffices to show non-identity, that sameness in that respect over a period of time is necessary to identity. Thus, Sir John Cutler's famous pair of stockings were the same pair all the time, although they started as silk and by much mending ended as worsted; people have found it hard to see this, because if at a given time there is a silk pair and also a worsted pair then there are two pairs. Again, it is clear that the same man may be in Birmingham at noon and in Oxford at 7 p.m., even though a man in Birmingham and a man in Oxford at a given time must be two different men. Once formulated, the fallacy is obvious, but it might be deceptive if not formulated.

'Why worry even about material continuity? Would not mental continuity be both necessary and sufficient?' Necessary, but not sufficient. Imagine a new 'Tichborne' trial. The claimant knows all the things he ought to know, and talks convincingly to the long-lost heir's friends. But medical evidence about scars and old fractures and so on indicates that he cannot be the man; moreover, the long-lost heir's corpse is decisively identified at an exhumation. Such a case would bewilder us, particularly if the claimant's *bona fides* were manifest. (He might, for example, voluntarily take a lie-detecting test.) But we should certainly not allow the evidence of mental connexions with the long-lost heir to settle the matter in the claimant's favour: the claimant cannot be the long-lost heir, whose body we know lies buried in Australia, and if he honestly thinks he is then we must try to cure him of a delusion.

'But if I went on being conscious, why should I worry which body I have?' To use the repeated 'I' prejudges the issue; a fairer way of putting the point would be: If there is going to be a consciousness that includes ostensible memories of my life, why should I worry about which body this consciousness goes with? When we put it that way, it is quite easy to imagine circumstances in which one would worry—particularly if the ostensible memories of my life were to be produced by processes that can produce entirely spurious memories.[2]

If, however, memory is not enough for personal identity; if a man's living again does involve some bodily as well as mental continuity with the man who lived formerly; then we might fairly call his new bodily life a resurrection. So the upshot of our whole argument is that unless a man comes to life again by resurrection, he does not live again after death. At best some mental remnant of him would survive death; and I should hold that the possibility even of such survival involves at least a permanent *capacity* for renewed human life; if reincarnation is excluded, this means: a capacity for resurrection. It may be hard to believe in the resurrection of the body: but Aquinas argued in his commentary on I Corinthians 15, which I have already cited, that it is much harder to believe in an immortal but permanently disembodied human soul; for that would mean believing that a soul, whose very identity depends on the capacity for reunion with one human body rather than another, will continue to exist for ever with this capacity unrealized.

Speaking of the resurrection, St. Paul used the simile of a seed that is planted and grows into an ear of corn, to show the relation between the corpse and the body that rises again from the dead. This simile fits in well enough with our discussion. In this life, the bodily aspect of personal identity requires a one–one relationship and material continuity; one baby body grows into one old man's body by a continuous process. Now similarly there is a one–one relationship between the buried seed and the ear that grows out of it; one seed grows into one ear, one ear comes from one seed; and the ear of corn is materially continuous with the seed but need not have any material identity with it.

There is of course no philosophical reason to expect that from a human corpse there will arise at some future date a new human body, continuous in some way with the corpse; and in some particular cases there appear strong empirical objections. But apart from the *possibility* of resurrection, it seems to me a mere illusion to have any hope for life after death. I am of the mind of Judas Maccabeus: if there is no resurrection, it is superfluous and vain to pray for the dead.

The traditional faith of Christianity, inherited from Judaism, is that at the end of this age Messiah will come and men rise from their graves to die no more. That faith is not going to be shaken by inquiries about bodies burned to ashes or eaten by beasts; those who might well suffer just such death in martyrdom were those who were most confident of a glorious reward in the resurrection. One who shares that hope will hardly wish to take out an occultistic or philosophical insurance policy, to guarantee some sort of survival as an annuity, in case God's promise of resurrection should fail.

NOTES

1. See Peter Geach, "Reincarnation" in *God and the Soul* for further development of these arguments.
2. Cf. the example of the mad surgeon's procedures in Peter Geach, "Reincarnation" in *God and the Soul*.

THE EXISTENTIALIST RESPONSE

Existentialism and the Fear of Dying

M.A. Slote

In this paper I shall present a fairly systematic "existentialist" view of human anxiety about death and human responses to that anxiety, based on the work of Pascal, Kierkegaard, Heidegger, and Sartre. My main purpose is constructive, rather than exegetical. What seems to me most distinctive and important about the work of these existentialist authors is their approach to the fear of dying—or at least the relevance of what they say to that subject, for sometimes, when they deal with other topics, what they say can (I shall attempt to show) be used to illuminate the nature of human responses to the fear of death. But I think that much of what these authors say about the fear of dying is inchoate, confusing, or incomplete, and requires supplementation, clarification, and systematization of the kind I shall be attempting to provide here.[1]

From *American Philosophical Quarterly,* Vol. 12, No. 1 (January, 1975), pp. 17-28. Reprinted by permission of the author and the editor.

I

Perhaps the central locus of discussion by an Existentialist, of human attitudes toward and responses to death is the section of Kierkegaard's *Concluding Unscientific Postscript* called "The Task of Becoming Subjective." According to Kierkegaard, becoming subjective is "the most difficult of all tasks in fact, precisely because every human being has a strong natural bent and passion to become something more and different." [2] But what is it to be subjective or to be objective, and why is the former so difficult and the latter so tempting? Part of Kierkegaard's explanation involves him in a contrast between the subjective and objective acceptance of Christianity. But Kierkegaard also applies the subjective/objective distinction to attitudes toward life and death generally. And what unites Kierkegaard in the "Becoming Subjective" section of the *Postscript* with such non-religious Existentialists as Heidegger and Sartre is the fact that he has something to say about human attitudes toward life and death that presupposes no particular form of religiosity and that has not, I think, been said by anyone outside the existentialist tradition. And it is this aspect of Kierkegaard's work that I shall be examining.

According to Kierkegaard, to have an objective attitude toward one's life is to have the kind of attitude toward one's life encouraged by an Hegelian view of the world. On such a view, one is part of a larger "world-historical" process of the self-realization of Reason or Spirit, and one's life takes on significance if one plays a role, however minor, in that world-historical process. One does not have to be an Hegelian to think in this kind of way. One can be thinking in a similar way if, as a scientist or philosopher, e.g., one devotes oneself to one's field in the belief or hope that one's life gains significance through one's contribution to something "bigger."

Kierkegaard says that people with such an attitude have an objective attitude toward their lives; and he wants each of us to dare to become subjective and renounce this "loftily pretentious and yet delusive intercourse" with the world historical.[3] Those who live objectively are, according to Kierkegaard, under a delusion or illusion, and if so, then surely he has a real argument in favor of being subjective. For Kierkegaard, at least part of the illusion is, I think, the belief that by living objectively, one's dividend, what (good) one gets from life, is greater.[4] In the first place even if a certain world-historical process of development is a great good, it is a good that is divided up among those participating in that development into many parts, none of which, presumably, is large in relation to the whole, and so perhaps the good to be derived from participating in that development will be less than the good to be gained by living subjectively. But Kierkegaard then seems to question whether indeed there is *any* good to be gained from living for some world-historical process, since one who does so may not be around when it comes to fruition. But it is not clear that the good of such a process of development must all come at the end of that development, so I think Kierkegaard has still not given us any very strong reason for believing that one who lives objectively is under some kind of illusion that his life is better.

However, in the *Postscript* Kierkegaard attempts to tie up his discussion of living objectively, i.e., of living for the world historical, with certain illusory "objective" attitudes towards death. One who lives world-historically will sometimes say: "What does it matter whether I die or not; the work is what is important, and others will be able to carry it forward." But this is to think of one's death as nothing special, as just one death among others, as a "something in general." And Kierkegaard seems to believe that one who thinks this way is under an illusion, the illusion that his own death has no more significance *for him* than the death of (random) others, or, to put it slightly differently, that he *should be* no more concerned about his own death than about that of others. However, various Stoic philosophers would, I think, tend to argue that it is Kierkegaard's belief that one should be especially concerned about one's own death that is an illusion, an illusion born of irrational self-centeredness. So it is not obvious that Kierkegaard is correct about the illusory nature of objective living, or about the advisability of living subjectively. In any case, the attitude of people who live for the world historical toward their own deaths is of some interest: they are, at least at some level, not as afraid of dying as they might be or as some people are. And I think there are interesting implications to be drawn from this fact that have some of the spirit of what Kierkegaard says in the *Postscript*.

II

Those who live world-historically for some enterprise like science or philosophy seem not to be very anxious about dying. And I would like to suggest, what Kierkegaard never actually says, that we may be able to *explain* the tendency to live for the world historical as resulting from our characteristically human fear of dying. For no one wants to live in fear, and since one who lives objectively, for the world historical, does not feel the fear of dying that some of us do, there is reason and motive for people who have experienced anxiety or fear at the prospect of dying to (try to) adopt an objective existence, including an objective attitude toward their own deaths. But what are the psychological mechanisms by which living world-historically assuages someone's fear of death. Here I can only suggest, not establish, an answer, and what I shall say is intended as exploratory and somewhat speculative.

Consider the claim that people who live for the world historical sometimes make that they will *be or become immortal through their works*, or that they will *live on through their works*. Why do people ever say such things; if what they are saying is just metaphorical, why do they use *that* metaphor and why do they seem to take the metaphor seriously? [5] It seems to me that such claims of immortality or living on are not (if there is no afterlife along traditional religious lines) literally true. It is not even literally true to say that part of one lives on in one's works, for books, e.g., are not literally parts of those who write them. Moreover, even if there is a traditional religious type of afterlife, one presumably does not live on *through one's works*.[6]

When we say that we shall live on or be immortal through our writings, e.g., I think we sometimes make that claim in a serious spirit. We are not just joking or deliberately speaking loosely. But when someone points out that what we are saying is not literally true, I think that most of us are willing to admit that what we have said is not literally true. How is this possible? It is my conjecture that someone who says he will live on, at least unconsciously believes that what he has said is (literally) true. Part of the evidence for the *unconsciousness* of the belief, if it exists, is the fact that when someone brings it to our attention that it cannot literally be true, we are ready, at least on a conscious level, to admit that this is so. What (further) supports the idea that the belief exists on some unconscious level is the fact that we at first express it in a serious vein and are not fully conscious that what we are saying is not literally true. We have to be reminded that what we have said is not literally true and in this respect are not like someone who says that a certain person has a heart of gold. In the latter case, one is quite clear in one's mind *ab initio* that what one is saying is not the literal truth. One is, I think, often less clear, and in some sense more confused, about the literal falsehood of what one says when one says that one will live on in one's works. And this unclarity or confusion, as compared with the "heart of gold" case, is some evidence that one who speaks of living on in his works unconsciously believes that he will do so, inasmuch as the existence of such an unconscious belief is one very obvious possible explanation of that unclarity or confusion.[7] But what lends the greatest support to the view that such an unconscious belief exists in those who live world-historically and say they will live on in their works is the generally accepted fact that human beings naturally tend to fear dying. It is to be expected that men will try to avoid that fear and repress it, if possible. One way of doing this would be to convince oneself that one was immortal through one's works, so that death was not really or fully the end of one's existence. It would be hard to convince oneself of such a claim on a conscious level, just because of its literal falseness. But such belief in one's immortality could perhaps survive on an unconscious level where it would be less subject to rational scrutiny, and perhaps be capable of counteracting one's fear of death. The unconscious delusion of one's immortality (or living on) through one's works can, if we adopt Freudian terminology, be thought of as an unconscious defense mechanism of the ego that protects us from conscious fear about death by repressing that fear and counterbalancing it in such a way that it for the most part remains unconscious.[8] And this would explain why people who live for the world historical are not consciously afraid of dying much of the time, and, in effect, why people so often live for the world historical.[9]

Let me carry my speculation further. At one point in the *Postscript* (p. 274) Kierkegaard says that to live for the world historical is to forget that one exists. This curious claim is, I think, more plausible or forceful than it may seem at first. Consider a person who lives objectively and unconsciously believes that he will live on through his books. Such a belief is not just false, but necessarily false, since it involves both the idea that one is alive and the idea that the existence of certain works like books is sufficient for one's continued existence; and nothing whose continued existence is entailed by the existence of such works can be *alive*. Moreover, the belief that one's books' existence is sufficient for one's continued existence seems to involve the idea that one has roughly the same kind of being as a book or series of books. So I think there is something to the idea that one who lives objectively somehow thinks of himself as not existing as a person, and as not being alive. But he presumably does not think this on a conscious level, for much the same reason that one does not on a conscious level think that one is going to live on through one's works. On the other hand, the *unconscious* delusion that one is not alive (or is of the same kind as a series of books) would seem capable of counteracting and allaying anxiety about dying just as easily as the unconscious belief that one is immortal through one's works does so. If one is going to live on in books, one is not going to lose one's life and there is nothing to fear from death, so that fears about dying may be prevented from becoming conscious by being allayed on an unconscious level. Similarly, if one is not really alive, or is of the same "stuff" as books, then one also has nothing to fear from dying; and one's ceasing to be, if it occurs, will be no more tragic than the ceasing to be of a book.[10] So if one believes this kind of thing on an unconscious level, it is again not hard to see how one's fear of death may be allayed and kept unconscious.[11] Thus it would seem that people so often live for the world historical because such living involves unconscious beliefs (delusions) that help them, more or less successfully, to avoid conscious fears about dying.[12]

According to Kierkegaard, however, not only does one who lives for the world historical forget that he exists, but such a person at least to some extent ceases to exist as a person, ceases to live.[13] For if we use our lives as a means to the existence of certain works and/or to be mentioned in some paragraph or footnote of some authoritative history of our field of endeavor, then we are valuing our lives no more than we value the existence of certain works or our being mentioned in paragraphs or footnotes. And when we unconsciously think of ourselves as immortal through our works, we are in effect thinking that what we lose when we die cannot be that important or valuable. And to do and think in this way is to put a low value on one's living. But if one places a low value on actual living, one will not take full advantage of one's life (living) and that is a bit like already being dead, or not alive. So I think there really is something to Kierkegaard's claim that to live world-historically is to some extent to cease to exist as a person, to cease to be alive. The claim constitutes not literal truth, but a forceful and penetrating metaphor.

It is well known that the fear of dying is a prime source of much of human religiosity. Belief in an afterlife of the traditional religious sort is one way that men can assuage their anxiety about dying. What is perhaps not so well known is how the fear of dying can give rise to (and explain) certain attitudes and activities of people who are not in any ordinary way religious and perhaps also certain attitudes and activities of religious people that are not generally associated with religion. What I have tried to show here is that there are in Kierkegaard's *Concluding Unscientific Postscript* insights about our attitudes toward life and death that can be used to help us understand how certain non-religious aspects of human life result from the fear of dying.

In doing so, I have assumed that people who live objectively and say that they are not terribly anxious about dying are nonetheless afraid of dying at some level. And this may seem high-handed. However, I am inclined to think that in general people living world-historically (who do not believe in some traditional religious type of life after death) continue to be subject to a certain welling-up of death anxiety that can overtake them in the midst of their daily lives.[14] Despite my own tendencies toward the world historical, I have often experienced this sudden welling-up of death anxiety, and I think that the fact that this phenomenon is widespread among non-religious world-historical people (and indeed among people in general) is evidence that fear of dying never entirely ceases to exist in (such) people, but always continues to exist at least on an unconscious plane. For it is easier to imagine such a sudden welling-up of fear as the "return of the repressed" and as indicating a certain inefficiency of one's repressive mechanisms than to think of it as resulting from the sudden regeneration of death fears within one. What could plausibly explain such a sudden rebirth of death anxiety *in medias res?* Moreover, the earlier-mentioned fact that world-historical people (people who live for the world historical) sometimes seriously say that they will be immortal through their works, without being clear in their own minds that this is just a metaphor, is, as I have already argued, evidence that such people unconsciously believe that they are immortal through their works (or that they are not alive). But why should they have such unconscious beliefs, except as part of a mechanism to relieve and keep repressed their fear of dying? So even such seemingly innocuous locutions as that we shall be immortal through our works indicate the existence of death fears even on the part of people who live for the world historical and claim not to be afraid of dying. Let us now turn to Pascal's *Pensées* to see how the fear of dying affects other aspects of human life.

III

There is a famous long passage in the *Pensées* where Pascal talks about diversion, its role in human life and its sources. Men "cannot stay quietly in their own chamber" alone and meditating, for any length of time.[15] We need or think we need diversion and activity and cannot be happy without diverting ourselves from ourselves because of the "natural poverty of our feeble and mortal condition, so miserable that nothing can comfort us when we think of it closely." [16] Now Pascal does not go on to decry the vanity of human diversion and claim that life would be less vain if we thought more about ourselves and our mortality. He is not arguing for the vanity of worldly human concerns in the time-worn manner of *Ecclesiastes*. He has an entirely new perspective on where the vanity of human life really lies. The vanity of our lives consists, for Pascal, in the fact that when we divert ourselves (from ourselves), we typically deceive ourselves about our motives for behaving as we do.[17] For example, a man who gambles often convinces himself that obtaining the money he is gambling for would make him happy (at least for a while). He focuses on the getting of the money and forgets that his real or main purpose is to divert himself. Thus if he were offered the money on condition that he does not gamble, he would be (at least temporarily) unhappy, because he seeks diversion. On the other hand, if he were offered the diversion, say, of playing cards without being able to gamble for money, he would also be unhappy. For it is not just diversion he seeks; he must also have some imagined goal that he focuses on in such a way that he does not see that diversion is his real or main goal. Pascal does not, however, explain why men cannot simply seek diversion without fooling themselves about their goal. But an explanation can be given along lines that Pascal might have approved. Imagine that we divert ourselves in order not to have to think of ourselves and also realize that this is so. Shall we not *ipso facto* be thrust back into that very awareness of self that we sought to avoid through diversion? To realize that one wants not to think of oneself because it is unpleasant to dwell on one's feeble and mortal condition is *ipso facto* to be thinking of oneself and opening oneself up to the very unpleasantness one wishes to avoid. And if those who want to avoid thinking of themselves must remain ignorant of that fact if they are to succeed in not thinking of themselves, how better to accomplish this than by focusing on something outside themselves and thinking of it as their goal?

This explanation of human striving and activity applies not just to gambling, but, as Pascal says, to the waging of campaigns in love or in war and to many other human activities. Many of us fool ourselves about our motives much of the time when engaged in such activities. One objection to this analysis, however, would be that to explain so much human activity in terms of the fear of, or desire not to be, thinking of oneself is to offer a gratuitous explanation of our behavior. Why not just say that as animals we have an instinctive desire for certain activities that typically involve a lack of self-consciousness and that are called "diversions"? But the instinct theory of the origin of our diversions has, as it stands, no obvious way of explaining the self-deception Pascal points out. If we simply have an instinct for certain activities, activities that in fact tend to divert us from ourselves, why do some of us much of the time and many of us some of the time deceive ourselves into thinking that it is winning a certain victory or honor or woman that is our main goal, when it is the diverting activity leading up to that winning that is our main goal? On the theory that we do not like thinking about ourselves, however, the fact of self-deception can be explained along the above lines; so the assumption of a desire not to think of oneself is not gratuitous.

Furthermore, there is good independent evidence that people do not like to think about themselves. There is, for example, an experience that I have sometimes had, and that I think the reader will probably also have had; in the middle of thinking about something else I have all of a sudden thought to myself: "All this is being done by *me* and all these people are talking about *me*." I hope this description will suffice to convey the kind of experience I have in mind. What is interesting, but also perplexing and distressing to me, are the following facts. When I have this experience of myself, there seems to me to be something precious about it; and I think: "This is the moment when I am most alive; it is very good to have this experience." (There is, after all, a long tradition in which self-consciousness is a great, or the greatest, good.) I usually also think that though I am at that moment too busy to prolong the self-consciousness, I shall definitely set aside a good deal of time in the future to take full advantage of this kind of experience of self-awareness. But somehow that never happens. And when I am again momentarily self-conscious in the way I have been describing, I again put off a long bout of such self-consciousness to the future, despite my typical accompanying conviction that the experience of being self-conscious is a wonderful one that I really should and shall take greater advantage of. All this needs explaining, and the obvious explanation, I think, is that I really do not like the experience of self-consciousness, as Pascal suggests.

But why, in the end, should we not want to think about ourselves? Pascal suggests that the reason is that thinking about ourselves makes us think of our feeble and mortal condition. He also says about man: "to be happy, he would have to make himself immortal; but, not being able to do so, it has occurred to him to prevent himself from thinking of death." [18] Presumably, then, Pascal thinks there is a connection between thinking about oneself and thinking unpleasant thoughts about one's death; and this seems to me to be quite plausible. For at least while we are absorbed in things outside us, we do not think of ourselves, or thus, it would seem, of our death; whereas if and when one does think about oneself, one might very easily think about one's death. It would seem, then, that the explanation of our diverting ourselves from (thinking about) ourselves is that this at least to some degree enables us to avoid thinking anxiously about our mortality. And so we have now clarified two general areas or aspects of human life in terms of the fear of dying. Let us turn next to Heidegger.

IV

Men's attitudes toward death are a major theme in Heidegger's *Being and Time*.[19] For Heidegger, in everyday life we exist in a mode that Heidegger calls the "they" (German: "das Man"). Heidegger characterizes this mode of existence as inauthentic, at least in part because in it, one is forgetful of the fact that death is one's ownmost possibility and cannot be outstripped. By this he means something close to the Kierkegaardian idea that one's own death has greater significance for one than does the death of others. Heidegger says that such a mode of existence is tempting because it tranquilizes one's anxiety in the face of death.[20] So it would seem that Heidegger can be thought of as providing a psychological explanation of certain aspects of human life, which he calls collectively "(being lost in) the 'they'," and thus that Heidegger is doing something similar to what we have seen Kierkegaard doing in the *Postscript* and Pascal doing in the *Pensées*.[21]

According to Heidegger, one important aspect of our average everyday lostness in the "they" is its typical modes of discourse, chatter, and idle talk, and the busy-body curiosity that characterizes such discourse. Heidegger points out that when people are idly and curiously talking about whether John and Mary will get divorced, the actual event, the divorce, if it occurs, actually disappoints the idle talkers; for then they are no longer able to conjecture about and be in on the thing in advance. The curiosity of everyday idle talk is concerned with the very latest thing(s), with novelty; and what interests in anticipation may be "old hat" or out of date when it occurs. Horse races and even pennant races in baseball seem to me to be good examples of this tendency. We have the keenest interest in who will win, but it is hard to maintain much interest in such races once we know their outcome; there is even a certain disappointment or "let-down" sometimes when the results of such things finally do become known.[22] Heidegger's discussion here seems to have a good deal in common with what Pascal says about diversion, for one way of diverting ourselves from ourselves would be to be constantly curious about the latest things. But why not be interested in things that are not new and be diverted by them? The answer here—though it is not one that Heidegger actually gives—seems to me to lie precisely in the desire not to think of oneself that Pascal lays such emphasis on. What is newer is less well known, and the more there is to learn about something, the less likely one is to get bored with it or to cease being absorbed in it, and so be thrust back into thoughts about oneself. Furthermore, our earlier discussion of Pascal can help us explain why we are sometimes let down when a certain event we have (only) conjectured about occurs, even though in advance we thought that "nothing would make us happier" than to know exactly when and how the event would occur. For if our goal is distraction from ourselves through conjecturing, we cannot very well admit this to ourselves without (running a grave risk of) defeating that goal; so we somehow fool ourselves into thinking that what we want is to know for sure about the character of the event we are conjecturing about, as a means to our real goal of diverting ourselves through conjecturing about something or someone outside ourselves; and when we cannot conjecture any more, then of course we are let down.

There may be a further reason why the desire for novelty is so pervasive in human life—though what I shall now be saying is perhaps more speculative than anything else I have to say here. As Heidegger says (p. 217), when one has the desire for novelty, it is as if one's motive were to have known (seen) rather than to know (see); for as soon as one has known (seen) something, one no longer wants to know (see) it. And there seems to be a certain vanity in such a way of dealing with things. Now consider what is implicitly involved in wanting, say, to have seen Rome, but not to see (keep seeing) Rome. There are tours whose advertising has the feeling of: "Come to Europe with us and you will see 8—count'em—8 countries in 8 days"; and such advertising and such tours appeal to many people who want to (say they) have been, e.g., in Rome, but who do not much want to *be* in Rome. When one makes such a tour, one often even wishes the tour were already over so that one (could say that one) had already been to Rome in Italy (and to the other seven countries). The actual touring, with its "inconveniences," is often not desired or enjoyed. But to want the eight days and the trip to be already over with is in a certain sense to want a part of one's life over with in exchange for a being able to say one has been. This desire is in many cases unconscious. Sometimes some of us say, with an air of seriousness, that we wish that a certain trip or period of time were already over. But when confronted with the implications of what we have said, we almost inevitably recoil from what we have said and say that of course we do not *really* want a certain part of our life to be already over, perhaps adding that we were only speaking loosely or jokingly in making our original remark. In that case our desire to have a certain part of our life over with exists, if at all, only on an unconscious level. Evidence that there *is* such an unconscious desire comes from the fact of our original serious-ness in saying that we wished a certain trip over with and from the fact that we are by no means clear in our own minds that we do not mean our statement literally, the way a hungry man is, for example, when he says that he could eat a mountain of flapjacks. I think this initial un-clarity is best explained by (and thus evidence for) the existence of an unconscious desire to have a certain part of our life over with.[23] And perhaps for the very purpose of keeping this desire out of consciousness, we convince ourselves at least temporarily that we really want to *be* in Rome, or *feel* its living antiquity, etc. But then, after we have spent the tour rushing about, impatient with tarrying in one place too long, we *may*, upon reflection, recognize that we wanted the having seen more than the seeing of the places, like Rome, that we visited.

The logical extension of the wish to have a certain portion of one's life already over with is the wish to have one's whole life over with, and I would like now very tentatively to argue that at some deep level many of us have this latter wish, and so want not to be alive. Part of the reason for thinking so consists in the way we deceive ourselves about the extent of our desires to have portions of our lives over with. We sometimes think: if only it were a week from now so that I knew whether *p*, every-thing would be all right. But then when the time comes at which every-thing is supposed to be going to be all right, we soon find another reason for thinking things are not all right and for wishing other parts of our lives over with. I think that the initially implausible assumption that some people unconsciously wish their whole lives over with, wish not to be alive, provides the best explanation of this whole perplexing phenomenon. For if one has the unconscious desire to have one's whole life over with, there will be mechanisms in force to prevent it from becoming conscious. If one were conscious that one wanted *many different parts* of one's life over with *seriatim*, one would be dangerously close to being conscious that one wanted one's *whole life* over with. So it might reasonably be expected that someone with the unconscious wish or desire that his whole life was over with would be (made to be) unaware of the extent to which he wanted particular portions of his life over with before they were lived. Thus I think there is reason to believe that people who deceive themselves in this way unconsciously wish not to be alive.[24]

It will perhaps seem more plausible to hold that such a wish exists if I can show how it is explained by our fear of dying. One way of allaying fear of the loss of something is a kind of denial that one might call the technique of "sour grapes in advance." We can convince ourselves that the thing we may lose is not worth having or that we do not really want it. (This recalls the studies psychologists have done on the resolution of "cognitive dissonance.") An unconscious desire not to be alive might, then, help us counterbalance or keep repressed our fear of dying. The existence of such a desire can thus be supported in various ways and fits well into the kind of theory about our attitudes toward death so far proposed. But there is no time to speculate further in its favor.[25]

We argued earlier that if someone thinks of himself as not alive, he will not take full advantage of his life and it will be as if he is not (fully) alive. The same can be said for someone who wants not to be alive. We saw earlier the force of the metaphor that some of us are dead. Since it is as if some of us are dead because of what we have, unconsciously, done to ourselves, there is also force to the metaphor that some of us have killed ourselves. To live for the having seen and known of things is, metaphorically speaking, not to be alive, and to have killed oneself.[26] And one can also say this about those who live for the world historical. I have a tendency to put myself entirely into my work and to live for something "bigger," philosophy. But sometimes I recoil from such an existence and from myself, and I feel that I have really just thrown my life away, have been personally emptied, through world-historical living. At such a time the metaphor of killing oneself seems particularly compelling.

We have thus far characterized those who live world-historically as assuaging the fear of dying via the *beliefs* that they are immortal and/or that they are not alive. But I think such people also sometimes unconsciously wish not to be alive in the manner of those who divert themselves with novelties.[27] (Of course, those who live world-historically can be diverting themselves as well, e.g., with busy research or advocacy of causes.) For one thing, as we have already seen, people who live world-historically unconsciously think that they are not alive. And they want to think this, at least unconsciously, as a means to less fear or anxiety. But presumably if one wants to think one is not alive, that is because one wants not to be alive. This kind of inference from what one wants to think to what one wants is surely *usually* in order. Secondly, there is evidence that world-historical people tend to want parts of their lives over with in much the same way that seekers after novelty do. Someone writing a book that is intended to advance some field in the long run will often wish that the next six months of his life were already over so that he could see the book in finished form and have the writing of it over with. If only this were possible, everything would start being all right, he thinks, and he would be ready really to live his life again. Such a person, however, will, in many cases, be fooling himself about the extent to which he wants to "put off living" by missing parts of his life. As soon as there is another book to write, or academic appointment in the offing, he may very well once again want some part of his life already over with. Saying that such a man really wants to live, but only wants to avoid certain tense or burdensome parts of life, does not really allow us to understand why he so often on such slight pretexts (is writing a book really so unpleasant and tense, considering the rest of the things that can be going on in one's life at the same time?) thinks up reasons for wanting to postpone living by omitting some part of his life. Just as a man who is always *just about* to take a vacation and really live (it up) for a change, but who never does, can be plausibly suspected of preferring his work to a vacation or to "life" despite his protestations to the contrary, the perplexing behavior of one who lives world-historically and keeps wanting parts of his life over with while remaining unconscious or unaware of the extent to which this is so can, I think, only be made sense of in terms of an unconscious desire not to be alive.[28] Such a desire is strange and perplexing, perhaps, but no more so than the behavior it is supposed to explain.

Heidegger says many more interesting things about the "they." Idle talk and curiosity seem to be interested in anything and everything, though in fact, unbeknown to us, limits have been set on what we are to be interested in. For example, one is not, in the midst of curious talk, supposed to bring up the tragedy of life or the inevitability of death. Anyone who brings up such things is told not to be "morbid." Heidegger suggests that idle talk and curiosity function as a way of keeping us from thinking of our own death. For one thing—if I may borrow again from our discussion of Pascal to supplement what Heidegger is saying here—the illusion of interest in everything is an excellent means for blocking off thought about dying and its consequent anxiety, since if we believed, while we were engaged in idle talk, that we were not supposed to be deeply talking about death, we might very easily be thrust back into the very anxiety that idle talk was supposed to avoid. Moreover, the very self-assurance and harshness with which someone who brings up death in the midst of idle talk is branded as morbid tends to encourage and rationalize our avoidance of the topic of death.

Another device by which everyday living in the "they" keeps us from fears of death is by branding such fears as cowardly. Heidegger, however, thinks that it is more cowardly *not* to face death anxiously. Now there certainly seems to be room for disagreement on this issue. Some of the Stoics seem to have thought that it was irrational, rather than courageous, to be anxious about one's own death because death was a matter of indifference. And this latter philosophy of death may be correct; but it might be interesting at this point to make some educated guesses about the psychology of those who have advocated the "Stoic" view of death. For to my mind there is something strange and suspicious about (holding) the view that one's own death is not an evil. I have already discussed the fact that despite our best repressive mechanisms, the fear of dying sometimes comes upon (some of) us suddenly in the midst of life. When others tell us that it is morbid or cowardly to worry about death, we are given an excuse or motive not to worry about death, and such advice may help us to get rid of the conscious fear of death at least temporarily. The philosophical view that it is irrational to worry about death because death is a matter of indifference may have a similar function to play in the psychic lives of those who propound it. Philosophers pride themselves on being rational, and by branding the fear of dying as "irrational," they may give themselves a motive for ceasing consciously to worry about death and actually help themselves get rid of the conscious fear of dying. I am inclined to think, then, that the view that it is irrational, and not courageous, to fear death, because death is no evil, may well be motivated, in many of those who propound it, by the fear of death itself, a fear that they are consequently able to repress, but not to get rid of. If so, then those who are helped to repress their fear of dying by holding a "Stoic" view of death are under an illusion when they claim as rational philosophers to be totally indifferent to death. But it might be better to live under such an illusion without consciously worrying about death than to know that one was not indifferent to death because one *was* consciously afraid of death. In the light of these complexities, it would seem hard to decide between Heidegger, on the one hand, and the Stoics and the "they," on the other, as to whether it is courageous to be (consciously) anxious in the face of dying.

Heidegger suggests yet further ways in which existence in the "they" tranquilizes our anxiety about dying. In the "they" there is an emphasis on keeping busy doing things, as the means to, or sign of, a full and good life. When someone suggests that one might do better to be more reflective and less busy, the response of the "they" is that by keeping busy, one is living "concretely" and avoiding self-defeating and morbid self-consciousness; this encourages the person who hears this to keep busy and not reflect on himself, and thus functions as a means to keeping us from the conscious fear of dying. (Consider, in particular, how the old, who are especially subject to fears of death, are told to keep busy and active.)

Heidegger points out that someone lost in the "they" will *admit* that death is certain and that one (everyone) dies in the end. According to Heidegger, in speaking of what happens to "everyone" or to "one" eventually, we "depersonalize" and "intellectualize" death. In thus depersonalizing death, it is as if the person were saying that death has nothing to do with *him right now,* and this enables him to talk about death without focusing on himself or having that particularly intimate experience of self-awareness described earlier or, thus, having fearful thoughts about death. Also talk about the inevitability or certainty of death, etc., may be part of a process of "isolation of affect" in which one intellectualizes (about) a certain phenomenon to keep away from (consciousness of) certain related feelings.[29] Heidegger also points out that social scientists often seek to create "typologies" and systematic theories about humanity in the belief that they are thereby penetrating to the deepest level on which one can understand humanity and oneself, but that such intellectual "hustle and bustle" may entirely ignore the question of the significance for men of their own death and death anxiety; such intellectualization, he suggests, may serve to keep one from anxious thoughts about death by convincing one that one has reflected as deeply as it is possible to do. And the very stuffiness and detachment with which some sociologists, psychologists, etc., sometimes declare their desire to plumb the depths of the human spirit is, I would think, some evidence that they have a deeper need to avoid the *feeling* of their own mortality.

An important further point that is due to Kierkegaard rather than to Heidegger is that one can even overintellectualize one's response to a work, like that of Kierkegaard or Heidegger, that attempts to reveal in an "existential" manner the importance of our attitudes toward dying.[30] Spinoza has said that "passive" feelings like fear tend to dissipate when we scrutinize them, and this may well mean that it is difficult at one and the same time both intellectually to focus on and learn the significance of death anxiety and to *feel* that significance. And so there seems to be a real danger that someone who reads the writings of Existentialists will only intellectually understand and agree with what they say, and thus fail to derive all the benefit one could or should get from reading them. Of course, Spinoza's dictum also implies that it is difficult to think intellectually about death anxiety while feeling such anxiety. And one reason why I and others may be interested in thinking and writing about death anxiety is that such thinking and writing may, in effect, involve an isolation of affect about death.[31]

In discussing Heidegger, we have brought in Kierkegaard and Pascal to help "deepen" his analysis of how death anxiety affects large portions of human life. I would like now to make use of certain ideas of Sartre's (in ways that Sartre undoubtedly would not approve) to point out yet another aspect of human life that can be explained in terms of the fear of dying. (However, I shall not discuss Sartre's own views on death, which in fact run counter to much of what we have to say on that subject.)

V

Being and Nothingness is perhaps most famous for its discussion of what Sartre calls "bad faith," which consists in being or putting oneself under the illusion that one is not free and cannot do other than what one in fact does.[32] For Sartre, one is in bad faith when one says: I have to get up and get to work; I can't stay in bed, I have a family to feed. Bad faith is involved because one does not *have* to get up and go to work.

Some people will immediately object to what Sartre is saying on the grounds that if determinism about human behavior is true and a certain person in fact will not stay in bed, then he is under no illusion when he says that he cannot stay in bed. Since, despite anything Sartre says, it is by no means obvious to me that such determinism is not (approximately) true or that human beings possess free will, I would like now to (re)interpret Sartre's "bad faith" in such a way as to avoid assuming either human indeterminism or human free will.

Someone who says he has to go to work in the morning will sometimes say: "I have no choice in the matter." But I think that he does have a choice, even if a determined and unfree one, and that if he cannot stay at home, that is in part *because* of his (perhaps determined and unfree) choice. Moreover, I think that someone who is reminded of these facts will typically be willing to take back his original claim to have no choice in some matter, will grant that he had been speaking loosely or metaphorically. But it seems to me that such a person will typically not have been clear in his own mind about all this at the time when he originally claimed to have "no choice." And for reasons we have already gone into at length, I think this indicates that the person making such a claim unconsciously believes that he has no choice in a certain matter, even though he really does have a (possibly determined and unfree) choice in that matter and can be brought to conscious awareness of that fact. Such a person is under an illusion about the part he (and his choosing or deciding) plays in certain events or situations, and it is *this kind* of illusion that *I* shall call "bad faith."

Bad faith in this new sense is clearly related to bad faith in Sartre's sense. And, assuming that the new kind of bad faith does exist, it would be good if we could give some sort of explanation of it. Sartre's explanation of bad faith in the old sense will not be of much help to us here, since it assumes not only that human behavior is undetermined but also (implausibly enough) that human beings basically realize (believe) that this is so. My suggestion is that we explain bad faith in my new sense in much the same way that we have been explaining various other phenomena, namely, in terms of the fear of dying. (Indeed, Heidegger hints at this idea in *Being and Time*, p. 239.) I think that we can explain bad faith in terms of the fear of dying, if we suppose that the illusion of bad faith helps to repress such fear and if we borrow one further idea of Sartre's. According to Sartre, someone in bad faith (in his sense) who denies his own freedom is, in effect, thinking of himself as a thing or object, since things and objects are unfree, etc. I would like tentatively to claim that people who unconsciously believe that they have no choice, say, about getting up in the morning are, in effect, thinking of themselves as things or objects,[33] since things and objects really do lack choice. If we make this assumption, we can explain how bad faith in my sense enables one to relieve or repress death fears. For objects cannot die, and so unconsciously thinking of oneself as an object is unconsciously to think that one has nothing to fear from death.[34] (And if one passes away but is a mere object, then that is no more tragic than the passing away of a rock.)

Bad faith in the new sense seems to have much in common with living for the world historical. In the latter case, one thinks of oneself as not alive; in the former, one thinks of oneself as a mere thing; and one might wonder whether there is much difference here either in the content of these unconscious beliefs or in the way they act on the fear of dying. Furthermore, just as one who lives for the world historical can aptly be described metaphorically as not alive [35] and as having killed himself, one who lives in bad faith is, metaphorically speaking, a mere thing and not alive, and since he has (unconsciously) done this to himself, he has, metaphorically speaking, turned himself into a thing. And given the fact that the only way a person really can turn himself into a thing is by turning himself into a corpse, it is perhaps metaphorically appropriate to describe someone who is (constantly) in bad faith as having killed himself. Sartre holds that someone who thinks of himself as a mere thing wants (among other things) to *be* a mere thing. And I think we could argue that people in bad faith in my sense sometimes unconsciously want to be things in something like the way we earlier argued that people living for the world historical want not to be alive. Furthermore, the unconscious desire to be an object would seem capable of countering the fear of dying in much the same way that the unconscious desire not to be alive does so, and so there is this further similarity between living in bad faith and living for the world historical.

VI

If what has been said here is on the right track, then it would seem that Pascal, Kierkegaard, Heidegger, and Sartre all describe phenomena that pervade our lives and that are best explained in terms of their efficacy in relieving or repressing the fear of dying. Our explanation has made use of a Freudian type of view of repression and of the unconscious. This will certainly make our arguments here suspect in the eyes of some people. I have in effect been "practicing" a kind of "existential psychoanalysis," and though this term is one that was originally used by Sartre in *Being and Nothingness* to describe some of his own procedures, it may well apply more accurately to the kinds of things I have been doing here. For Sartre does not posit an unconscious, but I have followed Freud in doing just that.[36] In any case, I hope that this paper may bring to light an area, or areas, where Existentialism and Psychoanalysis can be mutually enlightening.

Of course, in addition to using psychoanalytic ideas, I have also frequently appealed to my own experience and intuitions, to how things strike me and to the "feel" of certain ideas. Though some things, I trust, will strike readers the way they have struck me, this will no doubt not always be the case; and when it is not, my appeals to how things feel to me, etc., are bound to seem like special pleading. Perhaps I *am* guilty of this, but I do not know how to avoid it in a paper like this when personal experience may be more relevant to seeing certain points than abstract arguments. And perhaps some of the ideas or intuitions I have relied on will seem more palatable to the reader if he "lives with them" and takes the time to see whether they do not, perhaps, make sense in and of his experience of himself and the world. For it is in something like this way that many of the ideas and intuitions of this paper have become acceptable to me.

In this paper, I have pieced together various ideas from Pascal, Heidegger, Sartre, and Kierkegaard, as well as extrapolated beyond what any of them has said, to provide a fairly general picture of how the fear of dying accounts for many aspects of human life. The explanatory "theory" we have presented links together phenomena that the various Existentialists discussed separately, and as such should, given any standard account of scientific method, be more plausible than the accounts of the various Existentialists taken separately. So I hope I have helped to support and fill out the basically existentialist notion that the quality of a (non-religious) man's life greatly depends on his attitude toward his own death. And even if this idea is not particularly prevalent in Sartre, we can use things Sartre says to substantiate it.

Some people will complain that I have only been doing psychology, not philosophy. But it may not be important whether this accusation is true. And I also think that when psychology is general enough and speaks directly to the human condition, it can also count as philosophy. If, as we have argued, the main motive for world-historical (or busily self-distractive) participation in certain enterprises comes from (desire to avoid) the fear of dying, then a good many intellectuals, scientists, and others may be less pure in motive, less selfless, than they are often thought to be.[37] And this fact, if it is one, is surely very relevant to our understanding of the human condition, and so counts in favor of calling what we have been doing philosophy.[38]

NOTES

1. I shall by no means, however, be discussing all the things these authors say on the topic of death.
2. *Concluding Unscientific Postscript* (Princeton, 1960), p. 116.

3. *Ibid.,* p. 133.
4. *Ibid.,* p. 130ff.
5. Horace in the *Odes* (3, XXX) seems to be an example of someone who takes the metaphor seriously.
6. I think that people who talk of gaining immortality through their children also say what is literally false, and their psychology is, I think, significantly similar to the psychology of those who talk of living on through their books.
7. Kierkegaard hints at the idea that world-historical people believe they live on through their works when he implies (*Postscript,* p. 140) that such people need to be reminded that "in the world-historical process the dead are not recalled to life."
8. For examples of reasoning similar to that just used that appear in the psychoanalytic literature, see, e.g., S. Freud's "Splitting of the Ego in the Defensive Process" (in his *Collected Papers* [London, 1956], vol. 5, pp. 372-375) and Otto Fenichel's *The Psychoanalytic Theory of Neurosis* (New York, 1945, pp. 479-484). For another *philosophical* use of an argument like mine above, see M. Lazerowitz' *The Structure of Metaphysics* (London, 1955, p. 69ff.) and *Studies in Metaphilosophy* (London, 1964, pp. 225ff., 251). I am indebted to Lazerowitz' account for some of the structure of my own analysis.
9. J. P. Sartre (in *Being and Nothingness* [New York, 1956], p. 543) says that "to be dead is to be a prey for the living." And Thomas Nagel (in "Death," *Noûs,* vol. 4 [1970], p. 78) has tentatively claimed that a man can be harmed or unfortunate as a result of things that happen after his death, e.g., if his reputation suffers posthumously. I wonder whether these views are not, perhaps, indicative of some sort of unconscious belief that people live on in their works.
10. The unconscious belief that one is going to live on and the unconscious belief that one is not alive seem to counteract the unconscious belief or fear that one is going to die in contradictory ways, the former with the "message" that we are not really going to lose what we have, the latter with the "message" that we really have nothing to lose. But we have already seen that the unconscious belief that one lives on in books is itself contradictory or necessarily false, so it should not, perhaps, be so surprising that the unconscious uses mutually contradictory means to repress death-fears. On this see Freud's *The Interpretation of Dreams,* ch. 2. For similar use of the (metaphorical?) notion of unconscious "messages," see Otto Fenichel's *Outline of Clinical Psychoanalysis* (New York, 1934), esp. pp. 13, 30, 33, 52, 250, 260, 275f.
11. In "A Lecture on Ethics," *The Philosophical Review,* vol. 74 (1965), pp. 8ff. Ludwig Wittgenstein speaks of the feeling people sometimes have of being safe whatever happens. He claims that such a feeling or belief is nonsensical; but perhaps this occasional feeling is better thought of as the expression of a meaningful, but necessarily or clearly false, unconscious belief that we are safe whatever happens, a belief that counteracts the fear of dying and that is roughly equivalent to the unconscious belief that one is not alive. For one is absolutely safe (from death) if and only if one is not alive.
12. I do not want to claim that everyone dedicated to some "cause," to something "bigger" than himself is living world-historically. Such dedication may result from altruism or "conviction" and may not involve the world-historical psychology if it is not accompanied by delusions of immortality through one's works or actions, or the view that one's own death is unimportant.
13. *Ibid.,* pp. 118, 175, 271, 273.
14. See Heidegger's *Being and Time* (New York, 1962), p. 233f.
15. New York, 1958, p. 39.

16. *Ibid.*
17. *Ibid.*, p. 40.
18. *Ibid.*, p. 49.
19. Our discussion here will be based on sections 27, 35-42, and 47-53 of *Being and Time* (New York, 1962).
20. Heidegger uses "fear" only with respect to things in the world. For death "anxiety" is reserved; but this is not necessarily dictated by ordinary usage.
21. Of course, some philosophers will say that by treating Heidegger as an explanatory psychologist, I am treating him as if he were operating on the "ontic" level, whereas Heidegger thinks of himself as operating on an "ontological" level deeper than the "ontic" level on which science, psychology, and most pre-Heideggerian philosophy typically function. However, despite many efforts, I myself have never been able to make satisfactory sense of the ontic/ontological distinction. If the distinction is viable, Heidegger may have a good deal more to say than I shall be giving him credit for; but we can at least credit him with insights on a level with those of a Pascal or a Kierkegaard.
22. Of course, some people constantly dwell on past (sporting) events (and their part in them), but I do not think this is incompatible with the general tendency I am describing.
23. Compare here our earlier argument for the existence, in world-historical people, of an unconscious belief in their immortality through their works.
24. Our earlier argument that we do not like thinking about ourselves can be strengthened along the lines of our present argument for the existence of an unconscious wish not to be alive. Similar self-deception occurs in the two cases.
25. I have posited the wish not to be alive as an unconscious defense mechanism of the ego that responds to (prior) fear of dying. Freud, on the other hand, late in his career posited a basic (id-based) death instinct to account for various phenomena. See *Beyond the Pleasure Principle* (New York, 1950). The two sorts of views are incompatible, and so the explanation given just now in the text may be mistaken. However, there is some reason to prefer it. Our ego-theory of the death wish fits in better with our earlier-discussed theories about the ego's unconscious handling of the fear of dying. Moreover, other things being equal, it is better to treat a phenomenon as a derived phenomenon, within a theory, than to treat it as basic, within that theory. In addition, there is the sheer unintuitiveness of supposing that we have death wishes *ab initio*, rather than acquiring such (irrational) wishes in the *neurotic* process of repression. Finally, it is by no means clear that a basic death instinct is needed to account for clinical phenomena. On this see Otto Fenichel's "A Critique of the Death Instinct" in *The Collected Papers of Otto Fenichel*, first series (New York, 1953), pp. 363-372.
26. I think we have some inkling of this metaphorical killing when we speak of "killing time" at moments when we want to have something over with, want a certain (perhaps boring) part of our lives over with. Use of that phrase may be a disguised conscious expression of the unconscious desire not to be alive.
27. Kierkegaard's claim in the *Postscript* (p. 137) that one whose eye is on world-historical things has perhaps found "a highly significant way of . . . killing time" seems to indicate some awareness on his part that world-historical people want not to be alive and have, metaphorically speaking, killed themselves. Whose time, after all, does one kill except one's own? And one's time

is one's life. Incidentally, it is natural to say that world-historical people "bury themselves in their work," and this metaphor seems to suggest the very same things that our use of the metaphor of killing time does.

28. Cf. Emerson's remark in his *Journals* (13 April, 1834) that "we are always getting ready to live, but never living."
29. Cf. O. Fenichel's *Outline of Clinical Psychoanalysis, op. cit.*, p. 190f., for ideas about "isolation of affect" that are related to some of the things we have said here and earlier in the paper.
30. *Postscript*, p. 166f.
31. Heidegger also points out that the force of living in the "they" is such as to make people lost in the "they" scoff at his analysis of such lostness. Once one is aware of one's tendencies to cover up certain anxieties, it may be harder to use the mechanisms one has previously used in doing so; so one who wishes at some level to keep covering up his anxiety has a motive to reject Heidegger's analysis and, indeed, our analysis here.
32. See *Being and Nothingness* (New York, 1956), Pt. 1.
33. I hope I shall be forgiven for ignoring plants.
34. This recalls the Simon and Garfunkel song that goes: "I am a rock, I am an island; and a rock feels no pain, and an island never cries." The idea that we sometimes want to think of ourselves as things to avoid the pain of life or of facing death is not new or silly. Moreover, even if people in bad faith only think of themselves, unconsciously, as *similar* to mere things, that thought may itself be capable of relieving the fear of death.
35. Kierkegaard says that such a person is also a "walking stick," which suggests the similarity of such a person to someone in bad faith who exists as a mere object.
36. Sartre rejects the unconscious for reasons that seem to me to be interesting, but ultimately unacceptable.
37. This is not to say that such people should stop doing science, etc., with their present motives. They may be happier than they are otherwise likely to be, and may be contributing to the intellectual or practical good of other people. Also see footnote 12, above.
38. I am indebted to G. Boolos, E. Erwin, B. Jacobs, D. Lewin, S. Ogilvy, and M. Wilson for helpful comments on earlier drafts of this paper.

THE HUMANIST RESPONSE

The Meaning of Life

Richard Taylor

The question whether life has any meaning is difficult to interpret, and the more one concentrates his critical faculty on it the more it seems to elude him, or to evaporate as any intelligible question. One wants to turn it aside, as a source of embarrassment, as something that, if it cannot be abolished, should at least be decently covered. And yet I think any reflective person recognizes that the question it raises is important, and that it ought to have a significant answer.

If the idea of meaningfulness is difficult to grasp in this context, so that we are unsure what sort of thing would amount to answering the question, the idea of meaninglessness is perhaps less so. If, then, we can bring before our minds a clear image of meaningless existence, then perhaps we can take a step toward coping with our original question by seeing to what extent our lives, as we actually find them, resemble that image, and draw such lessons as we are able to from the comparison.

MEANINGLESS EXISTENCE

A perfect image of meaninglessness, of the kind we are seeking, is found in the ancient myth of Sisyphus. Sisyphus, it will be remembered, betrayed divine secrets to mortals, and for this he was condemned by the gods to roll a stone to the top of a hill, the stone then immediately to roll back down, again to be pushed to the top by Sisyphus, to roll down once more, and so on again and again, *forever*. Now in this we have the picture of meaningless, pointless toil, of a meaningless existence that is absolutely *never* redeemed. It is not even redeemed by a death that, if it were to accomplish nothing more, would at least bring this idiotic cycle to a close. If we were invited to imagine Sisyphus struggling for awhile and accomplishing nothing, perhaps eventually falling from exhaustion, so that we might suppose him then eventually turning to something having some sort of promise, then the meaninglessness of that chapter of his life would not be so stark. It would be a dark and dreadful dream, from which he eventually awakens to sun-

Richard Taylor, "The Meaning of Life" from *Good and Evil* (New York: Macmillan, 1970), pp. 256-268. Reprinted by permisson of the author and publisher.

light and reality. But he does not awaken, for there is nothing for him to awaken to. His repetitive toil is his life and reality, and it goes on forever, and it is without any meaning whatever. Nothing ever comes of what he is doing, except simply, more of the same. Not by one step, nor by a thousand, nor by ten thousand does he even expiate by the smallest token the sin against the gods that led him into this fate. Nothing comes of it, nothing at all.

This ancient myth has always enchanted men, for countless meanings can be read into it. Some of the ancients apparently thought it symbolized the perpetual rising and setting of the sun, and others the repetitious crashing of the waves upon the shore. Probably the commonest interpretation is that it symbolizes man's eternal struggle and unquenchable spirit, his determination always to try once more in the face of overwhelming discouragement. This interpretation is further supported by that version of the myth according to which Sisyphus was commanded to roll the stone *over* the hill, so that it would finally roll down the other side, but was never quite able to make it.

I am not concerned with rendering or defending any interpretation of this myth, however. I have cited it only for the one element it does unmistakably contain, namely, that of a repetitious, cyclic activity that never comes to anything. We could contrive other images of this that would serve just as well, and no myth-makers are needed to supply the materials of it. Thus, we can imagine two persons transporting a stone —or even a precious gem, it does not matter—back and forth, relay style. One carries it to a near or distant point where it is received by the other; it is returned to its starting point, there to be recovered by the first, and the process is repeated over and over. Except in this relay nothing counts as winning, and nothing brings the contest to any close, each step only leads to a repetition of itself. Or we can imagine two groups of prisoners, one of them engaged in digging a prodigious hole in the ground that is no sooner finished than it is filled in again by the other group, the latter then digging a new hole that is at once filled in by the first group, and so on and on endlessly.

Now what stands out in all such pictures as oppressive and dejecting is not that the beings who enact these roles suffer any torture or pain, for it need not be assumed that they do. Nor is it that their labors are great, for they are no greater than the labors commonly undertaken by most men most of the time. According to the original myth, the stone is so large that Sisyphus never quite gets it to the top and must groan under every step, so that his enormous labor is all for nought. But this is not what appalls. It is not that his great struggle comes to nothing, but that his existence itself is without meaning. Even if we suppose, for example, that the stone is but a pebble that can be carried effortlessly, or that the holes dug by the prisoners are but small ones, not the slightest meaning is introduced into their lives. The stone that Sisyphus moves to the top of the hill, whether we think of it as large or small, still rolls back every time, and the process is repeated forever. Nothing comes of it, and the work is simply pointless. That is the element of the myth that I wish to capture.

Again, it is not the fact that the labors of Sisyphus continue forever that deprives them of meaning. It is, rather, the implication of this: that they come to nothing. The image would not be changed by our supposing him to push a different stone up every time, each to roll down again. But if we supposed that these stones, instead of rolling back to their places as if they had never been moved, were assembled at the top of the hill and there incorporated, say, in a beautiful and enduring temple, then the aspect of meaninglessness would disappear. His labors would then have a point, something would come of them all, and although one could perhaps still say it was not worth it, one could not say that the life of Sisyphus was devoid of meaning altogether. Meaningfulness would at least have made an appearance, and we could see what it was.

That point will need remembering. But in the meantime, let us note another way in which the image of meaninglessness can be altered by making only a very slight change. Let us suppose that the gods, while condemning Sisyphus to the fate just described, at the same time, as an afterthought, waxed perversely merciful by implanting in him a strange and irrational impulse; namely, a compulsive impulse to roll stones. We may if we like, to make this more graphic, suppose they accomplish this by implanting in him some substance that has this effect on his character and drives. I call this perverse, because from our point of view there is clearly no reason why anyone should have a persistent and insatiable desire to do something so pointless as that. Nevertheless, suppose that is Sisyphus' condition. He has but one obsession, which is to roll stones, and it is an obsession that is only for the moment appeased by his rolling them—he no sooner gets a stone rolled to the top of the hill than he is restless to roll up another.

Now it can be seen why this little afterthought of the gods, which I called perverse, was also in fact merciful. For they have by this device managed to give Sisyphus precisely what he wants—by making him want precisely what they inflict on him. However it may appear to us, Sisyphus' fate now does not appear to him as a condemnation, but the very reverse. His one desire in life is to roll stones, and he is absolutely guaranteed its endless fulfillment. Where otherwise he might profoundly have wished surcease, and even welcomed the quiet of death to release him from endless boredom and meaninglessness, his life is now filled with mission and meaning, and he seems to himself to have been given an entry to heaven. Nor need he even fear death, for the gods have promised him an endless opportunity to indulge his single purpose, without concern or frustration. He will be able to roll stones *forever*.

What we need to mark most carefully at this point is that the picture with which we began has not really been changed in the least by adding this supposition. Exactly the same things happen as before. The only change is in Sisyphus' view of them. The picture before was the image of meaningless activity and existence. It was created precisely to be an image of that. It has not lost that meaninglessness, it has now gained not the least shred of meaningfulness. The stones still roll back as before, each phase of Sisyphus' life still exactly resembles all the others, the task is never completed, nothing comes of it, no temple ever begins to rise, and all this cycle of the same pointless thing over and over goes on forever in this picture as in the other. The *only* thing that has happened is this: Sisyphus has been reconciled to it, and indeed more, he has been led to embrace it. Not, however, by reason or persuasion, but by nothing more rational than the potency of a new substance in his veins.

THE MEANINGLESSNESS OF LIFE

I believe the foregoing provides a fairly clear content to the idea of meaninglessness and, through it, some hint of what meaningfulness, in this sense, might be. Meaninglessness is essentially endless pointlessness, and meaningfulness is therefore the opposite. Activity, and even long, drawn-out and repetitive activity, has a meaning if it has some significant culmination, some more or less lasting end that can be considered to have been the direction and purpose of the activity. But the descriptions so far also provide something else; namely, the suggestion of how an existence that is objectively meaningless, in this sense, can nevertheless acquire a meaning for him whose existence it is.

Now let us ask: Which of these pictures does life in fact resemble? And let us not begin with our own lives, for here both our prejudices and wishes are great, but with the life in general that we share with the rest of creation. We shall find, I think, that it all has a certain pattern, and that this pattern is by now easily recognized.

We can begin anywhere, only saving human existence for our last consideration. We can, for example, begin with any animal. It does not matter where we begin, because the result is going to be exactly the same.

Thus, for example, there are caves in New Zealand, deep and dark, whose floors are quiet pools and whose walls and ceilings are covered with soft light. As one gazes in wonder in the stillness of these caves it seems that the Creator has reproduced there in microcosm the heavens themselves, until one scarcely remembers the enclosing presence of the walls. As one looks more closely, however, the scene is explained. Each dot of light identifies an ugly worm, whose luminous tail is meant to attract insects from the surrounding darkness. As from time to time one of these insects draws near it becomes entangled in a sticky thread lowered by the worm, and is eaten. This goes on month after month, the blind worm lying there in the barren stillness waiting to entrap an occasional bit of nourishment that will only sustain it to another bit of nourishment until. . . . Until what? What great thing awaits all this long and repetitive effort and makes it worthwhile? Really nothing.

The larva just transforms itself finally to a tiny winged adult that lacks even mouth parts to feed and lives only a day or two. These adults, as soon as they have mated and laid eggs, are themselves caught in the threads and are devoured by the cannibalist worms, often without having ventured into the day, the only point to their existence having now been fulfilled. This has been going on for millions of years, and to no end other than that the same meaningless cycle may continue for another millions of years.

All living things present essentially the same spectacle. The larva of a certain cicada burrows in the darkness of the earth for seventeen years, through season after season, to emerge finally into the daylight for a brief flight, lay its eggs, and die—this all to repeat itself during the next seventeen years, and so on to eternity. We have already noted, in another connection, the struggles of fish, made only that others may do the same after them and that this cycle, having no other point than itself, may never cease. Some birds span an entire side of the globe each year and then return, only to insure that others may follow the same incredibly long path again and again. One is led to wonder what the point of it all is, with what great triumph this ceaseless effort, repeating itself through millions of years, might finally culminate, and why it should go on and on for so long, accomplishing nothing, getting nowhere. But then one realizes that there is no point to it at all, that it really culminates in nothing, that each of these cycles, so filled with toil, is to be followed only by more of the same. The point of any living thing's life is, evidently, nothing but life itself.

This life of the world thus presents itself to our eyes as a vast machine, feeding on itself, running on and on forever to nothing. And we are part of that life. To be sure, we are not just the same, but the differences are not so great as we like to think; many are merely invented, and none really cancels the kind of meaninglessness that we found in Sisyphus and that we find all around, wherever anything lives. We are conscious of our activity. Our goals, whether in any significant sense we choose them or not, are things of which we are at least partly aware and can therefore in some sense appraise. More significantly, perhaps, men have a history, as other animals do not, such that each generation does not precisely resemble all those before. Still, if we can in imagination disengage our wills from our lives and disregard the deep interest each man has in his own existence, we shall find that they do not so little resemble the existence of Sisyphus. We toil after goals, most of them—indeed every single one of them—of transitory significance and, having gained one of them, we immediately set forth for the next, as if that one had never been, with this next one being essentially more of the same. Look at a busy street any day, and observe the throng going hither and thither. To what? Some office or shop, where the same things will be done today as were done yesterday, and are done now so they may be repeated tomorrow. And if we think that, unlike Sisyphus, these labors do have a point, that they culminate in something lasting and, independently of our own deep interests in them, very worthwhile, then we simply have not considered the thing closely enough. Most such effort is directed only to the establishment and perpetuation of home and family; that is, to the begetting of others who will follow in our steps to do more of the same. Each man's life thus resembles one of Sisyphus' climbs to the summit of his hill, and each day of it one of his steps; the difference is that whereas Sisyphus himself returns to push the stone up again, we leave this to our children. We at one point imagined that the labors of Sisyphus finally culminated in the creation of a temple, but for this to make any difference it had to be a temple that would at least endure, adding beauty to the world for the remainder of time. Our achievements, even though they are often beautiful, are mostly bubbles; and those that do last, like the sand-swept pyramids, soon become mere curiosities while around them the rest of mankind continues its perpetual toting of rocks, only to see them roll down. Nations are built upon the bones of their founders and pioneers, but only to decay and crumble before long, their rubble then becoming the foundation for others directed to exactly the same fate. The picture of Sisyphus is the picture of existence of the individual man, great or unknown, of nations, of the race of men, and of the very life of the world.

On a country road one sometimes comes upon the ruined hulks of a house and once extensive buildings, all in collapse and spread over with weeds. A curious eye can in imagination reconstruct from what is left a once warm and thriving life, filled with purpose. There was the hearth, where a family once talked, sang, and made plans; there were the rooms, where people loved, and babes were born to a rejoicing mother; there are the musty remains of a sofa, infested with bugs, once bought at a dear price to enhance an ever-growing comfort, beauty, and warmth. Every small piece of junk fills the mind with what once, not long ago, was utterly real, with children's voices, plans made, and enterprises embarked upon. That is how these stones of Sisyphus were rolled up, and that is how they became incorporated into a beautiful temple, and that temple is what now lies before you. Meanwhile other buildings, institutions, nations, and civilizations spring up all around, only to share the same fate before long. And if the question "What for?" is now asked, the answer is clear: so that just this may go on forever.

The two pictures—of Sisyphus and of our own lives, if we look at them from a distance—are in outline the same and convey to the mind the same image. It is not surprising, then, that men invent ways of denying it, their religions proclaiming a heaven that does not crumble, their hymnals and prayer books declaring a significance to life of which our eyes provide no hint whatever.[1] Even our philosophies portray some permanent and lasting good at which all may aim, from the changeless forms invented by Plato to the beatific vision of St. Thomas and the ideals of permanence contrived by the moderns. When these fail to convince, then earthly ideals such as universal justice and brotherhood are conjured up to take their places and give meaning to man's seemingly endless pilgrimage, some final state that will be ushered in when the last obstacle is removed and the last stone pushed to the hilltop. No one believes, of course, that any such state will be final, or even wants it to be in case it means that human existence would then cease to be a struggle; but in the meantime such ideas serve a very real need.

THE MEANING OF LIFE

We noted that Sisyphus' existence would have meaning if there were some point to his labors, if his efforts ever culminated in something that was not just an occasion for fresh labors of the same kind. But that is precisely the meaning it lacks. And human existence resembles his in that respect. Men do achieve things—they scale their towers and raise their stones to the hilltops—but every such accomplishment fades, providing only an occasion for renewed labors of the same kind.

But here we need to note something else that has been mentioned, but its significance not explored, and that is the state of mind and feeling with which such labors are undertaken. We noted that if Sisyphus had a keen and unappeasable desire to be doing just what he found himself doing, then, although his life would in no way be changed, it would nevertheless have a meaning for him. It would be an irrational one, no doubt, because the desire itself would be only the product of the substance in his veins, and not any that reason could discover, but a meaning nevertheless.

And would it not, in fact, be a meaning incomparably better than the other? For let us examine again the first kind of meaning it could have. Let us suppose that, without having any interest in rolling stones, as such, and finding this, in fact, a galling toil, Sisyphus did nevertheless have a deep interest in raising a temple, one that would be beautiful and lasting. And let us suppose he succeeded in this, that after ages of dreadful toil, all directed at this final result, he did at last complete his temple, such that now he could say his work was done, and he could rest and forever enjoy the result. Now what? What picture now presents itself to our minds? It is precisely the picture of infinite boredom! Of Sisyphus doing nothing ever again, but contemplating what he has already wrought and can no longer add anything to, and contemplating it for an eternity! Now in this picture we have a meaning for Sisyphus' existence, a point for his prodigious labor, because we have put it there; yet, at the same time, that which is really worthwhile seems to have slipped away entirely. Where before we were presented with the nightmare of eternal and pointless activity, we are now confronted with the hell of its eternal absence.

Our second picture, then, wherein we imagined Sisyphus to have had inflicted on him the irrational desire to be doing just what he found himself doing, should not have been dismissed so abruptly. The meaning that picture lacked was no meaning that he or anyone could crave, and the strange meaning it had was perhaps just what were seeking.

At this point, then, we can reintroduce what has been until now, it is hoped, resolutely pushed aside in an effort to view our lives and human existence with objectivity; namely, our own wills, our deep interest in what we find ourselves doing. If we do this we find that our lives do indeed still resemble that of Sisyphus, but that the meaningfulness they thus lack is precisely the meaningfulness of infinite boredom. At the same time, the strange meaningfulness they possess is that of the inner compulsion to be doing just what we were put here to do, and to go on doing it forever. This is the nearest we may hope to get to heaven, but the redeeming side of that fact is that we do thereby avoid a genuine hell.

If the builders of a great and flourishing ancient civilization could somehow return now to see archaeologists unearthing the trivial remnants of what they had once accomplished with such effort—see the fragments of pots and vases, a few broken statues, and such tokens of another age and greatness—they could indeed ask themselves what the point of it all was, if this is all it finally came to. Yet, it did not seem so to them then, for it was just the building, and not what was finally built, that gave their life meaning. Similarly if the builders of the ruined home and farm that I described a short while ago could be brought back to see what is left, they would have the same feelings. What we construct in our imaginations as we look over these decayed and rusting pieces would reconstruct itself in their very memories, and certainly with unspeakable sadness. The piece of a sled at our feet would revive in them a warm Christmas. And what rich memories would there be in the broken crib? And the weed-covered remains of a fence would reproduce the scene of a great herd of livestock, so laboriously built up over so many years. What was it all worth, if this is the final result? Yet, again, it did not seem so to them through those many years of struggle and toil, and they did not imagine they were building a Gibraltar. The things to which they bent their backs day after day, realizing one by one their ephemeral plans, were precisely the things in which their wills were deeply involved, precisely the things in which their interests lay, and there was no need then to ask questions. There is no more need of them now—the day was sufficient to itself, and so was the life.

This is surely the way to look at all of life—at one's own life, and each day and moment it contains; of the life of a nation; of the species; of the life of the world; and of everything that breathes. Even the glow worms I described, whose cycles of existence over the millions of years seem so pointless when looked at by us, will seem entirely different to us if we can somehow try to view their existence from within. Their endless activity, which gets nowhere, is just what it is their will to pursue. This is its whole justification and meaning. Nor would it be any salvation to the birds who span the globe every year, back and forth, to have a home made for them in a cage with plenty of food and protection, so that they would not have to migrate any more. It would be their condemnation, for it is the doing that counts for them, and not what they hope to win by it. Flying these prodigious distances, never ending, is what it is in their veins to do, exactly as it was in Sisyphus' veins to roll stones, without end, after the gods had waxed merciful and implanted this in him.

A human being no sooner draws his first breath than he responds to the will that is in him to live. He no more asks whether it will be worthwhile, or whether anything of significance will come of it, than the worms and the birds. The point of his living is simply to be living, in the manner that it is his nature to be living. He goes through his life building his castles, each of these beginning to fade into time as the next is begun; yet, it would be no salvation to rest from all this. It would be a condemnation, and one that would in no way be redeemed were he able to gaze upon the things he has done, even if these were beautiful and absolutely permanent, as they never are. What counts is that one should be able to begin a new task, a new castle, a new bubble. It counts only because it is there to be done and he has the will to do it. The same will be the life of his children, and of theirs; and if the philosopher is apt to see in this a pattern similar to the unending cycles of the existence of Sisyphus, and to despair, then it is indeed because the meaning and point he is seeking is not there—but mercifully so. The meaning of life is from within us, it is not bestowed from without, and it far exceeds in both its beauty and permanence any heaven of which men have ever dreamed or yearned for.

NOTE

1. A popular Christian hymn, sung often at funerals and typical of many hymns, expresses this thought:
   > Swift to its close ebbs out life's little day;
   > Earth's joys grow dim, its glories pass away;
   > Change and decay in all around I see:
   > O thou who changest not, abide with me.

To Have and To Be

John Lachs

In an incident Aesop did not record, three animals were lamenting their fate. "If only I had more to eat," said the pig, and he imagined himself buried under an avalanche of fragrant victuals. "If only I had

From *Personalist*, Vol. 45, No. 1 (Winter 1964), pp. 5-14. Reprinted by permission of the author and the editor.

shorter hours and less work," complained the ass as he rubbed his aching back. "If only people had more things and I greater skill to steal them," whispered the fox for he did not want to be found out.

The God Zeus, known for his cruel sense of humor, heard their complaints and decided to grant the animals what they desired. The pig's larder was overflowing with food: he had so much that he had to ask the fox to store some of it for him. But soon the pig could no longer enjoy these good things. Eating too much had caused indigestion and he could not even think of cooking or of food. The ass's workday was reduced; his master bought a small truck to do his heavy work. But soon, instead of concentrating on all the important things he had said he would do, the ass fell asleep and spent his day in a stupor. The fox did not fall asleep, but once the initial glory and excitement of plucking defenseless chickens had abated, he grew indifferent to the charm of pillage. He was bored.

The fable has, of course, no moral for anyone who thinks that boredom, stupor and the glut that comes of overconsumption are integral parts of a good and human life. No good has ever come of the fanatic claim that only one's own ideas are right and only one's own values authentic: if there is anyone who wishes to adopt the fabled pig's desires or share the fox's fate, I will be glad to have him try. The ultimate test of living by the right values is satisfaction or equilibrium, and satisfaction is an individual matter. It is possible that undisciplined consumption is the good of some, while others find happiness in the indulgence of their orgiastic passions. Nothing could be farther from my intention than to censure such behavior. Nature continues to laugh in the face of those stern moralists who strain to set bounds to the plasticity of man.

I will, then, not condemn a way of life, and I will not categorically reject the set of values which it embodies. Nor will I recommend the universal acceptance of another, possibly quite dissimilar, set of principles or aims. I will restrict myself to a critical appraisal of some of the values by which some men in our society live, and for which too many may be willing to die. A critical approach need not lead to criticism: it is merely the dispassionate attitude of the investigator who attempts, in this instance, to determine the value of certain values. As sympathy can only be aroused in men who share a certain concern and possess imagination, values can only be discerned by persons whose natures coincide and who are endowed with sagacity and insight. For this reason, my conclusions will have no validity at all save for those whose nature—being similar to mine—prescribes for them a similar way of life, who are able to achieve the self-knowledge that is required to recognize this, and eventually perhaps to muster the courage to carry it out.

If the values of the pig, the fox or the ass satisfy you, I will not argue: surely, nature will out. Your satisfaction implies that in truth you are a human pig, or a human fox, or an ass. But what of the rest of us who live amidst the ruins of values that were our fathers'? Tossed in an ocean of conflicting obligations and alien pressures, many of us survive by makeshift, impermanent adjustments: we live without settled principles, without a private attitude to life, without a planned pattern to our being. We are not trained to divine the demands of our individual nature, and as a consequence many of us lack the inner unity that is the unmistakable feature of a *person*. There is nothing mysterious about this inner unity. Morality is a kind of hygiene: it is a cleanliness and unpromiscuity of mind. As the child learns the simple facts of animal hygiene—to eat only that which nourishes and to reject whatever does not agree with his nature—the adult has to learn, sometimes through tragic experiences, the importance of acting by a single principle and living by a single plan, assimilating and dismissing as his nature commands. A healthy conscience is but the inner demand for consistency which makes one's life the history of a person instead of a disconnected series of events.

There is a current fallacy whose prevalence I do not feel called upon to discuss. This specious but unuttered principle is best expressed in the phrase "To live is to make a living." All the values of our Consumer Age are implicit in this phrase. "To make a living," of course, means to earn enough to be able to purchase the goods necessary for life. But what are the goods necessary for life? According to what I shall, for short, call the Consumer's Fallacy about the Ends of Human Life, enough food to avoid hunger, and enough shelter and clothing to keep warm, are not enough to *live* in the full sense of that word. Implicit in the Consumer's Fallacy is the claim that we do not even begin to *live* until we have the right or approved kind of food bought in a good store, fashionable clothing, and a cave as good as our neighbors'. This, of course, is only the beginning. For there are characteristically human needs, such as the need for fast cars, the need for heartshaped bathtubs, and the need for the envy of one's fellows. We *live* when we have as many of these and other goods as our fortune will allow or our stratagems create.

The possession and the use of manufactured physical objects have become primary and fundamental facts in our culture and in our lives. They have penetrated our thought to such an extent that the attitudes appropriate to ownership and use have come to serve as the model for our attitudes to the world at large and to other human beings in it. Our attitude to almost every thing we have or wish for is the attitude of a consumer. We use not only cars and washing machines, but also reputation and the goodwill of our neighbors. We possess not only typewriters and television sets, but also security and the loyalty of our children. It is, of course, natural for the human mind to reify the intangible: to substitute images for attitudes and concrete objects for abstract relations. But when such conceptual aids cease to be merely that and begin to penetrate our mental life and to govern our actions, when human beings begin to be considered physical objects and human feelings things to be consumed, the result is that the good life becomes a life filled with goods, and our attempt to live it culminates in a rage of possessiveness.

At the basis of the Consumer's Fallacy is the supposition that a man is what he has: that happiness is a function of the goods we possess and the things we consume, that it is the result of urges satisfied. Thus Hobbes, an early exponent of the Consumer's Fallacy writes:

> Continual success in obtaining those things which a man from time to time
> desires, that is to say, continual prospering, is what men call FELICITY.[1]

If this is true, the introduction of mass advertising and of credit buying
are the two greatest steps ever taken to promote the happiness of man.
Advertisers create new desires, and consumer credit makes it possible for
these desires to be readily satisfied. The unbroken cycle of desires and
satisfactions guaranteed amounts to that "continual prospering" which
men call "felicity." Continual success, which is happiness, is the share of
the American who desires, purchases and consumes in proportion to the
installment payments he can meet. And lest my point be misunderstood:
what is purchased need not be a manufactured object, it may be love,
and the installment payment need not be a sum of money, it may be
time to listen to a woman's troubles, or a promise of security.

If Hobbes and his contemporary soul-mates are right and happiness is
but the satisfaction of desires on the basis of wisdom in trading, I wonder why so many Americans, shrewd businessmen at work as well as in
their private life, remain unhappy. If Hobbes's analysis were correct, the
successful consumption of physical objects and of human emotions
should suffice to make us happy. How is it then, that so many of us are
successful as owners and consumers, even as consumers of human feelings, but unsuccessful as men? The answer to this question is not to be
found by an examination of the means we utilize to achieve our ends: it
resides, instead, in the nature and inadequacy of our current ends. Similarly, the cure for human dissatisfaction is not by concentrating on increasing our possessions, nor again by concentrating on combating the
natural urge to have, but by relegating possession and consumption to
their rightful and limited place in a comprehensive scheme of human
values.

The Consumer's Fallacy and the accompanying tendency to treat human feelings as commodities and human beings as serviceable objects, is
closely connected with our current veneration of progress. Progress is a
kind of motion: it is motion in the direction of some desirable goal.
What differentiates progress from mere movement or change is its direc-
tionality. Direction, in turn, implies a fixed point of reference: some
state of affairs for which we strive, an objective that is deemed worth-
while. I do not wish to assail the apologists of progress on the issue of
mistaken standards: that some of the objectives in terms of which we
measure our 'progress' are insignificant or worthless is too obvious to
require emphasis. It is as easy to suppose as it is barbarous to assert that
the possession of two radios per family or the development of wash-and-
wear, warm-yet-light, no-ironing-needed underwear is the yardstick by
which human advance is to be judged. My immediate concern here is
not with such mistakes, but with two even more fundamental errors
which the indiscriminate veneration of progress promotes.

The first blunder is best expressed in the scandalous slogan "Progress
is our most important product." Progress, in fact, is a movement not a
product, and its sole importance derives from the importance and the

value of its goal. No progress is valuable in and of itself: only the end of progress is of any worth, and it is only by reference to this end that a change may be called "progressive." The value of progress is, in this way, entirely derivative: it is wholly dependent on the value of the fixed objective at which progress aims. This single reflection should eliminate the mistake of supposing that progress can or ought to go on indefinitely or, in other words, that progress can be its own end. Like all forms of transit, progress aims at a destination not at its own self-propagation: its object is a state where progress will no longer be because its goal will have been achieved. I am, of course, not denying that progress is a "good thing" in some sense of that ambiguous phrase. But good things are of two sorts: those which we want for their own sake or as ends, and those which we want for the sake of other things or as means. Comfort and pleasure may be things we want in and of themselves: if they are such *ends,* they are valuable. Coal and electrical generators are a *means* to these ends. They help to bring about our comfort and pleasure and while not intrinsically valuable, they are at least useful. Now progress is at best useful; it is not intrinsically valuable. It is good as a means but not as an end: it must have an end or objective other than itself. Hence progress can never be the goal of progress and no progress can be indefinitely sustained. Progress makes no sense at all without the possibility of fulfilment or attainment, and the more fervently we desire the attainment of our goals, the more we look forward to the time when progress, having got us our aim, will have ceased to be.

The sharp separation of progress from its goal is the source of the second mistake to which I alluded. We believe that it is important to progress and pride ourselves on being a "progressive" nation. We tend to overlook the fact that progress is not a term of unqualified commendation. Progress is movement in the direction of that which we do not have and which, at the same time, it would be good to have. Its existence implies a current lack along with the hope of future consummation. For this reason, any society committed to progress is at once also committed to the future, and whoever is committed to the future ceases to live in the present. But it is impossible to live in anything but the present. The person who attempts to live in the future ends up by not living at all: his present is saturated with a heavy sense of impermanence, worthlessness and longing for the morrow. His concentration on what is yet to come blinds him to the satisfactions that are possible now. His desire to come closer to his goal makes his present a chamber of horrors: by hastening the passage of the days he wishes his life away. And not only is his longing agonized, after such fierce desire each attainment is an anticlimax. Unreleased emotion paints in hues reality can never match. The object of desire once possessed is only a pale replica of what it was to be.

The meaning of life is not to be found in the future and the characteristically human malady of trying to find it there leads only to disappointment and despair. Caught between the incompleteness of striving and the essential insufficiency of the possessions which flow from desire and hard work, the future-directed man lives with a pervasive sense of insecurity, anxiety, defeat. The paradigm is the grotesque figure of the man who works so hard to provide for his retirement that he dies of a heart-attack when he is forty-two. I will call the belief, fostered by our veneration of progress, that the means and the end must be distinct and separated by time, the Fallacy of Separation. The combination of the attitudes of ownership and use implicit in the Consumer's Fallacy with this Fallacy of Separation issues in disastrous effects on the attempt to lead the good life.

The Fallacy of Separation is so deep-seated in our thinking that it is difficult for us to conceive and almost impossible to admit that means and end may coincide. But this admission is the foundation of all sound ethics and, accordingly, it is found on the first page of Aristotle's great work on the subject. There Aristotle says:

> A certain difference is found among ends; some are activities, others are products apart from the actions that produce them.[2]

As a result of our commitment to the future and of our interest in "products apart from the actions that produce them," the concept of *activity* has been virtually lost to Western civilization. An activity is a deed, any deed, that is performed for its own sake. It is an action done not as a means to obtaining some ulterior end or producing some product. Let me make my point with unceremonious simplicity: to engage in activity is to keep doing things without getting anywhere. But why should we wish to get anywhere if we are satisfied with whatever we are doing? The desire to get somewhere, our everlasting restlessness, betrays a sense of dissatisfaction with what we have and what we do and what we are. If we find something worth doing, it is reasonable to enjoy doing it and to ask for no more. If we are satisfied with what we do and are, it becomes unnecessary to look to the future and hope for improvement and progress.

Because the concept of activity is alien to us today, we tend to think that whenever change ceases, stagnation sets in. If this were true, no one would be more stagnant than the Christian God, who is free of desire and eternally changeless. However, to be without the striving that characterizes the infantile romantic mind is not necessarily to be static or inert. Striving might come to an end not only out of exhaustion or disgust, but also because the condition of all striving, the separation of means and end, of creative act and created product, is eliminated. Activity is not the sequestered sleep of the impotent: it is, instead, achievement unfailing and instantaneous, because in it alone the human act is its own reason for existence. I readily admit that all activity is useless, and hasten to add that this uselessness of activity is the best indication of its great value. The useful merely *produces* good things without being one. Activity, on the other hand, is good in and of itself. Too often our actions are useful to bring about ends that are worthless. When these actions cease to point beyond themselves, like poisoned arrows, when they begin to function as ultimate ends, they acquire a worth that places them in the category of what is useless but because of its intrinsic value also priceless.

If the good life is a happy life, the pig, the fox and the ass are guilty of two fundamental errors. The first is an error of attitudes, the second an error of aims. The Consumer's Fallacy prompted the animals to extend the attitudes of ownership, use and consumption to areas, such as leisure, happiness and the emotions of human persons, in which they are inappropriate. The Fallacy of Separation prompted the unfelicitous beasts to look for aims and goals that are other than activities, for products of the human act instead of the enjoyment of the act for what it is. In short, the pig, the fox and the ass all wished to *have* and not to *do*. But human beings are built to be bustling engines: they are agents and only action can satisfy them. Possession is not action, it is a passive state and as such at best a substitute for activity.

There is no clearer instance of a possession that functions as an activity-substitute than what is now commonly called a "status-symbol." To *be* a developed person is to engage in characteristic activity. Nothing is more difficult than this, since it involves self-knowledge, spontaneous action and self-control. Thus the majority of us settle for less, while we wish to appear as if we had not compromised. If we cannot *be* someone, we can do the next best and *appear to be*: and this is done by acquiring the possessions that seem to go with being a man of distinction or a developed individual. On the level of the popular mind the confusion is even clearer. Each status symbol reveals an attempt to substitute having for being, ownership for activity, possessions for character: each is a visible manifestation of our endeavor to be someone by having what he has.

A question spontaneously arises in my mind, and I am sure it has already arisen in yours. What cure can we prescribe for the three beasts? My answer to this is as simple as it is disarming. I cannot prescribe a cure for animals. If satisfaction attends their life, I congratulate them: if they do not interfere with mine, I will at least tolerate them. But how could I prescribe a mode of life for forms of life that are as alien from mine as oysters are from migratory mice? I can only speak for myself and for anyone else whose similar nature demands a similar fulfilment.

For us my counsel is to be. Life itself is an activity, and we should not approach it with the attitude of the devourer of experiences or with a possessive violence. We must develop attitudes appropriate to activity, to self-contained, self-validating human action: nothing short of this can make a life happy, spontaneous, and free. Finally, we must engage in appropriate activity. Which activities are appropriate for us is determined by our nature and may be discovered by self-knowledge. The two rules of the personal hygiene of the mind are to know oneself and to concentrate on the exercise of human powers for its own sake and not for its products or its usefulness. By knowing ourselves we will do the right things, by concentrating on the exercise of human powers for its own sake we will do them for the right reason. In this way, each moment of life acquires meaning and inalienable value. In this way, death cannot cut us off or leave our lives dismembered. For under these conditions each moment of existence shines like a total crystal: each is an appropriate, meaningful, and completed human act.

NOTES

1. Thomas Hobbes, *Leviathan* (London, 1943), p. 30.
2. Aristotle, *Nicomachean Ethics*, 1094a 3-5.

A FINAL REJOINDER

The Absurd

Thomas Nagel

Most people feel on occasion that life is absurd, and some feel it vividly and continually. Yet the reasons usually offered in defense of this conviction are patently inadequate: they *could* not really explain why life is absurd. Why then do they provide a natural expression for the sense that it is?

I

Consider some examples. It is often remarked that nothing we do now will matter in a million years. But if that is true, then by the same token, nothing that will be the case in a million years matters now. In particular, it does not matter now that in a million years nothing we do now will matter. Moreover, even if what we did now *were* going to matter in a million years, how could that keep our present concerns from being

From *Journal of Philosophy*, Vol. LXVIII, No. 20 (October 21, 1971), pp. 716-727. Reprinted by permission of the author and the editor.
* Presented in an APA symposium on The Meaning of Life, December 29, 1971.

absurd? If their mattering now is not enough to accomplish that, how would it help if they mattered a million years from now?

Whether what we do now will matter in a million years could make the crucial difference only if its mattering in a million years depended on its mattering, period. But then to deny that whatever happens now will matter in a million years is to beg the question against its mattering, period; for in that sense one cannot know that it will not matter in a million years whether (for example) someone now is happy or miserable, without knowing that it does not matter, period.

What we say to convey the absurdity of our lives often has to do with space or time: we are tiny specks in the infinite vastness of the universe; our lives are mere instants even on a geological time scale, let alone a cosmic one; we will all be dead any minute. But of course none of these evident facts can be what *makes* life absurd, if it is absurd. For suppose we lived forever; would not a life that is absurd if it lasts seventy years be infinitely absurd if it lasted through eternity? And if our lives are absurd given our present size, why would they be any less absurd if we filled the universe (either because we were larger or because the universe was smaller)? Reflection on our minuteness and brevity appears to be intimately connected with the sense that life is meaningless; but it is not clear what the connection is.

Another inadequate argument is that because we are going to die, all chains of justification must leave off in mid-air: one studies and works to earn money to pay for clothing, housing, entertainment, food, to sustain oneself from year to year, perhaps to support a family and pursue a career—but to what final end? All of it is an elaborate journey leading nowhere. (One will also have some effect on other people's lives, but that simply reproduces the problem, for they will die too.)

There are several replies to this argument. First, life does not consist of a sequence of activities each of which has as its purpose some later member of the sequence. Chains of justification come repeatedly to an end within life, and whether the process as a whole can be justified has no bearing on the finality of these end-points. No further justification is needed to make it reasonable to take aspirin for a headache, attend an exhibit of the work of a painter one admires, or stop a child from putting his hand on a hot stove. No larger context or further purpose is needed to prevent these acts from being pointless.

Even if someone wished to supply a further justification for pursuing all the things in life that are commonly regarded as self-justifying, that justification would have to end somewhere too. If *nothing* can justify unless it is justified in terms of something outside itself, which is also justified, then an infinite regress results, and no chain of justification can be complete. Moreover, if a finite chain of reasons cannot justify anything, what could be accomplished by an infinite chain, each link of which must be justified by something outside itself?

Since justifications must come to an end somewhere, nothing is gained by denying that they end where they appear to, within life—or by trying to subsume the multiple, often trivial ordinary justifications of action under a single, controlling life scheme. We can be satisfied more easily than that. In fact, through its misrepresentation of the process of justification, the argument makes a vacuous demand. It insists that the reasons available within life are incomplete, but suggests thereby that all reasons that come to an end are incomplete. This makes it impossible to supply any reasons at all.

The standard arguments for absurdity appear therefore to fail as arguments. Yet I believe they attempt to express something that is difficult to state, but fundamentally correct.

II

In ordinary life a situation is absurd when it includes a conspicuous discrepancy between pretension or aspiration and reality: someone gives a complicated speech in support of a motion that has already been passed; a notorious criminal is made president of a major philanthropic foundation; you declare your love over the telephone to a recorded announcement; as you are being knighted, your pants fall down.

When a person finds himself in an absurd situation, he will usually attempt to change it, by modifying his aspirations, or by trying to bring reality into better accord with them, or by removing himself from the situation entirely. We are not always willing or able to extricate ourselves from a position whose absurdity has become clear to us. Nevertheless, it is usually possible to imagine some change that would remove the absurdity—whether or not we can or will implement it. The sense that life as a whole is absurd arises when we perceive, perhaps dimly, an inflated pretension or aspiration which is inseparable from the continuation of human life and which makes its absurdity inescapable, short of escape from life itself.

Many people's lives are absurd, temporarily or permanently, for conventional reasons having to do with their particular ambitions, circumstances, and personal relations. If there is a philosophical sense of absurdity, however, it must arise from the perception of something universal—some respect in which pretension and reality inevitably clash for us all. This condition is supplied, I shall argue, by the collision between the seriousness with which we take our lives and the perpetual possibility of regarding everything about which we are serious as arbitrary, or open to doubt.

We cannot live human lives without energy and attention, nor without making choices which show that we take some things more seriously than others. Yet we have always available a point of view outside the particular form of our lives, from which the seriousness appears gratuitous. These two inescapable viewpoints collide in us, and that is what makes life absurd. It is absurd because we ignore the doubts that we know cannot be settled, continuing to live with nearly undiminished seriousness in spite of them.

This analysis requires defense in two respects: first as regards the unavoidability of seriousness; second as regards the inescapability of doubt.

We take ourselves seriously whether we lead serious lives or not and whether we are concerned primarily with fame, pleasure, virtue, luxury, triumph, beauty, justice, knowledge, salvation, or mere survival. If we take other people seriously and devote ourselves to them, that only multiplies the problem. Human life is full of effort, plans, calculation, success and failure: we *pursue* our lives, with varying degrees of sloth and energy.

It would be different if we could not step back and reflect on the process, but were merely led from impulse to impulse without self-consciousness. But human beings do not act solely on impulse. They are prudent, they reflect, they weigh consequences, they ask whether what they are doing is worth while. Not only are their lives full of particular choices that hang together in larger activities with temporal structure: they also decide in the broadest terms what to pursue and what to avoid, what the priorities among their various aims should be, and what kind of people they want to be or become. Some men are faced with such choices by the large decisions they make from time to time; some merely by reflection on the course their lives are taking as the product of countless small decisions. They decide whom to marry, what profession to follow, whether to join the Country Club, or the Resistance; or they may just wonder why they go on being salesmen or academics or taxi drivers, and then stop thinking about it after a certain period of inconclusive reflection.

Although they may be motivated from act to act by those immediate needs with which life presents them, they allow the process to continue by adhering to the general system of habits and the form of life in which such motives have their place—or perhaps only by clinging to life itself. They spend enormous quantities of energy, risk, and calculation on the details. Think of how an ordinary individual sweats over his appearance, his health, his sex life, his emotional honesty, his social utility, his self-knowledge, the quality of his ties with family, colleagues, and friends, how well he does his job, whether he understands the world and what is going on in it. Leading a human life is a full-time occupation, to which everyone devotes decades of intense concern.

This fact is so obvious that it is hard to find it extraordinary and important. Each of us lives his own life—lives with himself twenty-four hours a day. What else is he supposed to do—live someone else's life? Yet humans have the special capacity to step back and survey themselves, and the lives to which they are committed, with that detached amazement which comes from watching an ant struggle up a heap of sand. Without developing the illusion that they are able to escape from their highly specific and idiosyncratic position, they can view it *sub specie aeternitatis*—and the view is at once sobering and comical.

The crucial backward step is not taken by asking for still another justification in the chain, and failing to get it. The objections to that line of attack have already been stated; justifications come to an end. But this is precisely what provides universal doubt with its object. We step back to find that the whole system of justification and criticism, which controls our choices and supports our claims to rationality, rests on responses and habits that we never question, that we should not know how to defend without circularity, and to which we shall continue to adhere even after they are called into question.

The things we do or want without reasons, and without requiring reasons—the things that define what is a reason for us and what is not—are the starting points of our skepticism. We see ourselves from outside, and all the contingency and specificity of our aims and pursuits become clear. Yet when we take this view and recognize what we do as arbitrary, it does not disengage us from life, and there lies our absurdity: not in the fact that such an external view can be taken of us, but in the fact that we ourselves can take it, without ceasing to be the persons whose ultimate concerns are so coolly regarded.

III

One may try to escape the position by seeking broader ultimate concerns, from which it is impossible to step back—the idea being that absurdity results because what we take seriously is something small and insignificant and individual. Those seeking to supply their lives with meaning usually envision a role or function in something larger than themselves. They therefore seek fulfillment in service to society, the state, the revolution, the progress of history, the advance of science, or religion and the glory of God.

But a role in some larger enterprise cannot confer significance unless that enterprise is itself significant. And its significance must come back to what we can understand, or it will not even appear to give us what we are seeking. If we learned that we were being raised to provide food for other creatures fond of human flesh, who planned to turn us into cutlets before we got too stringy—even if we learned that the human race had been developed by animal breeders precisely for this purpose—that would still not give our lives meaning, for two reasons. First, we would still be in the dark as to the significance of the lives of those other beings; second, although we might acknowledge that this culinary role would make our lives meaningful to them, it is not clear how it would make them meaningful to us.

Admittedly, the usual form of service to a higher being is different from this. One is supposed to behold and partake of the glory of God, for example, in a way in which chickens do not share in the glory of coq au vin. The same is true of service to a state, a movement, or a revolution. People can come to feel, when they are part of something bigger, that it is part of them too. They worry less about what is peculiar to themselves, but identify enough with the larger enterprise to find their role in it fulfilling.

However, any such larger purpose can be put in doubt in the same way that the aims of an individual life can be, and for the same reasons. It is as legitimate to find ultimate justification there as to find it earlier, among the details of individual life. But this does not alter the fact that justifications come to an end when we are content to have them end—when we do not find it necessary to look any further. If we can step back from the purposes of individual life and doubt their point, we can step back also from the progress of human history, or of science, or the success of a society, or the kingdom, power, and glory of God,[1] and put all these things into question in the same way. What seems to us to confer meaning, justification, significance, does so in virtue of the fact that we need no more reasons after a certain point.

What makes doubt inescapable with regard to the limited aims of individual life also makes it inescapable with regard to any larger purpose that encourages the sense that life is meaningful. Once the fundamental doubt has begun, it cannot be laid to rest.

Camus maintains in *The Myth of Sisyphus* that the absurd arises because the world fails to meet our demands for meaning. This suggests that the world might satisfy those demands if it were different. But now we can see that this is not the case. There does not appear to be any conceivable world (containing us) about which unsettlable doubts could not arise. Consequently the absurdity of our situation derives not from a collision between our expectations and the world, but from a collision within ourselves.

IV

It may be objected that the standpoint from which these doubts are supposed to be felt does not exist—that if we take the recommended backward step we will land on thin air, without any basis for judgment about the natural responses we are supposed to be surveying. If we retain our usual standards of what is important, then questions about the significance of what we are doing with our lives will be answerable in the usual way. But if we do not, then those questions can mean nothing to us, since there is no longer any content to the idea of what matters, and hence no content to the idea that nothing does.

But this objection misconceives the nature of the backward step. It is not supposed to give us an understanding of what is *really* important, so that we see by contrast that our lives are insignificant. We never, in the course of these reflections, abandon the ordinary standards that guide our lives. We merely observe them in operation, and recognize that if they are called into question we can justify them only by reference to themselves, uselessly. We adhere to them because of the way we are put together; what seems to us important or serious or valuable would not seem so if we were differently constituted.

In ordinary life, to be sure, we do not judge a situation absurd unless we have in mind some standards of seriousness, significance, or harmony with which the absurd can be contrasted. This contrast is not implied by the philosophical judgment of absurdity, and that might be thought to make the concept unsuitable for the expression of such judgments. This is not so, however, for the philosophical judgment depends on another contrast which makes it a natural extension from more ordinary cases. It departs from them only in contrasting the pretensions of life with a large context in which *no* standards can be discovered, rather than with a context from which alternative, overriding standards may be applied.

V

In this respect, as in others, philosophical perception of the absurd resembles epistemological skepticism. In both cases the final, philosophical doubt is not contrasted with any unchallenged certainties, though it is arrived at by extrapolation from examples of doubt within the system of evidence or justification, where a contrast with other certainties *is* implied. In both cases our limitedness joins with a capacity to transcend those limitations in thought (thus seeing them as limitations, and as inescapable).

Skepticism begins when we include ourselves in the world about which we claim knowledge. We notice that certain types of evidence convince us, that we are content to allow justifications of belief to come to an end at certain points, that we feel we know many things even without knowing or having grounds for believing the denial of others which, if true, would make what we claim to know false.

For example, I know that I am looking at a piece of paper, although I have no adequate grounds to claim I know that I am not dreaming; and if I am dreaming then I am not looking at a piece of paper. Here an ordinary conception of how appearance may diverge from reality is employed to show that we take our world largely for granted; the certainty that we are not dreaming cannot be justified except circularly, in terms of those very appearances which are being put in doubt. It is somewhat far-fetched to suggest I may be dreaming; but the possibility is only illustrative. It reveals that our claims to knowledge depend on our not feeling it necessary to exclude certain incompatible alternatives, and the dreaming possibility or the total hallucination possibility are just representatives for limitless possibilities most of which we cannot even conceive.[2]

Once we have taken the backward step to an abstract view of our whole system of beliefs, evidence, and justification, and seen that it works only, despite its pretensions, by taking the world largely for granted, we are *not* in a position to contrast all these appearances with an alternative reality. We cannot shed our ordinary responses, and if we could it would leave us with no means of conceiving a reality of any kind.

It is the same in the practical domain. We do not step outside our lives to a new vantage point from which we see what is really, objectively significant. We continue to take life largely for granted while seeing that all our decisions and certainties are possible only because there is a great deal we do not bother to rule out.

Both epistemological skepticism and a sense of the absurd can be reached via initial doubts posed within systems of evidence and justification that we accept, and can be stated without violence to our ordinary concepts. We can ask not only why we should believe there is a floor under us, but also why we should believe the evidence of our senses at all—and at some point the framable questions will have outlasted the answers. Similarly, we can ask not only why we should take aspirin, but why we should take trouble over our own comfort at all. The fact that we shall take the aspirin without waiting for an answer to this last question does not show that it is an unreal question. We shall continue to believe there is a floor under us without waiting for an answer to the other question. In both cases it is this unsupported natural confidence that generates skeptical doubts; so it cannot be used to settle them.

Philosophical skepticism does not cause us to abandon our ordinary beliefs, but it lends them a peculiar flavor. After acknowledging that their truth is incompatible with possibilities that we have no grounds for believing do not obtain—apart from grounds in those very beliefs which we have called into question—we return to our familiar convictions with a certain irony and resignation. Unable to abandon the natural responses on which they depend, we take them back, like a spouse who has run off with someone else and then decided to return; but we regard them differently (not that the new attitude is necessarily inferior to the old, in either case).

The same situation obtains after we have put in question the seriousness with which we take our lives and human life in general and have looked at ourselves without presuppositions. We then return to our lives, as we must, but our seriousness is laced with irony. Not that irony enables us to escape the absurd. It is useless to mutter: "Life is meaningless; life is meaningless . . ." as an accompaniment to everything we do. In continuing to live and work and strive, we take ourselves seriously in action no matter what we say.

What sustains us, in belief as in action, is not reason or justification, but something more basic than these—for we go on in the same way even after we are convinced that the reasons have given out.[3] If we tried to rely entirely on reason, and pressed it hard, our lives and beliefs would collapse—a form of madness that may actually occur if the inertial force of taking the world and life for granted is somehow lost. If we lose our grip on that, reason will not give it back to us.

VI

In viewing ourselves from a perspective broader than we can occupy in the flesh, we become spectators of our own lives. We cannot do very much as pure spectators of our own lives, so we continue to lead them, and devote ourselves to what we are able at the same time to view as no more than a curiosity, like the ritual of an alien religion.

This explains why the sense of absurdity finds its natural expression in those bad arguments with which the discussion began. Reference to our small size and short lifespan and to the fact that all of mankind will eventually vanish without a trace are metaphors for the backward step which permits us to regard ourselves from without and to find the particular form of our lives curious and slightly surprising. By feigning a nebula's-eye view, we illustrate the capacity to see ourselves without presuppositions, as arbitrary, idiosyncratic, highly specific occupants of the world, one of countless possible forms of life.

Before turning to the question whether the absurdity of our lives is something to be regretted and if possible escaped, let me consider what would have to be given up in order to avoid it.

Why is the life of a mouse not absurd? The orbit of the moon is not absurd either, but that involves no strivings or aims at all. A mouse, however, has to work to stay alive. Yet he is not absurd, because he lacks the capacities for self-consciousness and self-transcendence that would enable him to see that he is only a mouse. If that *did* happen, his life would become absurd, since self-awareness would not make him cease to be a mouse and would not enable him to rise above his mousely strivings. Bringing his new-found self-consciousness with him, he would have to return to his meagre yet frantic life, full of doubts that he was unable to answer, but also full of purposes that he was unable to abandon.

Given that the transcendental step is natural to us humans, can we avoid absurdity by refusing to take that step and remaining entirely within our sublunar lives? Well, we cannot refuse consciously, for to do that we would have to be aware of the viewpoint we were refusing to adopt. The only way to avoid the relevant self-consciousness would be either never to attain it or to forget it—neither of which can be achieved by the will.

On the other hand, it is possible to expend effort on an attempt to destroy the other component of the absurd—abandoning one's earthly, individual, human life in order to identify as completely as possible with that universal viewpoint from which human life seems arbitrary and trivial. (This appears to be the ideal of certain Oriental religions.) If one succeeds, then one will not have to drag the superior awareness through a strenuous mundane life, and absurdity will be diminished.

However, insofar as this self-etiolation is the result of effort, willpower, asceticism, and so forth, it requires that one take oneself seriously as an individual—that one be willing to take considerable trouble to avoid being creaturely and absurd. Thus one may undermine the aim of unworldliness by pursuing it too vigorously. Still, if someone simply allowed his individual, animal nature to drift and respond to impulse, without making the pursuit of its needs a central conscious aim, then he might, at considerable dissociative cost, achieve a life that was less absurd than most. It would not be a meaningful life either, of course; but it would not involve the engagement of a transcendent awareness in the assiduous pursuit of mundane goals. And that is the main condition of absurdity—the dragooning of an unconvinced transcendent consciousness into the service of an immanent, limited enterprise like a human life.

The final escape is suicide; but before adopting any hasty solutions, it would be wise to consider carefully whether the absurdity of our existence truly presents us with a *problem*, to which some solution must be found—a way of dealing with prima facie disaster. That is certainly the attitude with which Camus approaches the issue, and it gains support from the fact that we are all eager to escape from absurd situations on a smaller scale.

Camus—not on uniformly good grounds—rejects suicide and the other solutions he regards as escapist. What he recommends is defiance or scorn. We can salvage our dignity, he appears to believe, by shaking a fist at the world which is deaf to our pleas, and continuing to live in spite of it. This will not make our lives un-absurd, but it will lend them a certain nobility.[4]

This seems to me romantic and slightly self-pitying. Our absurdity warrants neither that much distress nor that much defiance. At the risk of falling into romanticism by a different route, I would argue that absurdity is one of the most human things about us: a manifestation of our most advanced and interesting characteristics. Like skepticism in epistemology, it is possible only because we possess a certain kind of insight—the capacity to transcend ourselves in thought.

If a sense of the absurd is a way of perceiving our true situation (even though the situation is not absurd until the perception arises), then what reason can we have to resent or escape it? Like the capacity for epistemological skepticism, it results from the ability to understand our human limitations. It need not be a matter for agony unless we make it so. Nor need it evoke a defiant contempt of fate that allows us to feel brave or proud. Such dramatics, even if carried on in private, betray a failure to appreciate the cosmic unimportance of the situation. If *sub specie aeternitatis* there is no reason to believe that anything matters, then that doesn't matter either, and we can approach our absurd lives with irony instead of heroism or despair.

NOTES

1. Cf. Robert Nozick, "Teleology," *Mosaic*, XII, 1 (Spring 1971): 27/8.
2. I am aware that skepticism about the external world is widely thought to have been refuted, but I have remained convinced of its irrefutability since being exposed at Berkeley to Thompson Clarke's largely unpublished ideas on the subject.
3. As Hume says in a famous passage of the *Treatise:* "Most fortunately it happens, that since reason is incapable of dispelling these clouds, nature herself

suffices to that purpose, and cures me of this philosophical melancholy and delirium, either by relaxing this bent of mind, or by some avocation, and lively impression of my senses, which obliterate all these chimeras. I dine, I play a game of backgammon, I converse, and am merry with my friends; and when after three or four hours' amusement, I would return to these speculations, they appear so cold, and strain'd, and ridiculous, that I cannot find in my heart to enter into them any farther" (Book 1, Part 4, Section 7; Selby-Bigge, p. 269).

4. "Sisyphus, proletarian of the gods, powerless and rebellious, knows the whole extent of his wretched condition: it is what he thinks of during his descent. The lucidity that was to constitute his torture at the same time crowns his victory. There is no fate that cannot be surmounted by scorn" (*The Myth of Sisyphus*, Vintage edition, p. 90).